NATURAL
DISASTERS

EARTH is an epic publishing feat never to be repeated, proudly created by Millennium House

Locator box indicates location of map within world

Locator box indicates location of map within region

Color-coded bars make identifying each continent easy

Each page is edged with silver gilding to help in the preservation of the book over time

Comprehensive labelling with current data

Specially created state-of-the-art full-color background relief

Colored relief bar indicating elevation

Feature boxes throughout the book focus on milestone events in a country's history or take an in-depth look at a unique feature about a country

Exquisite full-color images are used throughout, with more than 800 images in total

Scale bar and map scale information

A profile of each country provides a snapshot of vital information, including official name, population, area, capital city

A map of each country shows the major cities, highest point, and neighboring countries

Handy map reference information will take you straight to the corresponding map for each country

A locator map pinpoints the location of the country within the region

This limited edition atlas—the world's largest modern atlas—is bound by hand in beautiful custom-dyed leather with silver-gilded pages for preservation and silver-plated corners for protection. *Earth* establishes a new benchmark in the world of atlases, with highly detailed mapping and comprehensive country profiles. With 580 pages, including 355 maps of 194 countries, more than 800 images, 4 breathtaking gatefolds, and information on every country, territory and dependency in the world, *Earth* will appeal to book collectors, libraries and institutions, map lovers, and anyone wishing to enjoy now, and preserve for the future, a record of our world today.

Earth can be ordered from all good book stores or contact Millennium House for your nearest supplier

www.millenniumhouse.com.au

NATURAL
DISASTERS
AND HOW WE COPE

Chief Consultant Robert Coenraads

MILLENNIUM HOUSE

First published in 2006 by **Millennium House Pty Ltd**
52 Bolwarra Rd, Elanora Heights, NSW, 2101, Australia
Ph: 612 9970 6850   Fax: 612 9970 8136
email rightsmanager@millenniumhouse.com.au

Text © Millennium House Pty Ltd 2006
Photos from Getty Images® 2006 except where otherwise credited

Reprinted 2009, 2010

ISBN 978-1-921209-65-9

Millennium House would like to hear from photographers interested in supplying photographs

Printed in China
Color separation by Pica Digital Pte Ltd, Singapore

PUBLISHER Gordon Cheers
ASSOCIATE PUBLISHER Janet Parker
PROJECT MANAGER Fiona Doig
CONCEPT DEVELOPMENT Fiona Doig, Robert Coenraads, Lena Lowe, Avril Makula
ART DIRECTION AND DESIGN Avril Makula
DESIGN ASSISTANT James Sdrinis
COVER DESIGN Lena Lowe
EDITORS Fiona Doig, Heather Jackson, Jody Lee, Matthew Stevens, Sarah Shrubb,
    James Young
PRODUCTION Simone Russell
PICTURE RESEARCH Bree Adams and Anne Cameron
MAP AND ILLUSTRATION RESEARCH Guy Freer
MAPS Damien Demaj
ILLUSTRATIONS Andrew Davies
INDEX Puddingburn Publishing Services

Contributors appear on page 522
Photo credits appear on page 524

Photos on cover and preliminary pages:
FRONT COVER Lava streams out from the summit vent of Sicily's Mt Etna.
1 This supercell storm spawned four tornadoes in Texas, USA.
5 Preparations for a candlelight memorial service, one year after the 2004 Indian Ocean tsunami.
6–7 A couple survey all that remains of their home following the 2004 tsunami in Sri Lanka.
8–9 A wildfire burns in Yellowstone National Park, USA, in 2001.

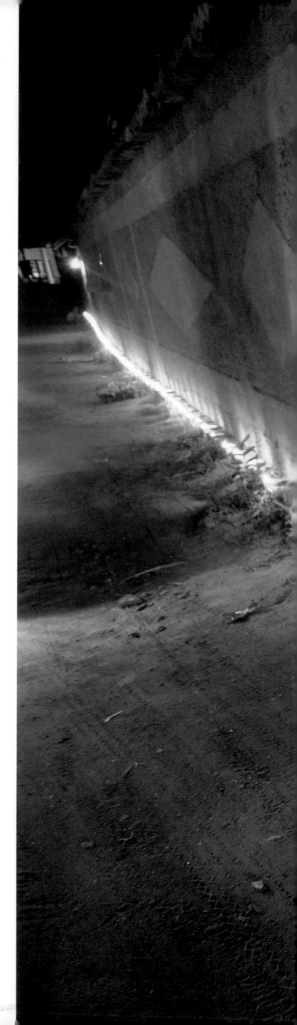

Contents

What is a Natural Disaster?

Just mentioning one of these words—volcano, earthquake, tsunami, drought, famine, hurricane, flood, avalanche, plague, wildfire, or pestilence—can strike fear into the hearts of ordinary people, especially those who are living in areas of the planet prone to unfortunate natural events. Although no part of our world is completely safe, some parts are definitely more susceptible than others.

Natural disasters roughly fall into three broad groupings: geological events, triggered by the internal workings of our planet; meteorological events, caused by variations in global weather patterns; and biological disasters, resulting from the actions of living agents such as diseases or insect pests. They can occur separately or together, and are generally, although not always, unrelated.

A deadly chain of events

Natural disasters are also known as "acts of God" because they can strike with little or no warning and without any apparent direct human involvement. Often one disaster will trigger a string of other disasters that can be as devastating as the original event. A big earthquake can rupture a city's gas and water lines. This occurred in San Francisco in 1906 and in Tokyo in 1923, causing massive firestorms that dwarfed the death and destruction caused by the earthquakes; firefighters then discovered they had little water to fight the fires. Volcanic eruptions can trigger mudflows, avalanches, landslides, flood surges, and fires. Eruptions and earthquakes at sea can send tsunamis on an ocean-wide journey of destruction. Hurricanes and typhoons can cause floods, leading to disease threats from bacteria and toxins in the unclean waters. Major outbreaks of infectious disease can also take their toll if basic needs such as clean water, food, shelter, and medical supplies are not restored quickly to a disaster zone.

Disasters caused by humans, on the other hand, have some element of human error, negligence, or intent. These types of disasters include nuclear accidents, transport disasters, wars, and terrorist attacks—and they can be equally as devastating.

Some of the world-scale disasters that face humanity today straddle the divide between natural and those of our own making. These include global climate shifts, together with general environmental degradation, which can induce floods, drought, or famine. The livelihoods of entire coastal nations are being threatened by a rise in sea levels caused by

FAR LEFT Iceland owes its existence to volcanoes, such as this one near the city of Vestmannaeyjar on Heimaey Island. But it is a precarious existence. In 1783, the 15-mile (25-km) long Laki fissure opened and poured out 3.6 cubic miles (15 km³) of lava, which covered 218 square miles (560 km²) of land. The enormous quantities of toxic gases that were released killed over half of Iceland's livestock, leading to famine and the death of over 20 percent of the country's population. The 1973 eruption on Heimaey destroyed one-third of Vestmannaeyjar.

LEFT Funafuti Atoll is home to nearly half of the nation of Tuvalu's entire population. But for how much longer? Global warming is raising the ocean's temperature, causing sea levels to rise. Higher sea levels will allow high tides to inundate these low-lying lands. The warmer water also generates more frequent and stronger storms in such low-lying island nations. Tuvalu is expected to be the first of many island nations impacted by global warming to need permanent evacuation.

RIGHT Bangladeshi flood victims, in boats laden with their possessions, navigate flooded city streets in Dhaka in 2004. These floods affected 30 million people and inundated nearly half of the capital. Floods bring much-needed nutrients to the fields, but are a double-edged sword for Bangladesh. The population of 145 million has little choice but to accept the inevitable.

global warming. Human activity and industry, being fossil-fuel dependent, are clearly bringing this about. Rather than being sudden and unexpected, these disasters are emerging slowly over decades, with their effects becoming increasingly apparent. Yet individuals feel powerless in the face of these global events, arising as they do from factors outside their control, and possibly even beyond the control of their governments.

The human population problem

Humans evolved on Earth over the last 5 million years and, like any other species, they have multiplied in number to fill almost every inhabitable part of the planet, as conditions permitted. During glacial periods, sea levels fell, allowing primitive groups to island-hop and cross land bridges in search of new territory. Later, as climate warmed, people moved northward, behind the retreating ice-sheet fronts. Population density maps reveal that the largest numbers of people live in areas abundant in natural resources—water, food, and a hospitable climate. As humans have become more ingenious, increasing numbers have spread into ever-more difficult and risky places in which to live, such as the desert and arctic fringes, and steep mountain slopes. With our rapidly rising population, the consequences of disasters, both natural and caused by humans, are affecting more and more individuals.

Why do people ignore the threat of natural disasters?

Humans are perfectly adapted to living in daily and yearly cycles of eating, sleeping, mating, planting, and harvesting. As Earth changes slowly, life adapts.

BELOW The volcano Vesuvius dominates the Italian city of Naples. Vesuvius erupted in 79 CE, burying the Roman cities of Pompeii (foreground) and Herculaneum, as recorded by the Roman historian Pliny the Younger. But volcanic ash generates good soil, so people returned. Today Naples has a population of around 3 million, some of whom live precariously on the flanks of the volcano. A recent study found that an eruption 3,780 years ago buried land and villages up to 15 miles (25 km) away. The last eruption was in 1944; no one knows when the next one will occur.

Natural disasters, however, recur over longer and more irregular time periods, or with random chance, and people tend to disregard them when planning their lives. Vesuvius is a volcano that has been continually active for at least 2,000 years—erupting in 1944, 1794, 1764, 1631, and earlier—yet people continually return to live in growing communities around it. Urban and industrial development continues unabated along the earthquake-prone San Andreas Fault in California, which slipped with catastrophic consequences in 1994, 1989, 1971, 1933, 1925, 1906, 1872, and 1857. Meanwhile, people in Indonesia, Sri Lanka, and Thailand plead with local authorities to be allowed to build new homes in exactly the same places where their old ones stood when the 2004 Indian Ocean tsunami destroyed them.

To understand why this is so, we need to take a more basic human perspective. A resident in a disaster-prone area may well think, "I need food, water, work, and my family. If my ancestors lived and survived here, then so will I. Besides, I don't know what else to do." Also, active volcanic slopes, continually top-dressed with nutritious volcanic ash, provide some of the best farming land; fishing communities rely on being near the sea; and southern California is the "in" place to live. Bangladesh's 145 million people risk yearly monsoonal flooding to make their living on the fertile soils of the massive Ganges–Brahmaputra delta.

Even in Tornado Alley, covering the central states of the United States, numerous deadly tornadoes can form each year. But storm funnels are narrow and generally only touch down for a mile or two, so the

probability of any individual's home being destroyed is very low. People are prepared to gamble on these odds in order to be able to live and work, and so houses continue to be built and rebuilt in Tornado Alley, and in other tornado areas.

Nowhere is safe

Even in areas of the planet thought to be relatively safe from natural disasters, dangers lurk. The world population has grown to 6.5 billion, and modern transportation and communication have enabled civilization to become increasingly interdependent. Today, pandemics such as bird flu could sweep the world with extreme speed; not many people remain who can remember the disastrous consequences of the last serious pandemic, the 1918–19 Spanish Flu, which killed between 40 and 100 million people.

Today, numerous varieties of staple food crops, such as potatoes and grains adapted to different regions, have been replaced by monocultures of high-production, genetically modified strains that feed large numbers of people. Nearly forgotten, however, are the hard lessons learned during the Irish Potato Famine of 1845–49. A simple airborne fungus caused the failure of three out of four of Ireland's essential potato crops during these years, and over 1 million people starved to death. Homeless families could only stand by and watch as their crops withered and turned black before their eyes.

Evolving to face new challenges

Humans evolved and became more intelligent over a long period of time in response to a changing environment. Those that survived because of useful

adaptations were able to reproduce and pass on their adaptations. The intellectual abilities of our species have now surpassed the basic need to survive, with extra brain capacity available to reflect on the very reason for being. As the trappings of modern civilization have, perhaps, removed the need for further physical adaptation, it is now the highest of human thoughts and principles, or the collective mind, that must evolve to lift society to its next level—to allow *Homo sapiens* to take hold of its own intellectual evolutionary process and push it in a positive direction. We must move beyond personal self-interest to the collective interest of the planet and deal with some impending natural disasters.

TOP Traffic works its way around flood damage in La Guaira, Venezuela, in January, 2000. Torrential rains left 30,000 to 50,000 people dead and affected the lives of nearly 1 million.

ABOVE This sign acknowledges the sponsors that helped rebuild Kodki, in the western Indian state of Gujarat, after it was destroyed by a massive earthquake in 2001; it killed over 25,000 people and left millions homeless.

Types of Natural Disasters

Several different types of natural disaster may befall Earth over the course of a human lifetime. These vary in their potential and historical severity. Fortunately for us, the deadliest type of natural disaster—meteorite strike—is also the least likely. Events with a higher probability tend to pose a lower threat to an individual; nevertheless they kill many thousands of people each year.

The following text discusses the different types of natural disaster, starting with the most cataclysmic, but least likely in a human lifetime, and continuing on to the least deadly, but most likely in a human lifetime.

Meteorite strikes

Impacts by comets or meteorites could cause the deadliest natural disaster. Hopefully by the time the next one comes, we will have systems in place to divert it. Evidence of such impacts on Earth is quickly obscured by weathering, erosion, and burial, and our atmosphere protects us from many smaller ones. However, one look at the cratered surface of the moon is enough to show the size of the bigger impacts, and there is ample evidence of massive impacts in prehistory.

The only significant impact event in more recent times was the Tunguska explosion in Siberia. It is believed that an extraterrestrial object about 330 feet (100 m) across exploded just before hitting the ground on the morning of June 30, 1908. It flattened about 800 square miles (2,072 km²) of Siberian forest, leaving all of the trees pointing radially away from the center of the blast. Fortunately it occurred in a relatively unpopulated area of the country, and only a few people were killed. Had it happened over a major city, millions could have died.

During his expedition to the area in 1930, mineralogist Leonid Kulik collected eyewitness accounts from people who lived nearby at the time. One of these was Sergei Semenov, who was 40 miles (64 km) from the blast. As reported in Astrobio.net news, he recalls, "I was sitting in the porch of the house at

LEFT Pontiac, an Ottawa Native American, confronts Colonel Henry Bouquet, who authorized his officers to spread smallpox among Native Americans by deliberately infecting blankets after peace talks in 1764. Disease often worked in favor of conquerors.

BELOW In 1991, a cyclone with winds up to 146 mph (235 km/h) hit Chittagong, Bangladesh, killing up to 138,000 people, robbing 4.5 million people of their homes or property, and causing US$2.7 billion damage.

about three sajenes [about 23 feet or 7 m] away from the porch and for a moment I lost consciousness … The crash was followed by a noise like stones falling from the sky, or guns firing. The earth trembled, and when I lay on the ground I covered my head because I was afraid that stones might hit it … Later we saw that many windows were shattered and some crops were damaged."

Smaller, insignificant meteorite impacts are recorded every few years, and, as a natural hazard, they pose less of threat than do lightning strikes. On June 12, 2004, the 2.9-pound (1.3-kg) Ellerslie meteorite struck a house in Auckland, New Zealand. It crashed through the roof, filling the house with dust, and was found lying on the sofa. The Peekskill meteorite was photographed coming in as a fireball over several eastern states of the United States on October 9, 1992. It broke up into fragments, one of which struck Michelle Knapp's car. When she went outside to investigate the crashing sound, she found the still-hot 27.3-pound (12.4-kg) meteorite in the trunk of her 1980 Chevy Malibu.

Plagues and pestilences

Pandemics rank as the most deadly natural disaster, causing some of the most savage death tolls ever recorded. The three worst-ever natural disasters were pandemics. The Plague of Justinian, which hit in 541–42 CE, killed at least 50 percent of the population of Europe. This first strike of the bubonic plague virus probably resulted in the collapse of the Byzantine Empire. The Black Death of 1347–50 killed at least 25 million—one in every three people in Europe—changing its social, economic, and political structure forever. The virulent Spanish Flu of 1918–19 reached all corners of the globe, killing between 40 and 100 million people.

Viruses rapidly mutate, enabling them to evade the human body's defense mechanisms; this creates a constant cycle of infection followed by immunity buildup. Modern city dwellers have finely tuned immune systems, but only short periods in isolation are enough to weaken this. Before they were linked to the outside world by air, residents of tiny Easter Island in the Pacific Ocean noted that when the supply ship from Chile arrived each year, they all got sick. A severe flu called the "coccongo" would rip through the small community, often killing the weak or the elderly. Longer isolation can lead to more disastrous effects. One little-remembered fact about the arrival of the first convict settlers in Australia is that the native Aboriginal society was largely destroyed by the introduction of diseases unknown to them. Smallpox, measles, colds, and flu were deadly ailments and led to so many deaths that a newspaper reported that "… bodies were to be found

TOP South Koreans cull ducks in 2003. Bird flu virus escaped tight quarantine in the north, striking birds 200 miles (120 km) away.

ABOVE Children beg for water in Kenya in 2006. Drought in the north of the country could lead to the deaths of thousands of people from starvation.

the trading station of Vanovara at breakfast time … when suddenly directly to the north, over Onkoul's Tunguska road, the sky split in two [about 50° up, according to an expedition note]. The split in the sky grew larger, and the entire northern side was covered with fire. At that moment I felt great heat as if my shirt had caught fire; this heat came from the north side. I wanted to pull off my shirt and throw it away, but at that moment there was a bang in the sky, and a mighty crash was heard. I was thrown to the ground

all around the shores of Port Jackson." Similar sad stories can be told about the first European contact with the Americas. Severe risk arises each time completely new strains of disease evolve for which nobody has immunity.

Famines and droughts

Famines occur when large populations become malnourished and die of starvation. They are often associated with crop failure due to drought or pestilence, but may also arise from human-related causes. Death tolls from famine can rival those of pandemics, particularly with rapidly rising population pressures in certain parts of the world. During the little-publicized "three difficult years" in China from 1958 to 1961, as many as 43 million people starved to death. The blame has been largely placed on the failure of Mao Zedong's great social experiment of 1958, when peasants were forced to set up communes as part of a radical advance toward utopian communism. Earlier, in 1907, a series of crop failures caused a massive famine that led to the death of 24 million people in China. In 1921, drought led to crop failure on about 20 percent of the Soviet Union's farmland. A combination of food shortages and poor political response resulted in the death of five million people.

Drought-related famines are particularly common in China, India, and Africa, where they may last up to several years and lead to severe land degradation. Essentially, the land in many of these high-population density areas has been pushed beyond its human-carrying capacity. It is particularly difficult for the international community to respond to famine disasters because of the enormous number of people affected.

Floods and storms

The world's worst floods occur regularly in the middle and lower reaches of China's major rivers due to heavy seasonal rainfall. Millions of the country's poor live in these areas, farming the river's fertile floodplain and delta soils. In 1887, flooding of the Yangtze River killed two million people; however, the most severe event was the July to August 1931 Yangtze flood. The river flooded along 900 miles (1,440 km) of its length. The flood affected one-quarter of China's population (51 million people) and resulted in the deaths of 3.7 million due to disease, starvation, or drowning.

Many of the devastating floods that occur in the Asian region are caused by typhoons or tropical cyclones. One such tropical system, the Bhola cyclone, hit the coast of East Pakistan (now Bangladesh) in the early hours of November 13, 1970. It was accompanied by an exceptionally high storm surge that flooded low-lying and densely populated coastal areas, drowning people as they slept. The official toll was 500,000 people killed and an additional 100,000 missing.

ABOVE A house is submerged on the waterfront of the Yangtze River in 2002 at Wuhan, in Hubei province, China. The Yangtze is being progressively dammed to provide hydroelectric power and to prevent such floods, but at enormous social and environmental cost: over 1 million people have had to be relocated; the huge amount of silt that used to reach the sea is already filling the new reservoirs; ocean fish that relied on the nutrients in the silt are now disappearing; and the rare Yangtze dolphin is threatened with extinction.

ABOVE August, 2002, saw the worst flooding in the Czech Republic in over a century, filling the Prague subway, and leading to the collapse of this house, built above the subway.

ABOVE RIGHT In 2005, fire raged across more than 4,000 acres (1,600 ha) of scrubland and threatened 200 homes in Ventura County, California.

FAR RIGHT Mt Merapi in Java, Indonesia, began a new eruptive phase in May, 2006. More than 22,000 residents were evacuated to camps, but many returned to live on the volcano's flanks.

Earthquakes

Again owing to its high population density, China has the unfortunate honor of hosting the world's top two most deadly earthquakes. The first took place on the morning of February 14, 1556. It was a powerful earthquake, with a magnitude of approximately 8, which struck Shaanxi Province near Mt Hua. At the time, millions of people were living in caves called yaodongs dug into cliffs of soft alluvium. Many of these collapsed or were buried by landslides during the shaking, killing an estimated 830,000 people, or about 60 percent of the region's population. China's next most devastating earthquake struck Tangshan in the early hours of July 28, 1976, killing 242,000 as they lay sleeping; the city was almost totally destroyed. It was thought to be in a low-risk area and its buildings were not earthquake-proof. To make matters worse, Tangshan was built on an alluvial plain, which magnified the shaking.

Tsunamis

In 2004 the Sumatra–Andaman Islands earthquake generated a devastating tsunami that swept onto the densely populated coastlines of the Indian Ocean, inundating tourist resorts and fishing villages alike. Coastal residents and visitors were totally unprepared, and as many as 300,000 were killed, necessitating an enormous international relief effort. The sheer magnitude of the casualties has spurred the global community into taking responsibility for the development of an advance-warning system for this kind of natural disaster.

Volcanoes

Explosive volcanoes have the potential to be highly destructive, but humans have not yet had to face the mightiest of these potential blasts, known as super volcanoes. The biggest eruption in recorded history was that of Mt Tambora, Indonesia, in 1815. After

TYPES OF NATURAL DISASTERS **19**

MEGA-DISASTERS

Mega-disasters are those that have the potential to change the whole course of human and even planetary evolution. Into this category fall the extremely rare but totally devastating giant meteorite impacts and massive volcanic blasts. During the entire course of our human evolutionary process we have, thankfully, not witnessed any of these—but they are clearly seen to have occurred on several occasions in Earth's geologic past. Careful study of the fossil record reveals that disasters such as these resulted in a dramatic drop in the number of living species; in fact, many lines ending simultaneously and abruptly. The way was then clear for new species to emerge and become dominant in the millions of years that followed.

Mega-disasters occurred 440 million years ago, marking the end of the Ordovician period; 365 million years ago, ending the Devonian; 248 million years ago, ending the Permian; 195 million years ago, ending the Triassic; and the most recent, 65 million years ago, ending the Cretaceous period. The most significant of these mega-disasters took place at the end of the Permian, destroying over 95 percent of life on Earth, possibly to due massive volcanic eruptions in Siberia and associated greenhouse gases causing global warming.

The Cretaceous extinction event was the next largest, in which 85 percent of all living things disappeared. Among others, all of the dinosaurs, winged pterosaurs, and marine reptiles died as a result of this disaster, leaving space for the rise of the mammals and the living things we know today. There are many theories, but widespread traces of the metal iridium indicate that a giant meteorite that hit Mexico's Yucatan Peninsula was the most likely cause of the extinction. It created the 112-mile (180-km) diameter Chixulub crater. Massive volcanic eruptions in the Deccan Traps in India, perhaps triggered by the impact, occurred at the same time, adding to the severity of the global catastrophe. Since far lesser eruptions are known to cause global temperatures to fall, this alone would have led to a volcanic "winter," quickly changing climatic conditions. The sedimentary record also tells of giant tsunamis radiating across the Caribbean and Atlantic as a result of the Chixulub impact.

quite a number of months' buildup, the volcano exploded, blowing about 19 cubic miles (50 km³) of material into the atmosphere. The blast was heard at least 1,000 miles (1,600 km) away, and scalding pyroclastic flows immediately killed about 10,000 people. The eruption and resultant atmospheric ash led to a lowering of global temperatures and made 1816 the "year without a summer." There were crop failures around the globe as a result. The death toll reached 92,000 due to subsequent loss of life from disease and starvation.

Fires, avalanches, and mudslides

Some of the most deadly fires, avalanches, and mudslides or landslides have been triggered by these other natural disasters; for example, fires following droughts, avalanches from earthquakes, mudslides from storms. Their deadly effects are usually summed with the toll of the causative disaster.

Surviving Natural Disasters

Surviving each type of disaster requires a different strategy. Many disasters are difficult, if not impossible, to predict, and even so there may not be much opportunity to act. Fate and chance play a very big role in determining the final outcome. There are, however, some simple precautions that individuals can take to maximize their chances of survival and these are applicable to most disasters.

It is vital to understand the potential dangers in the area in which you live and have your own personal emergency plans in place. Educating your family could save their lives. These plans may vary—from keeping a hidden, protected stash of food and water in order to survive several days in isolation in the event of a pandemic or a total breakdown of order in your city—to finding a rapid evacuation route in the event of a volcanic eruption, fire, or flood.

Be prepared for natural disaster

For anyone who lives in a natural disaster risk area, it is vital to make sure you and your family have studied a basic first-aid course. It is also important to ensure your home is made as ready as possible to withstand whatever natural disaster your region faces—be it earthquake, flood, wildfire, hurricane, or something else. Ensure that your house meets or exceeds local building codes.

Equipment that may be needed should be safely stored and easily accessible during an emergency. A battery-operated radio is an absolutely essential item to let you listen to updates and instructions from civil authorities following a natural disaster if the power fails. A comprehensive first-aid kit should also be kept containing emergency supplies. Mobile phones may come in handy; one survivor, trapped beneath rubble after the Kashmir 2005 earthquake, successfully used his mobile phone to call help.

Study carefully the plans and procedures that local authorities have in place for your area. Make sure that both you and your family know and practice the emergency drills. Joining and training with the volunteer emergency services in your area is a good way of improving your own survival skills as well as helping others. During a disaster or evacuation, obey the commands of civil authorities and emergency services. Even if such instructions seem inconvenient, their personnel are trained to save life before property. Many lives have been lost through wasting precious minutes in search of some "important" valuable. It is not worth the risk.

This book explores the causes and effects of natural disasters, both those long forgotten and those in more recent memory. It yields some forgotten stories behind the disasters: the true causes and consequences, the tragedies and triumphs in some remarkable stories of survival, and the ability of the human spirit to overcome extraordinary difficulties. Along with the tales recounted are captivating images of the disasters or their aftermath. The facts are often accompanied by stories from survivors, in their own words. Armed with this information, we can all better plan for and possibly survive future natural disasters—events that could befall us at any moment.

FAR LEFT Houses lie destroyed at Sirombu village in Nias, northern Sumatra, Indonesia. On December 26, 2004 tens of thousands of people were killed in this area alone after a massive undersea earthquake triggered a tsunami. A network of sensors has since been installed around the Indian Ocean to warn of future tsunamis.

BELOW LEFT Inhabitants of Las Cuchillas village, Solola department in Guatemala, search amid the mud for members of several families buried by a mudslide caused by heavy rains in 2005. Sixty-one people were killed, another 106 were injured, and 26,000 fled their homes.

BELOW RIGHT Avalanche rescue dogs in Utah. The Swiss Army began training search dogs in avalanche rescue in the 1930s. Many people owe their lives to these dogs and their handlers.

VOLCANOES

Volcanoes

Throughout history, stories of volcanoes have conjured vivid images. They are the point where fact meets fiction—the volcano has become associated with sulfurous witches, brimstone, bubbling cauldrons, fiery red and orange flames, hell, and eternal damnation. Watching the violent fury of a volcanic eruption by night reveals why volcanoes have become associated with such folklore.

Earth may seem solid and firm, but the planet is actually made up of a number of rigid crustal plates (the lithosphere) floating on a sea of semi-molten rock (the asthenosphere). These vast plates are relatively mobile and move around at a rate of several inches per year; roughly as fast as a fingernail grows. Volcanoes of various types erupt along the boundaries of these tectonic plates. Where the plates move apart, magma (molten rock) is able to well up in between and solidify, thereby adding crust as the plates continue to spread. Such boundaries are known as spreading margins.

Elsewhere, plates are forced beneath other plates where they heat up; the edges are then melted and destroyed. Such boundaries are known as subduction margins, and they host Earth's most violent and dangerous volcanoes.

This occurs in a continuous cycle, with Earth's crust being formed at the spreading margins and consumed in the subduction trenches.

Rift volcanoes

Although they are the most common type of volcano, rift volcanoes lie mostly out of sight at the bottom of the oceans. Along the sea floor, they form a line of continuous eruption thousands of miles long between spreading plates. It is only in rare circumstances that these mid-oceanic rift volcanoes become visible on land—in Iceland, for instance, where they run out of the ocean and right across the middle of the island. Icelanders have harnessed their abundant heat using thermoelectric power stations to supply their energy needs. Eruptions from rift volcanoes are usually gentle, but not always.

Composite volcanoes

Composite volcanoes are found at closely spaced intervals along every subduction margin, such as around the entire rim of the Pacific Ocean. It is often possible to stand on top of one volcano and see another, or several in a line. These volcanoes are the

LEFT Spectators watch the 1964 eruption of Irazu in Costa Rica. The sound of a composite volcano erupting is of such low frequency that it travels very slowly. A massive plume rises silently for many seconds before the sound reaches onlookers, who may be showered with ash.

PREVIOUS PAGES Indonesia's Mt Merapi erupting in 2006.

BELOW Volcanic ash blankets Heimaey, in Iceland. Ash travels far and wet ash is heavy; it can cause roofs to collapse. It is also highly abrasive, and will damage car engines. During an ashfall, stay inside and seal all openings.

ABOVE The volcano on Reunion Island in the Indian Ocean is a shield volcano, similar to those on Hawaii. In shield volcanoes the lava can flow so slowly that a person can easily out-walk it. When it hardens, this lava can pose problems, such as blocking roads.

product of the descending and melting plate mixed together with the seawater and ocean sediments, which have also been dragged down.

Deep trenches on the sea floor running parallel to the chains of volcanic peaks mark the lines along which plates are being forced beneath others and consumed. The viscous and highly gas-charged magma tends to erupt both explosively—as ash and various-sized pieces of broken rock (collectively known as tephra)—and as lava flows. Alternating tephra falls and lava flows build up a distinctive steep-sided cone known as a composite cone or stratovolcano.

Periodically these volcanoes explode with a massive venting of gas, steam, and tephra, ejecting this material high into the atmosphere as an eruption column or plume. This column collapses under its own weight, and the destructive, hot debris surges down the flanks of the volcano as a deadly pyroclastic flow—a dense, swiftly moving cloud of hot ash mixed with poisonous gases. After the

eruption, the summit, or even the whole cone, may have blown away, leaving a huge caldera. A new volcano then begins to slowly rebuild within the old caldera. Classic examples are Mt Fuji in Japan, Mt St Helens in the United States, and Anak Krakatau in Indonesia. All stratovolcanoes are potentially dangerous, even if they have not erupted for one or more lifetimes.

Shield volcanoes

This type of volcano occurs above specific hot spots in the mantle, where basaltic magma is able to find its way to the surface through a weakness in the crust. Erupting, flow after flow, for one or two million years, the runny, low-viscosity lava builds up an enormous broad, flat, shield-like volcanic edifice.

So heavy are these volcanoes that they begin to slowly sink. Eventually the moving plate severs the shield volcano from its feeder pipe so the lava flows stop and it can grow no further. Finally, after a few million years, the original volcano disappears

RIGHT The four main volcano types. From left to right: shield volcanoes punch up lava through weak spots in Earth's crust, such as in Hawaii; composite volcanoes erupt along plate edges such as the Pacific Ocean rim; rift volcanoes are most commonly found on the sea floor, but occur on land in Iceland; and cinder cone volcanoes, such as Mt Paricutín, in Mexico.

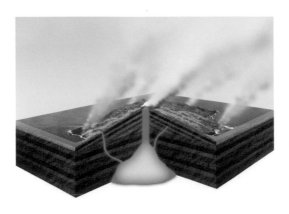

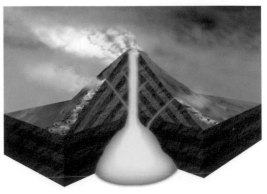

LEFT Ash pours out of Mt Paricutín in Mexico, circa 1950. This cinder cone volcano erupted from 1943 until 1952. The church in the village of San Juan was the only structure not to be destroyed; it still stands, buried in solid lava.

from sight beneath the waves. This mechanism is responsible for the many oceanic island chains, such as the Hawaiian chain in the Pacific, with the active volcano at the head of the chain. The big island of Hawaii is a classic example of a shield volcano: it stands 5 miles (8 km) tall as measured from the ocean floor. Another is Reunion, a French-governed island in the Indian Ocean. These gentle volcanoes do not often pose a threat to people living on them. Some of the very slow-moving lava—called "aa"— flows slowly enough to give people time to move historic buildings out of the way.

Cinder cones

Cinder cones are cone-shaped structures built entirely of volcanic bombs, cinders, and ash. They are the result of shorter-lived single events and rarely rise over 1,000 feet (305 m). A fire fountain of lava erupting may begin to "freeze" mid-air, before hitting the ground as solid fragments. Continuous explosive eruptions may also force huge amounts of cinders

ABOVE When a volcano explodes, its force is rated on the Volcanic Explosivity Index (VEI). This scale ranges from 0—for a non-explosive outpouring of lava, as seen in Hawaii—to 8 for a catastrophic explosion. The largest was Tambora, 1815, with a VEI of 7; the Mt St Helens eruption in 1980 had a VEI of 5. It destroyed vast tracts of forest in the surrounding region.

ABOVE Mt Arenal in Costa Rica is a typical composite volcano, erupting in spectacular explosive style. These stratovolcanoes hurl out lava and can eject boulders larger than a bus.

into the atmosphere. The larger pieces fall closest to the vent, eventually forming a cone with a bowl at its center. Paricutín in Mexico is a classic example. It started as a crack in a farmer's field in 1943, but by 1944 had buried the nearby village, leaving only the church steeple showing.

Such cones can also form from highly explosive, single cannon-blast-like eruptions that may bring diamonds to the surface from the mantle. However, such volcanoes have never been seen erupting. Cinder cones, being made up of loose fragments, erode away quite quickly. Composite volcanoes, with their alluring, classic pointy shape, are by far the most dangerous in the world. Unfortunately, their danger only becomes apparent every few generations or more, but it is then, during their explosive phase, that they can wipe out entirely the toil of all generations that lived since the last eruption. Entire Indonesian villages live around lakes, farming the fertile soils inside the craters of active volcanoes while new volcanic edifices grow noisily nearby. Entire cities are arrayed around the flanks of Mt Fuji. Even Mexico City, one of the largest urban populations, is located only 45 miles (72 km) from Popocatépetl volcano; in 2006 it is on yellow alert.

Styles of eruptions

Eruptions are named after volcanoes that exhibit characteristic styles. A Hawaiian eruption is a gentle outpouring of lava, while a Strombolian features fountains of lava. A Vulcanian explosively ejects fragments, such as blocks of lava. A Vesuvian features a vast cloud of violently discharged gases, laden with ash, resembling a cauliflower. This type is more usually called a Plinan eruption, named for Pliny the Elder, who died in the 79 BC eruption of Vesuvius. A single volcano can feature many styles.

WHAT TO DO DURING A VOLCANIC ERUPTION

1. BE AWARE OF THE VOLCANO ALERT STATUS Organizations such as the Smithsonian Institution and the United States Geological Survey maintain a global list of active volcanoes and their alert status is updated regularly; it is available online. If you live in a high volcanic-risk area or are visiting one on high alert, prepare an evacuation plan and an emergency communication plan, and have disaster supplies on hand and readily accessed: flashlight, battery-operated radio, emergency food and water, first aid kit, dust masks, and goggles.

2. EVACUATE QUICKLY Accounts of historic eruptions show that people and even civil authorities were often reluctant to leave despite extremely dangerous signs of volcanic activity, often to their peril. To leave one's home and comfortable surroundings is not an easy decision; make it well before disaster strikes so you can be prepared when it does.

3. BE AWARE OF ALL THE DANGERS Close to the volcano you may be affected by the direct effects of the explosions. Lava flows, mudflows, and floods will travel down river valleys and cover low-lying areas, so avoid these while moving away from the volcano.

4. BE PREPARED FOR ASHFALLS Ash poses a threat as it can travel hundreds of miles from an erupting volcano, blanketing downwind towns and cities.

5. IN THE EVENT OF AN ASHFALL It is best to remain inside and seal all doors, windows, and vents. The sharp jagged ash particles are extremely abrasive, so it is necessary to wear goggles and a dust mask outdoors, and to avoid using the car or other motorized appliances, as the ash will damage them. When there is adequate warning of an eruption, keep them covered.

6. KEEP THE ROOF OF YOUR HOME CLEAR OF ASH Wet ash is extremely heavy and even a buildup of a few inches can cause the roof to collapse. You may also need to assist neighbors.

LEFT Tranquil Mt Fuji in Japan is a composite volcano. Though inactive since 1707, it has erupted at least 16 times since 781 CE. Its two largest eruptions occurred in 930 BCE and 1050, with a Volcanic Explosivity Index rating of 5. The volcanic soils in the surrounding region have been cultivated into lush gardens and parks. In summer the volcano can become crowded with climbers wanting to make the 8- to 12-hour journey.

Keeping a check on the world's most dangerous volcanoes

Prior to an eruption, pressure begins to grow beneath the volcano as magma builds up in its subterranean chamber. Numerous micro-earthquakes accompany the upward movement of the magma as cracks and fractures open, and the mountain begins to swell. All this is imperceptible to the human eye and ear, but well within the capability of the sensitive seismometers and tilt meters that are arrayed on dangerous volcanoes.

Although the exact hour, day, or even week of eruption may not be known, many lives can be saved by having such a system of continuous monitoring and data collection in place.

An example of how effective this can be is evidenced by the 1980 eruption of Mt St Helens. Cooperation between scientific organizations and civil authorities meant that the warning signs were picked up early and protocols to restrict entry to the area were swiftly put in place. Despite mounting protests from logging companies, whose livelihoods depended on access to the tree-covered slopes of the volcano, and residents wishing to return home, the cordon remained firmly in place. As a result, on the morning of May 18, 1980, when Mt St Helens finally exploded, only 57 lives were lost. However, for many, and particularly those in developing countries where no monitoring or data collection systems exist, there may be no such advance warning. Death, for many, will probably be swift and sudden.

THE TEN MOST DEADLY VOLCANOES

APRIL, 1815	Tambora Volcano, Indonesia, erupted with the most deadly explosion in recorded history. Ashfalls and a tsunami, followed by disease outbreaks and starvation, resulted in a total 92,000 deaths (Volcanic Explosivity Index 7).
AUGUST, 1883	Krakatau volcano, Indonesia, exploded, turning day into night. The pyroclastic blast and tsunami stripped entire islands bare of vegetation, and killed about 36,400 people (Volcanic Explosivity Index 6).
MAY, 1902	A pyroclastic flow from Mt Pelée obliterated the town and harbor of St Pierre on Martinique Island in the Caribbean. Of the 29,000 inhabitants, only a handful escaped death by incineration and asphyxiation. Had there not been a forthcoming election, authorities might have been more stringent about heeding the clear warning signs (Volcanic Explosivity Index 4).
NOVEMBER, 1985	A devastating mudflow, spawned by melting snow and ice on the summit of Nevado de Ruiz volcano in Colombia, destroyed Armero and the surrounding towns, killing 27,000 inhabitants (Volcanic Explosivity Index 3)
MAY, 1792	The eruption of Mt Unzen on Kyushu Island was Japan's worst volcanic disaster. Dome collapses sent destructive ash flows sweeping down the volcanoes slopes, killing 14,500 people (Volcanic Explosivity Index 2).
1586	Kelut Volcano in Java erupted, emptying its large summit crater-lake, and sending a debris flow that killed 10,000 people. Tunnels have since been dug in an attempt to drain the lake (Volcanic Explosivity Index 5).
JUNE, 1783	Laki Fissure, a rift volcano in Iceland, spewed forth 3.6 cubic miles (15 km³) of basalt lava and sulfur-rich gases over seven months, causing extensive crop failure. The resulting famine killed 10,000 people—around 20 percent of Iceland's population (Volcanic Explosivity Index 4).
MAY, 1919	A sudden eruption of Kelut released lake waters, forming three major lahars, killing 5,000 people (Volcanic Explosivity Index 4).
DECEMBER, 1631	Mt Vesuvius erupted after a dormancy of 130 years. A summit explosion, followed by mud and lava flows, destroyed several towns over a three-day period, killing around 4,000 people and causing 40,000 to flee to Naples (Volcanic Explosivity Index 4).
AUGUST, 79 CE	The eruption of Mt Vesuvius buried several Roman townships on its flanks, including Pompeii, beneath cinders, ash, and mud. This eruption killed over 3,000 people (Volcanic Explosivity Index 6).

Mt Etna, Sicily, 1500 BCE to Present

Mt Etna, Europe's largest volcano, is one of the most studied volcanoes in the world. It is also the volcano with the longest historic record of eruptions. Thousands of people live nearby, seemingly oblivious to its destructive potential.

ABOVE An eruption in 2001 sent lava flowing from the Monti Calcarazzi fissure on the southern flank of Mt Etna. The lava flow threatened the town of Nicolosi, which lies below the volcano.

RIGHT Mt Etna during an eruption at night. Red-hot lava fragments can be seen falling to the ground around the vent, building up a spatter cone. The trail of white lights is car headlights as they venture away from the danger of the volcano.

Mt Etna has a more than usually complex geological history. It was born as a shield volcano at least 300,000 years ago, being built up by lava escaping from an extensional rift or fault in the ancient sea floor. Flow after flow of basaltic lava poured out, until the broad shield rose out of the water and reached a height of about 9,500 feet (2,900 m) above sea level.

Then, about 100,000 to 150,000 years ago, eruptive conditions changed, perhaps because of Mt Etna's proximity to the subduction zone where the African Plate is being pushed northward beneath the Eurasian Plate. More viscous andesitic magma from the melting plate was responsible for building the upper 1,200 feet (400 m) of the volcano. During this phase a number of more-explosive vents eventually coalesced to form a stratovolcano.

Today it is the largest volcano in Europe, with a base measuring about 36 by 24 miles (60 by 40 km). There are frequent periods of activity at the summit, and major eruptions from new vents occur on its flanks about every one to 20 years. Something in the order of 100 cinder cones dot the surface of Mt Etna as a result of this flank activity.

The people of Sicily do not generally regard Mt Etna as being particularly dangerous, and thousands live on its slopes and in the surrounding areas. Its fertile volcanic soils are perfect for agriculture, and numerous vineyards, olive groves, and orchards have been established on the mountain's flanks. Catania, Sicily's largest city (with a population over one million), also lies on the lower slopes of the volcano. Mt Etna can, however, be very destructive.

Etna's destructive past

Highly explosive eruptions occurred in 122 BCE and in 1500 BCE, the first historically recorded eruption. In 1500 BCE, the eastern flank of the mountain collapsed catastrophically in an enormous landslide. This event, recorded by historian Diodore of Sicily, would have looked quite similar to the Mt St Helens eruption of 1980. A scar in the side of the volcano

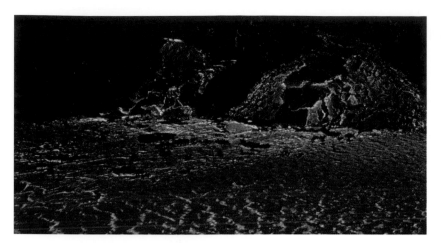

ABOVE Lava flows down the surface of Mt Etna during an eruption that continued over a 24-day period during 2002. The lighter red areas are the hottest; the darker red areas are cooler and reveal the first stages of a skin being formed on top of the molten lava flow.

ABOVE RIGHT The triangular-shaped island of Sicily at the foot of Italy is clearly seen from space. The enormous circular outline of Mt Etna dominates the island and a smoke plume can be seen rising from the volcano's summit.

remains, and is known as Valle del Bove (Valley of the Oxen). The Romans were also witness to eruptions, as recorded by the poet Virgil (70 BCE–19 CE):

The port capacious, and secure from wind,
Is to the foot of thund'ring Etna joined.
By turns a pitchy cloud she rolls on high:
By turns hot embers from her entrails fly,
And flakes of mounting flames, that lick the sky.
Oft from her bowels massy rocks are thrown,
And shivered by the force come piece-meal down.
Oft liquid lakes of burning sulphur flow,
Fed from the fiery springs that boil below.

One of the most dramatic eruptions of Mt Etna was that of 1669. On March 11, a 7-mile (12-km) fissure opened on the south flank of the volcano. Activity slowly moved down the flank, with the biggest vent opening up near the town of Nicolosi. Powerful explosions began to build a cinder cone

(now known as Mt Rossi); they were accompanied by voluminous outpourings of lava. Part of the town of Nicolosi and surrounding villages were quickly destroyed, though most of the villagers had already left their homes because of earthquakes in the two months prior to the eruption.

Lava flowed down the volcano's flank in two main branches, overwhelming numerous hamlets, villages, and towns in its path. Refugees fled ahead of its advancing front to Catania and were housed there. In early April, the lava reached the city wall on the western side of Catania and began piling up against it. The flows were initially deflected to the south, along the wall and began filling the city's harbor. Lava kept building behind the city walls, however. Eventually, on April 30, the pressure grew too strong and a section of the wall collapsed, allowing lava to enter the city. It destroyed monasteries and other buildings around the church of San Nicolò l'Arena.

Residents rallied and quickly built walls across the major roads leading down to the lower part of the city in an attempt to stop the flows. Although much destruction ensued in the upper part of the city, the strategy worked and more widespread damage was avoided. The eruption finally ceased on June 11.

Interestingly, there is another part to the story about the 1669 eruption. When the residents of Catania attempted to build a lava diversion much higher upstream to protect their city, they were prevented from doing so by armed residents of Paterno. They claimed a successful diversion to save Catania would help destroy Paterno. Whether this often-quoted tale was true or not, a law was enacted prohibiting the artificial diversion of lava; it was only repealed in 1983. The eruption of 1669 was the last to affect Catania, and it appears that the local population now has the false impression that eruptions like that of 1669 will not occur again. They generally refer to Mt Etna as a "good volcano."

The most destructive eruption of the twentieth century began on November 2, 1929. Explosions and

FACTS AND FIGURES	
DATE	Numerous eruptions have occurred since 1500 BCE
LOCATION	Catania, Sicily, Italy
DEATH TOLL	Less than 100 recorded
DAMAGE	Partial destruction of Catania in 1669
VOLCANIC EXPLOSIVITY INDEX	1 to 3 (5 in 1500 BCE and 122 BCE)
ERUPTION TYPE	Hawaiian/Strombolian to Plinian (in 122 BCE)
COLUMN HEIGHT	16 miles (26 km) in 122 BCE
MATERIAL EJECTED	In 1669, ¼ cubic mile (1 km³) of lava erupted; in 122 BCE, ¼ cubic mile (1 km³) of tephra was ejected
COMMENTS	The main cause of death during all the historic eruptions was due to ballistic impacts from small explosions

plumes were seen near the volcano's summit before activity began to move down the eastern flank. As fissures opened at progressively lower levels, activity at the higher level would cease. On November 4, the lowermost fissure opened and lava began pouring into a ravine above the town of Mascali. The following day, Mascali's 2,000 inhabitants were evacuated in an orderly manner. The lava flow, traveling at less than 1/3 mile per hour (3 to 5 m per minute), advanced slowly through the entire town, consuming buildings and cultivated land.

By the morning of November 7, the destruction of Mascali was complete. The town's cathedral was the last building to be consumed. On November 9, lava flows cut the main state railway line for eastern Sicily, and by the 11th, the flow, traveling more slowly now, began consuming houses on the outskirts of Carrabba. Movement continued to slow, and the eruption finally stopped on November 20. No one was killed during this one, and residents of Mascali had time to save household goods and even roof tiles.

Future eruptions

The volcano continues to be active and the most recent eruptions have been quite explosive. The Catania Section of the Istituto Nazionale di Geofisica e Vulcanologia (INGV) has sophisticated monitoring systems on the volcano to detect any sign of an impending eruption and track, in real time, subsurface movements of magma. In this way civil protection authorities can be given warning of an eruption days or even months in advance. Micro-earthquakes indicate that, since 1994, magma has

been rising from a chamber 4 to 9 miles (6–15 km) beneath the volcano and is filling a shallower chamber 2 to 3 miles (3–5 km) below the surface. The build-up in pressure in the shallow storage area appears to have triggered the eruptions that took place in 2001 and 2002. Volcanologists are therefore worried that this explosive pattern of behavior is likely to continue.

According to Dr Domenico Patanè of INGV: "The volcano is erupting more frequently now than during the previous three centuries, and magma output rate is increasing. At present, there is no reason to hypothesize that this trend will invert in the near future. Therefore, in the future, flank eruptions must be expected to occur at intervals ranging from one to three years, and some of them might be much more voluminous and probably explosive than in the past."

ABOVE A painting by William Hamilton in 1776 of Mt Etna and Nicolosi shows the rebuilt town which was nearly destroyed in a dramatic eruption from the volcano's southern flank a century prior, in 1669. Lava flows advanced on the city, breaching its walls and filling the harbor.

BELOW A scientist wearing a full thermal suit for protection from the intense heat prepares to measure lava temperature and collect samples of rock and gas from the flanks of Mt Etna.

Mt Vesuvius, Italy, 217 BCE to Present

Mt Vesuvius, situated near the city of Naples in Italy, is potentially the most dangerous volcano on Earth. Most famous for destroying Pompeii in Roman times, it has been erupting frequently throughout history.

The more severe Vesuvius eruptions occurred in 217 BCE, 79 CE, 203, 472, 512, 787, 968, 991, 999, 1007, 1036, 1631, 1660, 1682, 1694, 1698, 1707, 1737, 1760, 1767, 1779, 1794, 1822, 1834, 1839, 1850, 1855, 1861, 1872, 1906, and 1944. It is quite apparent that it is due for another explosive eruption anytime about now. Furthermore, the longer it takes to do so, the more explosive the impending eruption is likely to be.

Vesuvius is considered to be so deadly because the population in its immediate vicinity has grown to over three million, with some 600,000 people living within the immediate area of the cone or "red zone." The red zone is the area that would be destroyed in an eruption with a volcanic explosivity index of 4 (an order of magnitude smaller than the Mt St Helens eruption of 1980, which killed only 57 people because of its relatively isolated location.)

The catastrophic eruption that buried the towns of Herculaneum, Stabiae, and Pompeii beneath layers of cinders, ash, and mud occurred in 79 CE. About 2,000 people died in Pompeii alone. Just as people were gathering a few precious belongings, resigned to leave due to falling ash piling up against their homes, a deadly pyroclastic flow, or dense cloud of hot ash and gas, surged down the mountainside. People and animals were burned and asphyxiated where they stood, and those who went back inside were quickly suffocated by poisonous volcanic fumes. Following the surge, ash continued to fall, burying and perfectly preserving the people in their death positions. The fishing village of Herculaneum, which was much closer to the crater, was buried under 75 feet (23 m) of ash and mudflows. The abandoned towns lay buried and forgotten until their rediscovery in the sixteenth century.

The 79 CE eruption of Vesuvius was the first in history to be described in detail—in two letters by Pliny the Younger. He was accompanying his uncle, Pliny the Elder, a Roman naval commander and historian, on a scientific voyage that quickly developed into a rescue mission.

ABOVE A human skeleton that was preserved in the ash which fell from the 79 CE eruption of Mt Vesuvius. This was the eruption that buried the towns of Pompeii, Herculaneum, and Stabiae.

Pliny's eyewitness account

"My uncle Pliny ordered his ships to sail across the bay to rescue the people not only in Rectina's house, but in all the houses and towns that lined the shore near Mount Vesuvius. He hurried toward the danger that people were already running from. As he sailed, he dictated notes about what he observed to a scribe, who wrote them down. My uncle Pliny sailed so close to the mountains that the hot cinders from the volcano fell onto the ships. Besides the cinders, there were also big chunks of burning rock. The ships were in danger from the rocks, by the sudden retreat of the sea from the area caused by the volcano, and from the huge boulders that were rolling down the mountain. He thought about turning back, and the pilot of the ship he was on thought that was a good

idea. But my uncle said, 'Fortune favors the brave.' He ordered the pilot to steer toward Stabiae, which is the port of the city of Pompeii. Stabiae is about 10 miles [16 km] away from Mount Vesuvius."

Pliny then goes on to describe vividly how: "Broad flames shone out in several places from Mount Vesuvius, which the darkness of the night contributed to render still brighter and clearer."

As the catastrophic ashfalls that were burying the town of Stabiae worsened, Pliny and his crew had to make their escape, "… having pillows tied upon their heads with napkins; and this was their whole defense against the storm of stones that fell round them." Unfortunately, as they were returning to the shore to try to set sail, "… flames surged out of the volcano, and with them came a strong smell of sulfur. Everyone began to run, but my uncle had not taken two steps when he was overcome by the sulfur fumes and died."

The term "Plinian" is now used by volcanologists to describe explosive volcanic eruptions of this type—those that generate a high-altitude eruption column and blanket large areas with ash—based on Pliny's original description: "The cloud appeared to come out of the top of a mountain that was a long way away. The best way to describe it is to say that it looked like a pine tree. It shot straight up like a very tall trunk. At the top of the trunk, the cloud spread out like branches. Parts of the cloud were very bright, and parts were quite dark. The different colors were caused by the amount of cinders in the different parts of it."

ABOVE An engraving captures the terror of people fleeing Pompeii as they tried to avoid the deadly volcanic projectiles during its destruction in 79 CE. Most people were burned or asphyxiated by the pyroclastic surges of incandescent gas and the ash which buried the town.

ABOVE Vesuvius forms a vibrant backdrop to the city of Naples. Its next eruption may threaten the lives of its 1 million inhabitants.

BELOW A fresco depicting a prostitute and patron. Artwork such as this adorned homes and public buildings in Pompeii.

FAR RIGHT This eighteenth-century painting of Vesuvius erupting by Michael Wutky (1739–1822) captures the fury, essence, and drama of a night-time volcanic eruption. This painting now hangs in the Louvre Museum in Paris.

Another deadly eruption in 1631

Life went on, and over the centuries new towns grew around those buried and forgotten. New villages, farms, and vineyards pushed their way up the volcano's fertile flanks, ignoring its rumblings and occasional outbursts. Then in 1631, the area was devastated by another catastrophic explosion. About 4,000 people perished this time, as had the Romans a millennium and a half before them, asphyxiated and buried by pyroclastic surges of ash, pumice, and incandescent gas. It only took a few minutes for these destructive clouds to roll down the volcano's flanks and out over the sea.

Vesuvius is a composite or stratovolcano. This type of volcano is formed as a result of viscous volatile-rich andesitic magma rising from the melting African Plate as it is pushed northward and beneath the Eurasian Plate. Mt Etna, in Sicily, and Mt Vesuvius are the two main active volcanoes along this convergent plate boundary.

The Naples area has been volcanically active for at least 40,000 years. Present-day Vesuvius is actually only a relatively small and new cone that is still building itself to fill the caldera of the much larger and older Somma volcano, which formed between 25,000 and 19,000 years ago. Mt Somma exploded and collapsed catastrophically about 18,300 years ago. This and later giant explosive eruptions of Vesuvius 16,000, 11,000, 8,000, 5,000, and 3,800 years ago have been determined through the dating of distinct widespread pumice layers around the volcano. That is, a major explosive event happens about once every 2,000 to 3,000 years. The 3,800-year-old Avellino eruption buried several Bronze Age settlements, preserving their huts, cooking utensils, livestock, and even footprints of the people and animals abandoning the villages. These villages were only discovered in 2001. How many others remain hidden with their stories still untold?

The future of Mt Vesuvius

An evacuation plan has been formulated for the red zone around Mt Vesuvius based on the extent of destruction caused by the 1631 eruption. Even so, scientists argue that this plan does not go far enough, as the eruptions occurring every 2,000 to 3,000 years may be significantly worse than that of 79 CE and affect a larger area, including present-day Naples. Because the region is one of the most densely populated in the world, the current plan requires at least two weeks' advance warning to be effective. It will take at least this time to move the people out by car, bus, train, and ferry. The Vesuvius Observatory in Naples, with extensive networks of instruments recording the volcano's every movement, must provide sufficient advance warning.

People still live on and around the volcano despite the Italian government's efforts to discourage this: the summit of Vesuvius was declared a national park in 1995; illegal constructions are continually being demolished; and the government is offering financial incentives to families who are willing to move away from the volcano.

FACTS AND FIGURES

DATE	August 24, 79 CE
LOCATION	Bay of Naples, Italy
DEATH TOLL	3,360
DAMAGE	Herculaneum, Stabiae, and Pompeii destroyed
VOLCANIC EXPLOSIVITY INDEX	6
ERUPTION TYPE	Plinian/Ultra Plinian
COLUMN HEIGHT	20 miles (32 km)
MATERIAL EJECTED	1 cubic mile (4 km³)
COMMENTS	Duration of eruption: 19 hours

Krakatau, Sunda Strait, Indonesia, 1883

In 1883 the island of Krakatoa (now known as Krakatau), off the west coast of Java, was the scene of one of the world's most spectacular natural disasters. More than 36,000 people died in the volcanic eruption and resulting tsunami. Ash from the eruption circled the planet and lowered global temperatures.

RIGHT An 1888 lithograph shows billowing clouds of ash pouring forth from Krakatau on May 27, 1883, during the early stages of its eruptive phase. It culminated in the main eruption event in August, which destroyed most of this island.

BELOW An engraving shows a view of Krakatau before its massive eruption in 1883. The conical shape is typical of explosive volcanoes. The Indonesian archipelago is home to dozens of volcanoes of this type, with at least 100 of them being active at any given time.

The volcano lies in the Indonesian archipelago, one of the world's most tectonically violent areas. The risks to the people living there from volcanic eruptions, earthquakes, and tsunamis are higher than anywhere else on Earth.

Indonesia is an arc-shaped chain of some 130 closely spaced active volcanoes formed by the relentless downward-thrusting of the Indo-Australian Plate beneath the Eurasian Plate. Some of the largest volcanic eruptions of all time have occurred along this chain. Tambora, in the Lesser Sunda Islands, erupted in 1815 with a colossal explosion (Volcanic Explosivity Index of 7), ejecting some 19 cubic miles (80 km^3) of material, and killing 92,000 people. Then in 1883, Krakatau, in the Sunda Strait, erupted, killing 36,400 people.

Eyewitness accounts tell of continuous ominous rumblings from Krakatau, increasing in intensity during August 26 and culminating on the following morning in a series of deafening blasts. The resultant eruption columns spewed upward, darkening the sky from 11:00 a.m. until the morning of August 28.

Collapse of the eruption columns generated searing pyroclastic flows and a continuous rain of pumice and ash over a wide area.

Tsunami waves generated by the blasts radiated outward, wreaking havoc and destruction on the nearby islands and on the coastal lowlands of Java and Sumatra on either side of the Sunda Strait. A total of 165 villages were wiped out without a trace and a further 132 were significantly damaged by the tsunami.

Effects of the giant eruption

The five enormous explosions that took place on the morning of August 27 were the loudest sounds in recorded history. They were heard as far away as Rodriguez Island near Mauritius, a distance of 2,885 miles (4,650 km). The airwaves from these blasts traveled seven times around the world.

Black clouds of hot ash and gas, surging outward from the collapsing eruption columns, obliterated all life on the nearby islands. Interestingly, the flows appear to have been able to travel across the water by

ABOVE The original volcano consisted of three remnant islands, which the blast stripped bare. Anak Krakatau is just a tiny part of the remaining southern remnant of the original volcano's island, Rakata.

BELOW A map of Sunda Strait shows the original volcano, the remnant islands, and flooding from the tsunami caused by the eruption. The locator inset also shows Tambora, history's biggest volcanic eruption, in 1815.

riding on a cushion of steam created by their intense heat evaporating the sea surface. They remained hot enough to cause burn-related fatalities on Sumatra, some 25 miles (40 km) away. Mrs Beyerinck, wife of the Dutch Controller, described what happened in Ketimbang, Sumatra, that morning:

"Suddenly, it became pitch dark. The last thing I saw was the ash being pushed up through the cracks in the floorboards, like a fountain. I turned to my husband and heard him say in despair, 'Where is the knife? I will cut all our wrists and then we shall be released from our suffering sooner.'

"The knife could not be found. I felt a heavy pressure, throwing me to the ground. Then it seemed as if all the air was being sucked away and I could not breathe. I felt people rolling over me ... No sound came from my husband or children.

"I remember thinking, I want to go outside, but I could not straighten my back. I tottered, doubled up, to the door. I forced myself through the opening. I tripped and fell. I realized the ash was hot and I tried to protect my face with my hands. The hot bite of the pumice pricked like needles. Without thinking, I walked hopefully forward. Had I been in my right mind, I would have understood what a dangerous thing it was to plunge into the hellish darkness ...

"I noticed for the first time that skin was hanging off everywhere, thick and moist from the ash stuck to it. Thinking it must be dirty, I wanted to pull bits of skin off, but that was still more painful ... I did not know I had been burnt."

Farther away, the heat had dissipated. Crews on the ship *Loudon*, located about 37 miles (60 km) north of Krakatau, and the *W.H. Besse*, about 50 miles (80 km) east, were shaken but unharmed when struck by hurricane-force winds, heavy tephra, and the strong smell of sulfur.

The effects of such a large volcanic explosion were felt globally. Ash from the eruption column traveled as far as Singapore, 520 miles (837 km) to the north, the Cocos Islands, 716 miles (1,152 km) to the south-west, and fell on ships 3,767 miles (6,062 km) to the west. Rafts of floating pumice, thick enough in places to carry people, clogged the Sunda Strait and drifted around the ocean for years afterwards.

Minute particles of ash circled the equator in 13 days, causing exotic green or blue halos around the sun and moon. Three months after the eruption, its aerosol-sized products had spread to higher latitudes, causing vivid red sunsets, which continued for about three years. Global temperatures fell by as much as 2.2°F (1.2°C) in the year following the eruption and did not return to normal until 1888.

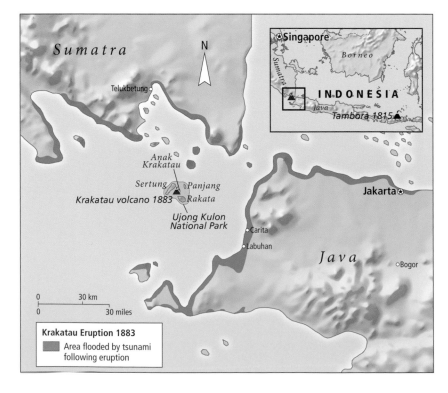

Krakatau Eruption 1883
Area flooded by tsunami following eruption

THE CHILD OF KRAKATAU

On December 29, 1927, a number of anglers from Java noticed plumes of steam and debris shooting from the sea. They were witnessing the birth of Anak Krakatau, the "child of Krakatau." Since then, a cone has emerged from the sea, built up from layers of ash deposits and andesitic lava flows. Since the 1950s, it has continued to grow at an average rate of 5 inches (13 cm) per week; in 2006 it was over 980 feet (298 m) high. Anak still has quite a long way to grow before reaching the height of its Krakatau parent, which stood at 2,720 feet (830 m) above sea level.

RIGHT A 1927 photo shows the start of a new volcano as Anak Krakatau begins its rise from sea; much of this eruption occurred under water.

Waves generated by the blasts reached heights of 130 feet (40 m) and heaved blocks of coral over half a ton (600 kg) in weight onto the shore. The tsunamis were recorded on tidal gauges 7,270 miles (11,700 km) away in the English Channel.

Captain Lindemann, of the passenger ship *Loudon*, which was moored in Lampong Bay near the village of Telok Betong, managed to pull out to sea as the first of several tsunami waves arrived:

"Suddenly we saw a gigantic wave of prodigious height advancing toward the seashore with considerable speed. Immediately, the crew … managed to set sail in face of the imminent danger; the ship had just enough time to meet with the wave from the front. The ship met the wave head on and the *Loudon* was lifted up with a dizzying rapidity and made a formidable leap …

"The ship rode at a high angle over the crest of the wave and down the other side. The wave continued on its journey toward land, and the benumbed crew watched as the sea in a single sweeping motion consumed the town. There, where an instant before had lain the town of Telok Betong, nothing remained but the open sea."

Had the crew not been so quick-thinking, their fate could have well been the same as that of the other ships caught in Lampong Bay. One of those, the steamship *Berouw*, was carried well over a mile (1.6 km) inland and dropped on a hill 30 feet (10 m) high; the entire crew of 28 was killed. The wreckage can still be seen there today.

Krakatau's volcanic cycle of fury

According to ancient Javanese royal scriptures, Krakatau erupted violently in 416 CE, destroying the original 6,500-foot (1,980-m) volcano. Its rim was marked by jagged island remnants. Between about 1680 and 1883, the volcano rebuilt itself into the island of Krakatau. The 1883 eruption blew several cubic miles off the summit, leaving only ocean. Two-thirds of the original island had vanished, believed collapsed into Krakatau's submarine caldera, which had been emptied by the powerful eruption. All that remained were three small islands—Rakata, Panjang, and Sertung—marking the edge of the submarine caldera. As in 416 CE, the volcanic cycle was again complete, with Krakatau's fury all spent.

FACTS AND FIGURES

DATE	August 26, 1883
LOCATION	Sunda Strait, Java, Indonesia
DEATH TOLL	36,400
DAMAGE	Ash covered 300,000 square miles (800,000 km²)
VOLCANIC EXPLOSIVITY INDEX	6
ERUPTION TYPE	Plinian/Ultra Plinian
COLUMN HEIGHT	22 miles (36 km)
MATERIAL EJECTED	4⅓ cubic miles (8 km³)
COMMENTS	Also caused tsunamis 130 feet (40 m) high

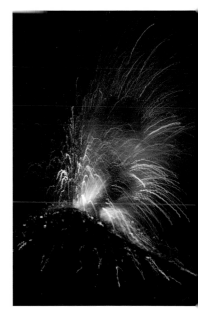

ABOVE The spectacular nature of a volcanic eruption is best witnessed at night. Here Anak Krakatau ejects streams of glowing lava and debris into the atmosphere. It has frequently erupted, usually every year, since its re-emergence in 1927.

La Soufrière, St Vincent Island, 1902

The 1902 eruption of the volcano La Soufrière killed some 1,600 people on St Vincent Island. The tragedy would have been far worse had not so many islanders heeded the warnings given by their volcano.

RIGHT The massive reddish purple cloud that MacDonald saw advancing toward his house on May 6, 1902, would have looked very much like this one, which was captured on film during the 1997 eruption on nearby Montserrat.

I n April 1901, it appeared to islander F.W. Griffith that earthquakes were becoming more noticeable than usual at Kingstown, St Vincent's main settlement. He suspected trouble was brewing, as had happened 90 years earlier, in April 1812, when his grandfather witnessed an eruption and described it in his diary. The rumblings increased and by May 1902 nearly everyone had evacuated the leeward (west) side of the island. Those on the windward (east) side, however, stayed put, assuming that the trade winds would be strong enough to carry volcanic debris away from them. This proved to be a tragic error of judgment.

Watching the eruption

Mr MacDonald witnessed the eruption from his estate at Richmond Vale, where he had a clear view of La Soufrière (French for "sulfur mine"). According to his meticulous notes, eruptions began on May 6 at 2:40 p.m. with an outburst of steam from the crater. Explosions continued throughout the night at two-hourly intervals and became increasingly frequent. By 10:30 a.m. on the following morning, the eruption was continuous, with a steam column rising to seven or eight times the height of the mountain, accompanied by tremendous roaring and a spectacular lightning display. He could see large stones falling from ascending clouds to windward.

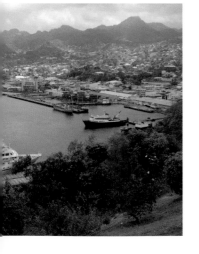

ABOVE A modern-day view of the town and countryside around Kingstown, the main town on the south coast of St Vincent. Though La Soufrière is on the northern end of the island, it was threatened by massive eruption in 1902.

FACTS AND FIGURES

DATE	May 6, 1902
LOCATION	St Vincent Island, Caribbean
DEATH TOLL	1,600
DAMAGE	US$200 million (in 2000 dollars)
VOLCANIC EXPLOSIVITY INDEX	4
ERUPTION TYPE	Vulcanian/Plinian
COLUMN HEIGHT	At least 6 miles (10 km)
MATERIAL EJECTED	9/100 cubic miles (0.38 km³)
COMMENTS	Duration of eruption: 13 days

Just before 2:00 p.m., Mr MacDonald recorded that a "terrific huge reddish and purplish cloud" was advancing toward his house. He managed to escape in a boat that he had in readiness for just this sort of situation. The boat was hit by "a great many rocks," but MacDonald survived.

This same pyroclastic flow killed 1,350 people on the windward side of the island, the trade winds being no match for the flow's force. People there died of asphyxiation or burns. Within a few minutes, the pyroclastic flow had stripped about one-third of the island bare of vegetation, leaving all of the affected areas a uniform dull gray.

Wise choices saved more lives

In total, 1,600 people perished in the eruption of La Soufrière. This compares well with the 29,000 lives lost during the simultaneous eruption of Pelée on the

nearby island of Martinique. Both volcanoes erupted with the same explosive force. More people died on Martinique partly because it was more densely populated than St Vincent, but mainly because the people of Martinique largely ignored the pre-eruption warning signs.

Almost all the people who survived the erupting volcano on St Vincent sought protection in cellars. This was recorded by E. O. Hovey in *National Geographic Magazine*, in December, 1902: "The most striking example of such protection was at Orange Hill, on the windward coast, two and one-half miles north of Georgetown where 132 persons were saved unharmed in an empty rum cellar … The only openings into the cellar were a door and two windows on the side opposite the crater, and these were provided with heavy wooden shutters which were kept closed during the fury of the eruption … The manager

of the estate, Alexander McKenzie, with his wife and a son, remained in the manor house, scarcely a hundred yards from the cellar, and were killed during the eruption, apparently by asphyxiation. The house had large windows, the glass of which was shattered by the projectiles from the volcano, permitting free entry to the deadly dust-laden steam and air."

Living with the volcano

La Soufrière is still a highly active volcano, along with all its companions that together form the string of islands that make up the Lesser Antilles. It erupted again explosively in 1979, but the people there were successfully evacuated with no fatalities. La Soufrière will continue to pose a threat, and those living in its shadow must be prepared for an explosive eruption about once every century.

Mt Pelée, St Pierre, Martinique, 1902

A prisoner in the jail at St Pierre, Martinique, was one of the few survivors of the eruption of Mt Pelée. He escaped the burning, choking cloud that incinerated the city within minutes. Tragedy could have been averted had warning signs been heeded; instead, political interest ruled the day.

The prisoner, 25-year-old Louis-Auguste Cyparis, was in solitary confinement in a small enclosed cell. He reported that while waiting for breakfast on May 8, 1902 he had been overcome by an intense blast of hot air and ash entering his cell through the small grated opening above the door. He held his breath, experiencing intense pain. After a while, the heat subsided. He was severely burned, but managed to survive for four days before being found by people exploring the ruins of St Pierre.

Cyparis survived because his windowless cell protected him from the full force of the volcanic blast. He was pardoned, and went on to join the Barnum and Bailey Circus, traveling the world and recounting his survival story to amazed crowds.

Volcanic jewels in the sea

Martinique is one of the many islands of the Antilles that lie in a great arc, like a giant necklace stretching across the Caribbean Sea from Cuba to Venezuela. These island jewels are all active volcanoes lining the eastern edge of the Caribbean Plate. They are being built from rising magma created by the melting of the westward-moving North American Plate as it plunges beneath the Caribbean Plate.

The great loss of life could have been averted had the warning signs of an impending volcanic eruption been heeded. What happened to St Pierre is a story all people in leadership roles can learn from.

The people of picturesque St Pierre, nestled at the base of Mt Pelée, never had any reason to fear the volcano. Its slopes were covered with tropical forest and the lake within its verdant crater was a popular place with the locals for outings. It had only rumbled once before: a long time ago, in 1851, when people awoke to find their houses lightly dusted with ash. From about mid-1901, however, the situation began to deteriorate.

Chronicle of a deadly eruption

May 1901: A picnic party to the summit crater of Mt Pelée notices a small, sulfurous jet of steam rising from one side of the crater lake scalding the surrounding vegetation.

BELOW Taken in May, 1902, 18 hours after the catastrophic eruption of Mt Pelée, this photograph shows destroyed ships lying half-sunk in the harbor in front of the ruined city of St Pierre, Martinique. Seen from the harbor, the still-smoking volcano forms a grim background to this scene of utter destruction.

LEFT Cloaked in verdant green vegetation, Mt Pelée today seems pleasantly tranquil. This scene does not hint at the horrific destruction that visited the town in 1902. It was the first eruption in over 50 years, and the volcano didn't erupt again until 1929. There has been very little volcanic activity since then. Scientists have determined that Pelée has erupted at least 30 times in the past 5,000 years, including 1792 and 1851, for which there are historic records.

April 2, 1902: Professor Landes finds some new steam fumeroles in the headwaters of a river near the crater—a sign of increasing sub-surface heat.

April 23: Mrs Prentiss, wife of the American Consul, writes about three slight tremors that rocked the house, rattling dishes on the shelves.

April 25: Smoke and steam are seen rising from the summit crater.

May 2: Ashes fall on St Pierre, giving the city a strange European wintry appearance.

May 3: The normally clear Blanche River becomes muddy and hot. That evening residents report that "flames accompanied by rumbling noises lighted the night."

May 4: Hot cinders continue to fall on the city. Many birds die of asphyxiation.

May 5: A mudflow sweeps down the Blanche River, reaching the sea. The Guerin Sugar Factory at the river's mouth is swept away, killing an estimated 150 people. The sea rises, covering the seafront of St Pierre, reaching the nearest houses. People panic and run for the hills, but the sea retreats again.

May 6: La Soufrière, on neighboring St Vincent Island, erupts. The people of St Pierre hope that this will "drain away hot gases from under Mt Pelée," but such hope is short-lived. Mt Pelée does not comply, instead exploding back into life. Trees break beneath blankets of ash and cattle die. Some people pack

VOLCANIC VERSUS POLITICAL PRESSURE

An election was scheduled for May 10, 1902, and it was important to the politicians that everyone remain in St Pierre so they could vote. The French Governor, Louis Mouttet, attempted to stop the general panic caused by the volcanic disturbances by declaring that the danger would not increase. Later, in order to stem a mass exodus, he sent a detachment of soldiers to set up roadblocks and prevent his officials and other government workers from leaving the city. The editor of Martinique's newspaper, *Les Colonies*, also a supporter of several candidates in the coming election, wrote for the May 7 edition, "We confess that we cannot understand the panic. Where would one be better off than at St Pierre?" The article concluded with an enigmatic quote from an interview with the well-respected Professor Landes, "Montagne Pelée represents no more danger to the inhabitants of St Pierre than does Vesuvius to those of Naples." That day, the Governor and his wife traveled to St Pierre to personally reassure the populace. They never left, and the election was never held.

RIGHT The sky was filled with red-hot cinders during the May 1902 eruption of Mt Pelée. It spewed out heated, poisonous gases that seared the lungs of those in the destroyed town of St Pierre, the largest on the island of Martinique.

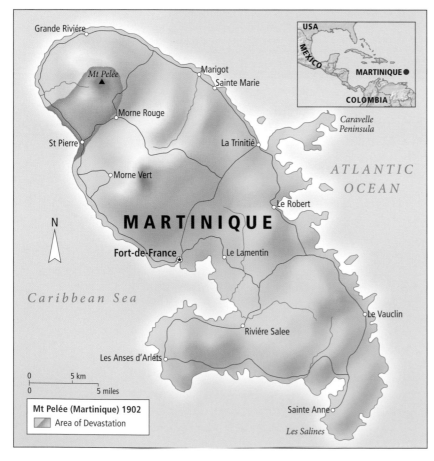

BELOW A map of the Caribbean island of Martinique, shows the location of Mt Pelée and the town of St Pierre. The area of devastation caused by the volcano is also indicated.

FACTS AND FIGURES

DATE	May 8, 1902
LOCATION	St Pierre, Martinique, Antilles
DEATH TOLL	29,000
DAMAGE	US$1 billion (2000 value)
VOLCANIC EXPLOSIVITY INDEX	4
ERUPTION TYPE	Vulcanian/Plinian
COLUMN HEIGHT	4 miles (6.5 km)
MATERIAL EJECTED	⅛ cubic mile (0.5 km³)
COMMENTS	The main cause of death: incineration or asphyxiation from the blast; the city of St Pierre was completely destroyed within three minutes.

their possessions and depart to neighboring villages on foot or by steamer to Port de France.

May 7: "Detonations like artillery" continue all day and are heard as far north as St Thomas and Barbados. A message received in St Lucia from the cable operator in St Pierre reads, "Red hot stones are falling here: don't know how long I can hold out." Later, all lines of communication with Martinique are severed. Italian captain Marino Leboffe pulls up anchor to leave port, even though his ship, the *Orsolina*, is only half loaded with its scheduled cargo. Amid threats of arrest by the St Pierre port officials, he states, "I know nothing about Mt Pelée, but if Vesuvius were looking the way your volcano looks this morning, I'd get out of Naples!"

May 8: At 7:45 a.m. a major eruption commences with four loud explosions. Pressure building in the volcano finally blasts out a plug of solidified magma blocking its throat. An eruption column rises from the mountain top followed by a blast from a vent in its side. The dense cloud of ash, hot gases, and superheated steam incinerates the entire city of 29,000 inhabitants in less than three minutes.

An eyewitness account from a ship at anchor

Assistant Purser Thompson witnessed the eruption from a Canadian passenger ship, the *Roraima*, which lay at anchor in St Pierre harbor; it was one of the ships emblazoned by the volcano's fury. He reports:

"I saw St Pierre destroyed. The city was blotted out by one great flash of fire. Of eighteen vessels lying in the road, only the British steamship *Roddam* escaped and she lost more than half of those on board. It was a dying crew that took her out … There was a tremendous explosion about 7:45. The mountain was blown to pieces. There was no warning. The side of the volcano was ripped out and there was hurled straight towards us a solid wall of

LEFT Ships sit at anchor in the harbor at St Pierre before the massive eruption. Scuba divers today visit the shallow waters to dive the many shipwrecks.

BELOW Not a building was left standing in St Pierre after the explosive eruption of Mt Pelée. It killed 29,000 people within the space of a few minutes; just two people in the town survived, plus a handful of others who were on boats during the eruption.

flame. It sounded like a thousand cannons. The wave of fire was on us and over us like a flash of lightning. It was like a hurricane of fire. I saw it strike the cable steamship *Grappler* broadside on and capsize her. From end to end she burst into flames and then sank. The fire rolled in mass, straight down upon St Pierre. The town vanished before our eyes.

"Wherever the mass of fire struck, the sea boiled and sent up vast columns of steam. The sea was torn into huge whirlpools which swirled under the *Roraima* and pulled her down on her beam end with the suction. The fire wave swept off the masts and smokestacks as if cut by a knife.

"Captain Muggah was overcome by the flames. He fell unconscious from the bridge and overboard. The blast of fire from the volcano lasted only a few minutes. It shriveled and set fire to everything it touched … The blazing rum set fire to the *Roraima* several times.

"Before the volcano burst, the landings of St Pierre were covered with people. After the explosion, not one living soul was seen on the land."

Eventually, visiting anglers and others rebuilt the town of St Pierre, and a small museum was dedicated to the disaster. But when the volcano erupted on September 10, 1929, and ash once again fell on the streets—this time there was no hesitation. The people evacuated immediately.

Heimaey Island, Iceland, 1973

The Icelandic island of Heimaey gained some fiery real estate in 1973. A towering new volcano, Eldfell, grew from the ground as lava engulfed part of the main town. The eruption began as a fiery curtain of lava that poured out over the land. It continued for five ash-filled months.

On January 23, 1973, a 1,300-foot (400-m) long fissure opened up in a grassy field on the outskirts of the pretty fishing port of Vestmannaeyjar on Heimaey Island. Resident Hjalmar Gudnason was one of the first to notice it, while walking home from his nightshift: "At first I thought a house was burning. But then I saw that it was beyond the edge of town and it was throwing sparks. I knew then that it was an eruption." He went quickly to raise the alarm, and within six hours most of the town's 5,300 residents had been evacuated to the Icelandic mainland by boat, plane, and helicopter. Only volunteers and members of Iceland's state civil defense organization remained.

Spatters of semi-molten lava falling to the ground quickly built up into ramparts around the edges of the crack. The edifice grew quickly and began engulfing outlying farmsteads and houses. Lava bombs thrown from the vent smashed windows and set some homes alight; ash rained down. Teams of volunteers fought back, nailing sheets of iron to windows and shoveling ash from the roofs of houses to prevent them from collapsing. Saving people's possessions was a priority: houses

that could not be saved were stripped of all their furniture and fittings before they caught fire and the residents' 800 cars were evacuated by ship.

Within two weeks, a 700-foot (210-m) tall volcano, named Eldfell, stood at the town's edge, disgorging flows of clinkery rubble, slowly demolishing block after block of houses. Lava was flowing into the sea, threatening to block the harbor.

FACTS AND FIGURES

DATE	January 23 to June 26, 1973
LOCATION	Vestmannaeyjar, Heimaey Island, Iceland
DEATH TOLL	1
DAMAGE	400 houses destroyed
VOLCANIC EXPLOSIVITY INDEX	3
ERUPTION TYPE	Vulcanian
COLUMN HEIGHT	5½ miles (9 km)
MATERIAL EJECTED	$^6/_{100}$ cubic miles (0.25 km³) of material erupted
COMMENTS	Duration of eruption: five months

BELOW Eldfell volcano as it erupted behind the houses of Vestmannaeyjar. A continuous rain of cinders and ash from the volcano slowly buried the houses and streets in the evacuated town. A number of houses were later dug out of the deep ash.

The people fight the volcano

On scientific advice, it was decided that the volcano could be fought using seawater. So thousands of gallons of seawater were pumped onto the front of the lava flows in an attempt to freeze the lava's advance. Amazingly, it worked!

The flows slowed down and began to thicken as lava piled up behind the hardened front. Water pipes and massive pumps were moved onto the flow itself. Amid the steam, workers directed water uphill to "freeze" a larger area of lava. Occasionally a deluge

A VOLCANIC ISLAND

Iceland sits astride the Mid-Atlantic Spreading Ridge. As the Atlantic Ocean slowly spreads, at about the speed a fingernail grows, the island is torn apart. As the pieces separate, basaltic lava from Earth's mantle wells up into the gap. Iceland came into existence only in the last 5,000 to 6,000 years. It emerged from the sea in much the same way as Surtsey Island, which appeared when a new rift opened in the ocean floor to the southwest of Iceland on November 14, 1963. Rift volcanoes generate voluminous amounts of lava but are rarely explosive.

of liquid lava would burst through the cooled lava exterior and pumps would be rushed to the spot to quell it. Lava entering the harbor was hosed with water cannons mounted on ships.

The fight would have been lost eventually, but the eruption finally stopped on June 26, 1973, five months after it had started. The campaign's delaying efforts saved Vestmannaeyjar and its harbor. The lava had destroyed one-third of the town's 1,200 houses, one fishing plant, and stopped 175 yards (160 m) short of closing the harbor. Only one person died, a fisherman overcome by toxic gases that had seeped into the basement of a house.

Coming home

Most of the residents have since returned to Vestmannaeyjar, the town has been cleared of ash and lava, and the fields are green again. Only the massive gray bulk of Eldfell looms in the background as a reminder of the people's fight. Today the volcano is an important tourist attraction, and its destructive energy is now being harnessed for the benefit of the town. Holes have been drilled into the volcano, into which water is pumped, generating steam to heat the buildings.

ABOVE The 1973 Heimaey eruption in progress. The red lines in the night sky show the trajectories of glowing volcanic bombs as they are violently blown from the volcano.

ABOVE Ash rises high into the sky following the 1973 eruption. Deep ashfalls bury the entrance to the island's cemetery.

Mt St Helens, USA, 1980

"Vancouver, Vancouver, this is the big one!" Such were the last words spoken by geologist David Johnston of the United States Geological Survey as he radioed his headquarters in Vancouver, a city on the Columbia River in Washington. His transmission came in at 8:32 a.m. on May 18, 1980.

ABOVE By May 23, 1980, the devastation was apparent—this ash-covered truck, and pine trees felled and stripped bare of their branches, were caught in the massive blast and pyroclastic surge from the 1980 eruption. Enough trees to build 300 new homes were destroyed.

RIGHT A Plinian column of hot ash and gas erupted skyward from the summit on May 18, 1980. The eruption was triggered by an earthquake which set off landslides on the mountain's northern face. The eruption sent masses of material surging into the valleys and rivers below.

Johnston, who was camped on Coldwater Ridge just a few miles from Mt St Helens, was witnessing the collapse of the entire north face of the volcano. The swollen and over-steepened north flank had been destabilized by a magnitude 5.1 earthquake. The giant avalanche, traveling at over 150 miles per hour (240 km/h), was immediately followed, and rapidly overtaken, by a massive explosion of escaping gas moving at about 300 miles per hour (480 km/h). Moments later, his transmission was cut. Johnston was completely obliterated by a menacing gray wall of hot gas, ash, rocks, and other debris.

Photographers face death

Geologists Keith and Dorothy Stoffel were in a light aircraft directly above the summit when the eruption took place. Running out of film probably saved their lives. They managed to dive steeply and swing their plane to the south, narrowly missing the rapidly rising vertical cloud column.

Elsewhere on the mountain, photographer Robert Landsberg also realized that there was no escape from the ground-hugging cloud flattening everything in its path. He continued to shoot the approaching cloud until the last moment. Just before the end, he quickly rewound the film into its canister in the camera, returned the camera to its case, placed it in his backpack together with his wallet, and then lay

on top to protect the film. Seventeen days later, the backpack and his body were recovered from the ash. Landsberg's heroic actions have left a photographic legacy so that future generations of geologists can study volcanic processes first hand.

Mt St Helens volcano in Washington State forms part of the Cascade Mountain Range. It is one of a chain of hundreds of active volcanoes that line the edge of the Pacific Plate. This circum-Pacific belt of intense volcanic and earthquake activity is aptly named the Pacific "Ring of Fire." Its volcanoes are constantly being destroyed and rebuilt by rising molten material called magma that is generated as the oceanic plates of the Pacific are forced beneath the continental North American Plate.

Youngest, most active major volcano

Louwala-Clough or smoking peak was the name for Mt St Helens used by the Native Americans of the Pacific Northwest. Its visible cone has grown up entirely within the last 2,200 years and the oldest volcanic ash deposits date back only 40,000 years, which makes it the youngest major volcano in the Cascade Range. As such, Mt St Helens' slopes are smooth and symmetrical compared with its older, glacially scarred, neighbors—Mt Rainier, Mt Adams, and Mt Hood. The volcano was intermittently active in the mid-nineteenth century between 1831 and 1857, but apart from some minor steam explosions, it had not been a hazard since that time.

As such, to the twentieth-century residents of the area, Mt St Helens was a serene, graceful, conical peak known as the Mt Fuji of America. Visitors came by the thousands, lured by the mountain's reputation for tranquility, to fish and swim in the clear water lakes, or hike and camp on its forested slopes. However, all of that changed in May 1980 when the upper 1,300 feet (397 m) of the mountain's summit was blown away, leaving a 1$\frac{1}{5}$ mile by 2 mile (2 km by 3.5 km) horseshoe-shaped crater.

The sudden pressure release due to the avalanche allowed the superheated groundwater around the volcano's magma chamber to flash to steam. It blasted laterally northward, out of the avalanche scar, and formed a hot, destructive, ground-hugging, gas-charged mixture of ash and debris. Immediately north of the volcano a once-productive coniferous

FACTS AND FIGURES	
DATE	May 18, 1980
LOCATION	Washington State, USA
DEATH TOLL	57
DAMAGE	Destruction included 153,000 acres (61,965 ha) of forest, 200 houses and cabins, 185 miles (300 km) of highways and roads, 15 miles (24 km) of railroad, and 27 bridges
VOLCANIC EXPLOSIVITY INDEX	5
ERUPTION TYPE	Plinian
COLUMN HEIGHT	16 miles (26 km)
MATERIAL EJECTED	$\frac{1}{3}$ cubic miles (1.2 km³)
COMMENTS	Duration of eruption: 9 hours

the volcano's magma chamber allowed the magma to de-gas violently—within minutes an enormous column of gas and ash rose vertically upwards from the summit (a Plinian eruption column), accompanied by huge lightning bolts. The column rose some 12 miles (19 km) into the atmosphere, where it began to flatten into a huge umbrella shape. At the same time, the column began to collapse on itself, raining down huge quantities of ash, pumice, and rocks. The whole eruption lasted for nine hours.

Additional hazards

The enormous black cloud of airborne ash released into the air was pushed eastward by fast-moving, high-level winds between 18,000 and 40,000 feet (5,490 and 12,200 m), and it was dispersed over central and eastern Washington State, Idaho, and Montana. It blocked the morning sun and turned day into night, grounding planes, and stopping trains and trucks. People had to wear masks to avoid choking while clearing the ash from their streets, roofs, drains, gardens, and crops. Fine airborne ash took three days to cross the United States and just 17 days to circle the entire globe.

Particularly destructive were the mudflows, caused by the avalanche dumping huge volumes of ash, snow, and ice into the headwaters of the rivers draining the volcano. The water-logged debris started to move down river valleys such as the Toutle and

ABOVE A minor eruption takes place inside the recently formed crater of Mt St Helens.

BELOW The eruption left Spirit Lake, where Harry Truman died, choked with mud and surrounded by acres of flattened trees.

forest was pyrolyzed (turned to charcoal). Giant trees were uprooted and laid down like matchsticks, while at greater distances trees were stripped of their leaves, branches, and bark. In six minutes, the blast leveled an area of prime forest in excess of 50 square miles (130 km^2). In total, some 3,700 million cubic yards (4,847 million m^3) of material was blown out by the explosion. Simultaneously, the unloading of

Cowlitz and continued for days after the eruption. Nine highway bridges, miles of highways, and many buildings were destroyed by these flows.

In total, 57 people lost their lives in the Mt St Helens eruption. These were mainly scientists working on the mountain, campers, a few logging company workers and a local man, Harry Truman, who consistently refused to leave his home, a lodge on Spirit Lake. The death toll could have been much higher had it not been for the actions of the US Geological Survey in placing a 20-mile (32-km) cordon around the volcano and restricting access to essential personnel.

As well as the human toll, it is estimated that the eruption also killed numerous animals: 5,000 black-tailed deer, 1,500 elk, 200 black bears plus unknown numbers of mountain lions, bobcats, rodents, birds, fish, and insects. Complete rebuilding of the local food chain may take over 40 years.

Current status
Mt St Helens has since become the most studied volcano in the world. Johnston Ridge Observatory (named after the geologist who lost his life there) has been set up by the US Geological Survey on a ridge 5 miles (8 km) from the volcano. The status of the mountain is constantly being monitored via a network of video cameras, seismometers, and other instruments covering its slopes.

Minute earthquakes signify the movement of new magma beneath the base of the volcano. Rising and swelling of the mountain indicates pressure buildup in the subterranean magma chambers, and herald the possibility of another eruption. These changes in the shape of the volcano are being mapped daily with inch-scale accuracy by Earth-orbiting satellites. With such monitoring systems in place, hazards can be assessed well before they pose a threat to life.

Future of Mt St Helens
Mt St Helens is on Alert Level 2 (Aviation Code: Orange). A new lava dome is slowly growing within the volcano's crater, accompanied by minor seismic activity and emissions of ash, steam, and volcanic gases. It has been at this level since it was downgraded from Alert Level 3 (Code: Red) in October 2004. Other Cascade Range volcanoes are Mt Baker, Glacier Peak, Mt Rainier, and Mt Adams in Washington state; Mt Hood, Mt Jefferson, Three Sisters, Newberry, and Crater Lake in Oregon; and Medicine Lake, Mt Shasta, and Lassen Peak in California. All are at normal levels of background seismic activity and pose no immediate threat.

Since the initial 1980 eruption occurred, viscous de-gassed magma in the central conduit of the volcano has been pushed from below into a lava

dome. This edifice has been partially destroyed by several smaller explosive eruptions but has continued to grow. It now stands at 1,363 feet (416 m) above the 1980 crater floor. It represents only 4 percent by volume of the original volcanic summit. However, if growth were to continue at the rates that had been recorded during the 1980s, it would take some 200 years to rebuild the volcanic cone.

It is not clear whether Mt St Helens will blow itself apart in another major eruption anytime in the near future or much later, after it has had the opportunity to build a majestic new cone.

ABOVE A mudslide covered this road after the eruption. Mudflows, made from mixtures of ash and melted snow, surged down valleys, destroying bridges and roads around the volcano.

BELOW Scientists must use specialized equipment to continually measure and monitor the new lava dome growing within the crater of Mt St Helens.

Nevado del Ruiz, Colombia, 1985

Of all the stories of volcanic eruptions, that of Nevado del Ruiz is perhaps one of the most tragic. It tells of a modern-day disaster that could have been avoided if attention had been paid to the warnings issued by scientists.

RIGHT Eruption clouds eject from the volcano in 1989. The heat from volcanic ash can melt the snow and ice that cover the peak, making Nevado del Ruiz, and others like it, a source of dangerous mudflows.

BELOW RIGHT Aftermath of an eruption: the ruined town of Armero as seen from the air in 1985. It was devastated by the mudflows created by the eruption of the volcano.

It was well known that Nevado del Ruiz, Colombia's tallest stratovolcano, was active. It had erupted numerous times before and, though not considered violent, the volcano posed a special danger: at 17,680 feet (5,389 m), Nevado's summit is always covered with snow and ice. As such, whenever the volcano erupts, its hot pyroclastic flows melt the snowpack, forming deadly mudflows known as lahars.

Following an eruption in 1593, lahars killed 636 people. Again, in 1845, the volcano sent mudflows into its surrounding valleys, destroying the towns of Armero and Ambalema, killing 2,000. The new town of Armero was constructed on top of the 1845 mudflows and by 1985 had grown into a vibrant town of 27,000 residents.

The 1985 eruption

During 1985, Nevado del Ruiz again began to show signs of life, with increased seismic activity, fumarolic activity, and sulfur emissions from its summit crater. This prompted the establishment of a network of seismographs in July 1985. A small eruption on September 11 resulted in ashfalls in the city of Manizales and minor lahars. By October 7, a volcanic risk map had been prepared for the area. It showed that Armero and other towns lay in the path of dangerous mudflows that would likely occur in the event of an eruption. Unfortunately, government officials considered this map to be "too alarming," which caused delays in its distribution.

By November 10, continuous earth tremors were occurring beneath the volcano. On November 13, a small steam eruption at 3:05 p.m. sent ash into the atmosphere that fell on Armero as a muddy rain about two hours later. Warnings were telephoned to Armero and the emergency sirens were sounded, but then fate took an unfortunate turn. Alarmed residents were calmed by messages from the mayor over the radio, and again at 8:00 p.m. by the local priest with a bullhorn, telling them not to worry about the ash, to close their doors and go to sleep.

At 9:08 p.m., the main eruption began. For about 30 minutes, pyroclastic flows blasted across the volcano's icy summit. About 10 percent of the summit icepack melted, sending torrents of mud down the side of the volcano. At 11:25 p.m., the first lahar hit the town of Armero. Geology student José Luis Restrepo, in town at the time, reported: "Suddenly, I heard bangs, and looking towards the rear of the hotel I saw something like foam, coming down out of the darkness … It was a wall of mud approaching the hotel, and sure enough, it crashed against the rear of the hotel and started crushing

FACTS AND FIGURES	
DATE	November 13, 1985
LOCATION	Armero, Colombia
DEATH TOLL	27,000
DAMAGE	Town of Armero destroyed
VOLCANIC EXPLOSIVITY INDEX	3
ERUPTION TYPE	Vulcanian
COLUMN HEIGHT	19 miles (31 km)
MATERIAL EJECTED	$\frac{1}{100}$ cubic miles (0.05 km³)
COMMENTS	Duration of eruption: 30 minutes

walls … the entire building was destroyed and broken into pieces. Since the building was made of cement, I thought that it would resist, but the boulder-filled mud was coming in such an overwhelming way, like a wall of tractors, razing the city, razing everything."

Within minutes, the town was destroyed and most of its inhabitants had been killed. The rescue teams arrived by noon the next day, but all that was remaining of Armero was the cemetery and a few of the houses on the highest ground.

Lessons from the tragedy

Government authorities are often slow to act, but it is up to every person living in a high-risk area to know what to do during an eruption event. As a direct result of this disaster, the US Geological Survey and the US Office of Foreign Disaster Assistance assembled a team of volcano specialists and equipment that can be quickly dispatched to an awakening volcano when needed.

Before the 1994 eruption of Rabaul in Papua New Guinea, the inhabitants attended numerous talks on their emergency plan, and were in the process of orderly evacuation well before an official alert was given. As a result, no lives were lost.

Mt Pinatubo, Philippines, 1991

Dormant for more than four centuries, volcanic Mt Pinatubo came back to life with a vengeance in 1991. The June eruptions killed hundreds of people, forced the evacuation of tens of thousands, wrecked the local economy, and disturbed Earth's atmosphere for years after its violent outpouring.

ABOVE A satellite photo of Mt Pinatubo taken in 2001 shows the rising waters in the new lake that had formed within its summit caldera. It had to be partly drained that year as it became a potential flooding risk.

Mt Pinatubo is a stratovolcano on the island of Luzon, 55 miles (90 km) northwest of the Philippines' capital city, Manila. On April 2, 1991, it awoke from 450 years of quiescence with a steam blast. Scientists reacted quickly, and within days had installed stations on the mountain to monitor seismic activity. On June 3, Pinatubo started ejecting ash, and a Level 3 alert warning was issued on June 5. By June 7, the number of micro-earthquakes had increased dramatically. The quakes were becoming shallower, indicating that magma was moving toward the surface.

The main eruption began at 6:00 a.m. on June 9, with an eight-hour ejection of steam and ash accompanied by minor pyroclastic flows. That afternoon the Philippine authorities increased the alert warning to Alert Level 5 (Aviation Code: Red), indicating an eruption in progress, and a 12 mile

(20-km) exclusion zone was established around the volcano; 25,000 people were evacuated. During the following days, a series of vertical eruption columns blew out of the volcano's summit. Collapsing under their own weight, they filled rivers and streams radiating from the volcano with cascading pyroclastic flows. On June 10, Clark Air Base evacuated its 18,000 personnel and their families. Then on June 12, the danger radius was extended to 19 miles (30 km) from the volcano, resulting in the evacuation of a total of 58,000 people.

Pinatubo blows its top

Three days later, on June 15, two explosions occurred at dawn, accompanied by incandescent pyroclastic flows. The flows reached up to about 4 miles (6 km) away from the center of activity. At 10:27 a.m., the violent climactic eruption ejected a 22-mile (35-km) high ash column; it was followed by five similarly strong explosions from 11:17 a.m. to 1:42 p.m. There were 19 eruptions that day, and almost 500 feet (150 m) of the volcano's summit was blasted away, creating a new summit caldera 1½ miles (2.5 km) across. After June 16, Pinatubo's activities began to wane. Then, from July to October 1992, a lava dome began to grow in the new caldera as fresh magma rose from beneath Pinatubo.

The eruption coincided with the arrival of tropical storm Yunya. Ash in the air mixed with the storm's water vapor to precipitate an extremely heavy "black ash" rain across almost the entire island of Luzon. The dense, wet mixture built up quickly, causing the roofs of many buildings to collapse on the people within. This sent the death toll much higher than it should have been.

The Philippine Institute of Volcanology and Seismology and the US Geological Survey managed the eruption well. They gave timely and accurate recognition of the warning signs. Evacuation of poor farming communities, dependent on their land for their existence, is a difficult exercise, as the case of Popocatépetl, Mexico, proved. To the indigenous Aeta, living on Pinatubo's densely rainforested slopes, the mountain is a sacred home to their god and departed spirits. Many farmers refused to go or tried to return immediately. The evacuation plan, however, saved at least 5,000 lives.

ABOVE One of the 19 eruptions that occurred on June 15, 1991, as seen from inside the almost-deserted Clark Air Base. This eruption has a classic mushroom-topped Plinian-style column that rose 22 miles (35 km) into the air.

LEFT During the 1991 eruption, indigenous Aeta people carrying their belongings fled their village of Botolan, which was in the danger zone on Mt Pinatubo's densely rainforested slopes.

ABOVE A girl carries her sister along a road that had become buried in volcanic ash following the eruption. Residents were evacuated from the area around the volcano, so relatively few lives were lost, but the loss of infrastructure had a huge impact on the economy.

Counting the cost

The long-term economic and humanitarian costs to the Philippines of Mt Pinatubo's eruption have been devastating. Property damage and economic loss amounted to nearly US$500 million. Dams, irrigation systems, power stations, transmission lines, roads, bridges, and schools were either destroyed or very badly damaged.

With no farms, shops, and factories, more than 650,000 people were forced out of work. About 80,000 people were left homeless, and roughly 20,000 Aeta highlanders were completely displaced from the slopes of the volcano by the eruption. Many will never return to the mountain.

The central Luzon area will possibly take several decades to recover physically. The bare ash deposits on the volcano's flanks are seasonally remobilized by monsoon and typhoon rains to form giant mudflows of volcanic materials known as lahars. Although most evacuees from the lowlands around the volcano have since returned home, many still face continuing threats from the lahars, which have already buried numerous towns and villages. These flows caused more destruction than the eruption.

In 2001, a further problem arose. A lake that had begun forming in the volcano's new summit caldera was rising by up to 30 feet (10 m) per year. The authorities, greatly concerned that the caldera walls could burst and flood the communities below with wet volcanic debris, had to construct a canal. Action was taken. About a quarter of the lake was drained into the nearby Maraunot River, relieving pressure on the upper caldera walls. The project was completed safely.

FACTS AND FIGURES

DATE	June 9 to 16, 1991
LOCATION	Luzon Island, Philippines
DEATH TOLL	722
DAMAGE	US$500 million property damage and economic loss; 1 million people displaced
VOLCANIC EXPLOSIVITY INDEX	6
ERUPTION TYPE	Plinian/Ultra Plinian
COLUMN HEIGHT	22 miles (35 km)
MATERIAL EJECTED	1 cubic mile (5 km³)
COMMENTS	Duration of eruption: 8 days

Global atmospheric impact

The eruption of Mt Pinatubo caused the greatest disturbance of the stratosphere since the eruption of Krakatau, Indonesia, in 1883. Suspended fine ash spread around Earth in two weeks, and within a year had covered the planet. This phenomenon caused global temperatures to fall by about 1°F (0.5°C) and is thought to have influenced such events as the 1993 floods along the Mississippi River and the drought in the Sahel region of Africa.

Pinatubo also ejected around 20 million tons (over 22 million tonnes) of sulfur dioxide into the atmosphere. The sulfur combined with atmospheric water and oxygen to form sulfuric acid, which fell as acid rain. Spectacular sunsets were witnessed around the globe for years following the eruption, and during 1992 and 1993 the ozone hole over Antarctica was much larger than normal.

Continuing dangers and the volcano's current status

Pinatubo is one of a chain of 22 active and over 200 dormant volcanoes running through the Philippines. The Philippines is a very seismically and volcanically active chain of islands which lie on a series of micro-plates that are being squeezed by converging oceanic plates on both sides.

On the eastern side of the island chain, the Philippine Plate is being pushed westward down the Philippine Trench, and on the western side the Eurasian Plate is being pushed into the Manila Trench. Melting of both these plates as they descend and heat up produces the magma that is rising to the surface to form the Philippines' volcanoes.

Mt Pinatubo has since 1991 been going through the usual volcanic cycle of explosive destruction and rebuilding. The largest eruption in the history of Pinatubo occurred over 35,000 years ago, destroying the ancestral cone, which may have risen as high as 7,550 feet (2,300 m) above sea level at that time.

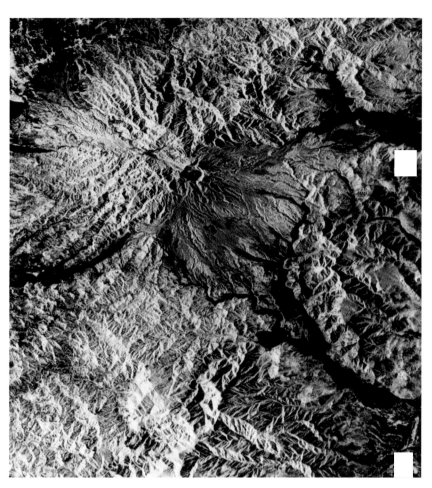

This eruption spread more than 320 feet (100 m) of ash and pyroclastic flow material around the edges of the volcano. It marked the birth of the modern volcanic cone. Remains of the ancestral volcano caldera are marked by several eroded volcanic plugs and vents surrounding the present-day cone. Present-day Pinatubo stands at 5,248 feet (1,600 m), which is only about two-thirds of its ancestral size.

ABOVE A composite satellite image of Mt Pinatubo in 1994 shows the landscape barely recovering from its eruption. Rougher ash deposited during the eruption appears red. Such images are used to identify the areas flooded by mudflows.

A PERILOUS ESCAPE AND A MYSTERY BABY

On June 24, 2001, the *Star Bulletin* in Honolulu, Hawaii, reported survivor Susan Kreifels' amazing story of her escape from the 1991 eruption of Mt Pinatubo in the Philippines:

"My Filipino assistant Virgilio Herrera and I were in Angeles, a city of 300,000 people outside Clark, when day turned into night and ash and small rocks started to pelt us. Although we couldn't see Pinatubo, we heard it booming and felt it shaking. Eerie orange flashes ignited the black skies. We didn't know what the volcano would do next. Our greatest fear was pyroclastic flows—gas, molten rock, and ash that could tumble down the mountainsides in excess of 100 miles per hour [160 km/h], incinerating everything in its path.

"We crammed his three children, wife, elderly mother, a nephew, and his eight-month pregnant sister into our small Mitsubishi, by then sputtering.

"Along the way we squeezed in an elderly woman who was barely able to plod through the ash. It was then that the crying baby was passed through my jammed window, a man's voice pleading from the darkness to take his child to safety. He disappeared before I could say anything."

Popocatépetl, Mexico, 1994 to Present

Mexican authorities are concerned about a major eruption of their most active volcano, Popocatépetl. It has erupted in the past, but now it would have the potential to affect the 30 million people living in the area surrounding the volcano, including the sprawling metropolis of its capital, Mexico City.

ABOVE The oldest villager of Xanizintla carries red flowers as a gift to Popocatépetl. People here believe these offerings will protect them from the volcano. On the feast day of St Gregory each year, residents climb the volcano, which rises more than 14,700 feet (4,500 m) above sea level, to present flowers and gifts, in a tradition dating back to the Spanish conquest of Mexico.

RIGHT The Popocatépetl volcano erupting on December 20, 2000, near the village of Cholula, one of 15 within the local area in the Mexican state of Puebla. The eruption caused small forest fires on its slopes. Thousands of residents were evacuated.

Popocatépetl is a beautifully symmetrical stratovolcano located 34 miles (55 km) southeast of Mexico City. It and the other volcanoes in Mexico's central volcanic belt are forming as a result of the Cocos Plate (part of the Pacific tectonic plate) being forced beneath the North American Plate. Popocatépetl has clearly been active in the past. Its Aztec name means "Smoking Mountain," and legends probably refer to its eruptions in 1347 and 1354. It is said that Popocatépetl hurled huge blocks of rock and ice at Xinantécatl in a fight over the love of Ixtaccíhuatl (which are both other nearby volcanoes).

The mountain is being intensively monitored, and authorities have an evacuation plan based on circular zones around the volcano. The area that is of the greatest danger from lava flows, pyroclastic flows, and mudflows is located within 12 miles (20 km) of the crater. The area of moderate danger extends up to a radius of 25 miles (40 km) from the crater and includes some larger centers of population. The outer zone, up to 50 miles (80 km) from the crater, is that which could be affected by extremely large eruptions. Within this zone lie cities such as Tlaxcala, Puebla, Cuautla, Cuernavaca, and Mexico City.

FACTS AND FIGURES	
DATE	1994 to present
LOCATION	Mexico City, Mexico
DEATH TOLL	5
DAMAGE	No significant damage
VOLCANIC EXPLOSIVITY INDEX	1 to 3
ERUPTION TYPE	Strombolian to Vulcanian
COLUMN HEIGHT	8 miles (13 km)
MATERIAL EJECTED	7/1000 cubic miles (0.028 km³)
COMMENTS	41,000 people evacuated in December 2000 and later allowed to return, when it was safe

The smoking mountain awakes

On December 21, 1994, Popocatépetl awoke from its dormancy after nearly 70 years of quiescence with a series of moderate explosions. Since then, ongoing eruptive activity has been interspersed with cycles of quiet dome-building within the crater followed by periods of explosive destruction, all leading up to a more explosive future eruption.

Although closed, on April 30, 1996, five climbers who ignored the warning notices were killed near the summit by a shower of incandescent bombs. On June 30, 1997, the largest ash emission during this episode occurred, with an eruption column rising 8 miles (13 km) above sea level during a 90-minute pulse. About two or three hours later, ash fell on towns around the volcano, including Mexico City. During December 2000, dome lavas began extruding at a faster rate, accompanied by increased seismic activity. Continuous tremors, some lasting 10 hours, were felt up to 9 miles (14 km) away. Pyroclastic flows began escaping from the crater.

Worried civil authorities defined a security radius of 8 miles (13 km) designed to include some of the most vulnerable towns. About 41,000 people were evacuated to emergency shelters; they were allowed to return to their homes after the danger passed.

THE SULFUR MINES OF POPOCATÉPETL

Members of the Tecuanipas tribe were the first to climb Popocatépetl, in 1289. The first European ascent of the mountain was an expedition led by Diego de Ordaz in 1519 to discover the source of its smoking plume. Two years later, the conquering Spanish had run out of gunpowder and a small party was sent to the mountain to find sulfur. The party leader, Francisco Montaño, was lowered several times 400 feet (120 m) into the crater in a makeshift basket to collect the bright yellow encrustations from around the fumarolic vents. Eighty pounds (36 kg) of sulfur was collected and the expedition was hailed a success.

Later, sulfur was mined using indigenous laborers until the end of the nineteenth century. It was dangerous work, made even more difficult by the high altitude and exposure. The miners would descend into the crater using ladders to reach the fumaroles. They carried the sulfur in baskets up to a point on the rim where it was sent down the mountainside in chutes to where a smelter had been set up on the volcano's flanks.

Merapi, Indonesia, 2006

Starting on May 13, 2006, Merapi was rocked by a series of spectacular eruptions and residents were ordered to evacuate potentially dangerous areas. Some completely ignored the order. Others complained of poor conditions and boredom at evacuation centers and, after a week or two, started to return to the volcano to resume their livelihoods. But the danger was far from over.

FAR RIGHT Merapi ejects hot lava, as seen from the village of Kemiri in the Yogyakarta province of Java on May 18, 2006. Despite the apparently subsiding activity, experts warned that the volcano remained highly dangerous.

BELOW Tens of thousands of residents were evacuated from the immediate danger zone around the volcano to wait in tented refugee camps. When the warnings were not followed by a significant eruption, many people became complacent and returned to their homes well before the alert level was lowered.

Merapi is an active volcano near Yogyakarta in central Java and part of the volcanic chain running the entire length of the Indonesian archipelago. It has erupted 68 times since 1548; in May 2006 it began building toward what threatened to be a major explosion event.

Dense vegetation covers the flanks of the volcano, but the top of the mountain is bare because ash continually falls there. A broad gouge funnels lava and ash flows from the top of Merapi down the south slopes of the volcano. Many farmers live in villages around the volcano as the volcanic ash makes rich soil for growing crops.

A dangerous place to live

Because of Merapi's violent past and its proximity to areas of high population density, it was designated a "decade volcano," as part of the International Decade for Natural Disaster Reduction (1990–2000) and it is the subject of close surveillance by the Volcanological Survey of Indonesia. Merapi has the unfortunate distinction of sending more deadly pyroclastic flows, or hot debris surges, down its flanks than any other volcano in the world due to collapse of its unstable summit lava dome. Of the 67 historic eruptions, 32 have had pyroclastic flows associated with them. Eleven of these eruptions resulted in fatalities.

A particularly devastating eruption, which killed 1,300 people, took place in 1930. Another, in 1976, killed 28 people and left 1,176 people homeless. In 1979, heavy rainfall turned lahar deposits into mudflows that surged 12 miles (20 km) down the flank of the volcano. Eighty people were killed. Again, in 1994, a dome collapse sent pyroclastic flows down the volcano's southern side, this time killing 43 people. Today, 50,000 people live on the dangerous southwest flank of the volcano, and the city of Yogyakarta lies only 22 miles (35 km) to the south.

Threat of a major blast

Early in April 2006, the volcano showed increasing seismicity, and a bulge was detected in its cone. By April 23, smoke plumes and numerous micro-earthquakes signaled subterranean movement of magma. Six hundred elderly residents and children were evacuated. On May 11, 17,000 people were evacuated from the area following a week of intermittent lava flows. On May 13 the alert status was raised to the highest level: Red Alert, and all residents were ordered off the mountain.

Volcanic activity had begun to calm by May 16, and villagers started to return to their villages to tend their livestock and crops. But then something unexpected occurred: on May 27, a magnitude 6.3 earthquake struck nearby, killing 6,200 people (see the earthquakes chapter). Microseismic activity jumped to three times its pre-quake level and Merapi became active again.

On June 1, Merapi sent 80 lava flows down its western slopes. The May 27 earthquake was blamed for the volcano's increased activity. Indonesian volcanologist Tri Yani said, "It is the first time that lava was seen flowing to the west." Scientists warned that the earthquake might have cracked the magma dome forming at the peak. It could collapse, spewing

FACTS AND FIGURES

DATE	May 13 to July 6, 2006
LOCATION	22 miles (35 km) north of Yogyakarta (population 500,000), Java, Indonesia
DEATH TOLL	2 (at at July 6, 2006)
DAMAGE	Damage from pyroclastic flows and ash to land, property, and forests on Merapi's flanks (July 2006)
VOLCANIC EXPLOSIVITY INDEX	1 to 2
ERUPTION TYPE	Strombolian to Vulcanian (as at July 2006)
COLUMN HEIGHT	0.8 miles (1.3 km) on June 1, 2006
MATERIAL EJECTED	Lava-dome volume 5 million cubic yards (4 million m³) June 2006
COMMENTS	The current eruptive phase began in 1987. The largest pre-2006 buildup event occurred in 1994.

ABOVE Farmers pick hot chilies covered with volcanic ash at a farm in Babadan, near Merapi, on May 18, 2006. Many of the local farmers ignored warning signs to tend to their crops or feed and water their livestock, remaining unconvinced the simmering volcano posed any danger.

out millions of cubic yards of volcanic rock and lava. On June 6, 11,000 people fled from Merapi as pyroclastic flows continually spilled down the volcano's upper slopes. Agung, a disaster relief official from Magelang district told the *TimesOnLine*, "It is no longer a mere call for the people to evacuate, they now *have to* evacuate. We are not taking any chances." By June 8, the volcano began spewing out massive clouds of ash. However, Merapi began to

settle and on June 12 the alert level was downgraded, meaning an eruption was no longer imminent. But it doesn't mean one will not occur in the near future.

The largest event prior to the 2006 buildup occurred in November 1994, when a lava dome collapse sent pyroclastic flows and surges 5 miles (7.5 km) from the summit and a plume 6 miles (10 km) high; 43 died and 6,000 were evacuated. Pyroclastic flows were the main cause of death.

Earthquakes

For many people, earthquakes are a commonplace occurrence; small tremors are felt on an almost daily basis in certain parts of the world—an imperceptible vibration in the ground causes the unnerving realization that Earth's crust, and everything on it, is not stable, but in constant motion. Many people in earthquake-prone regions live in resigned fear of the next big one.

Earthquakes result from sudden ruptures of Earth's crust. As the rigid crustal plates slowly move on top of the softer plastic mantle, they tend to build up stress—particularly around their edges, when those edges are forced against adjacent pieces of hard crust. Solid crust will crack rather than bend; such cracking to accommodate movement in the crust is called faulting. The energy released from the point of rupture, known as the earthquake focus, travels radially outward as earthquake waves. These destructive waves become weaker at greater distances from the focus. Earthquakes occurring beneath the ocean can also generate tsunamis.

Where do earthquakes occur?

Belts or zones of abundant and strong earthquake activity occur along the margins of tectonic plates, where the plates push or slide against each other. Around the edge of the Pacific Ocean, intense earthquake activity coincides with a belt of volcanoes known as the "Ring of Fire." Here, Pacific Ocean crust is being consumed (subducted) beneath the surrounding plates. Another belt of earthquake activity occurs along the major continental collision zone boundary marked by several mountain ranges—the Himalayas of Nepal and India, the Alps of Europe, the Zagros of Iran, the Sulaiman of Pakistan, and the Taurus Mountains of Turkey.

Styles of crustal faulting

There are three types of faulting of Earth's crust that generate earthquakes. Thrust faulting occurs when the the crust is under compression and cracks, allowing one piece to ride over the top of the other. This type of faulting is common around the Pacific margin and along continental collision zones, and is responsible for powerful earthquakes. Sudden crustal movements along enormous lengths of fault line, such as those that caused the Great Chilean Earthquake of 1960, are known as megathrusts.

Strike-slip faulting occurs where one plate slides horizontally against another with little or no vertical movement. Classic examples of this kind of movement are displayed by the San Andreas and North Anatolian faults. They generate large earthquakes such as those that occurred in San Francisco in 1906 and in Izmit, Turkey, in 1999.

Normal faulting occurs in areas where the crust is being stretched apart, such as along the mid-ocean spreading ridges. Classic examples are the East African Rift Valley and Iceland. Such faulting is associated with the upwelling of basaltic magma; it does not tend to generate powerful earthquakes.

Measuring earthquakes

There are many seismic observatories around the world dedicated to recording earthquakes. Early recording instruments or seismographs were no more than large weights suspended on a sensitive spring or pendulum, which remained static when the ground around them began to shake. The shaking was recorded as a wiggly line on graph paper turning on a revolving drum. By accurately measuring the arrival time of an earthquake at numerous locations, and triangulating that data, its point of origin on Earth's surface (the epicenter) can be accurately determined.

FAR LEFT Earthquake damage exposes interiors of apartments in a building in Mexico City, Mexico. On September 19, 1985, an earthquake registering 8.1 on the Richter scale hit central Mexico, causing damage to about 500 buildings in the city and killing over 8,000 people.

LEFT A satellite view of the southern tip of South America (Chile and Argentina). Along the western coastline is the Pacific margin, a continental collision zone that generates many earthquakes in the region.

PREVIOUS PAGES An aerial shot near Valencia, California reveals the damage on the I-5 caused by the Northridge earthquake on January 17, 1994. It occurred on a thrust fault, and though only moderate, there was exceptionally strong shaking. This resulted in several major freeways into Los Angeles collapsing or being damaged along with 11 major roads, creating gridlock traffic for commuters in the following days.

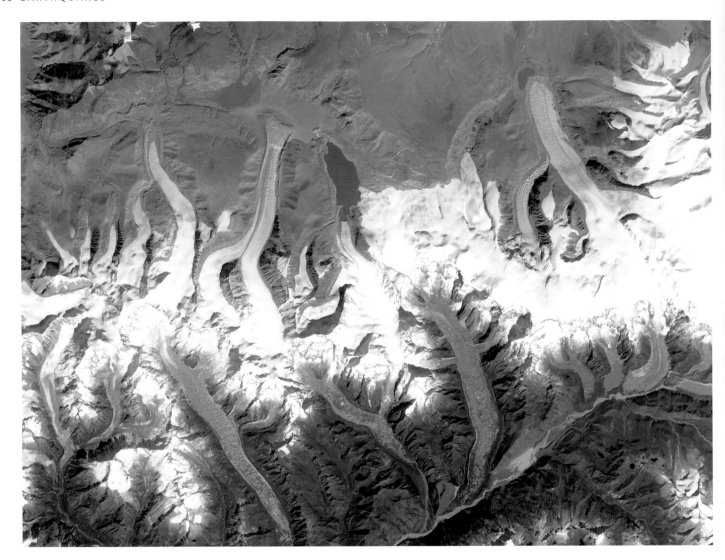

ABOVE A satellite view of the Himalayas in Bhutan reveals the extent of this vast continent-to-continent collision zone.

RIGHT An aerial view of the San Andreas Fault, a right-lateral strike-slip fault which is responsible for the numerous minor and major earthquakes that occur in California.

FAR RIGHT Thingvellir, Iceland, lies at the junction of two major tectonic plates, the North Atlantic Plate and the Eurasian Plate. It straddles the Mid-Atlantic Ridge, a normal fault, where crust is stretched apart. It is the site of many earthquakes, and the Meteorological Office monitors earthquake activity there.

MODIFIED MERCALLI INTENSITY SCALE

I People do not feel earth movement. **II** People at rest or in tall buildings may notice movement. **III** Many indoors feel movement. Hanging objects swing. Vibrations like a light truck. People outdoors may not feel anything. **IV** Most people indoors feel movement. Hanging objects swing. Dishes, windows, and doors rattle. Like vibrations from a heavy truck. A few people outdoors may feel movement. Parked cars rock. **V** Almost everyone feels movement; direction can be estimated. Sleeping people awakened. Doors swing. Pendulum clocks stop. Dishes break. Pictures move. Small, unstable objects move. Liquids are disturbed and may spill. **VI** Everyone feels movement. Many are frightened and run outdoors. People have difficulty walking. Objects fall from shelves. Pictures fall off walls. Windows, dishes, and glassware break. Furniture moves or overturns. Plaster in walls may crack. Small bells ring. Trees and bushes shake. Damage is slight in poorly built buildings. No structural damage. **VII** Difficulty standing; cars shake. Some furniture breaks. Chimneys, tiles, and plaster may fall from buildings. Damage slight in well-built buildings; considerable in poorly built buildings. Waves form on ponds. Water may become muddy. Large bells ring. **VIII** Difficulty steering cars. Houses not bolted down may shift on foundations. Tall structures, towers, and factory chimneys might twist and fall. Damage slight to moderate in well-built buildings; severe in poorly built structures. Branches break. Hillsides may crack if ground is wet. **IX** General panic. Considerable damage in well-built buildings. Houses not bolted down move off foundations. Underground pipes may break. Ground cracks. Reservoirs suffer serious damage. **X** Most buildings and foundations destroyed. Some bridges destroyed. Dams seriously damaged. Large landslides. Water thrown on the banks of canals, rivers, lakes. Ground cracks in large areas. Railroad tracks bent slightly. **XI** Most buildings collapse. Some bridges destroyed. Large cracks appear in the ground. Underground pipelines destroyed. Railroad tracks badly bent. **XII** Almost everything destroyed. Objects thrown into air. Lines of sight and level distorted. Ground moves in waves. (Adapted from US Federal Emergency Management Agency [FEMA] and Association of Bay Area Governments information.)

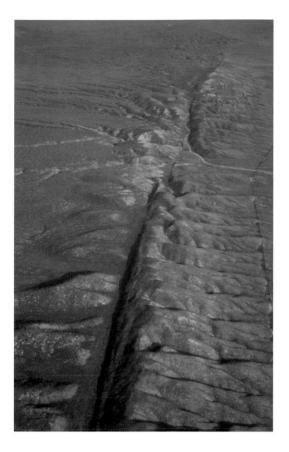

Quantifying the amount of energy released by an earthquake is achieved by measuring the amplitude of certain waves in its record or seismogram at various stations, taking into account the distance of the earthquake from the station. The magnitude of an earthquake is given using scales such as the Richter or the newer Moment scale. These measure earthquakes from those barely felt (less than 3.5) to the largest on record, which occurred in Valdivia, Chile in 1960 (Moment magnitude 9.5).

The Mercalli scale was designed to assign an intensity rating (which runs from I to XII) based on the severity of observed damage, rather than instrument readings. Intensity maps often appear as "bullseye" concentric zones of decreasing damage around the earthquake epicenter. Maps for some earthquakes, such as Mexico 1985, will also show isolated pockets of greater damage corresponding to areas of unconsolidated sediment that magnify the earthquake intensity. These maps are useful for town planning and for formulating building codes.

In the event of an earthquake

During a strong earthquake, many people's lives are going to depend on a number of simple but unpredictable factors, such as which city of the world it takes place in, and the time of day it occurs. Consider the effects of a severe earthquake under the following scenarios—each represents an increase in

TEN BIGGEST EARTHQUAKES BY MAGNITUDE

MAY, 1960	Magnitude 9.5 earthquake, generated by the longest fault rupture in recorded history, strikes Valdivia in southern Chile. The Pacific-wide tsunami was responsible for most of the 5,700 deaths (2,300 in Chile).
MARCH, 1964	Magnitude 9.2 "Good Friday" earthquake rocks Anchorage, Alaska, sending the suburb Turnagain Heights sliding into Cook Inlet. Shaking killed 15 out of a total of 125—the tsunami killed the rest.
DECEMBER, 2004	Magnitude 9.1 Sumatra–Andaman Islands earthquake spawned the infamous Indian Ocean tsunami responsible for widespread destruction and almost 300,000 deaths around the Indian Ocean.
NOVEMBER, 1952	Magnitude 9.0 earthquake off the coast of Russia's Kamchatka Peninsula generated a destructive Pacific-wide tsunami killing 2,000 people in the Northern Kuriles district and destroying the town of Severo–Kurilsk.
JANUARY, 1700	Slippage of the Cascadia subduction zone caused a 9.0 magnitude earthquake: the Washington State coastline sank 5 feet (1.5 m). A tsunami was recorded in Japanese and in Native American legends.
JANUARY, 1906	A 300-mile (500-km) segment of the Peru–Ecuador Trench ruptured, causing a magnitude 8.8 earthquake. The resulting tsunami killed between 500 and 1,500 people and reached Hawaii.
FEBRUARY, 1965	Subduction slippage in the Aleutian Trench near the lightly populated Rat Islands produced a magnitude 8.7 earthquake. A 35-foot (10.7-m) tsunami caused damage on Amchitka Island.
NOVEMBER, 1755	Catastrophic magnitude 8.7 earthquake and fire destroyed Lisbon, Portugal, and was felt throughout Europe. Survivors ran to the docks, only to be struck by a tsunami. A total of 100,000 people died.
MARCH, 2005	Magnitude 8.6 earthquake killed 290 people on the island of Nias, Northern Sumatra, Indonesia. Hundreds were trapped in collapsed buildings. Thousands of coastal dwellers fled but there was no tsunami.
MARCH, 1957	An earthquake of magnitude 8.6 occurred south of the Andreanof Islands, in the Aleutian Islands, Alaska. It triggered a Pacific-wide tsunami which caused damage in Hawaii. No lives were lost.

WHAT TO DO DURING AN EARTHQUAKE

Make sure that everyone is trained to act fast and automatically when the big one hits:

1. IF OUTSIDE Move quickly away from buildings and power lines and get into the open. If there is no open space, watch for falling masonry, tiles, and glass, and dodge them or get into or under a car. Entire building facades may collapse into the street, as occurred in the earthquake in Napier, New Zealand, in 1931.

2. IF INDOORS Do not try to run outside—you may be injured by falling glass, masonry, or awnings. Collapses of substandard buildings generally happen within seconds or, at most, minutes of a large earthquake, which is insufficient time to move to anywhere safer. Quickly drop to the floor and take cover under a sturdy piece of furniture such as a desk or table. Hold on to it tight and move with it. Remain there until the ground stops shaking. Stay clear of windows, fireplaces, stoves, and furniture that may topple over. In crowded areas, take immediate cover where you are. Stay calm and encourage others to do the same.

3. IF DRIVING Stop as soon as it is safe to do so, but not under trees, light posts, power lines, or signs. Stay inside the car. Keep clear of structures that may collapse, such as bridges, overpasses, and tunnels. Do not block the road with your vehicle, and if you have to abandon it, leave the keys in the ignition so that others can move it if necessary.

4. IF IN THE MOUNTAINS Watch out for falling rock, landslides, or avalanches that could be triggered by the earthquake. Get out of areas downstream from dams; ideally head uphill.

5. IF AT THE BEACH Be aware of the possibility of tsunamis generated by the earthquake and move quickly to higher ground, or as far as possible inland. A wave may hit within minutes.

6. AFTER THE EARTHQUAKE Assist others who may be injured. Check your home, and if it has been damaged, turn off the gas, electricity, and water at the main outlets. Fires due to leaking gas pipes or damaged electrical wiring often cause more damage than the earthquake itself, such as in Tokyo 1923 or San Francisco 1906. Extinguish any small fires quickly to stop them spreading. Do not use the telephone except in the case of emergency.

7. BEWARE OF AFTERSHOCKS Use extreme caution when entering buildings. Even if they look safe, there may be hidden damage. Buildings that have been damaged by the initial earthquake often collapse during aftershocks.

risk: inside a car parked on a flat open country road; relaxing in a single-story traditional Japanese wooden frame residential dwelling; working in a code-compliant well-engineered modern office building in downtown San Francisco; or sleeping in a multistory concrete and brick Soviet-style apartment block built to a minimum price using second-rate materials and ignoring local building codes.

Even in recent times, earthquake-proof building codes are ignored and construction is shoddy in poorly regulated countries. Such was found to be the case during recent earthquakes: Kashmir 2005, Iran 2003, Turkey 1999, and Armenia 1988. Many who were indoors during these earthquakes were killed within moments by building collapse. Earthquakes of similar magnitude in countries with strongly enforced building codes, such as Japan or the United States, kill relatively few people.

Earthquakes occur unexpectedly, but there are certain preparations that should be made by anyone in an earthquake-prone area. It is important to have a prearranged rendezvous point for friends and family as all communication lines may be damaged. A battery-powered flashlight and radio, and supplies of food and water are essential, as organized relief help may take days to arrive. A whistle on a chain around the neck can save your life if you are trapped by fallen debris—while it is only possible to shout for several hours, it is possible to blow on a whistle for several days. This simple, inexpensive purchase could save your life.

ABOVE People clear away debris in Sherman Oaks, California, after the Northridge earthquake in 1994. One of the worst-hit areas, it took this town 12 years to repair the infrastructure damage.

LEFT A damaged house sits precariously as earthquake aftershocks continue after a magnitude of 6.8 earthquake hit Nagaoka on October 23, 2004. This series of earthquakes rocked northern Japan, causing 35 deaths and 1,306 injuries. These traditional wooden buildings often remain intact, as wood flexes during shaking; they tend to leave their foundations if they are not anchored.

FAR LEFT, TOP A tricycle driver rides past destroyed houses in Kecamatan, Yogyakarta, after the devastating 2006 earthquake. As dawn broke over the Indonesian city, rescue workers searched for survivors of the 6.2 magnitude earthquake that killed at least 3,000 people. Whole villages were reduced to rubble.

Lisbon, Portugal, 1755

One of history's deadliest earthquakes, it resulted in the almost complete destruction of Portugal's capital city, Lisbon. About a third, or 90,000, of Lisbon's inhabitants were killed and a further 10,000 perished in neighboring Morocco. Lisbon was, at that time, the fourth-largest city in Europe.

It was reported that all of the city's finest and strongest stone buildings, such as the Santa Maria Cathedral, All Saints Hospital, numerous churches and even the brand-new Phoenix Opera House, were the first to fall. The Royal Palace was lost, together with its 70,000-volume royal library, as well as hundreds of works of art, including paintings by Titian, Rubens, and Correggio. The Royal Family themselves had a narrow escape; one of King Joseph's daughters had wanted to spend the All Saints' Day Catholic holiday in the countryside. The family had already attended a dawn Mass and left the city before the earthquake struck at 9:20 a.m. Survivors of the earthquake, the resulting tsunami, and the fire, struggled to escape to the outskirts of the city. Here, many were to stay for months in tents set up in the fields while their ruined city was being rebuilt.

James O'Hara managed to write to his sister about the disaster on November 12: "I sit down to relate to you the dreadful catastrophe that has befallen the once-flourishing city of Lisbon, now a scene of horror and desolation. On the first day of this month, at half past nine in the forenoon, a sudden earthquake shook its foundations, and laid it in ruins. At this fatal hour, the churches were crowded; and as their fall was momentary, and allowed no time for retreating, those who were in them were crushed to death.

"It is impossible to describe the affrighted looks of the inhabitants, flying various ways to avoid destruction. Numbers flocked to the river's side in hopes to save their lives by means of boats. The custom-house quay was imagined to be a place for safety; but unhappily it was soon inundated, and those who fled on it, only escaped from the falling city, to meet a watery grave. Fathers and mothers were seen seeking their children, and children searching for their parents."

The rebuilding of Lisbon

The King and Prime Minister Sebastião de Melo wasted no time in drawing up plans for the new city. With the assistance of the Portuguese Army, they conscripted able-bodied citizens from the tent cities to commence the clean-up effort. The remaining fires were extinguished, the dead were loaded onto barges and buried at sea, and rubble was cleared from the streets. Gallows were even set up to discourage looters who, it is said, were deliberately starting fires to create further confusion. Within a year, architects and engineers were already hard at work, constructing the new city of Lisbon with its grid of wide streets and earthquake-proof buildings built out of wood, the first of their kind.

FACTS AND FIGURES	
DATE	9:20 a.m., November 1, 1755
LOCATION	Epicenter in the Atlantic Ocean, 124 miles (200 km) from Cape St Vincent
DEATH TOLL	100,000
DAMAGE	City of Lisbon almost entirely destroyed by earthquake, tsunami, and fire; one-third of its population was killed
DURATION	10 minutes
MAGNITUDE	Richter scale 8.7
COMMENTS	The earthquake was felt throughout Europe and as far away as Finland and North Africa. It generated an Atlantic-wide tsunami.

BELOW This engraving by Laplante of the Fall of Lisbon in 1755 is from *Le Monde Illustre*. It records the horror as the majestic buildings of the capital and center of European commerce crumbled, while the harbor was lashed by a devastating tsunami that threw sailing ships around like corks. Meanwhile, a massive fire swept through the ruined city.

ENLIGHTENED VOLTAIRE WRITES

On November 24, 1755, the French philosopher Voltaire wrote a now-famous letter to Dr Theodore Tronchin about the Lisbon earthquake: "This is indeed a cruel piece of natural philosophy! We shall find it difficult to discover how the laws of movement operate in such fearful disasters in the best of all possible worlds—where a hundred thousand ants, our neighbours, are crushed in a second on our ant-heaps, half, dying undoubtedly in inexpressible agonies, beneath debris from which it was impossible to extricate them, families all over Europe reduced to beggary, and the fortunes of a hundred merchants—Swiss, like yourself—swallowed up in the ruins of Lisbon. What a game of chance human life is! What will the preachers say—especially if the Palace of the Inquisition is left standing! I flatter myself that those reverend fathers, the Inquisitors, will have been crushed just like other people. That ought to teach men not to persecute men: for, while a few sanctimonious humbugs are burning a few fanatics, the earth opens and swallows up all alike. I believe it is our mountains which save us from earthquakes."

ABOVE Lisbon today is a vibrant, high density city. The 1755 earthquake was a linchpin that turned the debate from disasters as acts of God to taking responsibility for future safety. The visionary king insisted on wide streets, realizing they would one day be narrow, and had the world's first earthquake-resistant wooden buildings constructed.

San Francisco, USA, 1906

On Friday, April 18, 1906, at 5:30 a.m., a 270-mile (434-km) segment of the San Andreas Fault suddenly gave way, releasing more than 150 years of pent-up energy. Any natural features and man-made structures crossing the fault were displaced by up to 20 feet (6 m) by a continuous rupture or tear in the ground surface that was visible for a distance of nearly 200 miles (320 km).

RIGHT Fires roar down the end of rubble-covered Sacramento Street, downtown San Francisco, while hapless residents stand by watching their city burn following the earthquake.

O n that fateful morning, residents in every city along the Californian seaboard, from Hollister to Fort Bragg, were jolted awake by the sound of crashing china, falling pictures, and plaster—and the roar of a magnitude 8.3 earthquake. A violent shaking lasted between 45 and 60 seconds, accompanied by streets moving in waves, behaving more like tides rolling in than solid ground.

Major destruction occurred in the city of San Francisco, and to the north in Santa Rosa, where the entire city center was leveled. To the south, San José and Stanford University were also badly hit.

Widespread panic ensued, as it was neither safe to remain indoors nor run into the streets. The walls of many buildings collapsed, showering the streets with bricks, tiles, and glass.

A major aftershock that followed at 8:14 a.m. caused further destruction and another outbreak of panic. Around the bay, areas of reclaimed swamp and other in-filled ground amplified the seismic waves, unleashing their most destructive force. Structures built on solid rock fared far better.

BELOW The city of San Francisco lies in ruins, still smouldering after the earthquake and subsequent fires. This scene is of Market Street, between Sacramento and Third Streets.

The city burns

Even as the tremors finally died away, fires were breaking out all around the center of San Francisco, fueled by ruptured gas mains. Some people were even setting fire to their own ruined homes. One US Army captain, Leonard Wildman, reported being told by a fireman that people were burning down their houses because their insurance only covered fire, not earthquake damage. The city fire department was powerless—the earthquake had also broken most of the water mains.

On April 18, Mayor Eugene Schmitz issued a proclamation to the people: "The Federal Troops, the members of the Regular Police Force and all Special Police Officers have been authorized by me to KILL any and all persons found engaged in Looting or in the Commission of Any Other Crime. I have directed all the Gas and Electric Lighting Co.'s not to turn on Gas or Electricity until I order them to do so. You may therefore expect the city to remain in darkness for an indefinite time. I request all citizens to remain at home from darkness until

daylight every night until order is restored. I WARN all Citizens of the danger of fire from Damaged or Destroyed Chimneys, Broken or Leaking Gas Pipes or Fixtures, or any like cause."

Police and the army were assigned to the streets to assist with the orderly evacuation of the city. They forbade the use of lit candles or matches in

FACTS AND FIGURES

DATE	5:30 a.m., April 18, 1906
LOCATION	Epicenter along the San Andreas Fault near San Francisco, USA
DEATH TOLL	Estimated at over 3,000
DAMAGE	San Francisco destroyed, with 225,000 to 300,000 people left homeless. Overall damage estimated at US$400 million (1906 value)
DURATION	1 minute
MAGNITUDE	Richter scale 8.3
COMMENTS	Fire was responsible for 80% of the total damage

any building. In San Francisco's museum, the account of DeWitt Baldwin, 10 years old at the time, is recorded. He recalls, "These rules were difficult to follow especially for families with babies or little children. Sometime during that evening Mother felt that she just had to have some warm milk for my baby sister, Virginia, who was just six months old. Cautiously Mother struck a match to light a Sterno. Soon enough an officer knocked at our door and ordered her to 'Madam, put out the light and if you do that again I have to shoot you.' She protested only to be told that such was the order." On the third day of the fire's advance through the city, the Baldwin family had to join the others evacuating their homes. Thousands carried or wheeled what few possessions they could in front of the rapidly advancing flames.

Refugees were directed to areas at the edge of the city where the army had made available tents, blankets, medicine, and food. The fires continued to rage for four days before the army was able to

ABOVE A dramatic illustration of the earthquake as captured by Italian artist Achille Beltrame. It appeared in an Italian newspaper, *La Domenica del Corriere*, on April 29, 1906.

ABOVE These typical wooden houses of the San Francisco bay area actually suffered very little damage, with even the glass in windows remaining unbroken. They had been built on soft, unconsolidated sediments that liquefied during the shaking, which allowed the buildings to sink and tilt at crazy angles.

bring them under control. They even resorted to dynamiting entire blocks of houses in order to create firebreaks and halt the advance of the fires. By the end, more than 3,000 people had died in the earthquake and fires, and 500 downtown city blocks were destroyed. This earthquake caused more loss of life and property damage than all the other previous earthquakes in California combined, and it was estimated that the fire was responsible for 80 percent of the total damage.

Life along a very active fault zone

The people of America's populous west coast, including the major cities of San Francisco and Los Angeles, are no strangers to earthquakes. The region lies along an earthquake-prone boundary between the Pacific and North American tectonic plates, known as the San Andreas Fault, where the plates grind continuously against one another, moving at about 1.3 inches (3.3 cm) per year. Earthquakes occur here when the plates, which periodically lock

JAGGED FENCE LINES
AND THE CASE OF THE ENTOMBED COW

The surface rupture of the San Andreas Fault passed just outside Skinner's Ranch. Horizontal movement of 15 feet, 9 inches (4.8 m) tore the front path away from the farmhouse steps, leaving the front door opening out directly onto the garden. Elsewhere around the property, fence lines were offset and a cow barn was torn in two. Due to the early hour of the 1906 event, many observations of damage and other earthquake effects in rural areas were made by farmers as they went about their morning chores.

There was even a report of a cow falling headfirst into a crevice along the fault, which closed moments later, leaving just the cow's tail visible above the ground. Today at Point Reyes National Seashore, north of San Francisco, the half-mile (0.8 km) Earthquake Trail follows the fault line. On this trail, visitors can see some effects of the 1906 earthquake, including the broken section of Skinner's fence, an offset creek bed, and the grave of the entombed cow.

RIGHT The 100-square-mile (259 km²) Point Reyes National Seashore in California straddles the western side of the San Andreas Fault. During the 1906 earthquake, the entire peninsula shifted 20 feet (6 m) north of the mainland. The fault zone can be explored along another short, signposted paved track that runs from near the Bear Valley visitor center.

up against one another for a while, suddenly snap free, releasing enormous amounts of stored energy.

The San Andreas Fault is part of the Pacific "Ring of Fire," a seismic belt responsible for about 80 percent of the world's earthquakes. California alone records thousands of shocks each year. Of these, 500 are large enough to be noticed by many people, the state averages about one earthquake of destructive magnitude every year. The biggest include southern California 1857, Owens Valley 1872, San Francisco 1906, Santa Barbara 1925, Long Beach 1933, San Fernando 1971, and Loma Prieta 1989. The 1906 earthquake was the worst natural disaster to strike a major city in the history of the United States. With west-coast populations increasing, the situation has now reached critical point—in San Francisco alone, the population had grown from 400,000 in 1906 to over 6 million by 2006. Notwithstanding preparations, the death toll during the next event could be horrendous.

Tragedy leads to preparation

Full attention is, however, galvanized on the earthquake problem in California. The 1906 event was directly responsible for the development of modern seismology. Instruments now measure ground tremors, slow creep of the fault, and strain buildup along the entire length of the fault. They are continually monitored by government and academic organizations in order to predict which portion of the San Andreas Fault system may fail next and how much stored energy could be released. However,

prediction of the exact timing of such events has still not been achieved. Building codes were completely rewritten after 1906, with all new structures in the region required to withstand significant earthquake-generated horizontal stresses. Today, older buildings of historic importance, such as the Los Angeles City Hall, are being upgraded. With their foundations set on a suspension system, earthquake-proof buildings are free to move independently from the ground during shaking. Earthquake drills are practiced regularly in schools and by emergency services in preparation for the next big event.

BELOW An abandoned buggy leans precariously into a crevice that has opened along the middle of a cobblestone street in San Francisco. Such crevices result from the movement of the soft sediment in the bayside areas.

Messina Straits, Italy, 1908

A massive earthquake took place before sunrise on December 28, 1908 in the narrow Messina Straits between the toe of Italy and the adjacent island of Sicily. At 5:20 a.m., a rupture began to propagate along a 25-mile (40-km) segment of fault line, starting beneath the Calabrian coast near Reggio, and finishing at Capo Peloro in Sicily.

The shaking devastated the Sicilian and Calabrian coastlines, especially Messina, with a population of 150,000, and Reggio di Calabria, with 43,000 inhabitants. Unfortunately, as it was still dark, many people were still in bed and were buried beneath rubble as their houses collapsed. Within 30 seconds of severe shaking nothing was left standing but a few walls here and there—90 percent of Messina was destroyed.

One survivor, who was interviewed by the geologist Charles Wright, reported hearing "a low whistling sound in the distance, which gradually grew louder and louder, and finally broke forth into a roar. The earth seemed to move in all directions at once, and it was impossible to stand."

About 70,000 people were killed and many more injured. The true death toll will never be accurately known, and some estimates put it at over 100,000, on par with the Lisbon 1755 earthquake. Survivors were said to be left wandering in a daze around the ruins, searching for missing family and friends.

Help delayed by broken communications lines

With communications cables across the Straits broken, the only way to contact the outside world was via boat to Calabria to find a working telegraph station. It took all day for news of the earthquake to reach Rome.

ABOVE Many survivors had to pack up what few possessions they still had and leave the ruins of Messina as refugees to start a new life elsewhere. Ahead of them lie the ruins of a church.

RIGHT Because it took a day for news of the earthquake to reach the outside world, survivors in Messina faced the difficult task of attempting to rescue those still trapped under the debris using their bare hands.

FACTS AND FIGURES	
DATE	5:20 a.m., December 28, 1908
LOCATION	Epicenter in the Messina Straits, Italy
DEATH TOLL	At least 70,000
DAMAGE	Extensive in Messina and Reggio di Calabria; many poorly constructed stone buildings along Calabrian and Sicilian coasts collapsed onto occupants
DURATION	30 seconds
MAGNITUDE	Richter scale 7.1
COMMENTS	The earthquake was felt across all of Sicily and as far north as Naples. It generated a tsunami in the Messina Straits (see separate entry in the tsunami chapter).

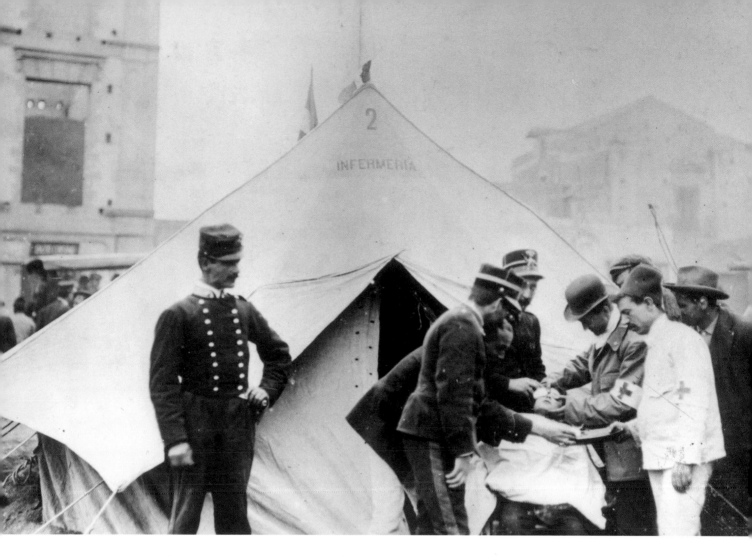

After hearing of the tragedy, thousands of emergency personnel were rushed to the region by ship. The most urgent tasks were to rescue those people still pinned under the rubble, and to house and feed others still searching for family and friends. Thousands of bodies had to be quickly recovered and buried in mass graves to prevent the spread of disease.

The government relocated many survivors to other Italian cities, while others emigrated to America. The clean-up took months, and repair of transport and coastal infrastructure far longer. Rebuilding of the cities had to conform to new codes for earthquake-resistant construction.

A survivor's tale

Ten-year-old Francesco Minissale and his two sisters were trapped beneath rubble for 18 days. They told their story to writer, Charles Wright, while en route to New York to be reunited with their father. In Wright's article, "The World's Most Cruel Earthquake (Messina)," *National Geographic*, April 1909, one of the sisters says: "We were sleeping in a large room on the ground floor. Our house collapsed killing our mother and imprisoning us. Providentially, in the same room there was

food, which we had purchased for the New Year's feast—figs, cookies, and a bag of onions, a bottle of vinegar and besides these there was a small barrel of water into which a large bottle of oil had tumbled and been broken, but the oil was not lost. On these provisions we lived but were never very hungry. Fresh water and fresh air were what we wanted most. The room was quite dark, and although we were there for 18 days it hardly seemed more than four Finally Francesco began pounding the plaster wall with a cobble stone, breaking it down bit by bit until there was an opening big enough for him to scramble into the adjoining room and up over the debris to the surface where he was hailed by an officer. He told his incredible tale and we were all rescued."

ABOVE Tented hospitals were set up among the ruins of Messina by the Italian Red Cross to attend to the injured survivors following the December 1908 earthquake.

A THIEVES' PARADISE

With the prisons in ruins, many of Italy's criminals were quickly back onto the streets, robbing the dead and living alike. Shortly after the shaking from the earthquake stopped, a group of them tried to rob the Bank of Sicily. Accessing the ruined building was easy, but fortunately they could not open the main safe, which had held firm. As the clean-up of Messina proceeded, soldiers were placing all valuables in boxes labeled with the house number and street name so that they could later be returned to the correct owners. Incensed by the number of thieves and their brazenness, orders were given by the authorities to shoot offenders on the spot.

Great Kanto, Japan, 1923

At around noon on September 1, 1923, a fault slipped beneath Sagami Bay on Japan's main island of Honshu. The movement generated an 8.3-magnitude earthquake that shook the surrounding Kanto Plains, including the built-up areas of the cities of Tokyo and Yokohama.

The effect was devastating due to the proximity of these large cities to the epicenter and the fact that they were built on loose, sandy river flats rather than on hard rock. These soft sediments amplified the earthquake's energy. However, it was the unfortunate timing of the earthquake that compounded the disaster.

Many people were indoors preparing their midday meal over charcoal fires or kerosene burners when the violent shaking collapsed their homes on top of them. Fires immediately started and were soon raging uncontrollably, burning most of what was not already destroyed by the earthquake. The rising heat formed its own winds that fanned the flames into huge firestorms. With most of the city's water pipes broken, firefighters waged a losing battle. Yokohama was completely destroyed, as was about 70 percent of Tokyo—mostly by fire rather than the earthquake. There was less damage and loss of life in surrounding rural areas. Over 300 aftershocks were felt in the day following the earthquake, adding to the panic and confusion. Japan's only other twentieth-century earthquake of comparable size was a magnitude 7.2 at Kobe, which occurred on January 17, 1995.

Other devastating effects

Movement of the Sagami Bay sea floor generated a tsunami, which struck Japan's shores within minutes of the earthquake in some places. Waves up to 40 feet (12 m) high surged into the bayside

BELOW The Nihombashi mercantile district of Tokyo lay in ruins following the September 1923 earthquake. Some makeshift shelters can be seen constructed along the edge of the canal in the foreground.

town of Atami, killing 60 people and destroying 155 homes. The earthquake also triggered hundreds of landslides, which buried entire villages, such as Nebukawa, killing hundreds more.

Many people fled down toward the harbor to get away from the fires but, by the second day, the water itself had become a flaming sheet when an oil slick caught fire. Boats were forced to head out to the open sea to avoid the flames.

Tragically, many of the survivors of the earthquake died when they took refuge in areas that were later consumed by the inferno. The greatest loss of life occurred at the Honjo clothing depot in Tokyo, where an estimated 40,000 people died in a suffocating firestorm. They had gathered in overcrowded conditions along with their bedrolls and other personal belongings salvaged from their homes, all of which further fuelled the flames.

The importance of reliable information

An unfortunate aspect of the earthquake was the civil unrest that grew in response to a number of false rumors that were spreading around the country, and even published in some newspapers. The most insidious of these were reports that groups of Koreans were rioting, starting fires, and poisoning wells. To the starving and thirsty survivors living among rubble, the rumors seemed reasonable.

Soon vigilante groups began taking the law into their own hands, stopping people at makeshift roadblocks and trying to determine if they were Korean by listening to their accent. Violence escalated and several thousand people were killed (including a number of Japanese with different dialects) before the army and police were able to bring the situation under control.

Today most Japanese earthquake educational posters remind citizens not to be misled by rumors and to carry a portable radio and use it to obtain reliable and up-to-date information.

Reconstructing Tokyo and Yokohama

The cities were quickly rebuilt, but it was not until 1981 that the stringent earthquake-proof building codes followed today were enforced. Numerous open-space public parks were established as places of refuge for future earthquakes.

Tokyo is now a city of over 12 million people, and September 1 is remembered nationally as Disaster Prevention Day. People are offered structural checks of their homes by their local government. Schools, the army, and emergency services practice their emergency drills, and everyone is reminded of the 70 percent probability that the next big earthquake will hit Tokyo within 30 years.

FACTS AND FIGURES

DATE	11:58 a.m., September 1, 1923
LOCATION	Epicenter in Sagami Bay, Tokyo, Japan
DEATH TOLL	143,000
DAMAGE	Over 570,000 homes were destroyed, with an estimated 1.9 million people left homeless; reconstruction costs estimated in excess of US$1 billion (2006 value)
DURATION	4 minutes
MAGNITUDE	Richter scale 8.3
COMMENTS	The earthquake triggered hundreds of landslides as well as a 40-foot (12-m) tsunami. Most deaths and damage were due to building collapse and fires in the major cities of Tokyo and Yokohama, leaving half the population homeless.

TOP A high-angle view of the area around the Azuma Bridge, which crosses the Sumida River, and the Honjo District of Tokyo. This area was damaged by fires following the earthquake.

ABOVE Around 2 million people all over Japan take part in anti-disaster drills on September 1 each year, the anniversary of the 1923 Kanto earthquake. These children wear flame-proof hoods during a joint disaster drill with the defense forces.

Napier, New Zealand, 1931

The freighter *Taranaki* was anchored in Hawke's Bay, about half a mile (800 m) off the city of Napier on New Zealand's North Island. HMS *Veronica* had just tied up in the inner harbor. It was a Tuesday morning, February 3, 1931, and Harbormaster H. White Parsons was on the *Veronica* with Captain H.L. Morgan. At 10:47 a.m. they felt a violent explosion.

At first both men thought the ship's magazine had exploded, but after looking toward the town they realized a far greater catastrophe was occurring—the buildings of Napier were crumbling and collapsing amid clouds of dust.

In his recollections of the event, Parsons later observed that, "The corrugated iron walls of the stores on the wharf were bursting asunder and disgorging bales of wool. The railway lines were twisting and bending under our eyes, and, with a crashing sound, the wharf a few yards in front of us gave way and fell into the harbour. The bed of the sea rose beneath us, and the stern wires gave way," according to an article by Matthew Wright commemorating the earthquake's 75th anniversary in the *New Zealand Herald*, May 1, 2006.

The floor of Hawke's Bay had risen suddenly about 6 feet (1.8 m). It hit the keel of the *Veronica*, lifting the ship, slamming it into the bottom of the *Taranaki* with "an ominous grating noise." Later, with its propellers churning in the mud, the *Taranaki* managed to push itself out to a distance of 3 miles (4.8 km) offshore before making deep water.

At 10:54 a.m. Captain Morgan tapped out a Morse code message advising his commander in Auckland of the massive disaster that had hit the town. He then sent teams of his men ashore bearing medical supplies, food, and rescue gear to assist at the scene of the devastation. By early that afternoon the New Zealand government had convened. They immediately ordered and dispatched two navy ships to the disaster zone.

BELOW A fire burns behind the S. Haddon Tailors building in Hastings Street, Napier's main street. All firefighting efforts were hampered by a lack of water as the earthquake had cracked the underground pipes. Also, the central fire station was destroyed, covering the fire engines in rubble.

ABOVE Blythe's Drapery Store (at left) in Emerson Street. With the water and sewage systems inoperable and the threat of disease, Napier was evacuated. Over half the people left within a week, ferried by bus and train.

LEFT Most of the buildings in the center of Napier were flattened. The city was rebuilt, and its Art Deco buildings now lure tourists.

RIGHT Several men look over a car in Napier's Alward and Bissell Service Station in Tennyson Street, near a burning building. Just minutes after the first tremor, the city gas supply was shut down. But this precaution was inadequate, as the fires began in pharmacies that were using flames to melt sealing wax to label their prescription bottles.

FACTS AND FIGURES	
DATE	10:47 a.m., February 3, 1931
LOCATION	Epicenter 9 miles (14.5 km) north of Napier, New Zealand
DEATH TOLL	256 (161 in Napier, 93 in Hastings, 2 in Wairoa)
DAMAGE	Downtown area of Napier destroyed by earthquake and fire; Hastings was also badly damaged
DURATION	2.5 minutes
MAGNITUDE	Richter scale 7.9
COMMENTS	The sea floor at Hawke's Bay was lifted over 6 feet (1.8 m)

ABOVE Dr Moore's Hospital was precariously tilted, sending patients' beds sliding across the floor. Like many partly damaged buildings, it was demolished due to concerns for safety in future earthquakes. Other hospitals fared worse. The Napier nurses' home collapsed and killed 12 night nurses trapped inside, and a nursing home was destroyed, killing 14 elderly residents.

FAR RIGHT A fire rages in the background in Hastings Street, viewed from the post office. Trams all over the city were halted when the power failed, and the city's tram tracks were buckled and bent out of shape by the earthquake. When the city was rebuilt, it was decided not to renew the tram service.

Destruction all around Hawke's Bay

Apart from Napier, the earthquake hit other towns around and near the bay, including Hastings, Wairoa, Waipawa, and Waipukurau. Most deaths occurred in Napier city center, where people were hit by falling masonry, either inside collapsing buildings or while running outside as building facades crumbled onto the streets. Timber-framed houses fared a lot better during the shaking, but the brick and stone buildings were clearly under-engineered for earthquakes.

Burning Napier rises from the ashes

Fires started almost immediately in Napier and Hastings due to electrical short circuits and gas leaks. Fire brigades in Hastings were able to bring the blazes under control, but in Napier there were too many outbreaks to deal with and, to make matters worse, the water pressure failed. The Napier brigades were overwhelmed, and turned their attention to rescuing people from ruined buildings before they burned. It is said that the town's people banded together, working quickly and without panic.

Napier and the surrounding towns now needed to conform to new national earthquake standards that were immediately brought into force. The town's ruined Victorian buildings were torn down, enabling the streets to be widened and better planned. Architectural firms in Napier came together to share facilities and unify the process of rebuilding the town. They designed new buildings to reflect the growing modern movement using Art Deco and Spanish Mission styles. It is said that they worked in shifts around the clock and that a new Napier rose "like a phoenix from the ashes" in an amazingly short time. The 1931 principal of Napier Girls' High School, Miss Spencer, told the *New Zealand Listener*, "Napier today is a far lovelier city than it was before."

New waterfront real estate

The earthquake destroyed many bayside landmarks, including Napier's popular Bluff Hill, which slid into the bay. However, the upward movement of Hawke's Bay caused a wide stretch of water to retreat from the coastline in a matter of minutes, resulting in 9,000 acres (3,645 ha) of new, dry land. While initially there were grave fears, it proved not to be a pre-tsunami retreat of the sea but a permanent uplift of the land. Today, housing and industrial estates and the town's airport have been built on this land.

Valdivia, Chile, 1960

The Great Chilean or Valdivia Earthquake of May 22, 1960, was a massive magnitude 9.5. That is the largest ever recorded since global seismographic monitoring began in the late 1800s. Its epicenter was in the Pacific Ocean near Valdivia, 435 miles (700 km) south of the capital, Santiago.

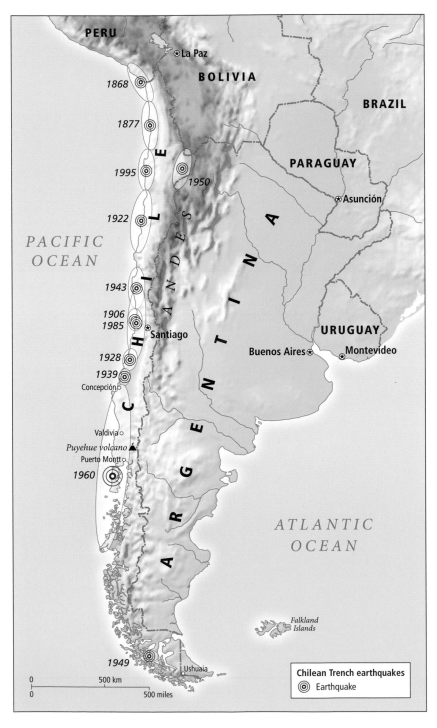

Chilean Trench earthquakes
◎ Earthquake

The region had been shaken earlier in the day by several precursor earthquakes, some as large as magnitude 8, so people were aware that something unusual and potentially dangerous was happening. Fortunately most of them were still out in the street talking about it when the main shock struck, half an hour after the foreshock. The wooden houses typical of southern Chile, being less prone to collapse, also helped keep the death toll down. The earthquake sent out a Pacific-wide tsunami with waves up to 80 feet (24 m) high, which caused severe damage as far away as Hawaii and Japan.

At 2:11 p.m. a highly stressed section of the Pacific sea floor—the Nazca Plate—suddenly broke free. It had been locked up against the edge of Chile—the South American Plate—building up stress for several centuries. As the Nazca Plate thrust suddenly eastward beneath the South American Plate, the sea floor tore to the north and south from the earthquake focus. It ran like a giant zipper, opening along a length of about 680 miles (1,094 km) parallel to the southern Chilean coastline. The Nazca Plate slid under for a distance of 66 feet (20 m).

The earthquake was felt throughout southern Chile, with the cities of Valdivia, Puerto Montt, and Concepción being the most extensively damaged due to their proximity to the epicenter. Many smaller towns and villages were also destroyed. In this area, 130,000 houses, or one in every three, were destroyed, gas and water pipelines were broken, roads, rail, and other communication lines were cut, and a large amount of coastal infrastructure was ruined by both the earthquake and the tsunami.

Particularly susceptible to the shaking were those settlements built on Chile's flat coastal plains. The unconsolidated water-saturated sands and gravels amplified the destructive seismic energy and liquefied, causing buildings to sink and topple. Whole sections of these sediment terraces slumped,

FACTS AND FIGURES

DATE	**2:11 p.m., May 22, 1960**
LOCATION	**Epicenter in the Pacific Ocean, near Valdivia, Chile**
DEATH TOLL	**5,700 (2,300 in Chile)**
DAMAGE	**US$550 million damage in southern Chile (1960 value)**
DURATION	**5 to 6 minutes**
MAGNITUDE	**Richter scale 8.6 (upgraded to 9.5 Moment scale)**
COMMENTS	**The earthquake also generated a very damaging Pacific-wide tsunami, which was responsible for most of the deaths (see separate entry in the chapter on tsunamis).**

causing drops in the elevation of the land and changes in the position of the shoreline. Part of Puerto Montt was permanently flooded by the sea.

Mountain landslides are triggered

The earthquake triggered numerous rockfalls and landslides in the Andes Mountains. One of these dammed the San Pedro River, requiring one of the Chile's largest emergency engineering feats. The lake was rapidly filling behind the rock barrier, so a drainage channel had to be opened up to avoid the flooding of prime agricultural and pastoral land, as well as an industrial area with a population of 100,000. To top off the disaster, the Puyehue Volcano in Chile's beautiful lake district erupted 19 days after the earthquake.

The Chilean navy was instrumental in assisting the people in the ravaged coastal towns and villages between Talcahuano and Chiloé. Ships anchored offshore sent teams in to provide assistance with the clean-up operations: to re-establish communications,

set up emergency water and food supplies, and evacuate people where necessary. Naval helicopters assisted with these rescue and salvage operations. Authorities had to redraw coastal charts for many areas due to dramatic changes in the sea floor caused by the earthquake.

CHILE PREPARES FOR THE NEXT BIG ONE

The 1990s were declared the International Decade of Natural Disaster Reduction, and a conference was held in Santiago in 1998 to raise awareness in all Pacific rim nations. Future earthquakes are expected along the Chilean coast, and these will undoubtedly trigger tsunamis. In anticipation, pressure sensors have been installed on the seabed just offshore to detect the passage of such waves. When this occurs, coastal sirens will sound along the Chilean coastline, giving people about 20 minutes to run for higher ground.

ABOVE Residents of Valdivia, Chile examine a deep crevice that opened in a cobblestone street following the 1960 earthquake. Settling of the soft water-saturated ground during the shaking caused this movement.

FAR LEFT The coast of Chile lies along an active fault zone that has been hit by many large earthquakes. Several of the largest events are indicated on this map.

Prince William Sound, Alaska, 1964

On Good Friday, March 27, 1964, the people of Anchorage were readying themselves for their evening activities when a magnitude 9.2 earthquake struck their city. It was the second-largest earthquake ever recorded on seismographs (the largest being in Valdivia, Chile, in 1960). The violent shaking lasted for about four minutes and triggered many landslides and avalanches but, of Anchorage's total population of 55,000, amazingly, there were only nine casualties.

ABOVE This sports car was shoved up under part of house.

BELOW These trees lining the Alaskan shore were killed during the earthquake and tsunami.

The majority of the 125 people killed died in other towns, including Valdez, Kodiak, Seward, and Crescent City, as a result of the tsunami that followed. The reason the earthquake death toll was so low was because most buildings in the Pacific Northwest are made out of wood. These tend to bend and flex in an earthquake rather than break.

Whole suburbs collapse into the bay

Massive slides occurred in the downtown business section, at Government Hill, and at Turnagain Heights. Great arc-shaped cracks appeared in the ground, ripping through houses and yards. People ran from their houses in panic as whole suburbs began to move and slump toward Cook Inlet. Huge blocks of land, some complete with houses still intact and windows unbroken, were rotated and tilted at crazy angles by the time the ground had settled.

The brand-new Four Seasons concrete apartment block had completely collapsed immediately next to still-standing older wooden houses. Fortunately it was still empty—residents were not due to move in until the following week. Certain areas of the city, built on thick alluvial glacial sediment layers, suffered worse shaking than others built on solid rock. In loose sediment, the grip between the individual grains is easily broken, allowing them to vibrate and move freely, thus amplifying the damaging vibrations of the earthquake. In Anchorage, most damage was due to landslides and the settling of the soft clayey glacial-alluvial deposits.

About 30 blocks were damaged or destroyed in the downtown area of Anchorage, including many multistory buildings. In the largest landslide, at Turnagain Heights, an area of about 130 acres (53 ha) was devastated. This slide destroyed about 75 homes and broke water, gas, sewer, telephone, and electrical lines throughout the area.

Reason for the earthquake

Anchorage is located along the Pacific "Ring of Fire," in an area where the Pacific plate is moving steadily to the northwest at 2 to 2¾ inches (5 to 7 cm) per year. It is slowly but relentlessly descending beneath the North American Plate. About a century and a half ago, however, the section of this plate around Anchorage jammed, and since that time it had been buckling and building up stress until the rocks suddenly ruptured and released their stored-up energy. The earthquake resulted from the sudden

FACTS AND FIGURES

DATE	5:36 p.m., March 27, 1964
LOCATION	Epicenter 75 miles (121 km) east of Anchorage
DEATH TOLL	15 due to earthquake; 125 total
DAMAGE	Alaska's fishing industry and most seaport facilities were destroyed; Oregon and Californian coastlines were also damaged by the resulting tsunami; the repair bill was US$300 to 400 million (1964 value)
DURATION	4 minutes
MAGNITUDE	Richter scale 8.4 (upgraded to 9.2 Moment scale)
COMMENTS	Shaking caused most extensive damage to buildings on loose glacial alluvial sediments. Felt as far south as Washington State. The earthquake generated a Pacific-wide tsunami, which was responsible for most of the deaths (see tsunami chapter).

slippage of the Pacific Plate about 30 feet (9 m) beneath the North American Plate.

In the three weeks following the earthquake, 20 aftershocks with a Richter magnitude greater than 6 were recorded, with 11 of those occurring in the first day while the stresses equalized across the descending plate. Many people reported wave-like movements of the ground, but Arthur Durant, who was skiing with his family at Elmendorf Air Force Base, had a particularly good view of the entire event. He wrote an account online (at www.vibrationdata.com/earthquakes/alaska.htm):

"Where we were, on a high hill outside Anchorage, allowed us to look over quite a long distance, all the way to Anchorage itself and the water beyond. The terrain was mostly white, either snow or frost covered all the trees and the rooftops. We could see huge waves move along the ground, starting from our right and spreading out rapidly in ever-widening circles to our left and away into the distance.

"We were actually watching the shockwaves as they spread out across probably a 12-mile [19 km] area of lower ground. One spectacularly large shockwave was enough to shake every last bit of snow off the trees and bushes. It was like watching a giant windshield wiper blade wipe across the city, changing it instantly from white to brown or green."

ABOVE Shops, bars and stores along the north side of 4th Avenue in downtown Anchorage dropped about 11 feet (3.4 m) after the Good Friday 1964 earthquake. The movement resulted from slumping and liquefaction of the soft clayey sediments on which this part of the city had been built.

Tangshan, China, 1976

Densely populated China has been home to some of Earth's most tragic natural disasters. Unfortunately, the country is also particularly prone to earthquakes. The Eurasian Plate, on which China sits, is being squeezed by the Indian continent driving northward into it, and by the Pacific Plate pushing westward beneath it.

According to official figures, deaths from the 1976 Tangshan earthquake are on par with those caused by the 2004 Indian Ocean tsunami. Both tolls are still well below the 830,000 lives lost in the world's most deadly earthquake, which occurred in 1556 in Shaanxi Province, China.

A complex set of causes

Tangshan's near-total destruction was compounded by several factors. As the city was thought to be in a low-risk area, the buildings were not earthquake-proof. It was built on an alluvial plain, which magnified the shaking. Also, the early hour of the earthquake meant everyone was indoors. In the city itself, over 90 percent of residential buildings collapsed, immediately killing one-third of Tangshan's sleeping inhabitants. The city's major hospital also collapsed, killing 2,000. Dazed survivors grouped together to dig for others beneath the rubble. A magnitude 7.6 aftershock made matters even worse.

Officials reject international help

The Chinese government brought relief supplies to the region by truck and plane, and began housing survivors in tents. Officials, however, rejected all international offers of help, stating that the people had enough food and clothing, and that there were enough doctors and medical supplies in the city. Rebuilding began quickly and the city has since grown to one million inhabitants.

China has long studied animal behavior and other phenomena as a means of predicting earthquakes, and has had some success in this inexact science. The day before the Tangshan earthquake, there were reports of dogs and chickens behaving strangely, water levels in wells changing rapidly, and strange lights appearing in the evening sky. It would be a brave official indeed who would try to alert a city of thousands on such evidence, but, in hindsight, that is exactly what should have happened in Tangshan.

Earthquake prediction in Qinglong

In neighboring Qinglong County, 60 miles (97 km) northeast of Tangshan, officials showed more foresight. They had spent the previous two years preparing for the event after being alerted by the State Council's Document No. 69, which endorsed a Chinese Academy of Sciences report dated June 15, 1974. The report cited increased micro-earthquake activity, changes in groundwater levels, increased

BELOW This map of China shows the locations of the Tangshan and Shaanxi earthquakes. The Tangshan earthquake also hit nearby Qinglong. The January 23, 1556 Shaanxi earthquake killed more people than any other in history; while not of the highest magnitude, many of the people killed in the 97 counties affected lived in caves hewn out of loess, which collapsed on them.

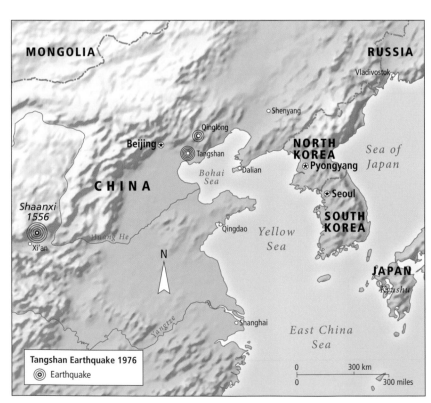

Tangshan Earthquake 1976
◎ Earthquake

LEFT People set about the task of rebuilding and repairing the structural damage in the Tangshan area, 100 miles (160 km) east of Beijing, after the devastating 1976 earthquake.

BELOW Transport infrastructure, vital to the industrial city of Tangshan, had to be returned to an operational state as quickly as possible following the earthquake. This railway carriage near Tangshan was derailed.

radon emissions, and changes in Earth's magnetic and gravity fields as evidence of a future earthquake. County officials handed out books and posters and gave slide shows to increase public awareness.

They set up an earthquake-disaster management committee headed by diligent 21-year-old Wang Chunqing. On July 16, two weeks before the earthquake, Chunqing attended a conference in Tangshan and wrote notes while listening to one particularly alarming presentation by the State Seismological Bureau. They stated, "There is a strong possibility of a magnitude 5 earthquake from July 22 to August 5, 1976, in the Tangshan region. A magnitude 8 is also likely in the second half of '76. Preparations should be made immediately."

This warning was taken seriously in Qinglong County and, over the next few days, school classes were moved outdoors. Students were asked to look for unusual phenomena. Some groups noted strange animal behaviors, particularly the sighting of nocturnal animal during the day. Another group reported that local spring water had become muddy and undrinkable.

On July 24, an official warning was broadcast to the people of Qinglong by the county government. Temporary earthquake tents were set up, and by July 26, over 60 percent of Qinglong County's 470,000 residents had moved out of their homes. Those who stayed were told to keep their doors and windows open at all times to avoid being trapped. When the earthquake finally struck on July 28, 180,000 buildings collapsed in Qinglong, but not one person was killed by debris.

FACTS AND FIGURES

DATE	3:42 a.m., July 28, 1976
LOCATION	Epicenter near Tangshan, Hebei Province, China
DEATH TOLL	242,419 (official figures); others report much higher casualties
DAMAGE	Most residential and commercial buildings in Tangshan over a 20 square mile (52 km²) area were destroyed
DURATION	15 seconds
MAGNITUDE	Richter scale 7.6 to 7.8 (official); 8.2 (other estimates)
COMMENTS	Most deaths and damage were due to building collapse in Tangshan.

Spitak, Armenia, 1988

On December 1, 1988, seismic stations in northern Armenia recorded a small earthquake (magnitude 3.5). A week later, after a long sequence of minor tremors, the water level in underground wells near Noyemberyan began to fluctuate. However, Armenia was clearly not ready for what came next.

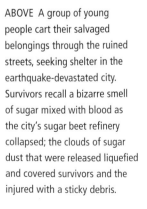

ABOVE A group of young people cart their salvaged belongings through the ruined streets, seeking shelter in the earthquake-devastated city. Survivors recall a bizarre smell of sugar mixed with blood as the city's sugar beet refinery collapsed; the clouds of sugar dust that were released liquefied and covered survivors and the injured with a sticky debris.

At 11:41 a.m. on December 7, when the earthquake hit, school children had just a few minutes of class time remaining before they would be going outdoors for their midday break. It was tragic—despite being a moderate 6.8 magnitude, the shaking collapsed most of Spitak's newer Soviet-style, concrete-framed apartment blocks, schools, and hospitals, as well as its historic buildings. It was followed just four minutes later by a magnitude 5.8 aftershock.

Almost two-thirds of the 25,000 deaths were of children. In the nearby city of Leninakan (the historic and cultural center of Armenia, now known as Gyumri), 80 percent of the buildings were destroyed or damaged, including the historic Holy Saviour Church. The industrial town of Kirovakan

(now called Vanadzor) was 50 percent destroyed or damaged. The unreinforced masonry along with a lack of a flexible steel frame were cited as the main reasons for the devastation—the heavy concrete floors of multistory buildings pancaked on top of one another, sparing no one inside.

With the hospitals destroyed and 80 percent of their medical staff dead, emergency medical services were unavailable at the time of greatest need, and any response was further hindered by roads being blocked by debris and clogged with traffic. Water, power, and communication lines were destroyed. Aftershocks and freezing conditions compounded the already difficult situation for survivors. Rescuers felt helpless and afraid to enter many damaged and twisted buildings for fear that they may collapse.

Help finally arrives

By the next day the military had arrived and begun assisting survivors digging for loved ones in the rubble, airlifting the wounded, and bringing in relief supplies. Cranes and other heavy equipment did not start arriving for another week, so most of the work of freeing people had to be done by hand. The available relief effort was minuscule compared with what was needed, so the Soviet Union invited foreign aid workers into the region to assist.

It was the first time since 1923 that international relief organizations had been allowed into the former Soviet Union, a decision that was later hailed as the "fall of the humanitarian wall." Soviet President Mikael Gorbachev cut short a meeting in New York to visit the disaster zone, pledging that no expense

FACTS AND FIGURES

DATE	11:41 a.m., December 7, 1988
LOCATION	Epicenter at Spitak, 15 miles (24 km) southeast of Leninakan (Gyumri), Armenia
DEATH TOLL	25,000 dead; 15,000 injured
DAMAGE	Spitak (population 25,000) and the surrounding villages were completely destroyed. Leninakan (population 250,000) was extensively damaged. Reconstruction estimated at US$14.2 billion (1976 value)
DURATION	40 seconds
MAGNITUDE	Moment scale 6.8
COMMENTS	Most deaths and damage were due to the collapse of poorly constructed Soviet-style buildings

ABOVE The family of earthquake victims bury their loved ones in a cemetery in the devastated Armenian city of Leninakan. Churches had to be rebuilt in record time just to keep pace with the thousands of funerals— one church was constructed in only seven weeks.

RIGHT A man stacks coffins into piles in the city streets for people to collect. A coffin shortage meant many people were buried without one. Spitak's soccer stadium was filled with thousands of coffins containing victims waiting to be identified.

FAR RIGHT Uzbekistani workers begin building new housing for Armenians who were left homeless by the devastating earthquake. The new buildings that were constructed with international help reflected the architecture of the countries that assisted—there are Italian, French, and Uzebekistani sectors, British and Czech schools, and an Italian hospital.

ABOVE A dazed woman sits amid the rubble of her home in the wake of earthquake that devastated Spitak. A ladder runs into a hole to her right, which was probably dug out to search for survivors.

would be spared in the rebuilding effort. Over 100 countries contributed supplies and personnel to the UNESCO-coordinated relief effort.

Reconstruction grinds to a halt

By December 18, a total of 70,000 people had been evacuated from the disaster zone and 514,000 were declared homeless. Swarms of aftershocks, some as large as magnitude 5.0, continued to plague the devastated region for months afterward. However, rebuilding was slow, and was hampered by political problems. The first two years went well, but with the fall of the Soviet Union in 1990, reconstruction

efforts ground to a halt. Russian workers returned home, leaving half-finished building projects in still largely ruined cities.

Even five years after the earthquake, many survivors were still housed in temporary emergency shelters unsuitable for Armenia's extreme weather. They could not afford new homes or building materials. Industry was operating at one-third of its pre-earthquake capacity, and many Armenians faced chronic unemployment. Most of the region's schools were still not operational. These depressing circumstances meant that many, particularly children, were still suffering psychological stress from the trauma.

Finally, in the late 1990s, a glimmer of hope came for the people—USAID (the United States Agency for International Development) and other international organizations provided needy families with housing purchase certificates, which meant many of those displaced could finally get a proper home.

Past lessons, readiness for the future

Armenia is part of a seismically active zone that stretches as far as India. It results from the Arabian and Eurasian plates colliding, which are pushing up the Caucasus Mountains. In 1988, increasing stress caused a 5-mile (8-km) section of a fault to rupture and break the surface near Spitak, creating a 5-foot (1.5-m) high escarpment. Historically, the 1988 earthquake is just one of a series that have occurred in the Spitak–Leninakan area: 1899 (magnitude 5.3), 1920 (magnitude 6.2, killing 40), 1926 (magnitude 5.6, killing 300 and causing extensive damage), and 1940 (magnitude 6.0).

There was, however, one positive outcome of the earthquake's devastation, and that was the formation of the Armenian National Survey for Seismic Protection (NSSP): its aim is to predict and plan for the next big earthquake. The NSSP prepares seismic risk maps, carries out real-time monitoring of Armenia's 150 seismic stations, identifies potential hazards—such as fire-prone or unstable buildings, or overcrowded areas—and prepares emergency responses to each hazard. It also implements new building codes, including reinforcement of existing buildings, broadcasts public awareness education, including TV and radio programs, and manages and trains disaster-response teams. NSSP teams now also take part in international relief efforts in other parts of the world.

Reconstruction in Spitak and Gyumri (Leninakan) has avoided known fault lines, and earthquake codes for new buildings are now strictly enforced. The new city of Spitak is only four stories high, and has much more steel and reinforcing in its buildings and other structures. Similar plans have also been drawn up for many other high-risk cities in the region, which also need to face their former Soviet legacy of artificially deflated earthquake-risk statistics and inadequate foresight in city planning. These include Baku, Tbilisi, and Yerevan.

RECOLLECTIONS OF THE TRAGEDY

It is impossible to understand the personal impact for each and every person involved in such a tragedy. Anileve posted her recollections on HyeForum on December 4, 2003: "This is the last thing I want to remember. It was the hardest winter of my life. I will never forget the faces of those young children … I remember my father returning from Leninakan, Spitak; he looked like he aged about 10 years with grey hair gracing his head full of dark black hair, and for the first time I saw him weep—not very typical of my macho father. One of the stories I heard [was] of how he was trying to save a child no more than five who was trapped under the debris, but there was no way of saving him. So after hours of trying, my father just sat there weeping, holding this boy's tiny fingers; he sat there listening to the boy's voice slowly fade away and his tiny fingers loosening. The things our nation went through and we are still surviving."

In Tigran Petrosyan's personal web page, he thanks the German doctors who helped his family: "At the time of the earthquake, in 1998, I was 12 years old. When the earthquake started, I was sitting in the armchair doing my geography homework, and my sister was playing the piano. At 11:41, everything happened in a blink of an eye: the earth and the sky started shaking. We didn't know what was happening. It seemed that everything stopped: life, and time. I don't think anyone could describe what happened, the terrifying feelings. Our building was completely destroyed. We stayed under the rubble for 13 hours. When my father, with the help of his brothers and other relatives, found us and took us out, I saw Spitak in ruins, in the dark. I was taken to an orthopedic hospital in Yerevan. My legs and my arms were hurt. That day, they operated on my leg. During those terrifying days, the whole world came to help Armenia, and the Germans were a part of that effort. Thanks to their great effort (especially Professor Domres) and despite countless difficulties imposed by Soviet officials, I was allowed to travel to Germany for treatment."

Izmit, Turkey, 1999

On August 17, 1999, heavily industrialized western Turkey was struck by a magnitude 7.4 earthquake, right where it was anticipated to occur. The epicenter was on a fault line at the head of Izmit Bay. It was the largest event to have devastated a modern, industrialized city since the earthquakes of 1906 in San Francisco and 1923 in Tokyo.

ABOVE An aerial photograph taken on August 23 reveals the extent of the damage in a residential area near the industrial city of Izmit. By then the Turkish government crisis center had counted more than 17,000 dead in the central and western Anatolian provinces.

RIGHT The day after the earthquake, a family camps in front of a wrecked house on one of the main avenues of the city of Izmit, where the death toll had already risen to at least 2,000.

FACTS AND FIGURES

DATE	3:02 a.m., August 17, 1999
LOCATION	Epicenter near Izmit, along the North Anatolian Fault Zone
DEATH TOLL	17,225 dead; 44,000 injured (official figures—others report over 30,000 dead)
DAMAGE	77,300 residential and commercial buildings were destroyed and 244,500 damaged; total cost estimated at US$6 billion (1999 value)
DURATION	37 seconds
MAGNITUDE	Richter scale 7.4
COMMENTS	Almost all fatalities were due to collapse of multistory residential buildings. Submarine slumping in the Gulf of Izmit generated a tsunami.

The rupture occurred over a length of 70 miles (113 km), with horizontal offsets of up to 16 feet (5 m) and vertical displacements reaching 10 feet (3 m), and with the north side of the fault dropping down. The timing of the earthquake meant that most people were at home sleeping when it occurred. It left them with little chance to get out of their multistory residential buildings, many of which collapsed completely. Deaths, injuries, and damage occurred over a wide region, including Izmit, Adapazari, Gölcük, Karamürsel, Yalova, Düzce, and Istanbul. The vertical drop, plus soil slumping, caused extensive and permanent flooding of large areas along the Marmara Sea coast in the vicinity of Gölcük.

The North Anatolian Fault Zone

The North Anatolian Fault Zone is a boundary between two tectonic plates that slide against one another, very similar to the San Andreas Fault of California in the United States. The Anatolian Plate, pushed by the African and Arabian plates, is sliding westward against the Eurasian plate at about ¾ to 1 inch (2–2.5 cm) per year. Earthquakes have been propagating from east to west along a 600-mile (965-km) length of this fault since the 1939 Erzincan earthquake. Others followed in 1942, 1943, 1944, 1951, 1957, and 1967. As an earthquake releases stress in one part of the fault, it places pressure on the next section of fault, further west, essentially "triggering" it to rupture. This allows a crude prediction to be made of where the next earthquake is likely to take place; unfortunately, no one is able to say exactly when it will occur.

Communications and roads down

When the earthquake struck, initially scientists and officials seriously underestimated the human loss and extent of damage. All telephone communication was cut and the main highway from Istanbul to Ankara was impassable. Other roads were choked with people trying to reach family and friends in the affected area. A fire broke out in Turkey's main oil refinery; it took six days to control. The fault

TSUNAMIS STRIKE THE MARMARA SEA COAST

Underwater slumping from the earthquake generated a tsunami that struck the coastline of Izmit Bay, a popular holiday area at the eastern end of the Marmara Sea (pictured). Eyewitnesses reported that minutes after the earthquake, the sea receded from the shore before returning as a 20 feet (6 m) tsunami, laden with yachts and cruise ships. It surged across the promenade and slammed into the seaside shops, hotels, and resorts.

Cengic Tayfur, a 26-year-old supermarket manager, working at the time, told Daniel McGrory about his experience (reported on the Pacific Marine Environmental Laboratory's Tsunami Research Program's website):

"It was like watching a whirlpool. It looked as if someone had pulled the plug out from the seabed. The sea was gurgling and then a wind came rushing at us, like a typhoon. The sea level dropped, but moments later a wave came rolling at us, getting bigger and faster all the time." He started to run up the stairs of an apartment block and remembers the sea gushing into the stairwell behind him. "A second or so later came another wave. Not quite as big, but I felt it pulling at my feet. The whole thing must have lasted no more than 10 seconds. After the two tidal waves, there must have been over 200 big waves that kept crashing on to the road … This effect was caused by the waves bouncing back and forth between the opposite shores of the narrow bay."

ripped through the navy base and ship-building yard at Gölcük causing extensive damage. At least 400 soldiers and officers were killed there.

Emergency response and aid

Emergency response teams rapidly swung into action. Tent cities for the homeless were quickly set up together with wireless communication to keep the residents informed of latest developments. Turkish Red Crescent, the country's largest aid agency, provided blankets, sleeping bags, food, mobile kitchens, and mobile hospitals. Thousands of heavy machines and operators were dispatched to the affected areas. Repair works on damaged

roads, water, and electricity lines began immediately. Guardianship was organized for children who had lost their parents. The Military Medical Academy set up a psychiatric therapy center to assist survivors suffering post-traumatic stress.

Within 48 hours of the earthquake, the risk-management company EQE International had a team of risk-assessment engineers in Turkey investigating the damage, and the US Geological Survey and Southern California Earthquake Center scientists had arrived to assist their Turkish colleagues map the surface rupture.

According to Peter Yanev of EQE, as quoted on PRNewswire, "Of the more than 70 earthquakes I've investigated this was, in many respects, the worst and in many respects the most important … This was the first earthquake with major faulting to strike through heavily populated areas. It is of particular interest to San Francisco because of the similar fault offsets between the 1906 event and Izmit … The lessons are an extension of what we expect to learn from a repetition of the 1906 San Francisco earthquake and the 1923 Tokyo earthquake."

Alarming deficiencies in modern building practice

A large percentage of the damaged or collapsed buildings were in the six- to eight-story range and were either still under construction or had been built in the last few years before the earthquake.

In some areas the contrast in structural performance was striking—in the town of Gölcük, for example, a very old mosque outperformed the modern buildings surrounding it, which were all supposed to have been built to an earthquake-

BELOW Oil slicks spread out from the shores along the Marmara Sea coastline at Izmit after the earthquake damaged oil and refueling facilities. The oil-covered waters hampered the operation of vessels in the area.

resistant code similar to that used in California. Even more alarming, however, was the observation that the newest of the modern buildings suffered the most collapses, indicating a deterioration of standards and quality control in today's Turkey, despite the earthquake code.

The findings of EQE International and other risk-management engineers were frightening. They found that most of the buildings did not meet the specifications of the earthquake code. Insufficient horizontal and vertical reinforcement had been used during construction, and the steel was of the wrong type—being smooth-surfaced rather than ribbed, it did not grip the concrete well. In addition, many of the buildings were made from low-quality and inadequate building materials, and the workmanship was very poor. As a result, many buildings failed where the vertical wall columns and horizontal ceiling beams meet.

Another contributing cause was the design: structural engineers for many buildings were not independent authorities, but employees of the actual building companies. As such, they did not inspect ongoing work or later design modifications.

One particularly serious modification involved creating more space on a building's ground floor to accommodate street-front shops—it was a huge mistake, as many of these buildings collapsed onto their ground floors. Additionally, in many cases the code was completely ignored and builders simply continued building the way they always had. Also, many structures were built without adequate foundations in areas of poorly consolidated beach sands or lake silts with high liquefaction potential. Some buildings even straddled active faults.

The predicted Istanbul earthquake

Attention is now being directed toward Turkey's next earthquake, which is expected within a decade or so. It is now the turn of the locked-up section of the North Anatolian Fault to the west of the Izmit section to rupture. This will occur near Istanbul, and the outcome for the populous capital will be devastating. Many tens of thousands will die and the country's economy will be severely affected. Many of Istanbul's buildings are old, and the newer ones are not likely to meet their code, so collapses will be significant. Fire may also be a serious problem in Istanbul's many older, wood-frame buildings.

ABOVE Many of the survivors attempted to reclaim what little undamaged property they could find, often with scant regard for their own safety. Eight days after the earthquake, a resident of Degirmendere returns, climbing through the precarious piles of rubble that were once his home.

Bam, Iran, 2003

Historic Bam, about 600 miles (965 km) southeast of Iran's capital, Tehran, is a 2,000-year-old red mud-brick walled citadel surrounded by desert. The city was a picturesque World Heritage Site—a jewel of Iranian culture visited by thousands of tourists each year. It was a thriving regional centre with a population of about 90,000 and the biggest adobe structure in the world.

RIGHT An aerial view of Bam reveals that the city was virtually leveled by the earthquake. Very few buildings were left standing, largely because their mud-brick construction was unable to withstand the violent shaking.

BELOW An Iranian man directs a Danish search-and-rescue team to a collapsed house in earthquake-striken Bam on December 31. Sniffer dogs and thermal imaging equipment were used to help locate survivors trapped under the rubble. One man survived for 13 days.

All this changed on Friday, December 26, 2003, when the city was struck by a magnitude 6.5 earthquake. Bam became a victim of its architecture. Its ancient mud-brick buildings were not built to withstand earthquakes, and a large part of the historic citadel was destroyed. Unfortunately, its newer buildings also collapsed, including two hospitals, the fire station, a bus terminus, and a prison. No part of the sleeping city was spared. Over one-third of the population was immediately killed, with a large number of the remainder injured.

The scene was one of confusion in the cold, dark, early morning hours. Survivors, covered in dust and blood, were desperately digging with their bare hands for loved ones in the dirt that had been their home. Tragically, few people trapped when their homes collapsed managed to survive. The mud-brick buildings disintegrated, suffocating people in dirt; there were not the air pockets normally found in a concrete building collapse. The few who did survive

were mostly dug out within the first few hours. Things were little better by Friday night, when temperatures again plummeted below zero. With no electricity or light, survivors had to stop digging, and most of them had few clothes other than those they were wearing at the time of the earthquake. Bonfires were lit everywhere to provide some warmth.

Help from outside the city

The city was powerless to help itself. With most government officials, doctors, and emergency personnel killed or injured, and their vehicles pinned beneath wrecked buildings, all help had to come from outside the city. National and international teams started to arrive on Saturday. The injured were transported by car, ambulance, or helicopter to hospitals in Kerman, 100 miles (161 km) northwest of Bam, and other cities. More than 8,500 relief workers were sent into the area, including 1,700 international workers from over 30 countries.

The Iranian Red Crescent Society set up a field hospital, basic health-care centers, and emergency water and sanitation units; they also coordinated international airlifts. The earthquake survivors were provided with food rations, bottled water, tents, blankets, stoves, hygiene kits, clothes, and kitchen sets. Over 111,000 people received medical treatment through Red Cross and Red Crescent emergency clinics. Construction of temporary emergency shelters began.

FACTS AND FIGURES	
DATE	5:28 a.m., December 26, 2003
LOCATION	Epicenter near Bam, Iran
DEATH TOLL	26,271 (official figures)
DAMAGE	80% of the mud-brick city destroyed, including its heritage-listed Arg-é-Bam citadel; total cost estimated at US$1 billion (2003 value)
DURATION	12 seconds
MAGNITUDE	Moment scale 6.5
COMMENTS	Almost all fatalities were due to the collapse of traditional mud-brick buildings or poorly made newer buildings in Bam

Hungry villagers rush to Bam

Anecdotal reports indicate that Bam's population rose to 120,000 after the earthquake and that over 110,000 tents were dispersed. Bam was the region's wealth center; the surrounding villages were much poorer. Apparently many more than just the earthquake-affected villagers were coming to Bam to take advantage of the food and aid handouts. Furthermore, many of the Bam survivors set up their tents near the ruins of their home rather than staying in the tent cities where aid distribution points were centered. This situation made it challenging for the government, in the months following the earthquake, to determine who was entitled to disaster aid and temporary housing and who was to be left without. In March, there were riots in the streets of Bam over the shortage of assistance.

Reconstruction begins

"The city of Bam must be built from scratch," its governor, Ali Shafiee, told the BBC News on December 27, 2003. The Iranian government, following a development plan that it drew up in the months after the earthquake, began reconstruction work in Bam and the surrounding villages. Houses have since then been built with lighter, safer components and designed to be earthquake resistant. Restoration of the historic citadel, vital to the city's livelihood, has been ongoing, with specialist assistance from the Ministry of Culture and help from a number of Japanese universities.

Building codes must be enforced

Professor Mohsen Aboutorabi of the architecture department of the University of Central England spoke with *The Guardian* about earthquake-resistant building codes in Iran: "There are building regulations, but they haven't been enforced except for high-rises. People are desperately in need of housing so the authorities overlook the code of building for earthquakes … On my last trip to Iran I banged two bricks together and they became like powder. Demand for materials is so high that manufacturers don't stick to any standards. The cost of cement is very high, so they don't use much."

Professor Aboutorabi explained that roofs of Iran's traditional buildings are supported by metal beams spanning brick arches. "The ends of the beams sit freely on the walls, so with any shake, if one goes, the whole roof collapses."

Of particular concern in such an earthquake-prone country as Iran is the new Russian-built nuclear power plant at Bushehr on the Persian Gulf. The city of Bushehr itself has suffered three destructive earthquakes in recent times (in 1877, 1911, and 1962), and German scientists responsible for the design on the plant claim that it is safe—they have engineered it to withstand earthquakes of up to magnitude 7.2. The results might be devastating if an earthquake is any bigger than that.

Iran considers moving its capital

Bam 2003, and other deadly earthquakes that have struck Iran throughout its history, are caused by stresses within Earth's crust as the Arabian Plate pushes northward against the Eurasian Plate at about 1 inch (2.5 cm) per year. The plates are crushing together, forcing up the Zagros mountain belt and deforming a broad area of crust that spans most of Iran. Strike-slip and reverse faulting within this zone of deformation are responsible for Iran's earthquakes.

The capital, Tehran, lies along the same series of high-risk faults as Bam. In an interview with Reuters, Dr Bahram Akasheh, geophysics professor at Tehran

BELOW Iranian rescue workers excavate a trapped woman from a collapsed house. The metal beam seen here was the type used to hold up roofs but, being unanchored, they shook loose and caused houses like this to collapse onto their occupants.

University, warned of the high probability that a large earthquake will hit Tehran in the future, although he cannot predict when that will be.

He advised that an earthquake of similar magnitude to Bam would be disastrous, as hardly any of the buildings in Tehran are made to withstand a major earthquake, despite the city's recent major construction boom. Many of its inhabitants would die in building collapses.

"We have to take the issue of earthquakes seriously," the professor said. "Tehran must be rebuilt; if not, it should be moved … Either we have to put up with millions of dead, millions of injured,

or we need to move the capital somewhere else and take steps to decrease the population here and make Tehran more resistant to earthquakes."

The professor wrote to Iranian President Mohammad Khatami proposing that the capital be moved to Isfahan, which is located in a less seismically active part of the country. He told an agency for BBC news: "Most people think that what God wills will happen. This is absolutely wrong. This thinking is poisonous." Professor Akasheh believes that Iranians should not be so fatalistic, and should use their God-given intelligence and resourcefulness to build homes that are resistant to earthquakes.

ABOVE A woman returning to her devastated house in Bam on December 31 manages to rescue a chicken, which survived the earthquake. She is holding onto one of the metal beams that originally held up the roof.

HOMELAND LOST IN RUINS

The citadel (pictured on December 31, five days after the earthquake) holds a great deal of significance to the Turkish people, including expatriates. Darius Bayat from Sydney, Australia, posted his opinion about its devastation on a BBC website. It sums up the tragedy and needless loss that occurred at Bam in 2003:
"I have spent many of my days in Bam as a youth. The beauty of the citadel brought tears to my eyes. It was a reminder of the glory of Ancient Persia and the kings of old, and it breaks my heart to see it in ruins … Why is it that a 6.5 earthquake takes only two lives in America while a 6.3 on the Richter scale kills 20,000 in Iran? My heart goes out to all the families robbed of loved ones. Please pray for the dead in Arg-é-Bam."

Kashmir, South Asia, 2005

The earthquake of October 8, 2005 that struck the very mountainous Kashmir region was indeed unfortunate in its timing. At 8:50 a.m., students had just gone to school and many people were still in their houses resting after the early morning Ramadan meal. Within minutes, severe shaking flattened shoddily constructed concrete and brick buildings over the entire region, which includes northern Pakistan, Afghanistan, and northern India.

Also called the Northern Pakistan or South Asia earthquake, it caused panic in Islamabad, the capital of Pakistan, where a 60-apartment residential tower collapsed. Falling schools, houses, and commercial buildings killed, injured, and disrupted the lives of hundreds of thousands of people. In Muzaffarabad, capital of Pakistan-administered Kashmir, 30,000 people died.

Why did the earthquake occur?

Kashmir is located in the Himalayan Mountains—the boundary between the colliding Indian and Eurasian tectonic plates. Both being continental crust, one plate will not slide beneath the other. Instead they are crushed and crumpled together, pushing up the most extensive and tallest mountain range in the world. This is a place where fossils of shells, once living in an ancient sea that lay between the two continents, are now found miles above sea level. It is a place continually wracked by earthquakes—and

also, unfortunately, one where poverty means that building and construction are of the poorest possible standard; this is deadly under such circumstances.

Balakot, once a pretty hilltop city with a population of about 40,000, and many hotels, restaurants, and souvenir shops bustling with tourists, was closest to the epicenter. It was entirely flattened. In one school alone, 600 girls were killed. The destruction was far greater than that caused by similar-sized earthquakes in Japan or the United States, where building codes are now strictly enforced. Panic ensued for a second time when a magnitude 5.7 aftershock hit an hour later.

Survivors cut off from help

When the dust finally settled, survivors left among the rubble found themselves cut off from the outside world. Landslides had blocked many of the roads in and out of the region, making it difficult to bring in heavy equipment to move the debris. Rescuers were

left using picks, shovels, and bare hands to try to dig out survivors. To make matters worse, freezing weather and winter snows were fast approaching. Survivors began trekking down the mountains from remote villages looking for assistance; it would take days or even weeks to come to them. Their numbers began to swell the devastated cities, where relief workers were unable to provide enough temporary

Tents stand among flattened structures in Balakot, Pakistan (above). Around 90 percent of the city was leveled by the earthquake. A group of men (far left) pray outside the destroyed Jama Haman Wali mosque in Muzaffarabad.

NOT ENOUGH, NOT FAST ENOUGH

The global response was admirable, but it was unfortunately not enough for the people on the ground. Supplies and shelter were insufficient. Tens of thousands of people with grievous injuries, particularly those in outlying regions, were not treated quickly enough, often making it necessary to amputate gangrenous limbs. Fortunately, the winter was milder than expected, but the return of summer and the monsoon brought a new set of difficulties. On April 8, 2006, the aid agency, Oxfam, reported to BBC News that six months after the event, thousands of victims still needed assistance. Muzaffarabad, Pakistan, needed to be rebuilt, and proposals for a new town near Balakot still needed to be put into action.

ABOVE Cars were flattened under the Margalla Towers apartment building complex in Islamabad, Pakistan. One block of 60 apartments in the ten-story twin complex collapsed, killing 56 people inside. Another 52 people were rescued.

shelter. Many whose houses did survive would not enter them, fearing that aftershocks would collapse the weakened structures. Mumtaz Rathore, who was living under a plastic sheet with his wife and four children, told CBS News: "Look at me, I have to live out here with my children. My house is full of cracks, and I won't go inside."

Tens of thousands were at risk of dying from starvation or exposure. The head of the United Nations' emergency relief effort, Jan Engeland, described the situation as worse than the 2004 Indian Ocean tsunami, stating on October 21, 2005, "We have never had this kind of logistical nightmare, ever." He called for an immediate emergency airlift effort of massive proportions.

International help comes by air

Dozens of countries supplied helicopters, the first arriving within 48 hours of the earthquake. They began flying in food, blankets, tents, and medical supplies to the stricken region and ferrying out the injured. It was the largest relief operation of its kind and would last nearly six months. Rescue and medical teams arrived with their own equipment, including sniffer-dogs to search the rubble.

The work was disheartening, punctuated by small miracles such as finding a 40-year-old woman, Naqsha Bibi, reported to be alive beneath rubble after 63 days. International medical teams from as far as Cuba, together with the local military, set up makeshift field hospitals and began treating the injured, under the most difficult of conditions. The Pakistani and Indian governments came together and

opened up crossing points through the otherwise militarily controlled Line of Control (LOC) between the two countries to facilitate the flow of relief goods and allow people to contact relatives. The building of shelters for the homeless continued throughout the cold winter months.

A very personal encounter

The true magnitude of the disaster is best felt through the words and experiences of those who were there, such as Karam Umrani, a 28-year-old member of the Islamabad police force. Here is what he told BBC News on October 8, 2005 at 6:30 p.m. from the police dormitory: "The cries of the people trapped in the debris haunt me. There are still many trapped there. I was on duty at the

FACTS AND FIGURES

DATE	8:50 a.m., October 8, 2005
LOCATION	Epicenter 12 miles (19 km) northeast of Muzaffarabad, Pakistan
DEATH TOLL	Over 90,000 dead; 106,000 injured
DAMAGE	Over 570,000 homes were destroyed; damages estimated in excess of US$5 billion (2006 value)
DURATION	1 to 2 minutes
MAGNITUDE	Moment scale 7.6
COMMENTS	Most deaths and damage were caused by building collapse, leaving 3.3 million homeless. The earthquake triggered major landslides, blocking access roads (see entry in chapter on mudslides and landslides).

time of the earthquake and close to Margalla Towers when it struck. I heard a blast. The ground shook violently and I saw only dust and mess everywhere. I was worried for my own life. At Margalla Towers, all I could see was rubble on the ground. I heard the cries of the people trapped inside there. I could only do one thing, which was to pick people out of the rubble and with my bare hands I started to dig. First, I pulled out one dead body—a man whose head had been badly injured. I couldn't save him. But then I managed to rescue somebody else. I followed the cries and the voices from inside the rubble and I kept digging and following them til I found their source. It was a man of 35. I carried him on my shoulders to the ambulance that was waiting. He had been inside the towers in an apartment. His head and legs were badly injured but at least he was alive. I kept on hearing only shouts and voices. Everyone was watching but we continued working, using what we had—our bare hands. I think I was in what was the basement of the building. We stayed for one hour and by that time all the emergency agencies had arrived. Now, I am in the police dormitory taking a

rest. I thought about my family. I was very worried for them—they are in the Sindh province. I live alone in these dorms. In about half an hour I have to go back to Margalla to continue the rescue effort."

Mobile phones cause life

At 11:30 p.m. Umrani spoke again with the BBC at Margalla Towers. "I am back on the spot now. But it has started raining here and that is hampering rescue operations. There are still 30 to 40 people inside the debris, including the assistant commissioner of municipal government in Islamabad, who lived in Margalla Towers. He's alive and speaking from a mobile phone from inside the debris. He says that he's in good condition and there are about 10 members of his family with him. They've got enough air. We have provided them with oxygen and we arranged water and other necessities for them and, Inshallah, they will be saved. Debris is being lifted by cranes and we are just continuing to talk to people. I will stay here until further orders from above. I am optimistic and I hope that within two or three hours everyone in the debris will come out."

ABOVE A tent camp with 1,500 tents was set up for over 700 families stricken by the earthquake in Islamabad. The Pakistani government urged earthquake victims to head south before winter set in.

Java, Indonesia, 2006

Early on the morning of May 27, 2006, a devastating magnitude 6.3 earthquake struck the Indonesian island of Java. The epicenter was just 10 miles (16 km) south of the region's largest city, Yogyakarta.

ABOVE Carved stones of the tenth-century Hindu temple at Prambanan were sent toppling during the earthquake. There are fears the stone foundations of this World Heritage site may now be greatly weakened.

The earthquake affected the densely populated region on the southern flank of the volcano, Merapi, stretching from Yogyakarta to the Indian Ocean. Known as the Bantul plain, the area is dotted with numerous small towns and villages surrounded by intensively cultivated rice fields. During the earthquake, tens of thousands of poorly constructed buildings collapsed, killing over 6,000 people and injuring more than seven times that many. The town of Bantul, closest to the epicenter, was worst hit, with 80 percent of its buildings destroyed. In Yogyakarta, many of the city's buildings suffered severe structural damage.

With the memory of the 2004 earthquake and tsunami fresh in their minds, coastal residents fled inland as soon as they felt the shaking. Fortunately, no tsunami eventuated, due to the smaller magnitude of this earthquake and the location of its epicenter onshore rather than in the ocean. Two aftershocks, of magnitude 4.8 and 4.6, followed several hours later, causing further panic among the survivors.

Many people were left without food or tents for the first few nights before help finally arrived. Children made up around 40 percent of those injured and displaced by the earthquake. Some had to resort to begging on the streets for food or money, a practice not normally seen in that part of Indonesia. Health authorities' first priority was to provide clean drinking water, as affected populations had limited access to stoves and kerosene to boil contaminated water taken from shallow wells. The first international airlifts arrived on May 29, bringing rolls of plastic sheeting for makeshift shelters, water containers, food, hygiene kits, medical teams, and field hospitals.

FACTS AND FIGURES

DATE	5:53 a.m., May 27, 2006
LOCATION	Epicenter 10 miles (16 km) south of Yogyakarta, Central Java, Indonesia
DEATH TOLL	6,200 dead; 46,000 injured
DAMAGE	67,000 houses were destroyed, leaving up to 200,000 people homeless; the Bantul region was the hardest hit
DURATION	57 seconds
MAGNITUDE	Richter scale 6.3
COMMENTS	As at June 2006, the Indonesian government had allocated US$8 million for emergency relief and US$107 million for the reconstruction; at that time it was expected to take one year

Government response too slow

Lack of clean water, electricity, food, shelter, and medical supplies were all issues facing survivors in the days following the earthquake. With hospitals overflowing and the injured waiting in queues for treatment, even lying on mats on the ground outside, there was some criticism leveled at the Indonesian government that their emergency response to the disaster should have been faster.

Jakarta's *Kompas* newspaper reported, "We accept the fact that ... most areas of our country are indeed prone to natural catastrophes ... Undoubtedly, volcano eruptions and earthquakes will become part of our daily life ... This natural reality should make us an intelligent and vigilant nation. Indonesia's nature requires us to have an active, sophisticated and capable disaster mitigation program."

Indonesian parliamentarian Wahyudin Munawir also spoke on the subject to Jakarta's *Republika* newspaper: "Mitigation efforts need to be made in order to increase society's ... preparedness in the face of a natural disaster, so that the impact can be reduced ... As a developing country, we perhaps need to learn from Japan about how to implement integrated mitigation plans to deal with the effects of a devastating earthquake."

Java's cultural loss

The temple at Prambanan, one of Asia's largest Hindu temple complexes, built in 850 CE and located 11 miles (18 km) east of Yogyakarta, was substantially damaged, with large carved blocks scattered over the ground. Also damaged was the Royal Graveyard of Imogiri, just east of Bantul. The World Heritage Buddhist stupa of Borobudur, dating to between 750 and 850 CE, was undamaged. Located 25 miles (40 km) northwest of Yogyakarta, it lay just outside the earthquake zone.

ABOVE Victims wait for help by the ruins of their totally destroyed homes in Klaten, 19 miles (30 km) northeast of Yogyakarta in Central Java. This photograph was taken four days after the earthquake from an Indonesian Air Force helicopter en route to a relief mission.

FAR LEFT Motorcyclists ride around a collapsed building in Yogyakarta on May 27, 2006, the day the earthquake hit.

WHY IS INDONESIA SO DANGEROUS?

Both Indonesia's numerous earthquakes and its active volcanic belt, including the volatile volcano Merapi, result from the continuous downthrusting of the Indo–Australian Plate beneath the Eurasian Plate. This takes place in the Sunda Trench, along the southwestern edge of the island archipelago, at a rate of about 2½ inches (6 cm) per year. Vast bursts of energy are released as earthquakes when the sea floor crust shudders, jerks, and cracks on its downward journey to ultimate destruction by melting.

Tsunamis

A tsunami, Japanese for "harbor wave," is perhaps one of the most unusual of natural disasters. Such a "freak" wave is an extremely rare occurrence and one can strike with little or no warning. A tsunami can cause damage thousands of miles from its origin, arriving several hours after its creation. It can devastate huge stretches of coastline around the ocean in which it formed.

Tsunamis or seismic sea waves are mostly caused by seismic activity in the ocean—an undersea earthquake. Submarine landslides, volcanic activity, and even large meteorite impacts can also generate tsunamis. Use of the term "tidal wave" is discouraged, as the tide plays no part in the creation of the wave. An upward movement of the sea floor generates a bulge of water that races outward, concentrically, from the earthquake epicenter, like ripples in a pond. If the sea floor moves downward, it is the trough part of the wave rather than its peak that moves outward first. In this case, the first sign of the tsunami people notice is the dramatic retreat of the sea from the shoreline. Eyewitnesses have reported that the surface of the sea may look as if it is boiling. This is caused by large quantities of gas bubbling to the water's surface. These gases, normally in balance under the sediment of the sea floor, escape due to the sudden drop in pressure as the sea retreats. Minutes or even hours later, a wave crest follows the wave trough of the tsunami.

The deceptive nature of a tsunami

In the deep ocean, tsunamis travel at high velocities, up to about 500 miles per hour (805 km/h), but they are barely noticeable by people at sea. This is because wave peaks may be hundreds of miles apart, but with a height difference of only a few feet between the peaks and troughs. Their passage through the ocean can only be detected by sensitive tidal gauges. It is only as the tsunami gets closer to the shore that friction against the seabed causes the wave front to become steep and break as the water further from the bottom overtakes the water closer to the bottom. Seen from the beach, a breaking tsunami may appear no bigger than a normal wave: photographs of the 2004 Indian Ocean tsunami show people calmly watching the oncoming wave from the sand. An aerial view of a tsunami, however, would reveal that the tsunami is a flat-topped wall of water, which doesn't drop down behind the crest like a normal wave. When it hits the beach it doesn't collapse and retreat but continues surging inland.

FAR LEFT Indonesian locals from the remote village of Lho Kruet on the island of Sumatra head back to their camp after being issued food and water rations. Assessment teams from the UN Health Organization surveyed and monitored the extensive damage caused here by the 2004 Indian Ocean Tsunami.

LEFT The "Byuo," one of the largest floodgates in Japan, is situated at Namazu Port in Shizuoka Prefecture. A massive 30-foot (9.3-m) high gate with a weight of 910 tons (925 t) automatically slams shut when a nearby seismograph detects a substantial ocean surge.

PREVIOUS PAGES Boats leave for Phuket, Thailand, filled with tourists and Thai workers. These tsunami survivors are being evacuated out of the wreckage left behind by the 2004 tsunami.

ABOVE Anglers try to salvage what they can from the boats that were piled up and destroyed by a tsunami that occurred in Nagapattinum, Tamil Nadu, in eastern India, in December 2004. This area was one of the hardest hit in the country, with about 7,000 people killed.

RIGHT Food supplies are unloaded off a longboat as Thai residents restock restaurants on the beach in the hope that tourists will return a month after the Indian Ocean tsunami. Many people from this region are still unaccounted for.

Unfortunately for tsunami victims, this realization comes too late. Amateur video footage of the 2004 Indian Ocean tsunami shows waves engulfing people as they try to outrun the foaming water while others just manage to scramble to safety on roof tops and balconies. Behind the beach, busy streets can be seen filling with torrents of water, sweeping along cars, trees, and all manner of debris.

How far inland is safe?

The distance that the wave will run inland depends on the shape of the coastline and the slope of the land. In areas where deep water abuts steep coastal cliffs, spectators have been known to gather on the cliff tops and watch the waves crashing harmlessly below. An offshore barrier or fringing coral reef will also help dissipate the energy of an incoming tsunami. However, if the slope is gentle, such as

where a river delta enters the sea or a broad tidal flat, there is nothing to block the tsunami's energy and it may travel up to several miles inland—as seen by the extent of devastation at Banda Aceh in Indonesia following the 2004 Indian Ocean tsunami. The shape of the coastline is also a critical factor in the impact a tsunami will have. A jagged coastline will cause the wave's energy to be distributed unevenly, often with disastrous results. Coastlines behind islands may have some protection, but even in these cases waves can bend around the island and reach the coast. Particularly susceptible are wide river mouths or funnel-shaped bays and harbors. As the wave moves in, its energy is concentrated, making it even more destructive. One of the most dramatic examples of this occurred at Valdez, Alaska in 1964. Here, the long narrow Valdez Arm fjord funneled the tsunami to an extraordinary height of 220 feet (67 m).

THE TEN MOST DEADLY TSUNAMIS

65 MILLION YEARS AGO	Taking first place for the honor of the world's greatest tsunami is the wave created by the massive 6-mile (9.7-km) diameter meteorite that hit Mexico's Yucatan Peninsula some 65 million years ago. Evidence from the sediments carried by the wave suggests that it must have been over half a mile (almost 1 km) high.
6100 BCE	Mega-tsunamis traveling across the Atlantic Ocean were caused by a collapse of a huge chunk of Norway's continental shelf in about 6100 BCE. Known as the Stroregga Slide, it ranks as one of the largest landslides in history.
1500 BCE	In 1500 BCE, Santorini Volcano in the Mediterranean Sea exploded and collapsed on itself, generating a mega-tsunami estimated to have been about 600 feet (183 m) high. It is speculated that the legendary city of Atlantis may have been sunk, along with Santorini Island.
NOVEMBER, 1755	A 16 to 33 feet (5 to 10 m) tsunami swept along the Tagus River into Lisbon, the bustling capital of Portugal. 100,000 people were killed and the city was so badly damaged that it was completely rebuilt.
DECEMBER, 1908	Towns and villages along Italy's Messina Straits suffered more damage and loss of life when a wave over 8 feet (2.4 m) high struck not long after a magnitude 7.1 earthquake. Waves along Calabrian and Sicilian coasts reached 15 feet (4.6 m), even traveling down the straits to Malta. Over 70,000 people were killed in the earthquake and the following tsunami.
OCTOBER, 1963	The reservoir behind the Vajont Dam in northern Italy was struck by an enormous landslide, which displaced water, causing a tsunami to sweep over the dam into the valley below. Almost 2,000 people were killed and the villages of Longarone, Pirago, Rivalta, Villanova, and Faè were destroyed.
AUGUST, 1976	An earthquake triggered a large tsunami in the Celebes Sea. This resulted in the death of more than 10,000 people in the Sulu Islands, North and South Zamboanga, North and South Lanao, North Cotabato, Maguindanao, and Sultan Kudarat, on the island of Mindanao to the south of the Philippines.
SEPTEMBER, 1992	An earthquake that struck Nicaragua on September 2, 1992, generated a tsunami with waves of up to 33 feet (10 m) along the Pacific coast of Nicaragua. Over 70,000 people living in the villages from San Juan Del Sur to Msachapa were affected by the tsunami.
DECEMBER, 1992	A series of tsunami waves arrived on the shores of Flores within two minutes of an earthquake occurring on the north coast of the eastern part of Flores Island. Over 1,600 Flores Islanders died, largely as a result of electrocution from fallen power lines, and approximately 18,000 houses were destroyed.
DECEMBER, 2004	An earthquake that had its epicenter in the Indian Ocean set off a series of lethal tsunamis on December 26, 2004, that killed approximately 275,000 people. This tsunami devastated areas in Indonesia up to the coast of Malaysia, as well as Bangladesh, India, Sri Lanka, the Maldives, and even as far away as Somalia, Kenya, and Tanzania in eastern Africa.

Which coastlines are most at risk?

The coastlines of the Pacific Ocean are most at risk, as the deep trenches running around its rim are sites of intense earthquake activity and more regularly generate tsunamis. The people living in tsunami-prone places such as Alaska, the western United States, Chile, and Japan are "tsunami ready." Other oceans are at less risk, but the people living along these coastlines can be caught unprepared, making the impact of a tsunami far more deadly, as was seen with the 2004 Indian Ocean tsunami.

Minimizing the power of tsunamis

Huge walls or tsunami barriers have been built in an attempt to dissipate the energy of incoming tsunamis, but the worth of this policy has been questioned. The 1993 Hokkaido tsunami reached 100 feet (30 m) and washed over the wall built

ABOVE An aerial view of Meulaboh in Sumatra shows the random nature of the destructive force of a tsunami. Some buildings have withstood the pummeling waves, but the rest of this village has been flattened.

to protect the Japanese port town of Aonae. After the 2004 tsunami, efforts were made by many governments to discourage people from rebuilding in coastal areas, but this, too, has met with limited success. Interestingly, however, it was observed that coastal areas with densely vegetated shorelines escaped relatively unscathed. It was found that stands of mangroves or coconut palms dissipated the energy of the incoming wave.

One of the most striking examples of this was seen in the southern Indian state of Tamil Nadu. The village of Naluvedapathy had planted a forest of thousands of trees on the shoreline in 2002 in order to enter the *Guinness Book of Records*. When the 2004 tsunami hit, the forest protected the village and there were only a few deaths and minimal damage.

As part of advance preparation and protection from tsunamis, it is now recommended that a high-density planting strategy be adopted along at risk coastlines.

Tsunami early warning systems

Tsunamis can be detected from merely minutes and up to a day in advance of their arrival. In the Pacific Ocean, a network of buoys constantly measure sea level, recording any unusual changes. The Hawaii-based network, established in 1948, forms what is known as the Pacific Tsunami Warning Center. A series of well-rehearsed international drills ensure that warnings can be received by local emergency services personnel and quickly relayed to the general public. Countless lives can be saved with even just a few minutes' warning. The December 26, 2004

RIGHT A. The subducting plate slides under the overriding plate, causing a build up of friction. B. This causes energy to accumulate, which is released as an earthquake. C. This forces the seabed above the overriding plate to shift suddenly upwards, pushing the seawater above it outwards in a circular pattern, creating a massive wave that moves out from the epicenter.

A

B

WHAT TO DO IN THE EVENT OF A TSUNAMI

1. PAY ATTENTION TO THE WARNING SIGNS. A strong earthquake or unusual rapid changes in sea level often herald a tsunami. On some tsunami-prone coastlines, people will run inland as soon as they experience a strong earthquake. Fishermen know to take their boats out to deep ocean if they suspect an impending tsunami. Animals may leave the area.

2. ACT QUICKLY. A few minutes may mean the difference between life and death. Resist the urge to look at the unnatural phenomenon. Many people make the mistake of walking toward the outgoing wave, onto the exposed sea floor, to collect shells or stranded fish. Warn others while moving quickly away from the beach.

3. MOVE TO HIGH GROUND. Choose where to go quickly and carefully. Waves reach heights of 10 to 12 feet (3 to 4 m) and can destroy non-substantial structures. Many people have survived by climbing nearby hills or to the upper floors and roofs of substantial buildings, such as hotels or office blocks. Although not an ideal solution, climbing a tall tree can save your life.

4. AVOID THE INITIAL SURGE. If you are caught at ground level, move behind any substantial object such as a concrete wall to avoid the initial surge. If caught in the current, don't swim against it. Far more dangerous than the fast-moving water is the tangle of roofing iron, trees, cars, and electrical wires carried in it. If possible, get onto a floating object, then get out of the water to avoid the rush of water as the wave heads back to the sea.

5. BE AWARE OF FURTHER WAVES. A tsunami is not a single wave but a series of crests and troughs. Do not return to the coast after the first wave. The second and third waves are often much bigger and therefore more deadly than the first.

BELOW This woodblock print by Japanese artist Ando Hiroshige (1797–1858) shows a massive wave that is reduced to a tiny hill when compared with the tsunami wave behind it. Tsunamis have been occurring in Japan for hundreds of years.

Indian Ocean tsunami highlighted the need for a coastal early warning system in all of the world's major oceans. Since then, there has been considerable international investment of time and funding into the establishment of the Indian Ocean Tsunami Warning System, with emphasis on the development of a multi-hazard approach to strengthen the capabilities of Indian Ocean regional governments to respond to all natural disasters, including tsunamis, cyclones, sea swells, floods, and earthquakes. This initiative was agreed to in a United Nations conference held in January 2005. The 2004 Indian Ocean disaster has also prompted a major review of early warning capabilities in the world's other seas and oceans. The Indian Ocean Tsunami Warning System became active in June 2006. It consists of 25 seismographic stations relaying information to 26 national tsunami information centers. Three deep ocean sensors have also been put in place.

It is difficult for people living in tsunami-prone areas to be on constant alert for an event they may never see. With some investment and cooperation between governments of coastal nations, warning procedures can be put in place to save lives.

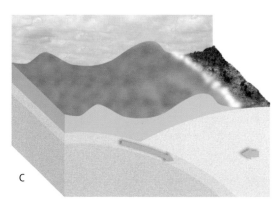

C

Kii Peninsula, Japan, 1498

One of the earliest recorded tsunamis, and also one of Japan's largest and most destructive, was the tsunami of 1498. On September 20 it struck the Kii Peninsular south of Tokyo, sweeping away thousands of buildings, and resulted in the loss of 31,200 lives.

Hanamako Lake was drastically altered by the tsunami, which shifted the position of its estuary mouth by about 2 miles (3.5 km). This changed the previously freshwater lake into a saltwater system. The 1498 tsunami is perhaps best remembered for washing away the temple building that was built around a revered 44 feet (13.4 m) high bronze Buddha statue that had been cast in 1252. Miraculously, the Buddha was left unharmed after the violent wave passed. To this day, the Buddha has remained exposed to the elements.

Living with tsunamis

For as long as the Japanese people can remember, they have had to deal with tsunamis striking their coastline. Tsunami warning signs along the beaches remind people of the danger, offering simple advice to those who might be caught by surprise: move to high ground as quickly and calmly as possible.

ABOVE The Great Wave of Kanagawa, from the series "36 Views from Mt Fuji" is a woodblock print that shows the size and scale of tsunami waves that have occurred throughout Japan's history.

RIGHT This map of tsunami waves reverberating out from the epicenter of an earthquake in 1944 gives information most likely to replicate the tsunami pattern that occurred in the same area in 1498. At that time, the Pacific rim was largely unmapped so there are no accurate records of the tsunami's ultimate reach.

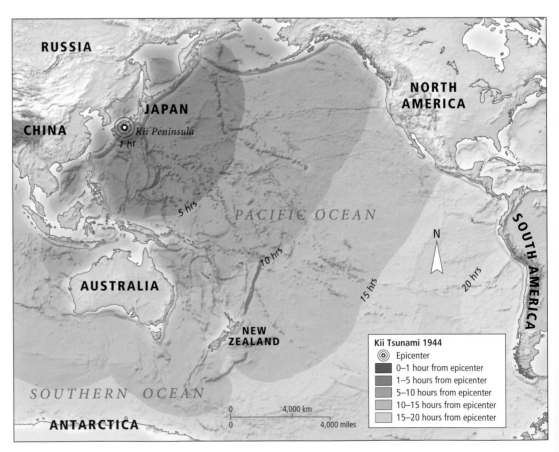

Kii Tsunami 1944
- ◎ Epicenter
- 0–1 hour from epicenter
- 1–5 hours from epicenter
- 5–10 hours from epicenter
- 10–15 hours from epicenter
- 15–20 hours from epicenter

The most dangerous part of Japan is its densely populated Pacific coast. Here, the Philippine and Pacific plates are descending beneath the Eurasian Plate along a line of deep trenches that lie just off the country's eastern edge. This subduction activity and melting are responsible for Japan being a volcanic island archipelago. Earthquakes and tsunamis occur because the passage of the descending plate beneath Japan is not smooth. The plate tends to jam for a while, building up stress, then suddenly moves a bit more when the breaking strain of the rocks is reached. This sudden release of stress is what generates earthquakes and tsunamis. So the longer an area goes without a substantial earthquake, the more at risk it becomes.

Japanese scientists have realized that there is a definite repeat-time interval between earthquake recurrences. Based on historic data from the Tokai–Nankai region, where there have been major earthquakes/tsunamis in 1361, 1498, 1605, 1707, 1854, and 1944, researchers have determined the repeat interval to be 100 to 150 years.

Furthermore, when stress is finally released on a certain portion of the descending plates it creates additional stress on the surrounding portions of the plate, which may then, in turn, fracture. This can happen almost immediately, as seen in the 1605 and 1707 earthquakes, or it may take a longer time, as was the case in the December 23, 1854 Tokai earthquake, which was followed 32 hours later by the Nankai earthquake. Or the stress release may take several years: the 1944 Tonankai earthquake was followed by one in the Nankai area in 1946. Most alarmingly, scientists have pinpointed a section of the descending plate in the Tonkai area that did not break during the 1944–46 activity, and has been jammed up since the 1854 earthquake. Scientists are predicting that a large earthquake and tidal wave could occur in the Tonkai region at any moment.

Japan's tsunami warning system

Japan is one of the Pacific Rim countries most susceptible to substantial loss of life, infrastructure damage, and economic setback as a result of earthquakes and tsunamis. But Japan is also the most disaster-ready nation in the world. People are aware of the particular hazards in their area and are prepared for any emergency.

Japan has a network of fiber-optic sensors that record any seismic activity around the archipelago. This information is transmitted to the country's Meteorological Agency, which estimates the height, speed, and arrival time of tsunamis and warns the coastal areas most at risk. The agency sounds an alarm within minutes of an earthquake being registered, giving people time to take preventive measures that will save lives.

ABOVE In Numaza, Shizuoka Prefecture, a residential area along the seaside, a seawall acts as a protective shield from potential tsunamis. There are four different tectonic plates situated underneath Japan, which cause disastrous earthquakes every 100 to 150 years.

FACTS AND FIGURES

DATE	September 20, 1498
LOCATION	Epicenter in Tokai–Nankai region, Shikoku Island, Kii Peninsula, Japan
DEATH TOLL	31,200
DAMAGE	Japanese Pacific coast towns and villages destroyed or extensively damaged
DURATION	Unknown
MAGNITUDE	Richter scale 8.7
COMMENTS	The tsunami severely altered Japan's Kii Peninsula coastline. Most deaths were caused by drowning or being hit by debris in the water.

Lisbon, Portugal, 1755

On the morning of November 1, 1755, a violent earthquake shook the city of Lisbon, at that time one of Europe's grandest cities. As the fine stone buildings and churches began to collapse, people ran for the open spaces of the docks, hoping to find safety. Many tried to board ships moored in the Tagus River, but could only stare in amazement as the sea began to recede, exposing lost shipwrecks and abandoned cargo lying on the sea floor.

Moments later, a massive wall of water could be seen on the horizon. It swept against the seawall and into the mouth of the mighty Tagus River, capsizing and sinking boats. The wave surged into the city, then just as quickly withdrew, dragging people and debris out to sea, again leaving large stretches of the bottom of the sea exposed. Two more enormous waves followed the first.

An eyewitness account

Reverend Charles Davy survived the earthquake and tsunami that followed it to tell his story: "You may judge of the force of this shock, when I inform you it was so violent that I could scarce keep on my knees; but it was attended with some circumstances still more dreadful than the former. On a sudden I heard a general outcry, 'The sea is coming in, we shall be all lost.' Upon this, turning my eyes towards the river, which in that place is nearly 4 miles (6.4 km) broad, I could perceive it heaving and swelling in the most unaccountable manner, as no wind was stirring. In an instant there appeared, at some small distance, a large body of water, rising as it were like a mountain. It came on foaming and roaring, and I rushed toward the shore with such impetuosity, we all immediately ran for our lives as fast as possible; many were actually swept away, and the rest above their waist in water stood at a good distance from the banks. For my own part, I had the narrowest escape and should certainly have been lost, had I not grasped a large beam that lay on the ground, till the water returned to its channel."

To make matters worse, a severe fire broke out and burned for days, completing the catastrophic and near-total destruction of Lisbon, the capital of the powerful Portuguese trading nation and one of the richest cities in Europe at the time.

Political upheaval and the birth of modern seismology

The terrible disaster caused a great uproar throughout Europe, as it occurred on All Saints' Day, a Catholic holiday. Many people were worshipping in churches when the buildings

THE REBUILDING OF LISBON

Sebastião José de Melo, the dynamic Portuguese Prime Minister of the time, oversaw the reconstruction of the harbor and the city of Lisbon following the catastrophic 1755 earthquake. Under his supervision, Lisbon was rebuilt in record time. The only contribution by this pragmatic and highly enlightened Prime Minister to the debate raging about God's role in the destruction of Lisbon was, in his dry sense of humor, when he asked why God had chosen to spare the city's red-light district while destroying all of its churches. He curbed the powers of the Inquisition by subjecting it to the King's authority and expelled the Jesuits from Portugal and its colonies. He also changed property laws to stop the Church accumulating wealth and power.

collapsed on them, and priests initially blamed the tragedy on all the "sinners" of Lisbon. Inquisitors roamed the streets looking for people to hang. It ignited spirited debate among Enlightenment philosophers about justice and the relationship between mankind, the natural world, and the divine. The grip of the medieval church on society was gradually weakened and eventually broke. The Prime Minister, Sebastião de Melo, reacted more pragmatically to the disaster with his now famous quote: "What now? We bury the dead and feed the living." He immediately embarked on an extensive program to rebuild the capital.

The Lisbon earthquake also led to the birth of modern seismology, as the forward-thinking Prime Minister ordered all observations of the disaster to be noted and documented. He asked questions about how long the earthquake had lasted, what happened in wells or waterholes, how many aftershocks were felt, what kind of damage was caused, and how animals had behaved. The newly built Lisbon was planned with wide streets and earthquake-proof buildings in its city center, which were tested by marching hundreds of soldiers around them.

It is believed that the 1755 Lisbon earthquake was caused by movement between the African and Eurasian Tectonic plates, a boundary known as the Azores–Gibraltar Fracture Zone. History shows that early warning systems are essential for saving lives.

ABOVE Earthquake, tsunami, and fire strike the city of Lisbon in the fateful year of 1755. Terror can be seen in the expressions of the people on the docks as the tsunami rushes into the harbor, while behind them the city burns.

FACTS AND FIGURES

DATE	9:20 a.m., November 1, 1755
LOCATION	Epicenter in Atlantic Ocean, 124 miles (200 km) west-southwest of Cape St Vincent
DEATH TOLL	100,000
DAMAGE	City of Lisbon almost entirely destroyed by earthquake, tsunami, and fire; damage around the Atlantic coast, particularly Portugal, Spain and Morocco
DURATION	10 minutes
MAGNITUDE	Richter scale 8.7
COMMENTS	The 16 to 33 foot (5 to 10 m) tsunami struck Portugal, southwestern Spain, Gibraltar, the west coast of Morocco, France, Great Britain, Ireland, Belgium, Holland, Madeira, the Azores islands, Antigua, Martinique, and Barbados

Messina–Reggio, Sicily, Italy, 1908

Before sunrise on the morning of December 28, 1908, a magnitude 7.1 earthquake shook the towns and villages of Italy's Messina Straits. Destruction was immediate and catastrophic due to the region's poorly constructed stone and brick buildings. A tsunami followed, hitting the already devastated Sicilian and Calabrian coastlines and killing more of the population.

ABOVE After the earthquake and tsunami struck Messina–Reggio, survivors were faced with the task of cleaning up the rubble. Workmen carry off debris and load it onto rafts ready to be shipped out to sea.

TOP RIGHT Collapsed buildings among others that are still standing show the need for standards of building design aimed to withstand quakes.

BOTTOM RIGHT Messina's destruction was so great that residents had to be relocated to safer areas of the city. Refugees were forced to camp on flat ground near the ruins.

A few minutes after the shaking had stopped, the sea retreated a short distance away from the shore, then quickly advanced in the form of a foaming wave. At Messina, the wave was 8 feet (2.4 m) high and washed over the neck of land that formed the harbor. It destroyed the breakwater and dragged fishing boats onto the beach. A 2,000 ton (2,032 tonne) Russian steamer sitting in the dry dock was carried out into the bay, where it quickly sank. The tsunami surged over the seawall and into the buildings along the waterfront. Only a few people on the waterfront were hurt. Due to the early morning timing of the earthquake, thousands of people were killed as they lay sleeping, buried under the rubble of their homes. There was more damage at Reggio di Calabria, where the tsunami reached heights of approximately 12 to 15 feet (3.7 to 4.6 m). The frightening first wave was followed by a number of smaller ones, gradually diminishing in size.

The tsunami rapidly raced southward along the heavily populated Sicilian and Calabrian coastlines to Taormina, Catania, and Syracuse. It finally reached Malta, arriving 113 minutes after the earthquake.

Damage compounded by gravel terraces

The coastline on either side of the Messina Straits is made up of a series of flat-topped terraces created from sediment washed down from the surrounding hills. On these flat gravel beaches many of the ports and fishing villages of Sicily and Calabria had been precariously built. Not only did the loose sediments amplify the earthquake's powerful and destructive energy, but the shaking also caused the unstable gravel terraces to slump dramatically into the Straits. Massive drops in elevation could be seen along the length of the coastline following the earthquake, with quays and wharfs dropping between 1 to 6 feet (0.3 to 1.8 m). Even though the fault responsible for this particular earthquake ruptured at a depth of at least 5 miles (8 km) and did not reach the surface, it was the collapsing terraces that caused the tsunami, and also broke Messina's submarine communications cable, the town's only contact with the outside world.

Slow economic recovery

Survivors of the earthquake and tsunami faced the bleakest of realities. Their homes and livelihoods were destroyed, and most were left searching for family members who were missing. The bustling city was reduced to rubble, with communication and transport infrastructure extensively damaged. Assistance to the disaster areas was not immediate as the only access was by sea, and organized help took days to arrive. It took months to clean up

FACTS AND FIGURES

DATE	5:20 a.m., December 28, 1908
LOCATION	Epicenter in the Messina Straits, Italy
DEATH TOLL	70,000 or more
DAMAGE	Tsunami damage to Calabrian and Sicilian coast minimal compared with the earthquake
DURATION	35 seconds
MAGNITUDE	Richter scale 7.1
COMMENTS	The tsunami struck the Calabrian and Sicilian coasts, reaching 15 feet (4.6 m) at Reggio. It traveled down the Messina Straits as far as Malta.

the debris. The destruction of the docks, ports, fishing fleets, and other coastal infrastructure by the tsunami was so great that the region did not fully recover for many years. The Italian government of the time took the decision to relocate many of the Messina survivors to different cities within Italy. Other refugees were forced to emigrate to America. The economic recovery of the region was further hampered by the onset of World War I. It is little wonder that so many families left southern Italy during the early decades of the 1900s.

A new bridge to economic growth

Interest in better understanding this particular earthquake and its associated tsunami has increased with a proposal to build the world's largest suspension bridge to connect the opposite shores of the Messina Straits. Although it is not anticipated that there will be any recurrence of activity along this fault for some time, any such structure needs to be able to handle whatever nature can throw at it.

Chile and Hawaii, 1960

On May 22, 1960, the largest earthquake of the twentieth century created a massive tsunami, which radiated out to all corners of the Pacific. The terrifying magnitude 9.5 earthquake occurred 435 miles (700 km) south of Santiago, off the coast from Valdivia in south-central Chile and, despite its size, it was not very destructive. Most of the damage was caused by the giant tsunami in those countries within and around the Pacific Ocean.

BELOW In Valdivia, Chile, a man prays among the ruins of his house, which was destroyed by the earthquake in 1960 that triggered the tsunami.

The earthquake was the result of the sudden release of built-up stress in the deep trench running down Chile's west coast. A violent down-thrusting of the Pacific Plate beneath Chile resulted in a vertical movement of the sea floor of approximately 30 feet (10 m). This generated a huge, spreading bulge of water. First hit was the Peru–Chile coastline, where there was major destruction of ports, fishing fleets, and other waterfront infra-structures from waves as high as 30 to 50 feet (10 to 15 m). About 2,300 people lost their lives within half an hour of the earthquake's impact.

The following tsunami surged across the Pacific, reaching Hawaii 15 hours later. Here, waves of about 30 feet (10 m) wreaked destruction in Hilo, killing and injuring people who had failed to evacuate low-lying areas in time. After 22 hours, the tsunami eventually reached Japan, where waves up to 20 feet (6 m) high flooded its coastline and killed 200 people. There was also damage reported in New Zealand, Samoa, the Marquesas, and the west coast of North America. Smaller waves continued to bounce backward and forward across the Pacific for about three days after the earthquake.

Chile: quick and wise decisions save lives

The most severe tsunami damage to the Chilean coast occurred between Concepción and the south end of Isla Chiloé. In the town of Valdivia, closest to the epicenter, people panicked after the severe earthquake and many, having no idea of what would come next, decided to run for the hills. This decision saved many lives when the tsunami surged in and completely destroyed the town's port and industrial area, then sucked back, dragging all manner of debris —including people calling for help from whole houses floating in the deluge. Along the coast of Chiloé Island, some of the inhabitants decided to seek refuge from the terrifying natural disaster in their fishing boats. About 10 to 15 minutes after the earthquake, the water began receding right along the coast stranding the boats on the sea floor—it was the first trough of the tsunami and would soon be followed by the crest. A sheer wall of water swept into the coast destroying all the fishing boats.

Meanwhile, near Queule, Mrs Vitalia Llanquimán had also felt the earthquake. A little while after the shaking stopped, a man came past her house on

horseback to tell her that the sea had disappeared from the shore. As the Llanquimáns lived about 1 mile (1.6 km) from the sea, Vitalia did not pay much attention to the stranger's story, but fortunately her husband realized that it was a warning. He said that when the sea came back it might surge inland. They gathered the family together and, with the two youngest children tucked under their arms, climbed a nearby hill, only moments before the tsunami wiped out their home in the valley below.

A quick decision to go to high ground or as far inland as possible can be a life-saving one, and time must never be wasted on trying to save material possessions, as Mr Ramón Atala, a wealthy merchant living in Maullín, discovered to his peril. Between the first and second waves, Mr Atala decided to go to his waterfront warehouse to get money he had left there. His wife tried to stop him, and he went to the warehouse. The second wave struck while he was inside and washed the building away.

ABOVE An aerial view of the southern section of the Peruvian coastline shows the houses on the shoreline completely submerged after the massive tsunami wave hit.

TOP The Pacific Tsunami Warning Center is in Hawaii. Data that is collected is processed in real time to give the position, direction, and the size of an incoming tsunami and alert all countries at risk around the Pacific rim.

ABOVE In the bottom left-hand corner of the picture, a man can be seen helplessly facing the oncoming fury of the tsunami breaking over Pier 1 in Hilo Harbor, Hawaii. Many went to watch it, unaware of the danger.

FACTS AND FIGURES

DATE	2:11 p.m., May 22, 1960
LOCATION	Epicenter in Pacific Ocean, near Valdivia, Chile
DEATH TOLL	5,700
DAMAGE	Estimated at US$550 million
DURATION	5 to 6 minutes
MAGNITUDE	Richter scale 8.6 (upgraded to 9.5 Moment magnitude)
COMMENTS	A tsunami up to 30 feet (10 m) high reached North America, Japan, and the Hawaiian islands. Most of the lives that were lost were not as a result of the initial earthquake, but in the tsunami.

A TIMELY WARNING TO MOVE TO HIGHER GROUND

In Onagawa, on the east coast of Honshu in Japan, fireman Kimura Kunio was on night duty beside the town's harbor when he noticed unusual motion in the water. He left his post and alerted the town's residents, telling them to make their way to the nearby hill. The last of the town's people just managed to arrive there by 4:45 a.m., as the first large wave entered town.

As a result of Mr Kunio's decisive actions, no one in Onagawa lost their lifes as debris-loaded waves measuring up to 14 feet (4.3 m) high pounded the town for several hours. Elsewhere along Japan's coast, those who did not have sufficient warning perished.

Hawaii: Hilo residents need more education to avoid mistakes

The residents of Hilo had many hours of warning in which to prepare and evacuate their town as the tsunami sped across the Pacific toward them. Yet some critical mistakes were still made that needlessly cost people their lives.

At 6:47 p.m. Hawaiian time, the US Coast and Geodetic Survey issued a warning to people that waves would reach Hilo around midnight, and at 8:30 p.m. they began sounding all the coastal sirens in Hilo every 20 minutes. Although about one-third of the population were evacuated, hundreds of people failed to understand the warning and were still on low ground when the wave struck as predicted. The first wave was only a few feet high, so people then began returning to Hilo thinking that the danger had passed. They were all caught unexpectedly when the highest wave of the tsunami struck at 1:04 a.m. on May 23.

The Brown family evacuated when they heard the sirens, but 16-year-old Carol Brown was one of those who came back too soon. She and her brother Ernest heard on the radio that a small wave had come into town; they had also met a police officer who had told them that the danger was over. So they went to their sister's house in a low-lying part of Hilo. Shortly after 1:00 a.m. they heard a low rumbling noise that started to get louder and louder, accompanied by crashing sounds. The next moment the lights went out and their wooden house was hit by the wave. It was lifted cleanly off its foundations and carried inland in one piece. Carol and her family were lucky, but 61 others perished and another 282 people were injured. Property damage in Hilo included 229 houses and 308 business and public buildings.

In the areas of maximum destruction, buildings of reinforced concrete or structural steel remained standing, proving that consideration needed to be given to building materials to prevent the loss of life that occurred from people being crushed by collapsing buildings.

Hawaii's Pacific Tsunami Warning Center

Being in the middle of the Pacific Ocean, Hawaii is susceptible to tsunamis from all points of the compass. The islands have been hit by six severe tsunamis in the past 60 years; they have come from the Aleutians (1946 and 1957), Kamchatka, Russia (1952), Chile (1960), Alaska (1964), and from an earthquake near Kalapana on the Big Island (1975).

Hawaii's main weapon against tsunamis is the DART (Deep-ocean Assessment and Reporting of Tsunami) buoy. Deployed all around the Pacific, these DART buoys consist of a float attached to a sea floor sensor that detects the size and position of an incoming tsunami. The sensor does this by measuring subtle changes in water pressure as the wave passes over. The information is relayed by satellite to the Pacific Tsunami Warning Center where the appropriate emergency response is made. Hawaii's tsunami experts regularly meet at the O'ahu Civil Defense office to study the different response possibilities for the next tsunami, and to review potential problems such as those that hampered the response to the Indian Ocean tsunami in 2004. Emergency personnel are drilled regularly. Tsunami

LEFT Military personnel carrying out one of many first aid evacuation drills. Tsunami emergency response teams practice regularly in Hawaii to minimize confusion and loss of life in the next big tsunami.

evacuation plans have been printed in the front of all Hawaiian telephone books. Emergency officials hope that all of this preparation is enough and the public will respond appropriately.

BELOW All Hawaiian beaches like Waikiki are at risk from tsunamis generated anywhere in and around the Pacific Ocean.

Gulf of Alaska, 1964

On Good Friday, March 27, 1964, tsunami waves radiated out into the Pacific Ocean from its north-eastern corner like ripples from a pebble thrown into a pond. The cause was an earthquake near Anchorage, Alaska, resulting from slippage along the Pacific rim subduction zone. Up to 50 feet (15 m) of the sea floor uplifted in the Gulf of Alaska over an area of about 200,000 square miles (520,000 km²), creating a massive bulge of water, that kept spreading over the Pacific.

FAR RIGHT, TOP A fishing village on Kodiak Island is strewn with debris. Geysers of water blow out from damaged fire hydrants.

FAR RIGHT, BOTTOM Fishing boats were tossed around like corks and smashed together when the tsunami hit the Alaskan coastline. Some ended up several blocks inland from the waterfront.

BELOW Kodiak after the tsunami. The first wave was small, giving residents time to escape to higher ground before the second and third waves hit.

Moving across the ocean at an incredible 500 miles per hour (800 km/h), the wave devastated Valdez, Seward, and several smaller Alaskan coastal communities. It took nearly two hours before it visited Kodiak Island with equal destruction. It reached Prince Rupert after 2 hours 40 minutes, Seattle after 3 hours and 20 minutes, Crescent City, California after 4 hours 30 minutes, Hawaii after 5 hours, Los Angeles after 6 hours, and finally Tokyo some 7 hours later than Los Angeles.

The destruction of Valdez

Valdez, a pretty Alaskan fishing town of about 1,100 residents, was the worst hit by the destructive force of the tsunami. The town lies at the head of a 30-mile (48 km) fjord, which appears to have channeled and funneled the wave, concentrating its energy and height. Witnesses tell of seeing a 220-foot (67 m) high mountain of water roaring up the fjord and hitting the Valdez pier. Most of the 31 people who died were working at the pier when the wave came in. A local resident, Jim Aubert, described the event to *National Geographic* writer, William Graves:

FACTS AND FIGURES	
DATE	5:36 p.m., March 27, 1964
LOCATION	Epicenter 75 miles (120 km) east of Anchorage
DEATH TOLL	125 (total), 115 (due to tsunami)
DAMAGE	Alaska's fishing industry and most seaport facilities were destroyed. The Oregon and Californian coastlines were also damaged. The repair bill was US$300–400 million.
DURATION	4 minutes
MAGNITUDE	Richter scale 8.4 (upgraded to 9.2 Moment magnitude)
COMMENTS	A tsunami up to 30 feet (10 m) high reached North America, Japan, and Hawaii. Most of the lives that were lost occurred in the tsunami rather than directly from the Anchorage earthquake that caused it.

"One second she was there, the next she wasn't. I saw maybe a dozen people turn and break for the beach, but she was a long pier—maybe a hundred yards—and they hadn't the littlest chance. She was sucked under all at once, like, well, like the bobber on a fishing line when the big one hits. My eyes can't seem to get rid of it."

More waves followed the first into Valdez harbor. Captain Bernard Whalen of the SS *Chena*, tied up at the pier at the time, reported that, after the first wave passed, his ship tore free of its moorings and plummeted vertically to the harbor floor. He ordered his crew to power up the engines to prepare for the next wave, so when it came in he would be able to turn the boat rousnd and head down the fjord to safety, but not before the boat dropped to the bottom two more times. Waves continued to arrive at about 30-minute intervals until 2:00 a.m. The dockside facilities in the town of Seward were swept away completely and 11 more lives were lost.

The fall of Kodiak

Two hours later it was Kodiak's turn. A dozen waves arrived with force with the second and third ones being the most destructive. The first was more like a rapidly rising tide than a wave. It served as a

warning to the people of Kodiak that the danger was imminent, and most of the town's 5,000 residents were quickly evacuated to the nearby high ground of Pillar Mountain.

Back at the waterfront, Captain Bill Cuthbert, on board the *Selief*, saw the entire crab-fishing fleet sitting on the dry harbor bottom after the first wave passed. The enormous second wave was a 30-foot (10 m) wall of water that picked up the boats and tossed them around like corks. The *Selief* and its crew were dragged back and forth several times, coming to rest inland in the town's school yard, several blocks from the waterfront. The main street of Kodiak became a jumble of wrecked boats, buildings, vehicles, and debris.

Towns along the Oregon and Californian coast also suffered damage. Crescent City was hardest hit, with its waterfront wiped out and 11 people dead. Santa Cruz harbor, San Francisco Bay, and marinas around Los Angeles were also damaged.

Hokkaido, Japan, 2003

At 4:50 a.m. on Friday, September 26, 2003, a powerful earthquake occurred in the Pacific Ocean, about 62 miles (100 km) off the coast of Japan's northernmost island of Hokkaido. Known as the Tokachi-Oki Earthquake, it was the largest in nine years to hit Japan. The shaking was strong in Hokkaido, and it was also felt on Honshu Island as far south as Tokyo.

About an hour later, a second earthquake measuring 5.8 on the Richter scale jolted Hokkaido, followed by a third measuring 7.0. The shaking triggered some landslides, and many roads in southeastern Hokkaido were damaged. Roof tiles were thrown from houses, some buildings cracked, gravestones toppled, a train was derailed, and an oil refinery was set alight. The worst damage was in the town of Kushiro, where the airport was closed, and more than 16,000 homes lost power due to a thermal plant shutdown. Most of the people injured were cut by broken glass or hurt by falling objects in their homes. One woman reported that the force of the quake made it impossible to stand up, so she stayed in bed until the shaking stopped.

BELOW A lone fishing boat sits on the ground after a tsunami hit the coast of Okushiri Island, which lies to the west of Japan's island of Hokkaido.

Officials issue tsunami alert

Immediately after the earthquake, Japan's high-tech Meteorological Agency issued a tsunami warning. Ten thousand families that were living in coastal areas on Hokkaido were put on an alert to evacuate. The warning was supported by seismologist Minoru Kasahara, of Hokkaido University, who appeared on television: "We should be alert for tsunamis for a day or two." Boats and ships started heading out from the Hokkaido coast toward open ocean before the tsunami arrived. The Japanese Red Cross prepared itself for an emergency situation, with their Disaster Management Division coordinating local government authorities, hospitals, and blood banks. The US National Oceanic and

Atmospheric Administration (NOAA) also issued a severe tsunami warning for Russia, and a lower-level tsunami watch for the Philippines, Taiwan, Hawaii, and many other Pacific islands.

Tsunami is surprisingly small and non-destructive

When the tsunami arrived, it was much smaller than expected, with waves only reaching 13 feet (4 m). The tsunami hit the southeastern coast of Hokkaido, where it washed away some parked cars and shipping containers, and beached a number of fishing vessels, but apart from that there was very little damage to port facilities. The impact of the tsunami was only felt locally. On Honshu Island it was measured at only 2 feet (60 cm).

This surprisingly small and localized tsunami shows how difficult it is to predict their destructive potential based on the magnitude of the earthquake responsible for them. This is because the amount of energy that an earthquake releases does not directly relate to the amount or type of sea floor movement. A fault with large amounts of sideways ground motion (such as the San Andreas Fault in California), or one that doesn't reach the surface, is much less likely to trigger a dangerous tsunami than one with a strong up-and-down motion.

A similar case of a non-performing tsunami occurred in 1994, when a magnitude 8.1 earthquake struck the Kuril Islands northeast of Japan. In Hawaii, Honolulu was evacuated in expectation of the tsunami, but in the end there was no wave. In contrast, a similar-sized earthquake west of Japan in 1896, generated a giant tsunami of over 70 feet (20 m) that struck an entirely unprepared population, wiped out entire villages on the north coast of Honshu Island, killing 27,000 people and destroying over 10,000 homes

The cause of the 2003 earthquake and tsunami

The earthquake was caused by the Pacific Ocean floor, which is moving westward at about 3 inches (8.2 cm) per year, being thrust beneath the Asian plate along a line marked by the deep Kurile Trench. This sudden movement between the plates occurred in the same place that ruptured in 1952, illustrating yet again that in most cases subduction is not a slow, continuous process. The plates do not move smoothly beneath one another, but grind together in a series of sudden jerks.

ABOVE Tsunamis have caused extensive damage in the region, and the damage they inflict can lead to the outbreak of fire. This one hit Okushiri on July 13, 1993.

BELOW Japanese Defence Forces personnel search through the debris in a residential area of Hokkaido after the tsunami caused its massive devastation.

FACTS AND FIGURES	
DATE	4:50 a.m., September 26, 2003
LOCATION	Epicenter was offshore, 85 miles (140 km) south southwest of Kushiro, Hokkaido, Japan
DEATH TOLL	Nil dead; 589 injured
DAMAGE	There was minor damage to roads and buildings in southeastern Hokkaido; the total damage was estimated at US$90 million
DURATION	40 seconds
MAGNITUDE	Richter scale 8.3 (Moment magnitude)
COMMENTS	A local tsunami of up to 13 feet (4 m) in height hit southeastern coast of Hokkaido, Japan. Most people who were injured in the earthquake were hit by falling debris and broken glass.

Indian Ocean, South and South-East Asia, 2004

At 07:58 a.m. local time, on December 26, 2004, a violent movement of the sea floor occurred off the west coast of northern Sumatra, where the Indo-Australian and Eurasian Tectonic Plates join. The sudden energy release resulted in a massive magnitude 9.1 earthquake, one of the largest on record, and triggered a lethal tsunami in the Indian Ocean.

RIGHT A mosque is the only building left standing on a strip of coastline in the province of Aceh in Indonesia. This was one of the worst-hit regions, with 50,000 people killed.

Traveling at speeds of around 500 miles per hour (805 km/h), the resulting tsunami took less than half an hour to reach the coast of Sumatra, where it struck with its greatest ferocity. Survivors reported waves of up to 30 feet high (9 m) moving as far as 1.5 miles (2 km) inland, and smashing everything in their path.

Within an hour of the earthquake, the coastlines of Thailand, Malaysia, and Myanmar were hit. In two hours it had inundated the eastern coasts of Sri Lanka and India. Finally, after eight hours, the wave reached Africa and Madagascar. In most reports the sea first receded, up to several miles in places. Unlike those living around the Pacific, where tsunamis are more common, most Indian Ocean residents did not recognize this warning sign and were unaware that the waves would soon follow. Many people were killed, particularly inquisitive children who went down to the dry sea floor to collect the stranded fish. In some coastal villages, all the children were lost. A number of unsuspecting local and international

BELOW Tourists run from the first of the six tsunami waves rolling toward Hat Rai Lay Beach near Krabi in southern Thailand, a popular tourist destination.

RIGHT The blue lines spreading outward from the earthquake epicenter show the time frame in which the tsunami waves hit.

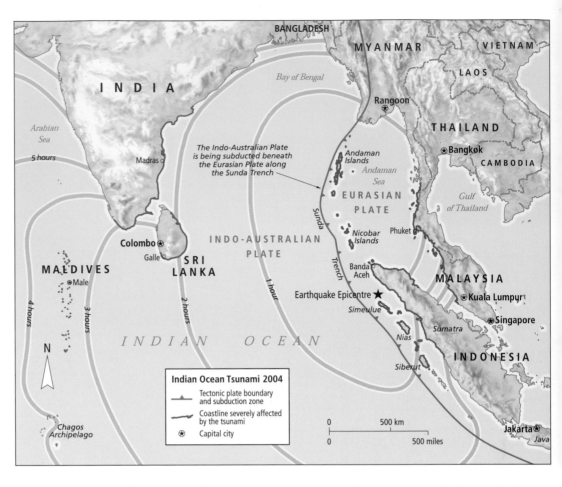

BELOW People grabbed whatever possessions they could as they searched for dry land away from the flood waters. A man, a girl, and their dog wade through the deep waters in Sirombu, on Nias, Indonesia. Nias suffered the most fatalities from the earthquake.

tourists vacationing in the many coastal resorts were also killed. The tsunami was made up of several monster waves, each one surging in followed by a retreat, with intervals of about 20 to 30 minutes between peaks. The third wave was the biggest, followed by smaller tsunamis throughout the rest of the day. Paul Kan, a tsunami survivor recalls the terrifying force and effect of the tsunami: "… a huge mass of mud-brown water hurtled forward with a loud crashing sound. I felt that I could hardly hear in that thunder, feeling a strange void of sound, no screams, no cries of help, just the thundering sound of trees snapping and the surging waters."

An unimaginable, uncountable toll

The final death toll will never be accurately known. The US Geological Survey estimates that close to 300,000 people across 12 countries were killed or went missing. In its destructive wake, the tsunami left a multitude of rotting corpses. Water and sewer lines were smashed, and pools of stagnant water were left behind. A lack of shelter left many people homeless. This factor, together with the remoteness of many coastal villages, led to grave fears that epidemics of diseases such as hepatitis, cholera, typhoid, malaria, and dengue fever, would kill thousands of weakened and dispirited survivors.

A massive international aid effort

With huge relief efforts swinging into effect almost immediately after the tsunami, those fears were never fully realized. Images of the devastation appeared on television screens around the world and millions of dollars were donated in response to the global aid campaign. Clean water or water-purification tablets,

food, and medical supplies were distributed to the battered regions—in many cases by air as roads had been destroyed. Emergency housing was set up, and spraying was carried out to control the increase in mosquito populations.

The enormity of the disaster sometimes led to some confusion between different authorities concerning important day-to-day risk-management decisions. For example, should one collect and store bodies in makeshift mortuaries for DNA sampling and fingerprinting, or bury the dead immediately to minimize the risk of disease to the vulnerable survivors? More than US$10 billion in aid was pledged by governments and organizations around the world to assist with the rebuilding process.

Most lives lost due to lack of adequate warnings

Following the Indian Ocean Tsunami many political questions have been asked about the extreme lack of preparedness of the civil authorities in all of the countries bordering the Indian Ocean. As there was approximately 15 minutes and 8 hours between the earthquake event and the tsunami, maybe something more could have been done to warn the many thousands living in coastal towns and villages. Why were people so inadequately educated in respect to this

type of natural disaster and unable to recognize what was going to happen to them, despite the obvious warning signs? The responses of richer countries around the Pacific Rim to earthquakes and tsunamis stood in stark contrast. The Japanese, in particular, are highly tsunami-ready. There are fewer tsunamis in the Indian Ocean than in the Pacific, but when they do occur they are far more deadly because Indian Ocean coastlines are so much more densely populated. Scientists manning and operating the efficient Pacific Tsunami Warning Center lamented that they were not able to reach the right authorities in that part of the world in the time available. As a

ABOVE Dozens of souvenir and gift shops that once stood next to the ferry jetty tumble into the sand. Picturesque Phi Phi Island in Thailand was regarded as a "paradise and a haven" for vacationers. It and nearby islands were used as the film location for the 2000 movie, *The Beach*.

AN UNLIKELY HERO SAVES PEOPLE FROM DROWNING

On the morning of December 26, 2004, ten-year-old Tilly Smith was holidaying with her parents at Phuket on the coast of Thailand when she noticed the sea recede from the shoreline, exposing unseen rocks, sand, and reef. She recognized this phenomenon as something her geography teacher, Andrew Kearney, had been teaching her class on natural disasters only weeks before. Tilly told her parents that within a matter of minutes their beach would be submerged by a returning wall of water. It took her a while to convince her parents that the situation was serious, and they ran from the beach. Tilly's desperate explanations convinced a Japanese chef at their hotel of the danger, and together with the security guard, they managed to clear about 100 people from the beach. The family sought safety on the third floor of their hotel, just as the terrifying tsunami swept up the beach.

FACTS AND FIGURES

DATE	7:58 a.m., December 26, 2004
LOCATION	Epicenter in the Indian Ocean, west of northern Sumatra
DEATH TOLL	About 300,000
DAMAGE	Extensive damage to coastlines all around the Indian Ocean, particularly in Indonesia, Thailand, Malaysia, and Sri Lanka
DURATION	7 minutes
MAGNITUDE	Richter scale 9.0 (upgraded to 9.1 Moment magnitude)
COMMENTS	The December, 2004, Indian Ocean earthquake produced the most deadly tsunami ever recorded in history

result, this tsunami has ignited a greater urgency toward setting up an international warning system in the Indian Ocean. At the 2005 United Nations (UN) conference in Kobe, Japan, it was decided that the UN would establish an Indian Ocean Tsunami Warning System as the first step in its warning program for all types of natural disasters. The cost of setting this up is expected to be around US$30 million—only a tiny amount of funding when compared with the level of damage caused by the 2004 Indian Ocean tsunami.

Education will save lives

There is no doubt that if more people had been able to recognize the natural phenomena that precede the arrival of a tsunami, thousands of lives could have been saved. There were instances where people with education, experience, or even knowledge of folklore made a difference to survival.

In the Andaman Islands, Abdul Rezzak, radio operator at the port of Teressa, saved hundreds of lives. He had felt the earthquake and had a rare premonition that tsunami waves would strike at any moment. He later told the *Deccan Herald*, "I used to see the National Geographic Channel, and am familiar with the expression 'tsunami' and also what it is all about. The earthquake was so heavy that I thought it might lead to some disaster. But that it would strike Andaman was something I never thought. The sight of the surging sea stirred me up." When Abdul saw the sea start to churn and recede from the port he immediately raced down the stairs shouting, "Oh my God! Tsunami is coming." He and his fellow workers started grabbing people on the street, telling them to spread the message around town as fast as they could. More people ran out of their homes, alerted by the shouting, and started following Abdul to higher ground. A short time later, violent waves struck the island inundating the port building and the police station.

On the Indonesian island of Simeulue, closest to the 2004 earthquake's epicenter, the shaking was so violent that people could barely remain standing. As soon as the earthquake finished, everybody grabbed what they could and ran for the hills. Many did not even know why or where they were running to, but their grandparents had always told them of giant waves that had come and killed thousands a long time ago (the 1907 earthquake and tsunami). Within 30 minutes, the villagers were in the hills watching as 33 foot (10 m) waves destroyed their village. This scenario was repeated all over the island. Because of this knowledge there were few casualties.

ABOVE Tsunami refugees wait in the rain to receive non-food relief packages during a United Nations High Commissioner for Refugees (UNHCR) distribution for families in a welfare center in Onthatchimadam, Sri Lanka.

FAR LEFT A Thai Buddhist monk walks past a boat swept up onto land at the devastated fishing village of Nam Kem in Panga province in Thailand.

WHAT CAUSED THE TSUNAMI?

Stretching along the southern side of the Indonesian archipelago lies a narrow, deep, oceanic trench—the Java Trench. Here the Indian Ocean sea floor (the Indo–Australian Plate) pushes northeastward at 2 inches (5.1 cm) per year, buckling and breaking as it is forced beneath the volcanic islands of the Indonesian archipelago, which lie on the edge of the Eurasian Plate. The sea floor is being consumed (subducted) not smoothly, but rather in a series of sudden movements. The descending Indo–Australian Plate drags the leading edge of the Eurasian Plate down into the trench with it. The edge is bent downward like an enormous spring, which, every few decades, snaps free and flicks back upward with incredible force.

On the morning of December 26, 2004, when the rupture along the contact surface between the two plates started it was 19 miles (31 km) beneath the seabed and tore along a distance of approximately 750 miles (1,207 km) within the space of a few minutes. It left the Indo–Australian Plate thrust up an additional 50 feet (15 m) beneath the Eurasian Plate over this entire length. The seabed was lifted up. As a result, some 7 cubic miles (30 km³) of water radiated from the zone as tsunami waves.

These sudden displacements in the ocean floor are known as megathrusts. The Prince William Sound, Alaska, "Good Friday" Earthquake of 1964 and the Great Chilean Earthquake of 1960 are other significant examples of megathrusts generating earthquakes and tsunamis.

Mudslides and Landslides

Landslides and mudflows are forms of mass wasting: the transport of soil and rock downslope under gravity. Mass wasting affects all surfaces of our planet that are not as flat as a pancake. It can range from the very slow movement of material downslope, called soil creep, to rapid and sometimes catastrophic movements such as rockfalls, rockslides, and debris flows.

Such rapidly moving masses of materials, sometimes including snow and ice in mountainous regions, are known as avalanches, and can reach speeds of over 300 miles per hour (500 km/h).

"Landslide" is both the accepted term for the downslope movement of soil, rock, and vegetation, and the name for the landform that results.

Debris flows or mudslides are rivers of water-saturated rock, earth, and other materials, and tend to flow in channels. They can flow rapidly, striking with little or no warning at avalanche speeds, and sometimes travel several miles from their source, increasing in volume as they pick up material, such as soil, boulders, trees, and houses, in their path.

Mass wasting is usually seen as disastrous, but it is a never-ending natural process that sculpts our landscapes: canyons, hillsides, valleys, and mountains. Mass wasting perpetually renews Earth's surface, creating the beauty that we admire and the fertile soils we depend on. It just happens to be disastrous for humans who live in the way.

What causes landslides?

There are many causes of landslides and mudslides, but all of them depend on the underlying bedrock and soil, the slope, and the groundwater conditions. These controlling factors can, in turn, be affected by changes in soil saturation through increased rainfall from storms or seepage from human activities; by earthquakes or volcanoes; by cycles of freezing and thawing; and by changes in slope through erosion, the removal of vegetation, or the construction of roads, railroads, or buildings.

Land mismanagement can be a particular problem. Land clearing can make land surfaces especially vulnerable to soil saturation by even relatively low rainfall, creating conditions conducive to landslides, particularly in mountain, canyon, and coastal regions. Land-use zoning, professional inspections, and proper design can minimize many potential landslide and debris flow problems.

Water that rapidly accumulates in the ground can result in a surge of water-saturated soil, rock, and

FAR LEFT Local residents and relatives of the victims watch as soldiers search for people buried by a landslide in 2005 in Lourdes, 12 miles (20 km) from San Salvador, El Salvador. Heavy rains and floods from Tropical Storm Stan were responsible.

LEFT Two homes slowly slide down a water-saturated hillside a month after record rainfalls in Anaheim Hills, California, USA. The recently built $2.5 million white house is pushing down and collapsing the brown house, which was under construction.

PREVIOUS PAGES Expensive southern Californian homes lie in ruins after a landslide sent structures crashing down a hill in Laguna Beach, California. Eighteen multi-million-dollar houses were destroyed.

RIGHT Landslides take many forms. Four of the more common types are illustrated here. Top left: a slide—movement parallel to planes of weakness and occasionally parallel to slope. Top right: a slump—complex movement of materials on a slope; note rotation of surface. Bottom left: a flow—viscous to fluid-like motion of debris. Bottom right: a mudslide—a sporadic and sudden channelled discharge of water and debris.

THE TEN MOST DEADLY MUDSLIDES AND LANDSLIDES

DECEMBER, 1920	On December 16, a magnitude 8.6 earthquake caused landslides that killed more than 180,000 people in Gansu province, northwest China.
JUNE, 1990	The Rudbar–Tarom earthquake (7.3) on June 20 in western Iran killed 40,000 to 50,000 people, many by landslides.
NOVEMBER, 1985	More than 27,000 people were killed in Armero, Colombia, when lahars swept down from the erupting Nevado del Ruiz volcano on November 13.
MAY, 1970	An earthquake-induced rock and snow avalanche on Mt Huascarán, Peru, on May 21 buried two towns and killed more than 18,000 people. The avalanche hit the towns at a speed of 100 miles per hour (160 km/h).
DECEMBER, 1999	Heavy rains set off thousands of landslides along the Cordillera de la Costa, in northern Venezuela. Debris flows and flash floods killed 30,000 people.
JULY, 1949	On July 10, an earthquake near Khait, Tajikistan, triggered a landslide near the summit of a mountain, killing 12,000 people in only a few minutes.
SEPTEMBER, 1618	A landslide in Chiavenna, Italy, killed 2,240 people from two villages.
NOVEMBER, 2001	Heavy rains combined with unregulated urbanization led to mudslides in parts of Algiers, Algeria, and the deaths of more than 800 people.
JANUARY, 1966	Heavy rains caused mountain landslides behind Rio de Janeiro, Brazil, taking 550 lives. The lives of another 4 million people were disrupted.
SEPTEMBER, 1806	On September 2, part of the Rossberg Peak in central Switzerland broke off and fell into a valley, sweeping away four villages and 500 lives.

The world's largest twentieth-century landslide occurred on Mt St Helens, USA, when in May, 1980, an earthquake dislodged 1.7 cubic miles (7.1 km³) of rocks and mud that slid down the volcano's flank. This released built-up pressure and produced the major eruption of May 18. The second largest was in 1911 in Usoy, Tajikistan, when an earthquake triggered a landslide, moving 1.5 cubic miles (6.25 km³) of material. It dammed a valley to 1,880 feet (573 m) (half again as high as the Empire State Building) on the Murgob River, forming a lake nearly 40 miles (64 km) long. The costliest in US history—exceeding US$400 million—was a slow-moving landslide in Thistle, Utah, in spring, 1983. It dammed the Spanish Fork River and buried a highway and a railroad.

debris that usually starts on a steep slope after being activated by other natural disasters such as earth tremors, volcanoes, or flash flooding.

Economic and social consequences

Landslides can have vast economic impacts. Should they cause serious damage to essential infrastructure, vital industries such as fishing, tourism, forestry, mining, and energy production, as well as general transportation, can be greatly affected, sometimes for years after the event.

Rapidly moving landslides and debris flows that inundate towns and villages cause varying degrees of trauma. Broken electrical, water, gas, and sewer lines can lead to electrocution, injury, or illness, and disrupted transportation systems can block access to urgently needed medical aid.

Where landslides occur

Areas where landslides have occurred previously are more vulnerable to repeats. However, built-up areas are also prone when vegetation has been removed and slopes have been altered by the construction of buildings and roads and the redirection of runoff.

Wildfires create potential hazards by destroying protective vegetation, putting naturally steep slopes and land at the base of slopes or canyons at risk in areas of high rainfall.

Minimizing landslide risks

Landslide risk management is improving through engineering and geological investigations, detection of slope hazards, and determination of the likelihood of landslide occurrence. This work can help engineers, developers, planners, and building inspectors avoid high-risk areas, and can contribute to improved zoning and community bylaws. In general, all construction close to steep slopes, mountain edges, drainage ways, and natural erosion valleys should be avoided, and steep banks should not be undercut.

It is important to check whether your area has a history of landslide activity. If it has, talk to your insurance agent about the risks, and minimize hazards around the home. For example, use flexible pipe fittings to help avoid gas or water leaks caused by the breaking of pipes. Sloping ground should be covered by plant growth and supported by retaining walls where possible. Construct channels and deflection walls around your property to direct flows around buildings. But keep in mind that you might be liable for damages if these modifications direct flow onto a neighbor's property.

The warning signs

There are sometimes indications of potential mass movement. Around the home, you might notice doors or windows newly jamming, or new cracks appearing in walls and foundations. Outside walls and patios might start to pull away from the main building.

In the land around you there might be changes in the patterns of water drainage on slopes, such as water seeping through the surface at new locations. Fences, retaining walls, utility poles, and trees might start to lean. Also watch for slowly widening cracks that might appear on the ground or on paved areas such as streets or driveways.

ABOVE A landslide on January 13, 2001, caused by a strong earthquake buried some 300 homes in Santa Tecla, a suburb of San Salvador, El Salvador. At least 400 people were killed.

WHAT TO DO IN A LANDSLIDE OR MUDFLOW

BEFORE If you suspect that a landslide is about to occur, make sure you contact your local emergency services and inform your neighbors, particularly those who might need help with evacuation. Getting out of the path of a landslide is the best protection, so evacuate if possible and move quickly, keeping clear of embankments, riverbanks, trees, and power lines and poles.
DURING Should you be caught up in a landslide when indoors, shelter in the least-affected part of the building under a strong table or bench, and if possible under protection such as a mattress. Hold on and stay put until all movement has ceased. If you are outdoors and near a watercourse, be alert for any sudden change in water flow and for a change from clear to muddy water. These signs could indicate landslide activity upstream and that you might be in the path of a debris flow. Be ready to move quickly. Save yourself, not your belongings!
AFTER Listen to local radio or television stations for the latest emergency information, and keep well away from the slide area in case there are additional slides or flooding. Check for injured and trapped persons near the slide, without entering the direct slide area, and check on neighbors who might need help with infants, or who are elderly or disabled. Direct rescuers to their locations. Look for broken electricity and gas lines and report them to the authorities.

FAR LEFT The aftermath of a landslide where a house slipped down a hill into another house in Tauranga, New Zealand, in 2005. A state of emergency was declared in parts of the Bay of Plenty area, southeast of Auckland, following extensive flooding after about one-third of the annual average rainfall fell in 36 hours.

LEFT Infrared image from 6,000 feet (1,800 m) showing the remains of the town of Yungay, Peru, following a massive landslide caused by an earthquake in 1970. More than 97 percent of the town's population of 17,000 were killed.

When a landslide starts it might be accompanied by a faint rumbling that becomes louder as it nears. Other sounds might include trees cracking or rocks colliding, indicating moving debris. It is possible for the ground to shift under your feet as it moves downhill. Avoid the tops and bases of cliffs and banks, especially where there are signs of loose rocks or debris. Never stand or sit on rock overhangs unless you are sure they can bear your weight.

When possible, remain aware of weather forecasts and warnings on radio or television. Be particularly alert if you are in a landslide-prone area and intense rain is forecast, especially if you suspect that the ground is already saturated from earlier falls.

If you are driving, watch the road for collapsed pavement, fallen rocks, or indications of debris flows. Embankments along roadsides are particularly susceptible, because quite often the anchoring toe of a slope has been removed.

TYPES OF MASS WASTING

Landslides or slope movements can be classified using criteria such as:
- rate of movement—from very slow (fingernail growth) to extremely rapid (highway traffic)
- type of material—bedrock, unconsolidated sediment or soil, and organic and other debris
- whether material slides, slumps, flows, or falls.

Using these criteria, geologists commonly use the following terms to classify landslides.

ROCKFALLS occur when masses of bedrock become unstable and crash to the ground below.

ROCKSLIDES move more slowly, with the broken rock mass moving together downslope as though down a ramp or a children's slippery slide.

SLUMPS are characterized by a shearing or rotational movement along a curved slip surface, tilting the slumped surface backward (and making trees, for example, lean backward).

DEBRIS FLOWS range from slow creeping movements to the very largest, nastiest avalanches. They consist of a mixture of materials, from fine particles of mud and silt to rocks and boulders. Vegetation and other materials can be collected and incorporated as the material flows, sometimes over vast distances and at great speeds.

LAHARS are debris flows that slide down the flanks of volcanoes.

AVALANCHES are masses of snow, ice, or rocks that fall rapidly down a mountainside.

Panama, 1904 to 1914

The 10 years of Panama Canal construction from 1904 onward were made all the more difficult by landslides. These contributed significantly to the deaths of as many as 27,500 workers and the massive overrun of the project's budget.

The building of the 48-mile (77-km) canal was plagued by problems of disease such as malaria and yellow fever, the unusual geology of the isthmus, and massive landslides. The problem of landslides had been largely ignored during the designing phase of the canal. Although the quality of the rock was known from core samples taken during the extensive drilling program, the effect of underlying strata on the overall strength of the rock had been totally misjudged.

These underlying strata contained bands of clay and iron pyrites, which break down when exposed to air and water through the removal of the overlying material. These, together with other soft rocks such as tuffs, shales, and mudstones, were involved in most of the landslides in the area during the canal's construction. The resulting additional excavation needed more than doubled the original volume estimated for the canal.

The Cucaracha landslide

The first major landslide occurred in 1907 at Cucaracha, when some 13.5 million cubic feet (382,000 m³) of clay moved more than 13 feet (4 m) in 24 hours. Removing it was fraught with difficulties; steam shovels couldn't handle the softened clay, and eventually it had to be removed by sluicing it with water from a high level. This slide caused many people to question the feasibility of the construction of the canal.

ABOVE Workers on the Panama Canal deal with a landslide, having to dig by hand in places inaccessible to steam shovels, which would sink in the mud.

RIGHT A pair of tugboats pull the SS *Kroonland* past the Cucaracha slide, heading south along Culebra Cut on the Panama Canal in 1915. The size of the ship gives an indication of the huge volumes of rock that had to be excavated from the cut.

FACTS AND FIGURES

DATE	1904 to 1914
LOCATION	Isthmus of Panama during the construction of the Panama Canal
DEATH TOLL	27,500 workers (from all causes, including landslides)
DAMAGE	Costs inestimable, but construction costs were increased by millions of dollars due to landslide activity, and many millions of dollars in shipping tolls were lost by the delay in opening the canal and by periods of closure due to landslides
COMMENTS	The landslides were triggered by various factors, such as improper excavation sequences, unpredictably high groundwater levels, and previously undetected geological conditions. Earthquake activity in the region has also been responsible for many massive landslides both during and after the construction of the canal

Associated with the slides were movements of the ground at the base of the cut. In some areas the ground subsided, and in other areas there was sudden upheaval. This was caused by the rock being so soft that it behaved like a fluid, reacting to various changes in pressure. Removing overlying material from the upper levels of the cut eventually reduced the pressure on the ground.

In 1913, the Cucaracha landslide became a problem yet again. On that occasion the flow reached right to the other side of the cut. The steam shovels excavated the moving material and in time won the battle. Nevertheless, a reactivation of the Cucaracha landslide in 1986 nearly closed the canal again.

Problems at the Culebra Cut

The most difficult area of excavation during the construction of the canal was the Culebra Cut, through the Culebra Mountain. Although this was the smallest mountain on the isthmus, it was the largest in the path of the canal. The notoriously heavy rainfall caused mudslides throughout the year, thus increasing excavation time and cost well beyond those estimated for Culebra.

Adding to the problem was that in the original design, the angle of slope of the cut and its height had been miscalculated. The rocks in this area were just too weak to support the steep slope. This exacerbated the landslide and rockfall problems so that it became necessary to constantly change the cross-section of the canal. Eventually a gradual slope was attained by the massive steam shovels working almost 24 hours a day.

The landslide problems that plagued the Culebra Cut necessitated the removal of five times the excavation volume originally estimated.

Economic woes at Gaillard

It was the excavation of the 7.8-mile (12.6-km) Gaillard Cut in the Continental Divide segment of the Panama Canal near its Pacific Ocean terminus that caused the greatest economic concern—and major construction problems. The slope failures and associated slides during the construction phase of this section of the canal constituted the world's most extreme case of damage to a transportation system. The slope failures not only severely disrupted construction, delaying the completion of the canal by some two years; they also closed the canal on seven occasions after it was opened to traffic in 1914. Landslides in the cut between 1914 and 1930 resulted in 1.4 billion cubic feet (40 million m³) of additional excavation. There was also a resurgence of landslide activity as a result of the first widening of the cut in the 1930s.

ABOVE The Panama Canal as it is today. This photograph shows the gentle slopes that are needed to prevent further mudslides and the shoring work required to keep the canal's cliffsides stable.

OVER 100 LANDSLIDES AT THE CANAL
In the National Academy of Sciences Report XVIII in 1924, US Geological Service geologist Donald F. MacDonald divided the Panama landslides into three classes: Class I involves a landslide where there is movement along a pre-existing plane or zone of weakness, inclined toward the canal; Class II is where there is movement along newly formed fractures or by flow, or the two combined; and Class III is a landslide involving the movement of surface material.

Between 1907 and 1916, the canal averaged more than 10 landslides a year; there were: 4 in 1907, 9 in 1908, 12 in 1909, 15 in 1910, 16 in 1911, 19 in 1912, 16 in 1913, 10 in 1914 (the year of official opening), 5 in 1915, and 3 in 1916, making a total of 109.

Surte, Sweden, 1950

On the morning of September 29, 1950, a massive landslide swiftly descended on Surte, a village of 2,600 people, northeast of Göteborg in Sweden. It destroyed 31 houses and 10 other buildings, transporting them up to 500 feet (150 m) downslope. Remarkably, the residents of some houses reported that they had felt no sensation of movement.

BELOW This house in Surte was uprooted by the 1950 landslide. Continuous heavy rain saturated the soil and allowed it slide on the underlying bedrock.

BELOW RIGHT The Göta River has two outlets to the North Sea. The slide blocked almost the entire width of the eastern channel at Surte. However, this caused only minor backing up of flow, because water was diverted through the second outlet to the sea at Kungälv, about 4 miles (7 km) upstream from Surte.

The landslide was about 2,000 feet (600 m) long, 1,300 feet (400 m) wide, and 65 feet (20 m) deep, giving it a volume of more than 140 billion cubic feet (4 million m³). The landslide covered 54 acres (22 ha). The saucer-shaped slide shifted suddenly when its toe, at sea level in the Göta River, failed. Its head was halfway up the valley side at an altitude of 65 feet (20 m) above sea level on a slope of only 7°. The slope of the valley walls in general was very low, varying from only 3° to 4° at midslope. It was the low-angled slope that made the Surte landslide unique; most landslides are usually associated with steep slopes.

Following the landslide, the relief between the head and toe was reduced from its original 65 feet (20 m) to just 20 feet (6 m), giving it an average slope of just 1°—anything but typical of a landslide. Another remarkable feature of the landslide was its rate of movement. Houses were moved 425 feet (130 m) in about three minutes.

Cause—the end of the last ice age

The type of low-angle sliding at Surte is common in Norway, Sweden, and eastern Canada, all of which were covered by ice during the last ice age some 18,000 years ago. In some parts of Sweden the ice sheet was 1 to 2 miles (2–3 km) thick, so thick that it depressed the underlying terrain significantly, some of it to below sea level. When deglaciation occurred and the pressure of the ice started to lessen, the land began to rise; it continues to do so at a rate of almost ⅓ inch (9 mm) per year in most coastal areas of Sweden, particularly in the south.

The sediments that were deposited and the changes to the landform during these times have resulted in gentle slopes made up of glacial silt and clay, mainly quick-clay (a very wet clay that is solid until disturbed, when it turns to liquid). The stability of these slopes is influenced by a number of factors, water saturation being the most important. Many of the potentially dangerous slopes are bordered by

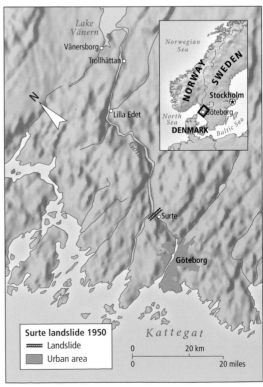

Surte landslide 1950
░░░ Landslide
▦ Urban area

open water—rivers or lakes—and water saturation from snowmelt, the thawing of frozen ground, or intense or prolonged rainfall results in sharp fluctuations in groundwater level. Other factors affecting the stability of the slopes include land uplift and human influences, such as construction activity that undercuts or overloads dangerous slopes. Warning systems that register movements in clay have been installed in the areas of important transportation links.

Shipping interrupted

The Surte landslide wreaked havoc on local commerce by disrupting the Göteborg–Vänersborg Highway, the Bergslag Railways, and the Göta River. The Göta River was 16 to 19 feet (5–6 m) deep and 500 feet (150 m) wide before the slide. It was the most important inland waterway for ships sailing from the North Sea at Göteborg to Lake Vänern, the largest lake in the center of Sweden. The channel was excavated to the west of the old, now filled, channel, so as not to decrease the stability of the slide.

FACTS AND FIGURES

DATE	September 29, 1950
LOCATION	Surte, a village of 2,600 people, northeast of Göteborg, Sweden
DEATH TOLL	0
DAMAGE	No estimation
COMMENTS	Unique landslide in gently sloping land resulting from postglacial activity

ABOVE These houses were destroyed in a landslide in Göteborg in 1977 that was like the landslide in Surte in 1950. The clay bed on which the houses were built gave way and flowed downhill. An area of 67 acres (27 ha) was affected.

EARTHQUAKES AND LANDSLIDES

Human interference has probably caused large landslides to become more common during the past century; however, there are many old landslide scars in glacial till in areas of northernmost Sweden. It appears that the slides occurred shortly after deglaciation and were triggered by earthquakes. During the melt, when pressure from the ice decreased, the underlying land began to rise, creating major faulting accompanied by earthquakes. Shaking from the earthquakes would have decreased the stability of waterlogged soils and mobilized them. Most of the slides involved gentle slopes with a fairly thick cover of overburden. In some cases considerable amounts of soil were displaced: 35 billion cubic feet (1 million m³) or more was not uncommon.

Aberfan, Wales, 1966

On October 21, 1966, a mountain of colliery waste surged down upon the village of Aberfan in the Taf River valley in south Wales, taking with it all the occupants of a little farm cottage, and 116 children and five teachers from the school that lay directly in its path. Altogether, 144 people died.

RIGHT Rescue workers toil into the night at the Welsh mining village of Aberfan. The school and 20 nearby houses were buried under mine waste.

For more than 50 years, waste slag from the coal mines in the Welsh mountains was dumped on a hillside above Aberfan, forming a mountain that towered above the village. Rain turned the slag into sticky black mud that would wash down into the streets of the village. Officials of the National Coal Board (NCB) said it "would be far too expensive to dispose of the waste in any other way," ignoring complaints from the villagers. In 1966, it took only a little more rain to lubricate the slag sufficiently for thousands of tons of it to slip down 600 feet (180 m) and sweep over the school and 20 buildings.

Early warnings were ignored

It was not as though the landslide had come out of the blue. Warnings of the potential danger had been reported as far back as 1927. Further, there had been earlier slips of slag heaps into the valley: one 5 miles (8 km) from Aberfan in 1939, and another in 1944 closer to the village. Injunctions and reports produced no reaction. There was even a mudflow into the streets of Aberfan in 1963. On that occasion it stopped just short of the school. But still the NCB officials took no action.

BELOW Volunteer rescuers clear debris and sludge near the wrecked Pantglas Junior School, which had stood at the base of the slag heap, on the edge of the village. The building remained standing, but was filled with mud.

La Conchita, California, 1995 and 2005

On Monday, January 10, 2005, a landslide struck the seaside community of La Conchita in Ventura County, California, United States, killing 10 people and destroying or damaging 36 houses. It was not the first landslide to hit the La Conchita region, and it is unlikely to be the last.

RIGHT Residents help neighbors sort through scattered belongings found on the first day they were allowed to return to their homes after the mudslide.

BELOW Dog handlers gathered on Highway 101 after a hillside shift had halted the search and rescue efforts in La Conchita. The dogs augmented the use of tiny electronic cameras that were inserted into cracks and crevices.

The community, which was established through subdivision in 1924, lies along a narrow coastal strip about 820 feet (250 m) wide between the shoreline and a 600-foot (180-m) sloping bluff. This bluff above La Conchita has been the cause of the landslide problem for a very long time. Geological deposits indicate a very large prehistoric event that affected the entire bluff. In more recent times, landslides around La Conchita have been a regular occurrence and the cause of extensive damage along the coastal strip.

The 1995 landslide

The March 4, 1995 landslide apparently occurred as a result of an extraordinarily wet year. Cracks, first observed in the upper part of the slope in

FACTS AND FIGURES	
DATE	January 10, 2005
LOCATION	La Conchita, Ventura County, California, USA
DEATH TOLL	10
DAMAGE	36 houses
COMMENTS	One of many landslides in the region; they date back to prehistory and will likely continue to occur

mid-1994, opened significantly when the rainy season began later that year. Several small landslides occurred right up until March 1995, when a large slide struck La Conchita. It destroyed or severely damaged nine houses, and a second landslide almost a week later damaged another five. It appears that rising groundwater levels provided lubrication for the landslide, but strangely, eyewitness accounts of the event describe dust in the air, and deposits that included some dry material. This suggests that most of the rain drained off the surface of the soil mass downslope, but upslope it soaked in and caused the groundwater level to rise.

Further problems were caused by the collapse of material supporting the sides of the deposit, allowing the main scarp and lateral margins to fail.

The 2005 landslide

The January 2005 landslide was also associated with high rainfall. It followed 15 days of record rain, and again much of the landslide deposit consisted of fairly dry material. A video made at the time showed dust in the air as the landslide flowed downslope. However, lush vegetation that had grown on some of the 1995 deposit indicated a concentration of water in the part of the material that failed in January 2005, and it is likely that the landslide moved on a saturated layer deep in the 1995 deposit. Once again, much of the material above the saturated zone was fairly dry and remained sufficiently intact to be able to raft vegetation along the surface of the rapidly flowing mass. This was further evidence that the landslide had been transported on a deep fluid layer.

The landslide rumbled down on La Conchita as a large chunk of the bluff broke free at the eastern end of the town. It carried trees, power lines, and thick

LANDSLIDE GEOLOGY AND HISTORY

Randall W. Jibson of the US Geological Survey visited the site. He concluded that the rocks of the bluff above La Conchita are poorly indurated (hardened) marine sediments. The upper part of the slope consists of alternating beds of siliceous shale, siltstone, and sandstone of Miocene age, and the lower part of the slope is siltstone, sandstone, and mudstone of Pliocene age. All the rocks are very weakly cemented. The two groups of rocks are in contact along the active Red Mountain Fault, which extends across the slope face. They are associated with extensive landslide activity throughout the region.

Thredbo, Australia, 1997

Shortly before midnight on Wednesday, July 30, 1997, a large section of steep mountainside collapsed immediately above Thredbo, a ski village in the New South Wales Alps. It killed 18 people and took with it masses of rock, earth, ski lodges, trees, and vehicles, making it one of Australia's most catastrophic landslides. The ultimate cause was water leaking from a pipe.

Witnesses reported hearing "a whoosh of air, a crack, and a sound like a freight train" when about 1,000 tons (1,000 tonnes) of debris came plunging down the steep slope from just beneath a major road, the Alpine Way. It sheared Brindabella Ski Club's four-story Carinya Lodge off its foundations and slammed it into the Bimbadeen Lodge, which also collapsed. A resident of Brindabella Ski Club and 17 residents of Bimbadeen Ski Lodge lost their lives. The Bimbadeen Staff Lodge was also hit, and it too collapsed. The multi-level buildings and a car park were completely crushed, along with many cars and trees, in the 1,300-foot (400-m) landslide.

Emergency procedures

BELOW Thredbo from above. A popular ski resort each winter, numerous ski lifts take visitors not only up to the numerous ski runs, but also to a raised walkway that leads eventually to the summit of Australia's highest peak, Mt Kosciuszko.

The first emergency calls were received within minutes of the landslide at the NSW Fire Brigades Communication Centre, some distance from Thredbo, and local fire brigades immediately responded to reports of a "small explosion" in the village, and 100 people trapped. Within an hour, police had evacuated the area and declared a regional disaster. Broken water, gas, and oil mains were secured by emergency services before a painstaking search and rescue operation was initiated.

Medical personnel were brought in from a number of centers, including Sydney, over 300 miles (500 km) away. Within three hours of the landslide, there were 100 professional services on the scene together with many volunteers from the various rescue organizations; in total, about 1,600 workers. Geophysicists examined the site and declared that although still very unstable, it was safe enough to begin an excavation of the top layers.

The rescue operation

Rescue efforts were hampered by the potential danger from the extremely unstable mass of earth, rock, shattered lodges, trees, and vehicles, the movement of any of which was capable of triggering further minor slides. Added to these difficulties were the below-freezing temperatures during the night and the steep angle of the debris that the rescue workers had to negotiate.

The first body was recovered late on the Thursday afternoon, and then on Friday another was found in the early morning and two others later that day.

Rescuers believed that many people might have been trapped beneath large slabs of concrete from the car park between the two lodges. These hampered access to the site and caused the delay in recovering bodies.

Locating survivors was a top priority, and rescuers used thermal imaging cameras and seismic listening devices in the hope of finding them. Just when it seemed unlikely that anyone would be found alive, a survivor was found buried in a void below three huge concrete slabs some 8 feet (2.5 m) below the rubble. Somehow he had endured three nights of below-freezing temperatures.

It took over seven days and nights of exhausting work before all of the 18 bodies were recovered.

Human error to blame

The official finding was that human error, not natural causes, was responsible for the landslide. Water from a leaking water main was judged to be the lubricating agent that allowed the road fill supporting the road to move downslope.

Further, the road was judged to have been poorly constructed. Much had been done over several years to keep the road open, even though it was recognized that landslides were a possibility and that these could cause death or injury if the road gave way under vehicles. It was not anticipated that damage to the buildings and their occupants on the slope below was also possible.

ABOVE Rescue workers attempt to free one of the victims of the Thredbo landslide. The route of the roadway that collapsed onto the ski lodges is just visible at the top of the photograph.

FACTS AND FIGURES

DATE	July 30, 1997
LOCATION	Thredbo, NSW Alps, Australia
DEATH TOLL	18, with one relatively uninjured survivor
DAMAGE	Many millions of dollars; AUD$40 million in out-of-court settlements was paid out to families of the deceased in compensation
COMMENTS	Human error was to blame

A MIRACLE OF SURVIVAL

On Saturday morning, sound equipment detected some movement underneath a concrete slab. After one of the rescuers called to check, a voice called back, "I can hear you." When asked if there was anyone else injured, the survivor replied, "None, but my feet are bloody cold!" He was identified as ski instructor Stuart Diver. He was pulled from the wreckage after having been trapped for 65 hours in a small space between two concrete slabs. He was beside the body of his wife, Sally, who had drowned in a deep flow of frigid water. Morale at the site increased and the nation watched on television as he was pulled from what almost became his icy tomb.

Caracas, Venezuela, 1999

During December 15 and 16, 1999, the Cordillera de la Costa in the state of Vargas, just north of Caracas, was hit by Venezuela's worst natural disaster of the twentieth century. Days of torrential rain (35.9 inches [911 mm] in three days) triggered avalanches comprising mudflows carrying boulders and other debris that killed as many as 30,000 of the several hundred thousand people who live along the narrow strip along the north coast of Venezuela.

BELOW Floodwaters rush through the slum area of Los Erasos on the fringe of Caracas, sweeping away makeshift houses and dragging tons of mud and debris. Local officials reported that dozens of people were killed in the capital and in eight states nationwide, and thousands more were left homeless.

The landslides were mainly debris flows that measured from a few yards or less in depth and up to hundreds of yards wide. Every year the hills of Caracas, the capital and largest city of Venezuela, are subject to landslides, most of which are associated with heavy rain that falls mainly from May to October in areas where annual rainfall averages 39 to 43 inches (1,000–1,100 mm).

Life in the barrios

The landslide problems of Caracas affect two different socioeconomic groups: residents of the modest to affluent areas, where loss of life might be low but the costs of property damage can be high, and the low-income barrios, where property damage might not be significant, but loss of life can be high. Quite often the barrios are constructed in ravines and along riverbanks. Of approximately 4 million inhabitants of Caracas, an estimated 40 percent live in low-income barrios, which have an annual population growth rate of about 20 percent.

Cleaning up the barrios

On the night of December 15, 1999, in keeping with other rivers along the northern coast of Venezuela, the Catuche River, which flows through a steep

FACTS AND FIGURES

DATE	December 15 to 16, 1999
LOCATION	Cordillera de la Costa in the state of Vargas, north of Caracas, Venezuela
DEATH TOLL	Estimated 30,000
DAMAGE	About 23,200 homes were destroyed and at least another 64,700 damaged. Economic losses of US$1.8–$2 billion.
COMMENTS	Venezuela has a long history of landslides because of its high annual rainfall and mountainous topography

ravine into the center of Caracas, rose rapidly to levels unseen in decades. It wiped out hundreds of homes with an unstoppable torrent of water, mud, rocks, and tree trunks.

However, unlike other Caracas neighborhoods battered by the floodwaters and debris flows, the Catuche barrio's unique history gave its residents a fighting chance to survive this disaster. As few as 15 people died there, a very small figure compared with other neighborhoods where hundreds lost their lives.

"The organization of the neighborhood and the solidarity of the people saved hundreds of lives in Catuche," said Manuel Larreal, director of Ecumenical Action/ACT, one of five Venezuelan church-related groups within ACT/Venezuela. ACT, Action by Churches Together International, is a global alliance of churches and related agencies working to save lives and support communities in emergencies worldwide.

The history of what made Catuche different begins in 1992, when Jesuit seminarians living there started organizing local residents in an effort to clean up the Catuche River. Unplanned development had allowed hundreds of families arriving from the countryside to build houses right up to the edge of the river—and in some cases directly on top of it, leaving just a small tunnel underneath for the passage of the water. Two years before the 1999 disaster, 36 families moved out of shacks above the river and into church-sponsored four-story apartment complexes overlooking the ravine. This saved their lives.

A HISTORY OF LANDSLIDES IN VENEZUELA

Venezuela has a history of landslides. At least a couple of severe flash floods with landslides occur every century along the northern coast. Records show that such events occurred in 1693, 1789, 1798, 1804, 1808, 1812, 1890, 1892, 1902, 1912, 1914, 1927, 1933, 1945, 1946, 1951, 1956, 1962, 1963, 1970, and 1987.

The 1970s were unique in having 13 severe events. In September 1987, when there was an unusually heavy rainfall of 6.8 inches (174 mm) in less than five hours 60 miles (100 km) west of Caracas, the rain triggered first minor slips of soil. These soon became high-velocity debris flows on the steep slopes and caused the worst landslide disaster in the history of Venezuela. The debris flows passed through the city of El Limón and small towns, damaging or destroying approximately 1,500 homes, 500 vehicles, 3 bridges, and 15 miles (25 km) of roads. About 210 people were killed and 400 were injured.

TOP Soldiers inspect the ruined barrio of San Bernardino in Caracas. A number of families were evacuated from their shacks along the banks of a drainage channel through the night.

ABOVE A man carries his bicycle across the main street of Macuto, a coastal town 9 miles (15 km) north of Caracas.

Bab El Oued, Algeria, 2001

On November 10 and 11, 2001, in the working-class district of Bab El Oued in Algiers, Algeria, a catastrophic debris flow took the lives of hundreds of residents. It was caused by record flooding from heavy rains that inundated the area within a few hours.

ABOVE A taxi lies on a flooded road in Dely Ibrahim, near Algiers, after fierce storms on November 10, 2001. The official casualty figures from more than a day of torrential rains and strong winds rose rapidly throughout the day.

Two months of drought in Algeria was broken by torrential storms that produced 38 inches (960 mm) of rain within a few hours and caused severe flooding. In Algiers, roads were flooded, trees were uprooted, and buildings collapsed as the storms took their toll. Altogether 1,800 housing units, 56 schools, and scores of bridges, roads, and public works were damaged.

The greatest devastation occurred in 12 or so municipalities in Bab El Oued, where the mudflows deposited 35 million cubic feet (1,000,000 m³) of debris up to 33 feet (10 m) deep in the streets. More than 350 cars, trucks, and buses with passengers were buried under the mud and debris. Storm drains in Bab El Oued were reported to have been blocked by the authorities as a countermeasure against possible attack by terrorists.

Urbanization—a contributing factor

In areas like Bab El Oued, urban development is a major factor in increasing the likelihood of severe flooding under the extreme weather conditions experienced in and around Algiers on November 10. Flash flooding is a growing problem, because the extensive use of concrete causes water to run off rather than soak into the ground. Other urban factors include the reduction in open spaces,

FACTS AND FIGURES	
DATE	November 10, 2001
LOCATION	Bab El Oued, a municipality of Algiers, Algeria
DEATH TOLL	Over 800 people killed; 350 injured
DAMAGE	Estimated at US$400 million, with 1,800 homes, 56 schools, and scores of bridges and roads damaged
COMMENTS	Greatest devastation occurred in 12 municipalities in the working-class district of Bab El Oued in central Algiers

engineering works that divert river flows, and city drainage systems weakened by neglect, lack of maintenance, and increasing population pressure.

There is also the problem of dwellings being built inappropriately on riverbanks or near deltas. Some houses are often badly built on or below steep slopes or on cliffs. Interfering with natural slopes and cliffs can cause rocks and soil to slide rapidly downhill with or without the help of earthquakes; storms, waterlogged soil, and heavy construction are also triggering mechanisms.

Overcoming the problem

Algiers took immediate emergency measures, with support from the national Civil Protection Agency, the military, the Red Crescent Society, health and sanitation workers, security forces, and the people themselves. Temporary relief for the affected population helped mitigate the immediate impact of the flooding. The government provided housing and financial assistance for those who had been left homeless by the storms.

The government recognized that there was an urgent need to introduce medium- and long-term disaster mitigation measures, particularly in Algiers, where the November 10 event highlighted the vulnerability of urban areas to natural disasters.

There was much restoration required: to basic infrastructure such as roads, water treatment plants, and distribution networks; and to social and cultural facilities such as schools, hospitals and health centers, training centers, sporting facilities, and cultural heritage sites. Urgent works were set up to refurbish or rebuild these services and facilities.

COPING WITH FUTURE NATURAL DISASTERS

As a result of the November 10, 2001 disaster, the Algerian government has established a project to work toward improving the ability of Algerian institutions at the national level to cope with natural disasters. They plan to do this by developing their monitoring capacity, an early warning system, and their understanding of the meteorological phenomena that led to the floods. They also plan to improve the means of intervention by social protection organizations, and to develop detailed plans to reduce the vulnerability of urban zones in and around Algiers.

They are specifically addressing the vulnerability of the urban zones most seriously affected by the flooding of November 10, 2001. The particular objective of the project is to reduce the risks incurred by the population of these zones—some 30,000 people—and to provide indirect protection to more than 250,000 people living in downstream districts, some of which are sites of ancient urbanization, in particular the ancient Casbah market district.

The measures will also contribute to the solution of the serious problems of pollution and erosion in accordance with one of the objectives of the Algerian government, which is to improve in a sustainable manner the conditions of life of the population affected by the disaster and of those located downstream that could face similar risks. The city is choked by pollution from many sources, including traffic, cement works, heavy industry, and a public waste dump.

ABOVE Algerians gather around a car covered by mud in the Bab El Oued area. Residents in Algiers and other towns in northern Algeria gloomily assessed the havoc caused by fierce rainstorms and mudslides, which officials said killed more than 800 people in two days.

LEFT A resident of the Bab El Oued district, standing in the rubble, echoes mounting anger expressed at the time that the Algerian government's inaction had let the crisis happen.

Kashmir, Pakistan and India, 2005

On October 8, 2005, the massive earthquake that shattered the region of Kashmir, an area disputed by India and Pakistan, also set off a number of devastating landslides, the two most significant occurring in Muzaffarabad and the Jhelum Valley. Communities already difficult to reach because of treacherous mountain terrain were cut off entirely when landslides slumped over roads.

RIGHT An aerial view shows a landslide blocking the main road linking Islamabad and Muzaffarabad, the day after the earthquake that triggered it.

BELOW Pakistani earthquake survivors walk through a landslide area in the Kashmiri town of Neelum Valley, near Muzaffarabad, the capital of Pakistan-administered Kashmir, two months after the earthquake struck. The inaccessibility of the area held up repair work.

The earthquake and more than 1,500 aftershocks triggered countless landslides which were funneled into tight canyons and down the steep rivers in the region. Northern Pakistanis tend to develop their communities in these narrow, steep canyons and live in traditional mud-built structures. These features create a deadly combination in a region of high seismic activity: more than 74,000 people died when the earthquakes struck and buildings collapsed under the landslides.

One of the largest landslides occurred southeast of the earthquake's epicenter, between Muzaffarabad in Pakistan and Uri in India, in the Pir Punjal Range of Kashmir. It was over 2,200 yards (2 km) long by over 1,600 yards (1.5 km) wide and blocked the convergence between two rivers to a depth of 820 feet (250 m). Almost immediately, lakes began to build up behind the debris and threatened to breach the earthen dam, thus creating a major flood hazard for up to 12,000 people downstream.

A satellite image of the landslide in Makhri, a village on the northern outskirts of Muzaffarabad, showed that the western face of the mountain had collapsed, sending a cascade of white-gray rock into the Neelum River. A number of landslides along the river made it almost unrecognizable after the earthquake: the usually blue waters turned brown from the mud and debris of landslides upstream.

Falls of large rocks or boulders were also common, and these caused considerable damage and disruption to roads and buildings. They also caused a significant number of fatalities.

FEATURES OF THE LANDSLIDES

The earthquake, which occurred as result of rupture in a zone of tectonic faulting, triggered a very dense band of landslides in the midslope areas. Fewer landslides occurred away from the fault rupture zone. Almost all landslides were shallow, disaggregated slides; there were only two larger ones. Owing to the generally arid landscape, liquefaction appeared not to be a factor in the mobilization of the slides.

The shallow landslides and rock falls on the steep natural slopes and in steep road cuttings posed the largest threat to mountain roads and structures at slope bases. Even though they were relatively small in scale, these shallow landslides contributed significantly to earthquake damage, particularly in the lower slopes inhabited by large human populations.

Many of these slopes, such as along the river terrace in Muzaffarabad, continue to pose a major hazard owing to the presence of large tension cracks, especially since emergency shelters were set up at the base of these slopes.

BELOW Pakistani survivors walk past a landslide in Chinari, some 40 miles (60 km) from Muzaffarabad, three weeks after the earthquake.

Rescue delayed by months

Rescue workers could not reach Pakistan's remote mountain areas for days after the earthquake, as roads to extremely remote earthquake-affected villages were made impassable by the landslides and rock falls. Even as long as three months after the event, several areas remained cut off via land routes, and power, water supply, and telecommunication services were down for varying lengths of time. People took shelter in tents or dwellings constructed of any remaining materials they could find. A number of refugee tent villages that were located in highly dangerous positions in river valleys vulnerable to landslides had to be moved.

The response of Pakistani and international relief agencies to the October 8 quake was remarkable, and a major international relief effort averted a feared second wave of deaths from cold and hunger during the winter that followed the quake.

Quick action required

An alarming consequence of the earthquake was the widespread instability of large tracts of land that presented the potential for fresh slides and flash floods. It was predicted that there would be a very high incidence of large-scale and destructive slip failures during the following monsoon season. Large numbers of people living on and beneath these slopes would have been under threat, with the possibility of substantial loss of life.

Professor Dave Petley of the International Landslide Centre in Durham University's top-rated Geography Department returned from the earthquake zone after a reconnaissance mission with an American colleague. They sent an urgent report to the Pakistan authorities with warnings and a list of required actions.

Professor Petley said at the time: "Although the national and international response to the disaster has been highly impressive there is a real need for the international community to take steps to help national organizations to prevent further tragedies in the coming months. The camps where people

FACTS AND FIGURES

DATE	October 8, 2005
LOCATION	The largest landslide occurred southeast of the earthquake's epicenter, between Muzaffarabad in Pakistan and Uri in India, in the Pir Punjal Range of Kashmir
DEATH TOLL	Toll due to landslides alone is not known, but over 90,000 were killed and 106,000 were injured following the events
DAMAGE	It is estimated that more than 780,000 buildings were either destroyed or damaged beyond repair
COMMENTS	Massive landslides were a particular feature of the earthquake

have lived since the earthquake could be hit by further landslips dislodged by the summer rains."

Professor Petley reported that the massive landslide in the Hattian area that had blocked two valleys to a depth of 820 feet (250 m) was probably the largest earthquake-triggered landslip anywhere in the world during 2005. The two lakes that formed behind it posed a serious threat, because previous studies showed that 70 percent of such landslide dams collapse and fail. He recommended quick action to assess the stability of the dam, and the creation of a spillway to channel water safely before the July monsoons filled the lakes, causing overflow and possible collapse of the dam.

Many other slopes in the area had been left cracked and unstable by the earthquake. Petley recommended that monitoring equipment be installed to assess the hazard and that people be moved out of some areas during the monsoon season.

Camps in highly dangerous positions

When commenting on some of the tented villages that had been built for refugees on the low terraces and alluvial fans, Professor Petley suggested that they were in "highly dangerous positions." Many were located at the bottom of slopes and close to rivers. "These are near-perfect conditions for the generation of debris flows and flash floods. Clearly the resistance of the tented villages to such events is

effectively nil. We anticipate the potential for large-scale loss of life if this issue is not addressed."

"We feel that urgent action is required and strongly urge the authorities to recognize that a policy of just monitoring is simply not adequate in this case," the report said.

Colonel Baseer Haider Malik, a spokesman for the Pakistani government's earthquake relief commission, said spillways—one of the recommendations of the report—had already been created to release water from the lakes. He was confident that other necessary work in the quake zone would be completed and that people would be moved from danger areas by the time of the summer rains in 2006.

ABOVE Clouds of dust billow out of a landslide in Chinari, some 40 miles (60 km) from Muzaffarabad, which occurred three weeks after a massive earthquake hit the region.

GEOLOGICAL HISTORY OF THE KASHMIR REGION

The Muzaffarabad landslide occurred in a dolomitic limestone unit that had previously failed and dammed the Neelum River for a day. There was evidence of a previous landslide in this formation that had also dammed the river. The enormous, deep-seated failure in the Jhelum Valley was 22 miles (36 km) southeast of the epicenter and within 2 miles (3 km) of the surface projection of the fault in a jointed sandstone unit. The landslide was over 1,100 yards (1.0 km) wide, and the distance between the top of the slip surface and the toe of the debris was more than 2,200 yards (2.0 km).

There were no specific geologic units or slope types associated with the many shallow landslides, which were no deeper than the root zone of the plant cover, anywhere from 1 foot (30 cm) to 3 feet (1 m) deep. These slides consisted of dry, highly disaggregated and fractured material that cascaded downslope to flatter areas at or near the base of steep slopes.

Panabaj, Guatemala, 2005

On October 5, 2005, in the Guatemalan village of Panabaj, about 1,400 people died under a huge mudslide triggered by torrential rains from Hurricane Stan after it made landfall. Although the hurricane soon fizzled out, it dumped enough rain to kill over 1,000 people.

ABOVE A policeman crosses a devastated area of the village of Panabaj. The mud was deep enough to bury houses. Panabaj was located on the edge of Lake Atitlán in the western highlands of Guatemala, to the west of Guatemala City.

By that time the storm was a low-strength Category 1, but the rain continued to fall on the already saturated regions of Central America and Mexico, flooding large swathes of land and initiating dozens of mudslides that hit mountain villages. It is not unusual for hurricanes and tropical storms to trigger devastating debris flows and landslides in Guatemala, and Hurricane Stan did just that, burying villages in mudslides and sending smaller debris flows down along the rivers into settlements. These are particularly vulnerable because so many people live in small, precarious, improvised dwellings built dangerously close to riverbeds and on mountainsides. Guatemala had only just recovered from the effects of Hurricane Mitch in 1998, which killed about 10,000 people in Central America, mostly in mudslides.

The worst of the landslides crashed down the flanks of the Atitlán volcano, carrying debris such as mud, rocks, and trees, which engulfed the Maya Indian village of Panabaj. In places the mud was 40 feet (12 m) deep and ½ mile (800 m) wide. Many villagers were buried alive when the wall of mud crushed their homes, but some families managed to escape when rumbling from the volcano's slopes awakened them in the middle of the night.

"If somebody had told us to leave, maybe the people would have got out. But they said nothing. Nothing!" screamed Marta Tzoc, who grabbed her five children from their home and fled just in time.

In addition to the mudflow that buried Panabaj, many small landslides occurred to the north and northeast of Lake Atitlán, a collapsed volcanic cone filled with turquoise waters 60 miles (100 km) west of the capital, Guatemala City. Lake Atitlán is popular with US and European tourists, scores of whom had to be evacuated on foot and by helicopter from towns cut off by the mudslides.

Loose soil on slopes

The flanks of the volcano comprise loosely packed volcanic sands, topped by soils that develop into impermeable clay layers covered in vegetation. These layers build up in cycles following volcanic episodes. During storms, water forms ponds trapped above

---

LANDSLIDES IN GUATEMALA

Debris flows can move at speeds of 30 miles per hour (50 km/h) over long distances, carrying large blocks of rock and tremendous amounts of debris. Such flows are very powerful and can be lethal. Anthony Crone of the US Geological Survey, who worked in the region after Hurricane Mitch, said, "Once they stop flowing, they set up like concrete."

Although Guatemala has been subject to many landslides caused by both heavy rainfall and earthquakes, damage from most of these events has not been well documented. The major exception has been the effects of landslides triggered by the 1976 magnitude 7.5 Guatemala earthquake. This quake generated more than 10,000 landslides throughout an area of 6,200 square miles (16,000 km²), causing hundreds of fatalities as well as extensive property damage.

The landslides disrupted major highways and the national railroad system. The railroad between Guatemala City (the capital) and Puerto Barrios (the Caribbean port city) was blocked in more than 30 places. The most extensive property damage and loss of life from landslides due to the earthquake occurred in Guatemala City. Although there were no exact figures, a conservative estimate was that there were at least 200 deaths, and 500 dwellings were damaged.

ABOVE Two inter-urban buses remain stuck in the mud, amid wreckage and debris left by the landslide in Panabaj, Guatemala.

LEFT Residents search for bodies in the village of Panabaj. Hundreds of people became entombed in the mud after an avalanche of rock and mud tumbled from the slopes of the volcano onto the towns of Panabaj and Tzanchaj, 112 miles (180 km) west of Guatemala City.

ABOVE Residents of the El Chile community in Puerto San Jose, 60 miles (100 km) from Guatemala City, isolated by water dumped by Hurricane Stan, gather to catch bags of relief aid thrown from a helicopter.

RIGHT Red Cross and municipal rescuers work on a slope covered by mud after a similar mudslide in El Salvador was caused by the same hurricane.

the clay soil. Once lubricated, the volcanic deposits perched on the steep hillsides fail and slide into the eroded river valleys, where many small towns and villages have been established. Most of the people are very poor and live without land-use planning. Their poverty gives them little choice but to live in the cheaper, high-risk areas.

Along the Pacific (southern) coast of Guatemala, the Nahualate River, fed from the slopes of the western ranges, broke its banks and created a new outlet to the sea, killing at least 20 people from a small seaside village.

Rescue efforts delayed by mud

Rescue workers took two days to reach Panabaj after struggling through roads blocked by mud. There they found the tops of lampposts and trees poking through the river of mud that covered the village. The only way rescue workers could block out the overpowering smell of death was by stuffing

their nostrils with herbs. Hundreds of rescuers dug through the sludge with hoes, shovels, and pickaxes.

Sniffer dogs trained to detect bodies had been promised, but failed to arrive in time to be of any help, and hundreds of Mayan villagers who had been swarming over the vast mudslides gave up when the task proved overwhelming. For health reasons a law puts a 72-hour limit on finding the dead.

The bodies that were found were piled up in morgues, while survivors sobbed, saying that they did not know what had happened to relatives. They were desperate for news. Many of the missing apparently will simply be declared dead, and the ground they rest in will be declared hallowed ground. About 160 bodies were recovered in Panabaj and nearby towns, and most were buried in mass graves.

"There are no children left, there are no people left," said teacher Manuel Gonzalez, whose school was destroyed. "There were only houses here, for as far as you could see … It makes you lose hope."

Behind a rope barrier, dozens of women dressed in the village's traditional purple blouses embroidered with birds and animals awaited news of missing kin. The survivors, who needed food and water, helped prepare lists of the dead and missing.

"We're more concerned with getting food to the people who are alive," a civil protection agency spokeswoman said.

Guatemalan rescue workers also were trying to restore access to 300 roads that had been blocked by fallen trees, flooding, and landslides, all of which made it difficult to bring in shipments of food. Eventually, when the weather cleared sufficiently, supplies were airlifted in. Officials said nearly 54,000 people had been evacuated to 370 shelters throughout the country, while the rains had affected 80 percent of the country's roadways.

There was a little joy amid the tragedy. Claudio Manchinel, from Iztapa in central southern Guatemala, was forced to walk for hours through rain and mud with his pregnant wife, Leticia. Upon reaching a highway, the couple stopped an ambulance, which took them to a naval base, where their son Claudio was born.

Guatemalan settlements buried under rivers of mud will be abandoned and declared graveyards.

FACTS AND FIGURES

DATE	October 2005
LOCATION	Guatemala, Central America
DEATH TOLL	About 1,400
DAMAGE	Not estimated
COMMENTS	Guatemala is particularly prone to mudslides because of its extremely high rainfall and volcanic terrain

HURRICANES AND LANDSLIDES

In October 1998, Hurricane Mitch, one of the most devastating storms ever to hit Central America and the Caribbean, caused major flooding and innumerable landslides in Belize, Costa Rica, El Salvador, Guatemala, Honduras, and Nicaragua. Although Honduras suffered the greatest landslide devastation, Guatemala was also hit hard, particularly in the Sierra de las Minas.

So people living in Guatemala in October 2005, and particularly those living on Atitlán's flanks, were probably aware of the risks they faced due to landslides and volcanic terrain. However, some mayors claimed that they did not receive evacuation alerts for this storm. There is also the problem of communication between villages and towns. The volcanic soils might be perfect for coffee and other crops, but the pockets of suitable soil can be some distance apart, so there is little discussion about past hazards and the risks involved.

It was reported that there were alerts out for new landslides and flooded rivers following the October storms. The warnings were for conditions similar to those that had already closed or destroyed dozens of highways and bridges.

Guinsaugon, Leyte, Philippines, 2006

On Friday, February 17, 2006, at 10:45 a.m., a low rumble was heard on the Philippine island of Leyte. It was the only warning residents of Guinsaugon had that a huge chunk of Mt Kanabag was about to break away and engulf their village in an avalanche of mud, water, and boulders.

ABOVE Guinsaugon villager Edna Bolagsac points to where she thinks her house was. Her parents, three brothers, and a sister were listed as missing. The burial of familiar landmarks made it virtually impossible for rescuers to know where to dig.

BELOW The site of the huge landslide as seen from the air. Approximately 6 million tons of rock and soil buried the village of Guinsaugon. This photograph was taken by the US Navy, which helped in the rescue efforts.

Between 3,000 and 4,000 people lived in and around the village, and it was feared that up to 30 feet (9 m) of mud might have buried more than half of them. Only three homes of the 375 families who lived in Guinsaugon were left standing; the rest were reduced to mud and rubble. The flow traveled at an astonishing 60 to 85 miles per hour (97 to 137 km/h). Houses, people, and personal effects were moved some 1,700 feet (520 m) downstream by the flow; remarkably, neighboring houses stayed adjacent to each other, almost as though they were sailing down the hill together.

It had been business as usual in the village that morning: 246 students were at the elementary school with their seven teachers; the shops were open and the men had gone off to work—some in the fields, others in neighboring towns. Around 100 visitors were at a women's celebration in the village hall, and other women were attending to family washing. They had taken advantage of some morning sun after a fortnight of torrential rains estimated to be four times more than normal: due, primarily, to the La Niña phenomenon. It appeared to be mostly women and children among the 1,400 believed buried beneath the mud. One policeman watched helplessly as the school housing his wife and four children was submerged in seconds.

FACTS AND FIGURES

DATE	February 17, 2006
LOCATION	Guinsaugon, Leyte, Philippines
DEATH TOLL	139 dead; 973 missing, presumed dead; 580 survivors registered
DAMAGE	350 houses destroyed; 3,314 evacuees homeless, including 648 from Leyte;
COMMENTS	Over US$3 million in foreign aid was given; the area hit was 3½ square miles (9 km²); the volume was almost 4 million cubic yards (3 million m³) of mud, rock, and debris in a debris avalanche; the greatest depth of mud was 98 feet (30 m); a total of 16 villages were affected; Guinsaugon is now gone from the map

One villager recalled how he had felt the ground shake shortly before the landslide struck: "I ran out in the street but fell to the ground along with my brother. There were big boulders, bigger than a house, and logs which rushed down." His wife and children were killed; he was unable to retrieve the bodies because of the danger of the moving mud.

Fifteen other villages in the area were also hit by the slide, but they suffered far less damage. Officials evacuated at least 11 of them. Residents were relocated to seven evacuation centers.

Mud-caked, gasping survivors

Rescue attempts were frustrated by not being able to use heavy equipment on the soft mud—there was a fear that it would cause the unstable mud to shift. Instead, rescuers had to rely on hands, shovels, and sticks, and as they dug, the mud would collapse back into their excavations. When the mud did begin to settle and consolidate, heavy machinery was brought in, but the backhoe had similar problems with sidewalls collapsing. One of the main frustrations was that no one was really sure where to dig. By evening, only 53 survivors and 19 bodies had been pulled from the wreckage of the village. Many of the survivors were mud-caked and gasping as rescuers carried them away.

All through the rescue operation there remained the danger of rescuers slipping waist-deep into patches of soft muck or being cut by jagged boulders or other sharp debris. Another danger was the possibility of further falls of mud, rocks, and debris from the mountain. Some little protection was afforded the rescuers when designated "watchers" were asked to give a shrill three-whistle warning

in the event of another flow so that everyone could drop what they were doing and run for their lives.

Rescue operations concentrated on locating the buried school, but it was difficult to know just where the school had been or whether it had been carried away. Rescuers had a 45-minute hike from the edge of the mud field to the suspected site of the school.

When no more survivors had been found after the first few hours of the landslide, hopes of finding others became less and less; finally, on Friday, February 24, rescue operations were called off. By then only 139 bodies had been recovered, and an estimated 915 were still missing. "The search and rescue phase is over. The decision was reached upon the recommendation of the experts," a local governor explained. The priority shifted to healing and rehousing the survivors.

Landslides are not new to Leyte

In November 1991, a flash flood and landslide from a nearby deforested mountain swept down into Ormoc city on the western side of Leyte, killing about 6,000. A landslide in December 2003 killed

ABOVE Rescuers dig through the rubble of what used to be a cluster of homes in the central Philippine village of Guinsaugon. Twenty-two people were pulled out of the landslide within hours, but only bodies were found in succeeding days.

ABOVE A view of the aftermath of the landslide. In 2003, government geologists listed more than 80 percent of Leyte Island as being prone to landslides. The island straddles the Philippine Fault, which zigzags through the Philippine islands archipelago. The landslides are aided by forest clearing.

133 in San Francisco, in southern Leyte. Seven road workers died in a landslide in Sogod town five days before the nearby Guinsaugon tragedy.

It wasn't that the residents of Leyte were unaware of the risks. Geologists had warned that villages near Guinsaugon faced danger from landslides, and government officials had ordered evacuation. However, many poor villagers said that they wouldn't know where to go, and if they were to move, their livelihoods would be at risk.

Because of the unusual rains in the weeks before the landslide, fearful residents around Guinsaugon had been evacuating the area at night, when the heaviest rain dramatically increased the risk of landslides and flash flooding. Many kept away for the entire week because of the freak rains. It was when the weather gave way to sunny mornings that people started returning and began to resume their village life. The Guinsaugon landslide was different—it happened in the morning, not at night.

LOGGING DESTABILIZES LAND

Unchecked logging activities have also been blamed
for this tragedy. Logging has been going on for the
past 30 years in this region—sometimes illegally and
sometimes using the devastating slash-and-burn system.
Widespread logging and clearing can cause instability
on denuded slopes. The government has been accused
of refusing to enforce a nationwide logging ban so that
measures can be put in place to protect communities like
Guinsaugon from flash floods and landslides.

It seems that a national geo-hazard map showing landslide-prone regions had been around for years, but without enough detail to indicate which towns faced danger. In 2003, government geologists listed 82.6 percent of Leyte as prone to landslides. In 2004, 100 potential landslide risks were identified by government agencies, in particular St Bernard, the closest town to Guinsaugon in Southern Leyte Province. In 2005, Philippine officials started a three-year program to create even more detailed maps.

The Philippines is undeniably a country prone to natural disasters. Leyte is an impoverished mountainous island 420 miles (680 km) southeast of Manila where high population density causes the movement of people to places vulnerable to disasters, including upland, geologically active areas.

A deadly combination of causes

Three factors—torrential rain, a geologically active tectonic structure, and rampant deforestation—combined to cause a huge chunk of Mt Kanabag to roar down into the valley below, burying the village of Guinsaugon.

During February 2006, a La Niña event caused higher than average rainfall in the Philippines. Four-and-a-half miles (7 km) from Guinsaugon, an official rain station recorded an accumulated rainfall of 25¾ inches (675 mm) in the period February 8 to 17; the highest amount of rain was 6¾ inches (171 mm) on February 12. Although only ¹⁄₁₀ inch (2.6 mm) was recorded on the disastrous day of February 17, the ground had already been thoroughly saturated by the daily average of 20 inches (500 mm). It takes only 4 inches (100 mm) of rainfall to activate a landslide in a terrain like that around Guinsaugon. Clearly there was more than enough reason to evacuate long before the disaster struck.

The record rains had fallen along a steep fault scarp, which is part of a major fault zone involved in tectonic plate activity. The entire length of the Philippine archipelago is located along a section of the Pacific "Ring of Fire," a sprawling region where

earthquakes and volcanic activity are common. Guinsaugon is located at the foot of a scarp directly affected by the subducting (descending) tectonic plate.

Also, at around 10:36 a.m. on the day of the landslide, the Philippine Institute of Volcanology and Seismology recorded a 2.6 magnitude earthquake in the southwestern portion of Southern Leyte. This earthquake would not have been strong enough on its own to trigger the landslide. However, combined with the other factors, especially heavy rainfall, it almost certainly contributed to the deadly landslide.

There are recommendations for an investigation into a reported drying up of the Himbangan River at the foot of the fault scarp days before the incident. Did the water go elsewhere, and did this event play a role in the landslide?

ABOVE US Marines work knee-deep in mud as they look for buried bodies in the still-shifting terrain. The US still maintains a military presence in the Philippines, which allowed it to respond quickly to the crisis.

BELOW A US Marine helicopter helps a Taiwanese search and rescue team, stuck in the mud in the middle of the wasteland of what is left of Guinsaugon, as they recover a landslide victim. The Taiwanese had to be rescued after they became marooned.

Hurricanes, Cyclones, and Typhoons

Hurricanes, cyclones, and typhoons are intense low-pressure areas—regions where the atmospheric pressure is lowest in relation to the surrounding area—that come from the tropics. They are able to produce tremendously strong winds and heavy rain. They are the most damaging large-scale weather systems in the world, and have been responsible for massive destruction and loss of life.

Hurricane is the word used in the Americas and the Caribbean to describe these storms; the term originates from a Central American Indian word *huracan*, meaning "God of evil." Over much of Asia, they are known as typhoons, a word that derives from the Chinese *t'ai fung*, meaning "great wind." In India and Australia, the term "tropical cyclone" is used. All this means that different names are used depending on the region they occur. It's a hurricane if it occurs in the Atlantic Basin or North Pacific Ocean, a typhoon if it's in the northwest Pacific west of the international dateline, and a tropical cyclone if it's in the southwest Pacific, southeast Indian Ocean, north Indian Ocean, south Pacific, or South Atlantic Ocean.

Hurricanes and tropical cyclones are an important mechanism of the global atmospheric circulation, and maintain equilibrium in the environment.

The components of a major storm

Hurricanes affect most tropical and subtropical parts of the world, including North America, the West Indies, the Indian subcontinent, Asia, and Australia. They begin as clusters of thunderstorm activity over warm tropical oceans where sea surface temperatures are in excess of 81°F (27°C). This happens most often during the summer and early autumn months.

If the storm clusters persist for a day or two, a slow rotation of the clusters begins that is enhanced by Earth's spin—the winds move clockwise in the southern hemisphere and anti-clockwise in the northern hemisphere. A roughly circular structure gradually develops, consisting of a small area of light winds and clear skies near the center (called the eye), and inwardly spiraling surface winds. Air then rises in massive thunderstorm towers that form a wall around the eye, and then spirals out from the top of

FAR LEFT In October, 1987, the southern coast of England was hit with gale-force winds. Kent, known for its country gardens, was faced with a massive clean-up operation after the storm. The woodlands around this country property were stripped bare by the terrifying 94 miles per hour (151 km/h) winds.

LEFT A view from space of a hurricane. The eye of the hurricane can be seen, formed by the slow rotation of clusters of thunderstorm activity. An eyewall surrounds the eye—it is made up of thunderstorms that spiral upwards to the top of the swirling air system.

PREVIOUS PAGES Hurricane Rita blew in with 165 miles per hour (265 km/h) winds and destructive force equal to that of Hurricane Katrina. The howling winds lashed the coast near Corpus Christi in Texas.

RIGHT The full strength of the Category 2 hurricane can be seen as a sturdy palm tree is blown in a fierce coastal hurricane. In these conditions, street signs are stripped off their poles and the roofs of houses begin to lift from their battens.

THE TEN MOST DEADLY HURRICANES, CYCLONES, AND TYPHOONS

NOVEMBER, 1839	A strong tropical cyclone produced a 40-foot (12-m) high storm surge across the coastline near Coringa, India. An estimated 300,000 people died.
SEPTEMBER, 1900	Galveston was devastated on September 8, 1900, by a powerful hurricane that leveled a large area of the city. The estimated death toll was between 8,000 and 10,000 people.
SEPTEMBER, 1928	A deadly hurricane cut a swathe of destruction across the Caribbean, Puerto Rico, the Bahamas, and Florida. More than 4,000 people died and the damage exceeded US$400 million.
AUGUST, 1969	One of the worst hurricanes in US history, Camille tore across the Mississippi Gulf coast during August 17 and 18, 1969. Winds of 190 miles per hour (306 km/h) were generated, together with a storm surge that was 25 feet (7.6 m) high; 250 people died.
NOVEMBER, 1970	One of the greatest disasters of modern history. Over 500,000 people died when a tropical cyclone hit Bhola in Bangladesh on November 13, 1970.
DECEMBER, 1974	Cyclone Tracy descended on Darwin, the capital of Australia's Northern Territory, on Christmas Eve, 1974. It moved across the city on Christmas morning, flattening over 70 percent of buildings and killing 71 people.
OCTOBER, 1979	Rated as one of the most powerful typhoons of history, Tip produced peak winds around 190 miles per hour (306 km/h) over parts of the Pacific on October 12, 1979. It caused 68 deaths and millions of dollars of damage.
SEPTEMBER, 1988	Hurricane Gilbert was a monster hurricane that cut a swathe of destruction across several countries during September, 1988. Jamaica, Haiti, and Mexico were devastated, with a final death toll of 318.
AUGUST, 1992	Packing winds of over 150 miles per hour (241 km/h), Hurricane Andrew left an enormous trail of destruction across southern Florida on August 24, 1992.
AUGUST, 2005	Hurricane Katrina was an incredibly destructive hurricane that devastated large areas of the coastlines of Louisiana, Mississippi, and Alabama. The damage bill was estimated to be over US$75 billion, with a death toll around 1,400 people.

HURRICANE CLASSIFICATIONS

Methods of categorizing the intensities of hurricanes vary around the world, but the Saffir–Simpson hurricane scale, as used in the United States, is broadly representative. It rates hurricanes from the least powerful (Category 1) to the most intense (Category 5).

CATEGORY 1 Winds between 74 and 95 miles per hour (119–153 km/h). Minor damage occurs to housing and infrastructure.

CATEGORY 2 Winds between 96 and 110 miles per hour (154–177 km/h). Roofing is peeled off houses and small trees are blown down. Small water craft are torn from their moorings.

CATEGORY 3 Winds between 111 and 130 miles per hour (179–209 km/h). Significant damage to housing and infrastructure occurs, plus an increasing storm surge in coastal areas. Large trees are blown down.

CATEGORY 4 Winds between 131 and 155 miles per hour (211–249 km/h). Major damage inflicted on housing and infrastructure. Extensive flooding occurs over coastal areas, through a rising storm surge. Widespread destruction of forested areas follows, with many large trees blown over.

CATEGORY 5 Winds greater than 155 miles per hour (249 km/h). Catastrophic damage occurs to buildings and infrastructure. Massive storm surge generates widespread flooding near the coast, and most trees and shrubs are destroyed. Loss of life is likely in populated areas.

the system, forming a disc-shaped three-dimensional structure that may be around 600 miles (965 km) across and 9 miles (14.5 km) high near the center.

Hurricanes usually move away from the equator and then hit either land or cooler areas of ocean waters. In both these cases, they weaken; after moving across land they form rapidly into rain depressions, which can produce extensive flooding on land masses.

If the hurricane moves out to sea again, it can re-intensify, build up momentum and follow a highly erratic and unpredictable trajectory. It is during this stage, when close to the coastline, that the danger to communities is highest.

Storm surges

As a hurricane approaches the coast, one of its first effects is the so-called storm surge, which occurs when strong and persistent winds blow from the sea toward the land, pushing ocean water toward, and then across, the shoreline, often moving further inland. The central pressure of hurricanes is normally very low, and this produces a lifting effect on the ocean, in much the same way as the reduced pressure inside a drinking straw lifts fluid upward. This lifting magnifies flooding from the sea. A storm surge is a particularly dangerous

phenomenon and has often produced more damage and loss of life than all the other effects of a hurricane combined.

Extreme weather conditions

The most common weather associated with a hurricane is the high winds, sometimes in excess of 174 miles per hour (280 km/h). These winds are powerful enough to destroy the average house and

ABOVE Hurricane Fran slammed into North Carolina's southern coast near Cape Fear in the United States in September, 1996.

BELOW On the Cayman Islands, cars were buried in sand after Hurricane Ivan swept through the Caribbean in September, 2004.

RIGHT A professional storm photographer is forced into a corner of a building in Gulfport, Mississippi, United States, by a rapidly rising storm surge caused by Hurricane Katrina in 2005.

BELOW Hurricanes need certain conditions to form. Seawater must be over 27°C (81°F) and 160 feet (50 m) deep. The air at the center must be unstable, causing high convection. In order to build, it must not be disturbed by windshear, and moisture needs to build up in the atmosphere to 2 miles (3.2 km).

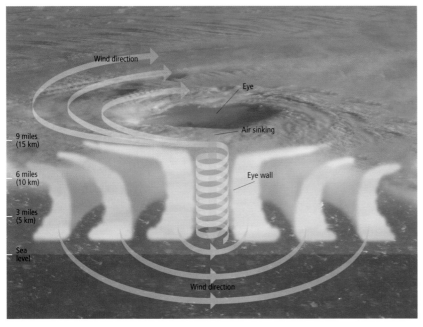

Wind direction

Eye

Air sinking

Eye wall

9 miles (15 km)

6 miles (10 km)

3 miles (5 km)

Sea level

Wind direction

WHAT TO DO DURING A HURRICANE

1. MONITOR THE MEDIA for any new warnings or developments with the hurricane. Be ready to evacuate should the need arise.

2. HAVE A BATTERY-OPERATED RADIO and fresh batteries ready in case the power fails.

3. IF YOU ARE IN A HOUSE, STAY INSIDE and shelter in the most secure part of the building, away from windows. Take cover under a mattress or rug if the building starts to disintegrate.

4. IF THE WIND DROPS don't go outside, as it may be the eye of the storm. Wait for official advice before leaving your place of shelter.

5. IF YOU ARE CAUGHT IN A CAR park well away from the sea or any watercourses, power lines, and trees. Stay inside the vehicle.

6. AFTER THE HURRICANE HAS PASSED help your neighbors. Don't go sightseeing. Keep the area clear for emergency vehicles.

flatten any surrounding structures. If a hurricane passes directly over a certain location, strong winds will be experienced from one direction, accompanied by heavy bursts of rain and often thunderstorm activity. The strongest winds normally occur just before the eye reaches an area. As the eye passes over an area, the winds suddenly drop and there is an eerie calm. The skies will often clear of storm clouds, making people believe that the hurricane has moved on and the danger has passed.

Depending on the size of the eye, and this can vary considerably, and the speed of movement of the hurricane, the calm weather can last for an hour or so. Then the wind, pelting rain and thunder will return with a similar ferocity, but from the opposite direction. This clears as the hurricane leaves the area.

The most destructive hurricanes are generally those that are both severe and also slow moving. This means that affected areas are exposed to the destructive conditions for an extended period of time.

During a storm surge, a hurricane moves out to sea, where it can re-intensify, build up momentum and follow a highly erratic and unpredictable trajectory. At this stage, it is close to the coastline and very dangerous to coastal communities, as it causes flooding from the ocean and destruction from rampaging winds.

If the hurricane moves inland, the increased friction of the wind movement across land, combined with a loss of its moisture source—the warm ocean waters—result in a rapid moderation of the winds. The system becomes a rain depression, capable of dumping massive amounts of water a considerable distance inland, causing flooding.

Detecting and tracking hurricanes, cyclones, and typhoons

Hurricanes are initially detected through satellite photography. They have a very distinctive appearance. there is a rough circular area of cloud that sometimes has the eye visible near its center.

Specialist meteorological teams monitor hurricanes in their developing phase, and once satisfied that the threshold intensities have been reached, a hurricane is declared and a name given. The naming of hurricanes comes from a list kept updated by the World Meteorological Organization (WMO)—they are carefully bestowed with male and female names alternating.

Warnings are issued to all the relevant areas, as well as to ships at sea and aircraft likely to fly over the affected zone. The hurricane is tracked using satellite photography, and by radar whenever the cyclone moves within range of a radar unit.

While these technological advances have greatly improved the monitoring of hurricanes, there has also been a considerable improvement in the prediction of their movement, using sophisticated computer algorithms.

Hurricane trajectories are notoriously erratic, ranging from moving in a smooth easily predictable path or trajectory to looping around and frequently

changing direction. Mathematical modeling of hurricane movement, taking into account the hurricane structure, together with its environment and surrounding sea surface temperatures, is providing increasingly valuable information, and this, in turn, improves the accuracy of hurricane warnings issued to the public.

A damaged beach house teeters on its supports in the aftermath of a hurricane (above). At Myrtle Beach, North Carolina, workers board up store windows in preparation for the landfall of Hurricane Fran in 1996 (below).

Bhola, East Pakistan (Bangladesh), 1970

On November 13, 1970, the deadliest tropical cyclone ever recorded struck East Pakistan, causing massive destruction and loss of life. The 1970 cyclone is one of the three most deadly natural disasters in modern history, along with the 1976 Tangshan earthquake and the more recent 2004 Indian Ocean earthquake and tsunami.

RIGHT For the survivors of the cyclone, hunger was the next danger facing their families. People search for rice and other grain in the flattened fields.

BELOW RIGHT Close to Sonapur, East Pakistan, villagers walk through a field of dead and bloated cattle. Livelihoods in the region hit by the cyclone were destroyed for many years to come.

BELOW Children on Bhola Island wade through murky and contaminated floodwaters. Orphaned children and distraught families were left to fend for themselves for weeks until foreign aid agencies came to their rescue.

Early on November 10, a tropical depression formed near the south coast of India. Slowly, it moved northward, gaining strength over the next couple of days; it developed into a tropical cyclone with strong wind gusts of over 100 miles per hour (161 km/h) as it headed into the Bay of Bengal. Inadequate and ambiguous warnings from the government left the residents of East Pakistan mostly unaware about and largely unconcerned with the storm.

In the early hours of November 13, the cyclone raged into the Bay of Bengal, swamping the bay islands with 15 to 20 foot (4.6 to 6 m) storm surges, before moving into the delta area. The Bhola Island region sustained the worst damage, with the towns of Charfasson and Tazumuddin completely destroyed. Twenty-five thousand of Manpura Island's 30,000 residents were killed when 20-foot (6 m) waves washed over the island. On the dozens of small islands in the mouth of the bay, there were no survivors. The storm also wreaked havoc in the mainland city of Chittagong as violent storm surges moved swiftly inland.

A ravaged nation

Bhola, at one square mile (2.6 km²) , is the largest island off the southern coast of East Pakistan. It lies near the Ganges River Delta along the Shabazpur Channel. The region's main source of livelihood comes from the fishing and farming industries, both of which suffered devastating losses from flooding, salt saturation, and pollution. In the aftermath of the storm, disease spread as a result of the numbers of corpses floating in and poisoning the floodwaters.

Nearly every building in the storm's path was damaged or completely flattened, along with fields where over 75 percent of the region's rice crop was ruined. Other crops in the region, including wheat, chilies and several kinds of nuts, were destroyed. Hundreds of fishing boats were swamped and over a million head of cattle drowned, plunging the already impoverished area into starvation. Water mains were damaged and, in the storm's aftermath, other water sources such as wells were polluted with seawater and rotting corpses.

The New York Times published the story of a rice farmer who watched helplessly as four of his five children were swept away by the waters. The fifth child also drowned elsewhere. The farmer managed to save his wife in the deluge, grabbing her as she was swept past him, and both were badly injured. Thousands of corpses littering the beaches and roadways and hanging from trees were buried in mass graves dug by survivors. People struggled to find grains of unspoiled rice and water. Some survivor stories were astonishing, including one tale

FACTS AND FIGURES

DATE	November 13, 1970
LOCATION	East Pakistan (Bangladesh)
DEATH TOLL	Approximately 500,000 dead; over 100,000 people missing
DAMAGE	Approximately US$5 million in aid; total cost unknown
CATEGORY	Unknown, probably reached 4
WINDSPEED	120 mph (193 km/h) highest sustained winds with higher gusts
BAROMETRIC PRESSURE	Unknown
COMMENT	Most deadly tropical cyclone ever recorded; the total death count is an estimate as the real death toll was never known

of two small girls found floating on a raft made of bloated corpses tied with palm fronds.

The Pakistani government in the west of the country, due to long-standing political issues, was slow to respond, delaying transportation of much-needed food and water, and did not send military aid. The recovery of the region was aided by foreign donations and military aid in excess of US$5 million. By spring, local unrest following the disaster developed into civil war. The bitter conflict eventually resulted in the separation of East and West Pakistan, with the East becoming the nation of Bangladesh.

Census estimates from the late 1990s revealed that about 5 million people lived in Bangladesh's high-risk tropical storm region. Despite being plagued by many dangerous storms every year, it was only after the 1991 Bhola Cyclone that the region began the necessary preparations and storm shelters that would preserve the population from future storms.

Tracy, Australia, 1974

Tropical Cyclone Tracy devastated Darwin, Australia, on Christmas Eve of 1974, with winds howling up to 135 miles per hour (220 km/h). This was the worst natural disaster that ever struck an Australian city. Cyclone Tracy killed 71 people even after city evacuations, and carved a swathe of destruction costing over US$3 billion. The residents of Darwin faced a very bleak Christmas.

RIGHT A street in an area of the city of Darwin looks more like a demolition yard than a suburban neighborhood. This was an all too common scene that faced survivors on Christmas morning.

BELOW RIGHT Cyclone Tracy breaks a man's heart. A Darwin resident, Jeff Casey, returned from his Christmas vacation to what was left of his family home.

BELOW The skeletal remains of a house on the outskirts of Darwin. Over 70 percent of the city's residences were destroyed, leaving more than 20,000 people homeless.

Early on December 21, a tropical low northeast of Darwin developed the pattern of swirling clouds that indicated a possible cyclone and the Weather Bureau issued major storm watch warnings. By 10:00 p.m., Tracy was declared a Tropical Cyclone 435 miles (700 km) northeast of Darwin. On December 24, morning weather reports announced that Tropical Cyclone Tracy would not be a danger to the city, but the cyclone made a sudden and dramatic 90-degree curve around Cape Fourcroy and turned directly southeast, on a collision course with Darwin.

Throughout the afternoon, with increasing wind, rain, and overcast skies, warnings and sirens announced the imminent disaster, but many of the unsuspecting residents of Darwin refused to believe that the storm would be a problem. The previous week, cyclone warnings had been issued for Cyclone Selma, which had dissipated over the water, leaving Darwin unaffected. On Christmas Eve, most of the city's nearly 45,000 population was busy with holiday preparations—another storm warning was not going to ruin their Christmas. In the harbor and boatyards, the warnings were received a little more attentively. By early evening, the harbor was emptying out. Only three uncrewed naval vessels remained; 27 ships left to ride out the storm at sea.

A Christmas nightmare

At 1:30 a.m. Christmas morning, hours before its predicted arrival, Tropical Cyclone Tracy hit Darwin directly, with strong winds up to 185 miles per hour (298 km/h) and torrential rain. While Tracy was the smallest tropical storm on record, having cyclone-force winds extending for only 30 miles (48 km) from the storm's center, it made Darwin look like a bomb had struck. Homes and buildings were torn off their foundations, office buildings crumbled, cars, trucks, railway engines, and airplanes were tossed about like toys, and trees and telephone poles were swept up and hurled everywhere. Of the 27 ships that had put out to sea, only six returned. The three naval vessels in the harbor were destroyed.

Survivors tell tales of huddling in terror in the darkness of laundry rooms, bathrooms, and closets while screaming winds dismantled their homes around them. Describing the sound of the winds as roaring, explosions and incoming trains, many hung on to shreds of buildings, clinging for their lives as they waited for momentary lulls in the storm's fury to seek better shelter. Many people fled into local hotels until those buildings were also destroyed by the storm's force.

Just before dawn, around the time Tracy had been predicted to arrive, the eye of the storm passed over

FACTS AND FIGURES

DATE	December 21 to 26, 1974
LOCATION	Darwin, Northern Territory, Australia
DEATH TOLL	71 dead; hundreds injured
DAMAGE	US$3.2 billion
CATEGORY	4 (possibly 5)
WINDSPEED	135 mph (220 km/h) sustained winds with 185 mph (300 km/h) gusts
BAROMETRIC PRESSURE	Unknown
COMMENTS	Worst natural disaster to hit an Australian city in Australian history. It has inspired songs such as Bill Cate's "Santa Never Made It Into Darwin," and a television mini-series called *Cyclone Tracy* about surviving the disaster.

the city. In the eerie calm, shell-shocked survivors watched barometric pressures drop right off the scales. Dazed, many wandered out to look at the devastation of their homes and take in the shocking sight of flattened neighborhoods. When the storm resumed with a sudden fury, dozens of people staring at the destruction were caught outdoors without being able to get to safety.

Christmas morning chaos
Early on Christmas Day, the survivors of Darwin began creeping out of their shelters to view what was left of their homes. Nearly every building had sustained major damage. The streets were littered with wrecks of vehicles, trees, and buildings.

In the aftermath of Cyclone Tracy, Darwin was also facing the additional danger of the potential spread of disease—20,000 homeless people were living in makeshift shelters without clean water, sanitation, or power. Arrangements were made to quickly evacuate the city for safety and health reasons. Three years later, Darwin was rebuilt to withstand a major cyclone, but the ghost of Christmas 1974 and Tracy still haunts the city.

Bangladesh, 1991

On April 29, 1991, southeastern Bangladesh was utterly devastated by a Category 4 cyclone with sustained winds up to 160 miles per hour (258 km/h) and storm surges over 20 feet (6 m) high. An estimated 138,000 people were killed, and more than 10 million were left homeless.

The storm originated some 20 days away from Bangladesh in the Pacific Ocean, approximately 3,728 miles (5,998 km) from the Bay of Bengal. By April 23, the tropical depression was tracked on radar; about two days later it had developed into a major cyclonic storm system as it moved swiftly across the dangerous Indian Ocean storm basin.

Despite having sufficient time before the storm struck, the warning systems in the southeastern Bangladesh region were inadequate and the people did not get advance notice of the storm's progress.

By April 25, the storm was bigger than the area of the entire Bay of Bengal. It was upgraded to a full tropical cyclone between April 27 and 28, with an overall diameter greater than 373 miles (600 km). On April 28, the cyclone turned on a northeasterly course; it headed directly into Chittagong harbor on April 29. Later that day, the storm had intensified to Category 4, with 160 miles per hour (257 km/h) winds. The cyclone made landfall at high tide that night, only slightly diminishing on impact. As it reached Chittagong, wind speeds were sustained at 155 miles per hour (249 km/h).

BELOW A young boy looks out at the devastated coastline of Chittagong. Corpses, livestock, and building materials were dragged from inland areas by massive storm surges.

Devastation on a massive scale

The storm relentlessly pounded the coastal region for over nine hours. Nearly 100,000 people were moved into existing storm shelters, but outlying areas and islands were completely flooded. Nearly two million homes were totally flattened, roadways were completely washed away, fresh water sources and wells were polluted with seawater and corpses, and entire crops for the region were destroyed. The

areas of Chittagong and Cox's Bazaar, both low-lying coastal urban centers prone to damage from flooding and storm surges, suffered the majority of casualties. Storm pattern analysts place the fatalities in these regions at up to 70 percent of their populations. On April 30, the storm raged inland and lost its power.

The combination of 155 miles per hour (249 kph) winds and the very low barometric pressure of the storm sweeping into the region at high tide carried the storm surges much further inland than ever had been predicted. Homes, structures, electricity poles, and trees were washed away as far as 6.2 miles (10 km) from the coast. The Chittagong harbor was chaotic, piled with the shattered remains of boats. Ships were tossed inland and wrecked, while several naval vessels were sunk. Bridges in the region were smashed by wreckage colliding with them. The Bangladesh Air Force Base was submerged in

ABOVE An aerial photograph of part of Chittagong illustrates how random the cyclone was in its destruction. Flattened houses stand next to others that appear to be relatively untouched. Most of the deaths occurred in this seaport, and many of them were of children or the elderly.

ABOVE Despite the heavy winds, a man emerges from a makeshift dwelling of coconut leaves and bamboo in Banshkali. His wife and their three children were killed during the cyclone.

15 to 20 feet (4.6 to 6 m) of water, with aircraft and fighter planes left floating. In Patenga, the Isha Khan Naval base was also completely flooded, and many of the ships sustained damage. Television, radio, and weather stations and towers were completely destroyed, which effectively severed the region's communications. Industrial and factory buildings were flooded or washed out, and there was no power throughout the entire area. Along the coastal regions, whole villages were either totally submerged or completely washed away.

The civil infrastructure of the region collapsed in the wake of trying to cope with the disaster. The ability of the newly elected democratic government was put to the test as it tried to handle a major disaster situation. With hundreds of cattle and livestock killed, and widespread destruction of crops and food sources, southeastern Bangladesh was plunged into

economic chaos. The farmers in these areas also had to face the desperate reality that their land was now salt-soaked and would be unable to yield sufficient crops in the near future.

Arriving by aircraft, rescue workers initially found no sign of anything living. Bodies of humans and animals were floating and trapped in debris or washed into depressions and canals. One rescue worker spoke of dropping available supplies to a group of survivors, and being overcome by the sight of mass suffering; starving people were fighting over the scant supplies. He assured the people that the aid workers would return with more supplies to ease their terrible plight. This became an all too common sight for many of the foreign aid workers who traveled across the country attempting to deliver as many supplies as they could to the large numbers of people trying to find areas of dry land.

In desperate need of help

The Bangladesh Army was able to provide reports and assessments of the total devastation, and gave recommendations as to how to best proceed with the rescue efforts and to get relief to the stricken population. They were mobilized with supplies and aid, especially water and precooked foods, to prevent further loss of life, and became the backbone of the rescue efforts. Prime Minister Khaleda Zia made worldwide appeals for relief and aid. International response was immediate. Britain, France, Italy, Australia, Sweden, Germany, Canada, Japan, China, Kuwait, and Saudi Arabia all responded. The US Government sent in the Marine Corps on the aircraft carrier the USS *Tarawa* to assist with rebuilding and rescue efforts, as well as providing supplies for the relief efforts. The US forces assisted the Bangladesh military in setting up a forward joint operation center at the damaged Chittagong Air Force Base. This center became responsible for organizing the relief efforts, and establishing satellite communications with the main rescue operations center in Tejgaon Thana Region Military Base. The Marines also helped establish communications with the isolated island regions, providing those areas with water purification and survival kits in close cooperation with the Bangladesh Army forces.

The survivors in the area rose to the challenge of the struggle to survive and rebuild. Communities and villages banded together to re-establish whatever was left of their homes and crops.

Where do tropical cyclones come from?

The Northern Indian Ocean hurricane basin, one of seven major tropical cyclone formation basins, produces the most deadly tropical storms in the world. Divided into two regions, the Bay of Bengal and the Arabian Sea, this region spawns the storms that affect India, Bangladesh, Pakistan, Thailand, and Sri Lanka. On rare occasions, these storms also affect

CYCLONE OF DEATH

Time magazine featured an article on the 1991 Bangladesh disaster called the "Cyclone of Death." In the feature, James Walsh wrote, "Twenty-foot walls of water. Demonic winds of crushing force. The horror left behind: 125,000 lives lost, and still counting. A world used to human-scale catastrophes—plane crashes, say, that kill a few hundred at most—cannot absorb the biblical dooms that visit Bangladesh. Straddling the conjoined mouths of the Ganges and Brahmaputra, two of the Indian subcontinent's mightiest rivers, the country is regularly drowned by flood crests surging downstream or scourged by whirlwinds from the sea. Of the twentieth century's ten deadliest storms, seven have devoured their victims at the head of the Bay of Bengal."

areas of the Arabian Peninsula. The Bay of Bengal region of the basin has over five times more storm activity than the Arabian Sea region.

Other tropical cyclone formation basins include the southwestern Indian Ocean basin, affecting places like Kenya, Mozambique, Madagascar, and Mauritius; the southeastern Indian Ocean basin, affecting Australia and Indonesia; the southwestern Pacific Ocean basin, affecting Australia and Papua New Guinea; the western-north Pacific Ocean basin, affecting China, Japan, Taiwan and the Philippines; the eastern-north Pacific Ocean basin, affecting Mexico, Hawaii, Central America, and California; and the North Atlantic basin, affecting regions next to the Caribbean Sea, the Gulf of Mexico, the eastern United States, Canada, and Nova Scotia. The North Atlantic basin produces the deadly Cape Verde-type hurricanes, and is the best-studied tropical cyclone formation region in the world.

BELOW Once the relief aid was coordinated, Bangladesh communities and rescue workers moved into action. These rows of water jugs are ready to be flown out to flood-stricken areas.

FACTS AND FIGURES

DATE	April 22 to 30, 1991
LOCATION	Bangladesh
DEATH TOLL	138,000 dead; those who survived were left homeless
DAMAGE	US$1.5 billion
CATEGORY	4 (possibly 5)
WINDSPEED	160 mph (260 km/h)
BAROMETRIC PRESSURE	898 mbar
COMMENTS	The worst natural disaster to strike Bangladesh since the 1970 Bhola Cyclone

Thelma, Central Philippines, 1991

On November 5, 1991, the relatively small Tropical Storm Thelma crossed the Philippine Islands. Although weak, the storm, which was locally known as Uring, brought torrential rainfall. In its wake, dams burst, rivers overflowed, and flash floods triggered landslides, killing over 4,800 people.

Toward the later days of October, one particular storm front, of what would become several significant tropical fronts, formed directly east of the Caroline Islands. Moving on a northwesterly course, by November 1 it had formed into Tropical Depression 27W. Gaining strength, it continued westward with increasing intensity until it was upgraded to the international designation of Tropical Storm Thelma on November 4. (It was also called Tropical Storm Uring for the purpose of Philippines warnings.) The storm reached its peak intensity with 50 miles per hour (80 km/h) winds and a central barometric pressure of 991 mbar.

On November 5, Tropical Storm Thelma arrived on the east Philippines island of Samar, dropping up to 6 inches (15.2 cm) of rain. Over the entire region, Thelma would dump more than 5½ inches (14 cm) of rainfall in less than 24 hours. The storm continued moving west, decreasing in power to approximately 40 miles per hour (64 km/h) as it crossed the islands, and headed out into the South China Sea. It was then weakened by opposing weather fronts and was downgraded back to a tropical depression by November 7. The remains of Thelma impacted on eastern Vietnam on November 8 before fading out.

Although Thelma was only a weak tropical storm, it dropped a massive amount of rainfall across the Philippines, most notably on Samar, Leyte, Cebu, and Negros. On Leyte, Ormoc City was affected.

BELOW Debris from the forest, which was carried by a flash flood, is piled up on houses. Thelma caused a dam to burst sending floodwaters rampaging through several villages in the central Philippines.

Deluge of disaster

Torrential rainfall began mid-morning on November 5, causing dams and rivers to overflow, triggering landslides and flash flooding. Due to heavy regional logging in the hills above and surrounding the city, the floodwaters slammed into the Ormoc City region. The river that runs through the city overflowed, and the entire city was flooded with up to 10 feet (3 m) of water, mud, and debris. Thousands of people were unprepared, and drowned in the deluge.

The storm moved over Cebu, swamping urban areas with similar flooding. In Negros, houses were ripped off foundations, and rivers overflowed their banks, running through the Victorias and Bacolod City. Bridges were destroyed, and more residents were drowned in the rising waters. The flooding

triggered landslides over the region from San Joaquin to Calinog in Iloilo, where the destruction of roads and bridges left entire communities isolated.

On Negros and Leyte, power and communications were cut. Lack of fresh water and food shortages became an immediate health danger in the storm's aftermath, along with widespread contamination from the debris, floodwaters, and corpses. Clogged roadways hampered many of the rescue and relief efforts. Rescue personnel and journalists present in the region described seeing Ormoc City as "a scene from the Holocaust, where dead bodies were stacked upon each other like logs or garbage." Despairing officials were forced to dig mass graves in order to quickly bury corpses littering the region and prevent the spread of deadly disease.

Over 4,800 people were confirmed dead, with another estimated 1,500 missing and over 3,100 injured. More than 45,000 people were left homeless, and an estimated 600,000 survivors were directly affected by the disaster. By November 10, the Philippines government had made an international appeal for aid. The United Nations (UN) contributed US$50,000 in emergency relief grants, while the international community and others offered practical aid, such as building materials and medical support. Government grants of nearly US$700,000 were allocated to internal relief funds along with another US$500,000 donated nationally. International aid exceeded $US5.5 million in addition to food, supplies, and personnel.

ABOVE Survivors in Ormoc City look for their lost relatives among the dead, whose bodies are lined up outside the front of a collapsed house.

FACTS AND FIGURES	
DATE	November 1 to 8, 1991
LOCATION	Philippine Islands, eastern Vietnam
DEATH TOLL	Approximately 4,800
DAMAGE	US$26.9 million
CATEGORY	Weak tropical storm
WINDSPEED	50 mph (80 km/h) sustained winds with higher gusts
BAROMETRIC PRESSURE	991 mbar
COMMENTS	The deadliest tropical storm in the Philippines in the twentieth century

Andrew, USA, 1992

On August 24, 1992, Category 5 Hurricane Andrew struck southern Florida with devastating force. With over 142 miles per hour (228 km/h) sustained winds and gusts higher than 200 miles per hour (322 km/h), the storm was compared to an incoming freight train. It destroyed Homestead, Florida City, and parts of Miami, with over US$30 billion in damage.

FAR RIGHT Wrecked boats sit on top of the sea wall at the docks of Dinner Key in the Coconut Grove area of the city of South Florida. Storm surges lifted these boats up there.

BELOW Bricks were scattered in the street after being blown off a building in Jennerette, a town in Los Angeles. This kind of damage meant that driving in the aftermath of the hurricane was extremely hazardous.

The casualties were officially between 25 and 65, while over 250,000 people were left homeless. The strongest hurricane to make landfall in the United States, Andrew caused four fatalities and millions of dollars worth of property damage, plus over US$1 million worth of damage to the Louisiana coastline. It left a legacy of terror that still haunts South Florida survivors.

A tropical depression formed on August 16, emerging from an African west coast weather front two days earlier. The front passed over the Cape Verde Islands and became organized enough to warrant tracking. It developed into Tropical Storm Andrew, then faltered, nearly vanishing.

On August 21, nearby weather fronts gave the storm a revival and Tropical Storm Andrew moved west. Over the next 36 hours, the hurricane increased in intensity and reached Category 5, with all peak winds at 175 miles per hour (282 kph). Then late on August 23, Andrew hit the Bahamas Eleuthera Island; it crossed the Berry Islands early on August 24 with wind gusts ranging from 150 and up to 160 miles per hour (241 and 257 km/h), until it finally lost its terrifying power.

As Andrew hit the Gulf Stream, it recovered its Category 5 strength. The storm's center then intensified and compacted just before making its landfall in South Dade on August 24. All the towns of Homestead and Florida City were directly hit. The central barometric pressure at landfall was 922 mbar, making it the third (at the time) most intense hurricane to strike the United States.

Andrew's path was traced crossing the southern tip of Florida, then roaring across the Gulf of Mexico, decreasing to Category 4 as it turned to northward. On August 26, the hurricane made its landfall near Morgan City, Louisiana, now Category 3 with winds sustained near 115 miles per hour (185 km/h). It continued northeast, and eventually dissipated into just another weather front.

A terrifying landfall

Southern Florida is a community that is well used to storm watches and warnings. In the early morning of August 23, the National Hurricane Center (NHC) issued a hurricane warning stating wind speeds of 120 miles per hour (193 km/h) that could increase as Andrew crossed the Gulf Stream, and a potential 8 to 12 foot (2.4 to 4 m) increase in tides. Approximately 700,000 people evacuated the entire region. Many only went a town or two away. But thousands stayed, stocking up on groceries and presuming the storm would swerve away like all the previous ones had. Earlier forecasts had predicted Andrew would make landfall in Florida's Broward County, between Fort Lauderdale and Palm Beach. However, the storm went directly westward and impacted Florida in the Miami-Dade County. By 11:00 a.m., with Andrew 500 miles (805 km) west of Miami, the upgraded warnings said "Dangerous Category 4 hurricane heading for South Florida … all precautions taken to protect life and property … should be rushed to completion."

At 3:00 a.m. on August 24, with Andrew only 40 miles (64 km) off the coast, the last bulletin, "extremely dangerous Hurricane Andrew closing in on southeast Florida … ", warned of winds of up to 150 miles per hour (241 kph), massive storm surges from 8 to 13 feet (2.4 to 4 m) at its landfall, and a possibility of isolated tornadoes. One resident remembers a television broadcast interrupting their program, telling them Hurricane Andrew had made an unexpected shift to the south and would strike South Dade and in five minutes, warning them to take cover, stay put and not attempt to evacuate.

Survivors tell of barricading their doors and sheltering in bathrooms and laundry rooms as the storm hit. They huddled in terror as their homes literally came apart around them. Many insist the feeling of the storm was "evil," and describe seeing

ENVIRONMENTAL IMPACT

Human lives lost and damage to property dominate the headlines in the wake of a hurricane. But the environment also takes a severe beating from the effects of wind and water. In the Biscayne National and Everglades Park, 70,000 acres (28,350 ha) of trees were affected. In a domino effect, toppled trees and stripped-off leaves and branches clogged the waterways with vegetation and debris. This resulted in oxygen depletion, which caused massive fish kills in south Louisiana's bayous and inland waterways.

ABOVE Despite a flattened front yard, crowded with fallen trees, a Louisiana house miraculously remains standing.

RIGHT A resident in the bottom right of the photograph looks out of his apartment, which had its walls blown away in the path of Hurricane Andrew.

swirling, dark cloudbanks flickering with eerie green lightning. The sound of the incoming hurricane has been described as "a freight train in the room," "a jet landing on the roof," and "a shotgun blasting away the house."

Max Mayfield, 2006 director of the NHC, was at the facility in Coral Gables in Miami. He recounted that the hurricane-shuttered windows were broken, and gusts of 164 mph (264 km/h) winds destroyed the center's radar equipment— something he noted was "not supposed to happen." Record wind speeds at the Fowey Station were up to 200 miles per hour (322 km/h) before the equipment was damaged. A meteorologist recorded a record 212 miles per hour (341 km/h) gust before his instruments were destroyed.

The storm surges in southern Florida reached a height of 14 feet (4.3 m). Over 82,000 business, 120,000 homes, and all but nine of Homestead's 1,176 mobile homes were totally destroyed. The US government allocated US$8 million in grants to help rebuild and re-establish the region. Ninety-seven percent of the Homestead Air Force Base was destroyed and its rebuilding took years.

Legacy of a disaster

Thousands of Florida residents left the region after Hurricane Andrew. Many who stayed behind were unable to forget what they all called "six hours of hell." The aftermath revealed entire neighborhoods smashed and flattened. Major General Richard Griffiths, on arriving with 23,000 emergency troops, said, "I had never seen a place completely leveled in all directions. There was a smell to it. A smell of utter destruction."

Emergency response to the area was slow, which attracted much criticism. Survivors waited seven to 10 days before receiving food, water, and

medical supplies. On August 28, *Miami Herald* headlines stated, "We need help—Bush sends in 2,000 troops—Metro blames feds for failure of relief efforts—More destruction than any disaster ever in America." Dade County Emergency Director Kate Hale made a national television broadcast begging for help, saying, "Where the hell is the cavalry on this one? They keep saying we're getting supplies. Where the hell are they?"

The unsolved equation

The fatalities directly and indirectly attributed to Hurricane Andrew vary between 25 and 65. There are a number of accounts from those who survived the disaster and rescue personnel that set the count much higher; the most extreme claim is over 1,000 deaths. Internet stories quote sources direct from the National Guard, the Coast Guard, the Red Cross, and others who claim that there was a military effort to keep the number of deaths quiet. Some theorize that this was an attempt to prevent widespread panic.

One survivor spoke of having looked up and seen "body parts flying around me," while other accounts tell of trucks arriving filled with body bags. One Red Cross volunteer described a wrecked mobile home site, saying, "the bodies and body parts were all over and the stench was getting bad. We were ordered to stop our food deliveries by the military after a few days because they claimed it was a health hazard ..." A rescue worker from the Federal Emergency Management Agency was quoted as saying "Andrew's wrath looks like Hiroshima."

These discrepancies may never be answered, and Andrew's legacy will never be forgotten.

FACTS AND FIGURES

DATE	**August 16 to 28, 1992**
LOCATION	**USA: Bahamas, Florida, Louisiana coast, and Miami**
DEATH TOLL	**65 (26 direct, 39 indirect), possibly far higher total deaths**
DAMAGE	**US$26–$30 billion in 1992; US$250 million in damages in the Bahamas**
CATEGORY	**Category 5; achieved twice in storm history**
WINDSPEED	**142 mph (228 km/h) sustained winds with higher gusts**
BAROMETRIC PRESSURE	**922 mbar; fourth lowest pressure in an Atlantic hurricane**
COMMENTS	**Fourth most intense hurricane at landfall as of 2005; four separate landfalls. Third Category hurricane in the United States, storm surges to 17 feet (5 m); highest wind gust was 212 mph (341 km/h), rainfall was 13.98 inches (36 cm). This was the second most costly hurricane ever recorded in the history of the United States.**

Mitch, America, 1998

In October 1998, the most deadly storm in nearly 200 years devastated Central America, bringing about 3 feet (900 mm) of rain and causing over 10,000 fatalities due to the floods and mudslides. Over US$6 billion in damages was caused across Honduras, Nicaragua, Guatemala, and El Salvador during the five days the storm hovered over the region.

ABOVE FAR RIGHT Homeless victims of Hurricane Mitch were living in makeshift shelters along the highway in El Progresso, Honduras, near San Pedro, one year after the disaster struck.

BELOW FAR RIGHT Already hit by massive floods caused by Mitch a year earlier, residents of El Progresso watch as the Ulva River rises again in October 1999.

BELOW San Juancito residents clear land for 52 new homes to be built in their town with the funds raised by their local and international rotary clubs.

The storm started on October 10, 1998 in the Atlantic Ocean. It moved into the Caribbean Sea and then was upgraded to a tropical storm when it neared the south area of Kingston, Jamaica on October 22. By October 24, Mitch was classified as a hurricane, reaching Category 5 two days later with a central barometric pressure of 905 mbar, the seventh-lowest pressure recorded. The hurricane held Category 5 strength for a day and a half. Wind speed was sustained at about 180 miles per hour (290 km/h) for nearly 15 hours.

Traveling parallel to the Nicaraguan coast, the hurricane crossed the Swan Islands on the morning of October 27 and turned in toward Honduras. Just off the coastline, the storm's momentum slowed to a stop, and it hovered there until October 29. The storm's fierce intensity dropped to Category 2 before it made landfall on the northern Honduras coast. On October 30, President Flores declared a state of emergency for the entire territory. Traveling over land, its initial power continued to decrease. It moved into Guatemala on October 31, at which time it was downgraded to a tropical depression.

By November 2, the storm regrouped over the Campeche Bay, again becoming a Tropical Storm 100 miles (160 km) south of Yucatan. It crossed the Gulf of Mexico and made final landfall as a Tropical Storm in Naples, Florida on the morning of November 5.

The aftermath

While the hurricane lingered menacingly off the coastline of Honduras, it caused massive flooding and devastation. This was the second most deadly hurricane to hit this area, killing over 5,600 people and leaving over another 8,000 missing. More than 50 rivers were flooded, destroying bridges and roads and nearly wiping out entire towns, along with over 70 percent of the country's crops.

In Nicaragua, there were over 3,000 fatalities — and many hundreds more people were unaccounted for. Hundreds of thousands were left homeless. During the hurricane's flooding, Chinandega also suffered an earthquake following the eruption of the Casita volcano.

Fifty thousand people in El Salvador were left homeless, and over 230 people were killed. Some towns and areas in the western part of the country were completely isolated or submerged in the floods.

Guatemala had over 250 fatalities, including 11 American tourists who were killed in a plane crash. Over 77,000 people were evacuated and dozens of bridges and roadways were completely destroyed.

Fatalities were also reported in Belize, Panama, Costa Rica, and Jamaica. At least six people were killed in the resort town of Cancun, Mexico. Two fatalities were reported in southern Florida. Damages

FACTS AND FIGURES

DATE	October 22 to November 5, 1998
LOCATION	Central America: Honduras, Nicaragua, El Salvador, Guatemala, and Belize; Cancun, Mexico; USA: the Florida Keys and Southern Florida
DEATH TOLL	Estimated 10,000 direct fatalities, possibly up to 10,000 more missing
DAMAGE	US$6 billion to US$7 billion
CATEGORY	Category 5
WINDSPEED	180 mph (290 km/h) sustained winds with higher gusts
BAROMETRIC PRESSURE	905 mbar (seventh lowest Atlantic hurricane pressure)
COMMENTS	Twenty-five towns destroyed in Honduras, rebuilding estimated to require 15 to 20 years. Between 200,000 and 800,000 people left homeless in Nicaragua. Eighty percent of crops were lost in El Salvador. Belize had 11 deaths. In Florida, 65 were injured from tornado-force winds.

were mostly limited to fallen power lines, building debris, and downed trees.

Analysts and experts have since claimed that the damage in such an impoverished region set economic development back by 50 years.

Amazing survival stories

In the wake of Hurricane Mitch, news broadcasts around the world told the story of Laura Arriola de Guity, a 36-year-old schoolteacher who survived for six days after being washed out into the Caribbean Sea. She witnessed her husband and three children carried away by the storm; her four-year-old son was torn out of her hands by the force of the water. She was rescued 75 miles (121 km) from her home, clinging to a makeshift raft of branches, tree roots, and a mortarboard. She suffered from dehydration, exposure, and hypothermia.

Award-winning journalist and author Jim Carrier wrote *The Ship and The Storm*, a dramatic account of the 282-foot (86 m) windjammer *Fantome* and her crew who vanished during Hurricane Mitch. Based on extensive research and interviews with the survivors, this real-life story gives a terrifying view of what it is like facing a Category 5 hurricane.

05B, Bay of Bengal and Orissa State, 1999

Early on October 29, 1999, a super-cyclone swept out of the Bay of Bengal and devastated the Orissa State coastal region. With some of the strongest winds ever recorded in the area raging up to 161 miles per hour (259 km/h) and storm surges up to 20 feet (6 m), Tropical Cyclone 05B was one of the worst storms in India's history.

Developing in the South China Sea around October 19 or 20, the very early stages of the storm crossed into the Andaman Sea, becoming a tropical depression near the Malay Peninsula on October 25. As it moved northwest, warmer waters and conditions caused it to intensify into Tropical Storm 05B by October 26. After rapidly gaining power, the storm moved to the Bay of Bengal the following day and was finally upgraded to a severe Tropical Cyclone.

By October 28, the cyclone became a Category 5 with sustained high winds of 160 miles per hour (257 km/h). Before making landfall, the intensity of the cyclone marginally dropped to 155 miles per hour (249 km/h). Stalling 30 miles (48 km) inland, it was downgraded to a tropical storm. The storm curved south back to the Bay of Bengal on October 31, and by November 3 no trace of a coherent storm front remained.

The day of reckoning

Tropical Cyclone 05B slammed into the Orissa coast slightly north of the cities of Bhubaneshwar and Cuttack at about 5:00 a.m. on October 29. The cyclone ravaged the area for nearly 24 hours. Over 1,500 villages were destroyed and more than 2 million people were left homeless.

The Orissa State economy is based on agricultural industry that accounts for approximately 80 percent of the population's livelihoods and provides over half of the state's income. The region's overall agricultural output makes up at least 10 percent of all the rice production for all of India. The massive tidal surge from Tropical Cyclone 05B reached approximately 9 miles (14.5 km) inland, destroying some 800,000 acres (324,000 ha) of crops and polluting soils with salt and debris in the process. Extensive flooding caused massive losses of livestock, vital to many families of the area.

FACTS AND FIGURES

DATE	October 25 to November 3, 1999
LOCATION	Orissa, India
DEATH TOLL	Over 9,900
DAMAGE	800,000 acres (324.000 ha) of crops, over 275,000 homes destroyed
CATEGORY	Strong Category 4
WINDSPEED	161 mph (259 km/h) sustained winds with higher gusts
BAROMETRIC PRESSURE	Unrecorded
COMMENTS	Deadliest Indian Ocean tropical cyclone since 1991 Bangladesh Cyclone. Flooding reached over 9 miles (14.5 km) inland from the coast.

The capital city Bhubaneshwar, known as the "Temple City of India," took the brunt of the cyclone's wrath; this was where the worst damage and losses occurred. In the capital and throughout surrounding areas, over 275,000 homes were damaged or destroyed. Roads were either blocked or washed away, and power and communications were disrupted for ten days. This made counting fatalities and assessing damage in the immediate aftermath of the cyclone close to impossible, causing serious difficulties for rescue and relief efforts.

The nearby port city of Paradip sustained heavy damages, with over 5,000 casualties. One 32-year-old farmer from the region told reporters, "When we found ourselves alive after the cyclone, we thought we were lucky. But now we think it would have been better had we died. Anything would have been better than the way we are living now." These words were echoed by many of the survivors.

Angry responses

The lack of fresh water, salvageable food, and the looming health threats from contamination and rotting corpses in the days after the cyclone hit led to hundreds more deaths by dehydration, starvation, and the spread of disease. Anger over the slow and inadequate government response to the crisis led to looting and riots among the remaining survivors.

When Bangladesh's Prime Minister Atal Behari Vajpayee visited Bhubaneshwar, he described the scene as "unimaginable. The rehabilitation of the people affected in the cyclone-hit areas will be a gigantic task." He released US$46 million from the National Calamity Relief Fund. Military troops were also sent to control the riots and restore order. This was seen as too little, too late, and much of the loss of human life was blamed on extremely poor emergency management and the absence of a clearly communicated and well-instituted evacuation plan.

ABOVE Fishermen in the Birupa River cast their nets to catch fish. After the cyclone the waters of the rivers were contaminated by debris and the corpses of humans and animals, and this impacted on their livelihoods.

FAR LEFT TOP Children play in front of a sea of plastic tents. Homeless people had to rely on foreign aid and supplies to help them build makeshift homes.

FAR LEFT BOTTOM A woman rummages through her damaged belongings trying to salvage whatever remains in her ruined thatched home.

Nabi, Japan, 2005

On September 6, 2005, Super Typhoon Nabi swept up the Korean Straits between Japan and Korea with winds up to 160 mph (257 km/h), destroying thousands of homes in Japan, causing widespread flooding, landslides and structural damage to buildings, killing 21 people and injuring 143 more. Fifty-five people were reported missing in Japan and South Korea, and over 300,000 people were forced to flee their homes in Kyushu, Japan.

RIGHT A roadside tree leans dangerously over a street in Kagoshima, Japan. Rushing home from work to get to the safety of their homes, people braved Nabi's torrential rain and powerful winds.

Early on August 29, a tropical depression formed off the eastern coast of Saipan, strengthening into Tropical Storm Nabi by midnight. By August 30, the storm had gained typhoon strength. It came into the range of the coastlines of Saipan and Guam on 31 August, causing tropical storm-force winds gusting up to 75 mph (121 km/h), bringing a rainfall of nearly 3 inches (76 mm). The typhoon continued past the Mariana Islands, rapidly intensifying to Category 5. By September 1, the storm attained the deadly Super Typhoon classification. As the storm entered the Philippines storm-tracking region on September 3, it was also assigned the name Typhoon Jolina for warnings to be broadcast in the Philippines.

Super Typhoon Nabi passed near the east coast of the Okinawa islands. The coastal region of the northernmost island, Amami Oshima, was swamped by storm surges up to 29 feet (8.8 m) high. The storm swerved northeast and was downgraded in its intensity as it headed closer to mainland Japan.

Typhoon Nabi made landfall in the Kagoshima Prefecture on September 6 at Category 2, with sustained wind speeds of 86 mph (138 km/h). Crossing the southern mainland Japanese island of Kyushu, Nabi rapidly moved up the Korean Straits and again made landfall on Honshu before turning northward. The typhoon crossed Hokkaido

NABI HITS THE MARIANA ISLANDS

Nabi impacted the coastline of the Mariana Islands on August 31 at a strong Category 5. The Mariana Islands are part of a submerged mountain range in the western Pacific Ocean near Guam and Japan and the northern islands comprise a commonwealth of the United States. After the impact of Typhoon Nabi, the region was declared a disaster zone. The head of the US Department of Homeland Security's Federal Emergency Management Agency (FEMA) made available federal disaster aid to supplement state and local recovery efforts in the area. The public property on Rota, Saipan, and Tinian, significant US military sites, was also repaired.

ABOVE The power of the typhoon can be seen by rocks and paving bricks that are torn up and hurled across a seaside promenade. Sheets of water can be seen rushing along the road.

overnight on September 7, and then moved out over the Okhotsk Sea early on September 8, dissipating into an extra topical low by 3:00 p.m. that afternoon.

Nabi moved very slowly, only up to 15 mph (24 km/h), and produced torrential floods due to an incredible amount of rainfall, lashing a region of over a 186 ½-mile (300 km) radius with 55 mph (88 kph) to 160 mph (257 km/h) winds for over an hour while it passed.

Floods that kill

The slow-moving typhoon impacted on 31 of the 47 prefectures in Japan. Thunderstorms caused by the typhoon pounded the mainland region near Tokyo

where heavy rainfalls of up to 4 inches (102 mm) per hour caused severe flooding and an estimated 163 landslides across the southern half of the island. By Tuesday, September 6, local Japanese governments had ordered over 100,000 people to evacuate and given strong advisories to another 250,000.

Flooding on the coastline of the southernmost island of Kyushu caused over 300,000 people to flee their homes, leaving precious belongings behind. Meanwhile, Tokyo dispatched around 1,500 military personnel to fortify and monitor the coastal regions and assist in the rescue efforts. The flooding and subsequent landslides caused the majority of fatalities. The rescue teams and local police reported finding most of the casualties in the aftermath of the landslides, especially the elderly. In Takachiho, a 70-year-old man was buried in one landslide. In Tarumizu, a 75-year-old woman was killed when her house was destroyed in another landslide. Two companions, both age 76, who had taken refuge in the house with her were found later, having been swept away in the destruction. Further landslides in the region claimed two other people, one aged 53 and the other aged 85. There were at least four persons missing in Kagoshima, and at least another eight in Miyazaki. One 61-year-old man was killed on a flooded roadway near Tokyo as he tried to start his car that was caught in the rising water. The initial rescue efforts reported a minimum of 20 people injured across Kyushu and Okinawa. Some of the survivors described winds and rain too strong to walk through, as well as flooded buildings and a lack of power.

Flooding affected many regions of Japan as the typhoon traveled further to the north. Predictions for Hokkaido, Japan's northernmost main island, estimated up to 10 inches (25 cm) of rainfall.

FLOODING AND LANDSLIDES

The Sanyo Expressway in Iwakuni, in the Yamaguchi Prefecture, lost a section to a landslide that crushed two nearby homes. The residents of these houses, a 70–year-old man, who was disabled, and his wife, age 65, along with an 81-year-old man were killed when the landslide hit. Also in Iwakuni, the wooden Kintaikyo Bridge (Brocade Sash Bridge) lost two of its five arch supports as a result of the flooding of the Nishiki River. This is the third time this historic bridge has suffered damage due to flooding, the other times being 1674 and 1950. A famous landmark of southern Japan, it was built in 1673 by Lord Kikkawa Hiroyoshi. It is known as one of the Three Bridges of Japan, and is the focus point for festivals and celebrations.

FACTS AND FIGURES

DATE	August 29 to September 6, 2005
LOCATION	Korea, Japan, and Philippines
DEATH TOLL	21 fatalities, 55 missing, over 140 injured
DAMAGE	Over 10,000 homes and 88 roadways destroyed
CATEGORY	Super (Category 5+)
WINDSPEED	160 mph (257 km/h) sustained winds with higher gusts
BAROMETRIC PRESSURE	898 mBar
COMMENTS	Majority of damage occurred in Miyazaki prefecture on Kyushu, fourteenth major storm in 2005 typhoon season, assigned name Typhoon Jolina on September 3 in Philippine warning area, caused 168 landslides in Japan. Nabi is the Korean word for butterfly.

Power cuts and rescue efforts blocked

In the Prefecture of Kagoshima, over 185,000 homes were without power, and another 170,000 homes were temporarily without electricity throughout Tottori, Shimane, Okayama, Hiroshima, and Yamaguchi. In Shiiba village in the Miyazaki Prefecture, which was drenched in over 3.3 feet (1 m) of rain, at least five houses were completely destroyed by mudslides, and three of the residents were never found. In the port city of Pohang, which lies near the mouth of Somjin River in Southern Korea, the storm surges drove a 5,400-ton (5,952 tonnes) Vietnamese cargo ship aground. Fortunately, none of the crew of the onboard was killed.

Transportation and regional access was widely disrupted by the storm. Rescue efforts were stalled or blocked by the lack of access due to flooded and damaged roadways. Some of the villages were isolated from access to rescue teams or evacuation. Hundreds of planes and scheduled trains were forced to cancel, leaving over 12,000 people stranded.

The severe weather conditions also kept the regional ferries from operating. On one of the last ferries that went into port at Takamatsu, one 37-year-old woman was thrown from the deck and drowned when strong winds hit the ferry. Over two-dozen flights were cancelled in South Korea, which was bracing for impact, along with coastal China. The last typhoon to impact the Korean Straits in 2005 was Typhoon Talim, which killed 95 people in China's Anhui province.

The rainfall from the typhoon also brought relief to the drought-stricken Shikoku region. Tosa's Samerua Dam reservoir, located behind the Sameura Dam in Okawa, is the largest dam and reservoir in western Japan. It supplies an extensive region

and is known as "the water jar in Shikoku." The banks of conifer trees that surround the reservoir contribute to its frequent low water levels, and one week before the typhoon hit the reservoir was nearly empty. The reservoir had not been at full capacity in nearly four months, however, following Typhoon Nabi it was reported to be at 100 percent capacity by the following Tuesday evening.

To avoid extensive damage to the very lucrative petroleum industry, oil refineries suspended production and shipping in preparation for Typhoon Nabi. This caused a slowdown of production to over 800,000 barrels of oil per day. The third largest refinery, Idenmitsu, reported no suspension of its refining operations, but did stop all waterway shipments for the duration of the storm.

ABOVE A television crew braves the weather conditions at a ferry port in Kagoshima. At this point, the powerful Typhoon Nabi was heading toward Japan's southern main island of Kyushu.

Katrina, USA, 2005

On August 29, 2005, Hurricane Katrina slammed into the Gulf Coast of the United States with 175 miles per hour (282 km/h) winds and huge storm surges of up to 34 feet (10 m). Massive flooding filled 80 percent of New Orleans, and washed away several small towns. After Katrina, 1,400 people were dead, with thousands more missing.

RIGHT US Coast Guards did aerial assessments to gauge the extent of the damage caused by Hurricane Katrina. Flooded roadways and suburbs can be seen throughout New Orleans.

At 5:00 p.m. on August 23, 2005, the National Hurricane Center made the decision to issue a major tropical storm and hurricane advisory warning for southern Florida. In just 24 hours, it became Tropical Storm Katrina. By 6:00 p.m. on August 24, Florida declared a state of emergency. By noon the next day, Palm Beach and several counties began evacuations and at 5:00 p.m. Katrina was upgraded to a Category 1 hurricane with a well-defined eye that was visible on radar. In two hours it made landfall, pounding southern Florida with about 80 miles per hour (129 km/h) winds and up to 5 to 15 inches (125 to 380 mm) of rain, causing extensive property damage, widespread power failures, and a confirmed 14 deaths.

Overnight, Katrina moved into the Gulf of Mexico, and by 2:00 a.m. on August 26 it had strengthened and turned toward the Gulf Coast.

The long-dreaded nightmare

Katrina was upgraded to a Category 3 on August 27, doubling in size after an eyewall replacement cycle.

A state of emergency was then issued for Louisiana, Alabama, and Mississippi. By 7:00 a.m. on August 28, Katrina had become Category 5, hitting peak intensity at 1:00 p.m. with sustained winds of about 175 miles per hour (282 km/h) and central pressure of 902 mbar, becoming the fourth most intense storm in American history.

Bulletins warned of the impending disaster, and New Orleans' Mayor Roy Nagin ordered a mandatory evacuation, establishing the Louisiana Superdome as an emergency shelter for people who were unable to leave. Eighty percent of the New Orleans population was evacuated before Katrina hit. Railway lines that went into the city and the nuclear power plant were shut down. Shops and residences were boarded up, and those left in New Orleans prepared themselves for their worst-ever nightmare.

On the morning of August 29, storm-force winds were experienced some 230 miles (370 km) away. A second eyewall replacement cycle had again nearly doubled Katrina's size, but it had also reduced its power. At 6:10 a.m. Katrina hit second landfall at Buras-Triumph, Louisiana as a Category 3, with up to 125 miles per hour (201 km/h) winds.

Katrina made its third landfall at 8:30 a.m. near the Louisiana–Mississippi border. Storm surges then swamped the coast, with heights ranging from about 13 feet (4 m) near Mobile, Alabama up to 34 feet (10 m) near Bay St Louis. Two holes were ripped in the Superdome as the storm passed over New Orleans.

New Orleans lies below sea level, protected by an intricate anti-flooding system. Storm surges caused areas of the levees to overflow. Three levees were breached by the combination debris, storm surges, and winds, resulting in flooding of 80 percent of the city from Lake Pontchartrain.

BELOW Days before the hurricane made landfall, the residents of Deerfield Beach in Florida were buffeted by fierce gale-force winds. This woman is bravely trying to get to her car.

NEW ORLEANS: DESIGN AND FLOOD PROTECTION

New Orleans lies in a bowl 6 feet (1.8 m) below sea level. Levees and floodwalls around the city prevent flooding from the Mississippi River, Lake Pontchartrain, heavy rainfall, and storms. It has a canal system to channel water as well as pumping stations that work 24 hours a day. A levee is a linear structure extending from high ground along one side of a river to another area of high ground on the same side. The New Orleans levees are structures of earth, sand, and shell. Floodwalls are barriers made of reinforced steel and concrete, used in heavily populated areas because they require less space. A levee failure, called a breach, is when there is structural damage or collapse. Failures are generally caused by water pressure over the design rating, poor maintenance, and erosion from extremely strong water flow.

Katrina continued past New Orleans well into Mississippi, finally losing power about 150 miles (241 km) inland near Clarksville, Tennessee. Part of the storm continued north into the Great Lakes and Canada, causing heavy rain and winds in Quebec. By 11:00 p.m., Katrina was gone.

Chaos in Katrina's wake

Along the Gulf Coast, Hurricane Katrina had caused over US$75 billion in damages. As at March 2006, the death toll was at 1,420, with about 2,000 people unaccounted for; 1,300 were believed lost in heavily damaged areas and possibly dead, bringing the final total to 2,720. This would make Katrina the second deadliest storm in US history.

Hundreds of buildings collapsed or were affected by structural damage or collapsed, roadways and streets were badly damaged or destroyed, and trees were uprooted. Worse still were the hundreds of casualties, human and animal, that could not be recovered. Electricity and plumbing were completely interrupted and few necessities were available. Thousands of survivors found themselves without food, water, power, or communication. Evacuation and rescue were crippled by a lack of access and equipment. Along the Gulf Coast, entire towns had been flooded out or washed away entirely; the list of missing persons continued to increase.

A serious concern facing the survivors and rescue personnel was the lack of sanitation and the resulting threat of disease. Because of the toxic mix of debris, corpses, foodstuffs, and refuse amid the flooding, in addition to dehydration and food poisoning there was a high risk of outbreaks of diarrhea and respiratory infections and the potential for cholera

FACTS AND FIGURES	
DATE	August 25 to 29, 2005
LOCATION	USA: Gulf states (Florida, Louisiana, Mississippi, Alabama, Georgia, Kentucky)
DEATH TOLL	1,422 dead; over 6,000 missing
DAMAGE	US$75 to $80 billion; the most costly storm in US history
CATEGORY	Sustained Category 5 for 15 hours
WINDSPEED	175 mph (282 km/h) highest sustained winds, with higher gusts
BAROMETRIC PRESSURE	Lowest: 902 mbar; sixth-lowest pressure in an Atlantic hurricane
COMMENTS	Third most intense hurricane at landfall; it made three separate landfalls. Sixth strongest US storm recorded, with peak winds at 150 knots, rainfall exceeding 1 inch (2.5 cm) per hour, storm surges of up to 34 feet (10 m). Third most deadly storm in US history (at March 2006; could become second after casualty count is finalized).

and dysentery. Local chemical refineries contributed toxins to the waters. The floodwaters also contained high levels of *E. coli* and other bacteria. The Center for Disease Control reported five dead from ingesting contaminated drinking water.

The human toll

Even though 80 percent of the population had been evacuated, over 100,000 people were still in the city when Katrina hit. The Superdome, prepared to support up to 75,000 people for perhaps four hours,

was already sheltering 10,000 (reports varied from 8,000 to 26,000) by late August 28. The US National Guard delivered supplies to support 15,000 for up to three days. Another 3,000 took refuge in emergency shelters. By August 29, over 27,000 evacuees were in emergency shelters. The *New York Times* reported that 70 percent of New Orleans nursing homes failed to be evacuated before the storm.

On August 29 it was apparent that the levees and floodwalls believed to have held through the storm had in fact failed in the storm surges and backlash

ABOVE The I-90 bridge over St Louis Bay in Pass Christian, Mississippi is folded back on itself and destroyed by high winds and waves.

FAR LEFT, TOP In this satellite image from the National Oceanic and Atmospheric Administration (NOAA), the eye of Hurricane Katrina can be seen over the Gulf of Mexico.

FAR LEFT, BOTTOM Homes are completely destroyed, reduced to looking like flattened cardboard. Recovering and rebuilding after the aftermath of this hurricane is estimated to take up to 10 years.

LEFT Hurricane survivors make their way up a flooded street by whatever means they can to find safety on higher ground.

ABOVE Debris clutters Canal Street in New Orleans. Hurricane Katrina made landfall east of the city early on the morning of August 29. Luckily most residents were indoors when the storm hit.

following the hurricane. As the hours went by, stories were reported of levees being breached and sections of the city being under water, with 12 to 14 feet (3.7 to 4.3 m) swamping neighborhoods. Miles of homes along the I-10 highway had only their roofs visible above floodwaters. Beams from flashlights shone from high windows where people were stranded and survivors were seen wading through shoulder-high polluted water.

On the evening of August 29, Mayor Roy Nagin addressed the public on television, where he broke down, barely able to finish. He said: "My heart is heavy. I don't have any good news to really share. Other than at some point in time the federal government will be coming in here in mass. But

the city is in a state of devastation. Eighty percent of it is under water, as much as 20 feet (6 m) in some places. There's an incredible amount of water in the city. Residents are on roofs and trapped in attics, awaiting rescue. Fire, police, and National Guard personnel are out rescuing those trapped right now. Both airports are under water. Twin spans [bridges] in New Orleans East are totally destroyed. Three huge boats have run aground. An oil tanker has run aground and is leaking oil. There is a serious [floodwall-levee] break at 17th Street Canal; the water continues to rise. Houses have been picked up off their foundations and moved … A barge has hit one of the main structures of High Rise [a bridge/span] and we're not sure that the High Rise is

SURVIVAL: VOICES FROM THE CHAOS

Numerous people had intensive discussions online talking about their experience of Hurricane Katrina. Here is a small sample of some comments from September 2005:

"NOPD [the New Orleans Police Department] is critical … Their command and control infrastructure is shot … The precinct is under water … The coroner's office is shut down so bodies are being covered in leaves at best or left where they lie at worst …" Interdictor.

"New Orleans is pretty well gone, as are the cities of the Mississippi gulf coast. There are miles upon miles of nothing but dirt and some debris where houses used to be … basically, it washed away several whole towns …" CotSurferB, Mississippi paramedic.

"He spent 24 hours in the Superdome on Wednesday after the storm … He told stories of major chaos, of how he watched people dying of things we could normally treat in the field under the right circumstances, people severely injured or dead secondary to violence, dodging bullets from gangs, and it just goes on and on …" NCMedic309, quoting a story he heard from a New Orleans paramedic who was at the scene.

"I'm from New Orleans and I was caught into the storm … they would not let us out … The army turned us around with guns … And I realized then that they really were keeping us in there … Four people died around me. One young woman couldn't survive it because of the dehydration … Murder, that's what I call it." Clarice B., a healthcare worker.

structurally sound. All of Slidell is under water. Most of Metarrie is under water. The list just goes on and on. There are gas leaks throughout the city. It's not a pretty picture. On the somewhat good news side, many people have survived. Uptown is pretty dry. The French Quarter and Central Business District are dry, but they also have buildings that look like a bazooka was shot through. There is no clear path in or out of the city, whether east or west. I-10 West is still full of water … The water system has been contaminated except for the Central Business District and Algiers. We have no electricity and they expect electricity to be out about four to six weeks."

The extent of the damage began to sink in for people across the United States. Tens of thousands

of homes had been destroyed, leaving people displaced, some permanently. Many were left homeless without means of support; many unable or unwilling to rebuild. Families were dismantled as a result of separation and death. Feelings of isolation and dissatisfaction with the government's response were eased by the warm welcome survivors received from many other states. Offers of homes, support, and medical care, poured in from Maine to California. Houston, Texas was lauded for its efforts in taking in the highest number of evacuees and providing the strongest response. Volunteers coordinated lists of survivors and databases to share information and messages to assist with reuniting families; especially reconnecting potentially orphaned children.

ABOVE Rescue workers pull a woman from the rapidly rising floodwaters. She was stranded on the rooftop that can be seen in the foreground.

Larry, Australia, 2006

Around 6:30 a.m. on March 20, 2006, Australia faced one of its worst natural disasters in 30 years. Cyclone Larry tore through northeastern Queensland, with winds gusting up to 180 miles per hour (290 km/h) and bringing 1 to 5 inches (2.5 to 12.7 cm) of rainfall. It caused over AUD$1 billion in damage to buildings, property, and crops, left at least 30 people injured, and thousands more homeless.

RIGHT A farmer takes stock of his banana plantation near Innisfail in Queensland. The Category 5 cyclone destroyed over 90 percent of Australia's banana crop; an acute banana shortage followed, sending banana prices all over Australia to unheard-of highs.

BELOW A tractor sits stranded in a heavily flooded sugarcane field. Cyclone Larry caused hundreds of millions of dollars' worth of damage to the all-important agriculture industry.

Cyclone Larry formed off the northwestern Australia coast early on March 18, 650 miles (1,046 km) east of the tourist resort city of Cairns. The first tropical cyclone warning for that area was issued before dawn. By around late March 19, the storm reached peak intensity, with buffeting wind speeds at about 115 miles per hour (185 km/h) and gusts of up to 143 miles per hour (230 km/h).

The cyclone then crossed the Great Barrier Reef at Category 4, making landfall to the south of Cairns on March 20. Larry pummeled coastal communities with intense wind gusts of approximately 180 miles per hour (290 km/h) and terrifying storm surges of 13 feet (4 m), causing massive damage from Cairns to Mission Beach. The storm moved inland toward Innisfail, Babinda, and the Atherton Table-land. The storm decreased in power as it traveled inland past Innisfail, rapidly falling to Category 2, continuing to weaken. Storm tracking of the cyclone ended around 10:00 p.m. on March 20, with the

ABOVE Just one of many thousands of homes that were torn apart by Cyclone Larry. People were left homeless and had to move to temporary shelters and refuges.

storm downgraded to a tropical storm with 46 miles per hour (74 km/h) winds slightly south-east of the Queensland town of Normanton.

Trail of destruction

The devastation in the wake of Cyclone Larry was compared with the fallout of an atomic blast. Damages ranged over an area about half the size of Tasmania, or 8,000,000 acres (3,240,000 ha). Entire regions were almost completely flattened, thousands of businesses and residences were damaged. Counts in the immediate aftermath of the storm estimated at least 7,000 people were left homeless.

Innisfail, a farming community with a population of 8,500, sustained the majority of the damage. While

CROSSING THE GREAT BARRIER REEF

The Great Barrier Reef lies off the northeast coast of Queensland, and is one of Australia's natural wonders and is a major tourist destination. The reef sustained a 30-mile (48 km) wide swathe of damage in the cyclone's passing, but experts say it could have been worse. David Wachenfeld, the director of Sciences for Reef Management, says the reef is over 1,200 miles (1,931 km) long and claims that the damaged section is both relatively small and lies in a less popular region, so it won't have a significant impact on the reef's tourist attraction. He noted that the damaged sections of the coral reef would take anywhere from 10 to 20 years to recover from the effects of the storm.

over 1,000 people were evacuated before the storm's impact, a significant number remained in storm shelters and in secured, shuttered buildings. Many experienced the storm's impact and were able to provide first-hand reports.

Amanda Fitzpatrick, the proprietor of Innisfail's Barrier Reef Motel, told Associated Press that when surveying the damage during the passing of the eye of the storm, it looked "like an atomic bomb had gone off." Resident Des Hensler described the storm's fury, saying, "I don't get scared much, but this is something to make any man tremble in his boots. There [was] a grey sheet of water, horizontal to the ground, just taking everything in its path."

From the safety of a neighbor's house, a sugarcane farmer from the region watched his home and his livelihood being totally destroyed. He told ABC News, "So far as the sugar crop's concerned, it is a catastrophe; it has been decimated. I think some farmers will give up."

Another farmer from the Tully banana district had 680 acres (275 ha) of his crops destroyed, forcing him to face the prospect of nearly a year with no source of income and having to lay off a substantial proportion of his workforce.

Kathryn Ryan working for the Emergency Services Department assessed damage to the area, especially in the worst-hit areas of Innisfail and Babinda. She told ABC reporters, "What I saw today is nothing like I've ever seen anywhere before. These communities have been completely gutted by this cyclone. Houses have been damaged—they've lost their roofs, their windows have blown out, some look like a bomb has exploded inside and shattered them to pieces. There's debris all over the roads, and trees have dropped everywhere; in some places it was really hard to get through because there were trees all over the road. There are wires and power poles down everywhere."

Innisfail Mayor Neil Clarke calls his region the tropical fruit bowl of Australia, but in the wake of the cyclone he said, "Every tree is flattened. It looks like an atomic bomb has hit the place." Ninety percent of the region's banana crop was damaged or destroyed. Along with the season's crop, the trees were flattened and damaged, resulting in a year or more of needed recovery before the region can produce again. As much as 10 to 20 percent of the sugarcane drop was also destroyed—an estimated 50 percent loss to industry revenues and a cost of over AUD$150 million to the Queensland economy.

The destruction extended beyond the town of Innisfail right down to the coastline. In Kurramine Beach, a motel owner described the destruction in her neighborhood to ABC reporters: "All the fibro houses have just disintegrated, a lot of roofs have gone off, especially the first three streets back from the beach. All the two stories—the top stories have gone. There's two houses across from the motel and one's just all caved in and the one beside it, the roller door has gone, the windows gone, roof gone. There's a house just down the road from us that's up on stilts … they came in yesterday and lowered it but it's fallen off the stilts and just disintegrated."

The cyclone caused havoc across the Atherton Tableland, the very heart of Queensland's dairy industry, causing damage to the infrastructure of many farms and cutting off power to the entire region. Wes Judd, president of Queensland's Dairy Farmers Organization, says that financial aid from groups such as the Dairy Farmers Co-op and other governmental assistance helped us to get power generators and mobile milking support to the dairy farmers as soon as possible so they could keep their businesses going after the storm hit.

Road to recovery
Queensland's worst natural disaster has left a legacy of years of recovery. Immediate relief efforts to the stricken area were decisive following the declaration of the region as a national disaster site. Australia's Prime Minister John Howard allocated funds for direct assistance for homeless residents. National Disaster Relief made provisions for business and farming industry recovery. AUD$100 million was allocated from governmental funds for the enormous rescue efforts.

On March 21, military rescue and relief efforts arrived via helicopter, as nearly every roadway and access route was damaged or blocked with debris. Medical teams were brought in to help with the damage evaluation.

Queensland's appeal for aid was met with an outpouring of national and international support. Donations came from communities and businesses all over Australia, providing supplies and funds of AUD$5 million, including a AUD$1 million relief donation from the Commonwealth Bank.

Queensland's Premier, Peter Beattie, visited the region on March 22 to assess the extent of the damage. He told *Queensland Register* reporters that "a massive number of people in the area depend directly on the sugar and banana industries, which have been literally flattened … Many of the shops and services have also been badly damaged and if they aren't doing business, there may be lots of people laid off—and so it goes on."

As of the end of March 2006, recovery and the rebuilding of the affected areas was beginning to get underway. Despite the ferocity of Cyclone Larry, an efficient warning system, careful preparation and what residents called "more than a little luck" resulted in no human fatalities.

FACTS AND FIGURES

DATE	March 18 to 20, 2006
LOCATION	Queensland, Australia
DEATH TOLL	Nil; 30 injured
DAMAGE	AUD$1 billion
CATEGORY	Category 4
WINDSPEED	115 mph (185 km/h) sustained winds with 180 mph (290 km/h) gusts
BAROMETRIC PRESSURE	No record available as of March 29, 2006
COMMENTS	1 to 5 inches (2.5 to 12.7 cm) of rainfall; storm surges up to 13 feet (4 m); storm damage across land region of 8,000,000 acres (3,240,000 ha).

ABOVE Freshwater crocodiles inhabit the ruins of the Johnstone River Crocodile Park, Innisfail, which was damaged by massive flooding and gale-force winds. Some of the escaped crocodiles were discovered in the rising floodwaters in a number of residential areas.

Storms

There are very many different types of storms, ranging from minor to totally destructive. A storm is any disturbed state of the atmosphere that affects Earth's surface. Some types of storms can be described as extreme, severe, or unique. They include thunderstorms, mesoscale storms with their associated exceptional hailstorms and derechos, tropical and extratropical storms, and dust storms.

The scale of weather systems varies greatly. Synoptic-scale (or broad-scale) weather occurs over wide areas (600 to 1,500 miles/ 1,000 to 2,500 km) on time scales exceeding 12 hours. Mesoscale systems, ranging from around 50 miles (80 km) to several hundred miles, are medium-size storms that range from squall lines and complexes of major thunderstorms to the very destructive tropical cyclones, known as hurricanes and typhoons in the northern hemisphere and cyclones in the Indian Ocean and Australia. Small-scale storms include localized thunderstorms.

Extratropical cyclones are the largest of all, and occur in the middle to high latitudes, sometimes spanning 1,200 miles (2,000 km). These synoptic-scale events, which form over land or water in all seasons, are usually characterized by a cold front that extends toward the equator for hundreds of miles. Extratropical cyclones come in two types. The first begins with a clash of warm and cold air and results in typical winter storms. The second forms when a tropical cyclone (hurricane, typhoon) leaves the tropics. Cooler air comes from the polar regions and clashes with the warmer mass of usually moist air to form a front commonly associated with destructive winds, flooding rains, hail, and snow. Some of the "Great Storms" of Britain and Europe, such as the Great Storm of 1987, had their origins in Atlantic hurricanes that left the tropics.

Subtropical storms usually form out of extra-tropical storms but are unusual in having a warm core like a tropical cyclone. They also develop an "eye" structure typical of tropical cyclones. As such they are considered hybrid storms. Wind speed often intensifies from gale force (39 miles per hour/ 63 km/h) to as much as 100 mph (160 km/h) as the storm's central pressure drops, frequently at an alarming rate. Consequently, what might have started as a lesser storm will rapidly intensify into a monster in less than a day. Such storms made disasters of two yacht races: the 1998 Australian Sydney to Hobart and the 1979 British Fastnet.

FAR LEFT The vertical cloud of a whirlwind (dust devil) rises from the desert. Whirlwinds form in areas of strong surface heating. This heating causes the air to rise, drawing in more heated air, which maintains the structure.

LEFT People watch the overflowing waters of the Choluteca River in Tegucigalpa, Honduras, in 1988. Heavy rains and severe flooding followed Hurricane Mitch. At least 70 people were killed.

PREVIOUS PAGES Time-lapse photography has allowed the photographer to capture several lightning strikes during a lightning storm off Sea Point, Cape Town, South Africa. In the United States, of the 100,000 thunderstorms that take place annually, around 10,000 are classified as severe.

RIGHT A lightning storm at night over the French Alps. Lightning bolts typically drop from a charged cloud to the ground, or to an object on the ground, but high-speed photography has shown that in the moments before a lightning strike, a "streamer" of positive electrical charge will snake up from the ground toward the negatively charged cloud. The lightning then travels down this streamer.

PRECAUTIONS TO TAKE DURING A THUNDERSTORM

1. LISTEN to weather updates for warnings about the severity of the storm and whether hail is forecast.

2. IF POSSIBLE, remain indoors and keep away from windows; they can be shattered by large hail.

3. IN THE CASE OF HAIL, close any window covers to reduce the risk of broken glass.

4. AVOID CONTACT with telephones and other electrical appliances (unplug them), metal pipes, and electrical wires—lightning can and does travel along these.

5. IF YOU ARE IN YOUR CAR, shelter in it with the windows up, and unplug any chargers.

6. IF HAIL IS FORECAST, park your vehicle in a garage or under shelter. Hail damage can be costly.

7. IF NO SHELTER IS NEARBY, stay away from trees, poles, and metal objects such as fences, sports equipment, or bikes; away from open ground, but if it is unavoidable, then try to minimize body contact with the ground by crouching with your arms around your knees and your feet together; stay away from bodies of water, like lakes or the ocean, which can conduct the electricity.

ABOVE A historic photograph of a towering thunderhead with an anvil top. The anvil top forms when a ceiling of colder air is reached and the cloud then spreads out sideways.

Thunderstorms can be relatively small-scale events that vary from short-lived single cells to destructive supercells. A thunderstorm, or electrical storm, is usually made up of one or more convective clouds with electrical discharge (lightning) that is heard as thunder. Cumulus and cumulonimbus convective clouds form when strong, warmer air currents move upward (as updrafts), carrying moisture high into colder layers of the atmosphere.

Their bases can range in height from 1,000 to 10,000 feet (300–3,000 m), and the cloud "tower" can rise as high as 59,000 feet (18,000 m). These thunderheads are often indicators of unstable air.

Nearly 2,000 thunderstorms producing some 100 lightning flashes per second are occurring worldwide at any one time, most frequently in rainforested areas. In temperate regions either side of the equator they are more common in spring and summer.

Types of thunderstorms

There are three main types of thunderstorms: single-cell, multi-cell, and supercell.

A single-cell thunderstorm forms when the wind speed and direction of the updraft (the wind shear) have relatively little effect, so the storm remains poorly organized and short-lived. The downdraft of cool air, which brings some rain, cuts off the storm growth cycle, so the storm typically lasts for no more than an hour.

Multi-cell thunderstorms form when the wind shear is of sufficient strength and persistence to increase the storm's growth cycle, giving it a more organized structure and a longer lifetime. They are made up of several cells one after another, lasting 30 to 40 minutes each. Severe multi-cell storms might have several cells operating at any one time.

Squall lines form sometimes through convective updrafts from an orderly lineup of multicell storms that can have gust fronts. Associated with squall lines are heavy rain and hail and damaging winds, particularly the derechos of North America.

The term "derecho," from the Spanish word for "direct," is used to describe straight-line winds, in comparison to the turning or rotating winds of a tornado. Derechos are very widespread, occurring over areas hundreds of miles long and more than 100 miles (160 km) across.

Supercells, although rare, are the most severe of all thunderstorms and are responsible for a remarkably high percentage of severe weather events—especially tornadoes, extremely large hail, and derechos. A supercell is caused by a persistent rotating updraft or mesocyclone. It can form from a multicell storm when there is sufficient directional wind shear to skew the updraft and so allow the cool downdraft to flow free of it. As a result, the main updraft can strengthen and start rotating.

Supercell fronts can take the form of a line of cumulus clouds that usually step up toward the tallest clouds near the main storm, or that produce gust fronts that form from the winds associated with downdrafts. Supercell storms can last several hours and spawn tornadoes, create wall clouds, and drop

ABOVE Hail stops play. Ground staff cover one of the tennis courts at Wimbledon during a heavy hailstorm. A recent decision to build a retractable roof over the famous center court by 2009 will consign such scenes to history, although the other courts will remain uncovered.

Pea: ¼ inch (6 mm)
Marble or mothball: ½ inch (13 mm)
Penny or dime: ¾ inch (19 mm)
Nickel: ⁹/₁₀ inch (22 mm)
Quarter: 1 inch (25 mm)
Half dollar: 1¼ inches (32 mm)
Walnut or ping-pong ball: 1½ inches (38 mm)
Golf ball: 1¾ inches (44 mm)
Hen's egg: 2 inches (51 mm)
Tennis ball: 2½ inches (64 mm)
Baseball: 2¾ inches (70 mm)
Tea cup: 3 inches (76 mm)
Grapefruit: 4 inches (102 mm)
Softball: 4½ inches (114 mm)

Lightning

Lightning causes an estimated 2,500 fatalities a year worldwide. It is caused by a difference in electrical charge between the top and the bottom of a thunderhead. Why the bottom of the cloud becomes negatively charged is not fully understood, but it is probably related to the rapidly rising moist air. Lightning is discharged within the cloud or from the cloud to the ground when the charge overcomes the electrical resistance of the atmosphere.

The lightning bolt superheats the surrounding air to temperatures of around 50,000°F (27,800°C)—hotter than the surface of the sun, which is around 9,000°F (5000°C). The violent expansion of the surrounding air causes the sound of thunder. A single lightning flash, which is often no more than 1 inch (25 mm) wide, carries an electric current as high as 300,000 amps, rather higher than domestic electrical wiring, which carries 10 to 20 amps. Well over 10,000 volts per yard or meter at ground level is sometimes reached during a storm.

ABOVE View of a developing mesocyclone. A mesocyclone is a region of rotating air that develops in the updraft of a thunderstorm supercell. Typically 2 to 6 miles (3–10 km) across, they can generate tornadoes under some conditions.

ABOVE RIGHT Hailstones as big as ping-pong balls. Hailstorms are usually very localized, but they can create serious damage to buildings, vehicles, and crops. When hailstones can be this size, this is not surprising.

very large hail (in rare cases up to 4 inches/ 10 cm across). The mesocyclone—the storm-scale region of rotation—usually measures around 2 to 6 miles (3–10 km) in diameter.

Thunderstorm severity and hail size

A thunderstorm is said to be severe when it produces either hail with a diameter of ⁸/₁₀ inch (2 cm) or more when it hits the ground; wind gusts at the ground of 56 miles per hour (90 km/h) or more; tornadoes; or very heavy rain with possible flash flooding.

The size of a hailstone depends on the strength of the updraft. The smallest hailstone requires an up-draft of at least 22 mph (36 km/h); those of golf ball size (1¾ inch / 44 mm diameter) require updrafts of around 55 mph (88 km/h); and the larger, softball-size hail needs updrafts of over 100 mph (160 km/h). In the United States, when weather warnings are issued, familiar objects are used for comparison:

LEFT Locals enjoy bathing under huge waves lashing the coastline of the port city of Mumbai, in India, during May, 2001. At this time, a severe cyclonic storm was moving toward the northeastern coastal areas of Gujarat state.

Hailstorms

Hail forms in thunderstorms when water droplets carried by updrafts freeze in the cooler upper air. The hailstones grow layer by layer as the updrafts repeatedly cycle them through the clouds. Usually, the stronger the updrafts, the more a hailstone will repeat this cycle and so the larger it will grow. Eventually the hail falls to the ground when it becomes too heavy for updrafts to keep it aloft.

Damaging hailstorms are frequent in various regions, including Europe, China, Russia, India, and Australia. In North America, hailstorms are most common on the plains of the United States, especially just east of the Rockies, and in Canada's "hailstorm alleys." Large hailstones can cause massive destruction to crops and property.

Tornadoes

A tornado is a tall, rapidly rotating column of air between 16 and 3,300 feet (5–1,000 m) in diameter that reaches the ground. It always starts with a funnel cloud, which usually hangs from the base of a cumulonimbus or large cumulus cloud. It is the most destructive of all atmospheric phenomena on a local scale and is accompanied by a loud roar. Tornadoes are covered in their own chapter.

Dust and sand storms

A dust storm is caused by strong winds sweeping dust through the air over extensive distances. The same winds can also carry sand, although the sand, being larger and heavier than dust, rarely rises above 50 feet (15 m) and is mostly confined to the lowest 10 feet (3 m). Major sand-dust storms occur when prolonged drought or overgrazing causes the unprotected soil surface to dry out.

TEN OF THE BLEAKEST STORMS IN HISTORY

JANUARY 16, 1362	Grote Mandrenke ("great man-drowning"). A southwesterly Atlantic gale swept across England, The Netherlands, northern Germany, and southern Denmark, killing over 25,000 people and changing the Dutch–German–Danish coastline by submerging many islands.
NOVEMBER 26, 1703	Great Storm of 1703. Severe gales affected the south coast of England. Over 8,000 sailors were lost.
JANUARY 6 TO 7, 1839	Night of the Big Wind. The most severe windstorm to hit Ireland in recent centuries, with hurricane-force winds, killed between 250 and 300 people and rendered hundreds of thousands of homes uninhabitable. Over 20 percent of all houses in Dublin were damaged.
DECEMBER 28, 1879	The Tay Bridge Disaster. Severe gales (estimated to be Force 10 to 11) swept the east coast of Scotland, infamously resulting in the collapse of the Tay Rail Bridge and the loss of 75 people who were on board a train crossing the bridge.
OCTOBER 14, 1881	Eyemouth Disaster. A severe storm struck the southeast coast of Scotland; 189 fishermen were killed, most from the village of Eyemouth. In Eyemouth it is still known as "Black Friday."
NOVEMBER 7 TO 13, 1913	Black Sunday Storm. This is one of the most severe Great Lakes storms on record. Winds of 87 miles per hour (140 km/h) swept over lakes Erie and Ontario, taking down 34 ships and 270 sailors.
JANUARY 31 TO FEBRUARY 1, 1953	A storm originating over Ireland moved down the east coast of Scotland and England and across the North Sea to The Netherlands, claiming over 2,000 lives. The storm surge caused the North Sea Flood of 1953, which is considered Britain's worst natural disaster of the twentieth century.
APRIL 10, 1968	Two violent storms merged over Wellington, creating a single storm that is the worst recorded in New Zealand's history. Winds that reached 170 miles per hour (275 km/h) in Wellington were the strongest ever recorded. The storm capsized the inter-island ferry *Wahine*, with the loss of 51 people.
OCTOBER 28 TO NOVEMBER 1, 1991	In the northwest Atlantic Ocean, extraordinary ocean waves and swells were caused by near-hurricane-force winds. Widespread destruction resulted from the waves and swells crashing into the coast of North America.
MARCH 12 TO 14, 1993	The Superstorm, or the US Storm of the Century, was one of the most intense storms ever to hit the eastern coast of the United States. It hit the Atlantic seaboard, the Gulf coast, Cuba, and northern Mexico, with wind gusts of up to 144 miles per hour (232 km/h) and a storm surge of 13 feet (4 m), causing 243 fatalities and US$2 billion in damage.

ABOVE A dust storm in Elkhart, Kansas, USA, 1937. A variety of causes, including drought, overgrazing, and falling crop prices, were responsible for hundreds of dust storms on the Great Plains during the Dust Bowl era of the 1930s.

RIGHT Vehicles with their lights on are directed by an Iraqi policeman through a sand storm in central Baghdad, Iraq, in 2005. The sand storm paralyzed the city, closing shops, and restricting traffic as a cloak of orange dust reduced visibility to a few feet (about a meter or two).

Sand particles range in size from around 2 to 4 hundredths of an inch (0.6–1 mm). Dust particles are smaller, in the nanometer to micrometer range.

Whirlwinds (dust devils in America, willy-willies in Australia) are a common occurrence in arid and semi-arid regions. They are mini tornado-like rotating columns of wind made visible by the dust that they carry. They typically last for only a few minutes.

Dust storms reduce visibility, form gritty layers on skin and clothes, permeate buildings, clog machinery, short-out electronic equipment, find their way into food and drinking water, and wear away protective outer wear and shoes.

During threatening weather, listen for dust storm warnings on radio or television. In the United States, a dust storm (or sand storm) warning means visibility of ½ mile (800 m) or less, and wind speeds of 30 miles per hour (50 km/h) or more.

Dust can cause respiratory failure, so stay indoors with the windows and doors closed.

If you are driving, pull over as far as possible when you see dust blowing across or approaching a roadway; stop and turn off your lights, or following drivers might try to follow you and run into you.

If there is nowhere you can pull over, then proceed at a safe speed, turn on your lights, and sound your horn occasionally. Use the painted centerline to help guide you. Look for a safe place to pull off the roadway. Never stop on the road.

Dust storms occur on Mars

Sometimes, though rarely, dust storms on Mars can be fierce enough to blanket the whole planet in a dusty haze for weeks, as the Mariner 9 spacecraft discovered in 1971. Local and regional dust storms are much more common and can affect the rate at which seasonal frost patterns evolve in polar regions.

The images obtained by NASA's Mars Global Surveyor showed the evolution of the 2001 great dust storm period. Several large storms would occur at the same time, and dust was kicked high into the atmosphere to obscure much of the rest of the planet.

ABOVE Two workers with the California Department of Transportation help a man whose car is stuck in a flooded section of road in Mill Valley, California, USA, in 2002. Severe storms hit northern California, bringing high winds and rain.

EXTRATROPICAL OR TROPICAL CYCLONE?

TROPICAL CYCLONES
• Form over tropical oceans, usually in summer and fall
• Have thunderstorms all around their center
• Have a center that is warmer than the surrounding air
• Have no fronts
• Have their strongest winds near the surface of Earth.

EXTRATROPICAL CYCLONES
• Form outside the tropics during any season
• Have thunderstorms where cold and warm air meet
• Take in cold, dry air from the outside into their center
• Have warm and cold fronts
• Have their strongest winds in the upper atmosphere.

Hailstorms, Worldwide

Nearly 2,000 thunderstorms are active around the world at any moment. Many of these produce hail. Hailstorms destroy on average one percent of all crops annually, and can cause millions of dollars' worth of property damage. They rarely kill people, but wildlife is particularly at risk.

Hail is formed in severe thunderstorms. Formation is enhanced by strong updrafts, a high content of supercooled liquid water (below freezing point), and a large vertical range of cloud height. Water needs a nucleus, such as a salt crystal or dust particle, on which to freeze, which is why supercooled water can remain liquid. A hailstone then acts as a nucleus for other super-cooled droplets, which slowly freeze onto it and thus build up the hailstone in layers. These layers often alternate between clear and opaque.

The size of a hailstone increases with the intensity of the storm cell. A hailstone the size of a golf ball requires over 10 billion supercooled droplets to be coalesced in the storm cloud for 5 to 10 minutes and be held in place by updrafts exceeding 55 miles per hour (88 km/h). Stones can weight up to 2 pounds (1 kg) and fall at 112 miles per hour (50 m/s). The average size is smaller than 1 inch (2.5 cm) across. The biggest hailstones tend to fall in India.

BELOW Emergency Brigade employees and civilians remove hailstones that block a street in Curitiba, southern Brazil. The severe overnight hailstorm blocked the streets of the city for several hours, wrecked the roof of the Pinheirão soccer stadium, and forced a cargo aircraft to make an emergency landing.

Hail damage and costs

The major damage from hail is to crops. Damage to vehicles, buildings, and landscaping leads the list of damage outside the agricultural sector.

Though not the most deadly storms, hailstorms can be the most costly. However, this is true only for the developed nations, where insurance claims are used to measure costs. The costs of hail damage in many developing nations might not reach internat-ional "record costs," but the damage is likely to cause a lot more human suffering and poverty.

Worst hailstorms on record

The deadliest hailstorm on record occurred in India on April 30, 1888, east of New Delhi. It killed 246 people and 1,600 head of livestock.

On July 19, 2002, in Henan province, China, giant hailstones, some egg-sized, killed 25 people and filled hospitals with people suffering from head wounds. The hailstorm uprooted trees, destroyed

LEFT Hail in Red Square, Moscow. Legend holds that it never rains in Red Square on May Day. To ensure that it doesn't, cloud-seeding is regularly used to encourage any rain or hail to fall before it reaches Moscow.

BELOW A Chinese farmer inspects a field of corn destroyed by hail in 2005. Damage can be much worse: in May, 1986, an intense hailstorm in China killed 100 people, injured 9,000, and destroyed 35,000 homes.

buildings, smashed car windshields, and cut off electricity. Locals described it as the worst hailstorm in at least half a century.

On July 12, 1984, a hailstorm struck Munich, Germany, injuring 300 people and causing a total estimated €1.5 billion worth of damage. Trees were stripped of their bark, and whole fields of crops were destroyed. The roofs of over 70,000 buildings were damaged, and around 250,000 cars were dented or worse by the egg-sized hailstones, some more than 3½ inches (9 cm) in diameter.

On September 7, 1991, the most costly Canadian hailstorm occurred, in Calgary, Alberta, causing an estimated C$360 million in insured damage and C$450 million in estimated total damage.

On May 5, 1995, Dallas, Texas experienced the most destructive hailstorm in North American history. It caused an estimated US$2 billion damage, and injured 510 people. This damage bill includes actual costs, not just insurance figures.

On April 14, 1999, a severe hailstorm struck the eastern suburbs of Sydney, Australia, causing extensive damage estimated in the billions of dollars. It became Australia's costliest ever natural disaster. This storm was highly unusual. Not only did it produce some of the largest hail ever recorded in Sydney, it also occurred at a time of year when severe thunderstorms are normally rare, and at a time of day when the probability of storms is low.

On Wednesday, May 16, 2001, a freak hailstorm wreaked havoc in Russia when hailstones the size of chicken eggs pelted down on houses, cars, and crops. Dozens of people suffering head injuries and fractures were hospitalized, and damage was estimated at 500 million rubles (US$17.2 million).

Most frequent hailstorms

Hail falls on Kericho, Kenya on 132 days a year, on average, making it the most hail-struck town on Earth. Hail is common also in the high plains of the USA and Canada, in central to eastern Europe, the Himalayas, southern China, and southeastern Australia.

THE COSTLIEST HAILSTORMS

The April, 2001, tri-state hailstorm that affected Kansas, Missouri, and Illinois, USA, resulted in the most costly losses on record, at US$1.9 billion. In 1998, severe storms in the Minneapolis–St Paul area, Minnesota, USA, caused insured losses of US$1.35 billion. The May 1995 Dallas–Ft Worth hailstorm in Texas, USA, cost US$1.135 billion in insurance. A hailstorm in Denver, Colorado, USA, on July 11, 1990, caused property losses of at least US$625 million. The July 12, 1984, hailstorm in Munich, Germany, produced insured losses of US$480 million. The April, 1999, hailstorm in Sydney, Australia, caused an estimated A$2.3 billion (US$1.5 billion) damage, which took months to repair. The cost of hail damage is usually measured in insurance terms, so these values are given here.

Severe Storms, Worldwide

A severe storm is defined as any storm that has wind gusts of 50 knots (58 mph [93 km/h]) or greater, drops hail ¾ inch (19 mm) or wider, or spawns a tornado. In general terms, it can be any destructive storm. As global warming increases, severe storms are likely to become more intense and more common.

FAR RIGHT This was the first lighthouse built on Eddystone Rocks in the English Channel, just off the English coast at Plymouth, Cornwall. Designed by Henry Winstanley as the first ever offshore light, it was completed in 1698, but was swept away in a storm in 1703, taking Winstanley and five others with it.

BELOW A policeman surveys the damage on a London road, where a tree fell during the hurricane that swept southern England in 1987. The huge numbers of fallen trees gave scientists a wealth of material for studying past climate and tree growth.

Severe storms can affect any place on Earth. For example, the extra-tropical cyclones that lash Europe in winter can have surface winds gusting at 80 to 100 miles per hour (130–160 km/h). The total losses from this type of storm are estimated to have been US$24 billion between 1985 and 2001.

The Great Storm of 1703

On November 26, 1703, the most severe storm ever recorded in the British Isles struck southern England and the English Channel. Raging until December 2, it wrecked many ships, caused about 8,000 fatalities, and felled 4,000 oak trees in the New Forest alone. This was the Great Storm of 1703.

The Great Storm was the only true hurricane ever to have made it all the way across the Atlantic Ocean at full strength. Barometric readings as low as 28¾ inches of mercury (973 hPa) were recorded.

The newly constructed Eddystone Lighthouse was right in the path of the storm, with its creator and builder, Henry Winstanley, in residence. He had made it known that he would like to be on the reef in the greatest storm that ever blew under the face of heaven so he would see what effect it would have on his building. He did not have to wait long. On November 27, the lighthouse was destroyed, and all six occupants, including Winstanley, died.

On the River Thames in London, around 700 ships were stacked together. Daniel Defoe's first book, *The Storm*, was based on the disaster.

Buildings, haystacks, and even people were whisked into the air by the roaring winds, estimated to have exceeded 120 miles per hour (190 km/h).

The Great Storm of 1987

From October 14 to 17, 1987, the southeast of England was struck by the worst storm since 1703. Some 15 million trees were uprooted, including one-third of those in the famous Royal Botanic Gardens Kew, and whole forests were wiped out. Ships were driven ashore, buildings were destroyed, and 16 people were killed.

Like the Great Storm of 1703, the 1987 storm started with an intense depression (28⅓ inches, or 960 hPa) that developed so rapidly that it was almost impossible to predict the track and ferocity of the storm. Three of four supercomputer storm models failed to predict the development of the storm. The one that did predict it was outvoted.

The strongest winds occurred in the early hours of the morning, when few people were about, so the death toll was comparatively low.

The Burns' Day Storm of 1990

On January 25, 1990, the Burns' Day Storm, one of the worst storms of the twentieth century and one of the top 15 storms on record, covered a much larger area of the United Kingdom than the Great Storm of 1987. It had one of the deepest depressions to affect the UK, falling to 28 inches (949 hPa) in pressure.

Gusts of up to 108 miles per hour (174 km/h) were recorded. Altogether, 97 people died throughout northern Europe, including 47 in the United Kingdom, 19 in The Netherlands, 10 each in France and Belgium, and 7 in Germany. The death toll was the largest from a storm since January 31, 1953, when a storm surge killed over 2,100 people.

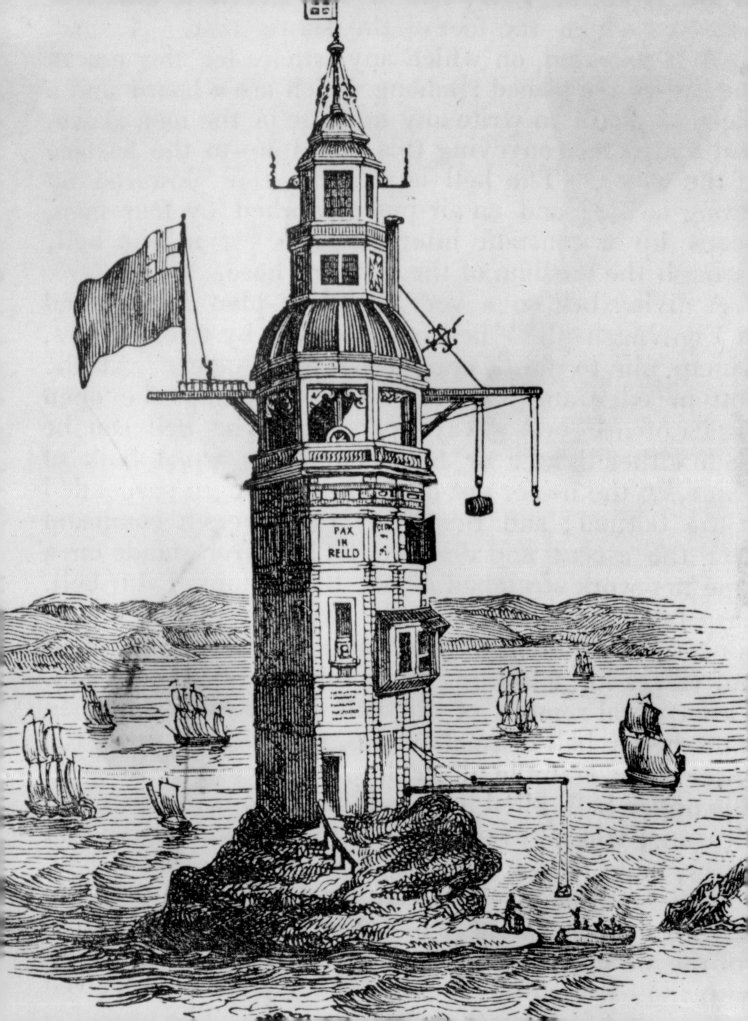

ABOVE Uprooted trees lie on the ground of the Vosges forest in France following the storm of December 1999. A week after, more than 300,000 households were still without electricity.

BELOW The Sydney to Hobart Yacht Race is one of the three toughest ocean races. Starting from Sydney Harbour annually on December 26, the boats are frequently hit by storms.

December 1999 storms, Europe

December 1999 was not a good month for Europe: fierce gales at the beginning brought the strongest winds for over a century to Denmark, and then from December 23 to 26 and again from December 25 to 28, 1999, when two depressions of unprecedented intensity developed in France. The storms caused €3.4 billion in forestry losses, and left 3.5 million people without electricity and 1 million without telephone lines.

The first storm brought a swathe of winds with gusts to 107 miles per hour (173 km/h). The second produced winds of similar strength along France's west coast, and spread a trail of destruction along the north coast of Spain and across many countries bordering the Mediterranean Sea. At least 79 people were killed, 34 of them in France.

European storm surge, 1953

On Saturday, January 31, 1953, a storm surge struck the east coast of England and the southwest coast of The Netherlands during the night, causing the worst natural disaster in northern Europe over the past two centuries. The surge coincided with a high tide, which devastated flood defenses in both countries and caused the worst damage seen since World

YACHTING DISASTERS FROM STORMS

On August 11, 1979, the Rolex Fastnet Yacht Race, organized by the Royal Ocean Racing Club, started in calm waters from Cowes on the Isle of Wight, United Kingdom. With little warning, three days later the fleet was hit by a freak storm that produced Force VII winds and whipped up mountainous waves, which caused 15 deaths and total chaos. Six lives were lost because safety harnesses broke; the others drowned or died of hypothermia. One of the few boats to reach the finish line was *Morning Cloud*, skippered by former prime minister Sir Edward Heath.

On December 30, 1998, a supercell storm whipped up massive seas in Bass Strait, between Tasmania and the Australian mainland, cutting through the fleet competing in the annual Sydney to Hobart Yacht Race. Six sailors drowned, 70 were injured, and seven yachts were abandoned at sea and lost. Only 44 out of 115 yachts finished the race. Thirty civil and military aircraft were involved in the daring rescues of 55 sailors from 12 stricken yachts. The cost was A$30 million (US$23 million). The coroner criticized the organizers and the weather bureau for inadequate warnings.

War II. Over 230 square miles (600 km²) of England was inundated, with the loss of 307 lives. In The Netherlands, 2,000 people died, up to 1,200 square miles (3,100 km²) was flooded, 3,000 homes and 300 farms were destroyed, and 47,000 head of cattle drowned. It was The Netherlands' worst disaster for 300 years. The seawater that entered the fields left farmland unfit for cultivation for many years.

Deadly US storms

On the afternoon of June 14, 1903, Willow Creek became a raging torrent 40 feet (12 m) deep as it struck the farming community of Heppner in Oregon without warning. Rescuers recovered 247 bodies, and about 150 residences were destroyed.

An immense cloudburst in the hills above the town followed a prolonged drought, so at first the buildup of clouds was welcomed. But as the clouds grew darker and thunder was heard, the town was hit by a massive hailstorm. Shortly afterward, heavy rain inundated the slopes and the upper parts of the valley. Reports estimated that an average of 1.5 inches (38 mm) fell over an area of 20 square miles (50 km²) in a short time.

The water rushed down the valleys toward the town, collecting debris along the way. At the end of the town, the debris built up, forming a dam. This breached when a building supporting it collapsed, releasing the massive wall of water that hit Heppner with a force unmatched in the history of Oregon.

On the afternoon of March 6, 2004, a cluster of thunderstorms moved through the Baltimore, Maryland metropolitan area, producing wind gusts of 40 to 55 miles per hour (64–88 km/h). A water taxi loaded with 25 people in Baltimore's Inner Harbor capsized in the winds, and five passengers drowned. Fortuitously, the others were saved by fireboat firefighters and navy reservists on training exercises within a few hundred yards of the taxi.

The rapid evolution of the unstable atmospheric conditions caught forecasters by surprise. A Special Marine Warning was issued in response to the increase in wind intensity, but sadly this came five minutes after the taxi had capsized.

ABOVE A rescue team uses a cadaver dog to search for the bodies of three missing people in the Baltimore Inner Harbor the day following the storm in 2004.

HOW STORM SURGES ARISE

A storm surge occurs when strong onshore winds and reduced atmospheric pressure raise the normal water level along a shore. The surge is at its most destructive when it coincides with a high tide, and can be the cause of most deaths from such storm events. It reaches widths of 50 miles (80 km) or more, with a height of 10 to 30 feet (3 to 9 m) at the coast. If the surge is funneled into a bay, its height can more than double. A look at an atlas reveals how the converging coastlines of England and The Netherlands funneled the water onto land in 1953.

Sand and Dust Storms, Worldwide

Parts of the world experience sand and dust storms—the Sahara Desert is an obvious example. But changing climate, increasing cultivation, and overgrazing are increasing the incidence of sand and dust storms worldwide. Many cities, notably Beijing, China, are regularly blanketed by choking dust that reduces visibility, clogs machinery, contaminates food, and even kills.

RIGHT A dust storm blows over the Red Sea. This satellite image shows the African countries of Sudan (top left), Ethiopia (bottom left), and Eritrea (between them, along the western coast of the Red Sea). Toward the right side of the image are Saudi Arabia (top) and Yemen (bottom) on the Arabian Peninsula.

There are five ingredients essential to the development of sand and dust storms: a source of fine dust or sand particles that can be lifted and transported; winds of sufficient force and velocity in a direction that will raise and carry the particles; weather conditions that can form convection cells of sufficient energy to develop the winds; landform features that help concentrate the force of the wind; and exposed soil surfaces susceptible to wind erosion, such as in deserts and overcropped and disturbed semi-arid lands.

Mounting global concern

The increasing frequency and severity of dust storms have raised concerns worldwide. "Over the last few years, there has been a growing awareness that air pollution from China is affecting us," said Russ Schnell, an official at the US National Oceanic and Atmospheric Administration, which tracks dust clouds. "Pollution is a global problem," he added, saying that when considering a storm such as China's 1993 "black windstorm", "Nature has sent us 'a perfect storm' to reinforce the fact that we are all downwind of someone else's pollution."

United States satellites show that thousands of lakes in the north of China have disappeared, and rapid industrial development has reduced forests and other vegetation that once provided moisture to the region and held the soil in place. In some areas the land is so devastated that farmers have abandoned their homes and fields. Sand dunes now cover them. Yields of crops where farming is still possible have shrunk, making harvests no longer profitable.

"The big risk is that it's going to push a lot of people into cities in a major migration," said Lester Brown, president of the Earth Policy Institute in Washington DC, which recently released an environmental alert on the problem.

Record dust storm in China

On May 5, 1993, northwest China was struck by a dust storm of record proportions. The "black windstorm," as it was called, caused 85 fatalities and serious economic losses through destruction and damage to property, and agricultural devastation.

Calamitous sand and dust storms are increasing in severity and frequency in China. They are both a symptom and a consequence of desertification—the changing of productive land into desert. The particle size of transported materials distinguishes dust storms from sand storms—dust is finer than sand—but they are known jointly as sand-dust storms. Sometimes these storms are a mixture of sand and dust in varying proportions, depending on

SAND VERSUS DUST STORMS

There are differences between sand and dust storms. A sand storm is basically a wind storm that carries sand through the air, forming a relatively low cloud near the ground. Typical sand storms reach heights of up to 50 feet (15 m), contain sand particles with average sizes between 6- and 12-thousandths of an inch (0.15–0.30 mm), have wind speeds exceeding 10 mph (16 km/h), and last as long as winds persist.

Dust storms are similar but have distinctly different characteristics. Dust storms form in semi-arid and arid regions where small dust (and sand) particles are blown into the air. Unlike in pure sand storms, dust particles are small enough to be lifted aloft by currents of turbulent air and carried in suspension for long distances.

As this picture on the left shows, dust seriously reduces visibility. Here, Haifa Street in central Baghdad, Iraq, is partially obscured by the dust from a sand storm that enveloped the city in 2005.

ABOVE A huge dust storm raged over a desolate Texas farm in 1955. In this year the county of Midland, Texas, formed the Sandstorm Advisory Board, whose one and only job was to name the storms.

the source area and the wind strength. In general, sand does not lift high into the atmosphere and it isn't carried over vast distances, because the particles are larger and heavier than dust.

Northwest China has all five ingredients essential to the development of sand-dust storms, most of which have been exacerbated by poor land management over decades. This in turn is the result of partial policies and uninformed human actions. The link between widespread desertification and the increase in the frequency and severity of dust storms has prompted investigation of the causes and mechanics of wind-related events.

Sadly, these investigations still have a long way to go before they can help to change the trend. Beijing was struck by 15 sand storms in 2001 and another 13 in 2002. The 2001 storms came mostly from deserts within China, whereas those of 2002 came mainly from China's neighbor to the north, Mongolia. It is predicted that Beijing will remain the recipient of dust storms for many years to come.

Impacts in China and beyond

The storms have heavy impacts on the environment and on the health of people and livestock, particularly when the dust combines with industrial pollutants as it passes through cities in eastern China. This combination has been blamed for the increasing rate of respiratory and skin ailments and for damage to the country's farming and industrial sectors.

Overplowing and overgrazing, coupled with drought periods, have led to the denudation of the land and thus have been blamed for the massive deterioration of China's agricultural resources. Dust and sand from the exposed soil are carried from the northwest by westerly winds as huge dust plumes that regularly travel hundreds of miles to Beijing and other cities in northeastern China. The plumes are often so thick that they obscure the sun, reducing visibility, slowing traffic, and closing airports. Residents caulk windows with rags to keep out the dust, and outdoor public facilities have to be cleaned repeatedly during the dust storm season.

China's neighbors, notably North Korea, South Korea, and Japan, have registered official complaints when the dust clouds have moved across them, and legislators from Japan and South Korea organized a tri-national committee with Chinese lawmakers to devise a strategy to combat the dust in response to pressure from their citizens.

During one of the 2001 storms, an unusually large dust cloud from northwest China drifted across the Pacific Ocean to the United States, where it hid views of the Rocky Mountains as it lingered over Denver, Colorado and other areas.

The Chinese farmers have been abandoning their unproductive, eroded land and migrating eastward as refugees, similar to the westward migration from the southern Great Plains to California during the United States Dust Bowl years.

China has lost up to US$3 billion a year over the past decade from the loss of land and productivity, threatening the livelihoods of 170 million people.

The United States Dust Bowl
From 1931 until 1941 the United States and Canada experienced a series of dust storms that earned the focal region the title of Dust Bowl. The storms were the result of a massive drought and decades of poor farming techniques, coupled with the severe windstorms that characterize the region.

Plowing exposed the fertile soils of the Great Plains by removing the grass cover. The soil dried out and turned to dust during the prolonged drought. The dust was picked up by the wind and blown to the east in very large black clouds. The clouds made the sky appear black all the way to the Atlantic.

This ecological disaster caused an exodus from the Great Plains region, where over a million Americans were made homeless. (The Dust Bowl is covered in more detail in the chapter on Droughts.)

The Dust Bowl should serve as both a warning and a source of comfort. Obviously, faulty land-use practices and inappropriate government policies can lead to an acceleration of land degradation in semi-arid lands. However, a solution can be found through careful analysis followed by a concerted effort by all stakeholders to seek a solution.

Australian dust storms
Late on the morning of February 8, 1983, a strong but dry cold front began crossing the state of Victoria, preceded by hot, gusty, northerly winds, which quickly picked up loose topsoil from western Victoria, where drought had held sway for some months. The soil formed a large dust cloud along the line of the cool change as it moved east.

In Melbourne, Victoria's capital city, the temperature rose to 110°F (43.2°C) as the north wind

strengthened, and reached a record February maximum by 2:35 p.m. A short time later, a spectacular red-brown cloud of dust was seen advancing on the city. It reached Melbourne just before 3:00 p.m., accompanied by a rapid temperature drop. The squally wind change that accompanied it was strong enough to uproot trees and unroof about 50 houses. Visibility plunged to 110 yards (100 m), and according to witnesses, "everything went black" as the storm struck.

On October 24, 2002, eastern Australia experienced one of the worst dust storms on record when thick dust swept in from the interior of the continent ahead of a strong southwesterly wind change. The dust cloud affected parts of inland South Australia, Victoria, New South Wales, and Queensland in a front stretching hundreds of miles.

ABOVE A dust storm billows across the western desert of Iraq in Al Asad in 2005. The storm was spawned near the border of Syria and Jordan. The wall of dust may have reached 5,000 feet (1,500 m) high, based on the height of the clouds above it.

CHARACTERISTICS OF DUST STORMS
A dust storm usually arises suddenly in the form of an advancing dust wall that may be many miles long and a thousand yards (1 km) or so deep. Ahead of the dust wall the air is very hot and the wind is light. The US weather watchers classify dust storms according to visibility: if blowing dust reduces visibility to between 5/8 and 5/16 mile (1.0 and 0.5 km), a dust storm is reported; if the visibility is reduced to below 5/16 mile (500 m), it is reported as severe.

Dust storm winds can also be associated with thunderstorm outflows and gust fronts. Vertical downdrafts of chilled air during thunderstorms may locally strike the ground with velocities of 25 to 50 miles per hour (40–80 km/h). Under such conditions, fine particles may also be swept upward hundreds or thousands of feet into the air.

The average height of a dust storm is 3,000 to 6,000 feet (900–1,800 m), and stronger storms have dust to 8,000–10,000 feet (2,400–3,000 m). Haze and dust from extreme storms have been documented as high as 35,000 to 40,000 feet (10,700–12,200 m). While these are often shorter-lived than wind-forced dust storms, they can be quite intense, with an impressive leading edge, called a dust wall. Dust storms on Mars can reach 130,000 feet (40 km) high.

RIGHT People in Beijing, China, battle their way through a dust storm in 2006. Residents found their homes, streets, and cars covered in brown dust. Experts advised residents to stay indoors or wear masks when going out.

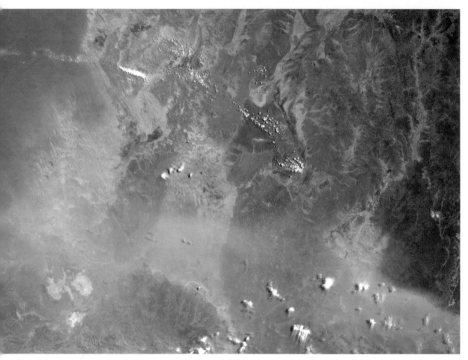

ABOVE Dust storms are common in Australia, the world's driest inhabited continent. This storm was recorded by NASA's MODIS satellite in January, 2003, as it tracked across the south-central part of the continent.

The huge dust storm was whipped up by winds blowing across farmland that had been so devastated by prolonged drought that it was totally denuded of vegetation. The winds carried away tens of millions of tons (tonnes) of the exposed topsoil—an estimated 2 million semitrailer loads of precious earth.

The dust storm extended 8,200 feet (2,500 m) into the atmosphere and reduced visibility in places to a few hundred yards (meters). The storm had a front measuring 930 miles (1,500 km) north to south and was 185 miles (300 km) deep. In the southwest of Sydney, Australia's largest city and the capital of New South Wales, a reading of 150 micrograms of dust per cubic meter of air was recorded; 50 is considered high. Health authorities warned people with asthma and breathing difficulties to stay inside.

Bureau of Meteorology records show that Sydney was affected by dust storms in April 1994, September 1968, December 1957, and January 1942, when the most severe dust storm to hit the city reduced visibility at Sydney Airport to 1,600 feet (500 m).

A global phenomenon

North Africa is a source of dust that is transported to southern Europe, and the Sahara region is the main global source of wind-blown dust. About 10 million tons (about 10 million t) of dust particles can be transported and brought to Great Britain from the Sahara Desert during a single dust storm. Great Britain has suffered 17 dust storms since 1900. Arid and semi-arid regions around the Arabian Sea are other significant sources of dust. India, Pakistan, Iran, and the Arabian Peninsula contribute to Arabian Sea dust deposition, and dust from China contributes to sediment in the Pacific Ocean.

Storms regularly occur in the arid and semi-arid regions of the Earth, particularly in subtropical latitudes. Sand and dust storms are natural events that have occurred throughout Earth's history. The geological record shows that changes in the growth and decline of desert sand surfaces over time are characterized by evidence of sand and dust storms, making the storms useful indicators of climate change during past eras.

In recent times the action of humans has greatly increased the desert sand surface area through poor land management, which has destabilized the desert margins. Such actions include overgrazing vegetation beyond its carrying capacity, gathering firewood for fuel, and clearing to plant crops. Corresponding to these areas of accelerated desertification is an increase in the severity and frequency of the many major sand-dust storms throughout several regions of the world. As in past geological eras, they could be considered indicators of current climate change.

Prevention efforts in China

The Chinese government has undertaken a large reforestation effort to combat the spread of deserts and to mitigate the effects of dust storms, particularly around cities. It has been investigating ways to make the arid land productive again. One strategy is to plant trees and tracts of grass in checkerboard patterns, so increasing vegetation coverage and reducing the buildup of sand dunes. As long ago as the late 1970s and early 1980s, a system of agricultural shelterbelts was implemented by reforesting large tracts of land in order to anchor loose soil and help stem the flow of dust across China.

Government reports indicate that some progress has been made in reversing the massive loss of productive land. Among the successful efforts cited, the buildup of sand dunes in some provinces has been reduced by as much as 64 percent, and total forest cover nationwide was increased by 14 percent in 1995 as a result of intensive planting.

Yet some people are concerned that the ever-more-intensive cultivation of land over the past decade has outpaced any progress. "If China cannot quickly arrest the trends of deterioration, the growth of the dust bowl could acquire an irreversible momentum,"

warned Lester Brown of the Earth Policy Institute. "What is at stake is not just China's soil, but its future."

"Desertification has become a bottleneck for the social and economic development and the improvement of people's living standard in some areas," declared Jiang Chunyun, vice premier of China's State Council, at a 1997 United Nations conference on desertification. "[In] other areas most severely affected by desertification, the problem of food and shelter for local residents remains unsolved."

To find a solution to desertification will require a shift of emphasis from the land to the people. Desertification control should be about the people who use the land, not just the land they use.

ABOVE A dust storm blows through Riyadh, Saudi Arabia. Such storms are getting worse. Natural desert soil is covered by a thin crust of algae, lichen, and pebbles. As more people are driving across these, the surface crust is becoming broken, allowing the underlying dust to be swept up into the air.

THE WORD: DESERTIFICATION

Desertification is a process by which land becomes increasingly dry until almost no vegetation grows on it, making it a desert. Desertification is often thought of as being associated with drought, but while land degradation might proceed more rapidly during drought, the real causes of desertification include natural climate variation, the overall inappropriate management of land (drought or no), ignoring normal climatic variability in land management, and the natural limitations of the land itself. In reality, drought is one of the risks associated with human occupation of arid lands where climate is largely unpredictable.

Boundary Waters Derecho, USA and Canada, 1999

On Sunday, July 4, 1999, thunderstorms that had occurred before dawn over portions of North and South Dakota came together to form a "bow echo," the term used to describe the curved front that typifies a derecho. This was the beginning of the "Boundary Waters–Canadian Derecho," which lasted for 22 hours over two days.

ABOVE The region struck by the Boundary Waters Derecho, as seen from space, looking southwest. The large lake to the right is Lake Superior, Lake Michigan is to the left, and Lake Huron is to the bottom left. The Boundary Waters Canoe Area Wilderness lies just beyond the long island (Isle Royale) on the right in Lake Superior. The derecho came from the top right part of the image toward the bottom right corner.

It traveled over 1,300 miles (2,100 km) at an average speed almost 60 miles per hour (100 km/h), and resulted in widespread devastation and many casualties in both Canada and the United States.

A derecho (pronounced "deh-*reh*-cho") is a widespread and long-lived windstorm that is associated with a band of rapidly moving showers or thunderstorms. The word "derecho" was first used by Dr Gustavus Hinrichs, a physics professor at the University of Iowa, in a paper published in the *American Meteorological Journal* in 1888. Dr Hinrichs chose this terminology for thunderstorm-induced straight-line winds as an analog to the word tornado. "Derecho" is a Spanish word which can be defined as "direct" or "straight ahead". "Tornado" is thought to have been influenced by the Spanish verb "tornar", which means "to turn."

Derechos are very severe convective windstorms with long damage paths. These storms arise from conditions that are uncommon in the upper Midwest and adjacent areas during the warm season.

The term "bow echo" is based on how bands of rain showers or thunderstorms "bow out" or curve when strong damaging downward winds reach the surface and spread out like pancake batter. The bowed rain band is near the leading edge of the damaging winds, and usually appears as a squall line (an organized line of storms in a cluster).

Derechos can be associated with single or multiple bow echoes. The bow echoes may vary in scale and may die out and redevelop during the course of derecho evolution. Derecho winds can be enhanced on a smaller scale by embedded supercells within the derecho-producing storm system.

Boundary Waters–Canadian Derecho

The very long-lived Boundary Waters–Canadian Derecho was one of the northernmost "progressive" derechos ever to have been recorded. It traveled through a large part of the boreal forests of North America, uprooting and breaking off hundreds of square miles of trees. Two people were killed and 70 were injured; almost all of these casualties (67) were the result of trees or tree limbs falling. Additionally, almost all of the victims were outdoors (camping, hiking, or canoeing), having taken advantage of the Independence Day holiday weekend. This includes one of the casualties that was not the result of a falling tree: this person's death was due to being blown off a boat and drowning, which is another of the types of casualties most frequently associated with warm-season derechos.

Most of the damage to homes and businesses occurred in areas of high population density, such as the Fargo, North Dakota, metropolitan area early in the event, and later on in south-central and southeastern Quebec. These areas contributed the most to the recorded property damage, which exceeded US$100 million (1999 value); over 700,000 households and businesses lost electrical power from this long-lived event.

The winds over the open waters of Lake Superior were estimated to have been greater than 100 miles per hour (160 km/h). Many boaters were besieged by the intense winds. Boaters are particularly at risk, because derechos form in weather that is conducive to sailing. A number of boaters had close calls, and were lucky to survive the fierce winds and huge waves as the storm roared through the area.

ABOVE A lighthouse marks the shore at Grand Marais, on Lake Superior, within the Boundary Waters Canoe Area Wilderness in Minnesota. Lake Superior, with the largest surface area of any freshwater lake in the world, is exposed to many sudden and severe storms, mostly from late October to early December; up to 10,000 ships have sunk in all five of the Great Lakes.

ABOVE The path of the July 4–5, 1999, derecho event. The curved lines show the approximate locations of the gust front (bow echoes) at three-hour intervals.

The main line of the Canadian Pacific Railroad was shut down between White River and Chapleau because of fallen trees blocking the tracks.

A near miss

Sarah Jamison, a National Weather Service meteorologist, was enjoying the Fourth of July holiday weekend camping and celebrating with family members and friends in the Rangeley Lakes region of western Maine. It was a very hot and humid day, with a high temperature near 90°F (32°C), just the weather for celebrating outdoors.

STORM IMPLICATIONS

The Boundary Waters–Canadian Derecho had very disruptive effects across northeastern Minnesota. Transportation was blocked in many areas along the storm path. Injured survivors had to be located and lifted out by helicopter over a period of a week. The remainder of the summer was spent opening up main roads, mainly along the Gunflint Trail.

There was insufficient communication with wilderness areas. While the National Weather Service at Duluth issued a number of warnings with significant lead-times along the entire storm path, there was not an effective means to get this warning to campers, hikers, and anglers. One of the wilderness areas was beyond the reach of NOAA Weather Radio transmitters, but this was rectified after the storm by the installation of three new transmitters in the area.

Another of the implications was the fire danger in and near forested areas destroyed by the storm. In the Boundary Waters Canoe Area Wilderness, 665,000 acres (269,000 ha) of forest was destroyed, leaving a dead fuel load averaging 60 tons per acre (22 t/ha). Worse are reports that very little of the fuel was in contact with the ground, and that most of it was not packed, but was exposed to the air. The idea of logging the area is fraught with political considerations and economic practicality. With such fuel availability, an intense wildfire is possible. And given the right conditions, such a fire could spread beyond the damage area.

When night fell, Sarah's parents slept on their boat near the docks, her brother slept in their car, and Sarah and her friends shared a tent. They had trouble sleeping because of the "stagnant" air, so at about 3 a.m. Sarah and a friend went out to get some fresh air. When they noticed lightning in the distance they returned to the tent to make it weather safe.

Sarah's mother also awoke and became concerned by the amount of lightning she was seeing as the storm approached. When she left the boat to warn the others, a gust front hit the campsite and the winds increased steadily. On reaching the tent, she started yelling for Sarah and her friends to get out but they were unable to hear her at first over the roar of the wind.

They had trouble rousing Sarah's brother in the car, but finally he unlocked the door just as the first tree was blown down in the campsite. Soon after, a much larger tree was uprooted and landed on the tent. Safely inside the car, they could see trees falling all around them during every lightning flash.

Within a half hour the storm had moved on. Fortunately, no one in the group was hurt. However, if Sarah's mother had not recognized the danger or had been a minute or two later arriving at the tent, things could have been much worse.

As is often the case in derecho events, the damage that hit Sarah's campground was linked to a narrow band of intense, very damaging downbursts embedded within the larger-scale, strong, but less severe winds associated with the derecho-producing system. The worst damage in the area extended

FACTS AND FIGURES

DATE	July 4–5, 1999
LOCATION	Across North America
DEATH TOLL	2 dead; 70 injured
DAMAGE	Exceeded US$100 million (1999 value)
COMMENTS	The distance it covered and the speed it traveled at made this derecho unique.

from an island in the lake, where every tree was snapped off or uprooted, across Sarah's and adjacent campsites. In Sarah's and two adjacent campsites about two dozen trees were blown down, several larger than 2 feet (60 cm) in diameter. One of these large trees and two smaller trees had fallen on Sarah's tent, crushing it. In Sarah's opinion it would have been impossible for them to have survived if they had stayed in the tent during the most intense portion of the storm.

After leaving the Cupsutic Lake campground, the derecho continued on, causing damage across southern Quebec and central and southern Maine. Finally, after traveling over 1,300 miles (2,100 km), the bow echo system weakened and the derecho ended, just before reaching the Atlantic coast.

Prescribed burns

About 40 percent of the forest in the Boundary Waters Canoe Area Wilderness was blown down, leaving five to 10 times as much fuel as before the storm. This amount of fuel could easily lead to uncontrollable wildfires. In 2000, foresters began a five- to seven-year program of prescribed burning in good weather to gradually reduce the amount of fuel. In an area 4 to 12 miles (6–19 km) wide and 30 miles (42 km) long, they will have their work cut out for them, especially as clear days are infrequent.

TOP Mudro Lake in the Boundary Waters Canoe Area Wilderness is one of hundreds of glacial lakes that lie along the boundary between Minnesota, USA, and Ontario, Canada.

ABOVE This type of damage to trees, in which they are snapped off above head height, is typical of a derecho. Trees were blown down over an area of 665,000 acres (269,000 ha) within the Boundary Waters area, necessitating several years of controlled burns to minimize the risk of wildfires.

HOW THE BOUNDARY WATERS–CANADIAN DERECHO FORMED

To be classified as a derecho, a storm must have a damage path of at least 250 nautical miles (463 km) in length. The Boundary Waters–Canadian Derecho had a damage path of about 6,000 nautical miles (11,100 km). As a progressive derecho, it caused serious wind damage over a very long path. Recorded wind speeds were as high as 91 miles per hour (146 km/h) near the beginning of the storm in North Dakota; many planes were overturned or damaged at the airport at Fargo. Damage was well in excess of F1 on the Fujita tornado scale along much of its length. The derecho moved very fast; it was traveling at 55 to 60 knots (100–110 km/h) when it entered northeastern Minnesota, and accelerated to 80 knots (150 km/h) after passing Ely, Minnesota. At no time while in northeastern Minnesota did the prevailing wind, at any level, equal or exceed storm speed. The storm traveled the 6,000 nautical miles in only two days.

A parent mesoscale convection system (MCS) existed more than six hours before the bow echo phase of the storm began, in eastern South Dakota. An MCS is a complex of thunderstorms which becomes organized on a scale larger than the individual thunderstorms, and normally persists for several hours or more. The bow echo phase of the storm began just after 5 a.m., a time window when very few derechos develop or remain in existence. The storm then maintained itself, around the clock, for two days, without break. It then evolved into an extremely dangerous bow echo. The tornadic portion of this configuration appeared to remain north of the Canadian border during the afternoon of July 4, 1999.

Tropical Storm Linfa, Philippines, 2003

On Tuesday, May 27, 2003, Tropical Storm Linfa (called Chedeng in the Philippines) smashed into the island of Luzon in the northern Philippines, killing 41 people, causing landslides, flash floods, and widespread flooding in five regions, and leaving a damage bill of nearly US$3 million.

RIGHT Workers clear their things from a bar on Roxas Boulevard in Manila as Tropical Storm Linfa batters the Philippines. The city is built on alluvial deposits and reclaimed land, making a great deal of it prone to inundation by storm surges and river flooding.

BELOW Commuters pile onto one of the few jeepneys willing to brave the floodwaters covering a street in the Philippine capital Manila, on the northern island of Luzon. Jeepneys developed as a popular form of public transport from US Army jeeps left behind after World War II.

The tropical storm passed directly over the Philippines during the last week in May, bringing heavy rains and the potential for flooding. Winds peaked at 65 miles per hour (105 km/h) as it as it slammed into Luzon, where it picked up sufficient strength to produce hurricane-force gusts of 80 miles per hour (130 km/h) over a 185-mile (300-km) radius. High winds cut off electricity to the region, and a landslide buried five houses in the town of Taytay, Rizal province, east of Manila.

Waist-deep floods swept through the northern Manila suburb of Valenzuela, displacing more than 600 families, and five others were rescued from a flooded district nearby. Many major streets in Manila were under water, and uprooted trees and fallen branches blocked some. Malabon mayor Amado Vicencio announced over the radio that 13 villages in his town were submerged in knee-deep floods.

The government warned that the Guagua River north of Manila and the Agno River in the north were in danger of overflowing after up to 4¾ inches (122 mm) of rain fell in 24 hours. Other places recorded up to 14 inches (350 mm), and Dagupan recorded 24¾ inches (629 mm) in 12 hours.

(The Philippine Atmospheric, Geophysical and Astronomical Services Administration uses its own naming scheme for tropical cyclones within its area of responsibility. These names are used along with the international names in the western North Pacific.)

Casualties—drowning and landslides

At the time of the storm the chief state weather forecaster, Prisco Nilo, announced that Linfa was the third weather disturbance to hit the country during the first half of 2003. He expected Linfa to continue to dump more rain before fizzling out.

"We expect improvement in the weather condition within the next two to three days," Nilo said. "We will still have rain but not as much as … we experienced for the past two days."

"I would just like to repeat that those that are living near a mountain should be alert, better still they should move to other areas because of a high probability of landslides," Nilo said. "Those in low-lying areas or near the [river] banks are advised against possible flash floods."

The Philippine Atmospheric, Geophysical and Astronomical Services Administration's weather

THE ECONOMIC DEVELOPMENT OF A COUNTRY DEPENDS UPON THE KIND OF ENVIRONMENT

FACTS AND FIGURES

DATE	May 27, 2003
LOCATION	The Philippines
DEATH TOLL	41 dead; 16 injured; 10 missing
DAMAGE	Infrastructure at 53.6 million pesos (US$1,017,463); fisheries at 38.7 million pesos (US$730,000); agriculture and livestock at 66.7 million pesos (US$1,275,334)
COMMENTS	Displaced 8,000 people; destroyed 286 houses; partially damaged 3,063 houses.

ABOVE A man crosses floodwaters in a village near the town of Calasiao, in the northern Philippines province of Pangasinan, with a freshly steamed pot of rice.

RIGHT Villagers aboard a raft check on neighbors stranded on the roof of a house near the village of Calasiao, Pangasinan province, north of Manila. The electrical wiring shown here is typical of that seen in many third-world countries, and poses a high risk of electrocution.

bureau raised typhoon alerts over the northern provinces of Pangasinan, La Union, and Ilocos Sur when the tropical storm appeared to be on course to hit these provinces directly. The areas experienced stormy weather with rough to very rough coastal waters that were dangerous to all types of sea craft.

Police in the central Bicol region said six people were killed, 67 were rescued, and another went missing after two small ferries capsized at sea off the coasts of Minalabac and Pilar towns at the height of the storm on the Wednesday.

Of the 41 fatalities, many had drowned, and others were caught by landslides. One man drowned in flash floods in the town of Masinloc, north of Manila, and a mother and her child were buried in a landslide in the northern mountain town of Tuba, according to the civil defense office. Three people drowned in flash floods in the northern province of Pangasinan, and a man was electrocuted in suburban Cavite, outside Manila. Ten others remained missing.

Although by May 28, Linfa had passed over to the eastern side of the Philippines and veered toward Japan, the government still advised people living near mountains that landslides and flash floods were possible. More rains, however, were expected after the weather bureau reported that a fresh weather disturbance had been spotted hovering above Pangasinan province. Linfa continued on to Japan, making landfall on May 31, and dumping up to 12 inches (300 mm) of rain in the south.

Damage to livelihoods

The agricultural department assessed the damage to fisheries at 38.7 million pesos (US$730,000). Rice yields were not affected, since most crops had been harvested. The National Disaster Coordinating Council (NDCC) estimated damage to infrastructure at 53.6 million pesos (US$1,017,463) and to agriculture and animal husbandry at 66.7 million pesos (US$1,275,334).

A total of 286 houses were destroyed and an additional 3,063 were damaged. Businesses remained closed in the towns of Urdaneta, Dagupan, Calasiao, and Santa Barbara, where a state of emergency had been declared because of storm damage. Many roads remained impassable for some time after the storm.

Evacuation and relief efforts

Hours after Linfa slammed into the Lingayen Gulf before dawn on Tuesday, President Gloria Macapagal-Arroyo shut down government offices and ordered city officials to use trucks to take stranded civil servants and thousands of other commuters to their homes. Over 2,500 people took refuge in 20 evacuation centers.

Press reports indicated that more than 8,000 people had been displaced by the floods, but according to the NDCC, 3,704 people were still sheltered in 31 evacuation centers for several days after the storm.

President Arroyo visited the town of Urdaneta, one of the worst-hit areas, on May 29 to assess the damage and to determine the assistance needed

TRACKING LINFA VIA THE NAVAL MARITIME FORECAST CENTER / JOINT TYPHOON WARNING CENTER

Tropical Storm Linfa (Chedeng/05W) formed west of Luzon, the Philippines, and intensified slowly as it looped counterclockwise in the South China Sea. Subsequently, the cyclone began to move east, toward Luzon island, in response to westerly steering flow.

The cyclone made landfall near Dagupan, the Philippines, weakened owing to land effects, and then moved east into the Philippine Sea. After moving back over water, the cyclone began to move north-northeast, with most of the heavy convection stripped from it. Subsequently, it began to slowly intensify, reaching a maximum intensity of 55 knots (102 km/h) as it tracked north, along the eastern periphery of the Ryukyu Islands of Japan.

On May 30, extratropical influences began to affect the cyclone, and it transformed into an extratropical cyclone shortly afterward in the Bungo Strait region between Kyushu and Shikoku islands in southern Japan.

by the people affected by the storm in Pangasinan. As a result, 15.7 million pesos (US$298,025) was provided at the time for relief assistance.

International aid came through a number of sources. The United Nations Office for the Coordination of Humanitarian Affairs served as a channel for cash contributions that were to be used for immediate relief assistance. They worked with other organizations in the UN system.

The NDCC provided 10 million pesos (US$191,205) and 800 sacks of rice for relief efforts. The regional health office allocated assorted medicines worth 602,087 pesos (US$11,512) to the provinces of Pangasinan and La Union and to the cities of Dagupan and Urdaneta.

KNOCK-ON EFFECT

Although parts of the Philippines had been declared drought areas during the previous months, the severity of Linfa, with its flooding and landslides, offered more rain than was bargained for.

In 2003, the drought and the SARS scare caused the Philippines' economy to shrink for the first time in three years. The Philippines had escaped the worst of the deadly SARS virus, with only 12 cases and two deaths, but thousands of Filipinos worked in some of the hardest-hit SARS locations, such as Hong Kong and Singapore. This meant that the remittances from overseas workers, which make up one-tenth of the Philippines' economy, fell significantly.

Besides SARS, the El Niño weather phenomenon caused grave problems. Agricultural output accounts for one-fifth of the economy overall, and the El Niño-related drought resulted in a considerable drop in production. So, after two months of dry weather, Tropical Storm Linfa turned the situation on its head. The storm at least brought the rain to beleaguered rice farmers, but at a considerable cost.

Tropical Storm Jeanne, Caribbean, 2005

On September 16, 2004, Tropical Storm Jeanne tore through Haiti, bringing heavy rains that caused severe flooding and mudslides in the Artibonite region in the north of the country. Jeanne is blamed for at least 3,000 deaths.

Jeanne affected about 80,000 of the 100,000 residents of the coastal city of Gonaïves, where 2,826 people died and another 2,601 were injured. The city was left without clean water and with limited medical supplies. Gonaïves, Haiti's third-largest city, was nearly washed away by floods and mudslides. The severity of the flooding and mudslides in Haiti was exacerbated by the lack of trees. Much of Haiti is deforested, leaving few roots to hold back runoff or mudslides, and few leaves to break the force of the rain. Most of the trees have been chopped down to make charcoal for cooking.

Although the floodwaters covered crops in the rural areas, they did not fully engulf homes, allowing dozens of families to huddle on rooftops to escape the high, muddy water. One teenage girl said that she, her mother, and six siblings spent the night in a tree. She also recounted seeing neighbors being swept away by the raging waters.

The origin of Jeanne

Jeanne formed as a tropical depression east-southeast of Guadeloupe on the evening of September 13, and strengthened to a tropical storm before crossing Puerto Rico on September 15. Winds as strong as 68 miles per hour (110 km/h) produced electricity outages for most of the island's 4 million residents.

BELOW Haitians ride trucks across a flood-submerged road in Gonaïves. Haiti was the first nation in the Caribbean to achieve independence from its colonial masters. Unfortunately, it remains one of the poorest nations on Earth.

Some 600,000 people were left without running water. The power outages were credited with indirectly causing three deaths and US$200 million in economic losses. Seven people were reported to have died in Puerto Rico as a result of Jeanne.

Landslides caused a large amount of damage to the lush vegetation in the Caribbean National Forest in Puerto Rico. US President George W. Bush declared the territory a federal disaster area and sent over US$2 million in relief.

The storm then moved toward Hispaniola, barely reaching hurricane strength before making landfall on September 16. It tracked slowly across the north coast of the Dominican Republic and Haiti, reaching hurricane strength just off the northeast tip of the Dominican Republic, with maximum sustained winds near 75 miles per hour (120 km/hr). During its slow progress over the northern Dominican

Republic, the storm damaged many homes in the town of Samaná and caused an estimated 18 deaths.

Jeanne weakened slightly while interacting with the high terrain of Hispaniola and as it tracked along the northern coast of Haiti. Even though it did not strike Haiti directly, the storm was large enough to cause flooding and mudslides, particularly in the northwestern part of the country.

Jeanne's unusually slow journey was caused by a weakening Hurricane Ivan. Ivan broke up a trough that was fueling Jeanne's steering currents. Interaction with Hispaniola caused it to degenerate into a tropical depression.

Disaster on top of riots

Gonaïves had suffered fighting during the February rebellion that led to the ousting of President Jean-Bertrand Aristide and left an estimated 300 dead;

SOME FACTS ABOUT JEANNE

Hurricane Jeanne was the tenth named storm, the seventh hurricane, and the fifth major hurricane of the 2004 Atlantic hurricane season. It was also the third hurricane and fourth named storm of the season to make landfall in Florida. The highest sustained wind speed measured 120 miles per hour (193 km/h). The lowest pressure was 28 inches of mercury (950 hPa). In eastern Puerto Rico, Jeanne deposited more than 24 inches (610 mm) of rain on the town of Naguabo.

Jeanne slowly tracked northward, waxing and waning in strength between a hurricane and a tropical depression. It brought flooding and high winds to the east coast of the United States, eventually leaving land at New Jersey. It finally headed off in the Atlantic Ocean east of New York on September 30.

ABOVE The flood damage in Gonaïves, Haiti. Although the storm center did not strike Haiti, heavy rain totaling about 13 inches (330 mm) caused severe flooding and mudslides in the northern part of the country.

ABOVE Haitians walk on a flooded road near Gonaïves. Tropical Storm Jeanne was blamed for the killer floods, but experts said poverty and deforestation also played key roles in the devastation. One of the world's poorest countries, Haiti also has the worst deforestation, depriving many areas of natural protection from flooding. Farmers struggling to eke out a living from badly degraded land chop down trees to make charcoal, which has a ready market in a country where most homes have no electricity.

and then in September the city was the hardest hit by the Jeanne tragedy, one of the many to beset Haiti in a year of revolts, military interventions, and further devastating floods, including one in May that killed more than 1,700 people in the country's southeast.

A World Health Organization worker, Pierre Adam, said he toured parts of downtown Gonaïves and saw people pushing wooden carts filled with bodies. "There is no life left in the center of town," reported Adam.

Residents told journalists that the floods caught the town by surprise on the Saturday night. Jean-Baptiste Agilus, a teacher, said he watched the water engulf houses in his neighborhood, filling some with 13 feet (4 m) of water. He saw one neighbor run

from his house, saying his wife and two children had been swept away in the flood. "The water rushed into their home, all the homes in the neighborhood," said Agilus. "It destroyed everything."

Many of the dead remained unburied for days, and relief workers had to bury bodies in mass graves in an attempt to prevent the spread of disease. Some bodies were washed out to sea and so have never been recovered.

In 2004, Haiti was supposed to be celebrating the 200th anniversary of its independence from France. It became the world's first black republic, as it calls itself, after being the first country to launch a successful rebellion against slavery.

Disaster relief and looting

The Associated Press reported that Prime Minister Gérard Latortue and his interior minister toured the area in a UN truck, but could not reach many areas because of flooded roads.

Latortue declared Gonaïves a disaster area and called on the international community to provide humanitarian aid. More than 3,000 peacekeeping troops, already stationed in Haiti, were able to help.

The United States offered the Haitian people aid to assist in their recovery from the disaster caused by Tropical Storm Jeanne. The Department of State provided nearly US$2 million in disaster relief to meet Haiti's urgent needs. This assistance included

FACTS AND FIGURES

DATE	September 16, 2004
LOCATION	Countries include the US Virgin Islands, Puerto Rico, Dominican Republic, Haiti, Bahamas, Florida; there was also flooding and damage in other eastern US states
DEATH TOLL	Over 3,000
DAMAGE	US$6.9 billion+
COMMENTS	Part of the 2004 Atlantic hurricane season, the storm formed September 13 and dissipated by September 30, 2004, having reached hurricane strength at times.

JEANNE'S FULL WRATH

The tenth named tropical system of the Atlantic basin began in the troposphere as a tropical wave that developed into a tropical depression on September 13 just east of the Leeward Islands. Tropical Storm Jeanne then tracked northward on September 18 and became a hurricane two days later, reaching Category 2 strength while over the western Atlantic.

The hurricane began tracking westward on September 23, reaching Abaco Island and Grand Bahama Island in the Bahamas on September 25, at Category 3 strength. Jeanne continued westward and made landfall at Stuart, Florida, near midnight on September 26, with Category 3 wind speeds of 120 miles per hour (193 km/h). Jeanne's landfall was almost exactly the same as that of Hurricane Frances only 20 days earlier. The storm moved northwestward, then northward through Florida, weakening to a tropical storm, and then tracked across Georgia and the Carolinas accompanied by heavy rain, finally exiting the coast just east of New Jersey on September 29. Jeanne is the first major (Category 3 or higher) storm to make landfall on the east coast north of Palm Beach, Florida, and south of the mouth of the Savannah River (between Georgia and South Carolina) since 1899. The final US damage was determined to be around US$6.9 billion, making it the 13th costliest hurricane in US history.

US$990,000 to the International Federation of the Red Cross; US$753,000 to the relief organization CARE for the distribution of emergency relief commodities; US$153,000 in direct relief supplies transported from Miami to Port au Prince for distribution by CARE in the city; US$100,000 in food aid and logistical support for the World Food Program in Haiti; and $50,000 which was made available following US Ambassador to Haiti James Foley's declaration of a disaster.

US Government personnel were quick to reach the disaster areas so they could assess Haiti's needs. The United States extended its condolences to the people of Haiti for the suffering they had endured, and reaffirmed its commitment to assisting them.

Various UN agencies also distributed food and medical supplies to the Haitians. Sadly, widespread looting was reported in the hardest-hit areas, and UN peacekeepers sometimes had to fight off armed crowds at relief distribution points. Street gangs, which have long ruled Gonaïves, mobbed relief workers and stole supplies. Trucks carrying aid were held up by men armed with guns and machetes.

An unusually high number of hurricanes lashed the Caribbean in 2004, causing casualties and damage from the United States to Trinidad and Tobago.

ABOVE A man in St Petersburg, Florida, braves a wave caused by the storm surge of Tropical Storm Jeanne. The storm made landfall in Florida on September 26, two weeks after it formed.

LEFT A family stand amid their partially destroyed home in Gonaïves, Haiti. Unlike wealthy Western nations, which can provide their own disaster relief, Haiti does not have the funds and has to rely on international aid in order to rebuild. In the meantime, many people shelter in huts built of rubble.

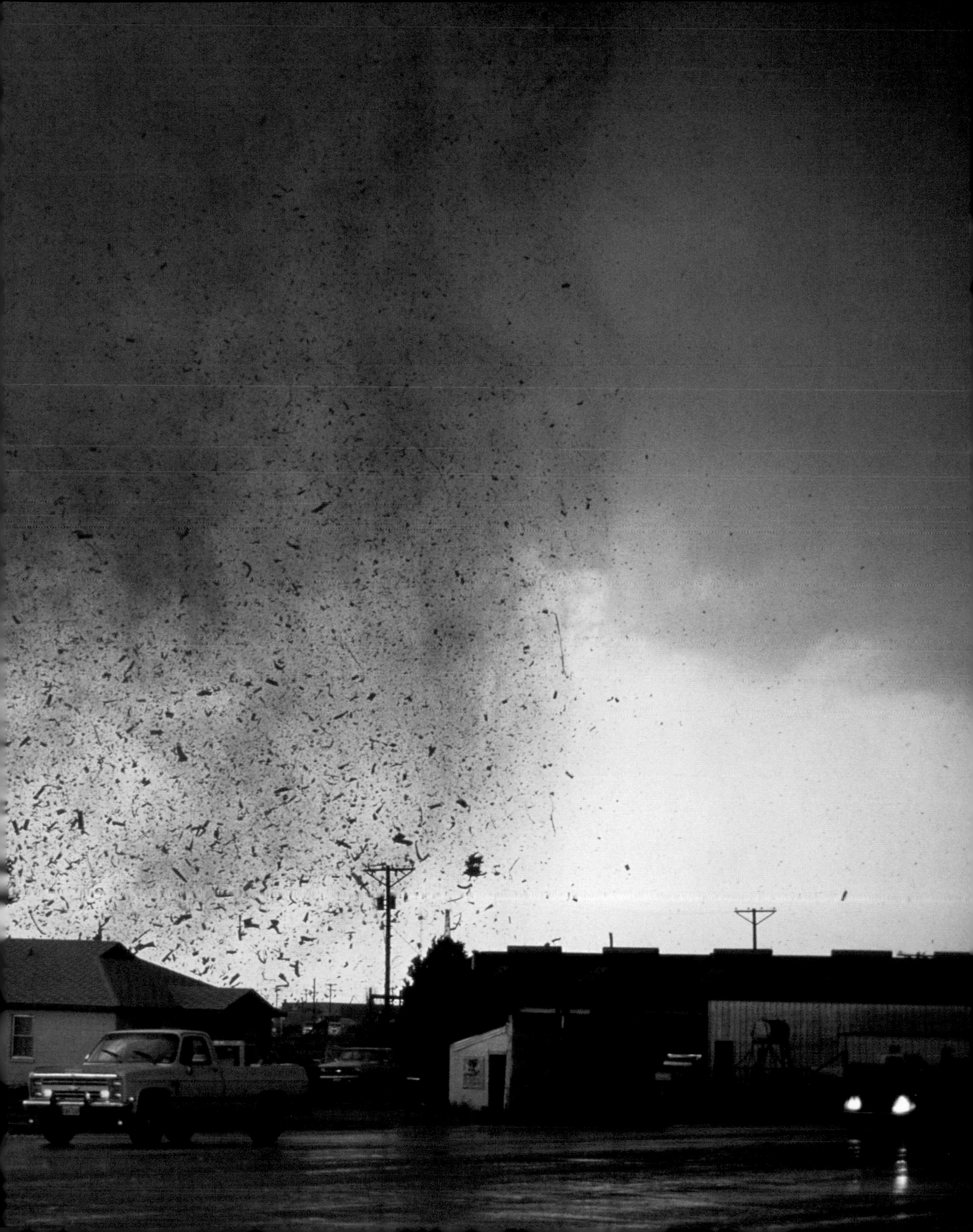

Tornadoes

Tornadoes, or "twisters," are nature's most violent storms. A tornado is a violently rotating column of air that usually extends from a cumulonimbus cloud to the ground with winds that can reach 300 mph (480 km/h). Damage paths can be in excess of 1 mile (1.6 km) wide and 50 miles (80 km) long. A tornado nearly always starts as a funnel cloud and may be accompanied by a loud roaring noise.

Tornadoes fall at the small end of the storm size scale, and arise from extreme atmospheric instability caused by clashes between air bodies with differing moisture contents and temperatures.

Wind shear is another essential ingredient in tornado development, and is responsible for spin. Wind shear occurs when winds are moving either in different directions or at different speeds at different heights in the atmosphere. This can cause rotation to begin in a funnel, which becomes a tornado when it hits the ground, or a waterspout on the water.

Most tornadoes rotate cyclonically—that is, counterclockwise in the northern hemisphere and clockwise in the southern hemisphere—but anti-cyclonic tornadoes do occur. Non-supercell land tornadoes and water spouts have been observed rotating anticyclonically.

Typically, a moderate thunderstorm of less than three hours' duration forms a single funnel. Occasionally, very destructive supercell thunderstorms, which are huge rotating storm systems, are capable of spawning families of tornadoes over several hours.

The when and where of tornadoes

Tornadoes mostly occur in spring and summer, when thunderstorm activity is at its highest. Although the United States has by far the most tornadoes in any one year, mainly in Tornado Alley, many other countries are also prone, and some have twisters to rival the nastiest of those in the United States. Most of these countries are in the mid-latitudes, between 20° and 50° on either side of the equator. Canada, which probably comes in second, has the same

LEFT A cloud sends down a small tornado funnel in a slate gray sky. It might be possible to outrun a tornado in a car in the open; it is not possible in a built-up area.

PREVIOUS PAGES A tornado strikes buildings in Pampa, Texas, USA. A typical violent whirling wind, accompanied by a funnel-shaped cloud, extends down from cumulonimbus cloud.

BELOW A tornado touches down on the North American prairie. The US receives the most tornadoes, but by no means all.

RIGHT A scene such as this, taken in the USA in 1919, may have inspired Victor Fleming, who directed the *Wizard of Oz*.

FAR RIGHT Near Manchester, South Dakota, an F4 tornado bears down on a storm chaser. A few storm chasers earn their living chasing storms—as scientists or photographers. Some do it for news coverage. Most do it for the thrill. Storm chasing is a dangerous activity.

TEN OF THE DEADLIEST TORNADOES

APRIL, 1989	Possibly the world's deadliest tornado on record struck the Manikganj area of Bangladesh, 50 miles (80 km) northwest of Dhaka, on April 26. At least 1,300 people were killed, 12,000 were injured, and 80,000 were left homeless.
FEBRUARY, 1884	Sixty tornadoes killed 600 to 800 people in Alabama, Georgia, South Carolina, and North Carolina, USA, between February 9 and 19. This outbreak was considered the largest until the Super Outbreak of April 3 to 4, 1974.
APRIL, 1936	Enormous tornadoes on April 5 and 6 took 455 lives and injured over 1,800 people in Mississippi, Tennessee, Alabama, Georgia, and South Carolina, USA.
MAY, 1896	On May 27, a tornado struck St Louis, Missouri, USA, killing up to 400 people and injuring 1,000. As many as 200 people simply disappeared, probably swept away in the river. Damage in St Louis alone totaled US$10 million.
MAY, 1840	On May 7, a single tornado struck the city of Natchez, Mississippi, USA, killing 317 people, mostly in boats on the Mississippi River, yet injuring only 109. This is the only tornado on record as having killed more people than it injured.
APRIL, 1903	On April 23 and 24, 16 tornadoes struck from Texas to Georgia, southern USA, killing 320 people. This event is known as the Dixie Outbreak. One tornado measured 2 miles (3 km) wide.
MARCH, 1932	Over 20 tornadoes in Alabama, Georgia, and Tennessee, USA, killed over 300 people on March 21, most of them in Alabama. Two separate waves of tornadoes struck, the first in the afternoon, the second after dark.
MARCH, 1917	A series of tornadoes from March 23 to 27 killed 211 people in four states of the US Midwest, most notably Indiana.
JUNE, 1953	On June 8, six tornadoes tore through 350 miles (560 km) of Michigan, USA, killing 116 people, injuring 844, and damaging 40 houses. The same weather system continued eastward, spawning another tornado that killed 94 people in Massachusetts.
MAY, 1985	More than 40 tornadoes swept through Pennsylvania, Ohio, and New York, USA, and southeastern Ontario, Canada, on May 31. They killed 88 people, 12 of them in Canada. Damaged exceeded US$450 million.

climate regime as the US, with the tornado season occurring mostly in summer, when storm fronts tend to move north from the southern Great Plains.

Some of the most violent and certainly the most deadly tornadoes occur in Bangladesh and eastern India. On April 26, 1989, the deadliest tornado on record killed about 1,300 people and injured another 12,000 in Bangladesh, where 80,000 people living in flimsy dwellings were left homeless. Unfortunately, there is no tornado warning system in Bangladesh.

Tornadoes have been recorded right across Europe, which would be the next most affected region in terms of number and intensity. The United Kingdom also has its share, with more than 30 tornadoes per year, which compares in frequency per unit of area with the Great Plains. However, the tornadoes are not spawned from supercell storms and so they are far less destructive.

Tornadoes are common also in the southern hemisphere: in southeastern and southwestern Australia; in northern Argentina, Uruguay, and southern Brazil; and in southeastern South Africa. The only continent where tornadoes have not been reported is Antarctica.

About 1,200 tornadoes occur annually in the United States, compared with 200 to 300 reported in the rest of the world. This is partly explained by the US having the only tornado reporting system.

Tornado warning system

Quite often before a tornado hits, there can be a calm, still period when the wind dies down. If a funnel or tornado is not visible, sometimes the first indication of its location is a cloud of debris. A few tornadoes are clearly visible with clear, sunlit skies behind them, but low-hanging clouds can obscure others. Tornadoes generally occur near the trailing edge of a thunderstorm and sometimes develop so rapidly that little advance warning is possible.

Before 1948 the only warning people had of tornadoes came by informal contact around small farming communities. Severe weather outlooks, tornado watches, amateur radio or spotter networks, community sirens, commercial television or radio alerts, and awareness programs were not available.

On the evening of March 25, 1948, two air force officers correctly predicted that conditions were ripe for tornadoes, which eventuated and caused major

ABOVE Ominous storm clouds gather over a field of grazing cattle in Nebraska, USA. Dark clouds above an oddly colored sky, sometimes with wisps of twisted cloud beneath, can signal an impending tornado.

258

TOP A tornado on the horizon of a wheat field. Anyone caught outside during such a storm should lie down in a ditch and watch out for flying debris.

ABOVE A tornado has stripped this tree of most of its leaves, broken off its tallest branches, and also wrapped a sheet of roofing iron around it. Flying debris can cause fatal injuries.

damage to their air base, but because of the warning there were no fatalities. This was the first time in US history that a tornado forecast was issued.

With technology now making it possible to effectively identify conditions and send out warnings, the death toll from tornadoes has been reduced considerably. The annual United States tornado death rate fell from 1.8 deaths per million in 1925 to only 0.11 per million in 2000.

Today tornado warnings are sent to the media and other agencies via various channels, and can be received on NOAA Weather Radio and the internet.

A tornado warning is issued when: a tornado is reported as being on the ground; a waterspout is headed toward land; a funnel cloud is reported; radar indicates a thunderstorm with a tight rotation signature; or a rotating wall cloud is reported.

A tornado warning means immediate danger—if not from the tornado itself, then from the associated severe thunderstorm. Anyone in the path of such a storm is urged to take cover immediately, as it is a life-threatening situation.

In contrast to a tornado warning, a tornado watch indicates only that conditions are favorable for the formation of tornadoes from severe thunderstorms. Therefore, a tornado watch also implies a severe thunderstorm watch.

Fujita Tornado Intensity Scale

The Fujita Tornado Intensity Scale (F-scale) infers wind speed from wind damage. All tornadoes, and most other severe local windstorms, are assigned a rating from 0 to 5. An accurate F-scale rating is important for historical, statistical, and climatological reasons and allows the public to get a sense of the storm's destructive force.

F0, 40 to 72 miles per hour (64–116 km/h)—light damage: some damage to chimneys; branches broken off trees; shallow-rooted trees pushed over; sign boards damaged. Also called "gale tornado."

F1, 73 to 112 mph (117–181 km/h)—moderate damage: the lower limit is the beginning of hurricane wind speed; surface peeled off roofs; mobile homes pushed off foundations or overturned; moving vehicles pushed off roads.

F2, 113 to 157 mph (182–253 km/h)—considerable damage: roofs torn off frame houses; mobile homes demolished; boxcars pushed over; large trees snapped or uprooted; small missiles generated.

F3, 158 to 206 mph (254–332 km/h)—severe damage: roofs and some walls torn off well-constructed houses; trains overturned; most trees in forests uprooted; heavy cars lifted off ground and thrown.

F4, 207 to 260 mph (333–418 km/h)—devastating damage: well-constructed houses leveled; structures with weak foundations blown some distance; cars thrown; large missiles generated.

F5, 260 to 318 mph (418–512 km/h)—incredible damage: strong frame houses lifted off foundations and carried considerable distance to disintegrate; automobile-sized missiles fly through the air in excess of 100 yards (90 m); trees debarked; steel-reinforced structures badly damaged; incredible phenomena occur.

The scale is named after the late Dr T. Theodore Fujita, a former professor of meteorology at the University of Chicago, USA. Although very useful, it has numerous shortcomings. The Enhanced F-scale, which is in planning, offers a much more precise way to assess tornado damage. It has been calibrated by engineers and meteorologists across 28 different types of damage indicators.

Tornadoes outside the United States

Tornadoes are not confined to the US and Canada. The Australian Bureau of Meteorology's database records 364 tornadoes across New South Wales from 1795 to 2003, and 160 in Victoria dating from 1918.

The most intense tornado recorded in Australia, at F4, occurred west of Bundaberg, Queensland, on November 29, 1992. Hail the size of cricket balls fell.

The British Isles actually experience more tornadoes per square mile (or per square km) than the United States, but most are far less severe than those in the US, so the damage is less noticeable.

In 1999 South Africa was struck by a tornado in the town of Umtata, killing 13 people. Another 150 people were injured.

LEFT A tornado in New Mexico, USA, high country. The typical twister descending from thick, dark cloud is clear in this shot, which also shows dust and debris being kicked up on the ground.

Tri-State Tornado, USA, 1925

On the morning of Wednesday, March 18, 1925, the weather forecast for the Midwestern United States was for "rains and strong shifting winds." By late afternoon, 695 people across Missouri, Illinois, and Indiana were dead, struck down by the United States' deadliest and most destructive tornado ever. Known as the Tri-State Tornado, it is listed as one of the top seven major catastrophes ever to hit the United States.

BELOW Minnie (left) and Rose Hawkins sit among the wreckage of their home in Murphysboro, Illinois, in the wake of the Tri-State Tornado, March 1925. This town alone suffered 234 deaths, giving it the largest recorded tornado death toll in a single city in the United States.

Because of its lethal combination of rapid movement, monstrous size, and long track, it managed to take hundreds of lives and injure thousands. The storm killed more than twice as many as the 1840 Great Natchez Tornado, the second deadliest. The Tri-State Tornado was indeed a rare event—an event that few people will ever experience in their lifetime and possibly one that occurs only once in a few hundred years.

The storm was first sighted around 1:00 p.m. Some said they had seen a typical funnel at that time, but other witnesses commented that the tornado had the unusual appearance of an amorphous rolling fog as it traveled along its path at near record speeds. The cloud, bloated with debris and tons of river mud, was very wide. This was possibly because the tornado was accompanied by extreme downburst winds generally throughout the entirety of its course;

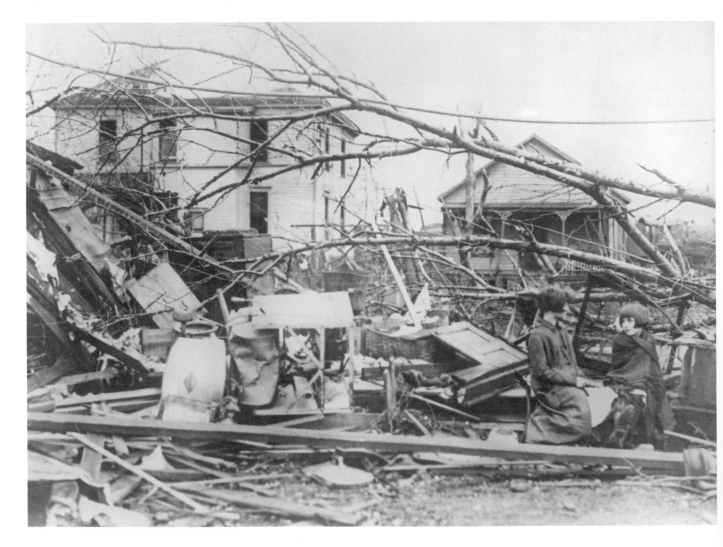

the tornado and downburst together caused damage at times 3 miles (5 km) wide, with the width of the tornado itself averaging a massive 1,000 yards (1 km). Usually the funnels of tornadoes are no wider than a block or two: 100–200 yards (100–200 m).

The path of the tornado

The 219-mile (352-km) path of the Tri-State Tornado remains a record. It started northwest of the town of Ellington in the southeastern part of the state of Missouri and sped to the northeast, killing two and causing US$500,000 damage to the village of Annapolis, 20 miles (32 km) away, and the mining town of Leadanna. Further on, 32 children were injured when two schools were damaged. Altogether 11 people died in Missouri.

The tornado crossed the Mississippi River near the city of Murphysboro in southern Illinois around 2:30 p.m., killing 34. It had an average speed of

60 miles per hour (100 km/h) as it cut a swathe almost 1 mile (1.6 km) wide through a number of towns, killing 541 and seriously injuring 1,423. One village, Parrish, was completely destroyed, and 22 were killed. The village was never rebuilt and today exists as a smattering of older homes a few miles northeast of West Frankfort in southern Illinois.

ABOVE Residents of Lorain, Ohio, search for valuables to salvage from the debris that remains of their house, which was wrecked when a tornado swept across the state. A tornado there in June 28, 1924, had killed 85 people.

THE AIR WAS FILLED WITH 10,000 THINGS

The Tri-State Tornado: The Story of America's Greatest Tornado Disaster, by Peter S Felknor, was first printed in the *St. Louis Post-Dispatch* newspaper of March 20, 1925. It reported: "All morning, before the tornado, it had rained. The day was dark and gloomy. The air was heavy. There was no wind. Then the drizzle increased. The heavens seemed to open, pouring down a flood. The day grew black … Then the air was filled with 10,000 things. Boards, poles, cans, garments, stoves, whole sides of the little frame houses, in some cases the houses themselves, were picked up and smashed to earth. And living beings, too. A baby was blown from its mother's arms. A cow, picked up by the wind, was hurled into the village restaurant."

RIGHT Inhabitants comb the wreckage of the town of Griffin, Indiana, in the wake of the Tri-State Tornado. The town was virtually flattened—all 150 homes there were destroyed, along with another 85 farms in the local rural districts. Deaths there included schoolchildren making their way home.

BELOW Several members of a county engineering committee pose for a photograph in southern Illinois where the Tri-State Tornado had passed through. They are showing a plank of wood which the winds had driven through this post.

Crossing the Wabash River into southwestern Indiana, the tornado struck the town of Princeton and traveled 10 more miles (16 km) to the northeast before finally dissipating, but not before 71 perished in Indiana. The tornado had covered a record 219 miles (352 km).

THE WALLS SEEMED TO FALL IN, ALL AROUND US

The *St. Louis Post-Dispatch* newspaper dated March 20, 1925 reported one girl's experience: "A Gorham schoolgirl tells of her experience as the tornado wreaked havoc at the Gorham school: 'Then the wind struck the school. The walls seemed to fall in, all around us. Then the floor at one end of the building gave way. We all slipped or slid in that direction. If it hadn't been for the seats it would have been like sliding down a cellar door. I can't tell you what happened then. I can't describe it. I can't bear to think about it. Children all around me were cut and bleeding. They cried and screamed. It was something awful. I had to close my eyes …'"

Streets strewn with wreckage

The days following March 18, 1925, were horrendous. In all, 695 died, mostly in Illinois, 1,423 were seriously injured, and thousands were left without shelter or food. The total damage was estimated at US$16.5 million. Looting and theft, particularly from the dead, were reported.

With so many fatalities, so many injuries, so much destruction, and so many lives torn apart, survivors had to face the soul-destroying task of restoring order. The few unscathed citizens were confronted by such complete destruction that it was hard for them to determine just where they had once lived. Their frantic search for family and friends was made all the more hellish when fires began to flicker through the ruins. The injured, dazed, and shocked wandered about with mud so thoroughly embedded in their skin that it was almost impossible to recognize them.

Throughout the night, relief workers and ambulances endeavored to make their way through streets strewn with wreckage, fallen telegraph poles and wires, and burning embers. The only light came from the fires. It took months to rebuild what nature had demolished within four hours.

Why so many fatalities?

The toll of 695 fatalities from the Tri-State Tornado remains a record. It is not hard to explain why this is so. There was no "Tornado Watch" or "Tornado Warning" system. People relied instead on the local newspaper, government mail, or word of mouth to relay messages or communicate current events from one town or family to another. So even if a watch or warning program had been in place, the message

would not have been disseminated in nearly enough time for people to have found suitable shelter.

Because the facilities for tracking extreme weather were poor, the exact conditions that preceded the Tri-State Tornado are not well known. However, based on the records from 1925 and our current knowledge, we can surmise that on March 18, 1925, there would have undoubtedly been a moderate to high risk of severe weather.

A question that many scientists often pose is whether the Tri-State Tornado was actually just one tornado or a family of tornadoes. Findings from modern weather records and research suggest that a tornado that endures as long as the Tri-State Tornado actually results from a cyclical supercell rather than one massive storm.

Despite all the uncertainties surrounding the nature of the 1925 Tri-State Tornado, one thing is certain—a storm like it will happen again. The only question is when and where.

ABOVE The destroyed seed store of Mr Mills, in which his wife was buried alive during the tornado that swept through three states. It began in Missouri, then hit Illinois, then Indiana, leaving devastation in its wake.

FACTS AND FIGURES

DATE	1:01 to 4:18 p.m., March 18, 1925
LOCATION	The three Midwestern states of Missouri, Illinois, and Indiana
DEATH TOLL	695 dead; over 2,000 injured
FORCE	F5
DAMAGE	US$16.5 million (1925 value) and 5,000 homes destroyed
COMMENTS	Records for longest track (219 miles, 352 km); widest track (1.5 miles, 2.4 km); speed of forward travel (62–73 mph, 100–118 km/h); lowest pressure (28.87 inches of mercury, 972 hPa)

"SHE SAW ME ABOUT THREE FEET IN THE AIR"

Geneva S. Nipper, then four years old, experienced the storm in Braden Valley Community. Her story is reported on the McLeansboro.com website: "The clouds began to move, the thunder roared and the green atmosphere remained. My mother took my brother out to the well in front of the store for a drink and I followed. Soon my dad rode up on a horse … I remember he said, 'It's going to storm and I must get my new saddle off the horse.'

I followed my mother and little brother inside. Mom went to the back of the store to a west or SW window. She screamed, 'My Lord, it's a tornado.' I had no idea what a tornado was except what I saw. It looked like a big black and green smoke, rolling on the ground as far as I could see in the valley, rolling trees and every thing in its path.

"[Dad] had my brother with one arm and picked me up with the other arm, feet dangling. He said 'Let's all go to [the] big ditch.' We all started but it hit as we got to the porch.

"I was loose from Dad when Mom said she saw me about three feet [1 m] in the air being twirled very fast around and around. When the wind released me it left me under the mules. Mom said she couldn't pick me up, [but one] of the teenage boys … did.

"It seems I awoke and looked to see Grandpa's house, barn and all were gone except at Grandpa's house, it was all gone except the upright piano was still on the floor [sic].

"We went on home. Our house was standing. The front bedroom window was out."

Woodward, Texas, Oklahoma, and Kansas, USA, 1947

On Wednesday, April 9, 1947, Oklahoma's most deadly tornado struck the city of Woodward, where its F5 violence caused massive destruction and numerous fatalities. Because it unleashed so much of its fury on Woodward, it became known as the Woodward Tornado.

TOP Many houses were destroyed in this town in Oklahoma. Woodward was among the worst hit.

ABOVE Most tornadoes have narrow paths. Little is left standing in the path of a tornado, yet buildings in the next street (behind) remain unscathed.

However, there is evidence to show that along its 220-mile (350-km) path, the tornadic event was probably made up of a number of tracks from a swarm of five or six tornadoes.

The storm began in the Texas Panhandle during the afternoon of April 9, and moved at around 50 miles per hour (80 km/h) northeast from Texas, through Oklahoma, and then to the west of Wichita in Kansas. In places, its massive path was 1.8 miles (2.9 km) wide.

The tornado first struck the towns of Glazier and Higgins in the far northeast corner of the Texas Panhandle, causing 69 fatalities and devastating both towns. When it first reached Oklahoma, it passed over farmlands to the southeast of a number of towns, which suffered no damage. However, even though no towns were struck, nearly 60 farms and ranches were destroyed, eight people were killed, and 42 more were injured. One more death was reported as the tornado continued along the ground uninterrupted for about 100 miles (160 km), eventually reaching Woods County, Oklahoma, 120 miles (190 km) northwest of Oklahoma City.

Tornado, fire, rain, and snow

Without warning, the tornado struck the western and northern sides of Woodward at 8:42 p.m., destroying over 100 city blocks with 1,000 homes and businesses. At least 107 people were killed and about 1,000 were injured in and around Woodward. The other side of the city was less severely affected.

In the aftermath, fires that started up added to the misery of the dazed survivors as they wandered confused and disoriented. Rain that followed the tornado soon had the fires under control, but the associated cold and snowy weather made clean-up efforts all the more miserable.

Beyond Woodward, the tornado lost some intensity, but it still managed to destroy another 36 homes and injured a further 30 people in Woods County before dissipating.

In all, at least 116 lives were lost in Oklahoma on that fateful night, making the Woodward Tornado the most deadly in that state's history.

FACTS AND FIGURES	
DATE	April 9, 1947
LOCATION	Texas, Oklahoma, and Kansas, USA
DEATH TOLL	181 dead; 970 injured
FORCE	F5
DAMAGE	US$7,700,000 (1947 value)
COMMENTS	Damage path 1,500 yards (1,400 m) wide and 170 miles (270 km) long

Good arises from bad

Like the many devastating tornadoes that struck the United States before the 1950s, the fatalities from the Woodward Tornado could be attributed to poor communications and the lack of a severe weather warning system. Following World War II, many new technologies became available, and some were adapted to keep watch on the weather. As early as 1953, and spurred on by the 1947 Woodward tornado, the Weather Bureau (now the National Weather Service) began a tornado watch and warning program. Tornado death tolls throughout North America have dropped dramatically since the implementation of the warning system.

ABOVE Falling masonry that has been dislodged by a tornado poses great risk to life and property. These cars were struck by debris in a town in Oklahoma that was hit by a tornado around the same period.

"I'D SAY, 'OH, BABY, LISTEN TO THE BIG WIND'"

Margaret Renton Chesney lived through the tornado that hit Woodward, Oklahoma, and surrounding areas on April 9, 1947, which she described in a letter to her mother, Meda Renton, in Portland, Oregon. Extracts from that letter describe the terror: "I was in the corner of the living room with baby in my arms … when … the weather … on the front of the house began to howl … [and] rose to a shriek … By now the lights were out. I … became terrified and heard the house cracking behind me … there seemed no hiding place so I tried to open the back door. The vacuum would only let it open several inches then it would slam again. Then the ice-box from the porch came crashing through and I was thrown into the center of the kitchen [where] Bob's table tipped onto the stove leaving a cozy nest for baby & me. The back wall caved in over this & the kitchen–dining room wall was supported by the buffet & dining room table. It seemed as if suddenly every thing was crashing down all around us. It seemed as if the next falling timber would crush our nest and finish us. I just squatted prayer fashion with Meda at my knees because I thought I'd have to get crushed pretty badly to flatten out that way. She was so cute! I'd say, 'Oh, baby, listen to the big wind' as if it were lots of fun & she'd just coo & gurgle … Bob … was frantic when he crossed the tracks & saw our house … Poor Bob was a wreck."

Judsonia and South-Central USA, 1952

The Arkansas weather report on the drab and colorless morning of Friday, March 21 was for a mostly cloudy afternoon and night with occasional thunder showers. By that evening, the worst tornado in Arkansas's history struck the town of Judsonia. It was one of a swarm of 28 tornadoes which caused 204 deaths over six states between 3:00 p.m. that day and 1:00 a.m. the next day.

ABOVE Students in Judsonia continued their lessons in a gymnasium after their school was destroyed by the tornado. They were among the luckiest, as other gymnasiums in the region were destroyed.

THE BLACKEST I HAVE EVER SEEN
Sam Womac's vivid recollections were reported online: "Late in the afternoon it was about as dark as night where I lived … in the Providence Community. The cloud was the blackest I have ever seen and appeared to have a green tinge to it. Sometime later someone drove by and yelled that a tornado had hit Judsonia. We … set out for there [and] I remember the trees, wires and houses down all over the place.

"Some say they felt three gusts of wind or three shocks, as if three [tornadoes] hit one after the other or the same one hit three times!"

The tornado reports started late in the afternoon and continued late into the night. The first tornado of the swarm struck a small lumber town in the southwest of Arkansas, 110 miles (177 km) from Little Rock, and followed what is known as the "tornado trail" from southwest to northeast, eventually reaching west Tennessee. All told, the twisters hit about 25 towns and rural communities in Arkansas, Tennessee, Missouri, Mississippi, Kentucky, and Alabama. In Arkansas, two or three tornadoes struck Judsonia at the same time.

The winds, spinning at velocities of several hundred miles per hour, picked up people as though they were leaves, shattered buildings with explosive force, and tossed automobiles about, according to reports from correspondents of *The New York Times*. During the night, yet another tornado rumbled high above Judsonia.

A strange eerie yellow twilight

And suddenly it was over. For some moments there was deadly silence and a strange eerie yellow twilight. Eventually survivors in Judsonia started to scramble from their hiding places—dazed by the immensity of the disaster as it became apparent. They climbed aimlessly over the massive piles of timber and bricks lying in the streets. Many of the survivors were injured. They dragged themselves along like zombies, with wide and staring eyes.

The heavy rains, plus hail, thunder and lightning, and floods and fire, that followed the tornadoes added to the plight of the survivors, many of whom found themselves homeless.

The worst damage was done within a six-block area through the central part of Judsonia. With the business section in a shambles, women were begging men to dig for husbands they feared buried beneath the wreckage of business houses.

As family members found each other, they cried with relief. The survivors started to stagger toward the Methodist Church, which was one of the few buildings left standing. Dead and injured were everywhere. Those who were able carried casualties to shelter from the rain on stretchers improvised from unhinged doors lying in the wreckage.

FACTS AND FIGURES

DATE	March 21 to 22, 1952
LOCATION	Arkansas (particularly Judsonia), Tennessee, and another four states
DEATH TOLL	204; over 1,000 injuries
FORCE	F4
DAMAGE	US$15 million
COMMENTS	Worst on record for Arkansas; first tornado watch issued by National Weather Service

Rescue efforts begin

Thirty minutes after the storm had subsided, a constant stream of traffic moved along the highway toward Jordania, in White County, Arkansas. Ambulances made many return journeys loading up the injured from the Methodist Church as rescue teams uncovered more people by digging into the piles of wreckage. At times they were directed by the voices of those who were buried.

Damage was massive

Property damage reached many millions of dollars in the six affected states. In rural areas whole towns were leveled, and apart from the homes and farm buildings that had been blown down or damaged, livestock were reported killed, power lines and communications were cut, and factories, shops, and other buildings were damaged.

Over on the railroad tracks at Judsonia, an automobile had jammed close against one of the oil cars parked on the siding. The rear wheels reached high up the side of the railroad car, and the car's headlights were a few inches above the ballast (gravel) of the track bed.

Most of the houses still standing had no gas, and none had electricity. To ward off the bitter cold, the National Guard set up braziers on street corners.

ABOVE Residents of Judsonia, dressed up for the photographer, try out a new storm shelter in preparation for the next tornado.

LEFT New buildings in Judsonia gradually replaced all those destroyed by the tornado, while empty plots waited their turn. All new houses incorporated a storm cellar, and many were rebuilt of bricks instead of wood.

Waco, Texas, USA, 1953

In Texas on the afternoon of May 11, 1953, a thunderstorm started to form after a very long period of drought. This was a welcome sight to those who had been living with scorching, sun-baked pastures for so long. But their elation was short-lived: soon after 4:00 p.m. a massive tornado struck Waco, killing more than 100 people and injuring nearly 600.

RIGHT Men search through the wreckage left by the Waco tornado for survivors. Makeshift lighting was pressed into service to allow work to continue through the night.

BELOW The search for survivors was hampered by the driving rain, which was already falling heavily while the tornado was still dying down.

The path of the developing storm had been carefully tracked by radar in Texas, and that morning a government forecast warned of possible tornadoes over an area in north-central Texas, with Waco at one of the four corners. This was the first year that tornado watches were issued.

Native American legend claimed that Waco would never be struck by a tornado because of its proximity to the steep banks of the Brazos River. Sadly, all 85,000 residents learned very quickly that this was not the case. Shortly after 4:00 p.m., a pouch of cloud briefly touched the ground 10 miles (16 km) south of Waco, then rose again. The funnel moved,

skimming above the ground and hanging with ominous intent as it advanced on the city. There, with a roar, it exploded into the heart of Waco, destroying about 200 business buildings and damaging about 400. One of the buildings destroyed was a large six-story furniture store. Its collapse filled the street 5 feet (1.5 m) deep in bricks, killed at least 30 employees in the store, and crushed two passing cars, killing a further five people.

An astonished store worker, holding a barometer with trembling hands, exclaimed, "It's gone to the bottom!" The sudden drop in air pressure shattered windows as the pressure inside became much greater

ABOVE A woman waits anxiously to hear the status of her missing husband in the wake of the Waco tornado. It took several days to remove the tons of rubble in places, so many had to wait some time to discover the fate of their missing relatives.

than that outside. Outside, buildings flew apart and telephone poles fell like bowling pins. Automobiles were blown along like tumbleweeds.

One driver jumped from his car when it began rolling backward. He crawled and rolled until he could hold on to the trunk of a plum tree, where he was whipped back and forth like a rag.

A reporter covering Waco for the *Dallas Morning News* had arranged for his wife and two children to pick him up from his office because it was evident that a bad storm was about to break. When he left his office it was very dark and the howling wind was blowing very heavy rain almost horizontally. As it turned out, he managed to leave downtown Waco less than 10 minutes before the tornado hit the spot where he had been standing, waiting for his lift. This

was the area that was hardest hit. He returned a short time later and saw the deadly aftermath. "It almost overwhelmed me," he said. "You couldn't get within about four blocks of the middle of town."

Large piles of debris downtown
Although the tornado demolished a number of houses both north and south of Waco as it moved northeast, the most detailed reports focused on the disaster it caused in Waco. About 150 homes were destroyed and 700 were damaged to some degree, and over 2,000 cars were damaged or destroyed.

A factor that made this tornado particularly notable was that it tore through the downtown of a city, and so created large piles of debris. Many victims had to be dug out. Survivors were buried for many hours, and several days were needed to remove the bodies buried under the tons of rubble. A switchboard operator who was buried under 15 feet (4.5 m) of rubble from the collapsed furniture store was trapped for 14 hours. She was eventually pulled out, and even with severe injuries, she had much to be grateful for: she was alive.

Afterwards, some victims experienced severe shock. A waitress was given a blue sports jacket by a rescuer for safekeeping—she calmly folded the jacket and put it in the refrigerator.

All in all, the tornado in Waco, Texas was a dramatic end to the spring drought of 1953.

A thousand rescuers
Very shortly after the tornado had vented its wrath, the students and staff of Waco's Baylor University volunteered for relief efforts. A thousand students worked in the largely destroyed downtown area. They joined campus maintenance workers, who had

---

FINDING A NEEDLE IN A BASEMENT
During the mopping up after the Waco tornado, two professors from Baylor University were asked to help with a somewhat dangerous rescue mission—the retrieval of a sliver of radium lost from a doctor's office in one of the buildings. The radioactive material belonged to a doctor who used it to treat cancer of the nose and throat. It was kept in a lead case when not in use, but on the afternoon of May 11, it had been removed from the case.

The doctor was treating a patient in a chair when the tornado struck, destroying the building and burying the two of them beneath the rubble. The pencil-length piece of radium was buried with them.

A couple of days later, when the seriously injured doctor regained consciousness, he began asking urgently about the radium needle. By this time much of the building debris had been transported to a dump, where the professors spent two days searching with a Geiger counter without finding the radium.

Finally, they returned to the area where the building had once stood, and at one end of the basement where the doctor's office had been there was a small pile of dust and debris. As they entered, the needle on the Geiger counter went off the dial. One of the professors turned to pick up a piece of string from the debris, and there on the other end was the radium needle.

FACTS AND FIGURES

DATE	May 11, 1953
LOCATION	Texas (Waco in particular)
DEATH TOLL	114 dead; 597 injured
FORCE	F5
DAMAGE	US$41 million (1953 value)
COMMENTS	Over 2,000 cars damaged or destroyed

been given permission to use the university's trucks and heavy equipment in the rescue efforts

What they found was chaos. There were the curious, attempting to enter the city, and others trying to sneak through alleys to get into buildings. Teams of students worked around the clock to control the traffic and possible looting.

Some of the students heard faint cries for help emanating from a demolished brick building. The students dug feverishly for hours, and eventually uncovered two adults and a child, all still alive. Others from the university were asked to take up posts downtown and prevent looters from ransacking the damaged stores.

Johnny Burress, a Baylor student, was one of many rescuers who worked downtown through the night of May 11 looking for survivors. In one of the demolished Austin Avenue buildings, he and his fellow rescuers uncovered the body of Ed Berry,

a popular Waco school board member. "I guess he must have been in his office," Burress said. "There were typewriters all around."

A number of Baylor women, including students from the School of Nursing, contributed to rescue efforts by making sandwiches and coffee for rescue workers, tending the wounded, and helping aid workers from organizations such as the Salvation Army and the Red Cross.

TOP Work to search for survivors continued throughout the night, with everyone pitching in, in spontaneous work brigades.

ABOVE Wrecked homes littered Waco and other towns, obscuring all trace of the buildings that originally stood there.

Palm Sunday Outbreak, Great Lakes, USA, 1965

On Sunday, April 11, 1965, many in the Great Lakes region of the United States were outdoors, eager to enjoy the day's beautiful skies and warm temperatures. With this unusually balmy weather, no one could have imagined it would end with such disastrous results—the 1965 Palm Sunday Tornado Outbreak. It was the second worst and deadliest tornado event to affect the region.

ABOVE What used to be inside was now outside. Twin tornadoes tore through Goshen, Indiana, destroying close to 100 trailer homes; this famous "double tornado" killed 36 people.

The Palm Sunday Tornado Outbreak crossed six American states, causing 271 deaths and more than 3,400 injuries. Over 50 counties had damage from the violent storms. US Weather Bureau offices were kept busy as the tornadoes swept through their warning areas. In the 12 hours the outbreak lasted, 51 tornadoes slammed through Iowa, then eastward 475 miles (765 km) to the east of Cleveland, Ohio, and from Bay County, Michigan, southward to just north of Indianapolis, Indiana.

FACTS AND FIGURES

DATE	April 11, 1965
LOCATION	Southern Great Lakes region and northern Ohio Valley; the worst-hit states were Michigan, Indiana, and Ohio
DEATH TOLL	271 dead; 3,400 injured
FORCE	15 at F1, 10 at F2, 5 at F3, 15 at F4, 2 at F5
DAMAGE	US$1.1 billion (2003 value)
COMMENTS	This was the second-biggest tornado outbreak on record, with 47 confirmed tornadoes over a 12-hour span

The first tornado of the day, rating F4, occurred early afternoon in Iowa. By late afternoon, the storm system had intensified over Indiana, where 11 tornadoes struck 20 counties, killing 137 people and injuring more than 1,700. Although many of the tornadoes were rated F4, there were two very destructive F5 tornadoes. Altogether the outbreak was Indiana's worst tornado disaster.

The cause of the outbreak

Before the tornado outbreak the day had been sunny and unseasonably warm, with storms developing in response to a strong low-pressure system that moved through Wisconsin, drawing warm, humid air into southern Michigan. Cooler and drier air at higher altitudes mixing with the moist, warm air near the surface caused the highly unstable conditions that generated the tornadoes.

Forecasters were advised that the jet stream had split into two branches over northern Illinois and southern Wisconsin, much like water in a river flowing around an island. It was this dividing effect that helped lift the air even higher in an already

unstable atmosphere, thus giving the upper level wind dynamics that would quickly raise storms to severe levels and start counterclockwise rotation.

As the day wore on, the skies across the lower Great Lakes region began to develop a somewhat hazy, unusual yellow pinkish color caused by topsoil from Illinois and Missouri being picked up by the strong jet stream winds.

It was at this time that Weather Bureau staff began to really worry. None of their forecasts had predicted severe weather; certainly not this widespread, or of this ferocity. They moved quickly and issued a tornado forecast to cover that area at 1:00 p.m. Unknown to the forecasters, the first tornado had already been on the ground for at least 15 minutes.

Why so disastrous?

When officials of the US Weather Bureau (known today as the NOAA National Weather Service) investigated the high number of fatalities, they were somewhat surprised by the reason—a failure in communicating the approaching storms to the public and community officials. The warning system had

failed. While the Weather Bureau did a good job in disseminating the warnings, members of the public never received them. This was partly a result of power outages and downed telephone lines caused by high winds, and partly because few radio stations were signed up to receive weather warnings. Another important reason was that many people were in church, celebrating Palm Sunday, an important event in the Christian calendar. With lines down, emergency staff in Elkhart, Indiana, could not warn southern Michigan of the approaching danger.

ABOVE "My advice, Sir ... seek shelter" would have been a more appropriate sign for this Great Lakes region gas station, which was toppled by one of the April 1965 tornadoes. In response to the failure of the warning system to alert people in time, the system of official weather warnings now in use was created after the Palm Sunday Outbreak.

SERMON IN A TEMPEST

The Manitou Beach Bible Church was built of stone in 1964 and dedicated in January 1965. It was destroyed by the huge F4 tornado as 50 worshippers were listening to a sermon. The first knowledge of any danger was a loud crash above their heads as the steeple became dislodged and tumbled down the roof. Some people in the back of the church went to investigate: they promptly returned, telling everyone to head for the basement.

Despite a rapid evacuation, nearly two dozen people were still upstairs when the south wall of the church disappeared. The entire building exploded, trapping some in the debris, while scattering others out into the church yard. Three people died later from their injuries.

Super Outbreak, USA and Canada, 1974

The Super Outbreak of April 3 to 4, 1974, was the most destructive tornado occurrence of the twentieth century. During a 16-hour period, 148 tornadoes hit 13 states in the United States and one province in Canada. This was the largest number within any 24-hour period on record. The tornadoes tore out a path of devastation that stretched 2,598 miles (4,181 km).

RIGHT A massive tornado bears down on Xenia, Ohio. It managed to overturn seven cars of the 47-car train that was passing through town at the time.

FAR RIGHT The bumper sticker on this car shows Xenia residents' determination not to be beaten, and to rebuild.

BELOW The Super Outbreak was more extensive than all other outbreaks. Of the 148 tornadoes known to have occurred during the outbreak, 118 had paths over a mile (1.6 km) long. The total path lengths were greater than 2,000 miles (3,200 km).

The 13 states affected were Alabama, Ohio, Georgia, Illinois, Indiana, Kentucky, Michigan, Mississippi, North Carolina, South Carolina, Tennessee, Virginia, and West Virginia, along with Ontario in Canada. The extremely large number of storms and their speed magnified the problems involved in determining the number and sequence of events. There was a rapid development of the tornado outbreak over an extensive area, with numerous tornadoes striking a number of states within a period of a couple of hours. At one stage there was a report of 15 tornadoes simultaneously touching ground. Six tornadoes with an intensity of F5 were also recorded that day.

The Xenia Tornado

Of the Super Outbreak, the most deadly tornado destroyed much of Xenia, a town of 27,000 in Ohio. In the nine minutes that it made contact with the ground, about twice the average, the tornado leveled half the town, destroying 300 homes. Its path varied from ¼ to ½ mile. The degree of devastation makes it the most destructive tornado in United States' history. The Xenia tornado remains a textbook case of the rare and most intense F5 tornado, and it is still studied by aspiring meteorologists in colleges. Apart from Xenia, in the rest of Ohio 12 tornadoes touched down, killing 41 people, injuring more than 2,000, and damaging about 7,000 homes.

Aerial survey of the aftermath

Not all the casualties and losses in the 13 affected states were due to the tornadoes alone. Large hail during the severe thunderstorms and tornadoes contributed considerably to the total damage. Also, straight-line winds rather than tornadic storms caused havoc, particularly to mobile homes. Some of the deaths reported by the Red Cross were caused by heart attacks, not by direct storm injury. The states of Alabama, Georgia, Tennessee, Kentucky, Indiana, and Ohio sustained the greatest storm activity and damage.

After the outbreak, an aerial survey team with up to five aircraft surveying the entire damage area found continuous damage paths up and down steep slopes, across mountain tops, and through deep gorges—types of countryside that tornadoes were formerly believed to circumvent.

Tornado warnings saved lives

In 1974, National Weather Service forecasters could not distinguish tornadoes from other storms on their radarscopes and had to wait for visual confirmation before issuing a tornado warning. On Monday, April 1, 11 severe weather watches were issued, and in that time more than 20 tornadoes developed, from Alabama and Mississippi through the central states into Indiana and Ohio. When on April 3 many people heard the watches and warnings of the possibility of widespread outbreaks, the impact of the April 1 storms was fresh in their minds. This gave them time to take protective action. In Alabama and Tennessee, where severe damage occurred on both days, many lives were saved because of this.

Midwest Tornado Super Outbreak 1974
— Path of individual tornado

Tornado Alley (Colorado, Iowa, Kansas, Minnesota, Nebraska, Oklahoma, South Dakota, Texas)

FACTS AND FIGURES

DATE	April 3 to 4, 1974
LOCATION	Ontario, Canada, and 13 US states
DEATH TOLL	315; 5,484 injured
FORCE	6 tornadoes at F5
DAMAGE	US$600+ million (1974 value)
COMMENTS	The Xenia Tornado was the worst to hit and has become the most studied tornado

While indications of the storms to come were accumulating, there was no prediction of their magnitude, extent, and intensity, or their precise timing and location. Two severe weather watches were issued during the pre-dawn hours on Wednesday, April 3 for portions of the lower Mississippi Valley, but little activity was noted in these areas. The National Severe Storms Forecast Center issued 28 severe weather watches covering almost the entire area from the Gulf of Mexico to the Canadian border and from the Mississippi River to the east coast. During this period, National Weather Service offices issued about 150 tornado warnings. The major activity occurred between 2:00 and 10:00 p.m. on April 3. NOAA's website reports one meteorologist's comments: "The storms were explosive. They would develop on radar and rapidly intensify and go from 25,000 feet to 50 and 60,000 feet [7,600–18,300 m] in height in a very short time. I have seen storms explode like that but not as many as during the super outbreak. It seemed like all of them did. The super outbreak of April 3 and 4, 1974 is by far the worst event that I have worked during my career."

"Deadly storms such as the 1974 super outbreak can and will happen again," said Ken Haydu, meteorologist in charge of the National Weather Service's forecast office in Wilmington, Ohio. "The people who experienced the super outbreak have an important story about tornado awareness and preparedness to pass on to later generations."

THE VIEW FROM THE NATIONAL WEATHER SERVICE

Bobby Boyd, a meteorologist with the National Weather Service in Tennessee, reported (on NOAA's website): "The nation's worst tornado outbreak occurred on April 3, 1974. I was working that day as a forecaster for the National Weather Service in Louisville, Kentucky. We were expecting a major tornado outbreak, and had issued a warning for our local area …

"Later that afternoon, about a half hour after the tornado warning was issued, we observed a thunderstorm approaching Standiford Field from the southwest. A lowered cloud base along the edge of the storm was clearly evident, but we did not see a tornado. The top floor of the terminal building offered an unobstructed view of the storm. As the lowered cloud base moved overhead, we first observed the funnel cloud forming and were able to even see small scale circulations within the descending vortex.

"Suddenly, an instrument shelter, which was bolted to a rooftop deck, collapsed on its side in front of our window. The tornado circulation had reached the roof without a visible funnel. We briefly sought shelter, then crossed the office to look toward the City of Louisville. The tornado was now clearly visible on the ground and was racing northeast into the densely populated city. An I-beam, ripped from the rooftop and thrown onto a car in the adjacent parking lot, marked the beginning of a trail of damage affecting 900 homes and causing millions of dollars of property loss.

"This tornado was one of 148 twisters recorded during the outbreak. For me, it was the most spectacular, since it was the first tornado I witnessed and the only one I have viewed from such a perspective."

Great Plains, USA, 2003

The tornado outbreak of Sunday, May 4, 2003, which caused 37 fatalities, was one of the deadliest in many years. But that Sunday was only the beginning of a week of devastation during which there were more severe weather outbreaks than during any other week in history. In the period from May 4 to 10, there were 393 tornadoes in 19 states, 1,587 reports of large hail, and 740 of wind damage.

RIGHT A home shows heavy damage from a tornado that touched down in the pre-dawn hours of May 5, 2003, near Clarksville, Tennessee. The outbreak began the night before and continued into the morning.

BELOW Linda Hinds looks over the rubble of her home in Pierce City, Missouri. The tornado that struck this city killed two people and left nine others missing. Several of the town's historic buildings were damaged.

There was a tornado outbreak every day during that week. Comparable events were recorded in 1917, 1930, and 1949 before the days of tornado detection, so these records lack the actual number of tornadoes. The week of the Super Outbreak (March 30 to April 5, 1974), which held the previous record for the most tornado reports in one week (245), still retains the record for having more significant and violent tornadoes than any other week in history.

On May 4 there were possibly as many as 80 tornadoes that touched down in eight states during the late afternoon. Of these, many were wide and long, and well documented by storm chasers.

A family of tornadoes passed west and north of Kansas City, causing one fatality. In southeast Kansas and southwest Missouri, a swarm of large, intense tornadoes produced three major damage tracks which wiped out hundreds of homes, dozens of farms, and several entire towns. Further north in Kansas a track moved northeast, killing three before crossing into Missouri, where four more were killed and the town of Stockton was virtually destroyed. The middle storm track caused three deaths in Kansas, and the southernmost track, which caused two deaths in Missouri, included one F3 tornado that almost destroyed Pierce City. There was further death and destruction to the east-northeast in that state.

Intense tornadoes occurred at night in western Tennessee. The deadliest, an F4, devastated the downtown area of Jackson and killed many.

Thus began the record-breaking week. On May 8, an F4 tornado hit Moore, Oklahoma, and portions of southern Oklahoma City, and the very next day, northern portions of the Oklahoma City metropolitan area were struck by a series of tornadoes. On May 10, a very large tornado outbreak struck Missouri and Illinois; the last major tornado

South Dakota, USA, 2003

On June 24, 2003, a total of 67 tornadoes touched down in South Dakota over a period of less than eight hours, equaling the record set in Texas on September 20, 1967 for a single 24-hour period. However, as a calendar day is the minimum baseline used by the Weather Service for its tornado statistics, it means South Dakota cannot claim this remarkable outbreak as a new record.

RIGHT The F4 tornado that destroyed Manchester, South Dakota, as it barreled down a rural road on its approach to the township. Manchester is just one of 13 townships in the county of Kingsbury, in central-eastern South Dakota.

"Everyone at the office knew we were going to have severe weather that day," said Greg Harmon, the meteorologist in charge of the Weather Service forecast office in Sioux Falls, South Dakota, "but I don't think anyone was expecting anything close to a record tornado event; especially since we live in an area that usually sees 24 tornadoes during a year."

More than 350 warnings issued

On the evening of Tuesday, June 24, there were severe thunderstorms across eastern South Dakota. There had been several days of hot, humid weather before the storm system developed. It first pummeled southeastern South Dakota and then redeveloped to produce heavy rain and high winds that damaged homes and farm buildings as it slashed through Minnehaha County. The heavy rains flooded rural roads in western and northern parts of that county. More than 350 warnings, statements, and storm reports were issued by the NOAA Weather Service offices in Aberdeen and Sioux Falls that evening.

The storms spawned a large F4 tornado that destroyed the small community of Manchester in

WEATHER WARNINGS BY THE DOZEN

The benefits of weather warning technology can only be appreciated when comparing the June 24, 2003 tornadoes with those of the first half of the twentieth century, such as the Tri-State Tornado of 1925. Through the evening and early morning hours of Tuesday, June 24, the National Weather Service had issued dozens of tornado warnings across eastern South Dakota in an area stretching from Aberdeen to Watertown and Huron to Sioux Falls. A severe thunderstorm watch had been in effect for 22 South Dakota counties that morning. A flood watch had been posted for the northeast.

It was also suggested that the outbreak of storms had been caused by an unusual jet stream. The jet stream had flowed further south than normal and had brought with it a mass of cool air. The storms were produced when the cool air mass collided with a front of hot moist air. There had been concerns that this unusual weather pattern might have persisted over the Upper Midwest for a considerable time, so residents were encouraged to remain prepared for the threat of further destructive storms.

ABOVE Another tornado, this one an F3, swirls across a South Dakota prairie. The dirt that it kicks up is clearly visible. An F3 tornado is actually capable of lifting cars off the ground.

Kingsbury County. It traveled along a path that was about half a mile (0.8 km) wide and an estimated 25 miles (40 km) long. The winds, which would have been 207–260 mph (333–418 km/h), caused damage extending from 1½ miles (2.4 km) south of Manchester, through the town, to about 2¼ miles

(3.6 km) north of Manchester. Four people were injured. The tornado warning issued by the National Weather Service in Sioux Falls would have given the residents of Manchester 28 minutes' alert—no doubt explaining why no lives were lost.

That no lives were lost during any of the storms is all the more remarkable given the stories of what happened during the night. As the storm hit, a couple heading for a basement managed to reach shelter, but the man was sucked out and carried a block away by the tornado. Two of the injured were in a mobile home that was demolished. Many of the injured had abrasions, deep cuts, and bruises.

"I've seen other tornado damage, but I've never seen farms where everything is gone. Usually, part of the house is standing," said Kingsbury County Sheriff Charles Smith. "It stripped it clean to the foundation. If anyone [had] been home at those places, they would have been dead." Smith reported that a shed was still standing in Manchester, but that every other building in town had been destroyed.

The rural areas north of Manchester were also badly affected by the storm. "There were two farms destroyed, but there weren't any injuries. The one

COMPUTER MODELING TO SIMULATE STORMS AND TORNADO FORMATION

A model called NCOMMAS (NSSL Collaborative Model for Multiscale Atmospheric Simulation) has been developed by Louis Wicker, a research meteorologist at the NOAA National Severe Storms Laboratory in Norman, Oklahoma. The aim is to computationally simulate thunderstorms and their associated tornadoes based on the June 24, 2003 F4 storm that devastated Manchester. The simulation begins with data describing the pre-tornado weather conditions—wind speed, air pressure, humidity, etc. From these initial variables, a virtual storm is born.

The simulation produces 650 billion bytes of data. The snapshots of the evolving storm consist of wind temperature, humidity, and precipitation data every few seconds for more than 3 hours. The resulting simulation takes shape with uncanny similarity to the real thing; eventually, the real and simulated storms will be juxtaposed.

NCSA's visualization team translated the data into a dynamic, high-definition, animated visualization of the tornado's birth and growth. Wicker and others are using the visualization to gain new insights into tornadoes—how and when they form, and why they become strong.

ABOVE This photograph was taken just minutes after the F4 tornado destroyed the town of Manchester, South Dakota. Virtually nothing was left standing in the town.

LEFT Roofing has been wrapped around the broken remains of a tree in the town of Manchester, South Dakota, after the tornado had swept through.

ABOVE What are the odds? Rescuers find a photograph of a tornado in the debris of a house in Manchester, South Dakota, that had itself just been destroyed by a tornado.

RIGHT An F4 tornado roars across a field near Manchester, South Dakota, just minutes after it had destroyed the town.

I went to, there was absolutely nothing left. A pickup up against a tree, a ball of metal. The house was spread across the field. There were pieces everywhere. The foundation was just sitting there. The other one we didn't go to because there was no one home," said Mark Hoek, a volunteer firefighter.

Hoek also spent a short time in Manchester: "That's a total loss. Buildings blown over, trees uprooted, cars smashed up, places where you knew were buildings, there was nothing."

There was a report of a startled basset hound found in the wreckage of a farm by some storm chasers. Somehow the dog had survived, perhaps under fallen debris. Its owners had left just minutes before the tornado leveled the house and farm.

FACTS AND FIGURES

DATE	June 24, 2003
LOCATION	South Dakota, and in particular the small town of Manchester in Kingsbury County
DEATH TOLL	0 deaths; 7 injured
FORCE	F0 to F4
DAMAGE	US$13.46 million
COMMENTS	67 tornadoes over 8-hour period; shares record with Texas for the most tornadoes ever to touch ground within 24 hours

Minnehaha County, South Dakota

Later on Tuesday night, straight-line winds were generated when rain-cooled air from one storm collided with another over Minnehaha County. The force of the wind drove the rain in horizontal sheets and extensively damaged property.

One person reported watching two clouds come together and swirl counterclockwise. From the swirling cloud dropped a tornado looking like a tail or snake that flopped around as would a length of rope hanging from a tree.

At the time, 12-year-old Daylyn Baysinger of Woonsocket took photos of the advancing storm cloud with his digital camera. He observed the storm from the front door of his home.

"It's kind of fun to watch it move and how fast it could go and that stuff was flying and how much damage it could do," he said.

Albert Overweg saw it coming. "The two clouds started coming together, and it started swirling counterclockwise. Then a tail dropped down. The last I saw it was just like a snake, a little tiny rope flopping like it didn't want to give up."

At one farm, there was absolutely nothing left. A ball of metal that used to be pickup up lay against a tree. The house was spread in pieces across a field, leaving just the foundations behind.

Freezes, Blizzards, and Snow Avalanches

When the air temperature at ground level falls below the freezing point of water, which is 32°F (0°C), it means much of the water on the surface will turn to ice, with often spectacular and dangerous results. Freezes, blizzards, and a buildup of snow that may lead to avalanches can form, and all of these have produced great loss of life and infrastructure damage throughout history.

A freeze can produce a magnificent glass-like panorama across the countryside, but its beauty masks a whole raft of dangers and problems. Freezes are generated when rain falls from a layer of air that is warmer than 32°F (0°C) into a layer of air close to the ground that has a temperature below freezing. This can produce sleet, which consists of pellets of solid ice or a kernel of water surrounded by a coating of ice.

A much more dangerous situation occurs when the cold layer near the ground is only just below freezing or is quite shallow. In this instance, it's possible for the rain to reach the surface in liquid form, and then freeze immediately, forming a layer of ice over all outdoor surfaces. When this type of situation continues for several hours, the ice accumulation can become considerable. Sometimes the term "ice storm" is used to describe freezes.

These large accumulations of ice are potentially dangerous for people on footpaths and roadways. Pedestrians can easily fall and break limbs, and there is also an immediate jump in motor vehicle accidents as slippery conditions create mayhem on the roads. As a result, there is dramatically increased pressure on ambulance services and hospital infrastructure.

Power and communications systems carried by overhead wires are particularly vulnerable to ice storms, as the ice accumulation can become heavy enough to snap the wires, or bring down trees that fall across them. This can seriously affect telephone and internet connections, cable television, and all household electricity supplies, including, of course, electrically powered heating devices.

Freezes or ice storms are a serious issue for areas of the northern United States, Canada, northern Europe, Russia, and parts of northern China.

FAR LEFT Frostbite and hypothermia can occur if there is prolonged exposure to the icy conditions of freezes and blizzards. Weather warnings suggest that people stay indoors and keep warm and dry.

LEFT Rapid snow melt from the US blizzard of 1996 caused massive flooding in parts of Frederick, Maryland, USA. The counties of Allegany, Garrett, Frederick, Washington, and Cecil were declared flood disaster areas.

PREVIOUS PAGES During freezes and blizzards, lack of visibility is termed a whiteout. Driving or walking in a whiteout is almost impossible. Residents who live in "snow-prone" areas tend to adapt to and learn to expect these extreme weather patterns.

ABOVE Heavy snowfalls and fallen tree branches weigh down power and communications lines, bringing them to the ground. In wet conditions, electrical lines can become dangerous, even lethal.

Dangerous avalanches

Another possible consequence of a big freeze is the much-feared avalanche. This is an accumulation of snow that has become detached from its area of origin, after which it slides downhill under the influence of gravity. It can be a localized phenomenon, involving only a small volume of snow moving a short distance, or it can involve huge masses of snow and ice moving at tremendous speed for several miles, turning into a destructive battering ram that flattens villages and buries the inhabitants. Historically, avalanches have caused substantial loss of life and property damage, so they are regarded as a real hazard in alpine areas all over the world, with the European Alps, in particular, considered a major danger zone.

Avalanches can come in two basic forms. They can consist of loose, powdery slides or a solid "slab," and both types can occur on mountain slopes varying from 30 to 60 degrees inclination. Normally snow cannot accumulate sufficiently on slopes that are steeper than this. The loose snow type normally starts at a single point and increase in size as it gains momentum down the mountain. The slab-type avalanche occurs when an entire slab of snow breaks away from the main mass and slides downhill; these can also grow in size very quickly.

Which type occurs depends very much on the history of the accumulation of snow. A heavy fall of fresh snow can result in a loose flow avalanche, and more than 12 inches (30 cm) of continuous buildup is regarded as very hazardous. Slab forms can result from the thawing and refreezing of an existing snow-pack, producing unstable, sliding layers of snow. If suitable conditions exist, an avalanche can be

WHAT TO DO IN A BIG FREEZE

1. **MONITOR** all weather warnings that are transmitted through the media, including radio, television, newspapers, and the internet.
2. **IF IN AN AVALANCHE AREA**, don't attempt to ski, hike, or drive without checking to see if warnings have been issued.
3. **STAY INSIDE** during, and immediately after, an ice storm. Both walking and driving will be quite dangerous.
4. **STAY INSIDE** if a blizzard is expected and prepare for a long wait. Make sure you have food and warm clothes available. Be prepared for power outages and have alternative heating and lighting ready for use.
5. **IF CAUGHT** in a motor vehicle in a blizzard, stay inside. Run the engine for around 10 minutes each hour with the heater on, but leave the window down a little for ventilation.
6. **IF CAUGHT** outside in a blizzard, prepare a windbreak or snow cave for shelter. It's most important to get out of the wind, and if possible, start a fire for warmth.

triggered by surprisingly small events. Sunshine can cause surface snow to melt, and the water produced can percolate through the snow cover and act as a trigger. Small vibrations caused by sound, or a skier or snowboarder traversing the area, can also cause a slide. Once under way, an avalanche can accelerate rapidly, building up millions of cubic yards of snow and reaching speeds of up to 125 miles per hour (201 km/h). In big slides, a massive air blast is generated ahead of the snow wall, and this can easily destroy buildings and trees before the snow arrives. In some countries, this wind is known as "the sigh of the avalanche."

After the avalanche has come to a complete standstill, the snow can set in a large, dense mass of ice that is rock-hard, making the rescue of buried victims particularly difficult. Victims are usually killed instantly, crushed by debris carried within the snow wall. Others who become trapped will succumb to suffocation and exposure within an hour. Rescuers, even if they are nearby, cannot hear cries for help, because snow acts as an excellent sound insulator. When searching for people trapped below, rescuers use dogs that "scent" for location, and metal rods or heat-sensing probes that are pushed vertically down into the snow.

The hazards of blizzards

The blizzard is another major hazard of the "big freeze" environment. This is a storm that contains strong winds and heavy snowfall, along with very cold temperatures. The combination of these

ABOVE This glacial avalanche in the Wrangell–St Elias National Park in Alaska, United States, shows the power and force of large amounts of crashing ice and snow. These types of avalanches usually occur as the edge of the glacier melts.

TEN OF THE WORST FREEZES, BLIZZARDS, AND AVALANCHES

JANUARY, 1922	In January, 1922, Washington experienced record snowfalls, with more than 2 feet (61 cm) of snow falling across the city in just 48 hours. The weight of the snow collapsed the roof of the Knickerbocker Theater, killing 98 people inside.
JANUARY, 1967	In January, 1967, a series of blizzards whipped across Chicago, bringing the city to a standstill for nearly two weeks with record snowfalls. Transport ground to a halt and people were unable to get to work. Stores were unattended for extended periods and widespread looting was reported.
DECEMBER, 1990	In what were the worst blizzards for around 20 years, large areas of the European Alps were badly affected in December, with 18 deaths recorded and transport disrupted across many districts.
MARCH, 1993	In March, 1993, a massive blizzard swept across much of the eastern United States, producing record low temperatures across many states, and closing every major airport along the east coast. The eventual damage bill exceeded US$10 billion.
JANUARY, 1996	The great blizzard of 1996 brought much of the eastern United States to a complete halt, and was responsible for over 100 deaths. Schools, offices and airports were closed for several days in some areas as roads became completely impassable.
JANUARY, 1998	One of the worst freezes in the recorded history of Canada occurred between January 4 and 10, when a massive ice accumulation spread across eastern Ontario, southern Quebec, southern New Brunswick and parts of Nova Scotia. Twenty-five people died as a result of the storm and the estimated damage bill was around C$2 billion.
FEBRUARY, 1999	Very heavy snowfalls, followed by a brief period of warming, generated what some experts called "the worst avalanche situation for more than 350 years" across parts of the European Alps during January and February. More than 70 people were killed in avalanches throughout resort towns in France, Italy, and Switzerland, as well as in other areas of Europe.
JANUARY, 2001	The worst blizzard in more than 50 years devastated western China's Xinjiang region, killing 31 people and causing major disruptions to the local infrastructure.
JANUARY, 2002	Much of central Europe, including large areas of Poland and the Czech Republic, was paralysed during early January by massive snowfalls that knocked out most of the road systems. Several people died in the resulting avalanches.
JANUARY, 2002	A massive freeze affected large areas of western and central Oklahoma between January 21 and 29, 2002. The worst icing occurred from west-central through to north-central Oklahoma, with local areas receiving a glaze of ice more than 1 inch (25 mm) thick on exposed surfaces.

FREEZE SEVERITY

The severity of a big freeze is often measured through the "wind chill" factor, which is a combination of temperature and wind speed. Wind carries heat away from the human body and produces a wind chill temperature that is less than the actual temperature.

RIGHT On Lake Superior, Ontario, Canada, a tugboat and freighter dock to wait out a snow storm during one of Canada's worst freezes ever recorded, in 1998. Weather storm watches were continuously issued to warn and prepare people for the severe storm conditions.

elements creates blowing snow; with near-zero visibility, deep snowdrifts, and potentially lethal wind-chill temperatures. A blizzard normally occurs at very low temperatures, and is worse when the existing snow cover consists of fine, light snow that is called "powder."

Blizzards are real hazards in any alpine locality, but are particularly severe in high latitude areas such as the northern United States, Canada, Siberia, and the polar regions. When there is an extensive cover of "powder," a phenomenon called a "whiteout" can occur, where the horizon, sky and ground all lose distinction, and the entire environment becomes a featureless white glow.

Blizzards create a whole variety of hazards for people, particularly hikers, skiers, and snow-boarders. The dangers posed include becoming lost and disoriented; and exposure to wind chill, hypothermia, and frostbite can be lethal. In urban environments, blizzards create dangerous road situations, with reduced visibility and treacherous, slippery driving conditions. Vehicle accident rates soar and parked cars are often either partially or completely buried during heavy snowfalls. As a result, people can become marooned on freeways, sometimes for several days, with potentially fatal results. Transportation systems, both sea and land, are disrupted or damaged by blizzards.

In certain conditions, blizzards will also produce heavy accumulations of snow on city power and communications lines, sometimes bringing them down, and this creates acute social problems because people may be without power and telephones during these very cold periods.

Freezes, blizzards, and snow avalanches can be responsible for triggering other natural disasters, such as landslides and flooding. When avalanches shift large amounts of rocks and debris, sloping ground surfaces can be made unstable, which can result in a landslide. In early spring, melting ice from extreme freezes and the snow from winter blizzards can flow into rivers and dams, causing drainage systems to overflow, creating flood conditions.

ABOVE LEFT In the ice-covered streets of New York, pedestrians walking along Roosevelt Avenue have covered their shoes with plastic bags. In January, 2005, many parts of New York received about a foot (0.3 m) of snow.

ABOVE The Karakoram Range spans the borders of three countries: Pakistan, China, and India. In the isolated area known as Nameless Tower, an avalanche thunders toward a mountaineering base camp.

Blizzard of 1888, USA

March 12, 1888, heralded "The White Hurricane"; one of the worst blizzards in United States history. More than 4 feet (1.2 m) of snow buried the Northeast with drifts up to 50 feet (15 m) deep driven by winds gusting to 80 miles per hour (129 km/h). About 400 people were killed, and property damages were an estimated US$25 million, equivalent to hundreds of millions in today's economy.

The storm began on March 11 following days of mild weather. Low-pressure fronts from the Gulf of Mexico and a western snowstorm converged over the Northeast, bringing torrential downpours. Overnight, the barometric pressures and temperatures dropped rapidly. The strong winds shifted northeast, velocities increasing as rain turned to heavy snow. The storm stalled over the region, braced by two high-pressure fronts over Newfoundland and off the Great Lakes, the second of which pulled cold air from Canada into the New York region. The storm, which struck with a sudden, intense fury, then hovered for more than 36 hours. There were still unbroken record 24-hour snowfalls in New Haven, Connecticut (28 inches/710 mm) and Albany, New York (31 inches/790 mm). An overall average of 40 to 50 inches (1.3 m) of total snowfall buried the northeast.

By 2:30 a.m. on March 12, New Haven had severe whiteout conditions. Just after dawn, those conditions spread to New York, New England, New Jersey, and the regions of Pennsylvania. Winds raged from 40 to 70 miles per hour (64 to 113 km/h) with stronger gusts, while temperatures fell to around 4°F to 5°F (-15°C) in areas. The whiteouts and freezing wind chills paralyzed transportation and caused deadly travel conditions. Communications lines were cut, isolating major cities from Maine to Washington DC. Rural regions were completely cut off. The *Bellows Falls Times*, a Vermont newspaper

FACTS AND FIGURES

DATE	March 11 to 14, 1888
LOCATION	US northeastern seaboard: New York, New England, New Jersey, Pennsylvania, Virginia, Washington DC
DEATH TOLL	Approximately 400
DAMAGE	US$25 million (1888)
WINDSPEED	70 mph (113 km/h) sustained winds with higher gusts to 80 mph (129 km/h)
RAIN/SNOW	40 to 50 inches (1 to 1.3 m) of snow
COMMENTS	One of the more intense blizzards ever recorded in US history. Transportation and communications were paralyzed.

founded in 1856 by A.N. Swain, published a poetic description of the experience: "No paths, no streets, no sidewalks, no light, no roads, no guests, no calls, no teams, no hacks, no trains, no moon, no meat, no milk, no paper, no mails, no news, no thing—but snow, always snow."

New York whiteout

Two of the 400 reported deaths were from New York. These people became lost and disoriented in the whiteout and died from exposure trying to get to jobs or obtain supplies. A famous account from feminist Nancy Sankey Jones outlines the storm's intensity as she watched from her window, as a man tried to cross 96th Street for an hour and a half. "We watched him start, get quarter way across and then flung back against the building on the corner. The last time he tried it, he was caught up on a whirl of snow and disappeared from our view. The following morning seven horses, policemen, and his brother charged the drift, and his body was eventually kicked out of the drift."

Hundreds of ships were damaged, at least 200 sank, and over 100 seamen were killed. Winds and low tides caused record lows in the Delaware

River, and ships ran aground. In New York and New England, snow drifts reaching up to 50 feet (15 m) created impassable walls and mountains.

Unbelievable damage

Prices of food, fuel, and coal skyrocketed as sources dwindled. Railways and shipping lines were halted. The New York-Harlem Railway attempted to punch through one massive drift, and four workers died. Other railways had similar problems. Two express trains collided at Dobbs Ferry without any fatalities, but another collision occurred in Huntington, Pennsylvania and claimed three lives. In Jersey, a snowplow and train ran into each other, causing three more deaths.

Many buildings suffered damage and collapse because of the heavy snow, strong winds, and flash flooding. Some factory roofs were distorted or caved in, and even undamaged buildings were forced to shut down through lack of coal or power. Homes lost roofs and windows; some were completely destroyed.

The "White Hurricane" paralyzed the whole of the northeastern seaboard for nearly a week. Storms of this magnitude, destructiveness, and power are only seen once every five centuries.

As trains pass by on either side, a lone person walks across the Brooklyn Bridge (above) after a blizzard left the bridge and tracks covered in snow. Throughout the blizzard people struggled to go about their daily lives in the freezing and treacherous weather conditions. All transport was hampered by the heavy snow and ice, from Park Row (above, left) to Madison Square (below, left) in New York City.

Alpine "Winter of Terror", Austria, Italy, and Switzerland, 1951

In the winter months of 1950 to 1951, the Swiss, Austrian, and Italian Alps suffered an incredibly intense period of extreme avalanches. While the region is prone to frequent snow avalanches, with several occurring every winter, this winter was particularly remarkable in its severity.

ABOVE In the surreal landscape, rescue workers clear debris and search for survivors well into the night. Since the 1951 avalanche, countries like Switzerland have invested in protective measures, such as heavy forestation and building avalanche barriers to limit the damage and loss of life.

RIGHT Young villagers carry wreaths to the local church for the funeral services of the 19 victims killed when avalanches hit and devastated the village of Vals in Switzerland.

During the course of a three-month period, almost 1,500 avalanches occurred. While some were probably small scale, some 1,000 to 1,100 of the avalanches were in the "damage-causing" classification. The worst of these occurred in January, causing massive damage in dozens of towns and killing more than 275 people.

Weather conditions throughout the region leading up to the avalanches were unusually severe. Warm air currents crossed in from the Atlantic and impacted with masses of cold polar air sweeping downward, causing a season of excessive rain, snowfall, and hurricane-force winds. Between January 15 and 22, snowfalls had dropped 7 feet (2.1 m) of snow on the ground. In the last week of January, the heavy rain and snowfalls caused a series of disasters. Avalanches swept down on over a dozen resort towns throughout alpine regions in Austria, Italy, and Switzerland. More than 45,000 people were trapped, and 240 people were killed as the massive snow slides swept through.

Deadly ice and snow

In Austria, which sustained the worst of the damage, the avalanches destroyed several villages along with thousands of acres of trees and forested land, as well as taking the lives of over 100 people. In Italy, the snowfall became excessive in early February. In the town of Bedretto, an average of about 4 feet (1.2 m) of snow fell on February 12. The result was the start of several large scale avalanches. The village of Airolo was wiped out and 10 people were killed.

In the Graubunden region of Switzerland, at least 650 avalanches were recorded, with a death toll of over 50. The town of Andermatt in Switzerland lies in the Central Spitsbergen region. On January 19, with some 18 inches (46 cm) of snow already on the ground, six successive avalanches struck the town in one hour. The only warning they received was a rush of gale-force winds strong enough to lift people off their feet and tear the roofs off buildings before the first avalanche struck, dumping over 30 feet (9 m) of snow. The last avalanche was followed by a blast of air that sounded like a loud thunder-crack.

The wave of snow barreled into an army barracks, and pushed 4-ton cannons (4.4 t) hundreds of yards down the slope. At least 13 people were killed in the massive slides of snow. Over 900 buildings were destroyed and 92 people were killed in other villages in the region. A number of buildings that had stood for nearly 500 years were destroyed. The series of avalanches that struck the town are referred to as wind-driven or wind avalanches. This is because they are comprised of light, powdery snow, and achieve airborne falls, instead of steady ground flow; they can reach up to 200 miles per hour (322 km/h) as they roar downward. The sheer pressure of the wind pushed in front of the wall of falling snow can throw heavy objects and tear buildings apart.

Learning from past disasters

Over the 50 or so years since the "Winter of Terror," authorities in the alpine regions of Europe have put in a series of warnings and snow blockades to help prevent avalanches. In addition to this, studies in avalanche dynamics and more accurate forecasting are helping to avert such large-scale disasters. Complex computer simulations are designed to predict the likelihood of avalanches in various areas by analyzing data such as total snow and rainfall, changes in weather patterns, and wind speeds. By comparing current data with conditions preceding avalanche disasters in the past, avalanche forecasters are hoping to gain a great degree of accuracy in their predictions and thus better protect life and property.

FACTS AND FIGURES	
DATE	December 1950 to February 1951
LOCATION	Swiss, Austrian, and Italian Alps
DEATH TOLL	More than 700
COST	Thousands of structures and villages were destroyed
RAIN/SNOW	7 to 10 feet (2.1 to 3 m) of snowfall in various regions
COMMENTS	The winter of 1950 to 1951 saw a record-breaking number of avalanches and disasters throughout alpine regions

Peru, 1962 and 1970

On January 10, 1962, tons of snow and ice hurtled down from the slopes of Huascarán Mountain in Peru, demolishing at least nine towns and killing up to 4,000 people in minutes. Eight years later, another avalanche hit Peru.

RIGHT In 1970, a massive avalanche plummeted down Huascarán Mountain, Peru, for almost 6 miles (9.7 km). It crushed the towns of Yungay and Ranrahirca.

A severe storm front on January 9 deposited a massive amount of snow atop Nevado de Huascarán, an extinct volcanic peak. With an elevation of over 22,000 feet (6,710 m), Huascarán is South America's second highest mountain.

By January 10, the run-off from the melting snow had accumulated beneath the ice of glacier 511, weakening the cliff face. In early evening, tons of ice, rock, and snow broke loose from the glacier. The avalanche fell over a mile in just minutes, gathering tons of snow and ice in its rapid descent before hitting Pacucco and Yanamachito, on the lower reaches of the slopes. Both towns were annihilated and nearly 1,000 people were killed. The avalanche roared through into the Santa River Valley canyon.

A terrifying wall of ice

A solid wall of ice and rock well over 40 to 50 feet (12 to 15 m) high and at least 1,000 yards (914.5 m) wide plunged down the valley at over 100 miles per hour (161 km/h). The pressure building up in front of the avalanche caused gale-force winds to precede it down the canyon, destroying buildings in several settlements minutes before impact. The water level in the Santa River rose 26 feet (7.9 m) as the avalanche screamed on.

Within only minutes of the beginning of the avalanche, the settlements of Calla, Chuquibannba, Huaraschuco, and Uchucoto were destroyed. The mass of water, snow, ice, and rock, and the remains of half a dozen villages, swept out of the mouth of the canyon and slammed into the river-plains town of Ranrahirca.

Casualties were estimated at between 2,500 and 4,000, but some think it may be even higher—the actual total is not known. Only 50 people from Ranrahirca survived. Mayor Caballero said, "In eight minutes, Ranrahirca was wiped off the map."

Emergency services director Colonel Umberto Ampuera called the disaster "a scene from Dante's inferno." While many victims were simply buried by the crushing wall of ice and rock that fell on their homes, some people were carried along by the swollen river tides that were up to 60 miles (97 km) downstream, to the coastline.

The Peruvian Air Force flew in supplies and rescue troops to search for survivors and bring aid to the isolated regions. The Acting Secretary-General of the United Nations, U Thant of Burma, offered any aid needed from the UN Children's Fund and the Technical Assistance Board to Peruvian President Manuel Prado. With assistance, Ranrahirca began the long road to recovery.

A repeat performance

On May 31, 1970 at 3:20 p.m., an earthquake that lasted for one minute, at a magnitude of 8 on the Richter scale, struck offshore near Chimbote on Peru's northeast coast, triggering the largest South American avalanche ever recorded. A massive cliff of ice and rock over 1 mile (1.6 km) long and more than 3,000 feet (915 m) wide broke free from the northern mountain face and roared down Huascarán.

ABOVE Only 400 survivors were left in the Ranrahirca region in the wake of the second avalanche in 1970. Mass funerals for the victims of the avalanche were held by the survivors and nearby townspeople.

FACTS AND FIGURES

DATE	January 10, 1962 and May 31, 1970
LOCATION	Huascarán Mountain, Peru
DEATH TOLL	2,500 to 4,000 (1962); 20,000 (1970)
DAMAGE	12 villages destroyed in the combined avalanches
WINDSPEED	100 mph (161 km/h)
RAIN/SNOW	Unknown
COMMENTS	Total death toll of both disasters is between 52,000 and 55,000 people

Plateau d'Assy, France, 1970

A short time after midnight on April 16, 1970, several hundred tons of rock, ice, and snow thundered down a mountain slope near Sallanches in the French Alps, slamming with devastating force into a children's hospital. One of the children's dormitories and a building housing hospital workers was swept away in its path. A total of 72 people were killed in the tragedy.

Plateau d'Assy is near Passy city in the Haute-Savoie area of the Rhône-Alpes region of France, and has an average altitude of about 1,831 feet (558 m), though its highest regions have an elevation up to 9,019 feet (nearly 3 km). Plateau d'Assy, a scenic alpine town that is popular with tourists and climbers, lies at about 3,281 feet (1 km). The historic alpine Martel-de-Janville Sanatorium in Plateau d'Assy is a hospital for children, specializing in the care and treatment of those trying to recover from tuberculosis. It lies under the mountain face Tête du Colloney, with an elevation of 8,832 feet (2.6 km). The sanatorium is a landmark building where climbers seek to start their climb; it is also the place they leave details of their intended route with the reception desk in case of emergency.

In the early morning hours of April 16, following a sudden and unpredictable thawing period, a massive snow layer broke loose at nearly 6,000 feet (nearly 2 km) elevation. The snow thundered down the mountain slope, collecting ice, mud, and rock into a several hundred-ton mass of debris falling at a speed of over 100 miles per hour (161 km/h). At 600 feet (183 m) wide and at least 60 feet (18 m) high, the solid, frozen wall roared down toward the sanatorium.

At the sanatorium, a "great boom" was heard; it sounded like the firing of a "huge cannon." Despite their best efforts, medical workers at the hospital were only able to evacuate the girls' dormitories in time. With the pre-dawn darkness, rocks, and ice working against them, they were unable to get to the other dormitories before the avalanche struck.

Tragedy strikes

The boys' dormitories, a concrete structure housing some 55 sick children all under the age of 15, was directly in the path of the hurtling wall of ice. The avalanche destroyed the building, and went on to flatten the chalet that housed at least a dozen-and-a-half sleeping members of the hospital's personnel.

Carrying the wreckage of these two buildings, the avalanche continued on, skimming the side of a hospital wing that housed over 125 patients and at least 70 more staff members. A number of

eyewitnesses said that the massive slide of snow and ice was terrifying, as it "moved at an incredible speed and carried each of the dormitories away like flimsy pieces of straw."

After cutting its 1,000 feet (305 m) swathe of total destruction, the avalanche had expended its energy. The devastating avalanche had claimed the lives of 72 victims. Contractors and rescue workers were immediately rushed in to clear the area and search for survivors, using shovels, earthmoving equipment and rescue dogs. After a grueling 18 hours of digging through the debris, they had recovered only 19 bodies. After days of digging and searching, the bodies of all the victims were finally retrieved and accounted for.

French government under fire

French Minister Boulin flew to Plateau d'Assy to visit the disaster site. He came under fire for ignoring what was considered an early warning sign two weeks earlier—a smaller avalanche in the vicinity of the hospital. Minister Boulin insisted that experts had conducted a thorough investigation and found that there were no signs that another avalanche was likely. He reassured the public that if there had been any such sign or danger, the children would have been evacuated. He said the event was "as unforeseen as an earthquake," that the incident had occurred without warning.

Many avalanche researchers believe that mountain regions which experience any sudden warming or thawing will have a strong likelihood of slides or avalanches occurring.

ABOVE Desperate rescue workers painstakingly search for any surviving children after an avalanche of mud, rocks, and packed snow smashed the health sanatorium at Plateau d'Assy in the French Alps.

FAR LEFT, ABOVE The picturesque apparently peaceful Rhône-Alpes region of France belies the horror and destruction that can occur when an avalanche sweeps through the area.

FAR LEFT, BELOW As twilight approaches and the daylight is disappearing, there is a race against the clock to retrieve the bodies and clear away any dangerous debris.

FACTS AND FIGURES

DATE	April 16, 1970
LOCATION	Plateau d'Assy, in the Haute-Savoie area of the Rhône-Alpes region, France
DEATH TOLL	72
DAMAGE	Damage and destruction of structures of the Alpine Martel-de-Janville Sanatorium
ESTIMATED VOLUME	Avalanche 60 feet (18 m) high, 600 feet (183 m) wide, moving at 100 mph (161 km/h).
COMMENTS	The Martel-de-Janville Sanatorium is a hospital specializing in the care and treatment of children with tuberculosis

East Coast of the USA, 1993

In March 1993, a super storm struck the US east coast, affecting every state from Florida to Maine. Hurricane-force winds and record lows plunged the east coast into massive blizzard conditions. Over 300 people were killed, billions of dollars worth of damages were incurred, and some 130 million people were affected by the storm's fury.

RIGHT Despite being spring, New York's financial district is swamped with snow. People rug up and face the unusual wintery conditions as they travel to and from work. In some cases, it was safer to walk than risk driving on the icy roads and freeways.

In early March, weather indications began showing the development of a powerful storm front. A low-pressure region formed into a cyclone in the Gulf of Mexico on March 12. Rapidly intensifying, it made landfall in northern Florida on March 13, causing excessive rainfall, winds of up to 110 miles per hour (177 km/h), and 13-foot (4 m) storm surges. Eleven tornadoes touched down in the southern region as the cyclone-driven storm raged across the country.

At the same time, over the Midwest, western airflows fed by chilled arctic winds had created a high-pressure system, which was pushed into the middle of the country by strong southward weather currents. The snow and rain then moved eastward from the west coast, mixing with an arctic weather system coming down from Canada.

A record-breaking storm front

The storm front moving northward from Florida provided the final ingredient in a recipe for disaster. All the factors ready to trigger a record-breaking nor'easter storm moved into place. Three fronts met over the Southeast, heralding one of the most frightening snowstorms ever to hit the coast.

Record temperatures plunged the coastline into a deep freeze from Kentucky to Maine. While not the

100-YEAR AND 500-YEAR STORMS

Storm models and theories are based off the probabilities produced from weather prediction models and the records of past weather patterns. Modern meteorologists are able to make better and more long-range predictions of upcoming storm fronts and patterns. The 100- or 500-year storm theory is based on these predictions and the analysis of climatic weather cycles for a region over an extensive period of time. A 100-year storm means the probability of the conditions that would create such a major weather event fitting the storm intensity category is only likely to occur once in 100 years. In any given year, a 1 percent chance exists of a 100-year storm event happening. The applies to a super storm, such as the Great Blizzard of 1993, which require conditions that are likely to occur only once in 500 years, or a 0.2 percent probability.

TOP United States Coast guards attempt to clear heavy snow deposits from the deck of their boat to prevent it from sinking into the icy waters of Scituate Harbor, Massachusetts.

ABOVE Whenever there was a break from the falling snow, people dug through record inches of snow and compacted ice. In severe snowstorms, drivers were forced to leave their cars and find shelter in nearby refuges to patiently wait out the storm.

most powerful or intense storm to strike the region, hitting only at Category 3 strength on the Safford-Simpson scale, it was the largest storm front ever recorded. Affecting 26 states and parts of Canada, the storm reached all the way to Texas. Along the coast, wind speeds were measured at anywhere from 99 miles per hour (159 km/h) to 120 miles per hour (193 km/h) and storm surges flooded coastal regions with 6 to 12 feet (1.8 to 4 m) of water.

From March 13 through March 15, the Great Blizzard held sway over much of the country. For the first time in history, every airport on the east coast between Georgia and Nova Scotia was closed due to the storm. Close to 60,000 lightning strikes hit as thunderstorms moved along the coast for three days.

Southern states completely unprepared for blizzard

States were blanketed with 5 to 50 inches (12.7 to 127 cm) of snowfall. In the South, Florida was hit with massive thunderstorms and tornadoes; approximately 44 people died. South of Tampa, the sea levels rose to more than 12 feet (4 m) and flooded the coast. Eleven people were swept out to sea by storm surges. These massive storm surges also collapsed and washed away coastal homes on the west coast and along the Outer Banks of North Carolina. In the north of Florida, snow and hurricane-force winds closed airports, schools, and public transportation systems, and left 10 million people without power in their homes.

In Chattanooga, Tennessee, massive snowfalls of up to 4 feet (1.2 m), shut down the city and outlying regions; they too were unprepared for an

FACTS AND FIGURES

DATE	March 12 to 15, 1993
LOCATION	United States and Canada, affecting 26 states from Texas to Maine
DEATH TOLL	More than 300
DAMAGE	Over US$10 billion
WINDSPEED	Peak winds recorded at 120 mph (193 km/h)
RAIN/SNOW	Highest recorded snowfall in a day was 56 to 60 inches (1.4 to 1.5 m)
COMMENTS	This super storm took people by surprise as it happened in spring and in conditions where people and forecasters didn't expect such a ferocious storm.

unprecedented accumulation of snow. The record snowfall to any area during the storm fell at Mt Leconte, Tennessee, where approximately 56 inches (142 cm) of snow was recorded. Newfound Gap, on the Tennessee and North Carolina borders, was buried in 5 feet (1.5 m) of snow.

London, Kentucky had some 22 inches (55 cm) of snow, while Perry County Kentucky suffered an all-time record high of 30 inches (76 cm). Heavy winds, especially in the flatlands, blew snows into drifts in excess of 35 feet (10.7 m). Throughout Kentucky, over 4,000 drivers were stranded and had to seek refuge in the emergency shelters that were set up in schools and public offices.

Across the southlands, buildings collapsed and snowdrifts caved in roofs and tore decks off houses. Over 200 people had to be rescued from the Appalachian hiking and vacation areas. More snow fell in the southern regions than the New England emergency snow management system could handle. Unused to dealing with heavy snows, the entire south was crippled for days. As a state of emergency was declared along the coast. Every interstate highway from Atlanta, Georgia north was restricted or closed. All secondary highways were inaccessible.

Storm tolls in the north

In the northeast, anywhere from 12 to 20 inches (30 to 51 cm) of snow fell over three days. This is not a significant amount by comparison to other nor'easters or northern blizzards, such as the legendary blizzard of 1978 that dumped record snows from New Jersey to Maine and paralyzed the entire northeast for over a week. However, combined with the storm conditions and widespread effect of the super storm, the snow caused much disruption to transportation and power.

Whiteout conditions varied along the coast. Grantsville, Maryland had 47 inches (119 cm) of snow, while snow levels in Syracuse, New York reached 43 inches (109 cm). In comparison, Roanoke, Virginia only received 16 inches (41 cm). The highest wind speeds of the storm were recorded on Mt Washington, New Hampshire. Hailed as the windiest place on Earth, gusts from the storm front topped at 144 miles per hour (232 km/h). Pittsburgh, Pennsylvania suffered a record temperature low of 1°F (-17.2°C), with snow falling at a rate of up to 3 inches (7.6 cm) per hour. The total accumulation in the region over three days was 24.6 inches (62 cm).

Legacy of a super storm

Almost 25 percent of the airline flights for the entire country were cancelled. Power and communications lines were torn down or destroyed. The freezing temperatures along the coast created dangerous

wind chills and prevented emergency management workers from clearing icy roads. Hundreds of homes were damaged or collapsed, and warehouses and factory roofs fell in due to the crushing weight of the heavy snow.

The total snowfall was calculated at a weight of between 5.4 and 27 billion tons (4.9 to 24.5 billion t) of snow. An estimated US$10 billion in damages and recovery costs were tallied up in the affected regions. The destructive storm was unique, a once-in-500-years phenomenon caused by a near-perfect alignment of weather patterns. Its massive scope and the widespread effect across so many US regions at once left an indelible mark on those areas.

ABOVE A snowstorm slows down traffic in New York streets. Even though it is daytime, drifts of swirling snow cast a darkening pall, adding to the disruptive effect of the super storm on the lives of people across many regions of the United States.

A STORM BY ANY OTHER NAME

It was springtime and no one expected a storm with the force of a hurricane to hit American shores. As this particular hurricane happened out of hurricane season it wasn't assigned a name, and it has since been called "the No-name Storm" or "the Super Storm." It is also referred to as the "Storm of the Century." Forecasters told people to expect some severe weather, but the weather was warm, so few people paid attention to the warnings.

Cotopaxi, Ecuador, 1996

On March 28, at 6:03 p.m. Cotopaxi Province suffered an earthquake that shook the mountain. Registering a magnitude 5.7 on the Richter scale, it affected over 70 local communities, 27 of which are built at altitudes averaging 9,840 feet (3,001 m). Latacunga and Pujili were among the most seriously hit. This earthquake triggered an avalanche.

RIGHT Search and rescue teams use metal probes to find any living survivors in the Cotopaxi avalanche. If a person is trapped in an air pocket of an avalanche, they can survive for several days.

In Latacunga, the earthquake killed 19 people, injured 58 and left over 1,000 homeless. Several of the affected communities had 75 to 100 percent destruction of houses and buildings, and over 3,200 feet (976 m) of water pipes were damaged, causing severe hardship in the region. In Pujili, thousands were left homeless and without power, clean water or means of heating. Most of the homeless were forced to live in temporary shelters and tents. Many people's livelihoods were affected and some were left with little hope for a future, as areas of farmland began to subside in the aftermath of the quake.

Cotopaxi claimed more lives the following week. The March 28 earthquake, combined with heavy spring snowfalls, created dangerous conditions on the slopes of the Cotopaxi volcano. A little more than a week later, on Easter Sunday, a group of climbers were visiting the mountain. The glacier face, de-stabilized by the earthquake and further weakened by runoffs from the heavy snowfalls, dislodged suddenly. The massive avalanche descended with crushing speed, killing between 8 and 11 tourists near a hotel's uphill courtyard as it thundered down the mountainside. Dozens more were trapped in the snow slide until rescuers could reach them.

BELOW Rising 19,388 feet (5,913 m) above sea level and towering above the Andean mountains, the Cotopaxi volcano is one of Ecuador's most active volcanoes. There have been more than 50 eruptions since 1738. Many of these eruptions have triggered devastating mudslides and avalanches.

A constant threat

Volcán Cotopaxi is located in the Eastern Cordillera in Cotopaxi Province, Ecuador. It is the tallest active volcano in the world. Cotopaxi, whose summit has an elevation of 19,388 feet (5,913 m), is a strato-volcano. A stratovolcano, such as Mt Fuji or Mt Shasta, is composed of alternating layers of lava and ash, bearing pyroclastic material (shards of volcanic rock, crystal, glass, ash and pumice) material. The nearly symmetrical cone is covered by a glacier starting at the 16,404-foot (5,003 m) line. Cotopaxi, which means "smooth neck of the moon," was first scaled by Wilhelm Reiss and Angel Escobar in 1872.

An eruption in 1877 caused melting snow and ice to flow over 60 miles (97 km) from the mountain. Its last recorded eruption was in 1904, though there are unconfirmed reports of a small eruption in 1942. Since that time, the volcano has had increasingly active steam emissions, slides of melting snow, and small earthquakes.

Latacunga, which translates literally as "God of the Waters" and more figuratively as "Land of My Choice," is the capital city of Cotopaxi Province, lying only 9 miles (14.5 km) southwest of Volcán Cotopaxi. Destroyed and rebuilt from volcanic eruptions and earthquakes 10 times, the mountain

FACTS AND FIGURES

DATE	March 28 and April 5 to 6, 1996
LOCATION	Cotopaxi Mountain, Ecuador
DEATH TOLL	11 (avalanche); 19 (earthquake)
DAMAGE	Extensive (buildings and water supplies)
WINDSPEED	not applicable
RAIN/SNOW	not applicable
COMMENTS	The March 28 earthquake destabilized the glacier face that collapsed in April.

is a constant threat to the residents of the city. The last disaster there was in Easter of 1996.

Cotopaxi's deadly charm

The adventurous spirit of many climbers, skiers, and winter sports enthusiasts cannot resist the natural beauty and allure of the slopes of the Ecuadorian volcano. Because the mountain has the highest number of clear days each year out of all the Ecuadorian Andes and a smooth and regular-shaped cone, it is irresistible for the thousands who brave the climb each year. Climbing activities on the mountain are an industry, and there are hundreds of guides and trails available. Below lies the expanse

of Cotopaxi National Park, where roundups for the Ecuadorian rodeo take place. There are also the numerous outposts and lodges along the bottom slopes, and the Quito metropolitan center is only about 24.8 miles (40 km) to the northwest.

Climbers, hikers, and skiers who are less familiar with the facts about how avalanches can be triggered are at constant, significant risk. The upsurge in the volcano's activity in the early 2000 also increases the risks of changes to the region and instability of snow layers. While guides are generally trained in how to avoid danger areas, such an active and highly frequented region puts a great many people in the path of possible future disasters on the slopes.

ABOVE Cotopaxi, with its spectacular national park surroundings, is a mountain climber's dream. It is situated in north-central Ecuador on the border of the Cotopaxi, Napo, and Pichinca provinces. Here a climber is crossing a crevasse on the climb down from the summit.

The Blizzard of 2003, USA

The two-part President's Day Storm of 2003 pounded the United States' midwestern and southern regions for days, reaching the east coast on February 15 with light snowfalls. The second part hit the northeast with the fury of a blizzard on February 16, soon becoming a deadly nor'easter with whiteout conditions, terrifying snowstorms, and dangerous wind chills.

Record snowfalls across the seaboard paralyzed major cities, and buried most of the United States northeastern states in snowfalls from 18 to 40 inches (45 to 120 cm). Gale-force winds blew the snow into high drifts, effectively shutting down coastal transportation. The blizzard caused 44 deaths, cost over US$65 million in repair and snow removal, and over US$1 billion in other damages.

By February 10 there were warnings that a major snow event would occur by the weekend, and that this would be brought in by two successive storm fronts. On February 14, the initial storm front began in the Rocky Mountains, causing heavy rain, snow, and freezing across the country. Iowa had approximately 11 inches (28 cm) of snowfall, and ice storms froze and shutdown Kentucky.

Snow started falling in Washington DC, Virginia, and Maryland on February 15. A low-pressure front

FACTS AND FIGURES

DATE	February 14 to 18, 2003
LOCATION	US northeast, midwest, and south from Tennessee through to Nebraska and from Maine to West Virginia
DEATH TOLL	44
DAMAGE	More than US$1.5 billion
WINDSPEED	60 mph (97 km/h)
RAIN/SNOW	16 to 40 inches (41 to 102 cm) of snow
COMMENTS	Even with the storm's passing, the conditions throughout the eastern seaboard remained dangerous. Travel conditions and transportation remained treacherous for days. Heavy equipment and manpower were in high demand.

formed in the Carolinas as the storm slowly climbed northward, creating very heavy precipitation from Tennessee to West Virginia. Overnight, the low front was impacted by a cold mass of air coming down from Canada, and just before dawn on February 16, heavy snow began falling at a rate of approximately 2 inches (5 cm) per hour across the DC metropolitan region. Over the next five hours, Washington DC became blanketed in almost a foot of snow.

Fueled by the cold air mass, the storm built up momentum quickly, dropping record amounts of snow. It fell up to 4 inches (10.2 cm) per hour as the storm headed into Philadelphia, with temperatures dropping to 15°F (-10°C).

The second storm strikes

By evening on February 16, the snow had become sleet and freezing rain in Delaware's south, and a state of emergency had been declared for Virginia, Pennsylvania, Maryland, and Delaware. Overnight, another low-pressure system off the Virginia coast, moving northeast, upgraded the storm to a nor'easter, and it struck New York and New England on the morning of February 17.

Snow stopped late that night in New York, but continued in Boston on February 18 before losing its intensity. Snowfalls ranged from around 16.7 inches (42 cm) at Reagan National Airport, Washington's fifth-highest amount on record, to 40 inches (102 cm) in Garrett County, Maryland. Boston had 27 inches (69 cm), while New York received 20 inches (51 cm), the fourth-highest total ever recorded in its weather history. With 27 inches (69 cm), Baltimore, Maryland had some its highest levels of snowfalls.

The State Department of Transportation of Rhode Island used its entire fleet of 400 snow-clearing vehicles to clear the roads for stranded commuters.

There were 44 fatalities across 13 states. In the state of Tennessee, a seven-year-old girl and her 12-year-old brother died after being swept away in a flooded stream. Four of the deaths in Maryland were also children, killed by carbon monoxide poisoning in snowbound cars. Major airports in Washington, Pennsylvania, and New York shut down and over 2,000 flights were cancelled. In Baltimore, the roof of the historic 1884 Baltimore and Ohio Railroad museum collapsed, destroying many of the valuable displays of railway artifacts. A roof collapsed at an Edison, New Jersey trade school, killing one man. The heavy snowfall and the extensive flooding from the melting of the snow caused structural damage across the affected regions.

The heavy snowfalls made driving near impossible (above). The residents of the US Northeast began digging out snowdrifts that were several feet high to clear the way for their cars (far left, above). Commuters frequently experienced vehicle breakdowns due to the severe conditions and many were forced to face the bitter outdoor conditions (far left, below).

WHAT IS A NOR'EASTER?

A nor'easter is a powerful storm that occurs in America between October and April, and has a counter-clockwise center of rotation like a hurricane, with winds from the northeast. Two elements create the necessary conditions—a warm low-pressure system from the Gulf Stream providing counter-clockwise winds, and a cold high-pressure system from Canada with a clockwise rotation. The warm air cutting up through the cold air creates an unstable front; the more disparate the temperatures, the faster and more violent the storm. A nor'easter brings immense dark storm clouds, heavy rain or snowfall, flooding, storm surges, and gale-force winds.

Boston, USA, 2005

In January 2005, the northeastern United States was hit by an intense nor'easter hailed as the most severe blizzard to strike the region since the 1920s. Airports and ground transport were halted across the corridor's metropolitan region as winds gusted up to the strength of a Category 1 hurricane, and pushed the snow into immense drifts.

A t least 20 deaths have been directly attributed to the blizzard. An average of 24 to 36 inches (61 to 91 cm) of snow fell rapidly in many regions. While the storm's ferocity was most focused on New England, the entire northeast felt the effects. Cold weather and deep freeze warnings were issued as far south as northern Florida.

In the early evening hours of Saturday January 22, 2005 snow began falling lightly across the region; it picked up as night fell. Between 10:00 p.m. and midnight, the low-pressure air was impacted by a high-pressure flow coming up the Atlantic coast, and the storm upgraded into a full-scale nor'easter. Massachusetts Governor Mitt Romney and Rhode Island Governor Don Carcieri declared a state of emergency.

While no widespread mandatory evacuations were issued, many weather-wise New Englanders evacuated themselves. In Scituate, Massachusetts, the US National Guard assisted in a partial evacuation in anticipation of severe coastal flooding.

BELOW In the deserted streets, a sole pedestrian struggles against the freezing gale-force winds that whistled through the city's central district. Many of Boston's residents were forced to stay in the city as the blizzard conditions made it impossible for them to return to their homes for days.

Regional disasters

In Maine, the wind-chill factor plunged temperatures down into a range of -27°F (-32.7°C) to -33°F (-36.1°C). Snowfalls across the northeast ranged from 21 inches (53 cm) in New Jersey to 24 inches (61 cm) in New Hampshire and 38 inches (97 cm) in Salem and Plymouth, Massachusetts. New York City received up to 15 inches (38 cm), and one fatality occurred there when a 10-year-old girl was hit by a snowplow.

Throughout early Sunday morning, the wind increased, and there was nearly a foot of snow on the ground by dawn. By 9:00 a.m., the storm's full force hit eastern Massachusetts, with whiteout and blizzard conditions that lasted more than eight hours. Snowfall increased, at 3 to 5 inches (7.6 to 12.7 cm) per hour. In Roxbury, a young boy was found dead from carbon monoxide poisoning in a car: the engine was still running and the tailpipe was snow-clogged. A 64-year-old retired reporter suffered a heart attack while trying to shovel snow in Brooklyn.

While Massachusetts was the worst affected region of New England, Cape Cod took the brunt of the storm. Wind speeds reached 55 to 78 miles

per hour (88 to 126 km/h) on the Cape, with gusts up to 84 miles per hour (135 km/h) recorded on Nantucket Island. The island also lost power from Saturday until Sunday night, and emergency crews struggled to rescue people isolated by snow drifts over 6 feet (1.8 m) high.

Transportation, too, was affected. Boston's Logan International Airport was shut down for 28 hours. While one runway reopened at 8:00 a.m. on Monday, a power loss that same afternoon delayed operations again. Nine hundred flights were grounded at New York's Newark, Kennedy, and LaGuardia airports. Philadelphia International was closed from Saturday into Sunday morning.

Boston's heavy winter

By Sunday morning, downtown Boston looked like an arctic ghost town. Mounds of snow piled from winds and plows loomed more than 5 feet (1.5 m) high along the sides of roadways. Winds roaring through the artificial canyons of downtown buildings were strong enough to push people off their feet at crossroads. Visibility was limited to a white, swirling wall of snow; the dim shadows of

buildings could barely be seen. While very few non-emergency vehicles braved the streets, one car spent over 20 minutes trying to traverse a single city block before skidding into a snow bank. A number of city residents and visitors were snowed in at downtown hotels, while hotel supplies slowly ran out.

FACTS AND FIGURES

DATE	January 22 to 24, 2005
LOCATION	Northeastern coast, New England region of the USA
DEATH TOLL	At least 20
COST	US$3 million
WINDSPEED	84 mph (135 km/h) gusts recorded on Nantucket Island
RAIN/SNOW	24 to 36 inches (61 to 91 cm)
ESTIMATED VOLUME	Snow drifts reached over 6 feet (1.8 m) in height
COMMENTS	For the first time in decades the entire northeastern corridor of the United States, including airports, transport, power, was shut down for nearly 24 hours, causing a total blackout.

ABOVE Boston looked more like Siberia than the east coast of the United States. Many office workers had to cross open park areas, which were very windy, in an attempt to keep out of the more severe wind and snowstorms in other areas.

Floods

A simple definition of a flood is the inundation of land by large amounts of water. Floods can be produced by excessive rainfall, causing rivers and waterways to overrun their normal channels and spread out across the adjacent countryside. It can also be caused by the ocean being driven inland across low-lying areas, usually by storm-force winds, such as those that occur in hurricanes.

Floods nearly always involve significant property loss, and in many cases, loss of life, and are often classed as natural disasters. However, in some areas, floods are a positive contribution. In the case of the Nile River, for example, floods have always sustained agriculture—and therefore civilization—for thousands of years. Many tropical regions depend on seasonal flooding to nourish crops and livestock, and to provide water that can be stored for the upcoming dry season.

The floods that tend to be the worst disasters are those which occur in areas where floods are not part of the normal climate, or, for flood-prone areas, those that are well above the usual scale of inundation.

The flash flood

A particularly dangerous form—flash flooding— occurs when intense, short-term rainfall events produce a larger amount of water than can be absorbed by the surrounding soil, or in the case of an urban environment, by the existing drainage system. The water then begins to run across the surface, and in some cases devastating floods can result.

The usual cause of flash flooding is intense, slow-moving thunderstorm activity, which is capable of dumping phenomenal amounts of water over a small area in a short time. These thunderstorms typically have a life cycle of only 1 to 2 hours, but during that time raging walls of water can result, often moving at high speed and causing massive property damage and loss of life.

In an urban environment, particularly a central business district, impervious substances, such as bitumen, concrete, and tiles, have replaced much of the natural soil and vegetation cover. This exacerbates the situation; with the water tending to rapidly overflow from drains, it is then channeled down the streets, spilling into low-lying areas.

LEFT In 1997, levees on the San Joaquin River in the California's Central Valley broke and flooded farmlands in the county of Tracy.

PREVIOUS PAGES Parked cars are partially submerged in floodwater outside homes in Tualatin, Oregon, USA.

BELOW In the aftermath of Hurricane Katrina in 2005, New Orleans, Louisiana, was left with streets that had become deep rivers as levee banks were breached. Debris was strewn in trees, deposited by the massive storm surge that accompanied the hurricane.

TEN OF THE WORST FLOODS

FEBRUARY, 1893	Phenomenal rain from a tropical cyclone caused the Brisbane River, which runs through Brisbane in Queensland, Australia, to burst its banks. Major flooding spread across much of the city, with colossal property damage resulting.
SEPTEMBER, 1900	A monster hurricane generating winds in excess of 120 miles per hour (193 km/h) drove a 15-foot (4.6-m) high storm surge across Galveston, Texas. Thousands died in what is still one of the worst natural disasters in the history of the United States.
JULY TO AUGUST, 1931	During the summer of 1931, particularly heavy rain along parts of the Yangtze River in China produced record floods across the area, with devastating results. It is estimated that over 3.5 million people died through drowning, disease, or starvation following the inundation.
JANUARY, 1953	An intense low-pressure cell produced a massive storm surge along the east coast of England, as well as a catastrophic breaching of the dikes in the Netherlands. Over 2,000 people died and thousands of acres of land were inundated with seawater.
NOVEMBER, 1970	A powerful tropical cyclone drove a huge storm surge across low-lying parts of Bangladesh, resulting in the deaths of 300,000 to 500,000 people. It devastated homes and destroyed farmland.
JULY, 1976	An intense, slow-moving thunderstorm dumped approximately 8 inches (20.3 cm) of rain in an hour at the head of the Big Thomson River canyon in Colorado. A massive flash flood swept down the river gorge, drowning 145 people and causing millions of dollars' worth of damage.
SEPTEMBER, 1980	During September and October of 1980, persistent heavy rain over a period of several days produced major flooding across northern and central Thailand, including the capital city, Bangkok. Massive evacuations followed, with over 200,000 people affected.
APRIL TO OCTOBER, 1993	Several weeks of high rainfall during the summer of 1993 resulted in massive flooding across the Mississippi River basin, producing a major inundation that lasted for a protracted period. A damage bill of around US$15 billion resulted.
AUGUST, 2005	The intensely strong Hurricane Katrina produced a deadly storm surge along the coastlines of Louisiana, Mississippi, and Alabama, resulting in the catastrophic inundation of New Orleans. More than 1,600 people died in the disaster.
JANUARY, 2005	During early January, 2005, heavy rain fell for nearly two days across the Cumbria area of northwestern England, resulting in some of the worst flooding in over 150 years. Mass evacuations followed, and more than 3,000 properties were flooded.

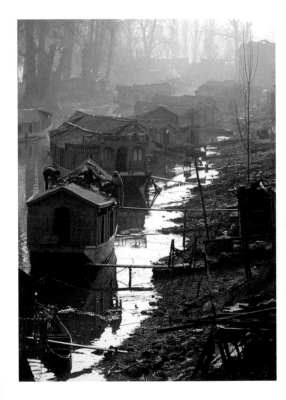

Flash flooding can also occur in deserts where the ground has become very hard, and in areas where rocky canyons or gorges confine the water to a narrow channel. An example of this occurred in the United States on July 31, 1976, in the Big Thompson Canyon, Colorado, when a heavy thunderstorm at the head of the gorge produced a huge wall of water that swept downward, killing 145 people. The force of the water was so great that large boulders lying on the canyon floor were rolled for miles downstream.

The flash flood tends to dissipate almost as quickly as it begins; it has a life of only a few hours.

Devastating broad-scale floods

Compared with the flash flood, broad-scale flooding generally has a much longer timescale. There is often a buildup period of several weeks, with several separate rain events gradually saturating the soil of a particular area.

Finally a major weather system, such as a low-pressure cell or hurricane, that produces a large amount of rain over several days, will trigger a flood. The surrounding soil, unable to absorb further water, becomes totally saturated, and water then begins to run across the surface. Watercourses such as rivers and creeks fill and overflow, with water then extending out across the surrounding countryside, further worsening the situation.

Unlike the flash flood, the broad-scale flood may last for weeks, particularly if the affected area is flat, and the water can only disperse slowly. In the case of a long river, the flood peak can travel downstream over a period of several months.

Monsoon rains in India and Bangladesh cause frequent broad-scale floods, often producing disastrous loss of life. But probably the most flood-prone river in the world is China's Huang He River (Yellow River), which is estimated to have flooded 1,500 times over the last 3,500 years. In 1887 and 1888, massive floods along this river resulted in the death of an estimated 2.5 million people, making them among the most devastating disasters in recorded history.

Storm surges and inland flooding

Widespread inundation of coastal areas can occur when strong and persistent winds blow from the sea toward the land, pushing ocean water toward the shoreline. This becomes apparent as an abnormally high tide, called a storm surge, which can extend for a considerable distance inland. Large waves accompanying the high water can also produce significant beach erosion, allowing water to encroach even further inland.

Intense low-pressure cells are the usual cause of these types of events, particularly of hurricanes moving across the coast. The central pressure of these systems is normally very low, and this produces a substantial lifting effect on the water. This effect, combined with the driving force of the winds, can result in massive seawater flooding along coastal areas, destroying communities and livelihoods.

FAR LEFT, TOP In Madras, India, seasonal monsoon rains make flooding a part of everyday life. The city's drainage systems are unable to cope with the large amounts of rainfall.

ABOVE People living in areas that have regular monsoon rains adapt their lives to suit the extreme weather conditions.

LEFT Over 2,500 people died in heavy flooding in North Pakistan and India in September 1992. Along the floodwaters, people moored their boats to whatever land they could. Crops, roads, and bridges were washed away.

ABOVE In February, 1996, a combination of record-breaking rain, warm temperatures, and the melting of a deep snowpacks led to severe flooding in the northern areas of Oregon, United States. The city of Tualatin experienced the worst flood in its history.

The severity of these events depends largely on the elevation of the coastal zone, and if this is only low, or even below sea level, the flooding can be particularly severe and extensive.

One of the worst examples occurred in 1953 in Holland, when a severe North Sea storm produced an ocean surge that breached the protective dikes along the Dutch shoreline. The resulting floods were a total disaster, with seawater extending as far as about 99 miles (160 km) inland. More than 1,800 people were drowned.

Modern-day flood predictions and weather monitoring

There has been significant improvement in the prediction of the various flood types over recent times, and this has enabled a whole variety of more effective responses to be engineered.

Perhaps the biggest single improvement has been in the area of weather forecasting, particularly in the time span out to one week ahead. This has been achieved through a wide range of activities, involving improved monitoring of the weather on a global basis, more efficient communication, particularly through the internet, and significant steps forward in mathematical simulations of the weather on computer.

Over the last decade or so, weather monitoring, particularly through remote sensing devices, has also improved significantly. There has been steady worldwide research and a proliferation of automatic

FLOOD CLASSIFICATIONS

The classification of flood, or the estimation of flood severity, differs in detail in various countries around the world, but they often contain the three descriptive terms of "Minor," "Moderate," and "Major."

MINOR FLOODING This produces nuisance inundation without substantial property damage. It may include water across roadways, and flooding of causeways and small, low-lying bridges.

MODERATE FLOODING This type of inundation will produce flooding of main bridges and adjacent low-lying areas. It may also result in the small-scale evacuations of housing and caravan parks along rivers and the removal of livestock to higher ground.

MAJOR FLOODING This is a major inundation of the countryside that causes significant disruption of transport and communications. Often widespread evacuation of houses is necessary, as well as the large-scale removal of livestock to high ground.

WHAT TO DO DURING A FLOOD

1. **MONITOR** news reports for any new warnings or developments in the weather. Be ready to evacuate should the need arise.

2. **TRY** to move your car to high ground and close all its doors and windows.

3. **BLOCK** the space under the doors and ventilator holes of your house with sandbags to minimize water entry. Tie curtains away from the floor and store electrical gear and furniture up as high as possible.

4. **STORE** food, water, and warm clothing in a high part of the house. Also, have a battery-powered torch and fresh batteries available in case of power failure.

5. **STORE** valuable documents and any medications in a dry and safe area.

6. **TURN OFF** electricity and gas supplies.

7. **PREPARE** as much as you can during daylight hours. Power failures at night can plunge your entire neighborhood into total darkness.

8. **DO NOT** walk or drive through floodwater.

9. **STAY CLEAR** of watercourses and drains.

ABOVE The Mississippi River flooded the city of Kaskaskia, Illinois, in the summer of 1993. The city had become an island after repeated floodings over the years. After this particular flood, the city did not recover; it is now almost deserted.

LEFT Volunteer workers in Granite Fall, Minnesota, use a water pump to keep the floodwaters from getting into a home. Floods in this area occur in the spring—they are caused by the melting of large amounts of winter snow.

weather stations (AWS), radar, drifting ocean buoys, and meteorological satellites, and this has enabled a far more comprehensive global weather picture to be assembled than was possible 10 years ago. Meteorological satellites, in particular, have become increasingly sophisticated, and early identification of potentially flood-producing rains is now routine, as is defining the limits of floods once they occur. This means that we are now aware of the onset of a heavy rain situation as it happens virtually anywhere in the world, which allows for very rapid responses to be set in motion. Many cities and towns that lie in floodplains or low-lying areas are well prepared, with flood prevention and protection strategies in place.

Johnstown, Pennsylvania, 1889

In 1889, Pennsylvania experienced days of heavy rainfall, between May 28 and 31. On May 31, the South Fork Dam broke, flooding Johnstown, Pennsylvania with over 20 million tons of water. More than 2,200 people drowned in the deluge and damages exceeded US$17 million.

RIGHT One of the best-known images of the Johnstown Flood is that of the John Schulz house. Pierced by a tree, the house became an icon and was a curiosity to those who traveled to view the devastation of this natural disaster. The Schulz family survived the flood.

At the end of May 1889, a major rainstorm hit Johnstown. The storm traveled east from the Midwest over two days, beginning on May 28. An estimated 6 to 10 inches (15.2 to 25 cm) of rain fell in the region in less than 24 hours. Overnight, the deluge caused creeks, streams, and rivers to flood, and washed out rail and telegraph lines. The Conemaugh River, which runs through Johnstown, was on the brink of breaking its banks. By mid-morning on May 31, there was already a few inches of water flooding the streets of the town.

The wave of death

At midday, the flooding in the region overwhelmed the South Fork Dam, located 14 miles (23 km) up the Conemaugh River from Johnstown, at the edge of Lake Conemaugh, a 3-mile (4.8 km) long lake containing over 20 million gallons (75.7 million l) of water. When the dam broke, the lake cascaded down the Conemaugh riverway into the town, unleashing a solid wall of water up to 60 feet (18 m) high that moved at speeds estimated to be at least 40 miles per hour (64 km/h).

As the flood surged into town, many of the Johnstown residents were caught unaware. Most were swept into the raging current, while others were crushed by debris or trapped in collapsing buildings. The wire factory, several miles upstream from the town center, had been flooded, and victims were caught in rolls of barbed wire floating in the floodwaters.

The Stone Bridge, an arched bridge over the Conemaugh River, erupted in a blazing fire that started in the accumulated flood

ABOVE *Frank Leslie's Illustrated Newspaper* ran a feature complete with detailed illustrations of the flood. This was the biggest news in America since Abraham Lincoln's assassination, and newspaper circulations skyrocketed. People were encouraged to donate to the relief fund.

debris trapped against the bridge. Eighty people were killed in the blaze, which burned for three days.

The deluge raged through the 4 square miles (10.4 km²) of downtown Johnstown, destroying the town center, including 1,600 homes. The property damage was worth US$17 million, and the town's clean-up and restoration took years to complete.

The decimation of a town

In 1889, Johnstown had a population approaching 30,000. It was a rapidly expanding industrial community founded by Welsh and German immigrants. A total of 2,209 people were killed in the disaster, including 99 families. Records show 396 of the victims were children, while another 100 children were left orphaned. More than 750 of the victims were unable to be identified and were buried in Grandview Cemetery in the Plot of the Unknown.

The Great Flood of Johnstown, one of the greatest natural disasters in United States history, it was also the first national disaster to receive relief efforts from the newly organized American Red Cross. Additional support was brought in from 18 other countries, including Russia, France, Great Britain, Germany, and Australia, and nearly US$4 million in relief funds were raised. The local efforts were run by Red Cross pioneer Clara Barton, who arrived in Johnstown on June 5. The army of relief workers she directed totaled more than 7,000 people.

South Fork club liability

The South Fork Dam, originally built as a reservoir for Johnstown in 1853, was later sold, first to the Pennsylvania Railroad, and later to private investors. These investors remodeled the reservoir so that it resembled a private lake resort. They raised the level of the lake and lowered the dam to create room for an access road. The South Fork Fishing and Hunting Club was born as a private retreat for the wealthy of Pittsburg Society.

After the Johnstown Flood, the club was accused of creating a greater flood threat through their land modifications, combined with a lack of proper maintenance of the dam. While lawsuits were filed against them, the courts upheld that the disaster was an act of God and dropped the charges, giving no compensation to the survivors.

FACTS AND FIGURES

DATE	May 31, 1889
LOCATION	Johnstown, Pennsylvania
DEATH TOLL	2,209
DAMAGE	US$17 million, an entire town destroyed
FLOODING	An excess of 20 million gallons (75.7 million l) of water
COMMENTS	One of the worst flood disasters in US history; one of the first relief efforts from the Red Cross Organization.

Seine River, Paris, 1910

On January 16, 1910, record rainfall in Paris, France, caused the Seine River to overflow its banks. The city was swamped with the worst flood in that had occurred in over 300 years. Approximately 10 feet (3 m) of water filled the city streets as the Seine rose 29 feet (8.8 m) above its normal levels, carrying mud and sewage through the streets of Paris.

Floodwaters took more than a month to recede, and the death toll still remains unknown.

When the Seine River started rising, spectators marvelled and were, at first, entertained by the changing river. A graphic eyewitness account of the rising Seine was recorded by Esther Singleton: "At ten minutes to eleven on the morning of Friday, January 21, 1910 ... the power station from which all the public clocks of Paris are worked by compressed air was flooded by the Seine. All the clocks stopped simultaneously with military exactitude, and with a start of surprise Parisians began to realize that the Seine in flood was not a harmless spectacle that could be watched with the cheerful calm of philosophic detachment, and that the river in revolt was an enemy to be feared even by the most civilized city in Europe.

"Crowds, it is true, had gathered on the embankments, admiring the headlong rush of the silent yellow river that carried with it logs and barrels, broken furniture, the carcasses of animals, and perhaps sometimes a corpse, all racing madly to the sea; they had watched cranes, great piles of stones, and the roofs of sheds emerge for a time from the flooded wharves and then vanish in the swirl of the rising water, while barges and pontoons, generally hidden from sight far below, rose gradually above the level of the streets, notably one great two-storied bathing barge, a vision of unsuspected hideousness, that threatened at any moment, moored as it was, to crash into the parapet." This was only the beginning of this major disaster. Soon, laughter was replaced by screams of terror as Paris residents realized what was unfolding.

Rising floodwaters inundate the city

The rains continued and the Seine overflowed the Left Bank, causing power failures and throwing public transportation into chaos. Areas along the riverbanks, such as wharves, cafes, businesses, and houses were affected first; water flooded the lower levels of buildings and continued to rise rapidly. Residents rushed to salvage what belongings they could, while boats became transport in the streets. Some residents close to the river desperately built walls to save their homes, but the rising floods covered them just hours after their completion.

BELOW A tree-lined avenue looks more like a desolate river, deserted but for the rising floodwaters. Two men paddle through the empty streets, avoiding the floating debris of destroyed buildings.

ABOVE Quai de la Conference and the fashionable avenue of Cours-la-Reine were deep in water, but sandbags and wooden screens kept back some of the surface flood from the nearby Seine. As the river rose, military engineers tried to pump out the water as they raised the areas along the embankments.

LEFT Onlookers in the Jardin des Plantes, the Botanical Gardens, watch fearfully as the floodwaters rise in the bear pits, home to the Paris Zoo polar bears. It is not known if the bears were rescued.

FACTS AND FIGURES	
DATE	January 16 to 29, 1910
LOCATION	Seine River, Paris, France
DEATHS	Unknown
DAMAGE	Repair and rebuilding cost Fr 200 million
FLOODING	The Seine River rose 29 feet (8.8 m) above normal levels
COMMENTS	Worst flood in Paris since the 1658 flood, which was the biggest on record, reaching 30 feet (9.1 m) above normal levels

ABOVE Outside the St Lazare Metro Station, floodwaters are held back by a wall of sandbags and rocks. The unfinished works of the Metropolitan railway looked like a subterranean river.

By January 26, along the quay, houses were flooded with more than 3 feet (90 cm) of water. The gas lamps that burned along the walkways continued to light underwater pathways.

Within two days, the floods had entered the city center. Railways and stations were flooded in up to 20 feet (6 m) of water. The Metro railway was turned into an underground river for nearly 2 miles (3.2 km), flooding St Lazare and St Michel Metro stations.

The bridges along the Seine were almost submerged, becoming dams for the debris swept along by the current. The few vehicles that were still in use were reluctant to cross the bridges, fearful of being washed into the raging river.

Some people were swept into the floodwaters and drowned. Others escaped drowning only to be crushed by debris or buried alive under collapsing structures. Rats, deprived of their normal food sources, attacked children. Tons of sewage and garbage were swept into the floodwaters, creating severe disease and health hazards. People were also injured from falling off the makeshift pathways.

The wall that saved Paris

As night fell on January 28, engineers worked desperately building up a barrier made of sandbags on the Right Bank, in an attempt to prevent the river from overflowing into that quarter as well. That single barrier kept more than 5 feet (1.5 m) of water from inundating the main boulevard and the Place de l'Opera collapsed, and to the horror of onlookers, the roadway on the south side of the Louvre began to sag under the weight of the overflowing drainage system. Crowds rushed to tear cobblestones out of roadways and build barriers to save the Louvre.

On Saturday, January 29, the rains stopped and the sun rose over the flooded city. Residents cheered as the Seine began to recede. The slow process of emptying the city of millions of tons of water began. Debris and carcasses were strewn through the streets, and repair and rebuilding to the cost of Fr 200 million was needed. Entire sections of the city were left uninhabitable due to water damage, mold, and disease. The clean-up and drainage of the city took more than a month.

Preparations for the next flood

The 1910 flood was not the biggest. In February 1658 the highest levels on record were measured at 13 inches (34 cm) above the 1910 peak. On average, there are about 10 large floods per century, but rather than being evenly distributed over time they tend to cluster together. In the seventeenth century there were three severe floods in the space of nine years. Since 1910, there have been two smaller floods, in 1924 and 1955.

Few preventative measures were taken after the 1910 flood—four reservoirs were constructed to store and release the river's water in a controlled manner, but these can only cope with a small rise. Urban development on the Ile-de-France floodplain has continued unabated. In between floods most people, including city planners, tend to forget about them, leaving today's Paris far more vulnerable than it was in 1910. Since then many new hospitals,

PREPARING FOR FUTURE FLOODS

Many Parisians refuse to be alarmed by the prospect of the Seine's next gigantic flood. As bartender Yves Thierry explained to *The Scotsman*:

"I'm not worried. In 1910 the flood stopped three doors down from here. I know how to swim—and a little bit of water never stopped anybody drinking."

Despite the light-hearted attitude, flood preparations including flood-warning systems, mapping of high-risk areas, and emergency response training are being put in place.

schools and other buildings have been constructed
within the flood zone, including hundreds of miles
of railway and thousands of underground car parks.
The city now has 1,300 miles (2,100 km) of sewer
pipes equipped with overflow pumps so that when
the sewers fill up during heavy rain excess water is
pumped into the Seine. One sewage worker told the
Reuters news service that the city's biggest problem
will arise when the Seine reaches street level: "If the
Seine flooded today like it did in 1910, there would be
problems. It would be a huge headache. Our pumps
are just not designed to cope with floods that big."

Severe flooding would leave a million Parisians
without telephones, 200,000 without electricity, and
80,000 without gas. With hundreds of thousands
of refugees needing food and shelter for several
weeks, all economic activity in the region would
be paralyzed, with government and municipal
authorities destabilized.

It was only in 2001 that civil authorities decided
to prepare an emergency response plan for the next
major flood. Huge warehouses to the northeast of
Paris are now being used for semi-permanent storage
of France's national treasures, after the supposedly
safe storage areas in basements of the Louvre and
other museums were threatened by a rising Seine in
2002. As government officials can only guarantee

an advance warning of about 72 hours, museums
have made the forward-thinking decisions to move
everything that could not be easily carried to the
upper floors within that time. The Musée d'Orsay, the
Louvre, the National School of Fine Arts, the Central
Union of Decorative Arts, the Georges Pompidou
Center, the Modern Art Museum of the City of Paris,
the Carnavalet Museum, and several libraries have all
taken part in this evacuation exercise.

For days, the residents of Paris
traveled the streets in flat-
bottomed boats, usually manned
by opportunistic boatmen (top),
or they walked along narrow
trestle bridges which were built
about 5 feet (1.5 m) above
ground level (above). These
bridges were not very safe.

North Sea, United Kingdom and The Netherlands, 1953

In late January, 1953, a once-in-250-years storm hit the United Kingdom and the Netherlands, causing hurricane-force winds, massive tidal surges, and widespread destruction. More than 2,300 people were killed and at least 100,000 were forced to flee in emergency evacuations. The 1953 North Sea flood is considered the worst disaster ever to hit northwestern Europe.

RIGHT Residents of The Avenue in Canvey Island, a town in Essex in the United Kingdom, are rescued from their flooded home. Over 11,500 people—the entire population of Canvey Island—were evacuated.

BELOW An aerial view of the flooding at the seafront village of Jaywick, Essex, in the United Kingdom. At least 35 people were killed here in the North Sea floods and 7,000 were left homeless.

On the night of January 31, 1958, a severe storm pounded the United Kingdom. Trees were downed all over Scotland, and the storm drove 11-foot (3 m) storm surges far along the eastern coastline. The storm devastated Canvey Island around midnight, before moving into the North Sea basin, bringing widespread flooding and casualties to the Netherlands.

Fifty dikes throughout the Netherlands were overwhelmed; islands and much of the mainland were flooded. Roozenburg, Rammekens, Ossenisse, Wolphaartsdijk, and Zeeuws-Vlaanderen all had breaches in dikes. Over 70,000 residents were forced to evacuate, and more than 1,800 were drowned or killed by debris. An estimated 10,000 domestic and farm animals were drowned and nearly 5,000 buildings were completely destroyed. Damages reached over £850 million.

Most of the regions of Zeeland, Noord-Brabent, and Zuidholland, were flooded. The islands of Ooltgensplaat and Tiengemeten were completely under water. Several major waterways flooded. More than 675 square miles (1,748 km²) of the country was submerged in floodwaters.

Flooding continues

Over 30,000 people were forced to evacuate the flooded regions in the United Kingdom. Twenty-four thousand homes were damaged or destroyed and over 300 people were killed. During the day

Ohio River, USA, 1997

On March 1, 1997, the Ohio River and its tributary streams flooded their banks. The flash-flooding reached levels not seen for decades, and caused widespread damage and destruction. Scores of river towns were inundated and 33 people were killed. Many areas were declared federal and state disaster zones and thousands of people were evacuated.

RIGHT Historically, the towns along the potential flood areas of the Ohio River are generally flood-ready. In brighter weather, a street in Harpers Ferry, West Virginia, becomes a watery playground for kayakers.

BELOW Floodwaters from the Ohio River swept through tributaries, including the Great Miami River. Without hills like those in Cincinnati, the cities of Columbus, Dayton, Hamilton, and Middletown were inundated.

Conditions were normal in the Ohio River basin before the heavy rains began—the new crop-planting season had not yet started, stream levels were well within their banks, and all the major rivers, including the Ohio, were at normal seasonal levels. Around late February 1997, the US National Weather Service began issuing flood warnings and notices. Using state-of-the-art technology, including radar and rain gauge networks, and recent satellite precipitation estimates, they could see that trouble was brewing in the Ohio Basin. Over a 48-hour period, a broad band of slow-moving thunderstorms dumped up to 12 inches (305 mm) of rain into the Ohio catchment area.

Water levels rise swiftly

Water levels in the Ohio rose unusually swiftly as a result of the heaviest rainfall occurring directly over the river. Large areas of unplanted ground also meant that there was little vegetation to slow down or absorb surface water runoff into the river. The gauging station at Portsmouth recorded a rise of 14 feet (4 m) within a 12-hour period. Most communities along the Ohio River were warned of the impending flood at least four to eight hours in advance, while some even received one or two days' notice from the National Weather Service. These timely warnings greatly minimized the loss of life, injuries, and damage to property. Engineers in Louisville had time to use the 45 floodgates had been installed after the historic floods of 1937. The most severe flooding occurred in Kentucky and Ohio with dozens of counties in these states declared natural disaster areas. The lives that were lost could have been saved had there been a better public education program—the most common cause of death resulted from people attempting to drive through heavily flooded river crossings and being swept away.

Major floods of the Ohio River valley

The Ohio River peaks seasonally each year between about January and April, and has overtopped its banks on many occasions. The accurate record-keeping of river levels began in 1831. At Cincinnati, the 1997 flood measured 65 feet (19.8 m) but it was by no means the biggest on record. As recorded at Cincinnati, four of the largest Ohio River valley floods are as follows: the flood of 1937 measured up to 80 feet (24 m); the 1884 flood measured 71 feet (21.7 m); the 1913 flood measured 70 feet (21 m); and the 1945 flood measuring 69 feet (21 m). The longest period between floods was 32 years (1964 to 1996) and the shortest was one year. Ohio River floods occurred in two consecutive years on two occasions, in 1883 and 1884, and in 1996 and 1997.

Life in the flood belt is not easy. After the 1997 flood, Hazel Godwin of Adams County told the *Cincinnati Enquirer*, "We didn't have much to begin with. Now we don't have a thing that we can call our own." A resident of Silver Grove, Myrtle Gross, who was affected by the 1964 flood, perhaps best sums up the feelings of many residents of low-lying areas within the Ohio basin: "Everything I owned washed away. If I could find a place on higher ground and could afford it, I would go."

Cincinnati Reds baseball season opens as planned

The National Weather Service was given credit for saving the opening day of the Cincinnati Reds' baseball season and, more importantly, the city's new US$2 million Cinergy Field "Astroturf" facility. Early warnings issued to management by the Ohio River Forecast Center allowed floodgates to be closed and pumps activated in time to keep the floodwaters out of the stadium and the game went ahead.

ABOVE The sun sets on the overspilling Maumee River in Grand Rapids, Ohio. Heavy rain caused many rivers in the northern parts of Ohio to swell. County officials hoped for cool weather to help slow down the runoff from the rains.

FACTS AND FIGURES

DATE	March 1997
LOCATION	Ohio River, USA
DEATH TOLL	33 (21 in Kentucky, 5 in Ohio, 4 in Tennessee, 3 in West Virginia)
DAMAGE	US$500 million across six states
FLOODING	Peak flow at Cincinnati was approximately 5 million gallons per second (20 million l/s)
COMMENTS	Close to 14,000 homes damaged or destroyed; 20,000 home and business owners applied for disaster relief

Asia, 1999

Floods are the most common disaster in the Asian countries, and their frequency has been increasing since the 1970s. Flood impact has become severe due to rapid population growth and urbanization. China, Korea, the Philippines, Indonesia, Bangladesh, Thailand, Vietnam, Cambodia, Sri Lanka, India, Pakistan, and Nepal are all affected.

The 1999 Asian flood began when heavy tropical cyclonic rain caused the Ganges, Brahmaputra, and Indus rivers to overflow, killing 300 in India, 100 in Nepal and 35 in Bangladesh. Further east, Typhoon Olga struck the coast of Korea in early August, followed closely by Typhoon Paul; together they caused the worst Asia-wide flooding in 30 years. Worst affected was China, where 725 people died. Torrential rain lashed the region, triggering massive landslides. In the Philippines, over 92 people were killed, South Korea 43, North Korea 42, Vietnam 37, Cambodia 8, Thailand 6, and Japan 2.

Why Asia floods each year

Flooding is associated with the June to September wet season monsoon. Each year moisture-laden winds are drawn from the sea into a low-pressure region over the Asian continent, caused by summer heating of the land. In the past, the agriculture-based populations accepted floods as a normal part of the seasonal cycle. Their arrival was essential and was celebrated with song and dance. Over the past few decades, however, land-use patterns have been changing with traditional fisher-farmer communities giving way more and more to industrialization and urbanization.

In these floods, the Mekong River basin of Cambodia and Vietnam was covered by 5.1 million acres (20,800 km²) of water. Even more devastating and extensive floods struck the basin again in 2000, this time covering 10.8 million acres (43,800 km²).

Unusual weather, climate change, and flooding

Minor changes in climate can upset the delicate balance during the wet season as swollen rivers flow inches below their levee tops. Critical areas include floodplains of rivers such as the Ganges, Brahmaputra, Mekong, and the Yangtze. Low-lying coastal regions, such as the Bay of Bengal and the South China Sea, are prone to flood after any unusual tropical storm activity. Slight rises in sea level as a result of global warming will have major consequences for these coastal zone deltas. Scientists predict that extreme rainfall and flooding will occur.

BELOW The Yangzte River in Chongquing (Chungking) in China, seen at low levels. In the flood conditions of 1999, the swollen Yangtze River pushed 1.8 million Chinese from their homes, leaving the Red Cross struggling to keep up with the cost of disaster relief.

China takes action

Over the years, poor Chinese farmers had moved into flood-prone and dangerous regions in order to make a basic living. One of these was Xu Songshun, a 39-year-old farmer living on a river islet near Wuhan in central China with his wife and two sons. During his 10 years on the islet, he rebuilt their meagre family home four times, because each time it was swept away by floods. The 1998 flood, the worst in nearly 40 years, was one in this long series

of growing annual threats by the Yangtze River to the people and their property. This all happened again in 1999. This time the Yangtze River inundated some 28 million acres (113,000 km²) of farmland, and China was forced to evacuate 5.5 million people from 23 states. Ambitious plans were then put in place, including the permanent resettlement of about 3 million people living in the lower Yangtze valley. According to Li Antian, head of Yangtze River Water Resources Committee, "It is the world's largest disaster-victim migration program, as well as the world's largest program for improving subsistence conditions and ecological environment."

Part of the program includes depopulating the lake-reclaimed farmland, allowing it to return to part of the natural drainage system, adding over 13 billion cubic yards (10 billion m³) of floodwater storage capacity to the Yangtze River. This, plus the construction of new reservoirs, will help ease the flooding. Farmers like Xu Songshun were resettled in new houses in villages built on higher ground. They can work their farms or raise fish after the land becomes flooded again. "We are now living a stable and promising new life," Xu told the *People's Daily*.

ABOVE The livelihoods of many depend on the bounty that the Yangtze River provides. The Three Gorges Dam project in China will purposely flood this area of the river. The continuing excavation and land clearing for the project is believed to be increasing the incidence of natural flood disasters.

FACTS AND FIGURES

DATE	June to August, 1999
LOCATION	China, the Philippines, Vietnam, Korea, Thailand, Cambodia, Indonesia, Sri Lanka, India, Bangladesh, Pakistan, and Nepal
DEATH TOLL	1,390 across Asia
DAMAGE	Extensive across Asia; repair bill unknown but well into billions of US dollars
FLOODING	Most Asian rivers, including the Yangtze, Mekong, Ganges, and Brahmaputra
COMMENTS	Tens of millions of people made homeless

Nepal, India, and Bangladesh, 2002

Massive flooding from tropical monsoons spread across South Asia in July 2002, killing approximately 1,000 people, affecting millions of lives, destroying crops, livestock, and homes, and costing millions of dollars in damage. In the early days of the disaster, reports of fatalities and damages fluctuated wildly as communications and power to the entire region were severed or impaired.

BELOW Two Bangladeshi girls collect drinking water in a flood-affected area of the capital, Dhaka, in 2002. The low-lying areas around Dhaka were in the grip of the flood as water rushed down to the Bay of Bengal from areas to the north.

Floods are common in the monsoon season in South Asia, but the storms of 2002 displaced thousands of people in India, Bangladesh, and Nepal. In the Indian state of Bihar, over 20 million people were affected and 293 died. In Assam, about 10 million people lost their homes. Bangladesh had over 19 million people affected by the disaster, and approximately 157 people died. In Nepal, 424 people were killed and 300,000 became homeless.

Deluge in Nepal

On July 21, 2002, the most severe rainfall in three decades began a three-day deluge in Nepal, causing sudden and deadly flash floods and triggering landslides. Riverbanks overflowed and thousands of acres of crops were inundated with floodwater and destroyed. Farming regions were contaminated by the debris-laden water, which had lasting effects on crop production.

Heavy flooding in the lowland areas and major landslides in the upper reaches of the country caused damage in 49 districts. Over 12,000 families were left homeless, more than 600 homes were destroyed, and more than 300,000 people lost their property or livelihood. Many of the main roadways and bridges were either destroyed or damaged. Power and communications lines were cut.

Helicopters rushed food, water, medicine, and emergency supplies to isolated survivors, but the contaminated waters remained a severe danger. "We are facing the threat of an outbreak of epidemics like cholera in the affected areas," Interior Ministry official Lekhnath Pokharel told reporters.

Downpours in Assam and Bihar

While the rains slackened off by July 24 in Nepal, the monsoon moved into India, bringing massive downpours across the eastern states of Assam and Bihar. Along with the rainfall, flooding from Nepal began seeping across the border, further inundating Bihar. Water levels in the Brahmaputra, Ganges,

FACTS AND FIGURES	
DATE	July 21 to 25, 2002
LOCATION	South Asia: India, Bangladesh, and Nepal
DEATH TOLL	Approximately 1,000
DAMAGE	Millions of dollars of damages, over 400,000 homes lost, extensive crop loss
FLOODING	Dozens of rivers overflowed; flash floods triggered mudslides; roads, bridges, and power lines were washed out
COMMENTS	The massive floods caused landslides that added to the destruction of lives, crops, and livestock.

Jamuna, and Maghna Rivers became dangerously high, contributing to concerns about flooding.

Crops were destroyed across Assam, with the worst damage occurring in the Morigaon district, which lost all its farmlands, and 81 percent of the population was left homeless. By July 25, three riverbanks had collapsed, increasing the flooding and putting large regions of Assam under water. Even the wildlife was affected. Panicked elephants ran out of the forests, blocking traffic and trampling people. In Guwahait, the overflow of the Brahmaputra River submerged sections of the city, causing 30 deaths from drowning. Nearly 100,000 people were taken to relief camps, which were also affected by flooding as the waters continued to rise. Fifty percent of Assam was under water at the height of the flooding.

The worst hit region of India was the state of Bihar. Over 350,000 homes were destroyed and more than 380,000 people were evacuated. Engineers and medical personnel rushed via boat to the Madhubani district, on the border of Nepal. Despite the rainfall

decreasing, river embankments were breached and riverbanks collapsed in Bihar, causing the flooding to move to previously less-threatened regions. Hundreds of villages across the state were completely submerged in the surging flood tides. Over 1 million acres (400,000 ha) of crops were lost and thousands of animals were drowned. It was estimated that over 80 percent of the northern part of the state was totally submerged in the muddy floodwaters.

Flash flooding in Bangladesh

In Bangladesh, flash floods triggered landslides that hit 30 districts and caused over 150 deaths. All of the four major rivers in the region, and most of their tributaries, overflowed, causing extensive property damage and leaving hundreds of thousands of people homeless. Affected residents fled to temporary shelters on any high ground possible, but the lack of fresh water and clean food led to nearly 32,000 people suffering from water-borne disease and needing urgent medical attention.

ABOVE This family in Dhaka is luckier than most—their floor remains above water level. Only two years after this flood, another one struck. In the Bogura district, 135 miles (215 km) north of Dhaka, at least five people drowned and 60 others went missing as suspected saboteurs cut open an embankment along the fierce-flowing Jamuna River, which wiped out a village of over 800 houses.

Europe, 2002

Several days of heavy rain resulted in massive flooding in several European countries in August 2002. Over 100 people were killed and tens of thousands were forced to evacuate. Damages ran into billions of euros. Old and historic buildings were ruined, and public transportation was severely disrupted.

What has been called a 100-year flood hit Europe starting around August 12, 2002. Storm fronts caused heavy rainfalls across the Italian, Bavarian, and Austrian Alps. The storms traveled across Bavaria and into the Czech Republic, causing massive flooding. The cities of Prague and Dresden sustained the bulk of the worst damage to buildings, infrastructure and transportation systems.

Evacuation of villages and cities

The storm's deluge soaked the Bohemian Forest, where the Elbe and Vltava rivers rise. The river surges caused massive rises in water levels through Austria and the Czech Republic as the rivers overflowed and the waterways expanded. In Northern Bohemia, Thuringia, and Saxony, several villages were swept away by the raging torrents of water. Saxony suffered nine casualties and nearly 20,000 people were evacuated by military and police.

At 4:00 a.m. on Wednesday, August 14, residents of Prague, in the Czech Republic, woke to find

ABOVE Residents of Prague in the Czech Republic adapt to life after the floods. Major structural damage was caused to buildings. Forty thousand people were evacuated from areas near the Vltava and Elbe rivers.

RIGHT People spent months cleaning up their businesses and properties after the flood. This man is emptying river silt, washed up on the promenade, back into the flood-swollen river.

firemen banging on their doors and ordering them to evacuate. Streets full of people fleeing with bundles of possessions in their arms was a sight that had not been seen since World War II. Over 50,000 people were evacuated while firefighters and emergency volunteers rapidly built barriers to minimize flood damage. Despite this, approximately 9 feet (2.7 m) of water washed through the Karlin district near the Old Town, sweeping away the sandbag walls and damaging historic buildings. The violent flood and overflowing rivers tore down bridges, submerged roads and railway lines, and carried away all manner of possessions, from furniture to vehicles. The Metro, an underground rail system, was disrupted and damaged by flooding. Millions of euros' worth of damage was caused and thousands of people were left homeless. However, thanks to efficient warning systems, much of the historic and culturally important art in the city was moved to higher ground long before the floods arrived.

Dresden, Germany was also forced to conduct massive evacuations. Over a quarter of the city's 480,000-strong population fled from the rising flood waters. The Elbe River surpassed a record high of 30 feet (9 m) on August 16, according to the Dresden Emergency Centre. As in Prague, numerous buildings were damaged as the floodwaters breached emergency retaining walls, forcing the rescuers to retreat further. The Zwinger Palace and neighboring Semper Opera opera house were also flooded. Across Germany, over 435 miles (700 km) of roadways and 180 bridges were destroyed.

Damages and disaster management

The Danube River also reached record-breaking levels, but minimal flooding occurred in Vienna due to extensive and effective flood management systems. In the worst-hit areas, the extent of the damage was attributed to the combination of towns built on floodplains and widespread deforestation that had occurred in recent years. The Regional Environmental Center for Central and Eastern Europe commented to reporters that, "The more

trees and plants that an area loses, the faster the run-off and the more water that ends up in the river. In the industrial north and mid-latitudes in the northern hemisphere, forest area, and vegetation coverage in general had shrunk rapidly every year due to acid rain and developments in industry, transport, and nature."

While the flood damage was widespread, there were relatively few fatalities due to good emergency management of the disaster situation. All of the evacuations were carried out in time following the reasonably accurate flood predictions. However, experts still insist that better pre-disaster planning is needed in more regions, along with redesign of areas to take massive flooding potential into account. In all, the 2002 flood resulted in damages and restoration costs exceeding 2 billion euros.

ABOVE A German fire brigade technician cleans a filter of a pump that is pumping water from a suburban street in Prague. Fire brigades traveled 435 miles (700 km) from Frankfurt am Main in Germany to help their Czech counterparts.

Haiti and the Dominican Republic, 2004

On May 24 and 25, 2004, massive floods hit Haiti and the Dominican Republic, leaving over 1,950 people dead and over 1,600 missing. There were also 1,500 homeless, and tens of thousands in need of food and emergency assistance.

Entire crop fields were flattened, and many of the more poorly constructed homes outside the city regions were destroyed. The threat of starvation, dehydration, and disease loomed large as rescue groups worked to clear debris and remove the dead before water-borne disease took hold.

From May 18 to 25, 2004, a low-pressure storm system rapidly crossed from Central America into the Caribbean, then moved into Hispaniola, causing heavy thunderstorms and massive rainfalls across the Dominican Republic and Haiti. In the border regions, an estimated 20 inches (51 cm) of rain fell. Jimani, in the southwest of the Dominican Republic, was swamped with more than 10 inches (25 cm) of rain in 24 hours. Hundreds of people were killed by drowning and landslides when the Solie River and Lake Enriquillo overflowed. Surging floodwaters rose to more than 15 feet (4.6 m). At least 300 people were found, their bodies crushed, drowned, and half-buried in mud.

The most severe flooding was along the rivers that drain from northern edge of the Massif de la Salle in Haiti. To the south of the Massif, widespread deforestation and heavy settlement on the river plain contributed to the scope of the disaster and losses. Flash floods and the accumulation of debris cut off roads and limited access for rescue and relief efforts.

Flash floods that kill

On the far side of the Massif are low-lying areas in Haiti. In the Mapou region, the three days of heavy rains drowned populations of entire villages and caused massive landslides. The flash flooding and pooling of water run-off from the Massif created a series of lakes, one of which nearly submerged Mapou. There were seven regions that turned into small lakes in the area.

Officials estimated at least 1,500 people were missing from the region and unaccounted for, while some 700 homes were destroyed. The final Mapou fatality count was over 1,000. Fond Verrettes also suffered severe flooding and landslides, with 158 reported dead. Two people were killed in Port-a-Piment. Across the southeastern region of the country, another 500 were found dead.

In Grand Gosier, Mayor Neddy Rabel helped bury 103 people, as well as another 176 in the town of Kadidier. He told reporters that at least 100 people were missing and presumed dead, and that many needy people were still waiting for aid.

A bulldozer was used to dig mass graves to deal with the piles of corpses. Search and rescue workers used dogs trained to sniff out bodies, while rescue teams wore masks to filter out the smell of flesh rotting in the tropical heat. Rescue personnel feared

BELOW Red Cross workers search for bodies in the floodwaters in Mapou, southeast of Port-au-Prince. The initial death toll in Haiti reached 996 with the discovery of 404 bodies in southeastern Haiti.

LEFT Flood victims wait for aid relief in Fond Verettes, east of Port-au-Prince in Haiti. These devastating floods and landslides killed up to 1,000 people. This large-scale natural disaster further complicated the efforts of the country's transitional government to recover from an armed uprising that occurred earlier in the year.

FACTS AND FIGURES

DATE	May 18 to 25, 2004
LOCATION	Haiti and the Dominican Republic, Hispaniola
DEATH TOLL	At least 2,000
DAMAGE	Over 1,000 homes destroyed, extensive crop losses
FLOODING	Up to 15 feet (4.6 m)
COMMENTS	Flash floods created small lakes in the Mapou, Haiti region; contaminated water raised the death toll after the floodwaters had receded

the death toll would rise due to the spread of disease from contaminated waters. Private companies and religious organizations offered assistance, sending food, medication, and relief workers to help prevent rising fatalities in the post-disaster period.

The international community rushes to help out

Over US$3 million in relief aid was raised with international support, including funds from the European Union, the United States, and Japan. Support troops, engineers, disaster management specialists and consultants were sent to the area, along with emergency packages of food, medication, blankets, and general supplies for all of the victims. New York City, which has a large population of Dominican Republic and Haitian natives, sent a

group of disaster management specialists to help make recommendations for better disaster control systems for the afflicted regions.

Some American troops were already present as a peacekeeping force following an internal political upheaval; they stayed on in the country until the end of June to assist with the relief effort. The few helicopters used by the marines in Haiti were utilized to reach inaccessible areas, to evacuate the injured, and to airdrop emergency supplies, food, temporary shelter, and fresh water.

ABOVE The height of the floodwaters can be seen on the tidemark of an abandoned house in the town of Jamini, 174 miles (280 km) from Santo Domingo in Haiti. An international rescue operation gathered pace as the death toll from floods in this country kept increasing.

Northeastern India and Bangladesh, 2004

The world's most at-risk areas for floods are the low-lying floodplains of the Ganges and Brahmaputra rivers. These giant rivers flow into valleys along the southern front of the massive Himalayan mountain range. They drain from the densely populated northeastern Indian states and join in Bangladesh to form a huge delta where they enter the sea.

RIGHT A man transports his wife and some of their belongings on a makeshift raft through the floodwaters. Their village, Sonapur, is some 16 miles (25 km) east of Guwahti in northeastern India.

This region receives most of its rainfall as a seasonal monsoon lasting from June to the end of September. Bangladesh, being at the mouth of the rivers, is generally affected by higher-than-normal rainfall anywhere upstream. The floods of 2004 began much earlier than anticipated, when northeastern Bangladesh and India experienced about 1½ times the average monthly rainfall for April. Most of this rain fell from April 11 to 20, resulting in severe flash floods. The Brahmaputra experienced flood peaks between April and July, and reached dangerous levels in the third week of July. The level of the Ganges River also rose. Maximum flooding was observed on July 24, inundating nearly 38 percent of Bangladesh.

In the capital Dhaka, 100,000 people were forced to abandon their homes to the rising floodwaters and crowd into emergency accommodation. Three-quarters of the city went under water. In India, hundreds of people had to wade through the floodwaters in search of dry land. Widespread flooding across south Asia caused over 1,100 deaths.

BELOW India's neighbor Pakistan also experienced major flooding in the city streets. In Lahore, vehicles and pedestrians battle the rising floodwaters. People use whatever transport they can find.

ABOVE An aerial view of the flood-affected Brahmanbaria area, some 107 miles (172 km) southeast of Dhaka, the capital of Bangladesh. Millions of people living here were left without adequate food or clean water so they had to face the risk of water-borne diseases.

Millions of homeless people face disease outbreaks

Millions of people were left homeless in India and Bangladesh. And the 2004 monsoon season had only just started. As the floodwaters receded, even more problems began to arise. It was still raining and pools of stagnant water lay everywhere filled with garbage, sewage, dead livestock, and other rotting debris. Fresh drinking water and dry food

were in very short supply. Hospitals and temporary medical centers in flooded areas reported treating more than 100,000 patients over a three-week period for waterborne diseases.

Bangladesh's Disaster Management Ministry said that most of that year's flood deaths were caused by diarrhea, snakebites, house collapses, and drowning. Most deaths from disease occurred in isolated areas where people could not seek immediate help. "Never

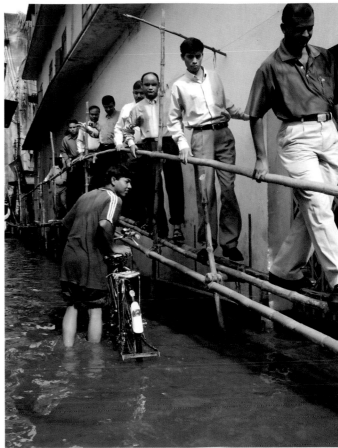

before had I seen such a devastation, especially in terms of scarcity of drinking water and dry food… I found it impossible to live there. So I fled with my only son," said Ferdousi Begum, a resident of flooded Dhaka. Other victims reported having to queue all day, sometimes standing in filthy floodwater, for handouts of fresh water, food, sheets of corrugated iron, tarpaulins or other relief supplies.

Aid agencies overwhelmed

International and local agencies tried to distribute aid and coordinate post-flood rehabilitation, but found they were completely overwhelmed by the mass of stricken humanity. Food and shelter supplies often ran out too quickly leaving many with nothing. One of these was 60-year-old Amiran Bibi. "I am in the shelter for a week now but have received nothing. I don't need rice or money. Please give me some dry or cooked food and some water for survival. Never in my life have I suffered so much," he said.

Bangladesh is used to flooding

Each year seasonal flooding, known as "barsha," inundates up to 20 percent of the country's land area. These annual floods are essential for the overall growth of the Bangladesh delta and maintain the soil fertility. People are accustomed to these floods and

have learned to organize their daily routines around them. It is part of the life/farming cycle here.

More threatening are the larger but less frequent floods called "bonna," which inundate over 35 percent of the land area. These floods disrupt many peoples' lives and threaten the country's economy. Bonna floods have occurred in 1954, 1955, 1974, 1984, 1987, 1988, 1993, 1998, 1999, 2000, and 2004. These particular floods have become more frequent and severe during recent years, and studies are being carried out to determine the reasons for this. Suspected causes are increasing population and changing land use practices within the catchment areas.

ABOVE Incessant monsoon rains caused the floods that covered these roads and partly submerged the buildings.

ABOVE LEFT People were forced to get around the city of Dhaka by boat, navigating the floodwaters or walking along temporary bamboo walkways.

FACTS AND FIGURES

DATE	April to August, 2004
LOCATION	Bangladesh, northeastern Indian states (Assam, Arunachal Pradesh, Bihar, Sikkim, Orissa, and West Bengal), and Nepal
DEATH TOLL	Over 1,100 across south Asia
DAMAGE	US$7 billion dollars in Bangladesh
FLOODING	Affected the Ganges and Brahmaputra rivers and their tributaries
COMMENTS	Millions of people were left homeless in India and Bangladesh

Maharashtra and Goa, India, 2005

In late July 2005, the western Indian coast had record rainfalls. The Indian states of Maharashtra and Goa experienced severe flooding, landslides, massive property damage, and the spread of disease. This was the worst rainfall experienced in the country in over 100 years and it paralyzed the entire region, bringing all public functions in Mumbai to a halt. Over 1,400 people were killed.

On July 25, 2005, a storm system that came in from over the Western Ghat Mountain Range caused continuous and heavy rainfalls in the Goa region and in western Maharashtra. Rainfalls triggered landslides, and 11 people were killed on National Highway 17 in Goa. By July 26, Maharashtra had severe, record-setting rains affecting the Mumbai metropolis, Chiplun, Kalyan, and Ratnagiri, among other regions. The accumulation of rain in Mumbai was at an all-time high, with up to 37 inches (94 cm) falling in 24 hours. The previous record for that region was 15 inches (38 cm) less than that. In the suburban areas around the city, a massive 37 inches (94 cm) of rain was also recorded.

The government announces a holiday

Power and communications were disrupted in many sections of the city as heavy rainfall and flooding overwhelmed the city disaster management program.

The sewage and drainage systems overflowed and contaminated all of the area's fresh water supplies.

The drainage system in Mumbai is only capable of handling 9 to 10 inches (22.9 to 25 cm) of water per hour. It is also affected, in areas, by blockages in the system. Many of the ocean drains lack floodgates, which causes sea water to back-up and flow into the system during high tide, decreasing drainage efficiency during heavy rainfalls. As the floodwaters rose, municipal workers closed down ocean drains to prevent the high tide from exacerbating the flooding, however, this left the already high waters with nowhere to flow to.

In a desperate attempt to try to keep the numbers of flood casualties down, the government declared a two-day state holiday on July 27 and 28 to force people to stay indoors. The rain lessened over the two days, but resumed its intensity on July 31. Police orders meant people were barricaded in their homes.

BELOW An aerial view from an Indian naval helicopter shows the flooded Karjat area on the outskirts of Mumbai. Rescue and relief teams evacuated thousands of people from low-lying areas, whose homes were threatened by overflowing dams and rain-swollen rivers and lakes.

On the morning of July 29, state official Chief Minister Vilasrao Deshmukh sent the military and home guard to assist with rescue and relief efforts. He told people to stay where they were and not to leave their homes, promising that rafts would be sent to rescue those who were stranded by rising floods.

Rescue efforts hampered

Landslides caused cave-ins and massive structural damages, killing and injuring hundreds of people. In apartment complexes, elderly residents were moved to top floors as floodwaters inundated first floor apartments. At the low-income region Lal Bahadur Shastri Nagar, there was a massive landslide. Rocks and boulders cascaded down from the slopes of Andheri, flattening four compounds, each of which had 12 homes. The houses housed between 5 to 10 people, and in the deluge, most of the residents were at home. The landslide deposited a layer of

ABOVE The Mithi River near Mumbai is flanked by slums. These areas were incubators for many water-borne diseases that occur after flood situations.

BELOW Indian social workers bring food to flood-affected villagers in Kalina, Mumbai. The Police Commissioner of Mumbai told people to stay home and keep off the streets.

ABOVE Outside a relief camp at Kurla in India's financial capital, flood-affected residents of Mumbai queue up with empty containers to be filled with kerosene for cooking.

CHILDREN TRAPPED IN FLOODWATERS

Across Mumbai on July 26, thousands of children were stranded in schools as floodwaters rose. School buses were swamped by the waters rising 1 to 2 feet (30 to 60 cm), forcing children to get out and walk home through knee- and waist-deep flooded streets, leaving frantic parents to look for them. One bus, trapped in rapidly rising water and strong currents, requested a local FM radio station to send an emergency call to the police to arrange a rescue for the schoolchildren.

debris 70-feet (21 m) deep, covering an area of some 538 feet^2 (51 m^2); volunteers could only dig with hand tools and carts to try to clear the disaster. One woman carrying an injured child, refused to leave the scene of the landslide-impacted wreckage of her apartment, believing her mother was trapped there. After she was finally convinced that her mother had been taken to the hospital morgue, her brother was sent to identify the body.

Mumbai brought to a standstill

An oil-drilling platform 100 miles (161 km) north of Mumbai caught fire, killing 10 and leaving another 14 unaccounted for. All public transportation ground to a halt. Buses, trains, and taxis were stranded in the rising floods and over 1,000 flights were cancelled between July 26 and 29. Over 150,000 people were stranded in railway stations in downtown Mumbai's financial district. The Mumbai-Pine Expressway was closed due to water and landslides. Banks and Automatic Teller Machines (ATMs) across the region were closed down for over a day because communications lines were disrupted, including those of India's main bank, the State Bank of India. Other institutions affected were Citibank, the HDFC Bank and the ICICI Bank. The Bombay Stock Exchange and the National Stock Exchange experienced disruptions and shutdowns as well. The financial systems of the region were estimated as suffering over a US$1 million loss.

Outbreak of deadly disease

Approximately 1,490 people died, with over 125 of those people killed in landslides and collapsed buildings. More than 450 died from the spread of disease from the contaminated floodwaters, caused by the backflow of sewage and the large numbers of human and animal corpses in the water. Sixty-six people succumbed to a disease suspected to be a severe bacterial infection called *Leptospirosis*, though the government flatly denied outbreaks of the fever. Another 750 people were taken to hospitals for

FACTS AND FIGURES

DATE	July 25 to 31, 2005
LOCATION	Maharashtra and Goa states, India
DEATH TOLL	At least 1,500
DAMAGE	Over US$1 million in business losses, thousands of buildings destroyed or damaged
FLOODING	37 inches (94 cm) rainfall overloaded drainage systems, caused landslides, flooded water supplies
COMMENTS	This flood resulted in the first-ever closure of all of Maharashtra's airports. A lack of preparation and insufficient flood warnings contributed to the high death toll.

LEFT Children search through a pile of wet rubbish dumped outside their house in Bharat Nagar, Mumbai. Under these conditions, many children were susceptible to diseases, such as malaria, typhoid, and cholera.

BELOW Indian policemen patrol Mumbai's Chowpatty Beach to prevent people from approaching the sea after the city's weather bureau issued warnings of high tides and heavy rains.

treatment of the same symptoms, with more than 40 of the cases in advanced and unstable conditions. Three districts were isolated with warnings that they were "hygienically sensitive" areas.

An irresponsible government

Maharashtra residents blamed the government for the inefficient warning systems and poor disaster management programs. Some said that no aid was given to the smaller coastal villages who were in dire need and the down-playing of the disaster in the media would restrict the generosity of foreign assistance offered to the stricken regions. Many local journalists tried to take the matter into their own hands and made online pleas to get the full story out to the international community that Maharashtra was suffering a devastating natural disaster and was in desperate need of help that the government was not providing them with.

Official analysis of the flood threats to the region cited a number of problems that aggravated the situation. Rapid growth in the suburban regions led to hasty and insufficient drainage systems that could not handle the overflow of water capable of backing up in the main city. Deforestation of the swamp regions that used to serve as a protective barrier from the sea has also increased the flood risk. Swamps along the Mahim Creek have suffered the systematic destruction of the natural mangrove ecology due to overwhelming construction demands, and the use of the area for dumping garbage and sewage. Over the previous 10 years, an estimated 40 percent of the mangroves had been killed or removed.

RUMORS CREATE PANIC AND RIOTS

By July 28, with massive flooding in the city, widespread rumors exacerbated the disaster situation. There were stories of tsunami warnings, and panic spread along the coast. In the Nehru Nager area, the tsunami rumor was aggravated by another one of a breach at Powai Lake. This caused a near riot among the people in the area. The resultant stampede killed at least 16 people, eight of whom were children. A local resident told reporters, "There were rumors that sea water was entering the land near Seven Bungalows. People were running helter-skelter, some even fell down." Police rushed to the scene to calm the crowd and dispel the rumors. Much of the lack of preparedness was blamed on Maharashtra's insufficient weather prediction equipment and radar, which made well-timed warnings impossible.

Droughts

When an area receives too little rain over a protracted period, a drought can result. Drought is by far the most serious hazard to world agriculture, and has a massive effect on national and world economies, as well as on the ability of a particular society to feed and clothe itself. Drought has such a severe impact on the landscape that plant and animal ecosystems can be changed irrevocably.

Unlike other weather disasters such as tornadoes, hurricanes, blizzards, floods or wildfires, drought is a slow and insidious phenomenon. Instead of lasting hours, days or even weeks, drought can last months and years, grinding away at agricultural production and infiltrating the fabric of society itself. The dollar damage done by an extended drought, although it is comparatively slow in accumulating, can be far higher than the spectacular damage trail produced by a hurricane or tornado.

Precise definitions of drought vary from country to country. For example in the United States, the term is sometimes used when an extensive area receives 30 percent or less of its normal rainfall over a minimum period of 21 days. In Australia, drought is defined in terms of rainfall deficiencies, with a severe deficiency occurring when rainfall over a particular area is in the lowest 5 percent of recorded falls for a minimum period of three months. In India, drought is declared if the annual rainfall over the area is less than 75 percent of the long-term average.

The different types of drought

Drought is usually a comparative term, referring to a rainfall deficiency relative to the normal, or usual rainfall, for the area in question. This is somewhat different from the areas of so-called permanent drought, which are the deserts of the world, where low rainfall is the norm. However, these are also areas of minimum agricultural activity, so the effect of this permanent drought on populations is not a major one. There are two types of drought that do affect human activity, and have far-reaching consequences for agriculture.

The first of these is the seasonal drought. This occurs in those areas of the world that experience a pronounced wet season/dry season climate.

FAR LEFT In drought-stricken outback Australia, many farming properties have been left to the elements as generations of farming families leave the land and search for work in regional centers and major cities.

LEFT Scattered bones bleached by the sun lie near an evaporating water hole. Drought leaves a devastating mark on wildlife, livestock, agricultural production, and food supplies.

PREVIOUS PAGES An Australian farmer checks the levels of his water tanks. The windmills pump borewater, but as the drought continues, the groundwater levels are dropping, making it harder to draw water. Many farmers have to buy in deliveries of water to keep their cattle alive.

ABOVE Near Semera, Danakil Desert in Ethiopia, a cloud of dust is kicked up by Zebu cattle, herded by the Afar people. Extreme drought causes soil erosion, leaching away soil fertility, and crops to fail.

RIGHT One-quarter of Earth's land is threatened by desertification. This is a process of land degradation in semi-arid and dry sub-humid areas that comes from extreme climate change, such as drought.

This covers many tropical and subtropical climate zones, including the northern regions of Australia, central Africa, and the India–Pakistan region, where agricultural activity is dependent on the onset of the wet season.

Because of its fairly regular nature, the seasonal drought is an inherent part of life for humans, plants, and animals in the affected areas, but real problems emerge if the onset of the wet season is late or if the wet season is weak and patchy. In these cases, extended drought results and the

WHAT TO DO DURING A DROUGHT
Governments around the world have developed various strategies for dealing with drought. These often involve water restrictions and financial relief packages for those worst affected.

Individual farmers usually look to agisting livestock, delaying the sowing of crops, and perhaps trucking in water to feed stock. In the city, residents may have to operate under water restrictions, and in areas where drought is periodic, perhaps augment their town water supply by installing water tanks. Some governments supply financial incentives to do this.

effect on agriculture can be catastrophic, producing widespread crop failures, famine, and loss of life.

The other type of drought is the contingent drought (meaning uncertain, or happening by chance, without obvious cause), which is possibly the most damaging form, because agricultural producers are frequently unprepared, and the consequences are therefore usually considerable.

Weather patterns hint at the start of a drought
The original term "contingent" drought is becoming somewhat of a misnomer, as our ability to understand the causes of drought is increasing. Scientists have been examining linkages between sea surface temperatures (SST) across the Pacific and Indian oceans and drought, and have discovered that for at least some continents, changes in the "normal" SST pattern can be associated with the onset of drought conditions.

The best local example of this is the El Niño phenomenon, where warmer than average SSTs develop across the eastern equatorial Pacific Ocean and produce a cascade of other linked phenomena which eventually impact as drought over much of eastern Australia, New Guinea, and Indonesia.

RIGHT Cornstalks dry and wither in the harsh, dry conditions. As food sources become limited, droughts contribute to major famines that can affect large numbers of densely populated areas, such as central Africa, China, India, and Pakistan.

TEN OF THE WORST DROUGHTS

1900 to 1903	A protracted period of dry weather around the time of Australia's Federation in 1901 caused the so-called Federation Drought. This led to huge stock losses followed by an almost total destruction of the national wheat crop for the year 1902.
1930s	An extended drought gripped the Great Plains area of the United States during the 1930s. Much of the Great Plains became a bleak and windswept "Dust Bowl," forcing many farmers off their land; huge agricultural losses resulted.
1968 to 1974	A series of dry years produced a massive drought across the Sahel region in Africa. Mass famines occurred, resulting in the deaths of hundreds of thousands of people.
1982 to 1983	Much of southeastern Australia was badly affected by a prolonged drought. Many areas received their lowest annual rainfall total on record, and severe wildfires followed in early 1983.
1984 to 1985	Severe drought over large tracts of Ethiopia, Kenya, and the Sudan led to an acute famine across the area, with one million people in Ethiopia dying from malnutrition and disease.
1988	Intense drought spread across the northern Great Plains area in the United States during the summer months, causing an estimated US$40 billion in crop losses.
2002	The worst drought in 27 years affected Vietnam, with only 25 percent of the annual rice crop being planted because of the acute soil dryness. Many villages experienced food shortages.
2003	Severe drought across eight southern provinces in China caused water shortages that affected more than 6 million people and nearly 3 million domestic animals. There were also power shortages and industry cutbacks because of a major reduction in hydroelectric power.
2005	One of the most severe droughts ever recorded in the Amazon, South America, saw several tributaries of the Amazon, and the surrounding wetlands, run almost dry. The river fish population was decimated, which caused severe hardship for the local population.
2004 to 2005	One of the worst droughts in the last 60 years severely reduced Spain's wheat and barley harvests. Reservoir levels reached historically low levels and wildfires scorched thousands of acres of forest, as well as killing 13 firefighters.

But El Niño is also associated with above-average rainfall in other areas, in particular Peru, so other explanations must be used to account for droughts in other parts of the world. However, it is likely that anomalous SST patterns will be implicated, and current research is investigating this approach in great depth. An El Niño condition can occur at irregular intervals of two to seven years, and it usually lasts one to two years.

Global warming, a much-debated but increasingly understood phenomenon, may also have a major impact on drought around the world, with some scenarios indicating an increase in its extent and severity across several continents.

The effects of drought

Drought, if it occurs over a protracted period across rural areas, certainly has the potential to force farmers off their land because of stock and crop losses. It also greatly increases the demand on water resources, and careful allocation has to be made to ensure equitable distribution. In urban areas, the results of drought are more indirect, including water restrictions and rising food prices.

The cost to governments can also be substantial, with financial assistance sometimes offered to farmers to get them through the difficult periods. A severe drought will have an impact on the national economy, chiefly because of the drop in rural activity. Shortages in hydroelectric power sometimes follow, causing widespread social inconvenience, as well as industry losses due to reductions in production.

LEFT A drought-dried stock tank and windmill in Rita Blanca National Grasslands, Texas. The National Grasslands began as a bailout program for the Dust Bowl farmers of the 1930s. Weather conditions on these prairie lands include severe winters and extreme drought.

In developing regions, such as Africa, droughts can be truly catastrophic, leading to widespread and protracted famine, with hundreds of thousands of people dying of starvation and disease. In the past, many millions of dollars have been spent in famine relief during these situations, but the problem can only be minimized, never solved.

Another major problem caused by drought is the wildfires that frequently follow. With the existing vegetation becoming tinder-dry during times of drought, the chances of wildfires developing are increased, and the severity of any such fire is also increased. An example of this were the notorious Ash Wednesday fires over southeastern Australia in February 1983, which occurred directly after the severe drought year of 1982.

Trying to predict drought

Because of its major impact across the whole gamut of human affairs, a great deal of international effort is being spent on drought prediction. To be able to predict the onset of a drought would produce immense benefits for the global economy. It would enable governments to prepare plans involving the stockpiling of food in affected areas, allow farmers to avoid wasting resources by not planting crops that are likely fail, and allow them to plan the movement of livestock into areas that are not expected to be severely rain deficient. The social and economic ramifications of such planning are enormous.

But can drought be predicted with accuracy? The short answer is no, but considerable progress is being made, and is realistically bringing accurate drought prediction into the realm of possibility.

One approach involves statistics, and links past rainfall with SST patterns at the time. This is used as the basis for looking into the future, taking into account the present SST conditions. Such an approach seems to be of some use, particularly in situations where a pronounced El Niño is evolving.

Another approach to drought forecasting involves the use of many dynamic mathematical models that simulate the movement of the Earth-atmosphere system. These have become increasingly sophisticated, and take into account meteorology, oceanography, land and sea ice, and even human interactions. They are called "coupled climate models," and they have the potential to produce even more progress in drought forecasting than the more widely used and orthodox statistical approach.

HOW DROUGHT IS MEASURED

The actual classification and measuring of drought varies from country to country, with Australia, for example, using three degrees of rainfall deficiency—serious, severe, and lowest on record.

In the United States, the Palmer Drought Severity Index (PDSI) is used. It employs past temperature and rainfall figures to determine environmental "dryness."

However, drought is increasingly being tracked internationally through satellite monitoring of vegetation cover, in which the density of green vegetation is measured and mapped through satellite imagery. A so-called vegetation index is calculated that quantifies the density of "green" vegetation right around the world. The Normalized Difference Vegetation Index (NDVI) rates vegetation cover from -1, meaning no cover, to +1, which means there is dense green growth. Most regions fall into the 0 to 0.6 range.

India, 1875 to 1900

A series of droughts in India between 1875 and 1900 killed 30 million people through consequent starvation, while the government exported wheat and rice. In the nineteenth and twentieth centuries, nine droughts were recorded in 44 years—that's one every 4½ years. Approximately one-third of the country is subject to regular drought. The drought of 1899 to 1900 is ranked as the fourth-deadliest disaster in India's modern history, and its second-deadliest drought.

RIGHT During the deadly famine in Ahmedabad, a province of India, the hungry wait to be given food handouts.

BELOW RIGHT A cartoon shows the British Empire donating small amounts of food to Indians starving after the drought.

BELOW Lucknow in India was just one example of the effects of a large population surviving on limited food supplies.

Before British rule, India managed to keep its people fed during times of famine—mogul emperors were responsible for distributing food in periods of drought until the rains returned. During British rule crops were exported for foreign income. Between 1875 and 1900, some 30 million Indians starved to death because they could not buy food because it was over-priced for export.

Droughts struck all of India in 1877 and 1899, but the worst hit region in the northeast experienced drought in 1884, 1891, 1892, 1896, and 1900. During the drought of 1899 to 1900, somewhere between 250,000 and 3.5 million people died. Up to two-thirds of the country was affected.

Why these droughts occurred

Drought in India results from failure of the monsoon. The Indian drought of 1899–1900 was the prompt for Sir Gilbert Walker (1868–1958), an English physicist and statistician who headed the meteorological service in India, to investigate why the monsoon sometimes fails. Walker discovered the link between barometric pressure in Tahiti and in Darwin, Australia: when the pressure is high at one, it is low at the other. The resulting seesawing of pressure is called the Southern Oscillation. Together with El Niño, it affects climate over much of the world. Sir Gilbert was able to link up weather records from India, Indonesia, Australia, and other countries, and found that heavy monsoon rain in India was associated with drought in Australia and mild winters in Canada, and vice versa.

El Niño events in 1876, 1877, 1888, 1891, 1896, and 1899 were responsible for below-average rainfall in the same years; those of 1877 and 1899 were responsible for the failure of the monsoon to arrive, and caused severe drought, with rainfall totaling as much as 30 percent below average rainfall.

Widespread famine and the decimation of crops

In 1876, the famine caused by drought spread from southeastern India to the west, then northward to the northwest. Peasant farmers sold whatever they could to survive the first year of the drought. But having sold their animals and farming equipment, they could not take advantage of the intermittent rain, and hundreds of thousands of people died in 1877. Millions more were left severely malnourished. By 1878, people were fighting over the dwindling supplies of food.

Heavy rains in late 1878 ended the drought, but brought hundreds of thousands more deaths from malaria, as mosquito populations exploded in the wet conditions.

With no farming animals or equipment, the surviving farmers had to plow with sticks. To add to their hardship, any crops they were able to sow and start growing were immediately eaten by locusts.

FACTS AND FIGURES	
DATE	1875 to 1900
LOCATION	India
DEATH TOLL	30 million
DAMAGE	Up to two-thirds of India was affected by this drought; it also extended to much of the world
COMMENTS	The number of famines in the 2,000 years before British rule was 17; the number of famines during 120 years of British rule totaled 31.

361

Political policy, not drought, was responsible
for the famine. The British rulers in India believed
that giving handouts encouraged shirking by Indian
laborers. They insisted on labor in exchange for food.
The amount given out provided fewer calories than
prisoners received in Nazi concentration camps in
World War II. The railways the British had built
across India did not transport food to the starving
population, but transported it to the ports for export
to Europe. Market forces determined grain prices,
leaving most peasants unable to buy the food that
they so desperately needed. Food that could have
fed 25 million people was exported; up to 10 million
tons (10.2 million t) a year by 1900.

Ukraine and Volga, 1921 to 1923

Drought in 1921 in Ukraine and the Volga and Caucasus regions of Russia precipitated the death by starvation of up to 2 million Ukrainians, not through lack of food but because of Soviet policy.

ABOVE Thousands of people abandoned their family homes in search of food for their starving children.

BELOW Ragged and barefoot refugees wait in an open-air area which used to be part of the Red Army military camp.

Drought is an occasional visitor to the Ukraine, and in preparation, farmers have traditionally kept grain in reserve for the lean times. But the drought that struck the region of western Asia in 1921, stretching from southern Ukraine through the Volga region of Russia to the northern Caucasus region led to the deaths of millions of people in the Ukraine. Their food reserves were forcibly taken, and they were left to starve while food was exported under Soviet directives.

During the drought, crop yields fell by as much as 85 percent. The drought was natural, but despite the low yields, the resulting famine was entirely human-made. Extreme drought in the Volga River valley and the northern Caucasus reduced Russia's food supply, which was already faltering under the effects of war and Bolshevik mismanagement. Faced with a food shortage, Russia, which had effectively annexed the Ukraine in 1920, instructed Ukraine to send grain to keep the major Russian industrial cities fed.

The drought lasted from 1921 to 1923. However, it did not affect northern Ukraine, which was able to keep growing enough grain to feed the entire population, if it had been allowed to send it south. Instead, in the first year of the drought, the grain went to Russia; in the second year, it was sold to the West. Russia appointed an All-Russian Committee to Aid the Hungry and accepted aid for its regions, but took eight months to let aid into Ukraine. Many who survived the famine succumbed to of cholera.

FACTS AND FIGURES

DATE	1921 to 1923
LOCATION	The Ukraine, the Volga, and Caucasus regions of Russia
DEATH TOLL	Up to 2 million Ukrainians, 2 to 10 million Russians
DAMAGE	Caused massive crop failures, including total crop failure of about 20 percent of Soviet farmland
COMMENTS	The severe consequences of this drought were more a "man-made" famine that caused the unprecedented starvation than agricultural devastation. People died from disease outbreaks.

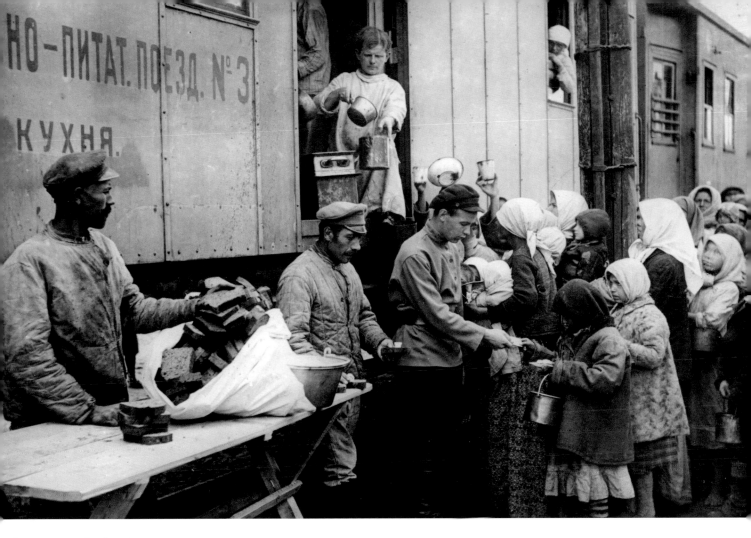

A man-made famine

The Russian government looked after its own population well, but at the expense of the 1.5 million to 2 million Ukrainians who died of starvation or disease.

Those who did not die escaped death by one of two means: they fled the Ukraine or they resorted to crime. The most desperate people resorted to kidnapping children to eat, and human flesh was commonly sold in markets. Those who fled the Ukraine camped out in disused railway carriages, or rode the freight cars, hoping to get to somewhere better. During the harsh winters, many of these refugees froze to death. In 1922, an official of the International Save the Children Fund was told that on two bitterly cold days the corpses of 400 frozen children had been removed from one train.

Aleksandra Rakhmanova, a Russian noblewoman who fled the Bolsheviks, wrote:

"August 15, 1921. The train moves slowly, passing endless deportation trains from the famine areas of the Volga and the North. The cattle trains are crowded with people, piled up like coal: men, women, children. But are these still people? Many of them lost their teeth, their gums are bleeding, their faces are green and ash-gray."

Although the Russian government was negligent in acting to ease its population's suffering, other governments were quick to respond. Hearing of the famine, the American Relief Association (ARA), headed by Herbert Hoover, sent immediate aid. The ARA gradually earned the trust of local authorities and saved 2 million people in the Ukraine and another 10 million in Russia from starvation. Others also contributed, notably emigrant Ukrainians, the American Jewish community, churches, and charities.

ABOVE American volunteers hand out much-needed food and seed grain supplies to the hungry from a traveling relief train that stopped at various towns in the Ukraine.

STORIES OF SURVIVAL

Lois Klaus of Oregon in the United States remembers that the effects of this drought lasted a lifetime: "My father went through the famine of the early 1920s. He told me about going through the markets and not finding anything to eat. When one did, you would hide it under your coat so no one would take it from you. When he finally came over to this country with his mother in 1924, and then got married in 1930, he would not let my mother cook *kartoffel und glase* [potatoes and dumplings] because that was all they had to eat for most of the two years."

Arthur Ransome, a reporter for *The Guardian* newspaper in Britain and author of several children's books, also wrote about the level of starvation that he saw in the Ukraine:

"We went down to the shore of the Volga, down a rough broken street, past booths where you could buy white bread, and, not a hundred yards away, found an old woman cooking horse dung in a broken saucepan. Within sight of the market was a mass of refugees, men, women, and children … still starving, listlessly waiting for the wagons to move them away to more fortunate districts. Some are sitting sheltered from the rain … I shall never forget the wizened dead face, pale green, of a silently weeping little girl, whose feet were simply bones over which stretched her dry skin that looked like blue-black leather. And she was one of hundreds."

Northwestern China, 1928 to 1930

"A human tragedy of unimaginable severity." This would have been the thoughts of those first on the scene of the drought that struck the northwest of China during the period from 1928 through to 1930. Communication with the outside world was limited and records kept by the local administrations were inadequate. As a result, the true extent of this tragedy will never be known.

BELOW The Xiahe grasslands in Gansu Province during times of normal rainfall are lush, fertile feeding grounds for livestock. During times of drought these grasslands become dust plains unable to sustain agriculture.

Demographers examining historical population records have estimated the death toll to have come to about 3 million. The worst-affected areas were the provinces of Henna, Anhui, Shaanxi, Gansu, and Guizhou, although the effects of the drought spilled over into neighboring provinces.

China is highly susceptible to drought, with the northwest being the driest region of the country. Meteorological records for the northwestern region during the period from 1928 through 1930 are scant, and the severity of the drought in comparison with other droughts in the region, in meteorological terms, cannot be accurately determined. However, it is known that this drought was prolonged, and affected a large proportion of the country. A recent study of the climate record puts this period in the top four driest periods over the last century.

The enormous death toll from this drought was the result of the effects of several factors. First, the regional grain storage facilities were grossly inadequate for the size of the population, and stores ran out during the early stages of the drought.

Second, regional governments were inefficient, and third, there were only a few relief organizations in existence. Finally, the drought occurred during a time of war between the forces of Chiang Kai-shek's Kuomintang and the opposing communist forces of Mao Zedong. This diverted internal and external attention from the victims of the drought, so very little external aid was provided.

Spread of the drought

During the summer of 1928, there was very little rain throughout the northwestern regions of China. This led to widespread crop failures. As communities exhausted their food stocks, they abandoned their homes and moved to nearby villages. The swollen populations of these villages meant that their food stocks too were quickly consumed. These villages, in turn, were abandoned. This process continued until large regions of the northwest of this populous nation had no food left at all. It was at this stage that the widespread deaths due to starvation and malnutrition-related illnesses started to occur. People took to eating anything they could find: plant, animal and mineral. There were fragmented reports and rumors of cannibalism.

Following the end of the 1928 to 1930 drought, one researcher undertook an investigation into what the survivors had been forced to eat in order to survive the harsh conditions. The investigations revealed that chaff, tree leaves, and bark, a powder made from edible wild herbs, poplar buds, corncobs, bleaching clay, sawdust, peanut shells, sweet potato vines, and even grass roots were eaten. In Shandong Province, a cotton-producing region of China, the villagers survived on a diet made up of cereal chaff and cottonseed. The local people were so dependent on the cotton plants for food that no cotton was sold on the market during this period of the drought. The Si Chuan Relief Association reported that tens of thousands of people ate *guanyintu*, a type of white clay, to help ease their hunger.

Lessons not learned

One researcher's estimate puts the total death toll from famines during the last century at close to 100 million. The drought of 1928 to 1930 followed China's drought of 1907, with estimated deaths of 24 million. In 1936, another severe drought hit China; it resulted in 5 million deaths. The drought of 1941 to 1942 led to a further 3 million deaths from starvation, and a combination of drought and political interference resulted in a massive death toll during the "hidden famine" of 1959 to 1962. It is only recently that the government and people of China have been able to prepare for, and withstand the ravages of the cycles of drought.

FACTS AND FIGURES

DATE	Early 1928 to late 1930
LOCATION	Northwestern China
DEATH TOLL	3 million
DAMAGE	Severe, but no accurate damage estimates have been made
COMMENTS	Further droughts of similar severity followed at intervals throughout the remainder of the twentieth century. The government and people are now able to prepare themselves for future droughts.

TOP An all-too-common sight throughout the provinces of drought-affected China. A man, unable to provide food for his family, grieves as his children watch their mother slowly dying from starvation.

ABOVE Refugees from Shantung during the famine barely survived on limited food supplies. People ate anything to ease their hunger.

Great Plains Dust Bowl, USA, 1930s

A severe drought in the breadbasket of the United States during the 1930s transformed productive farmland into gigantic clouds of windborne soil that blanketed everything in dust, forced the migration of hundreds of thousands of people across America, inspired *The Grapes of Wrath* and the songs of Woody Guthrie, and gave impetus to President Franklin Roosevelt's New Deal economic policies.

BELOW Early morning whirlwinds rise from the finely tilled soil on a farm in Walla Walla County in Washington DC, where dust lifted from the Dust Bowl region had been blown in by the wind, causing "black blizzards."

Following the end of World War I, the rebuilding of European economies gave new life to European agriculture, turning Europe from a net importer of food to a net exporter. Agricultural commodity prices in the United States, which had supplied a large part of Europe's food until then, began to drop. In response to the lower prices, American farmers planted more crops to compensate. But with the markets already saturated, prices dropped even further. This led to a vicious cycle of ever-increasing production and ever-diminishing returns.

The coincidence of this situation along with the drought resulted in the worst ecological disaster to occur in American history: the Dust Bowl.

The Dust Bowl centered on the Great Plains, which stretch from Canada in the north to Mexico in the south. This high plateau is characterized by flat plains and gently rolling hills, which were originally covered mostly by continuous grassland.

Until the late nineteenth century, the Great Plains were sparsely populated: in the entire region, the total population in 1880 was only 800,000 people, spread over an area of 1,125,000 square miles (2,900,000 km²). But by 1930, the population had increased over seven times that number.

Drought is a regular feature of the Great Plains. Tree-ring measurements, sediment, and other data show that droughts have occurred there three or four times a century for a very long time. For example, a particular drought in the late thirteenth and early fourteenth centuries lasted for 38 years.

The drought that began in 1931 continued for nearly 10 years. It became the worst drought on record in the United States. Farmers were hit hard by the dropping prices and their inability to grow anything to sell. Banks began to foreclose on farm loans and repossessed farming equipment. To make matters worse, overplowing and overgrazing had loosened the topsoil so much that even light winds began to pick it up and carry it away. As the drought worsened, all of the topsoil and its nutrients blew away, leaving farmers with nothing to grow crops in, even if rain had fallen. The Great Depression only exacerbated the problems.

What caused the Dust Bowl?

To understand the causes of the Dust Bowl, it is necessary go back a few years. The high grain prices during World War I encouraged farmers to plow up their pastures and plant large areas of wheat, cultivating land that would be recognized today as, at best, marginal. The recovery of post-war Europe and the falling US commodity prices spurred the farmers on to plow more land and grow more crops to make up the income shortfall. One irony of this scramble to produce more was that there was already too much food being produced worldwide and there was nowhere to sell it.

Clearing, plowing, and grazing played a large part in the creation of the Dust Bowl. The soils of the Great Plains, although fertile, are also fragile and fine. The native grasses put down very deep roots to tap the little moisture that the light soil can hold. These roots form a very dense, tough mat. Further, the herds of buffalo, which once numbered in their millions, had disappeared, and with them the fertilizer they deposited. The net result was a loss of the roots that held the soil together, and of nutrients.

When the drought struck in 1931, there was nothing to contain the soil, and it blew away.

How did the drought start?

Drought is a natural occurrence, and a feature of the Great Plains. Recent work by NASA scientists has pinpointed the likely cause of drought in this area. Writing in *Science* on March 19, 2004, Siegfried Schubert and colleagues reported how they used sea temperature records collected from ships, and

Vast quantities of topsoil were blown across the Great Plains, burying houses in mountains of dust (top). Farmers here were unable to work as their crops would not grow in the extremely dry, poor-quality soil (above).

THE ENDLESS CYCLE OF WIND AND DUST

During droughts, the native grasses gradually die off, leaving much of the soil surface bare. At these times, strong winds, unhindered by any natural windbreaks on the flat topography, can lift off some of the soil and cause dust storms, most often during spring. Newspaper and diary records from the nineteenth century show that long-term residents saw drought and dust storms as regular events, to be put up with. "The wind … filled the air with such clouds of dust that darkness of the 'consistency of twilight' prevailed. Buildings across the street could not be distinguished … The air was so filled with dust as to be stifling, even within houses."

land temperatures around the world, to reconstruct the weather patterns that occurred during the 1930s using a computer-generated model.

The key features of their findings are that lower-than-normal sea-surface temperatures in the tropical Pacific Ocean and higher-than-normal sea-surface temperatures in the tropical Atlantic Ocean shifted the winds that normally bring rain to the Great Plains. Normally, the jet stream—a low-level band of air driven by Earth's rotation—flows west from the Atlantic Ocean and over the Gulf of Mexico, where the mountains of Central America force it to turn northward. This air picks up moisture from the sea, which is deposited on the Great Plains. In normal circumstances, a higher surface temperature in the Atlantic and a lower surface temperature in the Pacific do not coincide. However, during the 1930s, they did: the differences in air pressure and the rate of evaporation combined to weaken the jet stream and divert it to the south, away from the Great Plains.

The location of the drought moved during the 1930s, as sporadic rains fell here and there. The US Soil Conservation Service defined the Dust Bowl then as the western third of Kansas, southeastern Colorado, the Oklahoma and Texas Panhandles, and northeastern New Mexico. This covered 100 million acres (more than 40 million ha). Beyond the core Dust Bowl area, drought affected all of the Great Plains and much of the rest of North America as well: in 1934, over 75 percent of the United States was in drought, and 27 states were badly affected.

Mass migration

The drought caused the biggest migration in American history. As much as one-quarter of all residents in the Great Plains region left; estimates vary from 300,000 to 2,500,000. Bank foreclosures on farms had already begun in the late 1920s because world oversupply meant that farmers were unable to keep up payments. The drought put the final nail in the coffin for many more. The lack of income meant that farmers were unable to pay their taxes, so county governments had to start laying off police and teachers, and cut back services. In some towns up to 60 percent of the population left.

The displaced population became known as Okies, from the nickname given to those from the Oklahoma Panhandle, even though most came from other states. Many went to California, which became enshrined in the folk songs of the time as a promised land. Some were able to find itinerant farm work there, being forced to move from place to place as the seasons and the crops demanded. With no money and little food, many itinerants set up camp alongside irrigation and drainage ditches

in Californian fields. As a result, outbreaks of malaria and other diseases created a public health problem. As the exodus continued, established residents began to resent the intrusion; some tried to prevent it. The police chief of Los Angeles even sent 125 officers, dubbed the "Bum Brigade," to the border to turn people away.

Collier's magazine in 1935 reported: "Very erect and primly severe, [a man] addressed the slumped driver of a rolling wreck that screamed from every hinge, bearing, and coupling. 'California's relief rolls are overcrowded now. No use to come farther,' he cried. … 'There really is nothing for you here,' the neat, trooperish young man went on. 'Nothing, really nothing.' And the forlorn man on the moaning car

FACTS AND FIGURES

DATE	1930s
LOCATION	The Great Plains stretch from Canada to Mexico; US: Montana, North Dakota, South Dakota, Wyoming, Nebraska, Colorado, Kansas, New Mexico, Oklahoma, Texas; Canada: Manitoba, Saskatchewan, Alberta
DAMAGE	All of the Great Plains—1,125,000 square miles (2,900,000 km^2), over 75 percent of the US and parts of Canada; up to 2,500,000 people were displaced
COMMENTS	Drought lasted for nearly ten years, up to 47 million acres (19 million ha) of crops failed. The fertility of the soil was greatly reduced.

ABOVE A family in Pittsburg County, Oklahoma, is forced to leave their home during the Great Depression because the drought had completely destroyed their livelihood.

FAR LEFT Some displaced farm workers from Oklahoma, often referred to as "Okies", stop at a "Road Information" sign on the Texas state border as they flee the Dust Bowl. Many such people walked for hundreds of miles to find work and shelter.

ABOVE Drought-affected farm workers were forced to move from their homesteads and settle in makeshift buildings as they searched for work.

looked at him, dull, emotionless, incredibly weary, and said: 'So? Well, you ought to see what they got where I come from.'"

In response to the flood of displaced citizens, President Roosevelt ordered the setting up of 13 camps, each housing 300 families in tents, in 1937. Finding that most of the farmland in California still belonged to corporations, many migrants gave up on farming and settled down in shacks built of scrap.

The new deal

When President Roosevelt took office in 1933, he acted quickly to stabilize the country. Congress passed the Emergency Banking Act, which balanced the banks with the backing of the Federal Government. Further legislation allocated $200 million to allow farmers to re-mortgage loans and avoid foreclosure.

The slaughter and disposal of 6 million pigs to stabilize prices was met with public outcry. In

response, Congress created the Federal Surplus Relief Corporation, which took food surpluses and distributed them through local relief agencies.

In 1934, the Farm Bankruptcy Act restricted the ability of banks to foreclose on any farmers experiencing hardship.

In 1935, the Drought Relief Service was created. The Service bought up cattle in drought-stricken areas, destroyed those that were in bad condition, and supplied the rest through the Federal Surplus Relief Corporation to the needy as food. Roosevelt approved the Emergency Relief Appropriation Act, providing $225 million in drought relief, and formed the Works Progress Administration, creating jobs for up to 8.5 million people and supporting families.

BLACK BLIZZARDS AND DUST BOWLS

The name "Dust Bowl" was coined in a newspaper report on April 15, 1935, the day after Black Sunday, when the worst "black blizzard" occurred. The black blizzards had begun in 1931, and they grew in strength and number, to 14 in 1932 and 38 in 1933. The worst one of these deposited dust as far as New York, Washington DC, and Chicago, where dust from a two-day storm in May 1934 fell like filthy snow. The dust banked up against houses, buildings, and fences, like snowdrifts.

US Congress created the Soil Conservation Service, which devised programs to reverse soil degradation and to restore productivity. Today it is known as the Natural Resources Conservation Service, and its work continues. Various Federal agencies bought up 11 million acres (4.5 million ha) of former farmland, which is currently leased to ranchers by the US Forest Service.

In 1937, Roosevelt established the Shelterbelt Program to minimize wind erosion. Under this specialized program, native trees were planted along property boundaries to cut the force of the wind and hold the soil. By 1938, this work and the various soil conservation measures had reduced the extensive amount of soil being lost by up to 65 percent.

Breaking of the drought

The drought finally ended in 1941, when heavy rain returned to the Great Plains. Modern-day soil conservation practices allow farmers in the Great Plains to farm as much land as was farmed in 1930. Droughts have occurred since, and dust storms are still a regular feature of the Great Plains, but the confluence of the events of the 1920s and 1930s has never been repeated.

The greatest legacy of the Dust Bowl is not the lesson to farm wisely, which continues to be re-learned, but the agricultural subsidies given by the US Federal Government to agricultural producers throughout the country to limit production; these now determine crop prices worldwide.

ABOVE A car full of "Okies", refugees from the Dust Bowl, look for work in San Francisco, California. Their belongings are strapped to the running board of the automobile.

India, 1965 to 1967

The failure of monsoonal rains in India can have dire effects on the Indian population. From 1965 to 1967, such a drought struck large parts of India, and a staggering 1.5 million people died. With a population of nearly a billion people, India was particularly vulnerable to such a crisis.

RIGHT A superstition in India is that in time of drought a neighbor's portable oven must be stolen, smashed, and the pieces soaked in water, to bring rain. This is a boon for manufacturers. Here, dozens of new portable ovens are waiting to be sold to replace those stolen.

FAR RIGHT, BOTTOM This map shows the path and timing of the monsoon rains that are expected to sweep through India annually. Between 1965 and 1967, the lack of these predictable rains caused widespread disaster.

It was the third catastrophic drought to afflict India during the twentieth century. It was the one that set in train measures to ensure that India would never be so unprepared again.

Approximately 80 percent of the annual rainfall over India occurs during the wet season, from June through to September, which is widely known as the southwest or summer monsoon. Two-thirds of the cultivated land in India is watered entirely by monsoonal rains during the Kharif season, which runs from June through to October. In the Rabi season that follows, spanning the October to March period, a combination of residual soil moisture and irrigation waters the crops. However, most of the irrigation systems are reliant upon monsoon rain-fed rivers. So when the monsoon fails, or is weaker than usual, drought has a major impact on food stocks. At the time of the 1965 drought, a large percentage of the population were subsistence farmers; few had any additional sources of income.

During the 1965 monsoon season, a staggering 47 percent of the country was drought affected, including 43 percent of the areas under cultivation.

An estimated 47.6 million people had to contend with a drought that reduced their grain production to close to 19 percent. This meant grain prices soared by 65 percent in one year. With half of the population living below the poverty line, many families were unable to buy food when crops failed: 37 percent of households were forced to survive with a daily calorific intake of only 500 calories, regarded internationally as the starvation threshold.

The aid available to the starving population was extremely limited. India was embroiled in a war with neighboring Pakistan, draining its foreign reserves, tying up its human and physical resources, and limiting its ability to respond. The government held only about 2 million tons (2.2 million t) of food in stock in 1965, well short of the needs of its people. Drought preparedness of the villages and at all levels of government was minimal.

The "Green Revolution"

The Green Revolution was a government initiative involving an effort to improve food self-sufficiency through developing technology and production in agriculture. The 1965 drought in India pushed the newly elected Prime Minister, Indira Ghandi, into action. The country's 14 leading banks were nationalized, making credit more freely available to agriculture and small industry. New drought-resistant grain crops were introduced and the areas under irrigation were expanded dramatically. Roads and transportation systems were improved in rural areas and the number of food distribution centers

RIGHT A baby sits on the roadside near the Ganges River as his mother begs for money during the famine that was a direct result of the drought.

FACTS AND FIGURES	
DATE	Started 1965, ended late 1967
LOCATION	India
DEATH TOLL	1.5 million
DAMAGE	The damage was severe, but accurate damage estimates have never been calculated; the extent of the drought meant that, in 1965, 47 percent of India was drought affected, including 43 percent of areas under cultivation
COMMENTS	As a result, the "Green Revolution" was put into action, making the country more able to withstand and survive its frequently occurring droughts.

escalated. Food stockpiles were built up during the years when there were abundant monsoonal rains. Successive governments have built upon these initiatives.

The 2002 drought: lessons learned

The dramatic improvement in the ability of modern India to withstand the effects of drought was highlighted during a drought in 2002. Meteorologically, this drought was a more severe event than the drought in 1965, with 263 districts, equal to 56 percent of the land area of India, receiving highly deficient rainfall, compared with 125 districts in the 1965 drought. The population directly affected by drought had grown to 300 million by 2002, yet there was a negligible number of deaths through starvation. The nation had proved that it was able to cope with a potentially catastrophic drought using just its own resources; no external aid was required. Gross Domestic Product (GDP) and the inflation rate showed a remarkable resilience to the drought, with the domestic price of goods barely changing.

Further to the Green Revolution, the Indian government has realized that there will be always be major droughts in the future, and money has been devoted for research into the life-giving southwest monsoon, so that it may be better predicted.

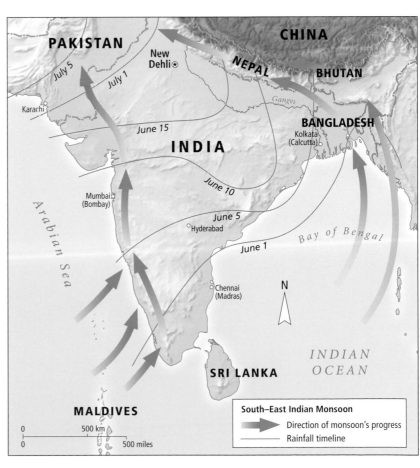

Sahel, Sub-Saharan Africa, 1968 to 1974

Always a fragile land perched on the edge of the vast, inhospitable Sahara Desert, the governments of the countries that comprise the Sahel region of sub-Saharan Africa—from Senegal in the west across some 2,795 miles (4,500 km) of the continent to Sudan in the east—were not prepared for the devastation wrought upon their people by a drought that was severe, even by their standards.

ABOVE The Emperor of Ethiopia, Haile Selassie, appeared to be unaware of the extreme impact of the drought on his people. This caused simmering unrest among the population. An army-led coup brought Selassie's almost half a century of rule to a dramatic end.

BELOW Famine relief, arriving in western Africa for the Mali tribes, is being loaded into sacks.

Although no accurate figures apparently exist, it is known that hundreds of thousands perished and whole tribes were forever displaced from their traditional lands.

The period immediately preceding the drought, from 1950 through to 1967, was the wettest period for the Sahel region during the past 120 years. Some say that this abnormally wet period exacerbated the drought as the economies of the sub-Saharan countries had become over-reliant on rain-fed agriculture and animal production. There was also a push, supported by governments of the area, for people to move northward, where the rainfall was higher. The increased population put pressure on grazing and land management. Then, in 1968, the rains began to fail over much of the central and western Sahel with drought conditions becoming more general across the Sahel in the ensuing years. This triggered a tragedy of unequalled proportions for the region. The years 1973 to 1974 were particularly harsh over the eastern countries. Millions of traditionally nomadic and subsistence tribes people were in dire straits. Crops failed, the water quality dropped, and diseases spread. Grazing lands turned to dust and domestic animals died in

their millions. Hundreds of thousands of people died from starvation and many more were permanently weakened from the effects of famine.

Always a climatically vulnerable region, many countries of the region also had to contend with warfare, government corruption and instability, and general mismanagement of already scarce resources. Their ability to cope with a major environmental disaster of this kind was severely hampered from the outset. External assistance was badly needed, but by the time the outside world was aware of the situation in the Sahel, it was far too late for many.

Bringing drought to the world

Few people in the western world even knew where the Sahel was in the early 1960s. All this changed in the latter half of the 1960s and the first half of the 1970s when journalists, investigating the devastating drought that spread from one side of Africa to the other, brought graphic pictures of millions of starving African people to newspapers and television sets across the globe. The shocking images jolted the wealthier countries into action. Food aid programs unparalleled in history were established, though they were too late for many victims of the drought. In the decades that followed, the relief programs have gradually evolved to become more sustainable schemes targeted to boost the capacity of key economic sectors of the affected countries. These strategies have enabled a greater degree of self-help, and more effective distribution of aid.

FACTS AND FIGURES

DATE	Early 1968 to late 1974
LOCATION	Sahel region of Africa
DEATH TOLL	Hundreds of thousands; 50,000 in Ethiopia
DAMAGE	Severe, but no accurate damage estimates have been made
COMMENTS	The start of a prolonged series of droughts across the region. Emperor Haile Selassie, said to have direct lineage back to the kings of biblical times, became the highest profile victim of the Sahelian drought when the army turned on him.

A complex cause

It was first thought that the degradation of land through the widespread destruction of vegetation across the region by overgrazing of large herds of goats and cattle, combined with the clearing of trees and moves to increase land cultivation, was the main cause of the prolonged Sahelian drought. However, more recent studies have shown that the processes contributing to drought in this region are far more complex than this.

Sea surface temperature anomaly patterns in the equatorial Atlantic, North Atlantic, and Indian oceans are strongly linked to drought and wet years across the Sahel. This means that, although the degradation of the landscape does increase the impact of the drought, reduce soil fertility, and decrease the quality of the remaining sources of surface water, the dominant causes of the drought are large-scale changes in the atmosphere and oceanic circulation patterns.

Satellite monitoring of suddenly decreasing vegetation cover across the region now provides advance warning of the onset of a drought, and is a significant indicator of an impending food shortage. The numerous governments, private sector traders, and aid agencies are now forewarned, and better able to assess, mobilize volunteers, and provide effective assistance during the earlier stages of drought.

What does the future hold?

Scientific evidence continues to indicate that the global climate is changing. What this change will mean in various regions is still the subject of research and debate. However, one recent finding is very encouraging for this part of the world. It arises from a study that uses state-of-the-art scientific climate prediction models to look at what is likely to happen in the greenhouse gas-induced warmer climate of the future. These models have predicted a reversal of the drying trend across the Sahel region as the global temperature warms over the next few decades. Predictions for decades ahead show an increase in rainfall in the southern parts of the Sahel.

There is also an understanding of the need to reduce the human-caused stress on the environment through improving soil and water conservation strategies, and building up stocks of fodder.

ABOVE A familiar scene during the Sahel drought. However, the devastating disaster did ultimately lead to some positive outcomes. Most countries in the Sahel now have sufficient resources and the experience of hindsight to help survive all but the most severe drought.

THE MOST SEVERE DROUGHT ON EARTH

This Sahelian drought was the third of the twentieth century but the first of several catastrophic drought events for this region in modern times. These events spanned the last two years of the 1960s through to 1974, then returned with even greater severity through most of the 1980s, 1990s, and half of the first decade of the twenty-first century. The rainfall decline over the 30-year period from 1968 to 1997, when compared with the 30-year period from 1931 to 1960, was a staggering 30 to 40 percent, the largest recorded anywhere on Earth.

South and Southeastern Australia, 1982 to 1983

Described as Australia's worst drought since Federation in 1901, the 1982 to 1983 drought was an economic and social disaster for the country. Never before had there been a drought that so seriously affected the entire country at the one time. Crop failures were widespread, with many farmers facing bankruptcy. Fires that occurred during the drought killed more than 70 people and destroyed 2,400 homes. The nation was plunged into a financial recession.

BELOW The desiccated carcass of a kangaroo lies by a fence at Teryanynia Station in Wilcannia, in outback New South Wales. Kangaroos and many other native wildlife species suffered during the drought which weakened their ability to search across wider areas for food.

Australia's most extensive and devastating drought had its genesis thousands of miles away on the opposite side of the vast Pacific Ocean. An immense pool of abnormally warm waters accumulated off the Peruvian coastline, triggering the strongest El Niño that meteorologists have ever recorded. During an El Niño, there is an eastward displacement of the normal rain-bearing region from over eastern Australia to the southwest Pacific region. In this particular case, the intensity of the El Niño was such that the drought was extremely severe and prolonged. Rainfall across the key grain-growing regions of South Australia, Victoria, and New South Wales was the lowest on record for the 11-month period from April 1982 through to February 1983.

Widespread disaster and devastation

Of critical importance was the complete failure of the winter and spring rains that normally support the growth of the main cereal crops, across almost all of southern and southeastern Australia. Crop failures became the norm in the usually reliable winter grain-growing belt of southeastern Australia. The almost total loss of feeding pastures also decimated the valuable sheep and cattle herds of these regions, and limited the productivity of irrigated crops.

Raging dust storms became commonplace through much of inland Australia as the parched soil turned to dust across vast agricultural tracts. The severity of the drought was dramatically brought home to those in the urban areas when a large cloud of dust smothered the city of Melbourne, an event that had never been experienced before. The high temperatures that accompanied this particular

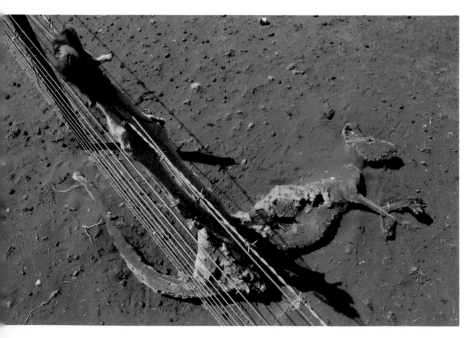

FACTS AND FIGURES

DATE	April 1982 to February 1983
LOCATION	Queensland, New South Wales, Victoria, South Australia, southern Western Australia
DEATH TOLL	76
DAMAGE	Approximately AUD$3 billion (1983 value); 2,400 homes destroyed by fire
RAINFALL	Lowest rainfall on record for the 11-month period from April 1982 through to February 1983 across the key grain-growing regions of South Australia, Victoria, and New South Wales
COMMENTS	Spurred on research into developing drought-tolerant crops. Also paved the way for research into efficient land management and ideal farm models.

drought are also thought to have increased the mortality rates of the frail and aged across the southeastern areas of Australia. Research following the event has revealed a steep increase in the death rate of the old and infirm over the three days following one extreme heatwave.

A cycle of natural disasters

One natural disaster can trigger another, and this was the case for the 1982 to 1983 drought. The prolonged hot and dry weather across the southeast of Australia turned the highly flammable forests and grasslands into a tinderbox. The approach of a strong frontal weather system on Ash Wednesday, 16 February 1983, caused temperatures to soar, and as a result, a series of massive, uncontrollable wildfires broke out, producing the most devastating outbreak of fire in Australia's history. Around 180 wildfires raged in South Australia and Victoria; they killed 76 people and left 2,400 families homeless.

The political impact

The impact of this natural disaster went well beyond affecting farmers and the agricultural industry who were reliant on the land for their livelihood. The political landscape of Australia was also changed as a result, bringing in a change of political parties. The prolonged drought is considered to have been a significant contributor to sending the Australian economy into recession. A failing economy and public dissatisfaction led to the ousting of the incumbent Liberal–National Party Coalition Government, and it effectively ended seven years of this party's political dominance. Drought-breaking rain across Australia during March 1983 signalled the arrival of the newly elected Labor Party back into power.

Learning to live with drought

A new sense of preparedness across Australia sprang from this drought. Intensive research efforts led to the development of new, drought-tolerant strains of cereal crops. Farmers and pastoralists accepted the inevitable; that there would be more droughts in the future. They began to adopt new measures to make optimum use and advantage of the available rainfall, and to minimize the problems associated with drought, including soil erosion, and degradation of the water quality of the river systems. Researchers were able to identify the strong relationship between El Niño and drought in Australia, with a result that seasonal climate predictions are routinely issued now to help the community prepare for developing droughts.

ABOVE LEFT An emaciated sheep stands in dusty field near Port Augusta in South Australia. A worsening of the drought conditions cut farm production revenue by billions of dollars.

ABOVE The gnarled remains of a mangrove tree stand as a testament to the devastating effects of salination. Although in the north of the country, the surrounding wetlands were impacted by the drought ravaging the southern states.

Australia, 2001 to 2006

Drought is a natural part of life in Australia, as *My Country*, the poem by Dorothea Mackellar, so famously immortalizes: "I love a sunburnt country, a land … of droughts and flooding rains." The drought that started in 2001 and did not end until the start of 2006 was as harsh as any recorded in Australia's rural history, affecting town and country.

During this five-year period, many parts of Australia experienced repeated crop failures, massive drops in farm income, wildfires, and water restrictions as severe as any imposed during the past 200 years. At its peak, a remarkable 98.6 percent of the entire continent received below average rainfall. However, drought management procedures and government support meant no lives were lost and rural communities, although hard hit, were ready to recover quickly once more favorable weather conditions returned.

Expansion of the drought

There was little warning of what was to become one of the most prolonged and extensive droughts in Australian history. The year 2000 ended with excessively wet conditions across most of the continent, making it the second-wettest year since 1900. During 2001, a sudden change in the rainfall patterns occurred across almost all of the states, particularly Queensland and New South Wales, but northern Victoria and the agricultural districts of southwestern Western Australia also experienced record low rainfalls. These areas included around 80 percent of the agricultural areas of Australia and significantly reduced the production of grain harvests across the country.

The drought reached a peak during the period from March 2002 through to January 2003. The rainfall deficiencies during this period ranked with the droughts of 1902 and 1982 to 1983, regarded

ABOVE Cracked earth appears as the water evaporates at Pejar Dam, one of the main water supply reservoirs of the town of Goulburn. This country town, with a population of 23,000 faced a severe water shortage.

RIGHT An outback farmer repairs water tanks on his property. The barren farmland shows the severity of drought in the rural areas of Australia.

FAR RIGHT A farmer sows grain seed. Many were frantically sowing crops after the drought broke with heavy rains on June 13, 2005.

Spain and Portugal, 2004 to 2005

From 2004 to 2005, the Iberian Peninsula was struck by the most severe drought since recording drought measurements began in 1947 in Spain. Portugal experienced its lowest rainfall since 1931. An estimated 70 percent of all agricultural land was declared to be drought affected. Drought-related damage in the livestock sector was estimated to have totaled €1 billion, with the agricultural sector experiencing an overall 12 percent drop in revenues compared with 2004.

At the drought's peak in Portugal, hundreds of farm animals and thousands of fish in reservoirs were dying daily. The Spanish olive harvest dropped from 850,000 tons (936,955 t) to 600,000 tons (661,380 t), forcing up the price of olive oil by 45 percent in Spain.

Rains started to fail across much of southwestern Europe during the 2004 winter. During the period from October 2004 through June 2005, rainfall was less than half the normal rate in areas as far apart as the south of the United Kingdom, western France, Spain, and Portugal. The hardest hit Spanish regions, those with less than 35 percent of their normal rainfall, were the west of Andalusia, the Guadalquivir, and the southeast of Castile. Across Spain, the water levels in reservoirs dropped to only 40 percent of their capacity, with those near the Mediterranean holding only 32 percent of their capacity. One-fifth of these were rendered unusable, as they held only sludge and brackish, undrinkable water. The limited water supply was exacerbated by a five-fold increase in demand during the peak summer months in the hottest and driest regions.

The Iberian drought is attributed, at least in part, to the fact that much of the North Atlantic Ocean temperatures were the warmest on record. The sea temperature anomalies in the North Atlantic Ocean led to the distortion of the Azores high-pressure system so that persistent hot and dry southerly winds from north Africa blew northward across Spain and Portugal, reaching France and southern England. The hot and dry conditions led to numerous and extensive wildfire outbreaks. Between July and the start of August, 13 Spanish firefighters were killed. During a major outbreak of fire in Portugal three major highways were temporarily closed, causing major traffic jams.

Travel warnings given

Not even the economically valuable tourism sector was spared the effects of the drought. Travel advisories were issued to those considering holidays in Spain, saying that in some southern areas, no water could be guaranteed for tourists and their activities. Some popular tourist resorts in the southern Algarve region tried to tap into underground water reserves.

BELOW A cow walks through barren pasture in Manzanares El Real in Spain. This became an all too common sight during the drought of 2005. Farmers had to handfeed livestock.

Heatwave alerts

Following the devastating European heatwave of the summer of 2003, a heatwave alert system was in operation across Spain. Frail and aged residents were forewarned when temperatures were forecast to exceed 104°F (40°C). Despite this newly installed system, the Spanish Health Ministry still logged 39 heat-related deaths in 2005.

Help for wild birds

The Doñana River and wetlands were particularly hard hit by the drought. River levels dropped in the three-year period leading up to the drought through the overuse of water from bores, many of which were illegally drilled. Approximately 7 inches (177 mm) of rain fell over the region in the 2004 to 2005 rain year, making this the second driest year since 1859. With the arrival of an estimated 100,000 wintering birds, park officers pumped water from underground aquifers into the "lucios" (pools) where the birds would gather during the winter months. This was in an effort to prevent the bird populations diminishing as a result of the extremes of the drought.

Swarms of insects

Infestations of insects in southwestern France added to the difficult conditions experienced during the drought. Any remaining pasture was stripped bare by locusts. This forced farmers to use their stores of winter forage to feed their starving cattle or face extra financial costs buying in extra stockfeed. Wasps, beetles, scorpions, and other insects appeared in huge swarms, invading houses, swimming pools, searching for water.

FACTS AND FIGURES	
DATE	October 2004 to September 2005
LOCATION	Portugal, Spain, western France, southern England
DEATH TOLL	13 Spanish firefighters were killed combating fires; 39 heat-related deaths occurred in Spain
DAMAGE	Livestock losses of €1 billion; a 12 percent drop in revenues for the Spanish agricultural sector
RAINFALL	Driest since records began in Spain and since 1931 in Portugal
COMMENTS	The drought had a severe impact on fish and wildlife.

ABOVE This cracked bed of the tributary of Llosa del Cavali, situated about 93 miles (150 km) northwest of Barcelona, normally flooded with water, is about three-quarters empty.

LEFT El Valdo's reservoir, near Madrid, dropped to 50 percent of its capacity at the peak of the 2005 drought. Despite the severe drought conditions, Spain continued to promote the area as a holiday destination to even up the fall in the economy.

Fires

Wildfires are the uncontrolled burning of natural vegetation. The two main types are forest fires and grass fires. They begin with some type of ignition process, such as lightning, accident, or arson, and can then spread uncontrollably, representing a significant threat to any community in the area. The traditional approach of suppressing all fires quickly can cause disaster by allowing fuel to build up.

The worst fires tend to occur in specific zones around the world, where large tracts of inflammable vegetation are subject to periodic drought and occasional bursts of hot and windy weather. These are the world's wildfire hotspots; they include parts of California, the French Riviera, and southeastern Australia. All these areas have suffered catastrophic blazes throughout recorded history, and during prehistory, as indicated by fossil deposits.

Wildfires (called bushfires in Australia) can start through lightning strikes or natural combustive processes, but just as often start through human activity, either accidental or deliberate.

How fires spread

Once under way, wildfires can spread in several different ways. They may start as surface fires, feeding off grass, surface plant matter, and low-lying shrubbery. They may begin as underground fires that travel along subsurface root systems or coal seams. "Crown fires" travel at high speed along the top of the forest canopy, while "spot fires" begin as burning debris that is carried aloft and then distributed downwind from the main fire, thereby starting new blazes. The rate of spread of wildfires varies widely, depending on several factors.

The amount of fuel available is a crucial factor. If existing plant cover is prolific, it means there is an abundance of fuel available, increasing the potential for a severe fire. This is more critical in areas with a dry season, but even rainforest will burn. Also relevant is the type and state of available fuel. California has extensive areas of highly inflammable vegetation, including pines, oaks, and chaparral. The French Riviera is home to various types of conifers and a dense shrubland called maquis. Over southeastern Australia, vast tracts of eucalyptus forest, full of oils, are an ideal fuel to feed any developing bushfire.

Obviously the dryness of the fuel is also a major factor. Soon after rain it is normally difficult for fuel to ignite, but during extended dry periods ignition is far more readily achieved, and can be followed by a rapid spread in the right weather conditions. For this reason, severe wildfires have often followed drought.

FAR LEFT A bushfire burns in a suburb of Sydney, NSW, Australia, in 2005. This photograph shows a crown fire, in which the fire has reached the top of the trees and leaps rapidly from tree to tree.

LEFT A destroyed bridge near Halls Gap, Victoria, Australia, in January 2006. Journalists reporting on the fire were unwillingly evacuated, while only a handful of residents of the tourist town remained behind on ember patrol.

PREVIOUS PAGES A forest fire burns in Idaho, USA. Poor management practices in Idaho forests, now being redressed, have increased tree deaths. In particular, early fire suppression policies resulted in the buildup of too much fuel, and fire-sensitive species were decimated.

ABOVE Smoke rises over an empty State Route 241, closed by a wildfire driven by high Santa Ana winds in February, 2006, near Orange, California; 1,200 homes in the fire's path were evacuated.

RIGHT A burned forest near Pampilhosa da Serra, central Portugal, in 2005. Over 220 people fought this fire, which burned on four fronts. Several dozen people had to be evacuated from their homes. Fire fighters suspected that the fire had been deliberately lit.

The surrounding terrain matters too. Fire tends to race up slopes because the flames can reach under the canopy of the trees further up the hill, increasing the chance of treetop ignition. Conversely, the rate of spread downhill tends to be somewhat reduced because of lesser exposure of the canopy to the flames. And hot air rises, including flames.

Individual weather components that are vital are humidity, temperature, and wind. Humidity is the moisture content of the air. When it is low, the rate of fire spread is increased. Contrary to popular belief, it is not necessary to have high temperatures to support a wildfire, and some severe fires have occurred in comparatively mild temperatures. However, high temperatures certainly raise the potential for severe blazes, because hot conditions assist in further drying out available fuel, and in the initiation of spot fires ahead of the main blaze.

The more the wind speed increases, the faster the fire will spread. Wind supplies more oxygen to the blaze, assists flames in reaching into adjacent vegetation, and enhances fire spotting, where burning debris is scattered ahead of the main fire front. It has been estimated that at a given temperature and humidity, doubling the wind speed will quadruple the rate of spread of the fire.

The mistral is a strong, dry wind that occasionally races across southern France, and can fan wildfires dangerously throughout the Riviera. Southern California is subject to the Santa Ana, a hot dry wind that has been a factor in many serious wildfires across the area. In southeastern Australia, strong, hot northerly winds often occur during the summer. All of these winds can be major factors in serious wildfire outbreaks.

In situations where high temperatures, low humidity, and strong winds coincide, any such blaze can spread rapidly, until it becomes an unstoppable monster, devouring everything in its path. Temperatures can reach 1,650°F (900°C), well above the temperature at which wood ignites (572°F [300°C]).

ABOVE A veld fire in Kruger National Park, Mpumalanga, South Africa. Such fires are a threat not only to people: 20 elephants were severely burned and one had to be put down after a veld fire at the Pilanesberg Game Park in South Africa in 2005.

FIRE DANGER CLASSIFICATIONS

Fire dangers are classified in slightly different ways in various countries, but the same broad principles are used. Fire dangers are calculated by taking into account past rainfall, air temperature, humidity, and wind speed. Present and forecast conditions are usually given.

Fire danger is commonly expressed according to the ratings Low, Moderate, High, Very High, and Extreme. Various fire restrictions or bans are usually attached to these ratings.

These ratings are normally included in weather bulletins, and are often displayed in signs alongside highways in rural areas. In many places there is no such thing as no fire danger.

RIGHT California Department of Forestry fire fighters supervise prison inmate fire crews, dressed in orange, as they hike to a fire front in Ventura County, California, United States.

FAR RIGHT A bushfire burns in the Grampians mountain range in Victoria, Australia. The leaves of eucalyptus trees contain oil, which burns easily, providing ready fuel for lightning-initiated fires. Fire is a natural part of the ecosystem in many parts of the world, but human interference can make the outcome worse.

RIGHT A plane drops fire retardant over the city of Sanary-sur-Mer, southern France, in April, 2006, to quell a fire. Fire retardant contains chemicals that are generally found in a broad range of agricultural fertilizers, and has no long-term ill effects on forest or grassland ecosystems.

WHAT TO DO IF CAUGHT IN A HOUSE WHEN A FIRE APPROACHES

- Shelter inside the house away from windows.
- Close all doors and windows to prevent the entry of embers, and block any gaps from the inside using wet towels.
- Take furniture away from windows and remove curtains from the windows.
- Keep children, elderly or infirm people, and pets inside the house. Make sure they have plenty to drink, and monitor their movements carefully. It is important that everyone stays together. Ensure that everyone is wearing long sleeves and long pants, to avoid burns to exposed skin.
- Turn off the gas supply at the main.
- Plug downpipes with tennis balls or rags and fill the gutters with water.
- Assemble an emergency water supply by filling the bath, basins, kitchen sink, and buckets.
- Drink plenty of water to avoid dehydration from heat and stress.
- Pack any items you may have to take away with you in the event of evacuation.
- Park your car in a clear area and close all doors and windows. Store some woollen blankets inside the car and leave the keys in the ignition—and remember to leave the doors unlocked!
- After the fire front has passed, exit the house and inspect the area for any small fires.
- If fires have started that cannot be extinguished, evacuate to a safe area.

Living through a fire

Large wildfires can produce a damage bill running into many millions of dollars, but even more significantly, they can result in large-scale loss of human life, livestock, and property.

No discussion of a fire can adequately capture the actual terrifying menace of a major blaze. The blazing heat from the flames and the thick, choking smoke can produce fear, disorientation, and panic among any people and animals in the path of the fire.

A little-known feature of a large blaze is the frightening noise of its approach. Survivors have described a terrifying roar, something like a jet aircraft taking off close by.

People who have managed to escape a large fire are often deeply affected psychologically by the sheer terror they have been exposed to, and take some time to recover.

The big fire killers

Wildfires can kill in three main ways: through radiant heat, dehydration, and asphyxiation. Radiant heat is the heat generated by the flames themselves, which can cook an unprotected person or animal in a matter of minutes. Dehydration, which is caused by excessive sweating in the very hot conditions, can result in collapse. Asphyxiation occurs through the inhalation of smoke, or hot fumes and flames.

If you are caught outdoors in a wildfire, escaping radiant heat is your first priority. Seeking shelter in a building or car is preferable to remaining exposed directly to the flames, as often the blaze will pass across quickly, allowing you to move outside again once the flames have cleared. Because hot air rises, you can often find breathable air at ground level.

Fight or flight?

When a severe fire approaches an area, police or fire fighting authorities may recommend or order that residents evacuate. In some countries it is mandatory to evacuate if instructed to do so by the authorities, but in others the decision is left to the occupant.

Whether you do evacuate or elect to stay and fight the fire is of course a major decision that is best made on the basis of being well informed and well prepared in the first place.

There is no definitive answer to the question of whether to fight or flee. Every situation is different; a variety of factors such as local vegetation, wind, intensity of the approaching blaze, and availability of fire-fighting equipment all have relevance.

Undoubtedly many houses have been saved by residents who stayed behind, just as many lives have been saved by evacuation. But research has shown that if you do stay behind to fight the fire, there is an increased chance that your house will survive. However, staying increases the risk to your own life.

The decision to evacuate or stay to fight the fire is one to consider well before a fire starts, but always be prepared to re-evaluate it to take into account any changing circumstance as the fire approaches. Either way, make sure everything likely to be needed is stored safely on hand, ready for action.

TEN OF THE MOST DESTRUCTIVE FIRES

OCTOBER, 1871	Northeast Wisconsin, USA, was devastated by a monster fire. Over 1,100 people were killed and 21.2 million acres (8.6 million ha) were scorched. The small town of Peshtigo was razed.
SEPTEMBER, 1894	Six towns were destroyed by a massive blaze in central Minnesota, USA, which killed more than 400 people and destroyed 260,000 acres (105,000 ha) of woodland.
JANUARY, 1939	The infamous "Black Friday" bushfires raged across Victoria, Australia. Seventy-one people died and 3.5 million acres (1.4 million ha) of forest were consumed.
AUGUST, 1965	18,500 acres (7,500 ha) of forest were destroyed around the Hyères to St Tropez area of the French Riviera. Thousands of holidaymakers were forced to retreat to the beach.
FEBRUARY, 1967	Massive bushfires surged across Tasmania, Australia, killing 62 people and destroying 618,000 acres (250,000 ha) of forest.
SEPTEMBER, 1970	The devastating Laguna fire raged over the San Diego County Mountains, California, USA, leaving six people dead and over 170,000 acres (69,000 ha) burned.
MAY, 1980	A monster blaze destroyed 108,000 acres (44,000 ha) of forest around Red Lake in Canada. Five thousand people were evacuated.
FEBRUARY, 1983	The "Ash Wednesday" fires blazed across parts of South Australia and Victoria, Australia. Seventy-five people perished, and around 618,000 acres (250,000 ha) of bushland were razed.
JULY–AUGUST, 2003	Huge wildfires devoured 133,000 acres (54,000 ha) of forest around St Tropez in the French Riviera. Five people died, including fire fighters, and 20,000 were evacuated.
OCTOBER, 2003	A massive wildfire outbreak devastated the Los Angeles to San Diego area, California, USA, a region spanning over 100 miles (160 km). Sixteen people died, and more than 500,000 acres (200,000 ha) were burned.

Chicago, Illinois, USA, 1871

Chicago in the late nineteenth century was becoming an important and great city. It had a large population for the time, of around 334,000 people. In October 1871, this was all changed as a fire swept through the metropolis, destroying everything in its path. This was a wildfire in the heart of a city.

The fire started on the night of Sunday, October 8 at around 8:45 p.m. in a barn on the alley behind 137 Dekoven Street, owned by Patrick and Catherine O'Leary, about a mile southwest of the then city. A story of a cow kicking over a lantern was made up by a journalist. The fire was probably started during a gambling game. It took two days and the eventual onset of rain for the fire to die out.

Chicago had grown very quickly in the early nineteenth century, and many of the buildings were constructed with wooden frames and straw-thatched roofs. Numerous barns were located throughout the city as well. Oil lamps provided the lighting at the time, so there was always the potential for a fire to start accidentally somewhere in the city.

BELOW A group of men stand with a wheeled wagon, surveying the damage in front of the Court House following the great fire of 1871 in Chicago. Situated on Clark, LaSalle, Randolph, and Washington streets, it was built in the 1850s. Extra wings were progressively added; they were fireproof but the original structure was not. Witnesses reported flames leaping a chasm of 200 feet (61 m) to the roof.

Everything went wrong

October 7 saw a large fire break out, destroying four city blocks before the Chicago Fire Department managed to contain it. The fire department consisted of around 300 firefighters scattered among various stations throughout the city. An alarm system was used to call these firefighters out, but its reliability was variable. After battling the October 7 fire, the firefighters were left under-equipped and exhausted.

When the second fire started it was late in the evening, and most people were at home. A small fire in a barn should have been easy to contain, but as a resident said at the time: "From the beginning everything went wrong." The alarm system was activated, and the fire department confirmed that a fire was burning, but the officer in one of the city's watchtowers guided the firefighters to the wrong place, thus delaying their arrival at the actual fire. By this stage nearby houses had caught alight.

Refuge by the lake

Residents began to panic as houses, shops, barns, and warehouses ignited. Chaos ruled the streets as many tried to escape the spreading inferno. Thousands of residents found refuge in Lincoln Park or along the shore of Lake Michigan. Superheated winds helped fan the fire onward. By 4:00 a.m. the following day, the Chicago Waterworks had been destroyed, leaving the water mains useless. Firefighters and residents then began frantically

FACTS AND FIGURES

DATE	October 8 to 10, 1871
LOCATION	Chicago, Illinois, USA
DEATH TOLL	Up to 300 believed dead (there are no accurate accounts from the time)
DAMAGE	2,000 acres (800 ha) burned (4 miles [6.4 km] long by ¾ mile [1.2 km] wide); 18,000 buildings were destroyed; US$200 million of property was destroyed; 100,000 residents were made homeless
COMMENTS	An inadequate fire alarm system and an overworked, under-equipped fire brigade allowed this disaster to grow to such proportions

collecting water from nearby Lake Michigan and the Chicago River in buckets to try to douse the flames.

The fire finally burned out on October 10, having destroyed 18,000 buildings and other property worth over US$220 million right down to the waterfront, over an area of 2,000 acres (800 ha). Even today, a century later, the rebuilt areas are sometimes still referred to as the "Burnt District."

In a final irony, the O'Learys' house was demolished in 1956 to make way for the Chicago Fire Academy, where a plaque records the event.

A NEW TOURIST ATTRACTION

After the shock wore off, the post-fire cityscape quickly came to possess a double fascination, both in itself and because of its association with what it suggested about the past and future of Chicago. The blocks of ruins became a popular subject for photographers and illustrators. "The town is beginning to fill with aesthetic sight-seers," the *New York Tribune* reported three days after the fire was finally extinguished.

ABOVE A man stands in front of the stone arch of the Second Presbyterian Church on Cullerton St, through which can be seen the remains of the Tribune Building and Court House. The church had been built only 20 years before. It was rebuilt between 1872 and 1874, but in 1900 its roof was destroyed by another fire.

Yellowstone National Park, USA, 1988

Yellowstone National Park in Wyoming has seen its fair share of fires over the years. In 1988, unprecedented dry electrical storms and human carelessness resulted in the largest blaze in the park's history, wiping out 1.4 million acres (567 million ha), or over half, of this famous park.

Yellowstone National Park is probably the best-known park in the United States. However, from August through November 1988, it gained notoriety as massive wildfires swept through it. The disaster reached an enormous magnitude when eight separate huge fires combined, taking out a staggering 1.4 million acres (567 million ha).

Plenty of fuel, then lightning

The summer of 1988 in Wyoming had been hot and dry. Storms passed over but brought little or no rain. Instead they produced many lightning storms, which were instrumental in setting off the chain of events leading up to the fires. An important contributing factor was the fire management regime that had been implemented in the park from 1880 to the 1970s: all that managers did was extinguish any fire outbreak immediately. This regime had left nine decades of fuel load in the park just waiting to burn. Human carelessness also contributed that summer.

On August 20, wind fanned one of the fires across 62,000 acres (25,000 ha) within the park. Several other blazes also started all around the park. With irregular fire intensity in each blaze, the focus of park managers had to shift continually.

BELOW Yellowstone National Park's chief ranger, Dan Sholly, stands amid barren trees, after the forest's consumption by fire. Yellowstone National Park was the world's first national park, proclaimed as a Federal (that is, national) reserve before this area of wilderness had been claimed by any state.

By September 6, over 9,000 firefighters were deployed, and eight of the major fires were linking up. The worst of these was taking a direct path toward the Old Faithful Inn. This was the largest log structure in the world, built in 1904, so every effort was put into saving it. Elsewhere in the park, however, firefighters could just stand and watch as walls of flame marched uncontrolled through the thick vegetation. The army had to be called in to help clear vegetation and construct fire breaks.

No evacuation for wildlife

The residents in the nearby cities of Cooke City and Silver Gate were evacuated as the fire looked as though it was going to reach them. Through luck and bravery only 10 houses were lost. However, the park was hard hit: countless animals and plants were destroyed. The animals that did manage to survive faced a stark winter without shelter and food.

Return of wildlife

After the first snows had helped bring the fires to a smoldering end, the impact could be seen. The patchwork countryside highlighted where the fires had burned to varying degrees. But the following spring and summer, wildlife had returned, much to the surprise of the locals. Biologists believe that the fire was actually a good thing for the park's ecological future and that everything will return to normal— even flourish—as a result of the devastation.

The fire that swept through Yellowstone National Park over a 3½-month period was the fiercest wildfire that Wyoming has ever seen. However, out of this fire came an important lesson to the park management: fuel loading needs to be checked and reduced with controlled burns. Strategies and action plans for park management and fire control are now in place, and the environment is recovering. Fire can be an enemy of the park, but it is also a necessary part of sustaining a healthy ecosystem.

ABOVE Firefighters watch a forest fire in Yellowstone National Park, Wyoming, USA. The 1988 fires were so huge they created their own weather—the enormous flames pushed air up, drawing in fresh air from ground level at gale force, which brought more oxygen to the fire and thus created even more flames.

FACTS AND FIGURES

DATE	August to November 1988
LOCATION	Yellowstone National Park, Wyoming, USA
DEATH TOLL	0
DAMAGE	1.4 million acres (567 million ha); 10 homes
COMMENTS	Countless plants and animals killed

A BRIGHTER FUTURE FOR YELLOWSTONE

The 90 years' buildup of debris no longer covers the ground, so it is unlikely that future fires would reach such catastrophic proportions. The burned patches of forest are now starting on a new cycle of growth. Sun-loving plants are blooming where shade ruled, and birds are now nesting in newly dead tree trunks. Because unburned and burned forest areas create a mosaic, plants and animals in Yellowstone now have a greater variety of habitats in which to live.

New South Wales, Australia, 1994

Late December 1993 and early January 1994 in New South Wales saw a bushfire crisis that lasted a horrifying 22 hot and windy days. Stretching from the Queensland to Victorian borders, a total of 2 million acres (800,000 ha) was burnt; 334 fire fronts were burning at the height of the emergency.

RIGHT A fire engulfs a recycling plant in Sydney's northern suburbs, where property damage cost millions of dollars. To have fires burning from one end of the state to the other, the city under direct fire attack, resource commitments stretched, and extreme weather conditions made this a major fire disaster.

The Australian summer of 1993–94 saw a hot, dry weather pattern that remained almost stationary over the state of New South Wales. Coupled with these hot conditions were westerly winds, which normally blow in winter or spring. These factors led to what became one of the state's worst bushfire emergencies of all time.

On December 27, with fires already burning in over 10 local government areas across the state, several assisting crews were sent to these areas from other parts of the state. These fires continued to burn as the weather conditions deteriorated. On January 5, the temperature climbed to 97°F (36°C) as the humidity dropped to only 16 percent. As any firefighter would be aware, this weather is synonymous with what is called a "blow-up" day. This proved to be true: the first major fire outbreak in the Sydney region occurred on the very next day, in Lane Cove National Park, right in the center of the metropolitan area. The firefight had now come to the city.

Total fire ban declared

The commissioner of the then NSW Bush Fire Brigades declared a statewide total fire ban on January 5; this was not revoked until the 14th. Statewide fire resources at this stage were becoming stretched as fires now burned over an area stretching from the Queensland border in the north to almost the Victorian border in the south (a distance of over 500 miles [800 km]). Interstate and military assistance then began to arrive to help local crews.

FACTS AND FIGURES

DATE	December 27, 1993, to January 15, 1994
LOCATION	New South Wales, Australia
DEATH TOLL	4
DAMAGE	2 million acres (800,000 ha) burned
COMMENTS	20,000+ firefighters; 2,300 fire appliances; all states involved; most of the firefighters were volunteers

The weather over the next few days was quite severe: January 5, 97°F (36°C), 16 percent relative humidity (RH); January 6, 99°F (37°C), 12 percent RH; January 7, 100°F (38°C), 8 percent RH; January 8, 99°F (37°C), 12 percent RH.

Winds during these days were predominantly hot westerly winds blowing at speeds of 25 mph (40 km/h), gusting to 40 mph (60+ km/h).

20,000 firefighters committed

By January 8 the commitment of firefighters across the state exceeded 20,000 personnel, using more than 2,300 fire appliances, including water-bombing helicopters. Fires had by this stage completely surrounded Australia's largest city, burning in Lane Cove, just north of the CBD, in the Blue Mountains to the west, in Gosford to the north, and in the Royal National Park to the south. The main freeway north from Sydney was closed on January 7 and was not reopened till January 9. Residents in Sydney and in many other areas of the state could only sit and watch as the fires marched on, and the firefighters, most of them volunteers, battled each blaze, trying to control it and limit property destruction. Eerie orange light bathed the state. This situation continued for four extreme days and devastated the landscape of New South Wales, including wiping out 98 percent of the Royal National Park.

By January 12 the weather conditions began to ease, and for the first time the firefighters gained the upper hand. Containment lines had been put in place, operations could begin to be scaled back, but vigilance on fires still burning was paramount. On Saturday, January 15, the state of emergency was ended, and interstate and military helpers were stood down to return home.

BELOW A firefighter watches as a trickle of water comes out of his hose as he tries to douse a bushfire near Newcastle in an attempt to save houses. Thousands of homes were threatened by the fires, some of which were caused by arsonists.

East Kalimantan, Indonesian Borneo, 1997 to 1998

Wildfire consuming the thick, dense, and usually wet tropical forests of South-East Asia seems an unlikely event. Yet in the lead-up to the summer of 1997, this is exactly what happened. Increased slash-and-burn clearing by farmers and large companies, along with a drought, saw fires rampant throughout Indonesia, particularly in the East Kalimantan region of Borneo.

In a region that is usually associated with high humidity, dense forests, and high rainfall, it is hard to imagine wildfire. In 1998, however, after a long drought, the forests had become dry, and uncontrolled fires affected not only the local area, but nearby countries as well, and caused health problems throughout South-East Asia.

Fires have been burning underground in this region in the natural peat and coal beds for years. But owing to the very dry spell from September 1997 through January 1998, these fires took hold at the surface and spread across Indonesia, in particular Borneo. Added to this source of fire was the practice of slash-and-burn agriculture. Fires lit to clear felled vegetation were not monitored very well, and many such fires escaped control lines.

Choking smoke and smog

As the fires continued to burn, the huge amount of smoke created an even greater problem. This smoke, heavily laden with toxic materials, drifted thousands of miles and badly affected many neighboring countries, particularly Singapore, Malaysia, and the southern Philippines.

The smoke caused thick smog over the region, creating respiratory problems for many people in Indonesia and beyond. People were forced to wear masks, which quickly became unavailable, whenever they needed to venture outdoors. The reduced visibility resulted in numerous collisions on land,

AN AREA THE SIZE OF BELGIUM

The fires in Indonesia destroyed 11,600 square miles (30,000 km²) of forest—an area roughly equivalent to the size of Belgium. Almost all of the Kutai National Park in the east of Kalimantan was destroyed, as well as the Wein River orang-utan sanctuary and unique limestone forests in the north of the state. Most of the fires had spread from oil palm plantations, where fires are a popular but illegal way of clearing land.

at sea, and in the air. Air pollutant indexes rocketed, at times reaching 900 micrograms per cubic meter (above 300 is considered unhealthy). The World Health Organization became involved. Many schools, factories, and offices were closed.

International assistance arrives

Many of the world's leading authorities on forest fire management, such as the NSW Rural Fire Service from Australia, offered assistance to Indonesia and its neighbors to help overcome the fires. In East Kalimantan alone, 253 fire appliances and 1,470 firefighters were mobilized to battle the fires. Cloud seeding was used to try to induce rain in the area. The areas worst affected were in the southeast of Sumatra and in the state of Kalimantan, Borneo. It was estimated that by February 1998 the fires had resulted in economic losses in East Kalimantan of US$10.5 million, not to mention the natural resources being destroyed.

The disaster has had extensive economic, health, ecological, and political impacts in both Indonesia

and neighboring countries. The fire and haze disasters caused untold damage, severely affecting numerous economic sectors, including all forms of transport, construction, tourism, and agriculture.

In some areas, the airports had to be closed, forcing the cancellation of numerous flights. Many places, including schools, factories, and businesses, were shut down. The international response and the commitment from all concerned since have seen more rigorous wildfire management procedures put in place, to reduce or prevent such occurrences in the future.

FACTS AND FIGURES

DATE	September 1997 to May 1998
LOCATION	East Kalimantan, Borneo, Indonesia
DEATH TOLL	2 from fires, but respiratory problems may have led to more deaths
DAMAGE	11,600 square miles (30,000 km²)
COMMENTS	Reduced visibility caused many collisions

ABOVE Haze covers the burned landscape near Samarinda, on the eastern coast of Kalimantan, in Indonesian Borneo.

LEFT Smoke haze and smog blankets the downtown skyline in Jakarta, Indonesia. Out-of-control fires set by farmers, plantation owners, and loggers to clear land on the islands of Borneo and Sumatra caused choking haze across parts of Indonesia, nearby Malaysia, and Singapore.

Southern California, USA, 2003

Wildfires in the southern parts of the United States are a common occurrence. California has seen its fair share of these fires, but nothing prepared Californians for what happened in October and November, 2003. A spate of terrible fires gutted the state, and showed nature at its destructive worst.

RIGHT A wildfire burns out of control near a house near Descanso, California, east of San Diego. The home survived when winds suddenly shifted.

BELOW Firefighters battle the Crestline fire in Los Angeles County. The fire, which was intentionally lit, destroyed 25 homes in the area.

From October 21, 2003, huge wildfires driven by very hot Santa Ana winds carved a destructive path through the southern California country-side. Wildfires are nothing new to this area of the world, but when fed by a thick, very dry fuel load, they created the explosive conditions that made this the largest recorded fire in California's history.

San Diego, San Bernardino, Los Angeles, and Ventura counties all had major destructive fires over this period, stretching the state's fire resources to the limit. President George W. Bush declared all four counties major disaster areas, opening the way for federal relief money. The fire in San Diego County on the worst day moved an incredible 20 miles (32 km) in less than 24 hours, making any tactical firefighting

FACTS AND FIGURES	
DATE	October 21 to November 8, 2003
LOCATION	California, USA
DEATH TOLL	16
DAMAGE	500,000 acres (200,000 ha); 2,500 homes; 900 other structures; US$2 billion+
COMMENTS	One town was completely leveled

near impossible, as well as unsafe. Residents in nearby towns were forced to evacuate, not knowing when they would be able to return, if indeed there was anything left to return to.

1,500 homes in one fire

In San Diego County, the major fire, dubbed the "Cedar Fire," destroyed some 300,000 acres (120,000 ha) of the countryside. This fire seriously threatened high numbers of lives and properties. Regrettably, owing to its sheer size and power, the threat became a reality as the fire marched through the lakeside town of Cuyamaca, completely leveling it. Several more towns in the fire's path were spared the same fate. In total, this one fire burned down 1,500 homes and killed 14 people. One resident observed, "We've been watching different crews drive around putting out hotspots, and I have never seen such an exhausted looking bunch of men."

Rugged terrain hampers efforts

Over in San Bernardino at the same time, three sizable fires were burning around the Big Bear and Lake Arrowhead regions into the mountainous countryside, where the rugged terrain meant it could take days, weeks, or even months to extinguish the fires. These three fires burnt an area of over 200,000 acres (80,000 ha), destroyed 1,000 homes, and killed two people.

The huge clouds of smoke obscuring the sky shut down small airports, and Los Angeles International Airport canceled or postponed flights during the worst of the fires.

As in other parts of the world, the California fires resulted from a high fuel loading, attributed to the quick dousing of fires in the past, and weather conditions combining at the worst possible time.

SPONTANEOUS DISASTER RESPONSES

People rallied around each other, helping any way they could. East of Temecula, Bryan Youst and his two teenage sons dragged out two women—an intellectually disabled young woman and her physically disabled grandmother, who relied on a walking frame and an oxygen tank—from their mobile home. Gerald Rauch shuttled his water truck between his house and a neighbor's, dousing flames while being directed through the smoke by an employee on a two-way radio. A stranger helped a family fight the fire and left before they could get his name. Brianne Yhlen and two friends, who were driving through with a horse trailer, headed into the fire zone without hesitation and ferried two loads of horses to safety. A ranch gave refuge to 200 evacuated horses, and local feed stores donated hay to feed them.

Southern Europe, 2003

Record heatwave temperatures across the whole of southern Europe in 2003 led to a series of fire emergencies in many countries. Portugal, Spain, France, Italy, Croatia, and Germany all had major fires burning. Many of these claimed property and, more tragically, lives were lost.

RIGHT Forest fires fanned by hot winds burn in St Tropez, on the French Riviera. The French weather bureau expected at least another week of abnormally high temperatures to follow.

From July through August, fire outbreaks became frequent. At least five countries declared states of emergency. Temperatures peaking near 120°F (49°C) and strong hot winds fan-forced these blazes across the countryside and across borders. Residents who up till now had only had to contend with the heat, which alone killed many thousands, now also had to face the onset of raging wildfires; they stood to lose everything.

Portugal hit hardest

The area hardest hit was Portugal, where a blistering heatwave set off a series of raging wildfires in the heart of the country which eventually crossed the border into Spain. At the same time, the searing heat set off similar blazes in nearby countries.

The fires burning in Portugal were described by the then interior minister as "one of the worst catastrophe situations in the last 20 years." As Portugal is covered with dense forests (accounting for about one-third of the country), this large-scale incident was truly worrying for the local people. A sense of unsettledness and fear was present in the country, especially in those who had to be

BELOW People watch the continuing fires from off the coast of Sainte Maxime, France. Forest fires nearby were being fanned by hot winds. Monsoon activity in sub-Saharan Africa, which poured hot desert air over Europe while keeping out cooler Atlantic lows, was blamed for the extreme heat conditions.

ABOVE A car passes by a burning forest in Vale Alto, Portugal. By August 7, firefighters had managed to gain control of wildfires which had ravaged Portugal for a week, killing 25 people and destroying thousands of acres of land.

evacuated from their homes. Over 20 major fires and hundreds of other minor fires were burning around the country. It became a mammoth effort for the firefighters, and the prime minister appealed to the European Union for assistance. It was as though the whole country were going up in flames. The disaster claimed the lives of 25 people and well over 960,000 acres (390,000 ha).

One firefighter, Pedro Carvalho, described the disaster succinctly: "This wasn't a fire, it was hell." Firefighters were stretched incredibly thin. Residents in some areas of Portugal became very irate when it seemed that they had been forgotten as flames encroached on towns and yet no firefighters could be seen, because they were committed elsewhere.

Across the border in Spain there was an equally grim outlook, as Spanish firefighters too became stretched to their limit. With 11 major fires burning across the country and soaring temperatures, the Spanish government began to evacuate residents in fire-affected areas, amid fears of losing lives. Sadly, in the northeastern part of Catalonia, a family of

five were killed when one of the uncontrolle surrounded their home while they were tryi flee. With over 314,000 acres (127,000 ha) Spanish firefighters were more than stretche they did manage to contain a lot of the blaze Unfortunately, one firefighter lost his life try to save those around him.

Criminal causes

Across the Mediterranean, Italy was under t with its own spate of major wildfires. Twen separate fires were burning uncontrolled th the country, the worst hit areas being Tusca Piedmont, Liguria, Lazio, and Campania. Bu Italians believed that the blazes had natural increasingly, they blamed criminal gangs in lowering property values to create redevelo opportunities. Water-bombing planes were effectively to combat these fires, and a requ Portugal saw one of the Italian planes sent with the fires still raging there.

Meanwhile, devastating forest fires swe through the Maures mountains near the Fre Riviera. Investigators found that Molotov c or gasoline (petrol) bombs, had been used the blazes, which killed at least four people destroyed 50 homes. One resident on the island of Corsica perished as he tried to pro property from a fire. This summer was the France since World War II. Further east, ir temperatures were the highest in over 100

ABOVE A car passes by a burning forest in Vale Alto, Portugal. By August 7, firefighters had managed to gain control of wildfires which had ravaged Portugal for a week, killing 25 people and destroying thousands of acres of land.

evacuated from their homes. Over 20 major fires and hundreds of other minor fires were burning around the country. It became a mammoth effort for the firefighters, and the prime minister appealed to the European Union for assistance. It was as though the whole country were going up in flames. The disaster claimed the lives of 25 people and well over 960,000 acres (390,000 ha).

One firefighter, Pedro Carvalho, described the disaster succinctly: "This wasn't a fire, it was hell." Firefighters were stretched incredibly thin. Residents in some areas of Portugal became very irate when it seemed that they had been forgotten as flames encroached on towns and yet no firefighters could be seen, because they were committed elsewhere.

Across the border in Spain there was an equally grim outlook, as Spanish firefighters too became stretched to their limit. With 11 major fires burning across the country and soaring temperatures, the Spanish government began to evacuate residents in fire-affected areas, amid fears of losing lives. Sadly, in the northeastern part of Catalonia, a family of

five were killed when one of the uncontrolled fires surrounded their home while they were trying to flee. With over 314,000 acres (127,000 ha) burned, Spanish firefighters were more than stretched, but they did manage to contain a lot of the blazes. Unfortunately, one firefighter lost his life trying to save those around him.

Criminal causes
Across the Mediterranean, Italy was under threat with its own spate of major wildfires. Twenty-four separate fires were burning uncontrolled throughout the country, the worst hit areas being Tuscany, Piedmont, Liguria, Lazio, and Campania. But few Italians believed that the blazes had natural causes: increasingly, they blamed criminal gangs intent on lowering property values to create redevelopment opportunities. Water-bombing planes were used very effectively to combat these fires, and a request from Portugal saw one of the Italian planes sent to help with the fires still raging there.

Meanwhile, devastating forest fires swept through the Maures mountains near the French Riviera. Investigators found that Molotov cocktails, or gasoline (petrol) bombs, had been used to ignite the blazes, which killed at least four people and destroyed 50 homes. One resident on the French island of Corsica perished as he tried to protect his property from a fire. This summer was the hottest in France since World War II. Further east, in Slovenia, temperatures were the highest in over 100 years.

FACTS AND FIGURES

DATE	**Late July and early August, 2003**
LOCATION	**Southern Europe—Portugal, Spain, Italy, France, Germany, Croatia**
DEATH TOLL	**36 directly from the fires; from the heat: 14,847 in France, 20,000+ in Italy, 907 in the United Kingdom—50,000+ in total**
DAMAGE	**1.2 million acres (500,000 ha) burned; numerous houses and other structures lost**
COMMENTS	**Record temperatures across Europe and arson contributed significantly**

In Croatia, as in most of southern Europe, major blazes were being battled. Temperatures here were well above 98°F (37°C), and the fires seemed to be creating their own weather patterns. The Croatian islands of Biševo, Brac, and Hvar were the worst hit in this region of Europe.

A major fire near the Bosnian city of Mostar continued burning for several days, as firefighters had to withdraw owing to the discovery of land mines in the area. These mines were believed to be remnants of the Bosnian war.

Germans, too, were thrust into danger as fires began popping up around Germany. A large blaze broke out about 40 miles (60 km) south of Berlin, forcing the closure of a major highway.

Death from heatstroke

It seemed as though the whole Mediterranean coast and southeast Europe were going up in smoke. Fires continued to grow in intensity, fueled by masses of dried timber and scorching heat. Weather patterns over southern Europe supported the fires, causing much angst and fear among authorities. People began dying from heat stress. The high temperatures and smoke haze were causing dangerous levels of ozone in several European cities.

The situation in France was the worst in all of Europe. It was partly created by the coincidence of the nation's vacations. Public offices, hospitals, and other services close during August, and many employees have no choice about when to take their vacations. In consequence, emergency services were too understaffed to cope with the huge numbers of people suffering from the heat. A coolstore had to be pressed into service as a mortuary.

Many people were away from home, and so were not even aware that relatives had died. Some of the dead may not even have had family—eventually, authorities in Paris buried 57 unclaimed bodies.

ABOVE This aerial view shows an isolated house in a carbonized forest in Les Issambres, in southeastern France, after it was gutted by a large fire that had started the day before.

WAS GLOBAL WARMING TO BLAME?

Many people were quick to blame global warming for the record heatwave. However, global warming is ultimately more likely to lead to a colder climate in Europe, rather than a warmer one. Global warming is expected to melt the summer North Polar ice cap within a couple of decades. Currently the year-round ice cools the water beneath it, causing that water to sink. This starts the "global conveyor belt," which carries water right around the globe, distributing heat. The best known aspect of the conveyor belt is the Gulf Stream, which carries water that was warmed in the Caribbean Sea north to the British Isles and the western coast of Europe. Without the Gulf Stream, the temperature in Scotland, at the same latitude as Alaska, would be a good 18°F (10°C) colder. If the global conveyor belt stops, this will make Europe a lot colder.

Okanagan Mountain Park, Canada, 2003

From coast to coast, Canadians watched with horror and sympathy as the town of Kelowna in British Columbia was assaulted by fire. The province was suffering one of its worst forest fire seasons in decades, with no major rainfall, and tinder-dry mountain forests exploding in flames.

RIGHT The wildfire burns in the Okanagan Mountain Park near Kelowna, British Columbia, Canada. The extent of the fire front is evident by the scale of the photograph.

BELOW RIGHT Firefighters dig out hotspots to prevent reignition of the fire. Hoses can also be used to douse embers in some of the more accessible areas.

The Okanagan Mountain Park fire was the most significant wildfire event in British Columbia's history. Much of BC was affected by fire, but the towns of Naramata and Kelowna suffered the most, with the evacuation of 33,050 people and the loss of or damage to 238 homes. The fire also claimed 12 historic wooden railroad trestles and damaged two other steel trestles in Myra Canyon. The trestles supported the historic Kettle Valley Railway as it wound through the rugged canyon.

South you lose, north we lose

As the fire grew, it became unclear where firefighting resources should be focused. The ever-changing wind offered the fire direct runs at either Kelowna or Naramata. Under a southerly wind, the people of Kelowna would find themselves in the firing line, and many large, expensive houses would be destroyed. However, if the northern winds prevailed, then the town of Naramata would become a casualty.

Firefighters managed to construct fire breaks by hand along the southeastern flank of the fire, as air crews began to water bomb the fire. The prevailing winds eventually made it clear that the main target of the fire was likely to be Kelowna, with a population of 96,000, at the northern end of the park.

A TREE CANDLE OVER 200 FEET IN THE AIR

A contributor to the Club Tread online forum described the spectacular sight of the fire:
"I truly hope no one here has fond memories of Okanagan Mountain Park; almost all of it was consumed today. I have never seen a more awesome sight than a tree candle over 200 feet [60 m] in the air. I just got into Oliver from Kelowna 15 minutes ago, and the wind was blowing from the southwest so that no smoke was obstructing the view from across the lake, and I have never seen anything more spectacular. We stopped on the side of the road for 5 minutes and could actually watch the fire spread at an alarming rate. At the time the front line was still a good 15 km [9 miles] from the edge of Kelowna, but that distance will shrink quickly if the wind keeps up (which it will; prevailing winds here come from the SW) ... I wouldn't be surprised if I return home from my short fishing trip to find the SE sections of my city under evacuation alert, if not already evacuated ..."

Rugged terrain, high alert

The fire continued to gain momentum in the rugged, inaccessible terrain of Okanagan Mountain Park. By August 17, the fire was just 2½ miles (4 km) from houses, and only 3¾ miles (6 km) from the heart of the city itself. Fire authorities therefore focused on the protection of life and property. Six homes were evacuated, and another 41 were put on high alert.

The next morning and throughout the day, containment lines were tested, and at times broken, as the fire marched on. By the time night had fallen on the 18th, the fire was less than 550 yards (500 m) from houses, and three small communities had to be evacuated. The Kelowna Fire Department put all of its resources into trying to protect residents under direct threat for the next three days.

On August 22, things took a turn for the worse when the fire blew up. Winds of 45 mph (75 km/h)

whipped the fire into treacherous conditions. Homes
were beginning to be lost, and crews were forced to
save what they could while letting other structures
burn. Eventually, 238 homes were lost.

The rugged terrain made control a challenge,
but finally, on September 6, the fire came to an end.
In all, 63,260 acres (25,600 ha) was burned. Since
then, there has been a spectacular rebirth of plants.

FACTS AND FIGURES

DATE	August 16 to September 6, 2003
LOCATION	Okanagan Mountain Park, BC, Canada
DEATH TOLL	0
DAMAGE	63,260 acres (25,600 ha); 238 homes; C$33.8 million
COMMENTS	Tens of thousands evacuated

Canberra, Australia, 2003

Saturday, January 18, 2003, is a day that residents of the Australian Capital Territory (ACT) will not forget in a long time. Australia's capital city, Canberra, was surrounded by a firestorm, which exploded out of the surrounding pine plantations and nature reserves directly into the heart of the suburbs. This prompted a state of emergency that lasted 12 days, and demonstrated the ferociousness that fire can display when it becomes uncontrollable.

The Australian summer produces hot and dry conditions across the country. On Friday, January 17, Canberra residents noticed smoke drifting into the city from fires that were burning in areas surrounding the ACT. They did not expect these fires to take a run directly into the heart of the Canberra suburbs the very next day.

As dawn broke over Canberra and surrounds the next day, the smoke present from the previous day was still evident, but was beginning to change color, growing darker and becoming thicker. The Bureau of Meteorology issued weather warnings for winds of the order of 56 miles per hour (90 km/h) and temperatures of 99°F (37°C). By mid-afternoon the sky was black, street lights were on, ash and embers were falling everywhere, and the sound of wailing sirens from fire trucks filled the air. By now the fire was only minutes from reaching homes.

Fight or flight?

Residents who chose to stay and fight instead of evacuating soon found that a garden hose was no match for the 100–130-foot (30–40-m) high flames, and soon abandoned hope, praying that what they had done to prepare their properties would be enough. The suburb of Duffy was hardest hit: several homes were fully engulfed in a matter of minutes. This was the site of the first fatality of the fire, when an elderly resident died of smoke inhalation as he tried to battle the fire in his backyard.

FACTS AND FIGURES	
DATE	January 18, 2003
LOCATION	Canberra, ACT, Australia
DEATH TOLL	4
DAMAGE	530 homes destroyed; 2,000 people evacuated; 4,200 head of livestock destroyed; Mt Stromlo Observatory destroyed; large numbers of native flora and fauna destroyed
COMMENTS	Most firefighters were volunteers; many of them had to travel very long distances to help out

Helping out strangers

The Australian ethic of "mateship" comes to the fore in emergency situations. One report told how a resident from the suburb of Duffy, on the Canberra outskirts, saved the lives of many of his neighbors. Aware that many of his fellow residents were elderly, or had no transport to escape the inferno, he collected them in the back of his pickup truck, and drove them to safety. This was not planned—he just reacted to the situation.

There were not enough fire appliances to go around, as new spot fires kept popping up throughout the suburbs faster than firefighters could react. The New South Wales Rural Fire Service sent many units from all over the state to help their ACT counterparts. Firefighters could only do their best, pushing themselves to the limit to save what they could. Property protection was the best they could do, the fire's intensity was so great; stopping it at this point was impossible. In the end, the insurance bill reached A$250 million.

As residents came to terms with what happened, they expressed their shock, disbelief, and sadness to friends, family, and the media. Many had lost everything. Firefighters continued mopping up the smoldering remains of the suburbs and surrounding forests. Twelve days after the fire had torn apart the Australian capital, the state of emergency was lifted.

PRIME MINISTER PAYS TRIBUTE

The Prime Minister, John Howard, paid tribute to the firefighters, as quoted in the *Sydney Morning Herald* of January 19, 2003: "Given the ferocity and the suddenness and the intensity of it, it is a miracle that more people didn't lose their lives and it's a huge tribute to the emergency services. The people have come together ... the volunteers ... everybody's pitching in, everybody wants to help, everybody wants to do something, everybody feels that there's somebody whose situation is a lot worse than theirs."

ABOVE An aerial view reveals the extent of fire devastation to homes. Pine plantations just across the road provided an easy path for the firestorm to jump to houses.

ABOVE LEFT The 74-inch (188-cm) telescope at the historic Mt Stromlo Observatory, built in 1922, lies gutted by the bushfires.

BELOW LEFT An aerial view of a fire-devastated pine plantation in the Stromlo Forest near the suburbs of Duffy and Chapman. These plantations will not regenerate, and must be either replanted with more pines or returned to native forest.

Southern California, 2005

Southern California, still recovering from the 2003 wildfires, was hit again only two years later. Wildfires began anew in the state on September 28, 2005, with a small brush fire northwest of Los Angeles. In less than two days the fire had spread to more than 17,000 acres (6,900 ha).

ABOVE A firefighting helicopter drops water to try to contain the Castaways Fire in Burbank, California. The fire burned over 1,100 acres (445 ha) and forced evacuations of homes in its path.

The blaze threatened homes and wildlife north of the Santa Monica Mountains. The Santa Ana winds and dry conditions encouraged the blaze, and the steep terrain made it extremely hard for firefighters to reach the fire fronts and avoid the destruction of homes that lie hidden in the canyons.

Heavy rainfall over the previous two winters allowed the undergrowth to became thick and dense. The scorching summer heat then drove all moisture from the new growth, creating the perfect fuel.

Authorities and residents alike were concerned that the fire could jump US Highway 101, endangering exclusive Malibu on the coast to the west of Los Angeles. If the fire jumped the highway, there would be no next fire break until it hit the shoreline of the Pacific Ocean to the south.

State of disaster declared

Los Angeles and Ventura counties each declared a state of local disaster. At least 1,500 residents of the area were mandatorily evacuated, as 3,000 firefighters from all levels—city, county, and federal—collaborated to battle this blaze.

A large smoke column could be seen from right across the Los Angeles basin. The fire was burning in the Chatsworth–Topanga area to the northwest of Los Angeles, and there were fears that it was going to hit Simi Valley to the north. These fears prompted firefighters to conduct a nighttime doorknock to wake residents so they would be prepared to evacuate if necessary. Authorities spent US$2.8 million bringing this fire under control. Many of the firefighters worked on constructing a 15-mile (24-km) fire break

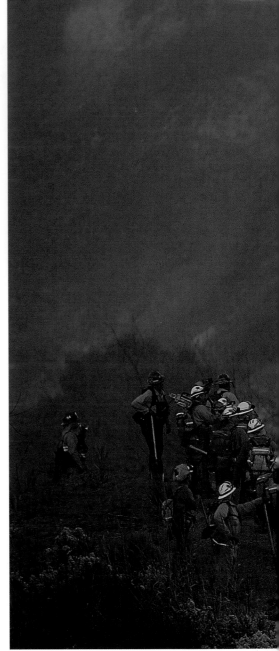

to halt the blaze. The total area that this fire alone consumed was 24,175 acres (9,783 ha) in just nine days, and at least 13 structures were destroyed.

A few miles to the east, a smaller fire in Burbank burned some 700 acres (280 ha), while 350 firefighters fought to control it. Fortunately, no homes were placed in jeopardy.

No fire without smoke

Many residents were overcome by the smoke and haze that hung over their cities and towns. The smoke has several effects on people, the most significant being health problems. Smoke can cause breathing difficulties, and people with asthma were strongly advised to stay indoors. Poor visibility became another concern: many traffic accidents occurred in areas blanketed by heavy smoke.

FIRE BREAKS WORK

Los Angeles County requires residents to clear plant growth from around their homes. Common sense says this is a good idea, whether it is legislated or not. Los Angeles County Supervisor Zev Yaroslavsky said residents who complied with this safety measure played an important role in preserving their homes: "You saw [on Thursday] night on CNN, homes that were within dozens of feet of the flames and the flames just came to a stop as though there was some supernatural force. The reason for it is there was nothing left to burn between the clearance area and the house and the house was saved."

With eight major fires burning in southern California during this time, all larger than 300 acres (120 ha) in extent, state officials, including California governor Arnold Schwarzenegger, reassured people that everything within their power was being done to battle the fires. Schwarzenegger had nothing but praise for the firefighters, saying, "You are willing to risk your own lives in order to save someone else's."

By October 8, the major threat had been eased, with most of the wildfires now under control and burning within containment lines. The fire season was officially ended on November 7, after rain fell.

ABOVE Prison inmates tend a backfire at the School Canyon Fire in Ventura, California. The late-season wildfire burned across an area of more than 4,000 acres (1,600 ha).

FACTS AND FIGURES

DATE	September 28 to October 8, 2005
LOCATION	Southern California, USA
DEATH TOLL	0
DAMAGE	100,000+ acres (40,000+ ha); 13 homes destroyed, countless damaged
COMMENTS	Second highest rainfall and second hottest year on record in Los Angeles

SANTA ANA WINDS DRIVE THE FIRES

In Southern California, the onset of the Santa Ana winds every October usually means fan-forced fires somewhere within the state. Around this time of year the normal offshore summer winds, which bring cooler moist air, swing around to produce a more easterly air flow, dragging hot dry air from the interior of the country. These winds can be ferocious, at times gusting to 75 mph (120 km/h). The winds suck the moisture right out of the fuel. This combination of ready fuel supply, the high temperatures ranging from 100°F to 110°F (38–43°C), and the low humidity always worries both residents and fire authorities.

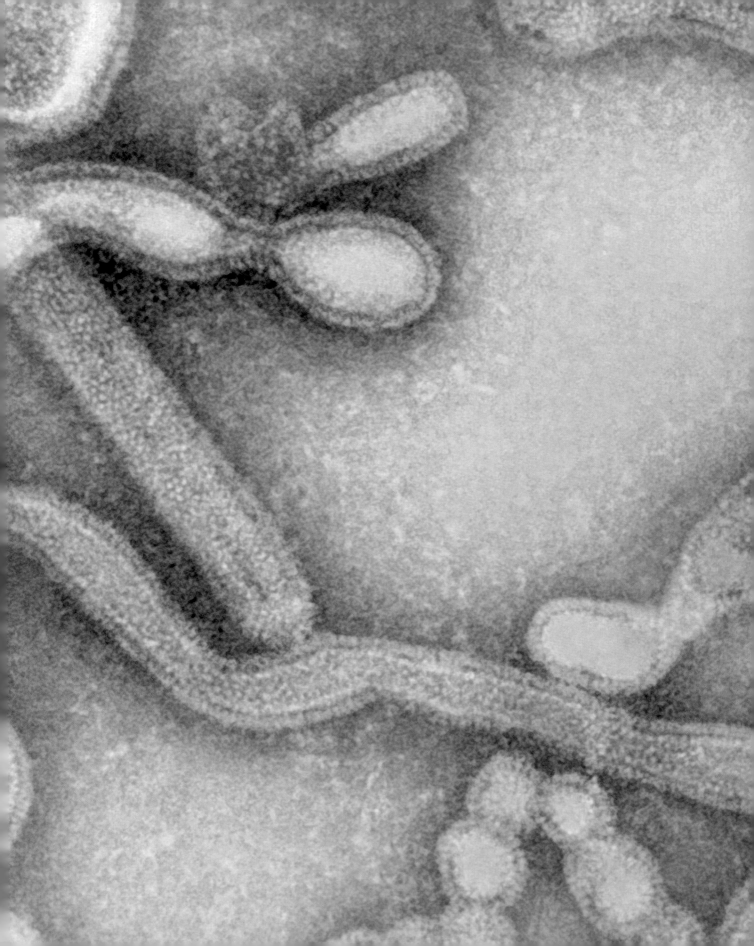

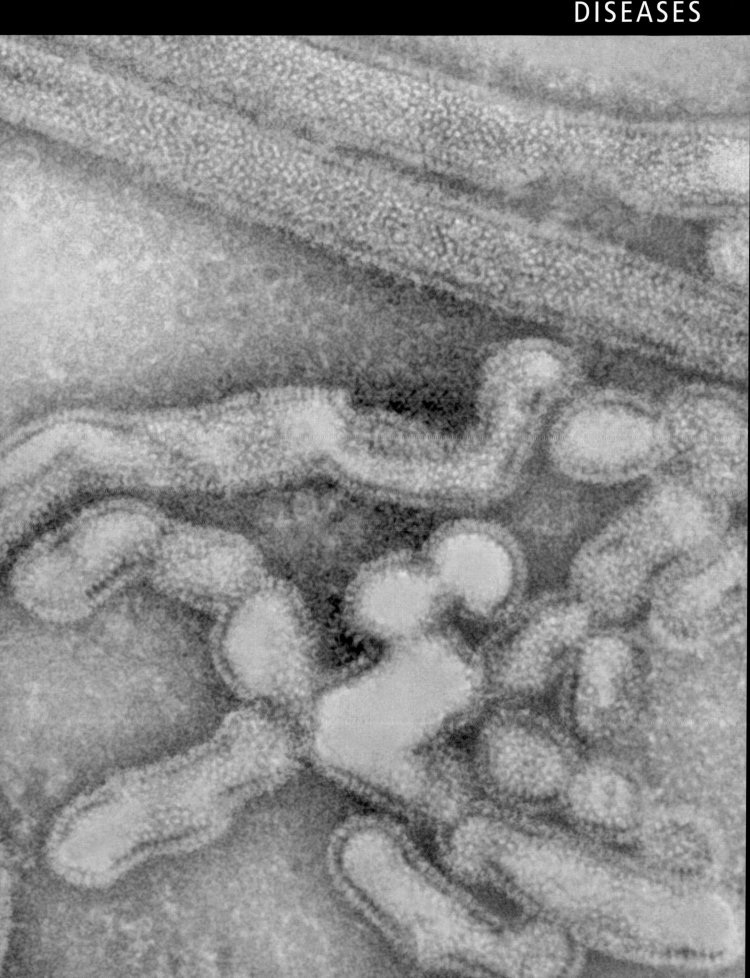

Diseases

Mention natural disasters and most people imagine devastating events such as earthquakes, floods, droughts, hurricanes, and volcanoes. These naturally occurring events can quickly be transformed by our delicate human condition into disasters of cataclysmic proportions, with significant consequences. The same holds true for diseases, the most deadly of all natural disasters.

Many factors can potentially affect the health of individuals and populations. Epidemiologists are scientists who study this field of medicine. They use state-of-the-art methods to rapidly identify and prevent potential sources of communicable diseases. Their surveillance techniques are one of the most effective means of mitigating disease outbreaks. Because of this, medical issues related to natural disasters tend to focus on health consequences—such as traumatic injuries, emotional stress, epidemic diseases, and indigenous diseases—as secondary outcomes of those disasters. But of course when a major disease outbreak threatens populations, disease can itself become a primary natural disaster event.

History is replete with epidemics and pandemics. These naturally occurring events can utterly devastate populations. At this scale, infectious diseases can wreak immediate havoc on a local, regional, or global scale and have severe long-term effects.

EPIDEMIC OR PANDEMIC?

The word epidemic (from Greek: *epi*, upon; *demos*, people) is an outbreak of an infectious disease that appears as new cases in a given human population, during a given period, at a rate that substantially exceeds what is "expected," based on recent experience. The number of new cases in the population during a specified period of time is called the "incidence rate." Pandemic (*pan*, all; *demos*, people) is an epidemic that spreads worldwide, or at least across a large region.

Quick and deadly

There are several important characteristics of epidemics and pandemics. First, they can be spread very efficiently by those who are infected, making it easy for otherwise healthy populations to become extremely ill. A quick onset is followed by quick burn-out of those infected if the source is

FAR LEFT Workers disinfect the waiting room of a Beijing railway station in the fight against SARS, in May, 2003. Beijing had seen a downward trend in the incidence of Severe Acute Respiratory Syndrome, and was confident that preventive measures helped stem the outbreak in China.

LEFT Bangladeshi flood victim Tahamina holds a packet of saline replenishment salts in her teeth as she swims through floodwaters in Dhaka, in August, 2004. A massive health crisis was looming in this South Asian country as sewage mixed with floodwaters, prompting the United Nations to warn that millions of people were facing a heightened risk of disease.

PREVIOUS PAGES A colorized microscopic view of the type A influenza virus. Influenza A subtypes have potential to be the world's deadliest pandemics.

ABOVE A policeman supervises a driver as he obeys the "Dip your feet" sign at Cockernach Farm in Hertfordshire, England. Disinfectant was used to contain the spread of an outbreak of foot-and-mouth disease in 1933.

RIGHT In September, 1994, residents of Surat, India could again walk around freely after health officials claimed that the recent epidemic of pneumonic plague, which took between 50 and 100 lives, was under control, and that it was safe for fleeing residents to return to the city.

determined to be a "point source," as was the case during the 1998 norovirus gastroenteritis outbreak that affected US Army trainees. But if a disease is spread in a communicable fashion—from person to person—it takes far longer for it to be curtailed. People who survive infectivity, and therefore the course of the disease, will develop antibodies that make them immune from future infections of the

same disease. This is why an outbreak of disease eventually dies out. Also, it is probably not in an organism's evolutionary interest to kill all its hosts.

With substantial increases in world population and quick and easy global transportation, the threat of a new pandemic poses an enormous challenge. It will greatly test our ability to effectively control it, and to respond in ways that mitigate its consequences. Modern life means more people are using more forms of transport at an ever-increasing rate—perfect conditions for a new global pandemic.

Should we be concerned about emerging infectious diseases? Will history repeat itself? Can modern medicine save us? These important questions are posed not only by scientists looking for ways to avert future biological catastrophes; they also confront the general public daily through newspapers, telecasts, and internet blogs.

The looming threat of outbreaks

The World Health Organization (WHO) recently sounded an alarm, saying that there is a substantial risk of an influenza pandemic within the next few years, one with the potential to create the worst-case scenario of any public-health emergency. The pandemic influenza outbreak in 1918–19 was the single largest recorded pandemic in human history, killing 40 to 100 million people globally. Dubbed the Spanish Flu, it affected rich, poor, young, and old, as well as disrupting postal systems and closing down transportation networks in India and Spain.

Most recently, one of the most dangerous possibilities is a highly pathogenic variation of the H5N1 subtype of Influenza A virus, which has the potential to rapidly mutate into a variation that could

LEFT Pedestrians fill the streets of Gulu in February, 2001. Gulu and its environs in northern Uganda were the epicenter of an outbreak of ebola, a virus that killed 173 people and infected almost 400 others from the fall of 2000 through January, 2001.

transmit easily from human to human. If such a mutation occurs, it might remain an H5N1 subtype, or it could shift subtypes, as H2N2 did when it evolved into the Hong Kong Flu strain of H3N2.

The WHO, the Centers for Disease Control and Prevention (CDC), and other world-renowned public-health leaders are in hot pursuit of answers to several important questions. First, can we determine the magnitude of a pandemic when we can't predict H5N1 virus mutations? Second, is there sufficient surge capacity throughout the global health care infrastructure to care for pandemic numbers of sick and dying patients? Third, can the global community coalesce into a united front and rally resources quickly enough, with common political and strategic aims, to prevent the disease from spreading? Finally, can global manufacturers speed up production for high-demand items, such as antivirals, antibiotics and critical equipment—for example, ventilators, masks, and other types of personal protective equipment? These questions must be answered in the affirmative if we are to successfully combat such an emerging disease threat.

Causes of diseases

Infectious diseases are caused primarily by bacteria, toxins, and viruses. Bacteria are living organisms that can, under certain conditions, multiply within a human host or outside the body (for example, in food or water). Examples include *Vibrio cholarae* (cholera), *Yersinia pestis* (plague), *Francisella tularensis* (tularemia), and *Rickettsia prowazekii* (typhus). Bacteria principally cause disease in humans by

either invading tissue or producing toxins—the second category of biological organisms. Toxins are essentially the chemical byproduct of some bacteria and fungi that can cause disease in humans. They occur naturally, originating from animals, plants, or microbes. One particularly dangerous toxin is botulinum, which causes botulism. Viruses are organisms that use human cells to reproduce themselves. They include influenza (caused by numerous viruses that mutate over time, producing different strains), *Variola major* (smallpox), and the

ABOVE Lines on a house in Ziltendorf, Germany, indicate the high-water level after devastating floods hit the Oder River Valley in 2002. Locals were vaccinated against typhus and hepatitis and water was pumped out of the flooded Ziltendorf basin, because it was contaminated with bacteria that could cause intestinal and urethral infections.

ABOVE New Yorkers line up for shots in a mass vaccination program after an outbreak of smallpox occurred in the city in April 1947. More than 6 million people were vaccinated at the time; by the late 1970s the virus had been completely wiped out, as a result of a worldwide immunization campaign.

Filo viruses, such as ebola and marburg. Of these three types of biological organism, viruses are by far the most difficult to control. This is mainly because of the challenge of producing effective counter-measures, such as antivirals and vaccinations, in the face of clever viruses that mutate to ensure that their variant strains survive. Although bacteria and toxins can produce severe consequences, if not identified and treated, viruses generally are believed to pose the greatest emerging pandemic risk.

Historic plagues, brutal deaths

History abounds with epidemics and pandemics. The first recorded outbreak of bubonic plague was in 541–42 CE, in Constantinople and Egypt. Known as the Plague of Justinian, around 25 million people died, 50–60 percent of the population. Earlier still, a plague, believed to be typhus, caused Athens' final defeat during the Peloponnesian War in 430 BCE. It killed a quarter of Athens' population—30,000, including soldiers. During the Antonine Plague (first outbreak, 168–80 CE; second outbreak, 251–66 CE), believed to have been smallpox, 5 million people in Rome died—over 508 per day during its period of 27 years. It claimed the lives of two emperors, Lucius Verus and Marcus Aurelius Antoninus. But perhaps the best-known plague is the Black Death (1346–52 CE), an outbreak of bubonic plague that affected 70 percent of European cities and killed 25 million people, or 33 percent of the population.

Twentieth-century virus outbreaks

The twentieth century was blighted by emerging strains of influenza. The Spanish Flu pandemic of 1918–19 (H1N1 virus) was the world's deadliest; in the United States alone, it is purported to have killed more citizens than all the wars fought in the twentieth century combined. It led to restrictions being imposed on public gatherings and travel. Between 1 and 4 million people were killed worldwide during the Asian Flu (H2N2 Virus) of 1957–58, while the Hong Kong Flu of 1968–69 (H3N2 virus) caused 34,000 deaths in the United States. It is the lack of an all-encompassing cure for influenza that makes the threat of new strains such as bird flu (H5N1) a serious threat to public health.

Smallpox was a major threat, which killed 300 to 500 million people worldwide. In 1967 alone, 15 million contracted it and 2 million died. This prompted the WHO to launch a worldwide mass vaccination program in 1967. Smallpox was deemed officially eradicated in 1977, when the last case of smallpox was reported in Somalia. More recently, the Human Immunodeficiency Virus (HIV), which leads to Autoimmune Deficiency Syndrome (AIDS), had killed approximately 25 million by 2006.

Practical strategies are vital

It is universally accepted that the basic practice of washing hands with soap and warm water is the *single most effective way of reducing the risks* of transmitting disease, either from one person to another, or from the site of the germs to a person. Hand washing should always be done before, during, and after preparing food, eating, and whenever coming into contact with someone who is ill. It should be done before playing with young children, feeding or nursing a child, or treating a cut or scrape. It should also be done after you use (or help someone else to use) a bathroom, cough or sneeze, change a diaper, handle money, handle trash, pet an animal, change a litterbox, do any work or activity that gets the hands dirty, or come into contact with any bodily fluids.

Wearing latex gloves provides a barrier between the wearer and the infected person or object. This is routine practice for those in health care. Nasal passages and eyes provide an easy point of entry of a pathogen into the body. Therefore, masks and eye protection can provide effective barriers to airborne particulates from or to the nose (mucous membranes) or mouth (saliva) or other bodily fluids or secretions, such as blood. Never share dishes, utensils, or linen. These can be sources of contamination. Transportation systems, places of public gatherings, such as schools and sporting events, are all areas where disease transmission occurs. It is important to pay special attention when going to these areas to reduce the risk of contracting any disease.

Widescale prevention is the key

Assessment, selection, and enactment of broad-ranging preventive strategies are what individual governments need to do to ensure the preparedness and safety of their respective populations. These strategies should include, but are not limited to, activities undertaken before the disease strikes that will help prevent, eliminate, or reduce its effects.

Medical surveillance is the best way to prevent a serious outbreak. It requires actively and systematically collecting, analyzing, and then interpreting data. Health authorities must constantly acquire information about health and the environment in which a disease occurs so that its diagnosis can be confirmed. Medical surveillance includes disease (syndromic) surveillance, epidemiological surveillance, clinical diagnosis, and environmental health surveillance.

Of course surveillance alone won't protect a population. Experience has proven that mass vaccination—medical prophylaxis—is the safest and most effective way to protect populations from serious infectious diseases. Enhancing the body's natural protection against sickness, disability, and death also significantly reduces the chances of spreading disease to others. Medical prophylaxis capabilities belong to two categories: pre-exposure measures (vaccinations and antibiotics) and post-exposure measures (antibiotics, antivirals, vaccines, and chemicals/antidotes). Pre-exposure prophylaxis is used to protect the population as a preventive and pretreatment method. The success of medical prophylaxis is directly dependent on the availability of approved or licensed vaccinations, which will vary from country to country.

Isolation and quarantine

Restricting the movement of people to or from suspected or confirmed contaminated areas can reduce the threat of continued exposure to others and prevent further spread of the disease. Such restrictions range from prohibiting personnel from visiting a specified country to imposing isolation or quarantine on a person, group, or entire population. Quarantine is a very strong consideration if a population is confirmed as having been exposed to a disease with epidemic or pandemic potential.

Knowing how pathogens behave and what can be done—as individuals or societies—gives us the capacity to reduce the likelihood of widespread outbreaks. Future outbreaks depend on the global community pooling resources and enacting agreed-upon strategies to combat disease, by far the most deadly of all the natural disasters.

BELOW A poultry vendor leaves a market in Hanoi, Vietnam, in 2004, where the H5N1 virus, also called bird flu, has been a serious threat. It has occurred largely in Asian countries but has also spread to Europe, the Middle East, and Africa. Massive control efforts have been made to avoid a major worldwide pandemic.

PANDEMIC ALERT STATUS

There are six World Health Organization virus pandemic alert phases, but in 2006 these were being rewritten in light of the challenges presented by H5N1 (bird flu) and the difficulty in distinguishing between certain phases, particularly 3 and 4, so these will change.

PHASE 1 No new virus subtypes have been found in humans; one may be present in animals but presents a low risk to humans.

PHASE 2 No new virus subtypes have been found in humans but a subtype animal virus presents a substantial risk to humans.

PHASE 3 A new virus subtype causes one or more human infections, but there is no known human-to-human spread or just a rare occurrence through close contact between people.

PHASE 4 Limited human-to-human transmission has occurred in one or more small clusters; it is highly localized, suggesting that the virus is not well adapted to humans.

PHASE 5 Human-to-human transmission occurs in larger clusters, but spread is still localized, suggesting that the virus is better adapting to humans, though it may not be fully transmissible.

PHASE 6 Full pandemic phase, where human-to-human transmission in the general population is increased and sustained.

The Black Death, 1347 to 1350

The Great Mortality or, as it was later called, the Black Death, was a lethal disease that swept through Europe, killing one-third of the population. Spread by a virulent bacterium, it was named for one of its symptoms—hemorrhages under the skin that turned the affected areas a purplish black.

Killing more people than any epidemic or war before 1347, the Black Death originated in China then spread through Asia. It was transferred to Europe when trading ships fled a siege of Caffa (in modern-day Ukraine) and sailed to Messina in Italy in 1347. On arrival, all crew members were either infected or dead. By the end of 1347, the disease had spread to Genoa and Venice; it had reached most of Western Europe by 1348.

Frightful symptoms and mass panic

The Black Death is now commonly believed to have been spread by a bacterium (*Yersinia pestis*) that lived in fleas carried by black rats (*Rattus rattus*). Infected people suffered from inflamed lymph nodes in the armpits or on the groin (these were very painful), hemorrhages under the skin that caused black or livid spots to appear, headaches, vomiting, and fever.

In the fourteenth century, the disease was all the more terrifying because no one knew its cause. People did not know how to avoid catching it, whether they would catch it, or when they would catch it. Parents fled towns and cities, abandoning their sick children.

Others buried their deceased families, knowing they too would soon be dead. The cautious locked themselves in their homes, attempting to escape infection, some forming communes of the healthy where they drank fine wines and diverted themselves with music. Fatalists took over taverns or looted houses, while frauds pretended to be doctors to extort money and even sexual favors from the dying.

Italian author and poet Giovanni Boccaccio wrote about the contagion in Florence, Italy, in *The Decameron*: "Many died daily or nightly in the public streets; of many others, who died at home, the departure was hardly observed by their neighbors, until the stench of their putrefying bodies carried the tidings; and what with their corpses and the corpses of others who died on every hand the whole place was a sepulcher."

Physicians were totally unequipped to deal with the disaster. Many believed the cause of the sickness to be bad air, known as miasma. They recommended driving out the infectious odors by burning various sweet-smelling twigs and herbs such as rosemary or, alternatively, inhaling the fouler stenches of a latrine.

BELOW This painting by Italian artist Lilio Andrea (1555–1610) depicts St Roch (1350–80), a hermit who caught the plague on a pilgrimage and was cared for by a dog in the woods. Legend has it that he recovered and went on to perform miraculous healings. He was so popular that many scoundrels attempted to pass themselves off as this saint.

FACTS AND FIGURES

DATE	1347 to 1350
LOCATION	Europe: the countries most affected were Italy, the United Kingdom, France, Spain, Portugal, Germany, and Scandinavia
DEATH TOLL	25 million people; countless domestic and farm animals
COMMENTS	The population of Europe did not regain its pre-Black Death numbers until the seventeenth century.

LEFT People pray for relief from the plague, in a lithograph by F. Howard, circa 1350. Many works of art from the time of the Black Death depict the suffering and agony of its victims. Some works were devotional; others suggested penitential remedies including fasting and prayer.

BELOW This map shows the progressive spread of the Black Death through Europe during the period from 1347 to 1350.

Others advised sleeping in different positions or sprinkling the body with rosewater and vinegar.

Bands of hooded men, believing that the Black Death was caused by the wrath of God, moved across Europe whipping themselves with iron spikes and sobbing, pleading for forgiveness from the Almighty.

Priests could not keep up with the increasing numbers of the dead, who were eventually thrown into mass graves. Entire populations of monasteries were often wiped out as monks cared for the sick after all the doctors had fled or died.

Even the rich were struck down. King Alfonso XI of Castile succumbed, and Joan, daughter of English King Edward III, died at Bordeaux, France, on the way to her wedding with Alfonso's son. England's Canterbury lost two successive archbishops, while the papal court at Avignon, France, was reduced by one-fourth. The mortality rate varied in the different regions, and was between one-eighth and two-thirds of the population.

Changing the fabric of society

After the plague had died down, the overwhelming feeling was one of utter powerlessness in the face of inescapable horror. The fear of God increased, with many paintings depicting rotting corpses and devils slashing the damned.

At the same time, people became more concerned with materialism, health issues, and making the most of the time they had left to live.

Rural laborers who survived the disease demanded higher wages, and if these were refused, they moved to towns to find jobs. Landlords who

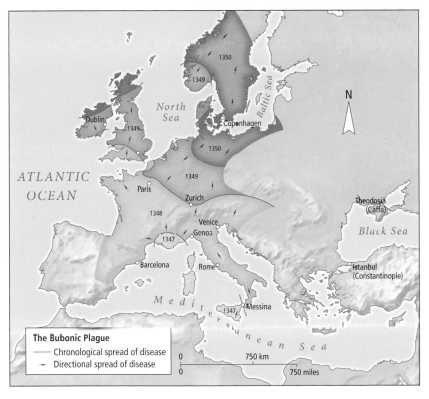

The Bubonic Plague
— Chronological spread of disease
→ Directional spread of disease

0   750 km
0   750 miles

were unable to find anyone to harvest their crops were ruined, and others suffered from the loss of their livestock—the Black Death also struck down sheep and cows. Statutes drawn up to fix maximum wages for peasants to prevent them bargaining for more money sparked revolt in France, England, and Italy. Europe was in physical and mental turmoil, and would never be the same again.

Smallpox, Central and South America, 1518 to 1600

Over 90 percent of Central and South America's indigenous populations were killed by the smallpox virus during the sixteenth century. Fascinating, powerful civilizations were lost forever as their populations perished from a lethal disease they had never before encountered.

ABOVE An engraving shows the first meeting between Hernán Cortés, the Spaniard who conquered Mexico, and ruler of the Aztecs, Montezuma II, at Tenochtitlán, now known as Mexico City. Cortés set up his army's headquarters in this city.

Before 1518, smallpox did not exist on mainland Central and South America. In that year, the Spanish soldier Hernán Cortés invaded Mexico, home of the Aztecs, with 500 men, at least one of whom was carrying the smallpox virus. In 1519, Cortés arrived at the Aztec capital, Tenochtitlán, a city of between 60,000 and 300,000 people. The Aztec ruler, Montezuma II, welcomed the Spaniard, but Cortés had his eye on the city's gold. He demanded treasure and, fearing an attack on his outnumbered forces, took Montezuma hostage. Six months later, the Aztecs rebelled. Although Montezuma died in the revolt, most of the Spaniards were killed; Cortés escaped.

An unknown killer

Cortés gathered new allies and besieged Tenochtitlán for three months, during which time smallpox killed most of the city's inhabitants. The survivors surrendered in August 1521. The signs of fighting and disease were everywhere. Cortés' chronicler, Bernal Diaz, wrote: "… all the houses and stockades in the lake were full of heads and corpses … we could not walk without treading on the bodies and heads of dead Indians. Indeed, the stench was so bad that no one could endure it …"

When a disease is introduced into an unexposed population, it kills all but the most resistant. As the deadliest strains die with their hosts, mild strains live on with the strongest survivors and are passed onto their children, who thus possess some immunity. Nearly all infected indigenous people died from the disease, whereas the death rate for smallpox among the Spaniards was only about 30 percent.

Heavenly wrath causes agony

Smallpox is spread by the virus *Variola major*, which is caught by inhaling droplets from an infected person. Symptoms include a high fever —102° to 106°F (39° to 41°C)—violent headaches, muscular pains, and vomiting. A skin rash on the face, chest, and back develops into pus-filled pustules. Death occurs from bacterial infection of the pustules, a heart attack, or shock.

An extreme form, known as "black pox," causes bleeding under the skin, giving the skin a charred, burned appearance and causing massive damage to internal organs. Victims bleed heavily from the mouth and other body cavities.

FACTS AND FIGURES

DATE	1518 to 1600
LOCATION	Central and South America
DEATH TOLL	About 20 million Aztecs in Mexico; 8 to 13 million Incas in Peru; 20 to 80 million in total in Central and South America
DAMAGE	Destroyed indigenous cultures throughout Central and South America
MORTALITY RATE	80% (Aztecs); 60–90% (Incas); over 90% (total Central and South American population)
COMMENTS	Eradicated in South America by 1971 and worldwide by 1977

LEFT Cortés and the Spaniards fighting the Aztecs, as depicted in an Aztec illustration. Unbeknown to Cortés, the invading Spaniards were wielding a secret biological weapon—smallpox.

The Native Americans believed that angry gods had inflicted this punishment, and had no idea how to treat the symptoms. When the disease hit a settlement, the survivors fled. Smallpox spread farther and faster than the Spaniards, who, on reaching towns with few people in them, just assumed they were sparsely populated.

For the next five years, smallpox annihilated most of Panama's population before crossing into South America. There, it wreaked havoc.

Early historical accounts, together with recent archeological finds of fertile farming soil, suggest that the Amazon Basin at this time was highly populated, with many villages and farms. It seems that smallpox reduced the population to such low levels that farming was abandoned and the rainforest took over.

End of the Incas

Smallpox reached the Incan empire in 1525. Within a few months, it had invaded their capital, Cuzco, in modern-day Peru. It killed the ruler, Huayna Capac, his son and heir, and 100,000 others, sparking civil war as the two remaining sons fought for leadership. The winner, Atahualpa, emerged in 1532.

Shortly afterward, Spanish soldier Francisco Pizarro landed in Peru with 180 men and conquered Atahualpa's stronghold in Cajamarca. After executing Atahualpa, he defeated the remaining Inca forces.

The gods have forsaken us

The Spaniards had destroyed the cultures of South and Central America, with smallpox, which was the invaders' deadliest, albeit unwitting, weapon. Native populations believed their gods had deserted them and that the Spaniards, being less affected by the disease, had supernatural powers. They continued to die from smallpox and other introduced diseases. By 1600, less than 10 percent of Central and South America's indigenous inhabitants remained alive.

BELOW The ruins of the ancient city of Machu Picchu lie high in the Andes Mountains in Peru near the capital, Cuzco. Built during the 1460s, the Incas living here at that time were hit hard by the smallpox virus, which wiped out half their population. The ruins of Machu Picchu were discovered in 1911.

Plague, England, 1665 to 1666

The last great outbreak of bubonic plague in England hit mainly the poverty-stricken, who did not have the means to flee. By September 1665 it was killing over 7,000 people a week in London. The rich left, the middle classes kept their distance, and the poor were locked in their homes and left to die.

BELOW A doctor wearing a mask during the plague. The "beak" of the mask was filled with pungent herbs—strong odors like hops or pepper were believed to ward off the plague.

The Great Plague spread to London in 1664 onboard Dutch ships carrying bales of cotton from Amsterdam. The winter of 1664 was freezing, which controlled the contagion. However, the spring and summer that followed in 1665 were very warm, allowing the disease to spread.

Rumors of pestilence

Treatment of bubonic plague had not advanced since the fourteenth century, though people knew they should avoid contact with the infected. Reporting had also increased in efficiency, with all parishes required to produce weekly bills of mortality detailing numbers of dead and cause of death.

The first reported case of plague was in May 1665—a woman named Margaret Porteous. People were immediately frightened. Samuel Pepys, a middle-class naval administrator, reported in his diary on May 24, 1665: "Thence to the Coffee-house … where all the newes is … of the plague … and of remedies against it …"

Attempts at containment

At first, most people tried to avoid spreading the contagion. Pepys wrote of the infected shutting themselves in their homes while neighbors left food on their doorsteps. Doctors visited, wearing long black gowns and beaked hoods filled with bergamot and aromatic spices. These actually helped to guard them against contagion as very little skin was exposed, restricting infected fleas from biting.

Doctors encouraged people, including children, to smoke tobacco, believing it prevented contagion. Others cut open patients' inflamed lymph nodes in their armpits or groins to purge their body of pestilential liquids. This would have been incredibly painful for the victims, who were also suffering from the other symptoms of the plague: hemorrhages, headaches, chills, vomiting, and fever.

The rich flee

By July, the contagion had spread rapidly, with 1,000 people a week succumbing to infection. The rich fled to their country estates. King Charles II moved to Oxford. The College of Surgeons left London, as did lawyers at the Inns of Court and the clergy. The Lord Mayor forbade anyone else to leave London unless they could provide a certificate of health. The rich and the middle class obtained certificates easily, buying forgeries if necessary, but the poor could not afford them and were unwittingly imprisoned in the capital.

LEFT An engraving by Peter Philippe of a banquet held at the Court of King Charles II of England, who reigned from 1660 to 1685. During the outbreak, he and his court were quick to flee London while the Lord Mayor and aldermen remained.

The plague of the poor

The authorities said the poor had brought the disease on themselves, using as proof the fact that outbreaks were centered in the most poverty-stricken suburbs, such as Westminster, Clerkenwell, and Southwark. Newspapers like *The Intelligencer* said the poor "hastened their own destruction," and the clergy, speaking from the safe distance of the countryside,

announced that the plague was God's punishment on them for their clearly immoral ways.

In reality, London's population had tripled since 1650, due to economic depression in the north of the country, which drove people to the capital to find work. The wealthy began to fear the "great unwashed" languishing on their doorstep, spreading disease everywhere. "Nothing is more complained

BELOW A broadsheet illustration of the time shows townspeople fleeing to the country to escape the threat of infection by the plague. Many illustrations from this period depict skeletons, here shown driving the carriage, as a reminder of the fragility of life.

Smallpox, North America, 1775 to 1782

Some historians believe George Washington's inoculation of his troops against smallpox was the most important decision of the American War of Independence, influencing the victory of the revolutionaries over the British.

George Washington (above), the President who eventually realized that inoculating his troops was worthwhile. The title page of a book (below) about the value of inoculating against smallpox, which was published in 1775.

Between 1775 and 1782, the smallpox virus swept throughout North America, killing approximately 130,000 people. The epidemic coincided with the American War of Independence, which was fought between Great Britain and 13 British colonies. Both loyalists and revolutionaries were struck down by the disease.

An Historical

ACCOUNT

OF THE

SMALL-POX

INOCULATED

IN

NEW ENGLAND,

Upon all Sorts of Perfons, *Whites, Blacks,* and of all Ages and Conftitutions.

With fome Account of the Nature of the Infection in the NATURAL and INOCULATED Way, and their different Effects on HUMAN BODIES.

With fome fhort DIRECTIONS to the UNEXPERIENCED in this Method of Practice.

Humbly dedicated to her Royal Highnefs the Princefs of WALES, by *Zabdiel Boylfton,* Phyfician.

LONDON:

Printed for S. CHANDLER, *at the* Crofs-Keys *in the* Poultry. M.DCC.XXVI.

Smallpox affects battle outcomes

Smallpox was present from the war's earliest skirmishes. The disease decimated British forces prior to battles in April 1775, and was a major cause of their subsequent retreat to Boston. American troops besieged the city. The Royal Navy supplied Boston by ship, but food was still in short supply. Still ill from smallpox and weakened by lack of food, the British suffered heavy losses when they attacked the Americans in June 1775 at the Battle of Bunker Hill. The Americans maintained the siege and the British were forced to leave Boston by ship.

Fortunes changed later that year. The Americans marched to Quebec, planning to persuade the Canadians to join the war, but smallpox cut swathes through their ranks. By the time these troops reached Canada in early November, only 600 of 1,100 men were left alive. Reinforcements arrived, but they also succumbed to the disease. On attacking Quebec, the Americans were soundly defeated by the British. Further attempts through 1776 to take the city also failed, ending the Americans' hopes of Canada rising in rebellion with them.

Throughout 1776, the British went from strength to strength, taking much of New York and New Jersey. The American army had dwindled by winter to 1,400 men. Morale was low. Smallpox continued to affect American forces, and the treatments used to combat it—ingesting mercury or applying leeches—only made the situation worse.

Inoculation boosts morale

Inoculation is a way of introducing a mild form of a disease into the system, so that antibodies will identify it as a hostile force, fight and kill it, and "recognize" the disease when it next enters the body. Although a medical vaccination for smallpox was not invented until 1796 (by English physician Edward Jenner), people had been inoculating themselves against the illness for several centuries. In China, physicians blew powdered smallpox scabs up the noses of healthy clients, and in India, the technique was to rub infected pus onto a metal pin before pricking the skin. By 1775, in Europe and the

United States, many people inoculated themselves by rubbing infected pus into a scratch or cut. This practise was risky: about 2 percent of inoculated people actually died from the disease.

Washington had delayed inoculating his troops because the outcome was hard to manage. The sick men would have to be locked away to prevent them spreading the disease, and could suffer for up to a month. In February 1777 Washington wrote that; "… should We inoculate greatly, the Enemy, knowing

it, will certainly take Advantage of our Situation." Eventually, however, he decided to proceed.

By doing so, he saved the lives of many men and greatly boosted the numbers of the fighting fit. Revolutionary confidence and determination saw the Americans beat the British at the Battle of Saratoga in October 1777, encouraging France, Spain, and the Netherlands to enter the war against Great Britain. The tide had turned, and the American revolutionaries eventually won the war.

ABOVE On June 17, 1775, British and American troops fought during a siege near Boston known as the Battle of Bunker Hill. Throughout the War of Independence, smallpox ravaged both sides; the British casualties from this battle alone were around 1,000 dead.

FACTS AND FIGURES

DATE	1775 to 1782
LOCATION	United States and Canada
DEATH TOLL	Approximately 130,000
DAMAGE	Near-defeat of both British and Revolutionary forces
MORTALITY RATE	30% in populations that have some immunity
COMMENTS	2% of people inoculated died from the disease

LASTING DISFIGUREMENT

Smallpox is quite an ancient disease—it was described as early as in 1122 BCE in China. Its mortality rate is around 30 percent in populations that have some immunity. The disease affects rich and poor alike. Some of the disease's more prestigious victims include Pharaoh Rameses V, Emperor Shunzhi of China, King Louis XV of France, and Tsar Peter II of Russia.

Between 65 and 80 percent of people who have succumbed to the disease are left scarred. Pockmarked survivors include Queen Elizabeth I of England, who covered her scars with thick white make-up, and Joseph Stalin, who had his photos retouched to hide his pockmarks. Sterility in men and blindness are some of the other unpleasant after-effects.

Tuberculosis, Worldwide, 1840 to 1940

Portrayed as a disease of passion contracted by geniuses, feared as the cause of vampirism, and regarded as a mark of refinement, tuberculosis was the most romanticized disease in nineteenth- and early twentieth-century Europe.

Throughout the 1800s and early 1900s tuberculosis (TB) ravaged the world, killing between two and three million people a year. TB was often misdiagnosed by early travelers to Africa and Asia as an exotic tropical disease. While those areas did not keep statistics on its prevalence, doubtless it had as big an impact on those nations as it did on North America and Europe, where it was one of the great killers. In England alone, 80,000 people died of TB in 1880, and it killed 100,000 French people a year before 1914.

In Europe, suffering artists were considered to have brought the disease on themselves. Their superior intelligence and creativity had produced "an excess of passion," their minds soaring to great heights as their bodies were consumed by fever. "Consumption," as TB was called, was the price to be paid for being talented. In reality, many artists contracted TB as they were living in overcrowded, unsanitary conditions, an ideal environment for the spread of the disease. Poor "untalented" people also succumbed in their droves, but older people, the middle-class, and the rich were also affected.

A romantic death?

New Zealand writer Katherine Mansfield, who spent most of her short life in England and France, said of her TB in December 1920: "I will learn the lessons [suffering] teaches … I must turn to work. I must put my agony into something, change it."

Female victims, looking pallidly attractive with their pale skins, eyes sparkling from fever, gentle cough, and resigned exhaustion, were seen as transcending their bodies and preparing for life in Heaven. English writer Charlotte Brontë wrote of her sister Anne's demise in 1849: "With almost her last breath she said she was happy, and thanked God that death was come, and come so gently."

At the same time, TB was dreaded for being the painful and agonizing disease it was. Charlotte wrote after Anne's death: "Papa has now me only … Consumption has taken the whole five … I

ABOVE An 1880 cartoon depicts TB as an evil serpent being conquered by bacteriologist Robert Koch after he isolated the tuberculosis bacillus.

am ordered to remain at the sea-side awhile …" Katherine Mansfield wrote in August 1920: "I cough and cough … I feel that my whole chest is boiling … Life is … getting a new breath. Nothing else counts."

Writers such as Fyodor Dostoevsky, Thomas Mann, Charles Dickens, and the Brontë sisters depicted their fictional consumptive characters as heroes and heroines. Pre-Raphaelite paintings showed pale, beautiful knights and ladies, while operas such as Puccini's La Bohème featured divas succumbing to TB on stage.

During the late nineteenth- and early twentieth-centuries, it became fashionable to adopt "the TB look." Women wore whitening powders, enlarged their eyes with black eyeliner, lost weight, and reclined gracefully on chaise longues. By turning themselves into dying heroines, they reflected a culture that was in love with female helplessness and hopeless romantic suffering.

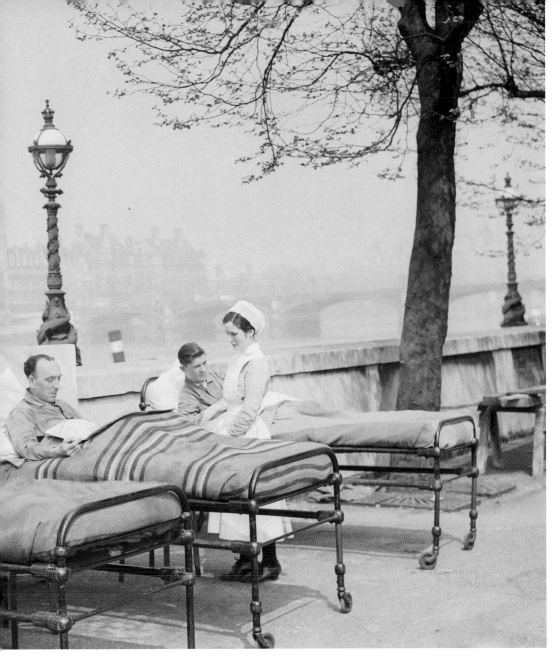

LEFT May 1936: TB patients from St Thomas' Hospital, opposite the houses of parliament in London, were put outdoors in the open air. At this time, the medical profession encouraged people to spend time in sunlight. As well as being therapeutic for TB and rickets, it was then also considered greatly beneficial for general health. The trend led to the quest for suntans and new architectural styles, such as summer houses.

The cause and cures

In 1865, French doctor Jean-Antoine Villemin demonstrated that TB could be passed from humans to cattle, and from cattle to rabbits. People had not previously believed that the disease was contagious. Robert Koch, a German scientist, then discovered the tubercle bacillus in 1882—*Mycobacterium tuberculosis*. He found that the bacteria caused fine granules to grow in organs of the body, damaging and destroying them.

TB commonly affects the lungs but also damages other organs, bones, and joints. It is spread by inhaling droplets from an infected person's coughing, sneezing, or spitting. The infection can wax and wane, with the damaged tissue healing before being attacked again by the bacteria, so some sufferers can live with TB for many years.

Some of the "cures" taken included smoking opium or cow dung, daily horseback riding, swallowing large amounts of cod liver oil, applying leeches, eating butter made from cows that grazed in churchyards, and ingesting a mixture of gold and sodium, a practise known as gold therapy.

The Polish composer Frédéric Chopin reflected people's lack of faith in the medical profession:

CURSE OF THE VAMPIRE

Among poor people in parts of nineteenth-century Europe, TB sufferers were believed to be vampires. Like vampires, TB sufferers were sensitive to bright light, had pale skin, and lost weight despite eating and remaining active. They coughed up blood; according to the prevailing belief, meant they had to replenish their supplies from feeding on other people.

If someone with TB died, and other family members soon after began to show signs of wasting away and illness, there was only one explanation: the recently deceased had made a nocturnal visit to drain blood from the hapless victim. The body was exhumed. If the corpse had not decomposed, the heart was removed and burned, or the whole body was set on fire. This gruesome practice was meant to kill the vampire … for good.

TB sufferers in outdoor school taking up art (above), at Dr Rollier's clinic at Leysin in Switzerland, 1925. He prescribed sun, good food, and exercise. A French advertisement (below), circa 1920s, outlines how to avoid contagion from TB.

"… one [doctor] sniffed at what I spat up, the second tapped where I spat it from, the third poked about and listened how I spat it. One said I had died, the second that I am dying, the third that I shall die …" Chopin did indeed die from TB, in 1849.

The most popular TB treatment from the mid-1800s to 1940 was to isolate patients from the rest of the population in sanitariums.

Suivez ces Conseils
VOUS VIVREZ LONGTEMPS

Vivez le plus possible au grand air

Dormez la fenêtre ouverte

Ne portez pas à la bouche les objets sur lesquels la salive des autres a pu se poser

Brossez-vous les dents avant de vous coucher

Tenez-vous droit à l'école

Prenez un bain au moins 1 fois par semaine

Lavez vos mains avant de vous mettre à table

Ne crachez jamais par terre

The success of sanitariums

In the 1850s, a German student suffering from TB, Hermann Brehmer, was told by his doctor to find a healthier climate, somewhere with fresh, dry air and low humidity. Brehmer went to the Himalayas, where he got better. After returning to Germany, he studied medicine and, deciding that TB was a curable disease, opened an inpatient hospital in Gorbersdorf, Germany. Here, his patients, surrounded by fir trees and plied with good food, were exposed to ample fresh air.

Other sanitariums followed, many serving large quantities of food, in an effort to build up patients' strength. But many sanitariums for the poor were more like prisons—75 percent of people died within five years, though some charitable organizations provided more comfortable facilities.

The wealthy paid for exotic but not necessarily effective treatments in luxury establishments. Sunny, alpine locations were very popular. In 1930, of the 5,698 people living in the Swiss town of Leysin, 3,000 were TB patients living in 70 clinics.

A popular sanitarium, Les Fernes, was set up in 1911 in Leysin by Dr August Rollier, who was internationally acclaimed as the Sun Doctor. He specialized in "heliotherapy" or sunlight treatment. He claimed a high cure rate, combining sunbathing

FACTS AND FIGURES

DATE	1840 to 1940
LOCATION	Worldwide
DEATH TOLL	1 billion
DAMAGE	Many people died from ineffectual and painful "cures"
MORTALITY RATE	60% to 80%
COMMENTS	TB was responsible for 500 out of 100,000 deaths in England in 1850 and 1 in 6 deaths in France in 1918

chest and head raised; and the "cure de silence," where she had to lie in bed and do nothing for two hours. To ensure total tranquility, the road in front of Les Fernes was closed at this time and local farmers were prohibited from working in the fields. Gandhi left Les Fernes in December 1940, still unwell.

In 1944, the antibiotic drug streptomycin was found to cure TB. The sanitariums closed down.

TB makes a comeback

Immunization against TB was developed by Albert Calmette and Camille Guérin in 1906. BCG (which stands for bacillus of Calmette and Guérin) was used in France from July 1921, but the rest of Europe did not adopt its use until after World War II. It was found to be quite effective in children but, unfortunately, less so in adults. A more comprehensive vaccine is being developed.

TB declined in the 1940s but made a resurgence in the mid-1980s. HIV-positive people are prone to TB and the disease has spread rapidly through developing nations in concert with HIV. TB is now the world's second-biggest fatal disease after HIV, killing around two million people a year.

Drug resistance is also a problem. Scientists are constantly developing new drugs to combat the resistant strains of TB that are emerging.

with good and plentiful food, breathing exercises, modern dance movements done in bed, light walking, and occupational therapy, including basket weaving, knitting, needlework, and typing.

Les Fernes contained a hall where films were shown and concerts held, a dining room, a ladies' salon, smoking room, and billiard room. Patients' rooms were centrally heated, large and airy, with views of the Alps.

Indira Gandhi, who later became Prime Minister of India, spent a year at Les Fernes from 1939 to 1940. She was subjected to treatments such as the "position ventrale," in which she lay on her stomach, propped up on her elbows and forearms with her

Malaria and Yellow Fever, Panama, 1882 to 1914

For mosquitoes at the turn of the nineteenth century, Panama was the ideal habitat. Constant high temperatures, a rainy season lasting nine months, and dense jungle provided ideal breeding conditions. Food was plentiful—Panama City and Panama's other major city, Colón, each supported about 30,000 people. Cesspools and swamps around both cities were perfect for mosquitoes.

ABOVE A yellow fever patient recuperates inside one of the portable isolation cages at Ancon Hospital during the construction of the Panama Canal. Such cages were purpose-built to keep out the two different species of mosquito that carry either malaria or yellow fever.

It was in this location that the United States went about building a thoroughfare between North and South America: the Panama Canal. They began construction in 1904. Between the end of the French endeavor, abandoned in 1889, and the beginning of the American project, the causes of both yellow fever and malaria had been discovered. Both diseases had completely disrupted the French construction. In 1897, Britain's Ronald Ross found that malaria was transmitted by *Anopheles* mosquitoes, and in 1900, US army surgeon Walter Reed proved Cuban Dr Carlos Finlay's theory that yellow fever was spread by the mosquito *Aedes aegypti*.

Causes and symptoms

Yellow fever is a virus transmitted by mosquitoes from monkeys to people. Symptoms include intense fever, muscle aches, headache and backache, bloody vomit, and sometimes jaundice through liver or kidney failure. Unlucky victims go into a coma, then die. Survivors develop immunity.

Malaria is a mosquito-borne parasite that enters the body through the mosquito's saliva, multiplies rapidly in the liver and invades red blood cells, which it destroys. Symptoms include fever, shivering, joint pain, vomiting and convulsions, an enlarged spleen, and renal failure. Survivors do not gain lifetime immunity; they can suffer relapses.

Neither disease had a vaccination or totally effective cure. Yellow fever was treated with bed rest, and malaria by taking quinine mixed with liquor, which sometimes killed the parasites but caused headaches and vomiting; especially in those over-enthusiastic about the liquor part of the remedy.

Gorgas' crusade

Doctor William Gorgas was employed to recommend measures to protect canal workers from both these diseases. He believed eradicating yellow fever would be like "making war on the family cat," whereas controlling malaria would be "like fighting all the beasts of the jungle." *Aedes aegypti* only lays its eggs

FACTS AND FIGURES	
DATE	1882 to 1914
LOCATION	Panama
DEATH TOLL	22,000 between 1882 and 1889 (not known between 1904 and 1914)
DAMAGE	The French government suffered a major embarrassment and lost millions of francs over its failure to construct a viable canal
MORTALITY RATE	Yellow fever: in 1904, 50% (in 2006, it was 5%). Malaria: death rate dropped from 11.59 per 1,000 in November 1906 to 1.23 per 1,000 in December 1909, and 0.30 per 1,000 by the end of 1913.
COMMENTS	The percentage of employees hospitalized in Panama dropped from 9.6% in 1905 to 1.6% in 1909. In 1914, the death rate among canal workers of 17 per 1,000 from all diseases was lower than the rate in many United States cities.

LEFT Vast numbers of workers were brought into Panama to build the canal, and all of them became exposed to malaria and yellow fever. The deck of the SS *Ancon* here is filled with some of the 1,500 laborers who were transported over from Barbados.

ABOVE Dr William Crawford Gorgas (1854–1920) had to appeal to President Roosevelt to get the supplies to eradicate yellow fever and control malaria.

in or near buildings occupied by people, in clean water in enclosed containers. *Anopheles* thrives in the jungle as well as in towns, and will lay its eggs in any still water in swamps, marshes, drains, or ditches.

To begin with, Gorgas ordered all workers to be provided with free hospital services and medicines, including quinine; he made sure all their quarters were screened with mesh. Diseased laborers were quarantined in structures that prevented mosquitoes from biting them and infecting other hosts.

In a massive infrastructure project, all buildings in Colón and Panama were also screened and given running water to eliminate the need for containers. Homes containing infected people were fumigated with burning pans of sulfur or pyrethrum.

Knowing that *Anopheles* mosquitoes must land before flying a certain distance, Gorgas ordered all the vegetation within 200 yards (183 m) of villages and 100 yards (91 m) of homes to be cut, and more than 100 square miles (259 sq. km) of swamp drained. To kill the mosquito larvae, workers placed dripping oil cans over waterways until films of oil spread over each stagnant pond, or applied a

larvacide made of carbolic acid, resin, and caustic soda. Cisterns and cesspools were oiled once a week.

Eradication and control

Gorgas' hard work eventually paid off and his methods proved to be highly effective. Yellow fever was completely eradicated from Panama by 1906, and has never returned. Incidences of malaria were drastically reduced. In 1914, the year the canal was opened, only seven employees died of malaria compared with 207 deaths in 1906.

A FRENCH FARCE

In 1882 France began work on building a canal between Limon Bay and Panama City. Laborers toiled waist-deep in stinking mud, hacking at virgin jungle with hand tools, wearing clothes that never dried due to the non-stop rain. Succumbing to yellow fever and malaria, which people believed were caused by toxic emissions from putrefying vegetation, workers were sent to the hospital in Colón, where the windows had no screens. To prevent patients from being bitten by ants, bed legs were placed in bowls of water—prime mosquito breeding grounds. Patients were grouped by nationality, not disease, leading to cross-infection. France's canal project was abandoned in 1889, by which time about 22,000 workers had died.

Spanish Flu, Worldwide, 1918 to 1919

In the years just following World War I, children chanted while skipping: "I had a little bird, its name was Enza, I opened the window, and in-flu-enza." The rhyme was written about the Spanish flu pandemic, which killed at least 40 million people—more deaths than had been caused by the war.

In 1918, the war raging in Europe had entered its fifth year. Years of rationing of foodstuffs and bad news from the front lines had already considerably worn down morale. Then a devastating form of influenza struck, affecting mainly healthy people in the 20- to 40-year age range (unlike other strains, which hit children and the elderly). Its origin is not known for certain. Some believe it began in France in the trenches, others in the United States in military camps, and others that it was a form of germ warfare developed by the Germans and spread from Germany. Wherever it came from, the disease was christened Spanish flu because Spain, which was neutral during the war, was one of the first countries to report it. The Spaniards called it the French flu.

Death by suffocation

The first outbreak was in March 1918. The symptoms included fever, muscle pain, headache, and sore throat. These progressed over five or six days to high fever, racking cough, loss of strength, and great difficulty breathing. Some people died horribly from suffocation, their lungs filled with fluid containing red blood and immune cells. Lack of oxygen caused their skin to turn purplish black, a condition known as heliotrope cyanosis.

Influenza is caused by a virus, which is spread from person to person by inhaling infected droplets from coughs and sneezes. The Spanish flu spread rapidly all around the world.

Many soldiers came down with the disease. Crowded military camps, trenches, and military transports were prime places for infection to occur. A doctor at a military camp in Boston, Massachusetts wrote in a letter to a friend: "One can stand it to see one, two or twenty men die, but to see these poor devils dropping like flies sort of gets on your nerves. We have been averaging about 100 deaths per day …" The countries hardest hit were Western Samoa, which lost 20 percent of its population, and India, which recorded up to 50 deaths per 1,000 people, a total of up to 16 million people.

BELOW Two men wearing and advocating the use of flu masks in Paris during the Spanish flu epidemic in March 1919. People are now concerned that avian influenza (H5N1) could have the same effect on the world today as Spanish flu did then.

Masks worn for protection

People locked themselves in their homes; theaters, schools, churches, and other public places were closed; and bodies were piled up outside houses to be collected in open carts. In North America, gauze masks had to be worn outside, public phones were doused with alcohol to disinfect them, and people were not allowed on trains without a health certificate. In Britain, streets were sprayed with chemicals and some factories changed their no-smoking rules, believing that tobacco fumes

could kill the virus. Hospitals were full of war wounded, and doctors and hospitals were pushed to their limits. The Red Cross recruited people to help with the nursing shortage. Some cities set up isolation hospitals to prevent the spread of infection. Exhausted military personnel survived the war to die from the disease, nurse their ill relatives day and night, or watch their spouses perish.

Porridge, sulfur, and kerosene

There was no cure known, so people developed their own preventative methods. *The News of the World* advised its readers in November 1918 to wash their noses, take lots of walks, and eat porridge. Some people sprinkled their shoes with sulfur, put vinegar packs on their stomachs, and tied cucumbers to their ankles. Others sat in baths covered in raw onions, ate lumps of sugar flavored with kerosene, or tied red ribbons round their arms. No one is sure what caused Spanish flu, why it had such a high mortality rate, or why it disappeared in mid-1919 as quickly as it had appeared. In 2001, three researchers theorized that the virus was a combination of an animal and a human virus, a new strain to which people had no resistance. Others believe the virus came from birds.

ABOVE American nurses caring for victims of the Spanish flu in Lawrence, Massachusetts, in 1918. Here it hit a large number of naval personnel, and navy nurses worked until dropping from exhaustion. Patients were kept outdoors in tents as part of an outdoor fresh-air treatment. The United States was not as badly hit as the rest of the world, but the 600,000 killed there was twice the number killed in battle.

FACTS AND FIGURES	
DATE	1918 to 1919
LOCATION	Worldwide
DEATH TOLL	Between 40 and 100 million including 500,000 in the USA, 228,000 in Britain, 400,000 in Germany
DAMAGE	Lack of productivity in factories and businesses due to many being closed down during the pandemic
MORTALITY RATE	2.5% (other influenzas have a mortality rate of 0.5%)

HIV Virus, Sub-Saharan Africa and Worldwide, 1959 to Present

Human immunodeficiency virus (HIV) kills more people worldwide than any other virus. By March 2006, over 40 million people were known to be HIV-positive. Africa south of the Sahara is the world's worst-affected region. The HIV virus attacks the immune system, and eventually leads to AIDS.

FAR RIGHT Eight-year-old Ruth Nakabonge throws earth over her father's coffin at his funeral in 2005 in Bambula, Uganda. He died from an AIDS-related infection after having already lost 10 family members to the illness.

BELOW The red huts on a map of a small village in Mozambique indicate families that have one or more members suffering from AIDS. The mortality rates for children are alarming: under a year old, 13 percent, and under five years, 20 percent.

HIV is a virus that originated in monkeys in Africa. The first recorded case in humans occurred in 1959, when a man died of a mystery illness in what is now the Democratic Republic of Congo. Later examination of a plasma sample taken at the time was found to contain HIV.

Through the 1960s and 1970s the virus spread, but the world did not know there was a new disease on the prowl until 1981, when in the United States several young homosexual men developed Kaposi's sarcoma, a rare cancer usually occurring in older people. Other people developed an uncommon lung infection, *Pneumocystis carinii pneumonia* (PCP). In Africa, people were dying of a wasting disease known locally as "slim." Scientists found that virological profiles in these instances were the same, and that a new pandemic had arrived.

The disease was given the name of Acquired Immunodeficiency Syndrome (AIDS) in 1982. Two years later, in 1984, researchers identified the HIV virus that causes AIDS.

Relationship between HIV and AIDS

Transmitted through blood, semen, vaginal fluid, preseminal fluid, and breast milk, HIV is caught by sharing infected needles; having vaginal, anal, or oral sex; having a blood transfusion; or an infected mother and baby exchanging fluids. By attacking the immune system, the virus exposes sufferers to infections and cancers, and affects internal organs.

AIDS develops from HIV when the immune system functions poorly or not at all. All HIV sufferers will eventually develop AIDS, unless they die first from other causes. People in developed nations with access to medication are living for 15 or more years with HIV without developing AIDS. For people without medication, the average time between contracting HIV and succumbing to AIDS is about 10 years. Once AIDS occurs, people in developing countries can die within a year due to lack of access to drugs and health care, and poor nutrition.

The symptoms of AIDS include cancers, serious brain infections, and infections of the throat, lungs, or bronchi. There is no vaccine for HIV (although scientists are working on developing one), and no cure. It is prevented by blood screening, using clean needles, and using a condom during sex.

Sub-Saharan Africa has the greatest HIV prevalence

Sub-Saharan Africa has just over a tenth of the world's population but two-thirds of the worldwide infected (25 million people with HIV and AIDS) and more than three-quarters of all HIV-infected women.

Several countries in this region are afflicted by droughts, wars, and poverty, so people have priorities other than health, such as avoiding hostile soldiers or simply finding food for their families. Many of them do not know about HIV and, if they do, have neither the time nor the money to go to a doctor, especially when the nearest medical facility can be many miles away and they have no transport.

Already suffering from starvation, malnutrition, or diseases such as tuberculosis, these people succumb quickly to HIV symptoms. Those aware of

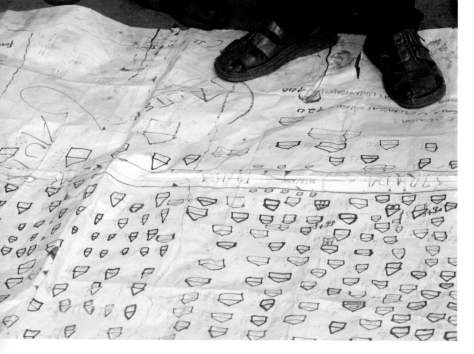

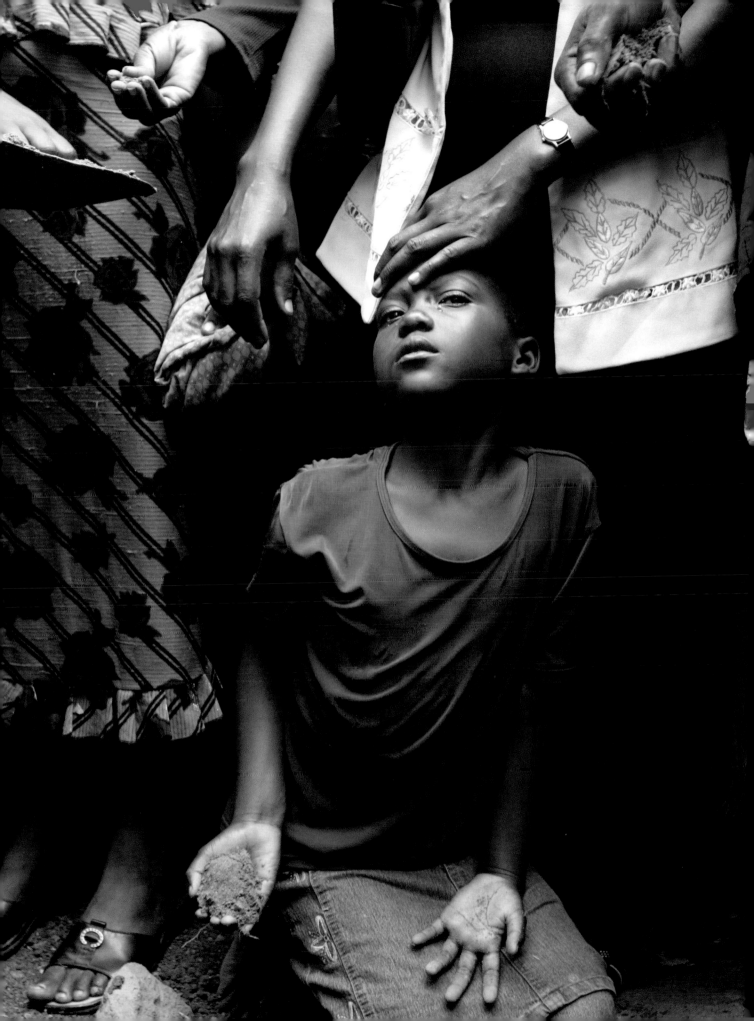

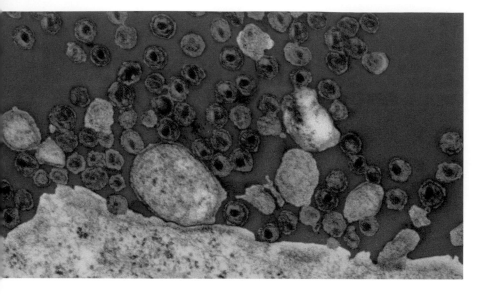

FACTS AND FIGURES

DATE	1959 to present
LOCATION	Worldwide, but at its worst in sub-Saharan Africa
DEATH TOLL	Over 25 million worldwide since 1981 from AIDS (3.1 million in 2005); this figure includes around 22 million in sub-Saharan Africa.
DAMAGE	As at March 31, 2006, 12 million children in sub-Saharan Africa have been orphaned by AIDS
MORTALITY RATE	100 percent (though some people live with HIV for many years but die from other causes)
COMMENTS	The Caribbean has the second-greatest prevalence of people with HIV, especially Haiti and the Dominican Republic

ABOVE A color-enhanced scanning electron microscope picture of the HIV virus shows it attacking human cells. The virus is highlighted in red.

BELOW A group of Malawi children orphaned when their parents died from AIDS. There are at least 1 million AIDS orphans in Malawi. In sub-Saharan Africa it is expected their numbers will rise to 18 million by 2010.

HIV are often reluctant to be tested when screening is available. Some rural community leaders or healers consider the disease a "punishment," and infected people and their families can be ostracized or even evicted from their villages. This attitude gives people an incentive to hide their HIV-positive status. For example, a woman who is HIV-positive should feed her baby formula rather than breast milk, but her relatives may force her to breastfeed so that village leaders will not discover her infected status.

Other factors assist the spread of the virus. Women in some African countries are not legally entitled to refuse sex with their husbands or demand that they use a condom. Many men view condoms with suspicion, as they believe they constrict and damage sexual organs. Rape, unfortunately, is common. In some cultures, there is no stigma against having several sexual partners, monogamy being the exception rather than the rule. Prostitutes will agree to have sex without a condom, as they can charge more for this service.

Health facilities are generally poor. Countries providing health checks and treatment programs do not have enough professionals to administer them, as medical workers are attracted by better conditions and higher wages elsewhere, or are themselves dying from HIV. Too few hospital beds means patients are admitted at the later stages of the illness, reducing their chances of recovery. In some countries, people can contract HIV through transfusions or needles being used on more than one patient.

Treatment is often hard to get

The main treatment for HIV is highly active anti-retroviral therapy (HAART), which consists of three or four drugs. HAART stops HIV replicating, enabling the immune system to recover.

In many countries, HAART is not available because the drugs are expensive, governments cannot afford to freely dispense them, and people cannot afford to buy them. In other nations, there is a limited selection of drugs, meaning people must be on the same ones for many years, during which time the virus has mutated to overcome their effects. In developed nations, HAART drugs are changed regularly to keep ahead of mutations.

It is also hard for people to get access to treatment. People in remote rural communities must find someone with a vehicle to take them to the nearest town, then pay the driver. "Businesspeople" taking drugs into these communities charge four or five times the official rate and have no idea how to prescribe them.

Finding a way forward

Rural families have drastically reduced their hours of agricultural work due to illness from HIV, so farms are not running at maximum capacity. Healthy relatives have to work twice as hard while the family income is declining. According to a United Nations report, one Zimbabwean woman now has to work in the fields instead of looking after her children. In the past, she hired others to weed her crops but now she has to do all the work herself. She is not alone.

Children, especially girls, are being removed from school to help out at home. Deprived of an education, their opportunities for productive work in the future have been severely curtailed. Some children whose parents have died from AIDS, who are living with their grandparents or other elderly relatives, are the household's main income earners.

Funerals are expensive, and can cost some families three times their monthly income. This means those still living must do without food and clothing in order to bury their dead.

Many African countries are working hard to improve the situation. In Uganda, HIV prevalence has decreased from 15 percent to 5 percent. A range of initiatives gets credit for this dramatic turnaround:

education programs that reduce the stigma of having HIV; persuading people to be tested and counseled; discussing sexual behavior openly; encouraging the use of condoms; and improving the status of women. Botswana routinely offers an HIV test at clinics and provides HAART via the public sector to needy citizens (it is also offered through the private sector).

ABOVE A billboard in Lagos, Nigeria, proclaims "AIDS is Real," a message that was also put on postage stamps in 2003 as part of an education campaign. Other African strategies include free condoms and raising awareness.

HIV SUFFERERS ARE NOT CRIMINALS

HIV sufferers in developed nations have better access to a greater range of medications and support groups than HIV-positive people in Africa. However, they share with their African counterparts feelings of isolation, frustration, and anger that they are at times treated like social lepers. One man, from London, who has been HIV-positive for 13 years, commented: "I have to say it's been tough to get to now. There have been serious problems with medications and I have continuing health problems. HIV has forced me to consider many different kinds of pain from the side-effects of drugs. Those of us with HIV can be refused entry to countries like the USA and Australia, must inform dentists and doctors of our status and are treated warily by colleagues. In the past five years, several men have been imprisoned for 'reckless infection with HIV.' The media portray such cases as the cloak and dagger stuff of melodrama, when they happen because of misinformation, poverty, low self-esteem, and isolation. These people need education and a cure, not punishment. Every media story diverts attention from the fact that governments, drug companies, and legal systems are treating people with the virus as sub-human."

H5N1 Bird Flu, Asia, Middle East, Europe, and Africa, 1997 to Present

Picture this: five million people have already died. Businesses, shops, and restaurants are closed. In their homes, people nurse ill relatives or stand by their locked doors with guns, threatening would-be looters. Hospitals have run out of beds and police patrol the streets in armed vans. Countries everywhere are unprepared for a virus that has swept the world like a mega-tsunami.

BELOW South Korean health officials wear full protective suits while burying ducks suspected of carrying H5N1 during a mass culling program that took place in 2003. The bird flu control program in South Korea was quick and aggressive.

This doomsday scenario is predicted by various officials worldwide who believe that H5N1, more generally known as "avian influenza" or "bird flu," will start spreading from person to person rather than from bird to person. They say once the virus mutates and starts jumping between humans, people will have no time to build up resistance and casualties will be similar to those from Spanish Flu in

1918. Governments around the world are scrambling to find a cure for a disease that has the potential to bring the world economy to a grinding halt.

H5N1 has already affected the lives of many people in South-East Asia. According to the Food and Agriculture Organization of the United Nations (FAO), one farmer in a village near Hanoi, Vietnam, had heard about bird flu on television. Yet when

WILL H5N1 BECOME THE NEXT PANDEMIC?

Influenza A viruses are capable of multiple mutations that allow the illness to cross species barriers and there is concern that H5N1 may become a worldwide pandemic. The first apparent human-to-human transmission was in June 2006 among five members of an Indonesian family who had the same strain despite having no contact with birds. However, it appears to not be easily spread and the few known cases were isolated. Researchers in Japan who have infected human tissue with H5N1 found that the virus would have to undergo key genetic changes to become more easily transmissible in humans and evidence suggests it is difficult for this virus to mutate. Because H5N1 does not infect nasal passages or other upper respiratory cells, it could not be spread among humans through sneezing and coughing, the usual way flu viruses are transmitted and spread among people.

his chickens refused to eat and looked ill, he did not know what was wrong with them. Shortly after, his four-year-old grandson developed a high fever. Burning up, he was taken to a hospital in Hanoi: he died just 12 days later from H5N1. The farmer's chickens were culled, so in the end he lost both his grandson and his livelihood.

"Chicken ebola" has already killed millions of birds

H5N1 has been present in birds for some time. Wild birds can carry and transmit—but do not seem to contract—the disease. They pass it on to domestic birds such as chickens, ducks, and turkeys, among which it is highly contagious.

Infected birds shed the H5N1 virus in their saliva, nasal secretions, and feces. Other birds contract H5N1 when they have contact with these secretions or excretions, or with surfaces contaminated by them, such as cages or water. Nicknamed "chicken ebola" because it causes massive internal bleeding, H5N1 has a mortality rate in birds of close to 100 percent.

Some people may not tell the authorities that they own sick birds because their flocks would be destroyed and they would lose their livelihood. Instead, they hide or sell them, which contributes to H5N1's transmission to new areas.

Usually, infected flocks are slaughtered. Disease and culls have already killed over 200 million birds in 32 countries. Some, such as China are vaccinating flocks, and this is the preferred method, for ethical reasons. But without appropriate monitoring and testing, seemingly healthy vaccinated birds can carry the virus and pass it on to others, so culling is the control method of choice used in most countries.

Until the end of 2005, H5N1 occurred mainly in South-East Asia. However, by the end of March 2006, wild birds in Europe, India, and Iran were found to be carrying the virus. Poultry flocks in Nigeria, Niger, Cameroon, Egypt, Jordan, and Azerbaijan had also been infected.

Human casualties

The first cases of human infection occurred in Hong Kong in 1997 when, following an outbreak of H5N1 in poultry, 18 people working closely with the infected birds developed the virus; six died.

No further human cases were recorded until 2003, when three people in Vietnam perished. By the end of May 2006, there were more casualties from H5N1 in South-East Asia: in Vietnam (93 cases,

ABOVE In a street in Kabul, the capital of Afghanistan, a poultry vendor holds chickens as she waits for customers. Afghanistan detected its first known cases of bird flu in birds, confirmed as the deadly H5N1 strain, on March 22, 2006. At that time it was also confirmed in humans in Azerbaijan; by April the virus had infected people in Egypt, and by May, in had hit Djibouti.

RIGHT A woman opens the door to her shed for Albanian health department workers to collect chickens for culling in Peze-Helmes, a village near the capital, Tirana, on March 23, 2006, after a second case of H5N1 was discovered in birds in Albania.

BELOW In March 2006, Dr Hadi Gourgouzou talks to residents of the village of Dan Barde in southeastern Niger. He is explaining why they must start slaughtering poultry to prevent the spread of bird flu. Niger was one several African countries to be hit by the deadly H5N1 strain of the virus at that time.

42 deaths), Indonesia (48 cases, 36 deaths), Thailand (22 cases, 14 deaths), China (18 cases, 12 deaths) and Cambodia (6 cases, 6 deaths). People have also died in Azerbaijan, Turkey, Iraq, and Egypt.

All those infected worked with poultry, or were family members of those who slaughtered and prepared birds for eating. Most were poorer people in rural areas. Nearly half of the fatalities have been under 25, many being young children.

People catch the virus through contact with the secretions and excretions of infected birds. Symptoms are fever, sore throats, chest or abdominal pain, coughs, bleeding from the nose and gums, difficulty breathing, and, in some cases, damage to the lungs, kidney, liver, or spleen.

There is no complete cure for H5N1, but antivirals help combat the disease. These include zanamivir (Relenza) and oseltamivir (Tamiflu). However, research in Vietnam indicates that some patients are partially resistant to Tamiflu. High doses of a trial human vaccine were showing promising signs of an immune response in March 2006.

People's lives are destroyed

Small-scale poultry farming was a good way of earning a living for many rural people in South-East Asia. Encouraged by various development schemes, they borrowed money from the bank to buy a few hundred birds and build shelters for them.

People only needed a little space in their yards to house the birds, which quickly produced eggs that fed the family or offspring that could be killed for meat or sold for profit. In Vietnam, for example, three out of four households owned chickens; the birds could bring a 700 percent annual return on the initial capital invested.

Some families had not broken even before their poultry was affected by H5N1 and destroyed. The Food and Agriculture Organization of the United Nations cited one case, a Ms Ninh in Vietnam, who owned her own broiler chicken business before H5N1 meant her flock had to be culled. The government provided some compensation but she could only afford 600 new birds (her original flock was 2,200). She then found that her ex-customers, scared of catching H5N1, were no longer eating eggs and poultry, instead eating fish and other meats.

Ms Ninh's income, along with her husband's salary, was paying for the education of her four children. She had a large bank loan that she did not know how she could repay. "I am having a hard time keeping the children in school … I keep raising chickens, but I'm not sure I can sell them," she said.

Some governments are trying to provide compensation, but this is only partial and is taking months to come through. Vietnam recommended compensating people 50 percent of the value of their birds. Thailand recommended 70 percent but has increased this to 100 percent in some cases. At the end of 2005, Cambodia was not planning any compensation. Banks are being urged to extend loans to prevent people sinking further into debt.

To prevent the further spread of H5N1, public education campaigns warning people to avoid contact with sick birds or carcasses and wash their hands after dealing with poultry have been implemented, and people are being advised to put nets over and fences around their coops, to decrease contact between wild and domestic birds.

Preparing for emergency

Governments in developed nations around the world are taking a number of precautions against an outbreak of H5N1 in humans. France, the United States, and Britain are all stockpiling antiviral medications. Australia is planning for quarantine centers near its international airports. Canada is considering border measures and surveillance

systems in airports and hospital emergency rooms. To guard against the spread of the virus in birds, countries such as Sweden and the Netherlands are plotting the movements of wild birds carrying H5N1, and asking their farmers to bring their poultry indoors, away from potential sources of infection.

FACTS AND FIGURES	
DATE	1997 to present
LOCATION	People: Asia, Azerbaijan, Turkey, Iraq, and Egypt; Birds: Afghanistan, Albania, Asia, Azerbaijan, Europe, Kazakhstan, Russia, Georgia, Ukraine, Middle East, Egypt, Djibouti, Nigeria, Niger, Cameroon, Sudan, Burkina Faso, and Côte d'Ivoire
DEATH TOLL	127 (110 in Asia) at June 1, 2006
DAMAGE	Vietnam: bird culls have affected the livelihoods of 124,000 people (FAO)
MORTALITY RATE	56.5% in humans (close to 100% in birds)
COMMENTS	Outside Asia: Azerbaijan (8 cases, 5 deaths), Turkey (12 cases, 4 deaths), Iraq (2 cases, 2 deaths), Egypt (14 cases, 6 deaths), at July 4, 2006

ABOVE In Bangkok, a worker disinfects poultry cages prior to their destruction at a Buddhist temple on January 29, 2004. By the end of that year, the virus had hit six more of Thailand's 76 provinces, bringing the number of people infected reported to the World Health Organization to 17. In 2005, there were just 5 cases there, and none in 2006 up to June.

Pest Plagues

Plague is used to describe the type of natural disaster that occurs when the population of an organism—animal, plant, or microbe—increases enormously. It then becomes a pest; something that can dramatically affect human welfare. Usually this is because it eats large amounts of a crop grown for human consumption. Plague pests can also carry disease, such as bubonic plague.

The effect of a pest plague can be measured in terms of loss of life or livelihood. If the effect of this plague reduces crop productivity or the increases the cost of pest control, this can have a significant economic impact as well.

The balance of nature

Nature exists in equilibrium. This means that organism populations are kept in balance, which allows for enough food for the population size. It is important to realize that the natural world is dynamic. An increase in the abundance of an organism requires favorable conditions such as weather and seasonal influences. For example, rain in an arid environment can result in a massive explosion of plant growth, which, in turn, will benefit a variety of animal species. These fluctuations do not necessarily cause a pest plague because the resulting increase of these species is usually kept under control by food limits and natural predators (restraining factors). For example, changes in the abundance of rabbits and rodents are closely followed by a similar change in the abundance of their predators, such as foxes and cats. Also, animals in large population densities are vulnerable to a higher rate of infectious diseases and parasites, especially when food sources become depleted; another effect on the balance of nature.

Natural disasters generally wreak havoc on the population of a particular species but sometimes these unusual conditions can improve a species chance of survival, and they are able to adapt to the change in the environment and may thrive under these circumstances, which will result in a population explosion. For example, blooms of algae can occur after flooding rains inundate normally arid regions. Or locusts can take advantage of drought-breaking rains to rapidly increase in numbers.

FAR LEFT Rabbits were introduced from Western Europe to many parts of the world by British colonists who wanted them for hunting purposes. Lacking the natural predators and diseases of their homelands, they increased to plague proportions. Despite various attempts at biological control, they are a recurring problem for pastoralists.

LEFT Two cricketers make their way through a swarm of Australian plague locusts (*Chortoicetes terminifera*) onto the oval at Dubbo, New South Wales, Australia in March, 2004. Australian farmers dealt with a locust plague over the summers of 2004 and 2005.

PREVIOUS PAGES The Dingo Fence was built in Australia during the 1880s to keep dingos out of the southeastern part of the continent. It stretched 3,300 miles (5,320 km) and was the longest artificial structure in the world. Similarly, three rabbit-proof fences were built in the early 1900s, stretching over 2,023 miles (3,256 km), to keep Western Australia free of rabbits. Unfortunately, the rabbits got through holes caused by erosion, broken wire, and gates left open.

RIGHT The third pandemic of bubonic plague in historic times began in China in 1855 and spread to all inhabited continents, mainly through infected rats on ships, and it killed more than 12 million people. Here in Peru people are mixing rat poison to help prevent its spread by killing the rats.

BELOW RIGHT People from Queensland in Australia are very familiar with cane toads (*Bufo marinus*). These ugly pest amphibians enter suburban homes in search of food, and are very partial to dog and cat food. Introduced to control the cane beetle they are now threatening many Australian species because their skin contains compounds that are toxic to predators.

TEN DEVASTATING PLAGUE PESTS

LOCUSTS	Locusts have always been a scourge to agriculture. There are three major species, distributed over Africa, southern Europe, and the Middle East, across India and southern Asia, to Southeast Asia and Australia.
RABBITS	European rabbits were introduced from Western Europe and northwest Africa to many parts of the world. In Australia, their numbers caused widespread destruction of arable land. The introduction of mixoma virus (1950s) and calici virus (1990s) helped, but resistance rapidly developed.
WEEVILS	There are many species that attack human crops. The cotton boll weevil nearly destroyed the economy of southern United States. The elimination of this pest is one of the few success stories in the fight against plague pests.
ARMYWORMS	These are the caterpillars of a large number of species of moths from all parts of the world. They attack pasture grasses, grains, and corn. Their common name is derived from the way they move across fields as a front.
POTATO BLIGHT	The destruction of the potato crop in Ireland by *Phytophthora infestans* between 1845 and 1849 resulted in widespread famine and mass migration of tenant farmers, particularly to the United States.
BIBLICAL PLAGUES	The 10 plagues that devastated Egypt around 1300 BCE have been interpreted as either an act of God to bring about the release of the Israelites or a coincident series of natural phenomena.
RODENTS	Due to a high reproductive rate rodents are common pest species. From Asia, house mice and rats have been introduced into most parts of the world; they transmit disease, eat stored grains, and foul dwellings.
QUELEA	The red-billed quelea is the most abundant bird in the world with a population count of 1.5 billion breeding individuals. They cause extensive damage to crops in sub-Saharan Africa.
RED TIDES	Red tides are caused by a large buildup of marine algae, which can result in the death of a huge number of marine creatures. They are responsible for the destruction of fisheries and can cause serious health risks to humans.
CROWN OF THORNS STARFISH	Over the last 50 years a number of plagues of crown of thorn starfish have devastated vast areas of the World Heritage-listed Great Barrier Reef in northern Queensland.

What makes a good pest?

To be a successful pest, an organism needs to take advantage of favorable circumstances quickly. To do this, they are usually of a species that produces large numbers of offspring that need very little parental care. These offspring must also reach reproductive maturity very early on in their life cycles. The organism must have effective ways of finding and taking over new habitats, such as moving in swarms or adapting to extreme or variable environmental conditions. Insects and rodents make particularly effective animal pests because they are able to move and colonize unfamiliar habitats quickly.

When does a pest become a plague pest?

A pest becomes a plague pest when its population increases beyond the normal "checks and balances" in nature. This means that an organism's food needs become greater than the rate at which the food is being produced. For example, weevils can affect cotton production dramatically because their population outstrips the number of cotton plants

At any one time, plague pests are not usually in plague proportions. Plague species multiply under favorable conditions and decline when conditions are unfavorable, making their surges in population episodic. While the favorable conditions may have been triggered by a natural event, such as appropriate rainfall, these conditions can be enhanced by human activities. Planting crops to coincide with the favorable rain conditions will also intensify population expansion of the plague pest.

Humans have been responsible for introducing organisms from one part of the globe to another. While many of these introductions have been accidental, others were moved to particular area for

some purpose, such as the control of another pest species. As a result of this, many introduced species now flourish as pests with numbers out of control.

Quite often there are no checks on the population growth that kept their numbers constrained in their countries of origin. An example of this is the cane toad (*Bufo marinus*) in Australia. Cane toads were used in the Caribbean islands and in Hawaii to combat the cane beetle, a pest of sugar cane crops. They were introduced into sugar cane fields in Cairns, North Queensland. This attempt at biological control of a pest backfired with dramatic consequences. With no natural population controls in Australia, cane toads have increased in population and have moved from the north of Australia toward the south. As they are extremely poisonous to native fauna, in some parts of Australia, large populations of native species of animals are suffering as a result of the increase in cane toads. They are an ugly, warty skinned pest and inspire revulsion in many people.

Whether or not plague pest species existed before humans began to modify the environment is difficult to determine. Plague pests have been documented in

ABOVE Black rats (*Rattus rattus*) often become plague pests. Other names for this species include Asian black rat, ship rat, roof rat, and house rat. Originating in tropical Asia, they spread through the Near East in Roman times before reaching Europe in the eighth century. This is the species that carried the infection that caused the bubonic plague. Today it is again largely confined to warmer areas, having been supplanted by the brown rat (*Rattus norvegicus*) in cooler regions.

WHAT TO DO TO PREVENT PEST PLAGUES

1. CHEMICAL SPRAYS AND POISON BAITS Be careful with these—although effective, they can have adverse environmental consequences on non-target species, including humans.

2. DIRECT KILLING This is effective against large pest species that can be culled by shooting from the ground or air. It often results in hostility from animal welfare groups.

3. TRAPS These can mechanically kill or immobilize the pest or they can contain a poison bait. They can result in the death of non-target species. The best insect traps rely on chemical lures that mimic those produced by one sex of a species to attract the opposite sex (sex pheromone).

4. BIOLOGICAL CONTROL Many pest species are introduced, but without naturally occurring predators from their area of origin. Identification of the most effective control organism requires research and caution due to the potential hazard of the introduction of yet another pest species.

5. CROP DIVERSIFICATION Agricultural pests are more likely to form plagues if their food crop is a monoculture that is planted year after year. This provides the pest with a plentiful and constant food supply. Crop diversification in time and space can break this cycle.

6. RESISTANT SPECIES AND STRAINS This involves cultivating a crop species that is unaffected by the pest or cultivating a resistant strain of a species normally affected by the pest.

FAR RIGHT Afghani men armed with insecticide prepare to march in formation through a locust-infested field in 2002 near Paiga Tash in Samargan Province.

BELOW Prickly pear (*Opuntia stricta*) became one of the most invasive plant pests of all time when it got into the Australian bush in the late 1800s. Luckily, scientists discovered a natural predator, *Cactoblastis cactorum*, a moth species whose larvae was very partial to it. The problem was under control in just six years—a spectacular example of biological control.

our earliest recorded histories so perhaps the answer depends on the actual plague pest in question.

Those that respond to particular favorable conditions will increase their numbers should these conditions be enhanced by human activities.

Locusts: the classic plague pest

About a dozen species of grasshoppers are commonly referred to as locusts. They are included within the Acrididae, a family that contains all grasshoppers with short antennae. Among these short-horned grasshoppers, locusts are distinguished by their ability to change their behavior in response to crowding. Under these conditions, they form rapidly moving swarms that consume every blade of vegetation over vast areas.

While all species of locusts belong to the one family, most species are not closely related to each other. This means that they have independently

evolved the survival strategy of swarming that has held them in good stead as creatures that thrive in some of the most inhospitable regions of the world.

The migratory locust *Locusta migratoria* and the desert locust *Schistocerca gregaria* are the most notorious plague pests. While the former has the widest distribution, ranging from the eastern Atlantic islands, through Africa, Eastern Europe, the Middle East, Asia, and into Australia, the latter is the more damaging pest. It has a distribution that does not extend as far eastward into Asia and Australia.

The last locust in North America

While it is alarming that in recent times so many plants and animals species have been declared extinct, it is with mixed feelings that scientists have determined that a previously very abundant species, the North American Rocky Mountain plague locust (*Melanoplus spretus*), has also been added to the list. Living specimens have not been sighted since 1902. This extinction is all the more remarkable in that these locusts ranged over most of the western half of the United States and Canada in the nineteenth century. Furthermore, it has been reported that a single swarm extended over an area of 198,000 square miles (512,820 km²), an area greater than California. The cause of the extinction is unknown, but if it were to be identified it could become the basis for eradication of other species of locusts. The passing of the Rocky Mountain locust leaves North America unique in being the only populated continent without an endemic plague locust.

What triggers swarming behavior?

Locusts have a remarkable response to crowding that is triggered by touch. There has been a lot of research carried out on locusts in an attempt to understand their biology; particularly what triggers their swarming behavior. Studies from the University of Oxford, in collaboration with other institutions, have shown that desert locusts in low numbers are shy, retiring creatures that actually avoid the company of other individuals except for brief encounters for mating. However, when the population reaches a threshold, they dramatically switch to being highly gregarious and form swarms. As juveniles, without wings, they move by crawling and hopping but when they become adults and develop wings they take to the air, reaching speeds of about 12 miles (20 km) an hour depending on the winds and travel over 60 miles (100 km) in a day.

This behavioral change is accompanied by a makeover in their personal image. As with all insects, locusts molt their exoskeletons in order to grow or to change in body form. As solitary individuals desert locusts are green. When they

prepare to swarm, juveniles change from green to the multicolored (yellow, brown, black and white patterned) gregarious form at their next molt. It has been suggested that this color change is adaptive; green when solitary to blend in with the vegetation and brightly colored to be a warning as unpalatable to predators when gregarious. This behavioral and physical change continues into the next generation as eggs laid by gregarious, multicolored females hatch as gregarious, multicolored juveniles.

This remarkable response to crowding is triggered by touch and particularly by individuals touching each other's hind legs as they jostle and bump into each other. Once the touch sensors on the legs have been stimulated, even by a researcher with a fine paint brush, chemical messages, called pheromones, are released and these are responsible for the changes in behavior and body color that subsequently take place.

Humans as plague pests
It has often been said that humans with our significant and fast population explosion and its consequent effects on the environment may actually be the most devastating of all plague pests. Are we

the worst "natural disaster" to have befallen planet Earth? When we consider all of the great pest plagues, many of these have arguably been caused by human activities that upset the general "balance of nature." Ultimately, it was we who gave them the opportunity of reaching their full potential as pests.

ABOVE Locusts will even try to eat thorns if that is the only food available. These are African desert locusts (*Schistocerca gregaria*) in their characteristic yellow and black gregarious form.

Biblical Plagues, Egypt, 1300 BCE

Around 1300 BCE, according to the Old Testament story in Exodus, an extraordinary series of natural disasters struck Egypt. The interpretation of these events continues to be the subject of scholarly controversy for theologians, ancient historians, archeologists, and scientists. Did the hand of God directly or indirectly orchestrate the plagues or were they a series of natural phenomena that occurred by coincidence at a particular time and place?

BELOW Aaron, the first priest of Israel and the younger brother of Moses, was asked by God to stretch his staff over the water of the Nile—and hordes of frogs came and overran Egypt.

The place was the city of Memphis, the center of cultural life in Egypt, situated on the Nile just south of present-day Cairo. The Israelite minority was enslaved by the Pharaoh to prevent a military threat. The story has it that God intervened on behalf of the Israelites, ordering Moses to demand their release. The Pharaoh refused and God sent a series of miraculous disasters to persuade him to change his mind. Finally, he reluctantly agreed.

The Israelites made their exodus out of Egypt but were intercepted by the Pharaoh's troops at the Red Sea. The waters miraculously parted and the Israelites were given safe passage. The waters returned, drowning the pursuing Egyptian soldiers.

The sequence of the Biblical plagues

The 10 plagues included: the waters of the Nile turning blood-red and killing all the fish; a plague of frogs; a plague of lice; a plague of flies; an epidemic of diseases of livestock; an outbreak of skin eruptions in humans and livestock; violent hailstorms; a plague of locusts; three days of darkness; and the death of all first-born male children and livestock.

Scientific interpretation

The 10 plagues have been interpreted by some as a series of natural phenomena, which obviously rules them out as being supernatural events. However, it still leaves open the possibility that God orchestrated the plagues through natural processes.

The change in the color of the Nile has been attributed to the red dust from a storm or a bloom of toxic algae, called a red tide. Either of these could contribute to a huge fish kill from asphyxiation or toxicity, and the decomposing bodies of the fish would have driven frogs from the water in plague proportions.

The subsequent mass mortality of the frogs encouraged the proliferation of disease-spreading insects. Precisely which insects increased is difficult to determine from the scriptures because of the

FACTS AND FIGURES

DATE	1444 BCE is favored by theologians and 1290 BCE is suggested by secular scholars
LOCATION	Memphis, Egypt
DEATH TOLL	Unknown number of Egyptians died from disease, famine, and drowning
DAMAGE	Unknown
COMMENTS	Scientists are unable to explain why the Hebrews were unaffected by the plagues that created such havoc for the Egyptians.

variability of common names for the different species of animals—particularly insects. However, a potential candidate has been suggested: blood-sucking gnats could have been the third plague, and these could have transmitted viruses responsible for the death of livestock (the fifth plague).

The fourth plague was also an insect plague, which might have been a swarm of stable flies. These could have transmitted a bacterial infection to both humans and livestock, which explains the sixth plague, the plague of skin eruptions or boils.

The Egyptians were then subjected to darkness, something that could possibly be due to a dust storm. This was followed by the destruction of crops by a severe hailstorm. The few crops that were left were consumed by a plague of locusts.

The death of first-born male children is an intriguing plague. It could possibly be explained by the custom of feeding the eldest child with double portions of food. If the stored grains were contaminated by a toxic mold, this extra portion would have been lethal.

Do the dates match?

A volcanic eruption on the Greek island of Santorini could possibly explain at least part of the Exodus miracles as a series of natural phenomena. The eruption might have polluted the Nile, turning its waters red; the three days of darkness could have

ABOVE The seventeenth-century painting, "The Passage of the Red Sea" by Jacob Willemsz de Wet, shows the Israelites watching in amazement as the sea closes behind them, engulfing the Pharaoh's pursuing army.

LEFT The sixth plague of Egypt was *Shkin*, a skin disease. God commanded that Moses and Aaron take two handfuls of soot from a furnace and scatter it in the Pharaoh's presence. Wherever the soot landed, people were afflicted. An angel walks among those succumbing to the plague.

been caused by ash in the atmosphere; and a tsunami may have caused the waters of the Red Sea to recede and advance. But the eruption of Santorini has been fairly accurately dated by scientific methods as having occurred in 1628 BCE. This effectively demolishes the volcanic explanation for some of the plagues: the Biblical plagues are dated some 300 years later.

Potato Famine, Ireland, 1845 to 1849

The Irish Potato Famine began in September 1845 with the sinister and sudden appearance of dark brown to black patches on the leaves of healthy potato plants almost ready for harvesting. This infection of the plants rapidly spread from one crop to another, instantly destroying the primary food source for the Irish population. The immediate effect on Ireland was devastating, and the long-term effects were enormous, changing Irish culture and tradition.

BELOW Irish tenants were evicted from their smallholdings and made homeless for the non-payment of rent during the Irish Potato Famine. The thatched roofs of the houses were removed to prevent them from being re-tenanted.

News spread almost as quickly as the disease. By October 1845, a Commission set up by the British Prime Minister, Sir Robert Peel, reported that the disease was likely to destroy a substantial proportion of the national harvest for that year. As it turned out, the blight all but wiped out the entire potato crop of Ireland for three successive seasons: 1845, 1846, and 1848. The Irish Potato Famine was the culmination of a social, biological, political, and economic catastrophe, caused by a mix of British economic policy and Irish farming practice.

Ireland before the famine

By 1840, the population of Ireland had reached a staggering 8 million, with a density of 700 persons per square mile (2.6 km^2) of cultivated land. This was among the highest population densities in Europe. The population expansion was largely confined to rural families, who were also among the poorest and least educated people in the Western world. Three-quarters of the population were illiterate. Most of the rural community lived in one-room cabins that would be home for up to

AN IDEAL CROP FOR IRISH CONDITIONS

The potato originally came from the Andes Mountains of South America. It was introduced to Europe by the Spanish in the sixteenth century and was rapidly assimilated into European agriculture.

The potato reached Ireland around 1600, and by 1800 it had become the staple crop for the poor tenant farmers for a variety of biological and sociological reasons. The cool and wet Irish climate provided ideal conditions for growing potatoes: 1 acre (0.4 ha) of fertile land could easily produce enough potatoes to feed a family of six for a year with some to spare. Furthermore, very little effort was required to plant a field of potatoes. The minimum requirement was to just leave some of the potatoes unharvested to produce the next year's crop.

A slightly more intensive approach to agriculture involved the laying out of rows of manure on which the seed potatoes were placed and then covered over with sods cut from the soil between the rows.

12 people. This meager housing was often shared with a pig and several chickens as there was not enough farming land to accommodate the livestock.

However, the Irish peasants were relatively healthy compared with their counterparts in the rest of Europe. This was due to their diet of potatoes, which provided a reasonable balance of proteins, carbohydrates, minerals, and vitamins, unlike a diet based on grains. Seven million tons of potatoes were consumed each year: a staggering 6 pounds (2.7 kg) per adult, per day.

The poverty of the rural Irish was the result of a feudal system imposed by the English, and dated back to Elizabethan times (1558 to 1603). Most of the Irish countryside was divided into enormous estates owned by English or Anglo-Irish landlords. These estates were maintained for their absentee landlords by Protestant middlemen who leased out parcels of land to the poor Catholic tenant farmers. A combination of the continual subdivision of the land by the middlemen to increase their rental income and the Irish practice of tenancy of land passing to all sons in the family resulted in tenant farms of less than 10 acres (4 ha).

Potatoes were the only crop that could provide a sustainable harvest on such a limited area of land. Any other income from cash crops or livestock paid the rent to the middlemen who, in turn, paid rent to the landlords. The system operated successfully, provided the potato harvest did not fail. The warnings of the dangers of so many people in one place, dependent on a single crop went unheeded. This was a disaster waiting to happen.

The famine hits hard

After the failure of the 1845 harvest, hopes were raised that 1846 would see the end of the blight. On the contrary, the diseased stock planted in the previous season was beginning to show signs of infection. This rapidly spread to any uninfected plants because ideal conditions were provided by the cool wet summer of 1846. Once again, the entire

ABOVE *The Illustrated London News* relayed the news of the widespread devastation the Irish Potato Blight was causing. An illustration from an 1849 issue shows a starving family desperately searching for potatoes in a stubble field.

ABOVE A traveling Catholic priest gives comfort to a farming family. Many accounts tell of priests turning up to give whole families the last rites. In some Irish counties, up to 25 people were dying daily.

crop was destroyed. One could hardly imagine a more desperate plight for the Irish peasants. To make matters worse, the normally mild Irish winter gave way to unprecedented gales, sleet, and snow. Without outside intervention, famine on an unprecedented scale was inevitable. However, aid was not forthcoming. A non-interventionist policy

on the part of the British government encouraged the setting up of local committees to raise funds to buy food. Even if there had been money available, there was little food to buy. Indeed, at the very height of the famine, any cash crops of locally grown grains were shipped out of Irish ports so that farmers could pay their rent and avoid eviction.

Eviction was inevitable as landlords sought to consolidate the smallholdings of the tenant farmers and convert their estates into growing wheat and grazing cattle and sheep. As the *Tipperary Vindicator* reported: "The work of undermining the population is going on steadily ... the fearful system of ejectment is a mockery of the eternal laws of God ... Whole districts have been cleared." Hundreds of thousands of these displaced farmers sought employment on the Public Works Relief Plan. They toiled in the harsh conditions of the winter of 1846 to 1847 on roadworks in remote rural areas for wages that were inadequate for preventing starvation. Poorly clothed and sheltered, malnourished and ill, these

THE CULPRIT—PHYTOPHTHORA

There are about 60 species of *Phytophthora*, most of which cause disease in plants, including several economically important crops. Some are also responsible for outbreaks of "die back" in native forests. While some species of *Phytophthora* can infect thousands of different host species, others infect only a limited number of host plants. *Phytophthora infestans* infects both potatoes and tomatoes; other plants are quite resistant. It has recently been discovered that the group of microorganisms to which *Phytophthora* belongs, the Oomycetes, are not fungi as had been believed, but instead are closely related to some marine algae, such as kelp. This would explain why the application of fungicide is ineffective in controlling the disease. The disease is kept in check by a variety of practices, including the development of resistant strains of the crop, use of early cropping varieties, and strict hygiene practices.

poor workers died where they worked. As reported by local newspapers, "Work on the public road is more destructive than fever." The dead workers were buried without ceremony in shallow and often unmarked graves.

A more interventionist change in government policy was initiated in the form of soup kitchens to feed the starving. One can only imagine what the soup may have tasted like when the smell alone was enough to induce violent gut eruptions. The watery concoction of bad meat, waste vegetables, and Indian corn only exacerbated weakened constitutions. A more substantial porridge brewed from Indian corn and rice and a slice of bread each day was considered marginally more nutritious, but it only postponed the inevitable starvation.

Immigration on a massive scale

Tenant farmers evicted from their cottages set off for the New World. First they traveled to the crowded port cities of Liverpool and Glasgow. From here they were herded onto overcrowded ships destined for Canada, the remaining British colony in North America. Their survival rate on the voyage was so low that these ships were known as coffin ships. From Canada, many of the immigrants crossed the border into the United States. They believed they would be welcome there, as the Irish and the Americans shared a hatred for everything British. However, they had not anticipated the strong anti-Catholic prejudice of the largely Protestant population. American ships transported Irish immigrants by the thousands; by 1850 they made up a quarter of the population of major cities on the eastern seaboard.

FACTS AND FIGURES

DATE	1845 to 1849
LOCATION	Ireland
DEATH TOLL	700,000 to 800,000, from starvation and disease
DAMAGE	Unknown
COMMENTS	An estimated 1 million emigrated to North America, Great Britain, and Australia. How many of them died in transit is unknown. Their struggle for survival was not over; they continued to be among the poorest of the inhabitants in their adopted country.

TOP As starvation took its toll on the nation, there were fewer and fewer people able to attend the funerals, and many people were buried without coffins, transported in open wagons.

ABOVE Workhouses were the only option left for the poor who had been evicted from their homes. Despite the desperate conditions, people were clamouring to get in.

Crown of Thorns Starfish, Great Barrier Reef, Australia, 1962 to Present

There have been three recorded series of crown of thorns starfish outbreaks from 1962 onward. The most recent one, which began in 1993, was yet another cycle of this rapacious pest that devastated the corals of the 1,250-mile (2,000-km) long Great Barrier Reef on Australia's far northeastern coast.

BELOW The crown of thorns starfish is one of the few animals that feeds on living coral. At low population levels the starfish is a normal part of the Great Barrier Reef's ecology. If it reaches a point where the starfish is eating more of the coral than is being reproduced, the reef system can be completely destroyed.

Crown of thorns starfish are potentially in outbreak proportions when there are as few as 12 mature specimens per acre (0.4 ha) of reef. During plagues, they can increase to hundreds of thousands, even millions. They often form a moving front of overlapping individuals with living coral ahead of them and a swathe of dead coral skeletons, like a demolition site, behind them.

Patterns of starfish outbreaks

The first two major outbreaks occurred between 1962 and 1976, and 1979 and 1991. Since underwater explorations on the Great Barrier Reef only really began with the advent of scuba equipment, outbreaks of crown of thorns starfish were not recorded until the early 1960s. This new equipment made data collecting more reliable. These outbreaks followed similar patterns, being first recorded in the reefs around Cairns in far north Queensland. In the following 10 to 15 years, the outbreaks moved to reefs further south, before dissipating in the region of the Whitsunday Islands. There is no evidence that starfish migrate from one reef system to another. The progression is due to the settling of larvae transported by the south-flowing eastern Australian current. Research showed that the second outbreak covered a wider geographic range than the first.

THE CORAL REEF

The framework that forms a coral reef is largely made up of the skeletons of coral polyps. New polyps then grow on this frame. The waters of the Great Barrier Reef support "gardens" of subtly colored corals populated with underwater organisms, including fish and shellfish of every color, shape, and size imaginable; crabs and shrimps; and a huge diversity of worms that use the corals for shelter. This delicately balanced system of life is easily disrupted by a variety of hazards—the crown of thorns starfish is just one of them.

Life history of the crown of thorns starfish

Adult specimens of the crown of thorns starfish, *Acanthaster planci*, usually measure 10 to 14 inches (25 to 35 cm) in diameter. These starfish glide over the surface of the coral, gently propelled by the coordinated efforts of thousands of tiny feet with suction-cap ends. *Acanthaster* can travel a record 65 feet (20 m) per hour and cover up to 1,800 feet (550 m) in a week.

The starfish feeds by pushing its stomach, containing strong digestive juices, out through its mouth, which is located in the center of the underside of the body. The digested coral tissue is then sucked back into the gut. Each day they can digest an area of coral equivalent to that of the undersurface of their body.

The 1,000 million eggs a female produces in a lifetime are released into the sea and then fertilized by sperm released from the males. The fertilized eggs develop into free-swimming microscopic larvae that eventually settle to the bottom of the ocean and transform into juvenile starfish. Their common name comes from spines covering their crown-shaped body. The spines can inject venom, giving *Acanthaster* protection from predators.

The cause of outbreaks

What causes the plagues of crown of thorns starfish is a question that continues to puzzle and concern marine biologists. There are three contenders. First, outbreaks may be due to natural cycles, such as fluctuations in temperature, salinity, and nutrient availability. Favorable levels of any of these could result in an increased survival of the settling larvae, and hence the number reaching adulthood. Second, while adult starfish have few predators, the removal of one, the giant triton, may have increased starfish survival. Third, runoff from land adjacent to reefs results in an increase in nutrients reaching the reefs. This promotes algal growth, which, in turn, provides food for developing starfish larvae.

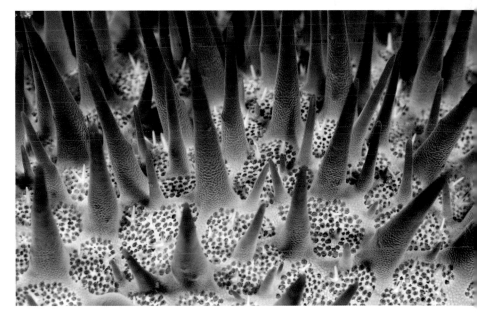

FACTS AND FIGURES

DATE	Recurrent in approximately 15-year cycles
LOCATION	Great Barrier Reef, Queensland, Australia
DEATH TOLL	Not relevant
DAMAGE	Major threat to marine ecology and the tourism industry; damage estimated at AUD$5 billion
COMMENTS	While many other plague pests directly affect human welfare, the crown of thorns starfish threatens the survival of one of the most important regions of animal diversity in the world, the Great Barrier Reef.

The crown of thorns starfish (top) is the largest in the world. Few sea animals are willing to attack its spiny and toxic covering (above). Natural predators of the starfish include the giant triton, and the humphead wrasse which feeds on starfish larvae.

Locust Plague, North Africa and Asia, 1986 to 1989

One of the most widespread and devastating locust plagues began in 1986 in Sudan and what is now known as Eritrea. Access to these areas to control the outbreaks was prevented by their remoteness and the civil war that was raging at the time. The United Nations Food and Agricultural Organization warned that an extensive outbreak of desert locusts in this region had the potential to dramatically affect the livelihood of 650 million people—one-tenth of the world's population.

FAR RIGHT Spraying for locusts is done by the national crop protection service or the military. Before 1980, toxic and long-lasting insecticides were used. Less damaging residual sprays are used these days but they need to be applied more often to control locust plagues.

BELOW Locust scourges have been mentioned in the Bible and the Koran. Desert locusts can consume the equivalent of their body weight, about 0.1 ounce (almost 3 g), each day in green vegetation. Nearly all crop and non-crop plants are at risk.

Because the outbreaks of the desert locusts began when the climatic conditions were perfect for their reproduction, swarms rapidly spread out. In all, 23 countries became affected, from West and North Africa to the Arabian Peninsula, the Middle East, and as far as Pakistan and India.

Famine, war, and plagues

History shows that famine and war are often bedfellows. The hardship caused by the locust outbreak of 1986 added another layer of misery to the seemingly endless civil war that was raging in the north of Ethiopia. The conflict was sparked by Ethiopia's annexation of Eritrea following Italy's withdrawal in 1962 as colonial ruler. Because of the conflict, locust control officers had great difficulty getting safe access to the sites of locust reproduction, which meant they were unable to target them. Consequently they went unchecked.

Outbreak control or crop protection?

In 1986, the African nations were unprepared for a locust plague. They had become complacent because the last major plague to affect the area had occurred 30 years before. The regional control organizations had been disbanded, and there was inadequate funding to maintain the required control infrastructures to monitor and prevent further locust plague outbreaks. Another contributing factor was the widespread distribution and remoteness of the outbreaks, which made it difficult to strategically target locations. Also, resources could not be sent out quickly enough to have any effect.

Targeting locusts before they swarmed was not feasible, so an emergency crop protection approach was put into action. The spraying of locust swarms is most effective overnight, during the roosting of the locusts, due to the concentration of numbers; during the day, the locusts are constantly on the

FACTS AND FIGURES

DATE	1986 to 1989
LOCATION	23 countries affected by major locust invasions across North and West Africa, the Arabian Peninsula, the Middle East, and Pakistan and India
DEATH TOLL	Difficult to assess due to other contributing conditions, such as famine and civil war
DAMAGE	US$300 million cost to international community besides the resources mobilized by the countries affected
COMMENTS	The cash cost of damage to the environment and to human health of the outbreak was never calculated. Large amounts of insecticide were released into the environment, and this may have caused long-term contamination.

move, searching for food. Spray units mounted on backpacks, trucks, and aircraft were used to spray insecticide early in the morning before the locusts became active. The short supply of key government crop protection specialists meant that brigades of farmers had to be rapidly trained and equipped. For example, Niger organized 10,000 of these brigades, each consisting of five people.

There is still controversy as to which is the more cost-effective way to treat locust outbreaks: direct action when required to protect valuable crops, or control when breeding populations reach maximum threshold levels. It has been argued that the massive crop protection costs during a plague like that of 1986 to 1989 are equivalent to the costs of 15 to 20 years of strategic preventive control.

The continual use of anti-locust sprays resulted in the fragile habitats and wildlife of Africa being adversely affected. More recently, projects to develop biological pesticides that kill locusts without harming the environment have been funded. Commercial manufacture and the use of these types of pesticides has already begun.

An ill wind blowing

After US$300 million was spent on control—and three years had passed—the plague was finally brought to an end. However, it wasn't just human intervention that was responsible: a change in the weather also played a major role. A storm front swept countless billions of locusts across the Atlantic in October 1988; an exceptionally cold 1988 to 1989 winter in North Africa and extremely dry weather conditions in 1989 also contributed to the ending of the devastating plague. Estimates show that approximately 80 percent of the locust plague was destroyed due to these climatic conditions. The other 20 percent was due to chemical intervention.

ENVIRONMENTAL AND HEALTH HAZARDS

The control of insect pests, particularly locust plagues, with chemical insecticides poses enormous environmental problems and health hazards to humans. This is especially true of the massive emergency applications of pesticides released during the more reactive strategy of crop protection. In the past, organochlorine compounds such as dieldrin were used to control insect pests, but they have now been discontinued because of the environmental longevity of these substances. The release of toxic chemicals tends to put more pressure on the environment, particularly in farming areas that are already under stress due to non-sustainable farming practices such as large-scale deforestation and overgrazing.

African Desert Locust Plague, 2003 to 2005

From 2003 to 2005, much of northern and western Africa was invaded by a plague of locusts. The locusts threatened to overwhelm the entire agriculture of the Sahel, the sub-Saharan region of West Africa. Farmers, herders, and governments were in despair, saying that without outside help, Mauritania's population would face catastrophe.

RIGHT In Dara, Senegal, villagers stand in a field invaded by swarms of locusts. Senegal needed US$100 million to battle the locusts, which devoured millions of acres of crops.

Swarm after swarm of desert locusts—some of them up to 25 miles (40 km) long and containing billions of insects—had already caused massive crop devastation.

Plagues are part of a repeating cycle of natural disasters: years of drought followed by floods, and then huge swarms of locusts descending onto the maturing crops just as they are reaching harvest time.

The long-awaited rain that had fallen in the mountains of northwest Africa in 2003 turned out to be a mixed blessing. Although it broke a harsh drought that had persisted for decades, it also initiated one of Africa's worst locust plagues. Enormous locust swarms moved across the Sahara to the Sahel. Exceptionally heavy rains maintained optimum conditions for a population explosion: moist sandy soil for egg-laying, and young green plants for food.

Mauritania and Mali were the most heavily affected, but there was also substantial damage in Senegal, Niger, and Guinea–Bissau—the locusts even reached as far as the Cape Verde Islands, 621 miles (1,000 km) off the Atlantic coast. In a single day, a swarm of locusts can fly 62 miles (100 km) in the

HELP FOR THE WORLD'S POOREST

The more than 65 million people in the nine Sahelian countries of sub-Saharan West Africa—Burkina Faso, Cape Verde, Chad, The Gambia, Guinea–Bissau, Mali, Mauritania, Niger, and Senegal—are among the poorest and least food-secure in the world. The region is marked by high rates of deforestation, soil degradation, erosion, and population growth, as well as by weak political and private-sector institutions and civil unrest. Libya and Burkina Faso have been accused of financing coup attempts in Mauritania, causing even more instability.

The United States Agency for International Development (USAID) provided support to the Sahelian countries through bilateral and regional assistance The United Nations also worked with Sahel governments, as well as with other donor governments. Direct assistance was given to Burkina Faso, Mali, Mauritania, Niger, and Senegal, which included funding for locust eradication programs in the region.

Senegalese children in Yoff (top). Densely packed swarms of up to 80 million insects per square mile (2.5 km²) are a common sight. A woman (above) removes the husks from grains of millet in the village of Sadongori Kolita near Maradi, Nigeria. The locust plague in nearby Niger caused a food crisis that affected 2.5 million people and their families.

FACTS AND FIGURES

DATE	2003 to 2005
LOCATION	Northern and western Africa
DEATH TOLL	Unknown
DAMAGE	US$60 million for fighting outbreak, with harvest losses valued at US$2.5 billion
COMMENTS	The international community was slow to recognize the plight of the people affected by the locust plagues; meanwhile people died from malnutrition and starvation.

general direction of prevailing winds, and consume their own body weight in food. Though each locust weighs less than 0.1 ounce (almost 3 g), even a small swarm could weigh as much as 1 ton (0.98 t) and so consume enough food to feed 2,500 people in that time.

The recent plagues marked the worst locust upsurges in 15 years. While Mauritania has suffered many locust plagues in the past, one senior locust survey officer couldn't recall such a dramatic upsurge. During late July 2004, he received reports of two to three sightings of swarms per day.

Locusts at the "grass roots"

In this region, subsistence farming means a delicate balance between crop production and famine, even at the best of times. While the start of the rainy season is a signal to farmers in the Sahel to plant crops of sorghum, millet, legumes, rice, and melon, it also provides ideal conditions for locusts to reproduce. Farmers work in their fields with hoes or horse-drawn plows even as swarms fill the sky above them.

"I can't just stand here with arms crossed— I have to plant my crops even if I know the locusts are going to come," says Jidhoum M'Bareck, a farmer near the town of Kaedi in Mauritania, who works a small field with a horse and plow. "Between 6 and 10 people depend on this field."

Another farmer, 82-year-old Amadou Binta Thiam, still tills his fields by hand. "I have a big family—20 people depend on me. I have no children working outside who can send me money. If locusts get my field, it is a real catastrophe."

The story of Diokam, a village consisting of a handful of huts surrounded by cultivated fields, is typical of the struggle against the elements these subsistence farmers face. An officer of the Catholic Relief Service of Senegal described the elation of the village chief when the rains ended the drought. A larger than usual harvest was anticipated. On a return visit two weeks later, the officer reported, "When I visited him this week, the sky was dark and the air full with swarms of locusts. Now only roots and stunted plants stood where the acres of green fields and maturing crops once lay." Devastated, the village chief seemed to have aged several years since the last visit only weeks ago. "I am afraid my son will once again miss school," was all he could say.

The devastating costs

The heavy damage locusts inflict on crops is devastating for subsistence farmers. The ongoing consequences continue to affect the lives of millions of people well after the event. The loss of cereal and other crops for human consumption and fodder crops for domestic animals has resulted in

LOCUSTS DESCEND ON THE CITY

In 2004, swarms of locusts descended on Mauritania's capital, Nouakchott, causing havoc to its residents. They filled the sky, bombarding residents going about their daily business. They ate what sparse greenery there was. The crackling from their fluttering wings and the rustle of their incessant munching drove residents into a frenzy.

Nouakchott's children took to swinging sticks like baseball bats, striking out at the swarms. After experiencing scratches from the locusts' sharp claws as they settled in hair and on shoulders, many people took to wearing upturned buckets on their heads when they went out into the open. For city dwellers, the locusts were a nuisance, but for 80 percent of Mauritanians, who make their living from farming or livestock, the plague was a catastrophe.

widespread malnutrition, starvation, and associated diseases. The locust swarms devastated nearly 4 million acres (1.6 million ha) of Mauritanian farmland, consuming half the country's cereal crop. In Niger, 40 percent of the fodder to feed livestock was consumed by the voracious swarms. These plagues also cause considerable social conflict, with subsistence farmers seeking work migrating en masse to urban centers that are already stressed by overpopulation and poverty.

It is not only food crops that are decimated by locusts; the cash crops on which many farmers depend are also destroyed. For example, in Guinea–Bissau, West Africa, desert locusts severely damaged the cashew crop on which the nation depended.

There are other less obvious costs, such as the damage to pastureland and fodder and the ability of land to recover after the plague has finished. Also, there are the costs of food aid from the international donor community, and other factors not directly associated with locust damage, such as secondary infestations of other pests and the cost to people's health and spirits from enduring years of hardship.

Mauritania, the country worst affected by this locust plague, is a case in point. From 2000 to 2005, the country faced a series of shocks. These not only compounded its tremendous poverty, but also caused extreme food insecurity. There have also been local famine conditions in some areas. From 2000, the population continued to experience poor agricultural production due to the effects of flooding (2001), drought (2002–03), and the combined effects of the widespread locust infestation and a premature end to the rainy season (2004). The current situation is the result of the combined effects of these shocks. They have progressively eroded the resilience of the population, leaving a large number of people destitute and highly vulnerable to famine. As a result, any further shock threatens to quickly reverse improvements in food security that followed the ongoing emergency response.

West African Locust Plague 2004
Area of locust plague

Control efforts

Millions of acres have been sprayed with pesticides to avoid a new round of breeding and migration of swarms. The affected countries have, to a considerable extent, financed these costly operations. Due to the size and number of the 2003–04 locust infestations, effective control could only be carried out using conventional pesticides. More than 10 million acres (4 million ha) were treated in Algeria, Morocco, Tunisia, Libya, and Mauritania.

It was hoped the heavy control operations in 2004 made an impact and another plague had been averted. However, the locust plague situation remained so serious that additional international aid was requested to supplement the major efforts already undertaken. Unfortunately, during 2005, the United Nation's Food and Agricultural Organization (FAO) warned that a new generation of locusts was maturing and taking to the skies, bringing yet again the risk of famine ever closer.

ABOVE This map shows the extent of the locust plague, which stretches from the north of Africa to the Cape Verde Islands.

Red Tides, Worldwide

Red tides are a natural phenomenon that can have a huge environmental and economic impact on many of the world's coastal regions. In November, 1946, the worst red tide on record appeared off the west coast of Florida, southeastern USA, and it persisted until September, 1947.

ABOVE The algae in red tides that are actually red have red photosynthetic pigments in their cells, which appears as a discoloration in the water.

FAR RIGHT A massive red tide swirls around islands in southeastern Alaska. People living on the coast near a red tide outbreak can be affected by exposure to the algae; it can cause breathing difficulties, eye and skin irritation.

Beaches from Tarpon Springs to the Florida Keys, a stretch of 150 miles (241 km), were littered with the bodies of thousands of dead marine animals, including bottlenose dolphins, sea turtles, and many species of fish. Researchers at the University of Miami identified the microorganism responsible for this and other fish kills along the Florida coast as *Karenia brevis* (*Gymnodinium breve*), a species of marine algae belonging to the group called the dinoflagellates. The red tide of 1946 to 1947 holds the record, but this type of natural disaster is not specific to Florida; it is being reported and recorded from other oceanic areas around the world.

What are red tides?

Red tides are not tides, nor are they necessarily red. They are actually marine algal blooms. Red tides can be many different colors from red through orange to brown and from green to blue; their color is determined by the predominant species of algae in a particular red tide event.

Life in the oceans ultimately depends on microscopic single-celled plants called algae, which float in the surface layer of the water. Algae are the basis of marine food chains and form vast blooms (a rapid increase in the algal population), enriching the surface waters of estuaries or oceans with nutrients. Normally these blooms are beneficial to fish and other marine life. It is no coincidence that the areas where blooms occur are also the most productive fishing grounds of the world's oceans.

However, these blooms can become concentrated, by a combination of tide, wind, and currents. Red tides produced by a diversity of algae have been reported from most oceanic regions of the world.

The effect on marine life

Red tides have an impact on marine life in a number of ways, depending on the circumstances and the species of algae involved. The sudden collapse of an algal bloom, which means that the algae die and sink to the bottom, can deplete oxygen levels of the water through lack of photosynthesis. Decomposition is another factor; it results in the depletion of oxygen due to the increase of bacteria that occurs with the breakdown of the algae cells. This lack of oxygen results in the death of other marine animals by suffocation. Fish are also suffocated through having their gills clogged by the massive number of algal cells in the water.

Many species of algae produce very potent toxins, which can affect the marine life that directly feeds on the algae. Some toxins associated with red tides can induce neurological damage and death in marine animals. These toxins can accumulate, becoming more and more concentrated as they pass up the food chain, becoming lethal to top carnivores, including humans. Shellfish feed by filtering algae from the surrounding water, and if they take in and accumulate toxic algae, bivalves—oysters, clams, scallops—become extremely toxic. Even though these toxins don't kill the shellfish, they make them potentially dangerous for human consumption.

What causes red tides?

Extensive research is being done on red tides to better understand their causes and effects. Increased nutrient levels in coastal waters, due to human wastes, have been strongly implicated in the apparent increase in the number and magnitude of red tides worldwide. Areas previously considered free of red tides are beginning to record and report outbreaks. This may be due to ships dumping ballast water that contains toxic algae in ports; this practice is a key factor in the introduction of a number of pest species that can threaten marine communities.

FACTS AND FIGURES

DATE	Red tides occur continuously
LOCATION	Worldwide
DEATH TOLL	Nil
DAMAGE	Red tides have enormous ecological impacts on marine life. They also have considerable economic effects on local fish and shellfish industries, and the tourist industry that sustains many coastal towns.
COMMENTS	The Florida red tide of 1987 to 1988 killed 740 dolphins, 50 percent of the entire Atlantic coast stock that migrates between New Jersey and Florida. In 1996, a red tide resulted in the death of 149 of the 3,000 Florida manatees (marine mammals also known as sea cows).

Cotton Boll Weevil, Southern USA

From its introduction from Mexico in 1892, boll weevils have wreaked havoc on the cotton industry in the United States. By the early twentieth century, cotton production had begun to dramatically decline. In Georgia alone, the crop fell from 2.8 million bales in 1914 to as low as 600,000 bales in 1923. This caused rural economic depressions and hardship, which lasted for many generations.

The decline continued over the next 60 years, during which time vast areas of southern United States, which were almost completely dependent on cotton production, underwent socio-economic decline. It has been suggested that the boll weevil is second only to the Civil War as an agent of change in the southern United States.

A radical approach was required to halt the seemingly unstoppable spread of *Anthonomus grandis*, the boll weevil—a grand name for a destructive but otherwise insignificant insect measuring only one-tenth to one-third of an inch (8.5 mm) in length. However, the snout, a characteristic feature of all weevils, is about half as long as the body—this may account for its impressive species name.

Aerial applications of highly dangerous pesticides, such as calcium arsenate, were only marginally effective and had extremely detrimental side effects on both the environment and human health. A major breakthrough in the control of the invasion came from research carried out in a collaborative effort by a number of institutions. The success of the boll weevil eradication program highlighted the invaluable role that focused scientific research can play in solving a practical problem of immense national significance.

A pilot study in 1978 on the Virginia–North Carolina border proved so successful that it led to full-scale eradication programs in 17 states and northern Mexico. These programs covered 10 million acres (4 million ha) of cotton fields. The boll weevil population was in rapid decline in 2006, with a number of states having been declared weevil-free. Consequently, cotton has once again become a flourishing industry in its traditional growing areas.

A biological approach to eradication

Basic scientific research on the biology of the boll weevil was the secret to a successful eradication program. The emerging over-wintering adults were considered the weakest link in the insect's life cycle chain. Researchers decided to target and effectively reduce the weevil population by interrupting this part of the insect's life cycle. This stage is when the boll weevils begin to lay eggs in large numbers,

Proper identification of the boll weevil is important. Along with the elongated snout, two sharp spurs are found on the club-shaped segment of the front legs (above). This tiny insect caused so much damage to the cotton industry (far right) that a Uniform Boll Weevil Eradication Act, declaring the weevil a menace and legislating full-scale eradication, was passed in 1975.

FACTS AND FIGURES

DATE	1892 to present
LOCATION	Southern United States
DEATH TOLL	Not relevant
DAMAGE	Estimates of yield losses and control costs due to the boll weevil total more than US$22 billion.
COMMENTS	The ongoing boll weevil eradication program started in 1978. Along with screw worm control, eradication of the boll weevil is a perfect example of the efficacy of scientific research in fully understanding the biology of the organism involved. Once this is achieved, the pest can be targeted at its most vulnerable point.

BOLL WEEVIL LIFE HISTORY

Boll weevils survive winter as dormant adults sheltering in the undergrowth on land that surrounds cotton fields. They emerge as the weather begins to warm, with a peak in late May but beginning as early as February in southern regions and extending through into early July further north. On emergence, weevils feed on cotton seedlings. They begin to lay their eggs when the flowers have developed. A single egg is deposited into each flower bud, but a female can lay many hundreds of eggs in her lifetime.

After an incubation period of two to four days, the eggs hatch as larvae, which feed voraciously, completing their development into pupae by 7 to 12 days. The pupae develop into adults in $3\frac{1}{2}$ to $8\frac{1}{2}$ days and begin the cycle over again, each generation taking a mere 12 to 24 days. Both larvae and, to a lesser extent, adults cause the destruction of the cotton flower and the cotton fibers. What the weevils don't destroy is often finished off by boll-rotting fungi, which enters as a consequence of the piercing of the flower buds and the activity of the weevil larvae.

which, of course, dramatically increases their population and chances of survival.

The eradication program depended on detecting weevils at the precise time they emerged after winter, then attacking them with carefully targeted insecticides. Detection was achieved by monitoring traps that contained an attractant.

As with many organisms, and particularly with insects, potential mates are detected by chemical odors produced by one sex for the specific purpose of attracting individuals of the opposite sex. These chemicals, also referred to as pheromones, are effective even in the minutest of quantities. After many years of painstaking research, four compounds were eventually isolated from the boll weevil males that, when combined, were extremely attractive to the female of the species.

About 100 pounds (45 kg) of boll weevil feces was needed to be able to extract a sufficient quantity to determine the chemical structure of the pheromone. Once this was done, the pheromone could be manufactured independently of the weevils. This synthesized pheromone was named "Grandlure," and became the sexy "aftershave" of the boll weevil world.

The next step was to design an effective trapping device. More than 20 million traps have been used in the United States since 1987. As soon as the time and place of the boll weevil's emergence in cotton fields was detected in the traps, they could be effectively eliminated by controlled use of insecticides. This has resulted in the progressive reduction of the use of insecticides as the eradication program continued to reduce the total population of boll weevils. The highly successful boll weevil eradication program has reinvigorated the ailing cotton industry. Its continued success is also based on the prohibition of unauthorized cotton growing and constant monitoring for new outbreaks.

The use of costly and dangerous insecticides was spiraling downward as eradication figures spiraled upward. Apart from the cost savings, there are additional benefits to a reduction of insecticide use. These include an increase in natural predators of the weevil, such as ladybirds, which now effectively function as biological controls. It is very possible that future generations of cotton growers may never have to spray for boll weevils. There has also been the introduction of genetically engineered cotton that contains a gene that codes for a plant-produced protein that repels a large number of cotton pests.

Agricultural scientists have almost succeeded in working themselves out of a job in the best possible way. However, there is no room for complacency, as pests have a habit of adapting to adverse conditions, and often return with renewed vigor.

GEORGIA, THE COTTON STATE

Georgia and cotton production have been synonymous since cotton was first planted near Savannah in 1733. The success of the boll weevil eradication program has played a major role in the recent revival of Georgia's cotton industry. In 1983, Georgia produced only 112,000 bales on 115,000 harvested acres (46,575 ha). The trapping and target-spraying regime of the eradication program began in 1987 and was completed in 1990. Since then, average yield has increased from 482 pounds (219 kg) per acre in the pre-eradication period (1971 to 1986) to 733 pounds (333 kg) per acre in the post-eradication period (1991 to 1995). Gross crop revenue has increased from US$70 million to US$400 million per year. In 1995, two million bales were produced, for total revenues of about US$720 million, the highest in Georgia's history.

Weevil worship

On December 11, 1919, the citizens of Enterprise, Alabama, now known as "Weevil City," erected a memorial to the boll weevil despite the damage it caused to their region.

The monument is of a woman dressed in a long, flowing white gown with arms stretched above her head. Built in Italy, she stands 13½ feet (4 m) above street level and cost US$3,000 (including installation), and is surrounded by a fountain.

The reason for this semi-deification of the boll weevil is that it provided a timely warning of the ecological dangers of single-crop cultivation. An Enterprise businessman, H.M. Sessons, reasoned that peanuts would provide a suitable alternative as they not only returned vital nutrients to the soil that had been depleted by the cotton but would also provide an alternative cash crop. The hard times brought on by the weevil forced farmers to diversify, which brought a new era of prosperity to the county.

FAR LEFT, TOP Cotton has been cultivated and used by people for over 7,000 years. The long white seed head, known as lint, grows into tubular fibers. After the fibers have been stripped from the plant, the remaining cottonseed is used to make oil and the cottonseed meal is used as feed for livestock.

Red-billed Quelea, Southern Africa

During November of most years in southern Africa, millions of migratory red-billed queleas descend on the precious cereal crops that have been planted to coincide with the rainy season. Quelea numbers are so vast that they have resisted and survived all attempts at control. These birds are regarded as a pest by farmers because of their greed, and are known as Africa's "feathered locust."

The red-billed quelea, *Quelea quelea*, is reputedly the world's most abundant bird species, with estimates of the adult breeding population at 1.5 billion individuals, and with a distribution that extends over much of southern Africa, to the south of the Sahara. They are highly gregarious and form colonies, reportedly containing as many as 10 million birds that extend over an area of up to 4 square miles (10 km²). They roost at night and feed by day, often targeting cereal crops that have replaced their natural seed-foraging grounds in grasslands and savannahs.

The sound of an approaching flock of red-billed queleas may be compared with that of an oncoming express train and, from a distance, it resembles a billowing plume of smoke rising up from a grass fire. A flock can be so vast that it can take 10 minutes for it to pass by. They behave like, and from a distance resemble, a plague of locusts.

The quelea colony

The red-billed quelea is a small bird, measuring around 5 inches (12.7 cm) in length and weighing only half an ounce (15 g). In the non-breeding season, both males and females look like any other species of little brown bird. Breeding plumage in males is quite variable, with a facial mask ranging from black to white, and breast and crown plumage varying from yellow to red. Individuals can display any combination of colors for these two regions of the body, making queleas one of the most variously colored of all birds. It is generally recognized that the function of male sexual ornamentation and color in birds is to provide females with a means of assessing the quality of a potential mate. However, a detailed study of male coloration in breeding queleas indicates that color variation in this species acts as an identity marker among males in densely packed colonies. Queleas are similar to quails in their appearance and feeding habits.

Quelea control

The extensive damage caused to crops by queleas has resulted in drastic action being taken to control their numbers. These strategies include the physical removal and destruction of tons of nestlings, along with the use of petrol bombing, flamethrowers, or the dynamiting of roosting colonies. In December 2005, spraying 77 gallons (350 l) of an organophosphate pesticide destroyed a colony of queleas in eastern Ethiopia, estimated to contain about 5 million birds. However, control measures have generally had little effect. The slaughter of at least 200 million birds each year in Africa has had negligible impact on the total

FACTS AND FIGURES

DATE	Annual and ongoing
LOCATION	Sub-Saharan Africa except equatorial West Africa and the southwestern tip of southern Africa
DAMAGE	Destruction of millet, wheat, barley, and sorghum crops. An average-sized flock can eat up to 60 tons (66 t) of grain per day.
COMMENTS	Perhaps one strategy to help control queleas would be to harvest them as a food source for protein-starved African nations. They could also be developed to export as a cash crop, as is done with quails. Queleas have few natural enemies; one is the crocodile, which hides in the queleas' drinking areas.

BELOW Flocks of red-billed queleas gather along the banks of the Khwai River in Botswana's Moremi Game Reserve, ready to roost for the night. Flocks can number hundreds of thousands of individuals, although they disperse into smaller flocks when they feed during the day.

population. There is concern about the long-term effects of chemical pesticides on non-target animals, including humans. Sub-Saharan Africa is also an extremely ecologically sensitive area because it lies in the path of hundreds of species of migratory birds. An integrated pest management program to reduce the numbers of queleas while also reducing the use of toxic chemicals is being developed. It includes monitoring breeding areas, modifying crop-planting time, substituting maize as a crop (it is unpalatable to queleas), and developing various devices to scare away or keep birds out of crop-planting areas.

Reproduction on the move

Queleas are members of the weaverbird family, Ploceidae, and construct elaborate nests from grass and straw in which a clutch of two to four eggs is laid. Incubation takes 12 days. The chicks are initially fed a high-protein diet of insects; they later move to a diet of grain. Juveniles leave the nest at about two weeks and become sexually mature in the following season. Queleas are serial monogamists: they swap partners after the colony has migrated to a new location. Migration follows the path of rain, which provides a continual supply of food.

ABOVE Red-billed queleas form dense, synchronised flocks that look like clouds of smoke. This cloud of queleas takes shape near Nionia, approximately 250 miles (400 km) northeast of Barnako in the interior Niger delta.

Mouse Plagues, Australia

Mouse plagues, in intense numbers and frequency, occur in the grain-growing regions of southern and eastern Australia. This area forms a belt from southeastern South Australia, through Victoria, into eastern New South Wales, and up into the regions of southeastern Queensland.

ABOVE Farm management practices have changed to incorporate techniques such as rotational cropping, diversity of crops, and extending crop seasons. This provides food and shelter for mice, creating the perfect conditions for mouse plagues to occur frequently.

The house mouse, *Mus domesticus*, was first introduced into Australia by the early European explorers and settlers, and has since spread over much of the continent. In urban areas, mice occur in relatively small numbers, as they are kept in check by pest control procedures.

However, in rural regions, mouse populations can dramatically increase to plague proportions, severely affecting the production and storage of crops. Mice also reduce productivity in pig and poultry farms through their continual harassment of stock. They cause damage to infrastructure and contaminate buildings and stored food stocks.

Frequency of plagues

Since the first report of a mouse outbreak in 1890, plagues have occurred nationwide on an average of once in every four years, and once in seven years at a particular locality. However, the frequency and extent of plagues has increased significantly since 1980, with outbreaks occurring at the same time in widely separated geographic areas. In 1980, mouse plagues erupted in a number of locations from South Australia (in the south) to southern Queensland (in the northeast). Unlike locust plagues, mice do not form a migrating front that travels over large distances. An individual mouse forages within a home territory that is no bigger than half a tennis court. Half a mile (1 km) would be an exceptional distance for a mouse to travel in its lifetime.

What causes a mouse plague to begin and end?

Mouse plagues occur over a wide range of climatic conditions, soil types, and agricultural practices. Hence different environmental conditions may trigger an outbreak in a particular region. Above average rainfall during the southern hemisphere winter and spring seasons (April to October) is believed to be a common trigger for an extensive mouse plague.

Prolonged rainfall results in the softening of soil for burrowing and the availability of high-quality food to sustain the massive reproduction of mice.

Recently sown and germinated seeds, and developing and harvested grain, are all preferred foods for mice. A full-blown plague can develop in about 9 to 18 months, depending on environmental conditions.

The "crash" of a plague is even more spectacular than its arrival. Plague densities that have reached almost 400 mice per acre (0.4 ha) in the fields and 1,200 per acre (0.4 ha) in grain stores can drop to less than 4 mice per acre (0.4 ha) within a few weeks. Plagues usually end in the southern hemisphere during mid to late winter (July and August). The "crash" often occurs, as it did in 1980, at the same time as other outbreaks are also crashing around the country, even though they may be hundreds of miles apart. Scientists are not entirely sure why this occurs but factors that may be responsible for the decline include disease, stress due to overcrowding, lack of food, and the increase of predators, such as feral cats.

Food and sex

With an abundance of food and nesting sites, the reproductive physiology of mice is geared toward rapid population increase. The breeding season can be as long as 10 months of the year. Females are sexually receptive soon after giving birth, so lactation and pregnancy can occur simultaneously. They have a gestation period of 18 to 21 days and give birth to up to 10 baby mice, which become sexually mature in five to six weeks.

Mice have a voracious appetite. Two hundred mice can consume 440 pounds (200 kg) of food per year, the same amount as one sheep. The end result of this binge eating is 18,000 fecal pellets per mouse per year. Together with the smell of their urine, this makes the presence of mice easy to detect.

Scientists are developing a genetically modified virus that affects mouse reproduction. It is hoped that this will reduce the problem.

FACTS AND FIGURES

DATE	Mouse plagues in Australia have been reported since 1890 at intervals of one every four years.
LOCATION	The grain belt of southern and eastern Australia. Mice plagues have only rarely been reported from the wheat-growing areas of Western Australia, possibly due to higher summer temperatures.
DAMAGE	AUD$35.6 million per year in lost production, together with cost of and environmental damage due to widespread use of rodenticides strychnine, zinc phosphide, and anticoagulants like warfarin.
COMMENTS	Apart from sporadic outbreaks in China and the United States, Australia is unique in experiencing regular and devastating mouse plagues. Perhaps the reason for this is that, in Australia, house mice are relatively free of predators and disease that would control their numbers.

ABOVE Rodent populations can sometimes become very large, and they can cause extensive environmental damage. This mound of mice is the result of four nights' trapping during a mouse plague in Victoria, Australia, in 1917.

Myths and Perceptions about Natural Disasters

Imagine living in a coastal area. Looking out the front door of your home, you see a wall of muddy water and debris encompassing your village. Neighbors are running away from the "new river," others are climbing trees and buildings to escape the rush of deadly debris. You take stock of the situation in seconds, though it seems like minutes, then race to get your family to safety.

BELOW The orderly tents of one of two refugee camps built to house nearly 3,000 local residents of San Giuliano di Puglia, Italy, after an earthquake on October 31, 2002. About 1,290 residents of San Giuliano were evacuated after a series of aftershocks in November continued to hit the region.

PREVIOUS PAGE Police officers stand by during a mock disaster drill in Union, New Jersey.

How confusing would it be to step into the scene of a sudden impact natural disaster? Most imagine a scene of mobs fleeing, looters smashing shop windows and stores adding $2 to the prices of water and milk. They anticipate schools or churches overflowing with injured people and bodies being dragged in off the street.

Unrealistic perceptions

Natural disasters have been affecting Earth since it formed: severe weather, earthquakes, volcanic eruptions, and tsunamis, among others. It is only very recently that the sociology of disaster behavior has been systematically studied. The results are quite a contrast to the myths of mobs and mayhem.

There are two types of disaster stories reported. Hard news stories stick to the facts—the type of disaster, area of impact, time taken to restore essential services, the duration, and related facts. Soft news stories rely on eyewitness accounts and interviews reporters orchestrate with people who might have seen or heard something relating to looting, panic, and price gouging.

Such stories are generally not collaborated. They appear as factual because people say what they believe has happened. Their interviews are directive and the people being interviewed are generally confused, dazed, and perhaps exhausted from lack of sleep and proper nourishment. News reporting at disaster sites is often over-dramatized and inaccurate.

In most cases, the media arrive following the impact. But as long as people are told a disaster is accompanied by a breakdown of behavioral and social norms, they will continue to expect authorities to call out the military to "restore" order. Planners will plan for looters, price gougers, a panicked public and reactions that are quite contrary to what actually happens at disaster scenes.

In fact, the best in people emerges when disasters strike. People go to the aid of their family, friends, neighbors, and strangers. Merchants do not price gouge their customers and people do not loot their neighbors' homes or local businesses. Shelters are usually orderly and not full. People look after one another, in and out of the rescue shelters, and food and water are shared.

Groups of survivors tend to gather at the site to begin looking for injured and dead. They help clear the debris and start the process of restoring *their* neighborhood. Police and fire service personnel also act heroically. Though their own families need them at this time, they stay on the job helping others in need. The image of firefighters risking their lives to save people and their property is compelling; yet few people realize the workers' families and property are also at risk in large-scale disasters.

People converge to help

Convergence is the phenomenon where people from surrounding areas come together at a disaster site. This is predictable following a disaster. It happens when situations become unmanageable, at this time, some of the myths and perceptions regarding disaster do become reality. However, the vast majority of people converge to render aid and help the victims. Sometimes warring countries have put down arms and reopened roads during natural disasters. Most recently, the Pakistan government offered security forces protection to non-government organizations venturing into the disputed Kashmir sector after the 2005 earthquake. It was soon discovered that these forces were unnecessary, so they were instead put to work building camps and supplying food and water.

ABOVE Students at the Silverton Avalanche School in Colorado, United States, form a line to search the snow for survivors and bodies using probes. The school teaches them how to organize a search and rescue operation. Following a natural disaster such as an avalanche, large numbers of people are needed to help with the rescue efforts and there is usually no shortage of volunteers who converge at the site to help. Graduates of this school will be able to guide volunteers in any rescues.

MYTHS IN PERSPECTIVE

Small percentages of people do exploit the situation. Price gougers sell water and food at high prices, and some out-of-town people may loot before order is restored. These isolated incidents are often what reporters see after the initial impact. Of course, the type of disaster and the levels of property and lives lost are variables in the equation. Sudden impact disasters, with little or no warning, have a different immediate effect on the people. People can expect others to converge. Most come to help; only a few come for the wrong reasons.

Natural Disaster Preparedness

Becoming prepared for a natural disaster is a positive way for people to take responsibility for their lives, their family's lives, their property, and the wellbeing of their community. To prepare means anticipating problems and taking steps to deal with them before they hit.

ABOVE A year after the 2004 tsunami, Phi Phi Island, Thailand is better prepared. Signs showing evacuation routes are displayed and tsunami drills are practiced.

RIGHT Firefighters in Tokyo, Japan, take part in the annual drill conducted by the Fire and Disaster Management Agency. This agency is also helping to install tsunami early warning systems in the Indian Ocean.

This needs to be done on a number of levels—family, community, and society—for events that require national and even international response and recovery. The general rule most experts agree on is that people need to make the necessary preparations to be able to live for three to five days without supplies, power, water, and sewage treatment. However, this rule depends on the location, size, and magnitude of a disaster.

Tools, plans, and exercises

The most basic tool for disaster preparedness is a comprehensive community education program designed for all levels of the community, from children to adults to seniors. Preparedness requires writing and exercising integrated disaster plans, sharing them with all involved, and receiving feedback. The man-made disasters in Three Mile Island, in Pennsylvania in 1979, and Bhopal in India in 1984, spurred national governments to seek ways to better prepare for, and respond to, large-scale disasters.

The planning process starts with hazard identification. That is, what type of natural disaster is most likely to occur? Is it an earthquake, hurricane, flood, severe winter storm or another disaster? Historic data is the first and best source of information. A contingency plan is needed for each hazard-based on the best estimates of which type is most likely to strike next. Some disasters provide adequate warning; others are sudden impact. Hazard identification provides a framework for plans.

The community disaster plan should be published and disseminated within the community it serves. This provides people with a context and some solid data points for planning their own family disaster plan. Warning and evacuation plans are a critical aspect of this preparedness activity.

The importance of preparation and making a safety plan

It is important to write and practice a family safety plan. This needs to complement the local community's disaster plan, which must in turn integrate into county, province, state, and also national plans. Mutual aid and support agreements must be in place and practiced as part of the overall preparedness plan from local to national levels. Emergency management staff carry out this work before a disaster strikes.

The basic community disaster plan provides an overview of the government's concept of emergency management. It shows who is in charge, who is responsible for which tasks, and how responding groups will work together. There are nine elements to the basic plan: introduction; the purpose; the situation and assumptions; a concept of operations; the organization and assignment of responsibilities; administration and logistics; plan development and maintenance (record of changes); authority and references; and definition of terms.

Once the plan has been staffed, the next step is for all participants to test the plan in an annual exercise. These exercises will show up any areas that need further attention and refining. After each disaster preparedness exercise, the plan should be revised using the lessons learned from the exercise.

MAKING A FAMILY PLAN

A family plan can be quite detailed; it depends on the family's size and the location of each member. The key elements of the most minimal plan include setting up the following:

- Family gathering (reunion) procedures, with separate plans for daytime and evening.
- An easily accessed household diagram that includes utility shut-offs (propane, gas, water, and electricity), location of any fire extinguishers, hoses, and outdoor taps. Any such paperwork needs to be kept where it is unlikely to be damaged by fire, water, or debris.
- Medical information, medical points of contact, and a medication list for each family member; again, kept in an easily accessible location, as well as copies kept offsite.
- Household inventory, along with insurance papers and, ideally, photos of valuables.
- Supplies of food and water for at least three days.
- Transistor radio and flashlight (with batteries), always kept in the same place.
- Contact numbers, along with local emergency phone numbers or radio call signs.
- Emergency contacts for friends, neighbors, out-of-area friends and family; utility companies; medical providers; work and school phone numbers.
- Pets and any working livestock list.
- Vehicle information, including numbers, types, and condition.

Keep copies of the plans and all information with out-of-area relatives or post it, along with photos of listed items onto your own website on an unlinked URL page, which can also include photos. Doing this means the information can easily be accessed if the home is destroyed.

Natural Disaster Mitigation

Following many devastating typhoons, cyclones, and hurricanes during the Middle Ages, it became apparent that merely reacting to a natural disaster was a woefully inadequate approach. Seawalls and barriers were built to hold back the tidal surges and huge waves generated by these devastating storms. As technology advanced over the centuries, stronger and better protection evolved.

BELOW Galveston, Texas, resident John McKenna runs along Seawall Boulevard before the arrival of hurricane Rita in September, 2005. The seawall, built after the devastating 1900 hurricane, has saved the city from the impact of hurricanes many times. With a million others, McKenna attempted to evacuate, but returned after 15 hours in traffic, having moved just 61 miles (98 km). The mass exodus emptied towns along Texas and Louisiana coastlines amid frantic last-minute preparations for the second super storm in a month.

Efforts to mitigate disasters are of two types: structural and non-structural. Non-structural mitigation includes such strategies as changing building codes and land-use policies, enacting tax incentives, and reducing insurance rates. For example, in the 1960s, the US government acted to reduce floodplain development through a series of incentives and programs that discouraged people from building on floodplains. Structural mitigation efforts include building dams, diverting rain, building seawalls and wind barriers, and building office complexes with special flexible foundations that withstand earthquakes.

However, technology alone is inadequate. The solutions proposed are not always adopted. It is also often not known if the structural projects will actually work. Some solutions, such as building dams which are poorly constructed, can even perpetuate existing problems. Many physical barriers can provide a false sense of security. A holistic approach is needed, taking into account social, economic, and political factors.

A new holistic approach

Gilbert White and J. Eugene Haas outlined such an approach back in 1975. They said it was necessary to change the focus, which at that time was on purely technological solutions, to a multi-disciplinary approach. They made recommendations. For floods, which are by far the most costly natural disaster, they proposed several tasks: improving control and prediction; warnings and flood-proofing; land management; insurance; relief and rehabilitation; and basic methods of data collection. They outlined similar approaches for 15 other natural hazards.

This novel approach embraced the concept of long-term community sustainability. The structural and non-structural tools for mitigation are combined in such a way as to allow a community to overcome damage, loss of productivity, and the reduced quality of life that follows a disaster. To provide this sustainability, a community takes responsibility for where, when, and how developments are permitted. Communities critically evaluate both their environmental resources and potential hazards,

and then choose where they are willing to accept losses and rebuild. This can only be accomplished by strong consensus that compounds locally as well as up the governmental chain. Mitigation activities must cross gender, income, racial, and age lines.

Mitigating is cheaper than reacting

Disaster mitigation has proven the most cost-effective way to save lives and property. This is because the cost of rebuilding a community is far greater than the cost of protecting a community. Any actions to reform policies and spend money on mitigating disasters are more likely to occur immediately following a disaster. Yet it is often the most contentious and difficult task a community faces. Property owners and developers are concerned about government interference, and want to rebuild immediately. Government officials, insurance companies, and concerned citizens often see building regulations, land-use reform, and insurance incentives as a critical part of disaster mitigation. Disaster recovery actually blends into mitigation issues as a community or society rebuilds.

Where people are allowed to rebuild and how the new structures are constructed can become a subject for public debate. Both residential and commercial property codes may be subject to change once the engineers' damage assessments have been made. Communities spending large sums of money on barriers, earthquake-proofing, and drainage projects is another part of the mitigation process that causes tension. For example, seawalls are still an important

part of disaster-mitigation projects. The seawall built around Galveston, Texas after the 1900 hurricane wiped out the city and killed over 6,000 people has saved the city time and again since that tragedy.

Communities need to foster a strong local economy that can quickly recover and support the population after a disaster has struck. Mitigation strategies that detract from the environment and from the quality of life of a community should not be implemented. The keys to mitigation are to set goals, define expectations, work with the resources available, build community awareness and support, use the tools in combination with one another, and prepare for the next disaster.

ABOVE The city of San Francisco is in the heart of earthquake country, and building codes in California are among the most seismically stringent on Earth. Even so, the USGS estimates that fewer than one-tenth of homes have been adequately secured to withstand shaking. In the bay area alone, there are eight faults with the potential for hitting over 6.7 on the Richter scale. Even strapping the water heater can reduce the chance of injury.

DISASTER WARNING CENTERS WORLDWIDE

There are monitoring stations for all types of natural disasters globally, and they work in the spirit of international cooperation. Seismographs (at right) are sited at monitoring stations in the world's seismically active areas; global information is regularly updated by the US Geological Survey. There are tsunami warning centers in Alaska, Hawaii, and Japan, and plans for an Indian Ocean system. Meteorological hazards are monitored in many countries by the meteorological bureau; the United States has a national hurricane center in Miami.

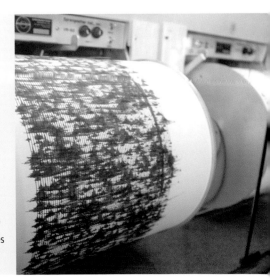

Emergency Response

When planning at a national or international level for a moderate or large-scale disaster response, inter-agency and inter-governmental coordination is the most vital element. Disaster response is not just the extension of existing emergency response processes and procedures. It is a specialist practice.

When a natural disaster strikes and the community infrastructure becomes overwhelmed, the response is directed by elected or appointed political authorities and, hopefully, disaster professionals. They all should have knowledge and training in how this coordinated effort must be orchestrated in order to mitigate the effects on the community. These are the people who will make the decisions that will save lives and property—or that will increase the death toll needlessly. They can even wipe out entire communities by making bad decisions or deciding not to do anything.

This is serious business, but questions related to the commitment, ability, and training of the officials who hold the responsibility are rarely asked prior to their taking office. It was not until recently that media reports began to focus on the ability of politicians and disaster experts to make these critical, time-sensitive decisions. The finger-pointing that was publicly played out over the loss of life and property in the United States city of New Orleans continued for months after Hurricane Katrina struck the city in 2005. The lesson here is that the level of commitment and expertise of elected officials and emergency management professionals is crucial to the overall impact of any natural disaster.

The vital practice of exercising plans

In the world of disaster response, plans and training must be based on what people are likely to do, not what they should do. The disaster plan is a living document that gets changed every time there is a an exercise or drill because first responders and decision makers learn new ways to coordinate, execute, evaluate, and cooperate during a meaningful disaster exercise. This continuous improvement process also facilitates the acceptance of the plan by first responders, decision makers, and the general public. In effect, the exercise process is just as important as the community's disaster plan.

There are five steps a community can take to exercise its disaster plan. The first step is to orient each functional group, such as medical, fire, logistics, by "walking them through" their role in the plan for each disaster contingency (for example, earthquake, flood, or typhoon). The annexures at the end of the disaster plan provide specific direction for each disaster contingency, and specific guidance for each functional support group. This low-stress walk-through shows each group how they must coordinate and respond with other support groups as well as what others expect of them.

The second step is an exercise—a drill. A drill involves actual field or facility response for an Emergency Operations Center (EOC) functional area. It requires performing each group's equipment procedures. Drills are particularly important if there is significant personnel turnover in a unit.

The third step is a tabletop exercise. It is where senior leaders and functional managers are given a series of problems inside a scenario to work out. The "game" is usually planned with a facilitator who sets the scene and provides problems for the group to work through. It is designed to elicit constructive and informal discussion so the participants can later examine and work through the problems it poses.

The fourth level is called a functional exercise. This is a fully simulated interactive exercise that tests the capability of an EOC to respond to simulated events in a time-sensitive manner without using the field equipment or deploying all the first responders. The exercise tests multiple functions of the response plan in real time. Each disaster plan has an annual "full-up" exercise where all the groups and the

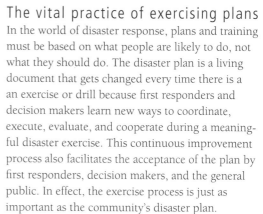

BELOW Sandbags are placed on the banks of the river to prevent further flooding on June 8, 2006, in China's Changting County, Fujian Province. China is prone to flooding disasters; with floods being the most costly of natural disasters, prevention can save money as well as lives. These floods and landslides killed more than 50 people and were estimated as the worst in three decades to hit China, with 16,000 people evacuated from their homes and villages.

equipment are exercised. At each point in this annual cycle, lessons are learned and the changes are noted and made in the disaster plan.

A disaster is a series of events

During a disaster it is not unusual for the communications systems to become clogged or overwhelmed, which results in uncertainty. Power, water, and sewage systems break, mass casualties occur, and transportation routes close. "Secondary emergencies" can occur: for instance, fires often burn down cities after earthquakes have ruptured gas lines. This is what destroyed San Francisco in 1906. Flooding results when hurricanes destroy dams and levies. Disease outbreaks occur when contaminated water is consumed following a landslide or severe storm. This means disaster response is a complex web of interconnected activities that can save lives and property, or compound problems in the field.

Who is in charge?

With limited resources, the authorities hopefully make decisions based on well-thought-out priorities that are sequentially correct and have been exercised. For example, emergency medical care cannot be rendered to save lives until the transportation routes are confirmed as being cleared, a crane to remove rubble from a fallen building that has trapped people is brought in, and search-and-rescue dog teams are dispatched to locate any trapped people.

Disaster response will usually include government agencies at local, state, and federal levels as well as a wide variety of non-government organizations that have separate plans that haven't been coordinated or practiced together. They have no idea what the others' capabilities are or how they operate. This leads to conflicting responses, misallocation of resources, and may lead to competition. More than likely, none of the groups has an overall grasp of

ABOVE School buses were used to evacuate Galveston residents from Hurricane Rita in September, 2005, along I-45. During such times, it is vital for residents to heed the local authorities' evacuation orders. School buses were also used to transport evacuees from New Orleans following Hurricane Katrina.

the immediate situation. The coordinated response of all agencies to the situations that come up from functional units like medical, logistics, public works, transportation, and security can be daunting.

First priority after a disaster strikes

The first task for emergency-response workers is to set up one or more command posts on site. If there is more than one command post and they are run by different groups, the problems are already compounding. Fire officials are normally the designated field commanders, but that is not always the case. In some countries, emergency managers take the lead in the field. Military units take the lead in others. The important issue is that a single, coordinated chain of command with operating communication systems is established as soon as possible. The incident-command structure is the most widely accepted in many countries.

The reasons for using this functional unified command structure are inherent in the nature of combating a disaster. It allows for close working relationships between diverse groups. It recognizes legal and fiscal authorities. It provides unit integrity by having people in the same agency work together. The structure has a manageable span of control and is modular, so each functional area can expand if required. Most importantly, it has an integrated communications system and comprehensive resource-allocation process built in. The Emergency Management Institute or the California Specialized Training Institute Information has online classes on this type of disaster-response structure.

Outlining the impact zone

Once the field command post is operational and communications are established, perimeters and impact zone areas are identified and cordoned off so that people do not inadvertently get in harm's way. Depending on the type and extent of the damage, first responders are trained to rescue people first

and save property second. That may mean fighting secondary effects such as fires and broken water or sewage lines that threaten people trapped in sectors they cannot escape from. Designating medical treatment areas in clinics, hospitals, gyms, or even out in the open is another first step out in the field.

At the EOC or major command level, large scale logistics will dominate the response. During the Indian Ocean tsunami in 2004, an assessment of the impact zones by way of satellite photos was one of the first steps taken to focus the relief efforts in the areas of greatest need. Mapping transportation routes to get supplies to the site is another activity requiring immediate attention. Roads, bridges, port facilities, and airstrips are key links. Setting up transportation, mapping routes, distribution methods, and looking for safe storage areas near the disaster zone are other immediate tasks.

It is easy to second-guess emergency response efforts. It is another thing to have to make life-and-death decisions without complete information in a fluid and rapidly changing situation.

ABOVE Relief supplies are flown in to Bagroo village, Bali Mang Chattar Plains, in the remote Pakistan-controlled Kashmir by a USAID helicopter during a Mercy Corps–USAID-sponsored distribution on October 29, 2005. With 3 million people without proper shelter, relief work was on a massive scale.

LEFT In Fort Pierce, Florida, power lines were toppled after Tropical Storm Jeanne slammed into the area. It knocked out power to most homes for many days after the storm hit on September 28, 2004. While apparently just an inconvenience, food spoilage resulting after even short power outages can lead to food poisoning.

THE VITAL MATTER OF MISSING PEOPLE

A Thai Buddhist monk scrutinizes hospital missing persons' notices after the 2004 tsunami (left). When searching for people, the two places to look are the nearest shelters and medical areas. Going back into impact zones is unwise until the areas are declared safe. People will frequently try to rescue their loved ones on their own. But in doing so they can clog transportation routes, get in the way of first responders, or even become casualties themselves. The best option for those seeking loved ones is to volunteer to search as part of the search-and-rescue teams, if that option is available.

Medical Response after Natural Disasters

Disaster situations involve treating large groups of injured or dying people in the field. When disaster strikes, unique protocols for medical treatment are necessary. Unless trained, medical people find it difficult to adjust to the new procedures. They mistakenly think it just means longer hours.

RIGHT Transport routes may be cut off, such as this highway during a freeze in the eastern United States in 2002. If no transport routes are open it may be difficult to obtain supplies. Communication nets and power sources are also critical during the initial response. The web of interconnected activities may fall apart unless training has been so extensive each group can function seamlessly with its counterparts.

BELOW A doctor from a Polish medical team offers first aid to an earthquake victim in Balakot, Pakistan, in 2005. With an overwhelming 106,000 injured and needing medical help, triage following this disaster led to a high rate of amputations.

Health professionals need to be trained for this type of care. The normal instinct is to spend time on the most severe cases. As a rule of thumb, when the number of injured people exceeds 120, onsite triage is necessary. This is simply sorting the injured into categories—usually urgent, immediate, minimal, and expectant. People are diagnosed, tagged, and treated in category order.

Triage at the disaster site

Injured people at a triage station may be surprised by who receives care first. First to be triaged but last to receive care are those in the expectant category. These are victims whose injuries are so severe that their chances for survival are extremely remote: they may be suffering the loss of one or more limbs, severe head injuries, or excessive loss of blood. They are not expected to survive field treatment and transport to hospital. They are made as comfortable as possible in a designated area. Some actually do live.

The urgent and immediate categories are cared for first and second. They are stabilized in the field and transported as soon as possible. Urgent

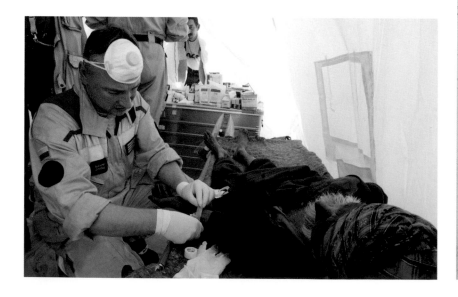

category people with significant injuries could die if left unattended for long. Those in the immediate category can survive for a while at the triage station but require attention and stabilization.

The minimal category includes people with insignificant injuries. They receive treatment from lay workers for cuts and sprains. After being treated, they can be put to work if physically able, carrying stretchers or supplies. They may be asked to sit with the dying to provide comfort.

Getting from the field to the hospital

Transportation of the sick and injured is a difficult task. Workers need to know where urgent and immediate care people can be taken and which hospitals and clinics can take in patients. Then the Emergency Operations Center (EOC) needs to know if transport is available to move the injured and which, if any, of the routes that are open will get them to the treatment centers. This can be complex or easy depending upon the level of devastation. Transporting the injured requires close coordination and communication between those in the field and the EOC. Without that coordination, people will die en route. The most critically injured have a chance to live providing they are treated soon after transportation, so there is no time to get diverted.

On arrival, triage is usually repeated. Getting supplies and medications is now vital—without

them, people will die needlessly. Painkillers and antibiotics are extremely important at the onset. Most hospitals do not keep enough supplies for large numbers of trauma cases. So tracking usage rates and informing the EOC of emerging requirements is vital.

Depending upon the magnitude of destruction, camps providing temporary shelter may be required. This will also include areas specifically designated for care of the injured, should there be no hospital or building left standing. Building a camp to house and care for entire communities is difficult, especially in mountainous terrain, deserts, equatorial jungles, or artic-cold temperatures.

Such a camp was built in the mountainous region of Kashmir following the 2005 earthquake. Thousands required temporary housing as winter set in; this was an enormous undertaking and required international intervention. In tough situations like this, there is an internationally recognized set of standards for carrying out massive projects. This is known as the Sphere Project.

Infrastructure damage and disease

Public health issues after a disaster strikes are complicated because the community's basic infrastructure is damaged. Water, sewage lines, power, and fuel sources can all be affected. This can quickly lead to cholera outbreaks, malnutrition, dysentery, dehydration, and diarrhea. Large numbers of displaced disaster victims can die if aid does not arrive quickly enough or is not set up to meet the emerging threat of disease.

The psychological impact of disasters

The psychological effects on large groups in the aftermath of a disaster is a relatively new field of study. There are two distinct groups to consider: victims and relief workers. Separate post-disaster approaches are needed.

Disaster victims are frequently victims of acute depression. They may have witnessed the loss of loved ones, homes, possessions, communities they have belonged to for many years, and be feeling powerless in the face of overwhelming devastation. This depression can lead to panic attacks, withdrawal, extreme aggressive behavior, and irritability. It can lead to physical ailments such as skin rashes and loss of bodily functions. Over time, people can manifest this psychological condition to extremes and suffer heart attacks, strokes, and high blood pressure. Some people who have a previous history of psychological treatment can become spontaneously withdrawn. This is called Wallace's Disaster Syndrome.

The problem of treating people is compounded because diagnosis is difficult in the midst of a chaotic situation. People are unlikely to refer themselves because they perceive others to be in greater need. Mental health workers must gain the confidence and trust of their patients, which is quite difficult in the midst of a disaster. The populations most susceptible to mental disorders during and just after disasters are the elderly, women, people who have just lost a loved one, people with pre-existing psychiatric illnesses, and people from lower socioeconomic groups who feel they cannot recover. Women are more prone to depressive and anxiety disorders after disasters, while men greatly outpace women in substance-abuse behaviors.

THE SPHERE PROJECT

In 1997, over 400 humanitarian and aid organizations from 80 countries developed a set of international guidelines and minimum standards of care for managing disaster victims. A definitive reference guide, the *Sphere Handbook*, dramatically changed disaster-relief operations, guiding thousands of humanitarian caregivers, planners, and workers. The project identified five areas to target—sanitation, nutrition, food aid, shelter, and health services. The book outlines the humanitarian charter, stating that the rights of disaster victims to life and dignity must be respected by all nations. Recently it tackled seven new areas of disaster-relief efforts for large populations—children, the elderly, disabled people, gender, protection/security, HIV–AIDS, and the environment. It is "Designed to be used in both slow- and rapid-onset situations in both rural and urban environments, in developing and developed countries, anywhere in the world. The emphasis throughout is on meeting the urgent survival needs of people affected by disaster, while asserting their basic human right to life and dignity." A person finding herself in a displaced persons camp today will see great improvements from even a year ago. With Sphere Project standards adhered to, more supplies, volunteers, and donations will flow into the impact zone and surrounding sites through coordinated efforts.

Aid workers can burn out

Relief workers often exhibit post-traumatic stress. Long hours under trying conditions can easily lead to breakdowns in the healthiest people. Critical incident stress is experienced by new workers who have never witnessed horrifying situations, where not only are death and destruction all around them, but body parts of people they knew as neighbors may be part of their experience. This trauma, in tandem with sleeplessness, can lead to breakdowns. The bottom line is that relief workers need to be well trained, and to get rest and comfort during the recovery process if they are to remain productive.

Decision makers and workers can make critical errors when they cross the line and neglect self-care. It up to the group to recognize this before workers make serious misjudgments that cost lives. Disaster syndromes include the Jehovah complex (overrating their ability to make decisions) and the Magna Mater complex (trying to solve too many problems at one time). This is a new field in disaster management.

BELOW Refrigeration for temporary morgues is particularly important in hot, humid climates like Thailand; after the 2004 tsunami, dry ice was brought in to help slow the rate of decomposition and stem the potential for disease outbreaks. One of the more difficult aspects of disaster relief is finding the balance between timely burial to avoid health problems and relieve the social anxiety, and the need to identify vast numbers of victims. There were added difficulties for these workers, such as flies and odors.

DEALING WITH THE DEAD

First priority in dealing with mass casualties is to find suitable locations for morgues—temples, schools, and gyms are often used. They are usually near medical treatment areas; body bags and refrigeration units are brought in if possible. Identifying victims can be difficult; bodies may not be identifiable by sight or may not be intact. Victim identification teams are set up—there were over 600 people in 30 teams in Thailand after the 2004 tsunami. Two types of data are collected. Primary data includes DNA samples, fingerprints, and dental information. Secondary data such as race, sex, age, hair color, and jewelry helps group victims. The information is carefully recorded according to special guidelines. It is then cross-checked against Interpol records for a match with information on missing persons which has been supplied by the relatives of missing people, embassies, or police, and compiled at an information center.

Support and Assistance after Natural Disasters

Volunteers are an invaluable resource during all phases of emergency management—mitigation, preparedness, response, and recovery. Volunteers tend to be representative of three primary sources: the local community, neighboring communities, and agencies that volunteer to help.

Volunteers are a great source of aid after natural disasters. French Red Cross members help clear snow from a tent used as a health unit (right). A volunteer from California (far right) collects clothing donated for displaced people in Gulfport, Mississippi. Clothes apparently just began showing up in this parking lot.

BELOW Animal control expert Alison Cardona of the American Society for Prevention of Cruelty to Animals rescues a dog from a flooded home in New Orleans. Following Hurricane Katrina, volunteers helped retrieve pets left behind by fleeing residents.

Most communities are not organized and prepared to deal with recruiting, training, mobilizing, and rewarding large numbers of volunteers at the time of a disaster. That means the mitigation and preparedness phases are the most important times to engage volunteers locally because it allows them to be effectively integrated and coordinated during the response phase, which is when the need is greatest. It is difficult, but not impossible, to design volunteer programs before a disaster strikes. Engaging the community in disaster-preparedness activities requires leadership, and educational and practical approaches to the local community situation.

People will come to help

Research is conclusive about the convergence factor. Large numbers of people will come to a disaster out of pure altruism. It follows that communities can plan to use these volunteers effectively. Some of the best ways they can be employed include assessing damage, communicating (ham radio operators), transporting victims and workers, removing debris, search and rescue, unskilled medical work—such as bearing stretchers, mortuary care, comfort for the injured and dying, and resupplying bandages and medicines. Local "runners" also play a vital role when regular communication methods are down. Volunteers can facilitate family reunions for those who become separated. This alleviates stress on the emergency operations center and field commanders, who have little time to search for individuals amid the chaos. While volunteers can be of great benefit, if mismanaged they can actually worsen a bad situation. They can cause miscommunication by spreading rumors, they can clog roads when vital supplies or the injured need passage, or become victims themselves by entering restricted zones.

International relief

On a large scale, there are national, international and religious groups that come to volunteer and provide support, and in some cases provide goods and services for a fee. Some non-government organizations (NGOs) provide a specific service or product, such as Doctors Without Borders (Medécins Sans Frontières), the International Medical Corps, the International Rescue Committee, and World Vision. Both the National Red Cross and National Red Crescent specialize in sheltering and mass care, while the International Committee of the Red Cross

MD 1389 BF

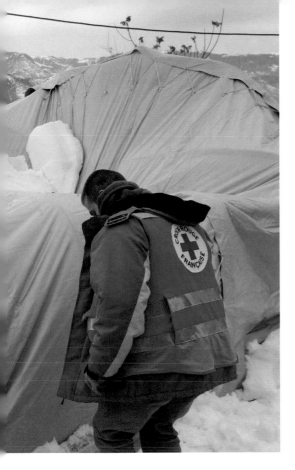

(ICRC) deals with human rights and legal issues. The United Nations plays a large role in organizing and funding large-scale disasters. The UN Office for the Coordination of Humanitarian Affairs (UN-OCHA) usually takes the lead. The United Nations High Commission for Refugees (UNHCR), the World Health Organization (WHO), the World Food program, and UNICEF, which focuses on children, are among the supporting agencies working with NGOs during disaster response and recovery. The United Nations will appoint a lead agent, depending on the nature of the natural disaster, which will then work with NGOs and other organizations to provide care.

Since the 2004 Indian Ocean tsunami, the United Nations has been reorganizing its disaster-response structure to deal with larger catastrophic events. One of the challenges arising from major events is when volunteers who become victims. A volunteer who is not part of a self-sufficient organization will need basics, like food, shelter, power, and water, which can burden the local populace trying to recover. Also, people who are inexperienced can get hurt in a disaster zone and overload local rescue operations and medical facilities.

The issues surrounding control of these groups by local and national authorities can also become contentious. Competition for funding among the groups is a relatively new angle in disaster-relief circles. Whoever gets there first and starts providing care has an inside track when a semblance of order is established and funding is dispersed.

DONATIONS CAN BE GOOD ... OR BAD

People are touched by misfortune and tend to want to give something to the victims. Their generosity sometimes leads to providing supplies in bulk that are not needed, or that can't be warehoused or kept safe from the elements. An example of this occurred after Hurricane Andrew wiped out Homestead, Florida, in August 1992. Tractor-trailer trucks full of winter clothes quite unsuited to the warm climate were donated from all over the United States. The Emergency Operations Center had to manage temporary storage, work out how to pay for this, and where to dispose of all the items. This was a monumental and expensive task added to providing short-term recovery of essential services to a devastated community.

The right donations at the right time can bring relief to victims. The wrong donations at the wrong time can divert efforts, waste time, and cost money needed to help the efforts already underway. Carefully managing donations and volunteers can enhance the recovery process. The best way to help is to send money to specific groups identified by the authorities. They can purchase items as they are needed without waste or excessive warehousing costs.

Recovery following Natural Disasters

As the residents of Darwin, Australia, surveyed their city on Christmas Day in 1974, just after Cyclone Tracy completely destroyed all in its path, they had to grapple with some tough questions. How quickly can we get back to normal? How much protection are we going to provide for the next generations so they don't have their city laid to waste?

RIGHT Darwin today is a vibrant city in Australia's tropical north. People ignore the wet season rains while strolling the streets on Christmas eve—a huge change from the chaos and despair of Christmas 1974, when the city was flattened by Cyclone Tracy. Building codes now require homes to have cladding to protect them from flying debris and their roofs tied to the foundations. There are also public cyclone shelters, a cyclone warning system, and cyclone preparedness campaigns.

S uch are the questions to be answered during the recovery and reconstruction phases. In Darwin, people had little left of their city. When Major General Alan Stretton, from the National Disasters Organization, arrived to start the recovery process, he found a city in ruins. Ninety percent of the town was flattened, 20,000 were homeless, there was no power or water, and the medical supplies were scattered to the winds. By some miracle, only 50 people died.

Other cyclones in Australia have claimed far more lives, but none has caused more damage to a population center—US$4.5 million in damage was sustained. For the short-term recovery, General Stretton called in the navy, because roads were choked and impassable. They brought in essential medical supplies, food, and water as they opened up the damaged port areas. The roads were cleared and aid from all over the country poured in to Darwin. International aid from New Zealand and the United States began to arrive. Thousands of people were evacuated; some never returned.

ODD BEHAVIOR CAN FOLLOW DISASTERS

The trauma experienced by people who live through life-changing disasters causes strain on relationships and some unusual behaviors. After Cyclone Tracy, one man cut down large trees because the wind blowing through the branches reminded him of the frightening sounds he had experienced during the cyclone. The sound of warning sirens is also a sound that brings people back to the terror of not knowing if they and their friends and family will live through the cyclone. Indeed, in the Museum and Art Gallery of the Northern Territory, where a darkened chamber replays a terrifying recording of the cyclone, there is a warning on the door to residents who experienced the cyclone. Other disaster survivors turn to to substance abuse and antisocial behavior out of fear, hopelessness, and anger following a life-changing event. Two teens began taking drugs then went on an irrational crime spree after a series of hurricanes in 2004. Others refused to leave home after a series of tornadoes destroyed their small town. They said they were disoriented and might get lost. After an earthquake in Los Angeles, people barricaded themselves at home, fearing looters would take their broken furniture and appliances. None came. People disabled their cars after Hurricane Katrina because they said they felt helpless.

ABOVE Crews clear away the rubble in Paso Robles after an earthquake hit the coastline of California on December 22, 2003. Such infrastructure damage can create chaos and require massive rebuilding programs.

FAR RIGHT, TOP One year after the 2004 tsunami, in Banda Aceh, Indonesia, rebuilding progresses slowly. While over 16,000 houses had been built for the survivors and a further 16,000 were under construction, about 67,000 people were still living in tents.

Recovery is a variable phase

As in all disasters where devastation is surrounding the survivors, some people take longer than others to recover. The work of rebuilding their community starts at an uneven pace as people realize the extent of the tasks ahead. Many Australians from Darwin returned and rebuilt because they just didn't want to feel defeated by the storm. Typical of this recovery spirit is Tony Pickering, a long time resident and businessman who stayed and rebuilt, saying, "Tracy was just piss and wind, and I didn't want to be defeated by it."

Darwin, like many places wiped out by disasters had a chance to rebuild for the better—and it was. Today Darwin is a thriving, high-energy metropolis. During the dry season there is an emphasis on tourism. The storm brought a new vitality, and self-government as a result of the rebuilding process.

Short-term recovery

One of the first issues to arise after a disaster is that of people wanting to return to their homes to protect what is left from looters, and to survey the remains of their property. And the opposite: people wanting and needing evacuation out of the impact zones. Managing this stream of people in and out of the area can be difficult. This may or may not be possible, depending on the extent of the damage to access roads and infrastructure. Safety is certainly a significant factor when considering whether or not people can be allowed back into the impact zones, as it is with evacuating them out. The process of cleaning up, removing debris, and restoring basic services also needs to be immediately started.

Short-term recovery is a complex process of bringing the basic needs aspects of the infrastructure back while providing food, water, clothing, and shelter to victims and aid workers. Many feel a strong need to restore the community to its original state as soon as possible. This is as a much a psychological need as a creature comfort desire, and is also good business for some. People want to get back to what they felt comfortable and secure with.

In this rush to rebuild and restore their community, property owners and developers will advocate strongly for reconstruction as things were. Typically, those arguing for a sustainable community in the future will want to examine and assess the disaster impact zones, and recommend strategies to mitigate future disasters. They rightly point out that disasters do have statistical and historical recurrence rates. A cyclone the size and strength of Tracy will hit the north coast of Australia

CRITICAL NEEDS FOR OPTIMAL RECOVERY

Rubin, Saperstein, and Barbee developed a useful framework for thinking about local disaster recovery in the early 1980s. Their research shows that the communities which recover soonest, and with the best results, do three things. First, they develop positive working relations with government institutions and effectively leverage those relationships post-disaster. Second, they compete for resources aggressively. Third, they manage the local decision-making processes effectively. To undertake these key tasks in less-than-ideal conditions requires strong personal leadership skills, the ability to act decisively, and the knowledge of what to do sequentially and comprehensively. For example, to act decisively, leaders must know the availability of local, state, and federal assistance, and have horizontal and vertical relationships in place to advocate effectively for them. Disaster recovery can carry on for years. Managing this process and building sustainable communities requires leadership that is proactive, intelligent, and committed to the long-term welfare of the community.

again. Darwin today is a city that planned ahead: it developed land-use policy, enacted building codes, and built community infrastructure that can withstand moderate-size cyclones.

The reconstruction phase

It is hard to define when response stops and recovery begins; when recovery stops and mitigation activities for the next disaster start. They blend together as a community recovers. The many participants in this process have varied agendas and skill levels. Managing so many people and organizations well signals the success of a community's recovery. There is quite a lot of research on disaster recovery models. There are indicators—quality and timeliness—for businesses, residential, government, and the general population.

For business, they include repairing or reconstructing economically viable commercial, industrial, and retail establishments, and restoring retail sales, business-related tax revenues and employment to pre-disaster levels. Residential concerns include repairing and reconstructing houses, home furnishings, and vehicles; temporary and permanent rehousing of displaced people; and settling insurance claims for property damage and personal items. Governments need to resume sewer, electric, water, telephone, public transportation, and other basic services that existed before the disaster. Long-term reconstruction involves restoring parks and recreational areas, repairing and reconstructing hospitals, libraries, police stations, fire stations, schools, and other municipal buildings. The general population has its own social indicators that can be monitored. They include birth rates, death rates, levels of alcoholism, child and spouse abuse, welfare payments, and crime rates. They also include implementing programs and projects that enhance a community's quality of life after a disaster.

So what are the indicators that distinguish one community's recovery from another's? Such knowledge will help people support local, regional and state-level disaster recovery planning. This is a relatively new area of work for disaster managers, business planners, and city planners. Business continuity planning is also a new part of disaster planning. These plans are designed to keep businesses afloat should critical infrastructure, information, and people sustain serious damage.

There are several functional areas for recovery that are commonly considered. These are: information gathering and assessment; organizational arrangements; resource mobilization; planning, administration, and budgeting; regulation and approval; coordination and intergovernmental relations; and monitoring and evaluation.

For example, in the early recovery stages, under organizational arrangements, ad hoc groups are formed to deal with the influx of donations and volunteers. Later, people are hired to administer and develop local recovery plans and implement state plans. Under information gathering and assessment, tasks in the early stages include: assessing damage relative to prior plans; determining the economic, social, and environmental impacts; determining the levels of disaster assistance needed and sources to use; and clarifying roles and responsibilities in terms of obtaining outside assistance.

As recovery shifts to reconstruction, damage assessment continues and competition for resources occurs at all levels of government, depending on the area and extent of the damage.

ABOVE St Ann's parade marches through the French Quarter of New Orleans on February 28, 2006. This is the first Mardi Gras since Hurricane Katrina devastated the city six months earlier. The rebuilding process is not without pain and struggle. Healing the external and internal wounds a devastating disaster can cause is vital. Returning to normal social functions helps heal some of the heartbreak accompanying loss.

The Way Ahead

Imagine ten years from now. What kind of place will our planet be? Will there be more natural disasters, brought on by the effects of global warming? This is certainly a subject of intense debate in the early twenty-first century.

RIGHT Rainfall in the Atacama Desert, Chile, has dropped 8 percent per decade, according to the United Nation's global deserts report. It says climate change has already affected desert areas which make up almost a quarter of Earth's surface. In the Dashti Kbir Desert in Iran, it has fallen by 16 percent; and in the Kalahari, in South Africa, by 12 percent.

BELOW Wilma, the 21st storm of the season, moves over the Gulf of Mexico—a particularly dangerous region in 2005. Coastal areas are more prone to natural disasters; as populations migrate there, disasters will yield more fatalities.

Natural disasters are Earth's way of releasing concentrated energy. There are four sources of energy that make the planet alive and active: The sun, Earth's internal heat, gravity, and an impact from an extraterrestrial body—something that happened with great frequency during Earth's early days. People cannot control these forces.

However, we can exacerbate them by creating a greenhouse atmosphere. The best available science indicates that we are in a global-warming cycle. This means Earth's energy concentrations will increase the size, frequency, and intensity of future natural disasters. Even just ten years into the future, we will be facing a fresh set of circumstances.

Migrating and growing populations

During the 1970s and 1980s there was a temporary lull in the number of severe storms that occurred throughout much of the world. At the same time, the world's interior populations began migrating toward coastal areas, where more frequent and more deadly storms occur. So future generations will face potentially greater losses of life and property in these densely populated coastal areas. These changes create a series of complex and contentious public policy decisions. While there are international organizations willing and able to take on these new challenges, they must be given the authority to do so by those in leadership positions.

From 1950 to 2000, Earth's population grew from 2.5 billion to just over 6 billion. Experts predict it will rise to 9 billion by 2050, with 80 percent of them living within 200 miles (322 km) of a coast. The predicted shift from the dry interiors is based on global warming turning farmland into deserts, a subsequent lack of agrarian work, and war and strife in marginal crop areas over scarce resources. A United Nations report released on June 5, 2006 says the growth of deserts was an increasing obstacle to ending global poverty and a possible threat to peace. More populations are moving away from drought-stricken regions and into areas that are at greater risk of natural disaster. This chain of events is leading the world down a dangerous path.

The results of global warming are clear. From the drought-stricken interior to coastal storms, 2005 was the worst storm season ever experienced in Central America and the US mainland. Water levels are rising and storm surges are going further inland because

the protective coastal wetlands and woods are being paved over by developers building as close to the ocean as possible. These developments affect the whole planet.

Preparing for future catastrophe

What, then, are some of the ways in which we are preparing for these tremendous releases of Earth's energy? There is an increase in the number of people becoming emergency management professionals. Universities now offer degrees and certificate programs. Some public officials promote regular community discussions so people do consider and debate how to protect themselves, their family, friends, the elderly, pets, and the community from disasters. This is a relatively new development.

It requires us to engage our leaders in debating these complex issues and to urge them to make some of the difficult choices. Information technology and communication advances have made responding to disasters more efficient in the short term. Well-engineered and constructed mitigation projects continue to save lives and property. Disaster planning and exercises are becoming more widespread and sophisticated, and well-defined recovery plans help rebuild sustainable communities.

Ultimately disasters are about people—the victims, rescuers, survivors, aid workers, public

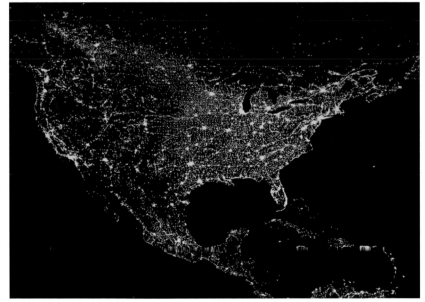

officials, and emergency managers. Technology does not solve the problems natural disasters present; people do. Ten years on, will we be reversing current trends, or will we be reacting to bigger, more frequent, and more intense disasters? You can make a difference by protecting yourself and your community. You can also raise your informed concerns with any level of government you wish to.

ABOVE Night lights over the United States, in a satellite image, show just how densely populated our planet really is. It also reveals how reliant we are on energy, much of it derived from fossil fuels, which contribute to a greenhouse planet.

Index

Page numbers in *italics*
refer to illustrations.

Contributors

ANDREW BATES

Andrew Bates is an affiliate faculty member at the College of International Studies at Hawaii Pacific University. He teaches international and domestic emergency management and is an emergency management consultant. He has spent most of his career in the Pacific region as a medical department officer in the US Navy, deploying field medical units to a variety of countries in support of humanitarian assistance missions. He spent two years as the program manager for the Center of Excellence in Disaster Management and Humanitarian Assistance. His broad knowledge of emergency management is condensed into the chapter on Dealing with Natural Disasters.

DR BRUCE BUCKLEY

Dr Bruce Buckley is a meteorologist whose varied career includes working in Australia for the Bureau of Meteorology, as a specialist United Nations adviser in Saudi Arabia, and as chief meteorologist for The Weather Channel Australia. With a PhD in numerical weather prediction, Bruce maintains an interest in the causes and prediction of extreme weather and climate events. His first-hand experiences in the hyper-arid conditions of the Middle East and across drought-prone regions of Australia, coupled with experience in coauthoring another four weather-related books, helped him write much of the chapter on Droughts.

SCOTT CALLAN

Scott Callan has encountered many wildfires and seen first-hand the devastation they can cause. He has been a volunteer firefighter since the age of 16 in 1993. In the Fires chapter, he highlights the fierceness of fire and its indiscriminate effects on people. He has shared the highs and lows of fighting wildfires, and has witnessed the devastation of the families who have lost everything to them.

DR ROBERT COENRAADS

Dr Robert Coenraads is a consultant geoscientist. He has led field trips to various corners of the globe, including the active volcanoes of the USA, Mexico, Chile, and the Pacific—in some cases narrowly avoiding natural disasters, such as the Mt St Helens eruption in 1980 and the Mexico City earthquake of 1985. His interest in natural disasters heightened after visiting the flood-prone areas of Bihar, India, in 2000, and again after finishing a project in Thailand just before the 2004 Indian Ocean tsunami. As chief author and consultant, he wrote the introduction to this book, the chapters on Volcanoes, Earthquakes, and Tsunamis and also several covered several other individual disasters.

FIONA DOIG

A natural history and travel writer and editor, Fiona Doig was project manager and one of the editors of *Natural Disasters*. She conceptualized the book with chief author and consultant Dr Robert Coenraads. Together they worked from the premise that the information in this book could save lives. Fiona's work includes dozens of natural history and travel publications, and seven years as managing editor of *Nature Australia* at the Australian Museum. She has experienced a few natural disasters: floodwaters have seen her bogged in mud in the Congo and stranded in Chiang Rai, Thailand, she has been bruised by hail, knocked over by blizzards, evacuated from wildfires, slept through earth tremors, and had her eyelashes covered in volcanic ash while watching Anak Krakatau erupt.

PHIL RODWELL

Phil Rodwell, who compiled the Gazetteer, has been researching and editing general interest books on topics as varied as gardening, history, motor touring, travel, heritage architecture, DIY, Australiana, and cookery for 30 years. After poring over a dozen volumes and consulting innumerable websites devoted to the multitude of catastrophes that have inflicted our planet since time immemorial, he is amazed that the human race has survived thus far.

DIANE ROBINSON

Diane Robinson has written on travel, health, and the environment for the *Sydney Morning Herald* and overseas magazines such as *Implosion*. She has always been fascinated by the more esoteric side of travel, winning a writing competition run by *Lonely Planet* for The Ten Most Morbid Sites Around the World. Her writing on health issues includes a training manual for audiologists for Cochlear Ltd. Writing the Diseases chapter allowed her to indulge her interest in the bizarre and increase her knowledge of health issues. Diane lives in Sydney, Australia.

PREVIOUS PAGES A man empties water from his boots in his daughter's flooded kitchen as she wades past her floating fridge to rescue a picture of her dog. The major floods in Yorkshire, England occurring in November 2000 hit the town of Barlby hardest, which has greatly improved its flood barriers in more recent years.

STEWART SMITH

Stewart Smith holds graduate degrees in Public Health, Management, and Policy from the Yale School of Medicine, Department of Epidemiology and Public Health, and the US Naval War College in National Security and Strategic Studies. He is a Doctoral Candidate in Complex Emergencies and Disaster Management at Tulane University, and holds Adjunct Professor appointments at the Uniformed Services University of the Health Sciences and Tulane University. Stewart was selected as the first American to chair the North Atlantic Treaty Organization's (NATO's) Biomedical Defense Advisory Committee (BIOMEDAC); its prime task being to enhance and expedite the work on biological warfare/infectious diseases medical countermeasures for NATO allies. He held this position from 2003 to 2005 while assigned to the United States Department of Defense Staff and United States Northern Command. Stewart wrote the introduction for the Diseases chapter.

MATTHEW STEVENS

Matthew Stevens works as a scientific editor in Sydney, Australia. He knows about droughts, having lived through many, and having worked with government on strategic plans for water conservation. He wrote part of the Droughts chapter and edited several others. He has written also for *New Scientist*, has co-edited academic books, and has written a book on scientific editing. He sat through an F1 tornado in his home in 1994, has walked through the crater of an active volcano in New Zealand, and spent a week cut off from the world by bushfires.

ROBYN STUTCHBURY

Robyn Stutchbury has spent much of her life in and around the waters of Sydney Harbour. Sailing small boats was a favorite activity since childhood, and it gave her the opportunity to closely observe variations in weather—essential knowledge for anticipating wind change and threatening storm activity. A science degree in geology included studies in meteorology and mass-movement processes, such as landslides. Her lifetime of experiences helped form the basis of the Mudslides and Landslides, Tornadoes, and Storms chapters.

DR NOEL TAIT

Noel Tait began his natural history education fossicking in coastal rock pools after school. After leaving school he extended this passion into an academic career in zoology. With a PhD from the Australian National University, he joined Macquarie University in Sydney, where he taught and researched various aspects of the biology of invertebrate animals. These make up 99 percent of the animal world and include a significant proportion of species that have become pests. From this wealth of knowledge, he wrote the Pest Plagues chapter and introduction.

LORI J. E. TURI

Lori J. E. Turi is a freelance writer who specializes in world history and mythology research. As a sixteen-year resident of the New England region of the USA, she has extensive familiarity with blizzards, nor'easters, winter storms, and floods. Lori worked as a volunteer providing aid and relief to Hurricane Katrina survivors. She wrote the chapters on Freezes, Blizzards, and Snow Avalanches; Hurricanes, Cyclones, and Typhoons; and much of the Floods chapter. The sections on US blizzards include her first-hand accounts.

RICHARD (DICK) WHITAKER

Dick began his career in meteorology when he started with Australia's National Weather Service, the Bureau of Meteorology, in 1971, after a two-year stint in the army. Working his way through the ranks, he was a Senior Forecaster for a nine-year period before becoming State Manager of the Bureau's commercial arm in 1993. Dick left the Bureau in 2002, but never lost the weather bug and came out of retirement to begin his own meteorological consultancy business. He is very interested in meteorological education, particularly through television, radio, and books, and has authored, coauthored and edited eight meteorological publications, including books for *Time-Life* and *Reader's Digest*. Since 2004 Dick has been Consulting Meteorologist to Australia's "The Weather Channel" and is a regular weather presenter on both radio and television. He wrote the introductions to Floods; Droughts; Fires; Freezes, Blizzards, and Snow Avalanches; and Hurricanes, Cyclones, and Typhoons.

Acknowledgments

Natural Disasters has been designed in order to convey an extensive and eclectic array of information. Due to layout limitations specific to text, some duplication of specific wording and phrasing from source material may have unintentionally occurred. Every effort has been made to clear copyright on original material. The publishers would be pleased to hear from anyone who feels their copyright may have been infringed.

Natural Disasters contributors sourced data and images from a broad range of sources, including web sites, printed material, and a variety of published visual media. While the authors, publishers, and other representatives of *Natural Disasters* have made every effort to provide accurate information and to verify sources, the publisher specifically disclaims that the material represents research from first sources in every case.

Much of the material and personal accounts in the articles on the Conlen Tornado (page 280) and the Boundary Waters Derecho (page 240) was sourced from the US National Oceanographic and Atmospheric Administration and is thus in the public domain. Therefore, any material in this story that is substantially the same as the source material is not subject to copyright protection.

Picture Credits

The Publishers would like to thank the following photographic libraries and sources of photographic material, especially Getty Images for their assistance in sourcing most of the images for this book. All pictures appearing in the book are by Getty Images®, with the exception of:

p. 33: top, The Art Archive / Peter Fabris
p. 67: courtesy of NASA Goddard Space Flight Center
p. 68: courtesy of NASA
p. 74: bottom left, The Art Archive / National Archives Washington DC
p. 75: bottom right, The Art Archive / Domenica del Corriere / Dagli Orti
p. 82: Hawke's Bay Museum
p. 83: top, Hawke's Bay Museum; bottom, postcard from the Publisher's collection
p. 84: postcard from the Publisher's collection
p. 85: Hawke's Bay Museum
p. 126: center, courtesy of NOAA
p. 159: Fairfax Photos / The Age / Craig Sillitoe
p. 187: top, National Library of Australia / Alan Dwyer
p. 187: bottom, National Library of Australia / Herald and Weekly Times / Bruce Howard
p. 222: center, courtesy of NOAA
p. 238: center, courtesy of NASA Goddard Space Flight Center
p. 243: center, Craig Perreault, Minnesota Department of Natural Resources
p. 262: center, courtesy of NOAA
p. 275: top left, courtesy of NOAA
p. 426: The Art Archive / Galleria Nazionale delle Marche, Urbino / Dagli Orti
p. 430: The Art Archive / Museo Correr Venice / Dagli Orti
p. 431: top, The Art Archive / Peter Philippe
p. 431: bottom, The Art Archive
p. 482–3: courtesy of Peter Brown, CSIRO Rodent Research Group
p. 507: bottom, courtesy of NASA Goddard Space Flight Center